Maritime Economics
Second edition

Martin Stopford

ROUTLEDGE

First published 1997 by Routledge
11 New Fetter Lane, London
EC4P 4EE

Simultaneously published in the
USA and Canada by Routledge
29 West 35th Street, New York,
NY 10001

Reprinted 1999, 2000 (twice)

Routledge is an imprint of the Taylor & Francis Group

Typeset in Janson by
Ponting–Green Publishing Services,
Chesham, Buckinghamshire

Printed and bound in Great
Britain by
TJ International Ltd, Padstow,
Cornwall.

British Library Cataloguing in Publication Data

A catalogue record for this book is available from the British Library

Library of Congress Cataloguing in Publication Data

A catalogue record for this book has been requested

ISBN 0–415–15309–3 (hbk)
ISBN 0–415–15310–7 (pbk)

Contents

6 Financing ships and shipping companies 193

7 The economic principles of maritime trade 225

8 The global pattern of maritime trade 253

Illustrations

Figures

Tables

Boxes

Preface to the second edition

This book is an introduction to shipping market economics. It aims to explain how the shipping market is organized and to answer some basic questions about how it works: How are prices and freight rates determined? Are there market cycles? What determines a shipping company's ability to survive depressions? How are ships financed? What factors influence ship design? Is it possible to make reliable forecasts?

Although mainly a textbook, I hope it will also be useful to practical people in the shipping business. The first edition started life as a series of lectures I gave at Cambridge Academy of Transport and the City University Business School while working for British Shipbuilders. Work on the second edition, a major revision of the first, started when I was at Chase Manhattan Bank and was finished at H. Clarkson & Co. the shipbroking company. These two new perspectives led to extra chapters on ship finance, the operation of shipping markets and sea trade. As a result *Maritime Economics* now has fourteen chapters, as summarized on the following pages.

In producing the two editions I received help from many people. For the first edition I would like to repeat my thanks to Ian Buxton of Newcastle University, Professor Costas Grammenos of City University Business School and Peter Douglas of Chase Manhattan Bank, Professor Harry Benford of Michigan University and Professor Rigas Doganis, John Evans, Brian Yolland, the Rt Hon. Gerald Cooper, Dr John Doviak of Cambridge Academy of Transport, Professor Henk Molenaar, Mona Kristiansen of Leif Hoegh & Company, Phillip Wood of Transport and Trading, Jim Battersby, J. Graham

Day, and Alan Adams of Shell, all of whom provided admirable comments, suggestions and criticisms.

For help with the second edition, thanks are due to Richard Hext of China Navigation Co., Rogan McLellan of P&OCL, Mark Page of Drewry Shipping Consultants, Professor Mary Brooks of Dalhousie University, Bob Crawley and Betsy Nelson of Chase Manhattan Bank, Peter Stokes; Merrick Raynor, Jonathan Tully and Robert Bennett of H. Clarkson & Co; Michael Tamvakis (Chapters 7–8), John Ferguson of Lloyds Register, Rear Admiral Mitropoulos of IMO, and Paul Stott. Finally, thanks to my wife Anne for putting up with it . . . again!

Martin Stopford
London, May 1997

Synopsis

Chapter 1: The economic organization of the shipping market

We start with an overview of the market covering the transport system, the demand for sea transport, the merchant fleet, how transport is provided, the role of ports, shipping company organization and political influences.

Chapter 2: The shipping market cycle

Shipping market cycles dominate the industry's economic thinking. A discussion of 'shipping risk' leads on to a review of how, over the last century, experts have defined the shipping cycle. The thirteen cycles since 1869 are identified from statistical series and contemporary market reports. A brief account is provided of each cycle, drawing attention to the economic mechanism which drove the market up or down and the underlying secular trend. The chapter ends with some thoughts on the return on capital in shipping and the prediction of shipping cycles.

Chapter 3: The four shipping markets

Now it is time to see how the markets actually work. Shipping business is conducted through four related markets dealing in different commodities, freight, second-hand ships, new ships and ships for demolition. We discuss the practicalities of each market and the dynamics of how they are connected by cash-flow. As cash flows in and out of shipowners' balance sheets it influences their behaviour in these markets.

Chapter 4: Supply, demand and freight rates

We take a more detailed look at the economic model of the shipping market which underlies the cyclical nature of the business. The model consists of three components, supply, demand and the freight rate mechanism. The first half of the chapter discusses the ten key variables which influence the supply and demand functions for the shipping industry. The second half examines how freight rates link supply and demand. Emphasis is placed on market dynamics.

Chapter 5: Costs, revenue and financial performance

Turning to the microeconomic side of the business, this chapter discusses the costs and revenues of operating merchant ships. Costs are divided into voyage costs and operating costs. Capital costs are also discussed, though the main review of financing is contained in the next chapter. The final section focuses on techniques for cash-flow analysis.

Chapter 6: Financing ships and shipping companies

Finance is the most important item in the shipowner's cashflow budget. The chapter starts with a review of the many ways ships have been financed in the past, followed by a brief explanation of the world capital markets, showing where the money comes from. Finally, the chapter discusses the four main ways of financing ships, equity, debt, newbuilding finance, and leasing.

Chapter 7: The economic principles of maritime trade

Shipping depends on trade, so we must understand why countries trade and why trading patterns change. We start with a short summary of trade theory, identifying the various explanations for trade. This is followed by a discussion of the supply/demand model used to analyse natural resource-based commodity trades. Turning to the actual sea trade of 105 countries, we review the evidence for a relationship between trade and land area, population, natural resources and economic activity. Finally we review the 'Trade Development Cycle' and the relationship between sea trade and economic development.

Chapter 8: The global pattern of maritime trade

There is a physical dimension to shipping economics, so we must be aware of the geography of the world in which trade takes place. Today's trading world has evolved over many centuries and history demonstrates that the regional centre of sea trade is constantly on the move – we call its path the 'Westline'. By examining the trade of the Atlantic and Pacific Oceans we can see where the 'Westline' is today.

Chapter 9: Bulk cargo and the economics of bulk shipping

The widespread use of bulk transport systems to reduce the cost of shipping raw materials has reshaped the global economy in the twentieth century. The first part of the chapter analyses the principles of bulk transport and bulk handling. It covers the transport system, the transport characteristics of commodities and the development of transport systems for bulk handling. This is followed by a brief account of the various commodities shipped in bulk, their economic characteristics and the transport systems employed.

Chapter 10: The general cargo and the economics of liner shipping

Containerization of liner services is one of the great commercial innovations of the twentieth century. Faster transport and lower costs have made it possible for businesses to source materials and market their products almost anywhere in the world. This chapter discusses the organization of the liner system, the characteristics of demand and the way the liner business deals with the complex economic framework within which it operates.

Chapter 11: The economics of ships and ship designs

In this chapter we discuss the design of merchant ships. The aim is to focus on the way designs have evolved to meet technical and economic objectives. The chapter starts from the three objectives of ship design, efficient cargo containment, operational efficiency, and cost. There follows a discussion of each of the main categories of ship design: liner vessels, liquid bulk, dry bulk, specialist bulk, service vessels.

Chapter 12: The regulatory framework of maritime economics

This chapter examines the impact of regulation on shipping economics. We identify three key regulatory institutions, the classification societies, the flag states and the coastal states. Each plays a part in making the rules which govern the economic activities of shipowners. The classification societies, through the authority of the 'class certificate', supervise the technical safety of the merchant ships. The flag states make the laws which govern the technical, and commercial activities of shipowners registered with them. Finally, the coastal states police the 'good conduct' of ships in their waters, notably on environmental issues.

Chapter 13: The economics of shipbuilding and scrapping

The shipbuilding and ship scrapping industries play a central part in the shipping market model. This chapter starts with a regional review of the location of shipbuilding capacity. This is followed by a discussion of shipping market production and prices cycles. A section on the economic principles is followed by a discussion of the technology of the business. Finally, there is a section on the ship scrapping business.

Chapter 14: Maritime forecasting and market research

The 'forecasting paradox' is that businessmen do not really expect forecasts to be correct, yet they continue to use them. There are two different types of 'forecasts' used in the shipping industry, market forecasts and market research. Market forecasts cover the market in general, while market research applies to a specific decision. Different techniques are discussed covering each type of study. We conclude with a review of common forecasting errors.

Appendix 1: An introduction to ship market modelling

Appendix 2: Tonnage measurement and conversion factors

Abbreviations

ABS	American Bureau of Shipping
ACF	annual cashflow analysis
AWES	Association of Western European Shipbuilders
bcm	billion cubic metres
BCV	barge carrying vessel
bt	billion tons
btd	barrels per day
btm	billion ton miles
CGM	Compagnie General Maritime
cgrt	compensated gross registered tonnage
cgt	compensated gross tonnage
CIF	cost, insurance, freight
COA	Contract of Affreightment
DCF	discounted cashflow analysis
dwt	deadweight tonnage
ECGN	Export Credit Guarantee Department
ECNA	East Coast North America
EEC	European Economic Community
FAK	freight all kinds
FEFC	Far East Freight Conference
GATT	General Agreement on Trade and Tariffs
GDP	gross domestic product
GNP	gross national product

GRI	general rate increase
grt	gross registered tonnage
gt	gross tonnage
ha	hectares
IACS	International Association of Classification Societies
ILO	International Labour Organization
IMCO	Inter-governmental Maritime Consultative Organization
IMO	International Maritime Organization
ISIC	International Standard Industrial Classification
ISO	International Standards Organization
ITF	International Transport Workers' Organization
kt	thousand tons
LCM	lateral cargo mobility
LNG	liquefied natural gas
lo-lo	lift on, lift off
LPG	liquefied petroleum gas
LR	Lloyd's Register of Shipping
lwt	lightweight
MSC	Maritime Safety Committee (of IMCO)
m.dwt	million tons deadweight
mgt	million gross tons
mt	million tons
NIS	Norwegian International Ship Registry
NPV	net present value
nrt	net registered tonnage
OBO	oil/bulk/ore carrier
OCL	Overseas Containers Ltd
OECD	Organization for Economic Co-operation and Development
OPEC	Organization of Petroleum Exporting Countries
PCNT	Panama Canal Net Ton
POSCO	Pohan Steelworks
PSD	parcel size distribution
RFR	required freight rate
ro-ro	roll on, roll off
ROI	return on investment
SBT	segregated ballast tanks
SCNT	Suez Canal Net Ton
sd	standard displacement
SDR	Special Drawing Right
SMM	Shipping Market Model
SOLAS	Safety of Life at Sea Convention
SPC	self polishing paint

STCW	Standards of training, certifications and watchkeeping for seafarers
TAA	Trans Atlantic Agreement
TACA	Trans Atlantic Conference Agreement
TDC	trade development cycle
TEU	twenty-foot equivalent unit
THC	terminal handling charge
tm	ton mile
TPDA	Trans Pacific Discussion Agreement
ULCC	ultra large crude carrier
UN	United Nations
UNCLOS I	first UN Law of the Sea Conference
UNCLOS II	second UN Law of the Sea Conference
UNCTAD	United Nations Conference on Trade and Development
VCF	voyage cashflow analysis
VLCC	very large crude carrier

Glossary of liner shipping terms and note on the tables

Breakbulk general cargo, manhandled into the ship's hold pre- or on- carrying vessel servicing mainline vessels with transshipment.
Fixed day weekly service with a sailing on the same day each week.
Homogeneous container capacity expressing capacity or volume in a way that permits combination of 20' and 40' containers to create a single homogeneous tally (e.g. forty × 40 ft plus twenty × 20 ft containers would be the equivalent of 100 TEU or 40 FEU). European based trades are more usually nominated in TEU; American lines and American based trades show some preference for FEU tallies.
Insulated containers containers that rely on an external source for their refrigeration.
Integral reefer containers containers with internal refrigerating machinery, not requiring an external cooling source.
Intermodal the ability to move between different modes of transport (ship/truck/train) with minimal disruption to the speed of through transit.
lo-lo Lift on, Lift Off description of a ship in which containers are worked vertically either by an on-board crane or, more usually, by a quayside crane.
Reefer refrigerated cargo.
Reeferpoints (also plugs) power outlets in ship or shore facilities to which integral containers can be connected. Alternatively, for containers without their own refrigeration plant, ducts to a central cooling system.

ro-ro Roll on, Roll off a description of a ship in which cargo is worked horizontally on wheeled vehicles via a ramp and through doors in the ship's wall.
Sequential routeing: routeing embracing multiple end-to-end trade routes, usually undertaken to optimize the use made of ship space by restricting legs on which either discharging or loading, but not both, are undertaken.
Slot the space, within a ship, for the carriage of a container; usually expressed as TEU (twenty foot equivalent container unit); FEU (forty foot equivalent unit).
Standing slot ships and fleets' capacity is usually indicated in terms of standing slots, i.e. in terms of the immediate capacity of the ship/fleet, without reference to the running capacity generated by voyages.
String/loop the fleet of containerships required to provide a required capacity and service frequently on a specific route.

Containers

Dominant leg the heavier of the two legs in terms of container requirement.
Imbalance the difference between container volume in opposite directions on a trade route.
Imbalance correcting the way in which the shortfall is made up, very often by moving empties back to the stronger demand area.
Leasing company a company leasing containers to liner operators, either on a long-term, master lease basis, or on spot terms.
Light leg the less heavy leg.
Standard container: This is 20' (length) × 8'0" × 8'6" (height); 40' containers usually have the same square, but hi-cubes are 9'6" high. There is a move towards a 45' length; 9'6" is their usual height.

Facilities

ICD Inland container depot, usually with Customs clearance facility.
Consolidation the process of combining less than container load parcels, to optimize use of containers.
Container freight station (CFS) area in which breakbulk cargo is received, to be loaded into usually consolidated containers.
Container terminal ship/shore interface, usually with several kinds of lifting equipment (gantry cranes, straddle carriers, etc.) mobile equipment for transferring containers within the yard, and from yard to shipside, etc., and gate facilities for receiving and delivering containers from/to customers' transport.
Container yard (CY) area in which containers are marshalled for onward movement in the transport chain, usually, but not exclusively, part of terminal facilities.
Van pool yard in which empty containers are stored.

Inland transport

Block train/stack train trains, with flatbeds, dedicated to the carriage of containers.
Chassis skeletal flatbed, on wheels, with capability of locking container mounted on it, for carriage, but requiring a Prime Mover i.e. a truck head, to provide motion capability.
Corner casting steel flanges at the eight corners of the container into which the crane or straddle carrier twist-locks fit, and lock, for lifting, which allow containers to be secured to each other, and lashed to the ship's deck.
Double-stack train (DST) train with flatbeds capable of carrying containers two-high.
Drayage inland haulage of containers.
Portainer crane gantry crane, usually with liftable outreach, for servicing container ships.
Post-Panamax crane gantry crane capable of servicing ships of dimensions too large to transit Panama Canal – usually up to seventeen containers across the ship's beam.
Straddle carrier a vehicle with high legs capable of lifting, and carrying containers around a container yard, and of lifting one container on top of and over, at least one other.
Transtainer a very large mobile crane, with four wheeled legs, capable of traversing a stack of containers, and providing yard container movement, usually on rail but sometimes independently (when it is known as a Rubber Tyred Gantry).
Twist-lock steel projection which fits into the aperture on a corner casting, of which the head turns, locks and provides the ability to lift the container.

Pricing

Basic service rate (BSR) sea freight element of the tariff.
Bunker adjustment factor (BAF) element in the tariff to cover swings in bunker prices.
Conference association of lines, grouped together primarily to create and maintain a joint tariff.
Currency adjustment factor (CAF) element in the tariff, to cover significant swings in the currencies in any particular trade in which expenses are incurred.
Demurrage charge levied on cargo for delayed receipt of container held in facilities at which the line incurs a consequential cost.
Detention charge levied on cargo for delayed return of a container within customer control, usually due to slow packing or unpacking at customers' facility.
Freight all kinds (FAK) standard rate, regardless of commodities loaded in a container.
Full container load (FCL) a cargo for which the exclusive use of the container is booked, usually rated at a lower rate than an LCL.
Less than container load (LCL) cargo delivered to the point of loading in breakbulk form, usually consolidated with other Less than container load cargoes in a single container, but at operator's convenience.
Terminal handling charge (THC) charge levied separately for the work performed for cargo in the terminal at either end of routeing.

Consolidators

Consolidator similar to a groupage operator, the consolidator specializes in fitting different client shipment requirements together to produce optimally cost-effective through transport.
Group operator forwarder, or consolidator, soliciting cargo, and consolidating lots to create economies in container utilization.
Non-vessel operating common carrier (NVOCC) American phraseology for an entity providing international shipping services, but buying in the ocean transit from vessel operators.

Note on the tables

Where the data used in tables has been produced by means of multiple calculations involving large numbers there are inevitably rounding errors. This is particularly the case with percentages, where totals may not always equal exactly 100.

Chapter 1

The economic organization of the shipping market

Shipping is an exciting business, surrounded by many false beliefs, misconceptions and even taboos . . . The facts of the matter are straightforward enough and, when stripped of their emotional and sentimental overtones in clinical analysis, are much less titillating than the popular literature and maritime folklore lead one to expect.

(Helmut Sohmen, 'What Bankers Always Wanted to Know about Shipping but were Afraid to Ask', Address to the Foreign Banks' Representatives Association, Hong Kong, 27 June 1985. Reprinted in *Fairplay*, London, 1 August 1986.)

1.1 The economic role of the shipping industry

The economic importance of shipping

The story of the shipping industry since the first steamships were built more than a century ago has been one of ingenuity, professionalism, fabulous profits and some disastrous miscalculations. It includes the drama of the supertanker,[1] the meteoric rise of shipping superstars like Niarchos and Onassis, and some equally dramatic scandals such as that involving Tidal Marine, which built up at 700,000 dwt (deadweight tonnage) shipping fleet in the early 1970s and was subsequently indicted, with a number of bankers in New York, on charges of fraudulently obtaining more than $60 million in loans.[2] There was the great asset play market of the 1980s when ships bought for a few million dollars increased in value by 600–800 per cent, making the lucky few investors some of the wealthiest men in the world. Among the miscalculations, at the forefront must be the remarkable episode in the tanker market in 1973 when orders were placed for over 100 m.dwt of supertankers, for which the demand never materialized, with the result that some went from the builder's yard straight into lay-up, and few ever operated to their full economic potential. In short, shipping is a 'larger than life' industry.

Our task in this book is to understand the economics of the industry. To do this we must step back from these day-to-day events, however fascinating they may be, and try to filter out the essential mechanisms that make the market-place operate. Even shipping magnates are subject to the laws of supply and demand. However, in carrying out our economic analysis we must not neglect the fact that the shipping market is a group of people – shipowners, brokers, shipbuilders and bankers – who together carry out each year the Herculean task of transporting more than 4,000 bt of cargo by sea and who may see shipping as much more than just a business.[3]

Shipping is one of the world's most international industries and in studying maritime economics we are drawn into a discussion of the world economy as a whole. Seaborne trade is, in a sense, at the apex of world economic activity. The first reaction of shipowners on hearing of some global event, such as a nuclear disaster in Russia or a change in the price of oil, is to consider what effect this will have on the shipping market. Many shipping fortunes have been made from political conflict, notably those brought about by the closure of the Suez Canal in the 1950s and 1960s. We cannot afford to ignore the political aspect of the maritime market. Nor should the strategic importance of shipping be underestimated. As business has become more international and newly industrializing countries have taken their place alongside the OECD countries,[4] the maritime industry has provided the vehicle for an extraordinary growth of trade. If we are to understand the economic and political forces that mould developments in the shipping market, we must appreciate the two-way interaction between developments in shipping and developments in the world economy.

In his book *The Economic History of World Population*, Carlo Cippola suggests that the transport industry has been one of the prime forces responsible for shifting the world from an essentially national system to the global economy that exists today.

> Fast and cheap transport has been one of the main products of the Industrial Revolution. Distances have been shortened at an astonishing pace. Day by day the world seems smaller and smaller and societies that for millennia practically ignored each other are suddenly put in contact or conflict. In our dealings, in politics as in economics, in health organisation as in military strategy, a new point of view is forced upon us. At some point in the past people had to move from an urban or regional point of view to a national one. Today we have to adjust ourselves in our way of thinking to a global point of view. As Bertrand Russell wrote, 'the world has become one not only for the astronomer but for the ordinary citizen'.[5]

The progression from a world of isolated communities to an integrated global community was made possible by shipping and sea trade, but this has been a two-way exchange which has, in turn, forced major adjustment on the maritime industry itself. At the forefront in recent years must be the US Oil Pollution Act (1990), a unilateral act by the US Congress which imposed stringent anti-pollution regulations on shipowners operating in US waters.

The role of seaborne trade in economic development

The idea of shipping as the catalyst of economic development is not new. Adam Smith, often regarded as the father of modern economics, saw shipping as one of the stepping stones to economic growth. In chapter 3 of *The Wealth of Nations*, he argued that the central economic force in a capitalist society is the division of labour, and the extent to which this can be practised depends crucially upon the size of the market. A business working in a country town without links to the outside world can never, he argued, achieve high levels of efficiency because its very small market will limit the degree of specialization.

Adam Smith saw shipping as the source of cheap transport which can open up wider markets to specialization, by offering transport for even the most everyday products at prices far below those that can be achieved by any other means. This proved to be a profound insight. Economic development has gone hand in hand with sea trade for sound economic reasons, a process which Adam Smith explains in the following way:

> As by means of water carriage a more extensive market is opened to every sort of industry than what land carriage alone can afford it, so it is upon the sea-coast, and along the banks of navigable rivers, that industry of every kind naturally begins to subdivide and improve itself, and it is frequently not until a long time after that those improvements extend themselves to the inland parts of the country . . . a broad wheeled wagon attended by two men and drawn by eight horses in about six weeks time carries and brings back between London and Edinburgh nearly 4 tons weight of goods. In about the same time a ship navigated by six or eight men, and sailing between the ports of London and Leith, frequently carries and brings back 200 ton weight of goods. Since such, therefore, are the advantages of water carriage, it is natural that the first improvements of art and industry should be made where this conveniency opens the

whole world to a market for the produce of every sort of labour.[6]

Technology has moved on since Adam Smith wrote these words in 1776, and the economically developed countries now have a massive inland transport infrastructure, but technology in the shipping industry has more than kept pace. Since the mid-1960s, two dramatic developments in the economic organization of the shipping business – unitization and bulk shipping – have played a major part in opening up a truly global market for both manufactures and raw materials.

Two technical revolutions in shipping

The most important technical development was the unitization of the liner shipping business. During the 1960s the traditional system of 'break bulk' liner shipping became increasingly unable to cope with the escalating volume of world trade, and industry observers could see that 'the old methods had reached the end of the line'.[7] To overcome these problems, palletization and containerization were introduced to speed up the flow of cargo. Putting general cargo into standard units had more wide-ranging effects than even its most ardent advocates anticipated. In the early 1960s, goods shipped from Europe to the United States could take months to arrive, but twenty years later, just a few days after leaving the factory in the Midlands of England, a container wagon could be arriving at its destination in East Coast USA with its valuable cargo safe from damage or pilferage and readily transferable to rail or barge with the minimum of delay or manual effort. In short, the shipping industry used organization to solve its own fundamental problems and, in doing so, opened the floodgates for the development of the global economy.

The bulk shipping revolution was no less wide-ranging in its effects. Bulk transport of raw materials by sea was, for the first time, viewed as part of an integrated materials handling operation in which investment could improve productivity. By employing economies of scale, investing in high speed cargo handling systems and integrating the whole transport systems, bulk transport costs were reduced to such an extent that it is often cheaper for industries to import raw materials by sea from suppliers thousands of miles away than by land from suppliers only a few hundred miles away – for example the rail freight for a ton of coal from Virginia to Jacksonville, Florida, was almost three times the sea freight from Hampton Roads to Japan, a distance of 10,000 miles.[8] Bigger ships played a central part in this process. Over a period of 50 years from 1945 to 1995 oil tankers became twenty times bigger and dry bulk vessels ten to fifteen times bigger. Improved cargo handling in ports and better integration with land transport completed the transformation.

The cost of sea transport

The shipping industry has been so successful at exploiting these technical developments that the cost of sea transport has hardly increased. Coal and oil cost little more to transport in the mid-1990s than in the late 1940s (Figure 1.1). In 1950 it cost about $8 to transport coal from East Coast North America to Japan.[9] In 1996 it costs $12.7. Along the way there were seven market cycles, peaking in 1952, 1956, 1970, 1974, 1980, 1989 and 1995, but the average transport cost was $10.9 per ton. The cheapest year for shipping coal was 1972 when it cost $4.5/ton, while the most expensive was 1980 when it cost $24/ton. The oil trade shows the same long-term trend, with transport costs fluctuating between fifty cents and one dollar per barrel. The highest cost was during the 1956 Suez crisis when the cost went up to $2.1 per barrel. In four years, 1949, 1961, 1977 and 1994 it fell to $0.5 per barrel.

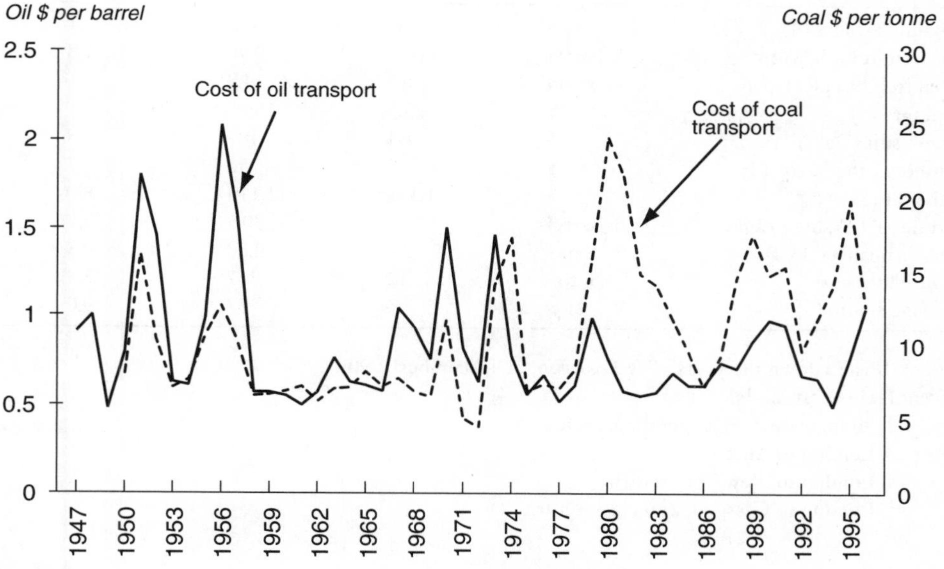

FIGURE 1.1 Transport cost of oil and coal 1950–95
Source: Compiled by Martin Stopford from various sources

Compared with other sectors of the economy, the bulk transport industry's achievement is exceptional. Average dollar prices in 1990 were nine times higher than in 1960 (Table 1.1).[10] A basic Ford motor car had increased in price from $1,385 to $11,115; the UK rail fare from London to Glasgow from $23.5 to $106; the price of a ton of domestic coal from $12 in the UK to $217; and the price of a barrel of crude oil increased from $1.5 to $20.5. The three products with the smallest increase in prices are air fares, seaborne oil freight and dry bulk freight all of which approximately doubled. The fact that air fares head the list provides an insight into why shipping lost the passenger transport business during this period. With this exception the shipping business has been very successful in maintaining costs during a period when the cost of most commodities increased by ten or twenty times. One consequence is that for many commodities freight is now a much smaller proportion of costs than it was thirty years ago. For example in 1960 the oil freight was 25 per cent of the cost of a barrel of Arabian Light crude oil delivered to Europe. In 1990 it had fallen to less than five per cent. Ironically this made the tanker business much less important to the oil companies. This impressive cost performance was achieved by a combination of economies of scale, new technology, better ports and more efficient cargo handling. These are the topics which we will address in the remainder of this chapter.

TABLE 1.1 Cost changes 1960–90

		1960	1990	Increase
Atlantic air fare (4)	$	1.5	1.8	1.1
Oil freight Gulf/West	$/barrel	0.55	0.98	1.8
Coal freight H.R/Japan	$/ton	6.9	14.8	2.1
Rail fare (5)	$	23.5	106.1	4.5
Men's suit (Daks)	$	84	484	5.8
Dinner at the Savoy (2)	$	7	52	7.7
Ford car (1)	$	1,385	11,115	8.0
Crude oil (Arabian Light)	$/barrel	1.5	20.5	13.7
Bread (unsliced loaf)	cents	2.4	42.0	17.5
Household coal	$/ton	12	217	18.3
Postage stamp (3)	cents	4	67	19.0

Source: 'Prices down the years', *The Economist*, 22 December 1990
Notes: 1. cheapest model
2. Soup, main course, pudding, coffee
3. London to America
4. London to New York return
5. London to Glasgow, 2nd class, return

Shipping – how many markets?

To understand the economic mechanisms that have brought about these changes one must step warily. While the shipping market is in some senses a single economic unit, there are important subdivisions. We have already referred to the liner and bulk industries, and probably the most striking aspect of the shipping business to an outsider is the totally different character of the companies in these sectors. Liner companies and bulk shipping companies belong to the same industry, but they seem to have little else in common, a fact we shall discuss more extensively in later parts of the book. The Rochdale Report commented on these divisions within the industry as follows:

> Shipping is a complex industry and the conditions which govern its operations in one sector do not necessarily apply to another; it might even, for some purposes, be better regarded as a group of related industries. Its main assets, the ships themselves, vary widely in size and type; they provide the whole range of services for a variety of goods, whether over shorter or longer distances. Although one can, for analytical purposes,

usefully isolate sectors of the industry providing particular types of service, there is usually some interchange at the margin which cannot be ignored.[11]

This suggests that there are several important ground rules for approaching shipping economics. First, it emphasizes the importance of the commercial divisions within the shipping market – the liner business carries different cargoes, provides different services and has a different economic structure from bulk shipping. Second, it acts as a reminder that shipping is in another sense a single market. Some shipping companies are active in both the bulk and liner markets and many ships are designed to operate in several different markets; indeed, this is one of the important shipowning decisions that we shall discuss in chapter 7. Consequently, we cannot afford to treat the market as a series of isolated compartments. We must recognize that, particularly in a depressed market, owners can move their investment from one market sector to another in order to avoid problems.[12] As a result supply/demand imbalances in one part of the market can ripple across to other sectors.

The final point is that, however hard we might try to develop the analysis in economic terms, shipping is an international business and the economic forces that make it so significant in economic terms also make it the subject of national and international political intervention. The Rochdale Report concluded its definition of the shipping industry with the comment that 'Most of the industry's business is concerned with international trade and inevitably it operates within a complicated world pattern of agreements between shipping companies, understandings with shippers and policies of governments.' Such matters cannot be ignored. Since the mid-1960s the maritime industry has seen an escalation of political involvement, ranging from the efforts of the Third World countries to gain entry to the international shipping business through the medium of UNCTAD, to the subsidizing of domestic shipbuilding; the regulation of liner shipping and the increasing interest in safety at sea, pollution, and crew regulations. Just as these subjects cannot easily be understood without some knowledge of the maritime economic framework within which the game is being played out, an economic analysis cannot ignore the political influences on costs, prices and free market competition. These are all subjects that will be discussed in some detail in later chapters. In this chapter we shall concentrate on discussing the shipping market as a whole. The aim is to show how the different parts and institutions within the shipping market – the liner business, bulk shipping, the charter market, etc. – fit together, and to examine the basic principles of how freight rates and ship prices are determined. From this foundation we discuss the components of the market in greater detail.

1.2 The international transport system

Transport modes and intermodalism

Shipping is only one link in the transport chain, so we must look beyond the narrow maritime perspective. The aim of the shipper is to obtain better and cheaper transport over the whole distance from origin to destination. To meet this need, in recent decades the world has evolved a transport system which provides fast and cheap access to almost every corner of the globe. The system consists of roads, railways, inland waterways, shipping lines and air freight services. In practice the system falls into three zones, inter-regional transport, short sea, and inland transport.

BOX 1.1 International transport zones and available transport modes

Zone	Area	Transport sector	Vehicle
1	Inter-regional	Deep sea shipping	Ship
		Air freight	Plane
2	Short sea	Coastal seas	Ship/ferry
3	Land	River and canal	Barge
		Road	Lorry
		Rail	Train

Although statistics are patchy, it seems that in 1990 air freight was 31 btm, rail 3,853 btm and sea trade 12,056 btm. In terms of volume this makes shipping roughly four times as important as rail and four hundred times as important as air freight. As we shall see, shipping has, to a large extent, created its own markets by reducing the cost of transport.[13]

Transport between regions

For most inter-regional cargoes deep sea shipping is the only economic transport between the continental landmasses. It is the main subject of this volume. Traffic is particularly heavy on the routes between the major industrial regions of Asia, Europe and North America. There are about 20,000 ships in this trade, offering services ranging from low cost bulk transport to fast regular liner services.

Air freight started to become viable for transporting high value commodities between regions in the 1960s. It competes with the liner services for premium cargo such as engineering goods, processed textiles, livestock and automotive spare parts. Shipments have grown rapidly, reaching 12.9 btm in 1982, and 31 btm by 1990. Despite this growth, air freight still accounts for only 0.1 per cent of the volume of goods transported between regions. Its contribution has been to widen the range of transport services available by offering the option of very fast but high cost transport.

Short sea shipping

Short sea shipping provides transport within regions. It distributes cargo delivered to regional centres such as Hong Kong or Rotterdam by deep sea vessels, and provides a port-to-port service, often in direct competition with land based transport such as rail. This is a very different business from deep sea shipping. The ships are generally smaller than their counterparts in the deep sea trades ranging in size from 400 dwt to 6,000 dwt, though there are no firm rules. Designs place much emphasis on cargo flexibility.

Cargoes shipped short sea include grain, fertilizer, coal, lumber, steel, clay, aggregates, containers, wheeled vehicles and passengers. Because trips are so short, and ships visit many more ports in a year than deep sea vessels, trading in this market requires great organizational skills. As Tinsley (1984) comments

> it requires a knowledge of the precise capabilities of the ships involved, and a flexibility to arrange the disposition of vessels so that customers' requirements are met in an efficient and economic way. Good positioning, minimisation of ballast legs, avoiding being caught over weekends or holidays and accurate reading of the market are crucial for survival.[14]

Short sea shipping is subject to many political restrictions. The most important is *cabotage*, the practice by which countries enact laws reserving coastal trade to ships of their national fleet. This system has operated for many years in the United States and in some countries in Europe.

The inland transport system consists of an extensive network of roads, railways, and waterways. It is linked to the shipping system through ports and specialist terminals.

Competition and cooperation in the transport industry

The companies in the transport system operate in a market governed by a mix of competition and co-operation. In many trades the competitive element is obvious. Rail competes with road; short sea shipping with road and rail; and deep sea shipping with air freight for higher value cargo. However, a few examples show that the scope of competition is much wider than appears possible at first sight.

For example over the last fifty years bulk carriers trading in the deep sea trades have been in cut-throat competition with the railways. How is this possible? The answer is that users of raw materials such as power stations and steel mills often face a choice between use of domestic and imported raw materials. Thus, a power station at Jacksonville in Florida can import coal from Virginia by rail or from Columbia by sea. Where transport accounts for a large proportion of the delivered cost, there is intense competition.

Cost is not the only factor, as shown by the seasonal trade in perishable goods such as raspberries and asparagus. These products travel as air freight because the journey by refrigerated ship is too slow to allow delivery in prime condition. However, the shipping industry has tried to recapture that cargo by developing refrigerated containers with a controlled atmosphere which prevents deterioration, thus permitting them to compete for this cargo.

Although the different sectors of the transport business are fiercely competitive, technical development depends upon close cooperation. Indeed the development of

Integrated Transport Systems[15] in which each component in the transport system is designed to fit in with the others has been one of the dominant themes of international transport in the last 20 years. There are many examples of this co-operation. Much of the world's grain trade is handled by a carefully controlled system of barges, rail trucks and deep sea ships. The modal points in the system are highly automated grain elevators which receive grain from one transport mode, store it temporarily and ship it out in another. Similarly, coal may be loaded in Columbia or Australia, shipped by sea in a large bulk carrier to Rotterdam, and distributed by a small short sea vessel to the final consumer. The containerization of general cargo is built around standard containers which can be carried by road, rail or sea with equal facility. Often road transport companies are owned by railways and vice versa.

The driving force which guides the efforts of the transport system is the quest to win more business by providing cheaper transport and a better service. We will explore more thoroughly how the industry does this in section 1.5 below. First, however, we turn to the demand for sea transport.

1.3 The demand for sea transport

The nature of transport demand

The primary task of the shipping industry is to move cargo around the world. Although this is the correct starting point for studying ship demand, as an economic definition it is too narrow. From the customer's viewpoint, shipping is a service. Saying that the shipping companies move cargo around the world, is rather like saying that restaurants cook food. There are sandwich bars, fast food chains and cordon bleu restaurants. Like the restaurateur, shipping companies provide a variety of services to meet the specific needs of customers. These needs may involve a whole range of factors, of which the most important are:

1 *Price*: The freight cost is always important, but the greater the proportion of freight in the overall cost equation, the more emphasis shippers are likely to place on it. For example, in the 1950s the cost of transporting a barrel of oil from the Middle East to Europe represented 49 per cent of the CIF cost. As a result, oil companies devoted great effort to finding ways to reduce the cost of transport. By the 1990s the price of oil had increased and the cost of transport had fallen to just 2.5 per cent of the CIF price so transport cost became less important.

2 *Speed*: Time in transit incurs an inventory cost, so shippers of high-value commodities value speed. The cost of holding high-value commodities in stock may make it cheaper to ship small quantities frequently even if the freight cost is greater. On a three-month journey a cargo worth $100,000 incurs an inventory cost of $2,500 if interest rates are 10 per cent per annum. If the journey time can be halved it is worth paying up to $1,250 extra in freight. Speed may also be important for commercial reasons. A European manufacturer ordering spare parts from the Far East may be happy to pay

ten times the freight for delivery in three days by air if the alternative is to have machinery out of service for five or six weeks while the spares are delivered by sea.

3 *Reliability*: With the growing importance of 'just in time' stock control systems, transport reliability has taken on a new significance. Some shippers may be prepared to pay more for a service which is guaranteed to operate to time and provide the services which it has promised.

4 *Security*: Loss or damage in transit is an insurable risk, but raises many difficulties for the shipper, who may well be prepared to pay more for secure transportation of his product without risk of damage.

Each part of the business provides for a different combination of needs. In studying how this business is carried out, we need to be aware of the different demands which commodities place on the transport system, and to understand how the system has evolved to meet these needs. As we consider the part played by cargoes and ships in the following sections we must not lose sight of the needs of the customers who use the transport system.

What commodities are traded by sea?

In 1995 merchant ships transported about 4 bt of cargo. The trade consisted of many different commodities. Raw materials such as oil, iron ore, bauxite and coal; agricultural products such as grain, sugar and refrigerated food; industrial materials such as rubber, forest products, cement, textile fibres and chemicals; and manufactures such as heavy plant, motor cars, machinery and consumer goods. It covers everything from a 4 million barrel parcel of oil to a cardboard box of Christmas gifts.

The prime task of the seaborne trade analyst is to explain the growth and development of seaborne commodity trades, and to do this each commodity must be analysed in the context of the world economy. Where commodities are related to the same industry it makes sense to study them as a group so that inter-relationships can be seen. For example the crude oil and products are interchangable – if oil is refined before shipment then it is transported as products instead of crude oil. Similarly, if a country exporting iron ore sets up a steel mill, the trade in iron ore may be transformed into a smaller trade in steel products. To show how the various seaborne trades inter-relate, the main seaborne commodity trades are shown in Figure 1.2 arranged into six groups reflecting the area of economic activity to which they are most closely related.[16] These groups can be summarized as follows:

1 *Energy trades*: Energy dominates bulk shipping. This group of commodities, which accounts for 45 per cent of seaborne trade, comprises crude oil, oil products, liquefied gas and thermal coal for use in generating electricity. These fuel sources compete with each other and non-traded energy commodities such as nuclear power. For example, the substitution of coal for oil in power stations in the 1980s transformed the pattern of these two trades. The analysis of the energy trades is concerned with the world energy economy.

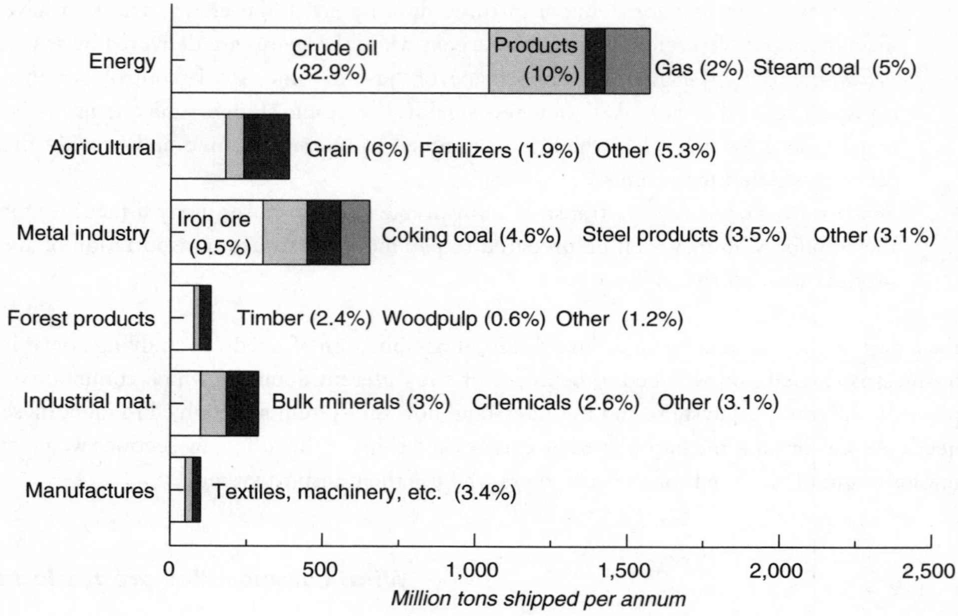

FIGURE 1.2 Seaborne trade by economic activity

Source: Compiled by Martin Stopford from various sources

2 *Agricultural trades*: A total of twelve commodities, accounting for 13 per cent of sea trade, are the products or raw materials of the agricultural industry. They include cereals such as wheat and barley, animal feedstuffs, sugar, molasses, refrigerated food, oil and fats and fertilizers. The analysis of these trades is concerned with the demand for foodstuffs, which depends on income and population. It is also concerned with the important derived demand for animal feeds. On the supply side, we are led into the discussion of land use and agricultural productivity.

3 *Metal industry trades*: This major commodity group, which accounts for 25 per cent of sea trade, represents the third building block of modern industrial society. Under this heading we group the raw materials and products of the steel and non-ferrous metal industries, including iron ore, metallurgical grade coal, non-ferrous metal ores, steel products and scrap.

4 *Forest products trades*: Forest products are primarily industrial materials used for the manufacture of paper, paper board and in the construction industry. This section includes timber (logs and lumber) woodpulp, plywood, paper and various wood products, totalling about 145 mt. The trade is strongly influenced by the availability of forestry resources.

5 *Other industrial materials*: There are a wide range of industrial materials such as cement,

salt, gypsum, mineral sands, asbestos, chemicals and many others. The total trade in these commodities accounted for 9 per cent of sea trade. They cover a whole range of industries.

6 *Other Manufactures*: The final trade group comprises the remaining manufactures such as textiles, machinery, capital goods, vehicles, etc. The total tonnage involved in this sector accounts for only 3 per cent of sea trade, but many of these commodities have a high value so their share in value is probably closer to 50 per cent. They are the mainstay of the liner trades and their impact upon the shipping industry is much greater than the tonnage suggests.

Viewing the trade as a whole, over 70 per cent of the tonnage of seaborne trade is associated with the energy and metal industries so the shipping industry is highly dependent upon developments in these two industries.

Although these trade statistics help to convey the scale of the merchant shipping business, they disguise its physical complexity. Cargo may appear in any of eighty countries which have maritime trade, for consignment to any other country. Some shipments are regular, others irregular; some are large, others are small; some shippers are in a hurry, others are not; some cargoes can be handled with suction or grabs, while others are fragile; some cargo is boxed, containerized or packed on pallets, while other cargo is loose.

The parcel size distribution function

To explain how the shipping industry approaches the task of transporting this complex mix of cargoes, we need to introduce a concept that is central to the economic organization of the shipping market, the parcel size distribution (PSD) function. A 'parcel' is an individual consignment of cargo for shipment. For a particular commodity trade, the PSD function describes the range of parcel sizes in which cargo is transported. If, for example, we take the case of iron ore shown in Figure 1.3, we see that individual shipments ranged in size from under 40,000 tons to over 100,000 tons, with the majority concentrated in the upper size range. A similar analysis for grain in the same figure shows a very different parcel size distribution, with grain shipments concentrating in the under 80,000 ton category, and only a few of over 100,000 tons. In short, for any commodity shipped by sea we must expect to find cargoes appearing on the market in a wide range of parcel sizes.

The precise shape of the PSD for each commodity is determined by the characteristics of demand. The market has sorted out the economic balance between large and small parcels. These are all subjects that we discuss more extensively in chapters 7 and 8; for the present, we simply establish the principle that the same commodity may be shipped in many different parcel sizes.

The importance of the PSD function is that it helps to answer the central question 'which cargoes go in which ships?' In practice, different sizes of cargo parcel require different types of shipping operation. One important division is between 'bulk cargo', which consists of cargo parcels big enough to fill a whole ship, and 'general cargo', which consists of many

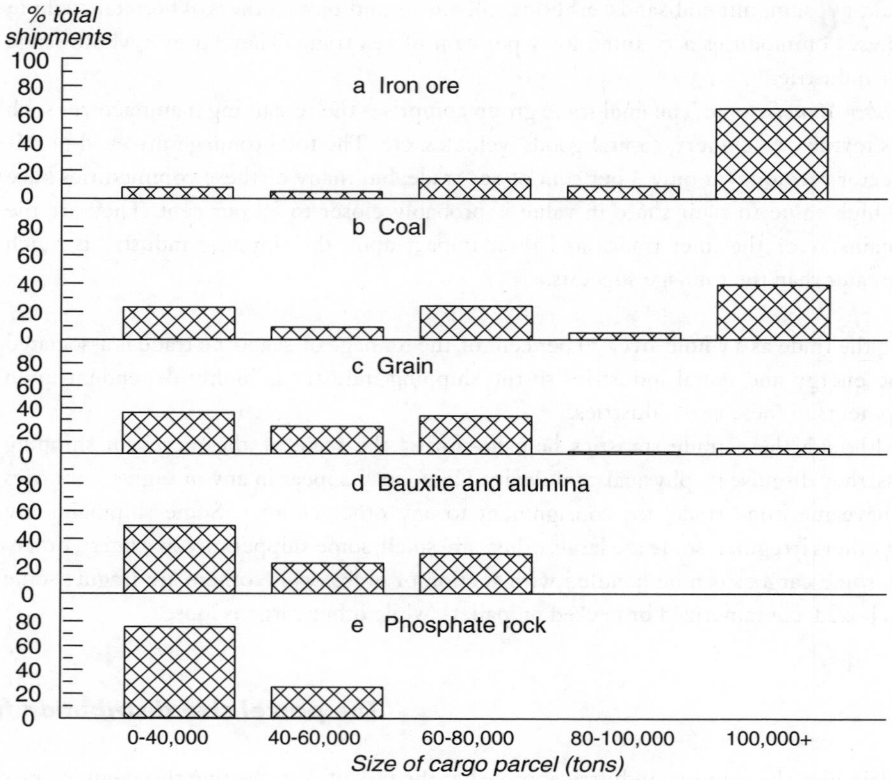

FIGURE 1.3 Parcel size distribution
Source: Fearnleys, *World Bulk Trades*

small consignments, too small to fill a ship, that have to be packed with other cargo for transport. Another is between the size of ships used. Some bulk cargoes travel in small bulk carriers, while others use the biggest ships available. Analysis of the range of commodity trades shown in Figure 1.3 shows that each has its own distinctive parcel size distribution, with individual consignments ranging from the very small to the very large.[17]

For many commodities the parcel size distribution contains some cargo parcels that are too small to fill a ship – for example, 500 tons of steel products – and that will travel as general cargo, and others – say 5,000 tons of steel products – that are large enough to travel in bulk. As the trade grows, the proportion of cargo parcels large enough to travel bulk may increase and the trade will gradually switch from being a liner trade to being predominantly a minor bulk trade. This happened in many trades during the 1960s and 1970s, and as a result the bulk trade grew faster than general cargo trade. Because many commodities travel partly in bulk and partly as general cargo, commodity trades cannot be neatly divided into 'bulk' and 'general' cargo. To do this it is necessary to know the PSD function for each commodity.

Parcel size and transport mode

The parcel size distribution provides the basis for explaining the micro-economic organization of the shipping market, the main elements of which are summarized in Figure 1.4. Starting at the top of this diagram, world trade splits into large parcels and small parcels, depending on the PSD function of each commodity. Large parcels are carried by the bulk shipping industry and small parcels by the liner shipping industry; these represent the two major segments within the shipping industry.

This distinction may appear slight when put in such abstract economic terms, but there is no doubt about its reality. Bulk and liner shipping are as different in their character as it is possible for two industries to be, as will become clear when we discuss the matter in detail in Chapters 9 and 10. Finally we note that the ships to carry the cargo are supplied partly from fleets owned by the bulk and liner industries, supplemented by vessels obtained from the charter market, as shown at the bottom of the diagram. This distinction between the operation of the vessel in the bulk or liner trade, and its ownership is important.

Definition of 'bulk cargo'

There is a long history of carrying cargo in shiploads – Roman grain ships, tea clippers, bulk timber and the fleets of colliers in the nineteenth century are examples – but bulk shipping did not develop as the major sector of the shipping industry in the decades following the Second World War. A fleet of specialist crude oil tankers was built to service the rapidly expanding economies of Western Europe and Japan, with smaller vessels for the carriage of products and liquid chemicals. In the dry bulk trades, several important industries, notably steel, aluminium and fertilizer manufacture, turned to foreign suppliers for their raw materials and a fleet of large bulk carriers was built to service the trade. As a result, bulk shipping became a rapidly-expanding sector of the shipping industry and bulk tonnage now accounts for about three-quarters of the world merchant fleet.

Most of the bulk cargoes are drawn from the raw material trades such as oil, iron ore, coal and grain, and it is common to describe these as 'bulk commodities' on the assumption that, for example, all iron ore is shipped in bulk. In the case of iron ore this is a reasonable assumption, but many smaller commodity trades are shipped partly in bulk and partly as general cargo; for example, a shipload of forest products would be rightly classified as bulk cargo but consignments of logs still travel as general cargo in a few trades. There are four main categories of bulk cargo:

- *Liquid bulk* requires tanker transportation. The main ones are crude oil, oil products, liquid chemicals such as caustic soda, vegetable oils, and wine. The size of individual consignments varies from a few thousand tons to half a mt in the case of crude oil.
- *The 'five major bulks'* covers the five homogeneous bulk cargoes – iron ore, grain, coal, phosphates and bauxite – which can be transported satisfactorily in a conventional dry bulk carrier or 'tweendecker stowing at 45–55 cubic feet per ton.

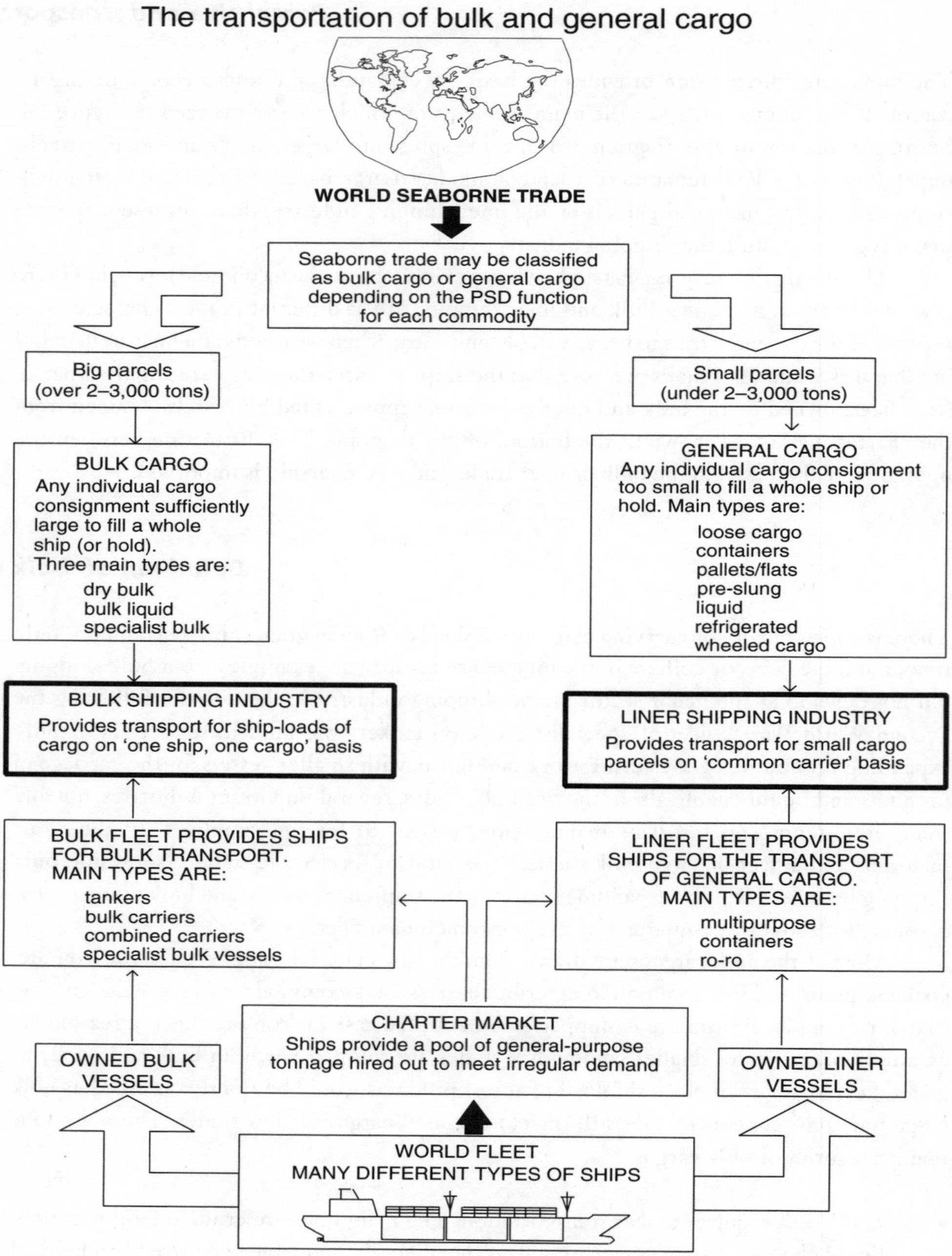
The transportation of bulk and general cargo
WORLD SEABORNE TRADE
Seaborne trade may be classified as bulk cargo or general cargo depending on the PSD function for each commodity
Big parcels (over 2–3,000 tons)
Small parcels (under 2–3,000 tons)
BULK CARGO
Any individual cargo consignment sufficiently large to fill a whole ship (or hold).
Three main types are:
dry bulk
bulk liquid
specialist bulk
GENERAL CARGO
Any individual cargo consignment too small to fill a whole ship or hold. Main types are:
loose cargo
containers
pallets/flats
pre-slung
liquid
refrigerated
wheeled cargo
BULK SHIPPING INDUSTRY
Provides transport for ship-loads of cargo on 'one ship, one cargo' basis
LINER SHIPPING INDUSTRY
Provides transport for small cargo parcels on 'common carrier' basis
BULK FLEET PROVIDES SHIPS FOR BULK TRANSPORT. MAIN TYPES ARE:
tankers
bulk carriers
combined carriers
specialist bulk vessels
LINER FLEET PROVIDES SHIPS FOR THE TRANSPORT OF GENERAL CARGO. MAIN TYPES ARE:
multipurpose
containers
ro-ro
CHARTER MARKET
Ships provide a pool of general-purpose tonnage hired out to meet irregular demand
OWNED BULK VESSELS
OWNED LINER VESSELS
WORLD FLEET
MANY DIFFERENT TYPES OF SHIPS

FIGURE 1.4 Transport of bulk and general cargo

Source: Martin Stopford, 1997

- *Minor bulks* covers the many other commodities that travel in shiploads. The most important are steel products, cement, gypsum, non-ferrous metal ores, sugar, salt, sulphur, forest products, wood chips and chemicals.
- *Specialist bulk cargoes* includes any bulk cargoes with specific handling or storage requirements. Motor vehicles, steel products, refrigerated cargo and special cargoes such as a cement plant or prefabricated building fall into this category.

Definition of 'general cargo'

The transport of general cargo is a very different business. General cargo consists of consignments of less than ship or hold size and, therefore, too small to justify setting up a bulk shipping operation. In addition there are often high-value or delicate cargoes that require a special shipping service and for which the shipper requires a fixed tariff rather than a fluctuating market rate. There are no hard and fast rules about what constitutes general cargo – boxes, bales, machinery, 1,000 tons of steel products, 50 tons of bagged malting barley are typical examples. The main classes of general cargo from a shipping viewpoint are:

- *Loose cargo* individual items, boxes, pieces of machinery, etc., each of which must be handled and stowed separately. All general cargo used to be shipped this way, but now almost all has been unitized in one way or another.
- *Containerized cargo* standard boxes, usually 8 feet wide, often 8 feet 6 inches high and 20, 30, or 40 feet long, filled with cargo. This is now the principal form of general cargo transport.
- *Palletized cargo* cargo packed onto a pallet for easy stacking and fast handling.
- *Pre-slung cargo* small items such as planks of wood lashed together into standard-sized packages
- *Liquid cargo* travels in deep tanks, liquid containers or drums.
- *Refrigerated cargo* perishable goods that must be shipped, chilled or frozen, in insulated holds or refrigerated containers.
- *Heavy and awkward cargo* large and difficult to stow.

Until the mid-1960s most general cargo travelled loose and each item had to be packed in the hold of a cargo liner using 'dunnage' (pieces of wood or burlap) to keep it in place. This labour-intensive operation was slow, expensive, difficult to plan and the cargo was exposed to the risk of damage or pilferage. As a result, expensive cargo liners spent two-thirds of their time in port and cargo-handling costs have escalated to more than one-quarter of the total shipping cost.[18] As the volume of cargo increased, liner operations found it increasingly difficult to provide the service that shippers required at an economic cost and their profit margins were squeezed.[19]

The shipping industry's response was to 'unitize' the transport system, applying the same technology which had been applied successfully on the production lines in manufacturing industry. Work was standardized, allowing investment to increase productivity.

Since cargo handling was the main bottleneck, the key was to pack the cargo into internationally accepted standard units which could be handled quickly and cheaply with specially designed equipment. At the outset many systems of unitization were examined, but the two main contenders were pallets and containers. Pallets are flat trays, suitable for handling by fork-lift truck, on which single or multiple units can be packed for easy handling. Containers are standard boxes into which individual items are packed. The first deep sea container service was introduced in 1966 and in the next twenty years containers came to dominate the transport of general cargo, with shipments of over 50 million units per annum.

Limitations of seaborne trade statistics

An obvious question is: 'What is the tonnage of bulk and general cargo shipped by sea?' We have already encountered the problem of obtaining statistics about the commodities shipped by sea and, unfortunately, there is another statistical problem in determining how the commodities are transported. As we have seen, the volume of trade in general cargo cannot be reliably identified from commodity trade statistics. For example, we may guess that a parcel of 300 tons of steel products transported from the UK to West Africa travelled as general cargo in a liner, whereas a parcel of 6,000 tons from Japan to the USA was shipped in bulk, but there is no way of knowing this for certain from the commodity statistics alone. As we have already noted, some commodities (such as iron ore) are almost always shipped in bulk and others (such as machinery) invariably travel as general cargo, but many commodities (such as steel products, forest products and non-ferrous metal ores) straddle the two. In fact, as a trade flow grows it may start off being shipped as general cargo but eventually become sufficiently large to be shipped in bulk.[20]

TABLE 1.2 Seaborne trade 1987–94

	mt 1987	1994
Bulk cargo		
Oil	1,080	1,586
Dry bulk over 50,000 tons	679	875
Dry bulk under 50,000 tons	570	579
Total bulk cargo	2,329	3,040
Other cargo	1,132	1,466
of which: containerized (est)	190	336
Total seaborne cargo	3,461	4,506

Source: Fearnley's Annual Review 1995, Table 1, and World Bulk Trades (1985 and 1995), Table 1

Note: Dry bulk in vessels under 50,000 dwt estimated on the basis of a fleet of 105.3 m.dwt transporting 5.5 mt per annum. Derivation of the estimate of containerized cargo can be found in Table 10.5

The difficulty of identifying bulk and general cargo trade from commodity trade statistics is very inconvenient for shipping economists, since seaborne trade data are collected mainly in this form and very little comprehensive information is available about cargo type. The only regular source of information about bulk cargo shipments is World Bulk Trades, published annually by Fearnleys of Oslo. On the basis of these statistics we can estimate that, out of a total seaborne trade of 4,506 mt in 1994, approximately two-thirds was bulk cargo and one-third was general cargo (see Table 1.2) although, since general cargo has a higher value and volume, its importance to the shipping industry is certainly understated by these statistics.

Although the distinction between bulk and general cargo is blurred in statistical terms, in the shipping market there is no such lack of clarity; the industry has evolved a totally different approach to the shipment of bulk cargo from that used to transport general cargo.

1.4 The world merchant fleet

The world merchant fleet grew from 9 m grt in 1860 to over 491 mgt in 1995 (Figure 1.5). In December 1995 the world fleet of self propelled sea-going merchant ships over 100 gross tons stood at 82,890 vessels with a capacity of 491 mgt. Within this total cargo-carrying vessels account for 95 per cent of the gross tonnage (465 mgt) but only 53 per cent of the numbers (43,802 vessels). The remaining 39,088 non-cargo-carrying vessels included 23,929 fishing boats, 2,845 offshore support vessels, 7,721 tugs, 818 research vessels, 1,125 dredgers and 2,650 other non-cargo vessels.

Types of ship in the cargo fleet

What sort of cargo carrying ships does the fleet consist of? During the last century there has been a steady flow of new ship designs developed to carry particular types of cargo, with the result that today there are many different categories of specialized vessels used in the shipping business. A few of the major innovations are shown in Figure 1.5, starting with the first bulk carrier in 1852. However, although some ship types are well defined, it is surprisingly difficult question to divide the fleet into clearly defined categories which provide a sound starting point for analysing supply. Merchant ships are not mass-produced like cars or trucks and few ships in the fleet are precisely the same. Most are designed to meet a specific owner's needs, so classifying ships into types relies on selecting distinctive physical characteristics which serve to identify the 'type' of ship when it is built. This approach has its limitations. For example oil tankers are readily identifiable from their hull structure, but 'products tankers' are not clearly defined as a separate group because they do not have any distinctive hull characteristics.

Lloyds Register of Shipping divide the cargo fleet into sixteen main categories of ship, mainly determined by the characteristics of the hull, as shown in Figure 1.6. The four biggest groups, which account for 78 per cent of the tonnage, are oil tankers, bulk carriers, general cargo ships and container ships. The eight other groups cover more specialized vessels, including combined carriers (which can carry oil or dry bulk), chemical tankers, gas tankers, ro-ro vessels, and refrigerated cargo vessels. The characteristics of these merchant ships is discussed in greater detail in Chapter 11.

However there is much more to analysing the supply of merchant ships than identifying ship types. Since ships have a life of twenty or thirty years, the fleet trading at a particular point in time is a diverse mixture of technology representing the cumulative investment decisions of several generations of shipowners. In recent years the design of ships has advanced enormously as technology has been adapted to improve the efficiency of vessels in these trades. Four aspects of this evolution deserve special mention, shipbuilding technology, economies of scale, cargo specialization and cargo handling. Each of these has played an important part in the industry's response to the challenge of providing cheaper and better transport.

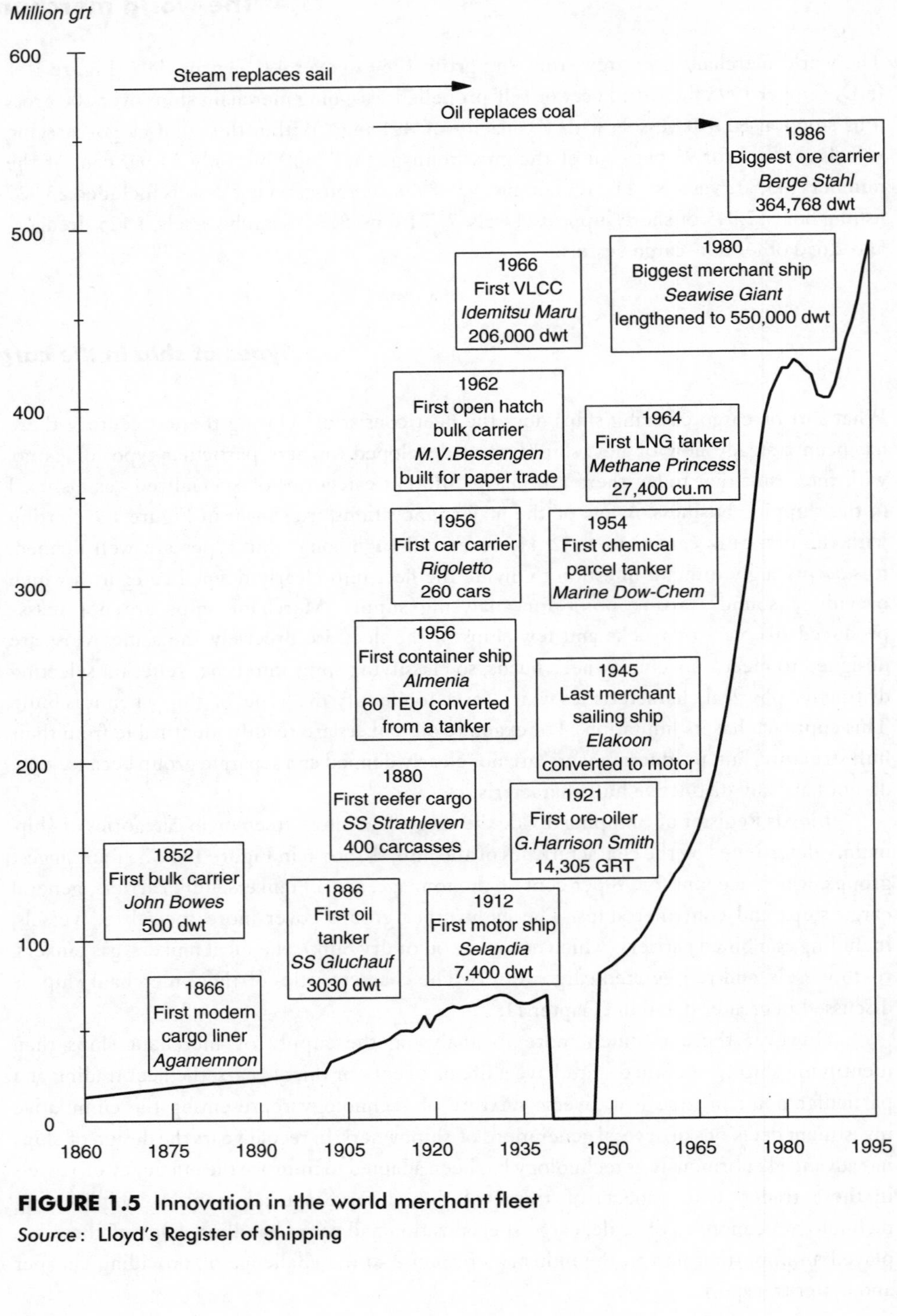
Million grt
600
500
400
300
200
100
0
Steam replaces sail
Oil replaces coal
1986
Biggest ore carrier
Berge Stahl
364,768 dwt
1980
Biggest merchant ship
Seawise Giant
lengthened to 550,000 dwt
1966
First VLCC
Idemitsu Maru
206,000 dwt
1962
First open hatch
bulk carrier
M.V.Bessengen
built for paper trade
1964
First LNG tanker
Methane Princess
27,400 cu.m
1956
First car carrier
Rigoletto
260 cars
1954
First chemical
parcel tanker
Marine Dow-Chem
1956
First container ship
Almenia
60 TEU converted
from a tanker
1945
Last merchant
sailing ship
Elakoon
converted to motor
1880
First reefer cargo
SS Strathleven
400 carcasses
1921
First ore-oiler
G.Harrison Smith
14,305 GRT
1852
First bulk carrier
John Bowes
500 dwt
1886
First oil
tanker
SS Gluchauf
3030 dwt
1912
First motor ship
Selandia
7,400 dwt
1866
First modern
cargo liner
Agamemnon
1860
1875
1890
1905
1920
1935
1950
1965
1980
1995

FIGURE 1.5 Innovation in the world merchant fleet

Source: Lloyd's Register of Shipping

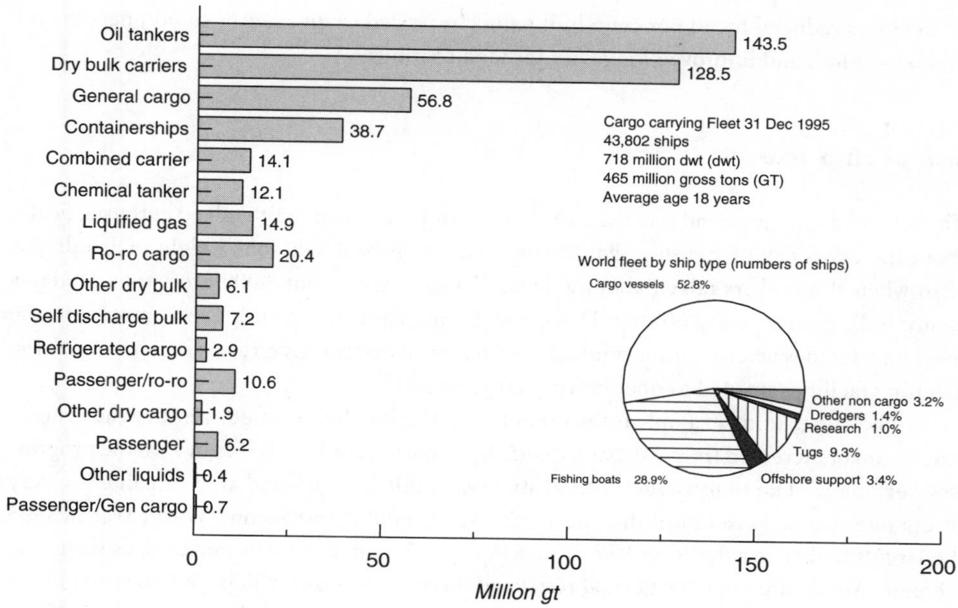

FIGURE 1.6 Ship types – cargo-carrying ships 31 December 1995
Source: Lloyd's Register of Shipping 'World Fleet Statistics'

Developments in ship design

The technical efficiency of merchant ships has grown with the technical capability of the shipbuilder, who constructs the hull, and the marine engineering industry which supplies machinery and equipment. Modern shipping started in the 1860s when shipbuilders were first able to build a commercially viable iron hulled steamship.[21] More efficient compound steam engines permitted long voyages and the iron hulls were more consistently watertight than their wooden predecessors. For the first time shipping became a business that could be planned and run to a timetable. Between 1880 and 1914 the steamers drove out the sailing ships. It was a hard fought battle spread over thirty years, with steamers forcing the sailing ships to the secondary routes and finally to the scrapyard. There were other technical changes along the way, though none so fundamental. The first deep sea diesel-powered ship, the *Selandia* went into service in 1912 and over the next fifty years the diesel engine replaced the steam engine, except in the largest ships. Welding started to replace rivets in hull construction and automation halved the number of crew required to man a deep sea vessel.

More recently the improvements, though less dramatic, have been equally real. Hatch designs, cargo handling gear, and navigation equipment all improved in efficiency. During the 1980s the fuel efficiency of diesel engines increased by 25 per cent. Shipbuilders became more adept at fine tuning hull designs, with the result that for some ship types the tonnage of steel was reduced by 30 per cent; hull paints improved to give better smoothness for the submerged hull and improved longevity for tank coatings.

The growth of ship size

The second dominant trend is in the size of ships. In 1776 Adam Smith talked enthusiastically about the efficiency of the ship that 'carries and brings back 200 tons weight of goods.' By 1876 when shipbrokers talked about a 'handy' vessel they meant 3,000 gross tons. Today a handy bulk carrier is 45,000 dwt. However, the increase of size has been greatest in the specialized trades where transport integration has provided the investment in ports and cargo handling facilities needed to operate very large vessels.

The outstanding example is the oil industry. During the twentieth century the average size of tanker increased from 4,000 tons to 95,000 tons (Figure 1.7). To begin with the progress was very slow. The *Narraganset,* 12,500 dwt was built in 1903 and this remained a very acceptable size of vessel until the late 1940s. At the end of the Second World War in 1945 the largest tanker was the *Nash Bulk* of 23,814 dwt. Then in the 1950s tanker sizes started to increase. At this time the Suez Canal restricted the size of tanker which could be used in the Middle East to Europe trade. The closure of the canal in 1956 and the rapid growth of the Japanese trade finally undermined this barrier to size and in the 1960s tanker sizes shot upwards. In 1959 the largest tanker afloat was the *Universe Apollo* 122,867 dwt. The first Very Large Crude Carrier (VLCC) the *Idemitsu Maru* followed in 1966 and the first Ultra Large

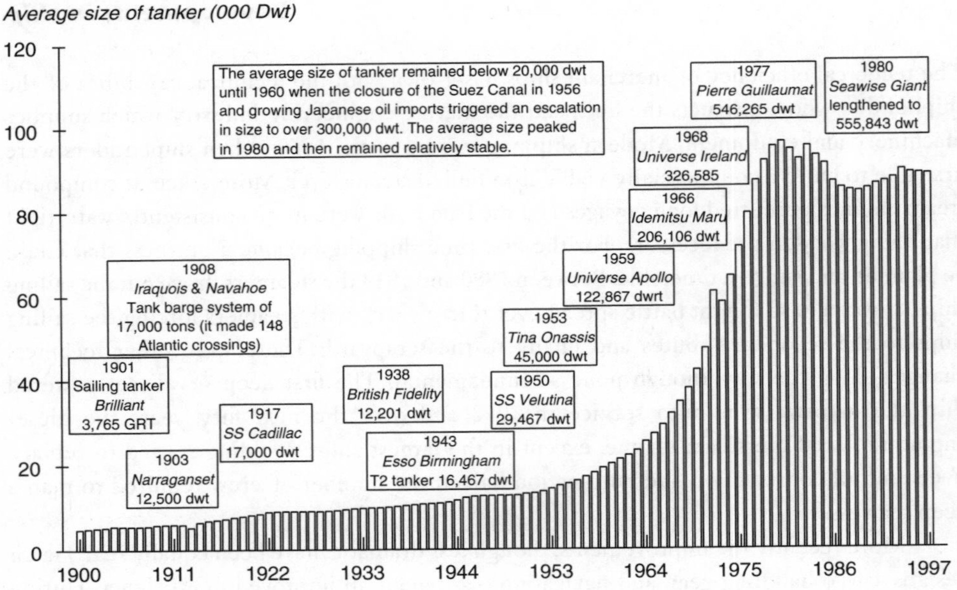

FIGURE 1.7 Average size of tanker 1900–97
Source: Compiled by Martin Stopford from various sources

Crude carrier (ULCC) in 1968. This upward trend reached its peak in 1980 when the *Seawise Giant* was extended to 555,843 dwt.[22] This increase in ship size had the effect of reducing unit shipping costs by at least 75 per cent.

In dry bulk shipping, the move into large bulk vessels was equally pronounced. Iron ore bulk transport started in the 1920s with the use of 24,000 dwt ore carriers.[23] By the 1970s vessels of 200,000 dwt were widely in use on the volume routes, while the first generation of 300,000 dwt vessels started to come into service in the mid-1980s. There was also a steady upward movement in the size of ships used for the transport of commodities such as grain, sugar, non-ferrous metal ores and forest products. Taking the grain trade as an example, in the late 1960s most of the grain shipped by sea was in vessels under 25,000 dwt.[24] It seemed inconceivable to shippers in the business that vessels of 60,000 dwt could ever be used extensively in the grain trade, although by the early 1980s this is precisely what had happened.

By capitalizing on economies of scale and developing integrated transport systems, bulk shipping has reduced transport costs to such an extent that it is often cheaper for industries to import raw materials by sea from suppliers several thousand miles away than by land from suppliers only a few hundred miles away.

Cargo specialization

Specialization is the cornerstone of economic development and this is precisely the path followed by the shipping industry. With each decade new ship types were developed to improve the transportation of specific cargoes, as shown in Figure 1.5. The first bulk carrier was designed in 1852, the first tanker in 1886, the first refrigerated vessel in 1880, the first combined carrier in 1925, the first chemical tanker in 1956, the first car carrier in 1956, and the first deep sea cellular container ship in 1965. All of these vessel types are represented in the fleet today in substantial numbers.

Some of the specialist vessels did not last the course. The outstanding example is the passenger liner, designed to carry passengers and mail at great speed. These vessels started to be built in the second half of the nineteenth century and reached their peak immediately before the First World War when cargo liners of 800 feet in length and capable of crossing the Atlantic in four days were constructed. After the Second World War this market was lost to air transport and the passenger liner disappeared from the seas. If nothing else, this illustrates the continuous ebb and flow of specialization within the shipping market.

The cargo handling revolution

Getting cargo in and out of the ship has always been a problem area, and one where major improvements have been made. New cargo handling techniques revolutionized the liner and bulk trades. Usually the cargo handling technology is more evident in the ports where investment in specialist terminals using high-speed cargo-handling gear forms an important part of the automation of cargo-handling systems. However in some trades the introduction of improved cargo-handling technology has resulted in a major change in the design of the ships.

The biggest change was in the liner trades where cellular container ships and, to a lesser extent, ro-ro vessels replaced conventional cargo liners. The container ships have box-shaped holds and cell guides which allow the containers to be dropped into place below deck, reducing loading times to a matter of minutes. Ro-ro ships provide access to the cargo holds by ramp, allowing wheeled vehicles such as fork lift trucks to load cargo at high speed.

Design changes in bulk shipping have been less spectacular, but just as important. Steel hatch covers with hydraulic opening mechanisms replaced the old system of canvas and batons. On some ships holds were widened to allow stowage of unitized bulks such as packaged lumber, steel coils, paper and cotton bales. Cranes replaced derricks.

Ageing, obsolescence and fleet replacement

The continuous progress in ship technology, combined with the costs of ageing which grow more evident over the twenty- or thirty-year life of a ship, present the shipping industry with an interesting economic problem. How do you decide when ships should be scrapped? Ageing and obsolescence are not clearly defined conditions. They are subtle and progressive. A great deal of trade is carried by ships which are obsolete in some way or other. It took fifty years for steam ships to drive sailing ships from the sea. Yet somehow the industry has to decide when to scrap the old ships and order new ones.

This is where the sale and purchase market comes in. When an owner has finished with a ship he sells it. Another shipping company buys it at a price which he believes he can make a profit. If no owner thinks he can make a profit, only the scrap dealer will bid. As the ship grows old or obsolete it trickles down the market, falling in value, until at some stage, usually between twenty and thirty years, it hits the demolition market. This whole process is eased forward by shipping market cycles. By driving freight rates and market sentiment sharply upwards (when new ships are ordered) and downwards (when old ships are scrapped) the cycles make poorly defined economic decisions much clearer. In case there is any doubt, it reinforces economics with sentiment. The decision to scrap a ship is much easier if the owner feels gloomy about the future. Thus, cycle by cycle, fleet replacement lurches forward. We discuss cycles in Chapter 2 and the four markets which are involved in the fleet replacement process in Chapter 3.

1.5 The supply of sea transport

How does the shipping market use all the ship types discussed in the last section to transport all the cargoes described in section 1.3? At first sight it is tempting to answer this question in terms of ship types – to say that bulk cargo goes in bulk carriers and general cargo goes in cargo liners. However, this answer would be highly misleading, since, as we shall see in the review of the world fleet in Chapter 11, shipping companies use the ships that are available and that offer the best profit. In fact one of the main functions of the shipping market mechanism is to match a sub-optimal fleet of ships to an ever changing pattern of cargo flows, with the minimum of waste.

The shipping industry unit cost function

Cost dominates the supply side of the shipping market and economies of scale dominate say that bulk cargo goes in bulk carriers and general cargo goes in the cost equation. An insight into the economics of providing sea transport can be obtained from the *unit cost function*, defined in the following terms:

$$\text{Unit Cost} = \frac{LC + OPEX + CH}{PS} \qquad \text{E1(1)}$$

The unit cost of transporting a ton of cargo in a particular ship depends on the capital cost of the ship (LC), the cost of operating the ship over its life ($OPEX$) and the cost of handling the cargo (CH) divided by the tonnage of cargo it can carry (PS). Unit costs generally fall as the size of the ship increases because capital, operating and cargo handling costs do not increase proportionally with the cargo capacity. For example a 280,000 dwt tanker only costs twice as much as an 80,000 dwt vessel but it carries more than three times as much cargo (we examine this in more detail in Chapter 4). Thus the cost of carrying very small cargo parcels is much higher than the cost of large parcels and economies of scale dominate shipping economics. As parcels become too small to occupy a whole ship the cost escalates further because of the high cost of handling and packing small parcels. For example, crude oil can be transported 12,000 miles from the Arabian Gulf to the USA for less than $1 per barrel using a 280,000 dwt tanker, whereas the cost of shipping a ton of lubricating oil from Europe to Singapore in a small parcel can be over $100.

The shape of the cost function is illustrated in Figure 1.8 which relates the cost per ton of cargo transported on the vertical axis to the parcel size on the horizontal axis. The shape of the cost function also shows how unit costs escalate as the parcel size falls below the size of a ship and the cargo slips into the liner transport system. There is clearly a tremendous incentive to ship in large quantities and it is the slope of the unit cost curve which creates the economic pressure which has driven parcel sizes upwards over the last century.

Liner and bulk shipping companies, who operate at opposite ends of the unit cost function, carry out fundamentally different tasks. Liner companies have to organize the transport of many small parcels and need a large shore-based staff capable of dealing with shippers, handling documentation and planning the ship loading and through transport operations. The bulk shipping industry, in contrast, handles fewer, but much larger cargoes. A large shore-based administrative staff is not required, but the few decisions that have to

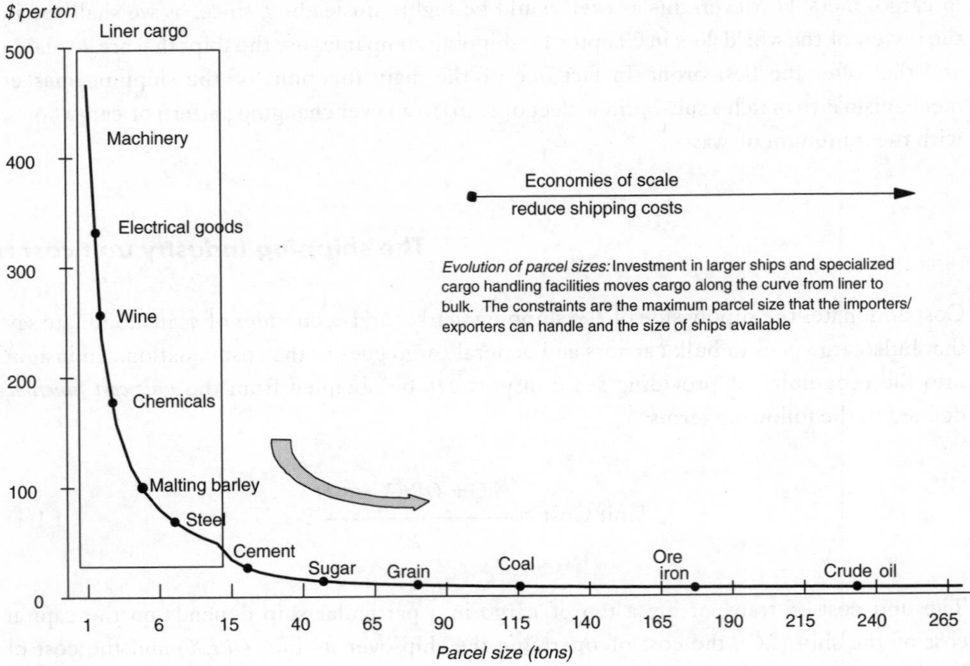

FIGURE 1.8 Shipping cost function
Source: Martin Stopford, 1997

be made are of crucial importance, so the owner or chief executive is generally intimately involved with the key decisions about buying, selling and chartering ships. In short, the type of organizations involved, the shipping policies, and even the type of people employed in the two parts of the business are quite different. The nature of the liner and bulk shipping industries is discussed in detail in Chapters 5 and 6, so the comments in this chapter are limited to providing an overview of these two principal sectors of the shipping market.

These differences in the nature of demand provide the basis for explaining the division of the shipping industry into two quite different sectors, the bulk shipping industry and the liner shipping industry. The bulk shipping industry is built around minimizing unit cost, while the liner shipping industry is more concerned with speed, reliability and quality of service.

The bulk shipping industry

The bulk shipping industry provides transport for cargoes that appear on the market in shiploads. The principle is 'one ship, one cargo', though we cannot be too rigid about this.

Several different bulk cargoes may be carried in a single ship, each occupying a separate hold or possibly even part of a hold in a traditional 'tramping operation', though this is less common than it used to be. A shipper with bulk cargo to transport can approach the task in several different ways, depending on the cargo itself and on the nature of the commercial operation – his choices range from total involvement by owning his own ships to handing the whole job over to a specialist bulk shipper.

Large companies shipping substantial quantities of bulk materials often run their own shipping fleets to handle a proportion of their transport requirements. For example, in 1995 the major oil companies collectively owned approximately 22.5 m.dwt of oil tankers, representing 8.5 per cent of the tanker fleet.[25] Steel companies in Japan and Europe also run fleets of large bulk carriers for the transport of iron ore and coal. This type of bulk shipping operation suits shippers running a stable and predictable through transport operation.

One of the first examples of modern dry bulk transportation was the construction for Bethlehem Steel of two ore carriers to carry iron ore from Peru to the newly constructed coastal steel plant in Baltimore, USA (see Chapter 9). The whole transport operation was designed to minimize transport costs for that particular plant and this pattern is still followed by heavy industrial operations importing bulk cargo. Similarly in the 1970s, two 90,000 dwt bauxite carriers were purpose-built to carry bauxite from Australia to a newly constructed alumina plant in Sardinia, Western Europe. In both cases the ships were optimized to provide precisely the material flow required by the plant at the minimum cost. However, industrial conglomerates do not necessarily become shipowners just to optimize the shipping operation. It is also necessary to ensure that basic transport requirements are met at a predictable cost without the need to resort to the vagaries of the charter market. The main problem is the capital investment required.[26]

If the shipper has a long-term requirement for bulk transport but does not wish to become actively involved as a shipowner, he may charter tonnage on a long-term basis from a shipowner. Some companies place charters for ten or fifteen years to provide a base load of shipping capacity to cover long-term material-supply contracts – particularly in the iron ore trade. For example, the Japanese shipping company Mitsui OSK ships iron ore for Sumitomo, Nippon Kokan and Nippon Steel on the basis of long-term cargo guarantees and operates a fleet of ore carriers and combined carriers to provide this service. In the early 1980s the company was carrying about 20 per cent of Japanese iron ore imports.[27] In such cases, the contract is generally placed before the vessel is actually built. Shorter-term time charters for twelve months or three to five years would be obtained on the charter market.

However, many shippers have only a single cargo to transport. This is often the case in agricultural trades such as grain and sugar where seasonal factors and the volatility of the market make it difficult to plan shipping requirements in advance, or the cargo could be a consignment of prefabricated buildings for the Middle East or some heavy plant. In such cases, bulk or multi-deck tonnage is chartered for a single voyage via some market such as the Baltic Exchange, where the shipper can hire a ship for a single voyage at a negotiated freight rate per ton of cargo carried.

Finally, the shipper may enter into a long-term arrangement with a shipowner who specializes in a particular area of bulk shipping supported by suitable tonnage. For example,

Scandinavian shipowners such as Star Shipping or the Gearbulk group are heavily involved in the carriage of forest products from West Coast North America to Europe and run fleets of specialist ships designed to optimize the bulk transportation of forest products. Similarly, the transportation of motor cars is serviced by companies such as Wallenius Lines, which runs a fleet of pure vehicle carriers servicing the Japanese car export trade.

The service offered in specialist bulk trades involves adherence to precise timetables, using ships with a high cargo capacity and fast cargo handling. Such an operation requires close cooperation between the shipper and the shipowner, the latter offering a better service because he is servicing the whole trade rather than just one customer. Naturally, this type of operation occurs only in trades where investment in specialist tonnage can provide a significant cost reduction or quality improvement as compared with use of general-purpose bulk tonnage.

Many different ship types are used for bulk transport but the main ones fall into four groups: tankers, general-purpose dry bulk carriers, combined carriers and specialist bulk vessels. The tankers and bulk carriers are generally of fairly standard design, while combined carriers offer the opportunity to carry dry bulk or liquid cargo. Specialist vessels are constructed to meet specific characteristics of difficult cargoes. All of these ship types are reviewed in detail in Chapter 11.

The liner shipping industry

Liner services provide transport for cargoes that are too small to fill a single ship and need to be grouped with others for transportation. The ships operate a regular advertised service between ports, carrying cargo at fixed prices for each commodity, though discounts may be offered to regular customers. The transport of a mass of small items on a regular service faces the liner operator with a more complex administrative task than the one facing the bulk shipowner. The liner operator must be able to:

- offer a regular service for many small cargo consignments and process the associated mass of paperwork;
- charge individual consignments on a fixed tariff basis that yields an overall profit – not an easy task when many thousands of consignments must be processed each week;
- load the cargo/container into the ship in a way that ensures that it is accessible for discharge (bearing in mind that the ship will call at many ports) and that the ship is 'stable' and 'in trim';
- run the service to a fixed schedule while allowing for all the normal delays – arising from adverse weather, breakdowns, strikes, etc.; and
- plan tonnage availability to service the trades, including the repair and maintenance of existing vessels, the construction of new vessels and the chartering-in of additional vessels to meet cyclical requirements, and to supplement the company's fleet of owned vessels.

All of this is management intensive and explains why, in commercial terms, the liner business is a different world from bulk shipping. The skills, expertise and organizational requirements are very different.

Because of their high overheads and the need to maintain a regular service even when a full payload of cargo is not available, the liner business is particularly vulnerable to marginal cost pricing by other shipowners operating on the same trade routes. To overcome this, liner companies developed the 'conference system', which was first tried out in the Britain to Calcutta trade in 1875. In the 1980s there were about 350 shipping conferences operating on both deep sea and short sea routes. However, the prolonged market recession in the 1980s, the changes brought about by containerization and regulatory intervention weakened the system to such an extent that liner operators started to look for other ways of stabilizing their competitive position. Liner operations are discussed extensively in Chapter 10.

1.6 The role of ports in the transport system

There is a third component in the transport system which is just as important as the merchant fleet. Ports are the crucial interface between land and sea. It is here that much of the real activity takes place. In the days of cargo liners and tramps the activity was obvious. Ports were crowded with ships and bustling with dockers loading and unloading cargo. Artists loved to paint these busy scenes and the waterfronts were famous for the entertainment they provided to sailors during their long portcalls. Anyone could see what was going on. Modern ports are more subtle. Today, ships make fleeting calls at highly automated and apparently deserted terminals, sometimes stopping only a few hours to load or discharge cargo. The activity is less obvious but much more intense. Cargo handling speeds today are many times higher than they were twenty or thirty years ago.

Before discussing ports we must define three terms 'port', 'port authority' and 'terminal'. A *Port* is a geographical area where ships are brought alongside land to load and discharge cargo – usually a sheltered deep water area such as a bay or river mouth. The *Port Authority* is the organization responsible for providing the various maritime services required to bring ships alongside land. Ports may be public bodies, government organizations or private companies. One Port Authority may control several ports, e.g., Saudi Ports Authority. Finally, *terminal* is a section of the port consisting of one or more berths devoted to a particular type of cargo handling. Thus we have coal terminals, container terminals, etc. Terminals may be owned and operated by the port authority, or by a shipping company which operates the terminal for its exclusive use.

Ports have several important functions which are crucial to the efficiency of the ships which trade between them. Their main purpose is to provide a secure location where ships can berth. However, this is just the beginning. Improved cargo handling requires investment in shore-based facilities. If bigger ships are to be used, ports must be built with deep water in the approach channels and at the berths. Of equal importance is cargo handling, one of the key elements in system design. A versatile port must be able to handle different cargoes

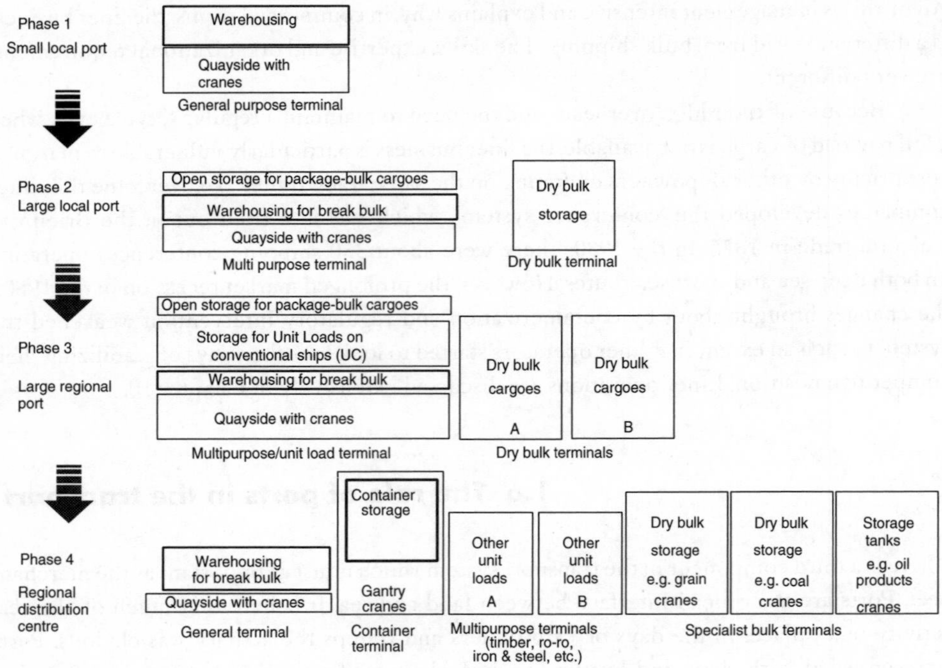

FIGURE 1.9 Four levels of port development
Source: Martin Stopford, 1997

– bulk, containers, wheeled vehicles, general cargo and passengers all require different facilities. There is also the matter of providing storage facilities for inbound and outbound cargoes. Finally, land transport systems must be efficiently integrated into the port operations. Railways, roads and inland waterways converge on ports and these transport links must be managed efficiently.

Port improvement plays a major part in reducing sea transport costs. Some of this technical development is carried out by the shipping companies who construct special terminals for their trade, or shippers such as oil companies and steel mills. For example, the transfer of grain transport from small vessels of 20–30,000 dwt to vessels of 60,000 dwt and above depended upon the construction of grain terminals with bulk handling and storage facilities. Similarly the introduction of container services required container terminals. However the port industry provides much of the investment itself. It has its own marketplace which is every bit as competitive as the shipping markets. The ports within a region are locked in cut-throat competition to attract the cargo moving to inland destinations or for distribution within the region. Hoong Kong competes with Singapore for the Far East container distribution trade. Rotterdam has established itself as the premier European port in competition with Hamburg, Bremen, Antwerp and, in earlier times, Liverpool. Investment in facilities plays a key part in the competitive process.

The facilities provided in a port depend on the type and volume of cargo which is in transit. As trade changes, so do the ports. There is no such thing as a typical port. Each has a mix of facilities designed to meet the trade of the region it serves. However, it is possible to generalize about the type of port facilities which can be found in different areas. As an example four types of port complex are shown in Figure 1.9, representing four different levels of activity. In very rough terms, the blocks in these diagrams represent, in width, the number of facilities or length of quay wall, and in height, the annual throughput of each.

- *Type 1 Small local port*: Around the world there are thousands of small ports serving local trade. They handle varied cargo flows, often serviced by short sea vessels. Since the trade volume is small the facilities are basic, consisting of general purpose berths backing on to warehouses. Only small ships can be accommodated and the port probably handles a mixture of containers, break-bulk cargo plus shipments of commodities in packaged form (e.g. part loads of wheat in bags, or oil in drums) or shipped loose and packaged in the hold prior to discharge. Cargo is unloaded from the ship on to the quayside and stored in the warehouses, or on the quayside until collected. Ports like this are found in the developing countries and in the rural areas of developed countries.
- *Type 2 Large local port*: When cargo is higher, special investment becomes economic. For example, if the volume of grain and fertilizers increases a dry bulk terminal may be constructed with the deeper draft required to handle bigger bulk carriers (e.g. up to 35,000 dwt), a quayside with grab cranes, apron space to stack cargo, railway lines and truck access. At the same time the break-bulk facilities may be expanded to handle regular container traffic, for example, by purchasing container handling equipment and strengthening the quayside.
- *Type 3 Large regional port*: Ports handling high volumes of deep sea cargo require heavy investment in specialized terminal facilities. Unit loads such as pallets, containers or packaged timber are handled in sufficient volume to justify a unit load terminal with cargo handling gear such as gantry cranes, fork lift trucks and storage space for unit load cargo. For high volume commodity trades, moving in volumes of several mt a year, special terminals may be built (e.g. coal, grain, oil products terminals) capable of taking the bigger ships of 60,000 dwt and above used in the deep sea bulk trades.
- *Type 4 Regional distribution centres*: Regional ports have a wider role as distribution centres for cargo shipped deep sea in very large ships, and requiring distribution to smaller local ports. This type of port, of which Rotterdam, Hong Kong and Singapore are prime examples, consists of a federation of specialist terminals, each dedicated to a particular cargo. Containers are handled in container terminals; unit load terminals cater for timber, iron and steel and ro/ro cargo. Homogeneous bulk cargoes such as grain, iron, coal, cement and oil products are handled in purpose built terminals, often run by the cargo owner. There are excellent facilities for trans-shipment by sea, rail, barge or road.

Ports and terminals earn income by charging ships for the use of their facilities. Leaving aside competitive factors, port charges must cover unit costs and these have a fixed and variable element. The shipowner may be charged in two ways, an 'all in' rate where, apart from some minor ancillary services, everything is included; or an 'add-on' rate where the shipowner pays a basic charge to which extras are added for the various services used by the ship during its visit to the port. The method of charging will depend upon the type of cargo operation but both will vary according to volume, with trigger points activating tariff changes.

1.7 The shipping companies who run the business

Who makes the decisions?

Perhaps the most striking aspect of the shipping business to an outsider is the totally different character of the companies in different parts of the industry. For example liner companies and bulk shipping companies belong to the same industry, but they seem to have little else in common, a fact we shall discuss more extensively in later parts of the book.

Within the bulk and liner shipping industries there are many different types of business, each with its own distinctive organizational structure, commercial aims and strategic objectives. Consider the examples in Box 1.2. This is by no means an exhaustive account of the different types of shipowning companies, but it illustrates the diversity of organizational types to be found and, more importantly, the different pressures and constraints on management decision-making.

The Greek shipowner with the private company runs a small tight organization over which he has total autocratic control – he makes all the decisions and has a direct personal interest in their outcome. In fact, the number of important decisions he makes is quite small, being concerned with the sale and purchase of ships and decisions about whether to tie vessels up on long time charters. He is a free agent, dependent on his own resources to raise finance and beat the odds in the marketplace.

The other examples show larger structures where the top management are more remote from the day-to-day operation of the business and are subject to many institutional pressures and constraints in operating and developing the business. The container company has a large and complex office staff and agency network to manage, so there is an unavoidable emphasis on administration. The oil company division reports to a main board, whose members know little about the shipping business and do not always share the objectives of the management of the shipping division. The shipping corporate is under pressure from its high profile with shareholders and its vulnerability to take-over during periods when they market does not allow a proper return on capital employed. Each company is different and this influences the way it approaches the market.

1.8 Politics versus economics in shipping

Finally, however hard we try to develop the analysis in economic terms, shipping is an international business and the economic forces that make it so significant in economic terms

Box 1.2 Examples of typical shipping company structures

Private bulk company A tramp company owned by two Greek brothers. They run a fleet of five ships, three products tankers and two small bulk carriers. The company has a two-room office in the West End of London run by a chartering manager with a telex and a part-time secretary. Its main office is in Athens where two or three staff do the accounts and administration and sort out any problems. Three of the ships are on time charters and two are on the spot market. One of the brothers is now more or less retired and all the important decisions are taken by the other brother who knows from experience that the real profits are made from buying and selling ships rather than from trading them on the charter market.

Shipping corporate A liner company in the container business. The company operates a fleet of around twenty container ships from a large modern office block housing about 1,000 staff. All major decisions are taken by the main board, which consists of twelve executive board members along with representatives of major stockholders. In addition to the head office, the company runs an extensive network of local offices and agencies who look after their affairs in the various ports. The head office has large departments dealing with ship operations, marketing, secretariat, personnel and legal. In total the company has 3,500 people on its payroll, 2,000 shore staff and 1,500 sea staff.

Shipping division The shipping division of an international oil company. The company has a policy of transporting 30–40 per cent of its oil shipments in company-owned vessels, and the division is responsible for all activities associated with the acquisition and operation of these vessels. There is a divisional board, which is responsible for day-to-day decisions, but major decisions about the sale and purchase of ships or any change in the activities undertaken by the division must be approved by the main board. Each year the vice-president is responsible for submitting a corporate plan to the board, summarizing the division's business objectives and setting out its operating plans and financial forecasts. In particular, company regulations lay down that any items of capital expenditure in excess of $2 million must have main board approval. Currently the division is running a fleet of ten very large crude carriers (VLCCs) and thirty-six small tankers from an organization that occupies several floors in one of the company's office blocks.

Diversified shipping group A company which started in shipping but has now acquired other interests. It runs a fleet of more that sixty ships from offices on the outskirts of London, where it was relocated when the group sold its prestige City office block. The company is quoted on the London Stock Market and the majority of shares are owned by institutional investors, so its financial and managerial performance is closely followed by investment analysts who specialize in shipping. The company is organized into divisions, with a bulk shipping division, a liner shipping division and a division running cruise ships. In recent years the problems of operating in the highly cyclical shipping market have resulted in strenuous efforts to diversify into other activities. Recently the company was the subject of a major takeover bid, which was successfully resisted but management is under constant pressure to increase the return on capital employed in the business.

Semi-public shipping group A Scandinavia shipping company started by a Norwegian who purchased small tankers in the early 1920s. Although it is quoted on the Stock Exchange, the family still owns a controlling interest in the company. Since the Second World War the company has followed a strategy of progressively moving into more sophisticated markets, and it is involved in liner shipping, oil tankers, and the carriage of specialist bulk cargoes such as motor vehicles and forest products, in both of which markets it has succeeded in winning a sizable market share and a reputation for quality and reliability of service. To improve managerial control the tanker business was recently floated as a separate company. The company runs a large fleet of modern merchant ships designed to give high cargo handling performance, and is based in an Oslo office with a sizable staff.

also make it the subject of national and international political intervention. The Rochdale Report we referred to in section 1.1 concluded its definition of the shipping industry with the comment:

> Most of the industry's business is concerned with international trade and inevitably it operates within a complicated world pattern of agreements between shipping companies, understandings with shippers and policies of governments.[28]

Such matters cannot be ignored. Over the last hundred years the maritime industry has seen an escalation of political involvement. From the Plimsoll Act (1870) which stopped ships being overloaded, to the US Oil Pollution Act (1990) which set out stringent regulations and liabilities for tankers trading in US national waters, politicians have sought to limit the actions of shipowners. Interest in subjects such as safety at sea, crew regulations, environmental pollution and the physical condition of ships have all increased in the 1990s.

Just as these subjects cannot easily be understood without some knowledge of the maritime economic framework within which the game is being played out, an economic analysis cannot ignore the political influences on costs, prices and free market competition.

1.9 Summary

In this chapter we have concentrated on the shipping market as a whole. During the last fifty years the cost of transporting major commodities by sea has fallen steadily. Our aim is to show how this has been achieved and how the different parts of the shipping market – the liner business, bulk shipping, the charter market, etc. – fit together. We have discussed market organization and the economic mechanisms which match a diverse fleet of merchant ships to an equally diverse but constant changing pattern of seaborne trade.

Because shipping is a service business, ship demand depends on several factors including price, speed, reliability and security. It starts from the volume of trade and we discussed how the commodity trades can be analysed by dividing them into groups which share economic characteristics such as energy, agricultural trades, metal industry trades, forest products trades and other industrial manufactures. However to explain how transport is organized we introduced the parcel size distribution. The shape of the PSD function varies from one commodity to another. The key distinction is between 'bulk cargoes', which enters the market in ship size consignments and 'general cargo', which consists of many small quantities of cargo have to be grouped for shipment.

Bulk cargo is transported on a 'one ship, one cargo' basis, generally using bulk carriers. Where trade flows are predictable, for example, servicing a steel mill, fleets of ships may be built for the trade or vessels chartered in on a long-term basis. Some shipping companies also run bulk shipping services geared to the transport of special cargoes such as forest products and cars. For trades such as grain where the quantities and routes are unpredictable, tonnage is drawn from the charter market. To meet marginal fluctuations in demand, or for trades such as grain where the quantities and routes over which cargo will be transported are unpredictable, tonnage is drawn from the charter market.

General cargo, either loose or unitized, is transported by liner services which offer regular transport, accepting any cargo at a fixed tariff. In the mid-1960s the liner trades were containerized, which turned loose general cargo into a homogeneous commodity which could be handled in bulk. This changed the ships used in the liner trades, with cellular container ships replacing the diverse fleet of cargo liners. However the complexity of handling many small consignments remained and the liner business remained distinct from the bulk shipping business. They do, however, go to the charter market to obtain ships to meet marginal trading requirements.

Sea transport is carried out by a fleet of 80,000 ships, of which about 25,000 carry cargo in the deep sea trades. Since technology is constantly changing and ships gradually wear out, the fleet is never optimum. It is a resource which the shipping market uses in the most profitable way it can. Once they are built, ships 'trickle down' the economic ladder until no shipowner is prepared to buy them for trading, when they are scrapped. The management of the supply of sea transport falls into two industrial segments, the bulk shipping industry which transports ship-sized parcels, and the liner shipping industry which transports small cargo parcels. They have different tasks, which they approach in totally different ways.

Ports play a vital part in the transport process. Automation of cargo handling and investment in specialist terminals have transformed the business.

Finally, we discussed the organization of the companies that run the business. They have very varied organization and decision-making structures, a fact which market analysts are well advised to remember.

Chapter 2

The shipping market cycle

The philanthropy of this great body of traders, the shipowners, is evidently inexhaustible, for after five years of unprofitable work, their energy is as unflagging as ever, and the amount of tonnage under construction and on order guarantees a long continuance of present low freight rates, and an effectual check against increased cost of overseas carriage.

J.C.Gould, Angier & Co, 31 December 1894

2.1 Shipping cycles and shipping risk

The market cycle pervades the shipping industry. As one shipowner put it 'When I wake up in the morning and freight rates are high I feel good. When they are low I feel bad.'[1] Just as the weather dominates the lives of seafarers, so the waves of the shipping cycle ripple through the financial lives of shipowners.

Considering the sums of money involved, it is hardly surprising that the shipping cycle is so prominent. If we take the transport of grain from the US Gulf to Rotterdam as an example, a Panamax bulk carrier of 65,000 dwt trading on the spot market could have earned, after operating expenses, about $1 million in 1986, $3.5 million in 1989, $1.5 million in 1992 and $2.5 million in 1995. The ship itself, a five-year-old Panamax, would have cost $6 million in 1986 and $22 million in 1989. Yet in 1994 it was still worth $22 million. In such a volatile environment the timing of decisions about buying, selling and chartering ships are crucial.

This is not just a problem for shipowners. Businesses with cargo to transport face the same risks. The cost of transporting about half a mt of grain from the US Gulf to Japan increased from $5.2 million in 1986 to $12.7 million in 1989. A very substantial increase.

The definition of 'shipping risk'

An important first step in understanding the shipping cycle is to recognize that it is there for a purpose. Cycles play a central part in the economics of the shipping industry by managing the risk of shipping investment in a business where there is great uncertainty about the future.

The whole process starts from the question: 'Who takes the shipping risk?' A merchant ship is a large and expensive item of capital equipment. In a world where the volume of trade is constantly changing, someone has to decide when to order new ships and when to scrap old ones. If ships are not built but trade grows, eventually business will grind to a halt. Oil companies could not ship their oil, steel mills run out of iron ore and manufactured exports would pile up in the factories and ports. The lucky owners of the few available ships would auction them to the highest bidder and make their fortunes. However, if ships are built and trade does not grow, it is a very different story. With no cargo, the expensive ships sit idle while the unfortunate investors watch their investment rust away.

This, in essence, is 'shipping risk' and it is what the shipping cycle is all about. When the risk is taken by the cargo owner this leads to an 'industrial shipping' business in which shipowners are subcontractors and cost minimizers. When the 'shipping risk' is left to the shipowner, the business becomes highly speculative. It is the world's biggest poker game, in which the ships are the chips. The analogy with poker is in some ways very appropriate. Players must know the rules, and later chapters are devoted to the economic rules of the shipping game. However winning at the shipping game, like poker, also depends on probability, strategy, psychology and luck. This chapter is devoted to these commercial realities of the game.

'Industrial shipping': the shipper takes the shipping risk

When shippers are confident about how much cargo they will need to transport in future, or if they feel that transport is of too great strategic importance to be left to chance, they may decide to take the shipping risk themselves. Shipping operations may be carried out with an owned fleet, or by pre-construction time charters with independent shipowners, if this is found to be a more cost-effective solution. With the assurance of cargo, the owners purchase ships and try to make a living by keeping costs below the contract margins.

This type of operation is often known as 'industrial shipping'. Raw materials such as iron ore, coal, bauxite, non-ferrous metal ores and coal for steel mills and power stations are shipped in this way. A common arrangement used by the Japanese in developing their heavy industry was the 'tie-in' ships or *shikumisen.* Japanese shipping companies arranged for ships to be built for foreign owners in Japanese yards. The companies then chartered the ships on a long-term basis.[2]

Industrial shipping is a policy, not a requirement. The oil industry provides a good example of how policies can change with circumstances. In the 1950s and 1960s it was the policy of the major oil companies to own enough tankers to cover between one-third and two-thirds of their requirements and to charter tankers long-term to cover most of the balance. This left only 5 to 10 per cent of their needs to be covered from the voyage charter market.[3]

After the oil crisis in 1973 the oil trade became more volatile and much of the oil transport passed to oil traders who had little incentive to plan for the future. As a result of these changes oil shippers started to rely more heavily on the voyage market. The amount of oil cargo shipped in vessels hired on the freight market increased from 10–15 per cent in the early 1970s to 50 per cent by the late 1980s and the proportion of independent tanker owners trading as subcontractors (i.e. on time charter) fell from 80 per cent to about 25 per cent.

Industrial shipping makes shipowners subcontractors rather than risk takers. This was the view of Xannetos (1972) who commented that 'I know of few industries that are less risky than the oil tankship transportation business. Relatively predictable total requirements, time-charter agreements, and, because of the latter, availability of capital mitigate the risks involved in the industry.'[4] In this business the challenge is to win the contract and deliver the service at a cost which leaves the shipowner with a profit. Although the shipowner is freed from market risk, that does not remove all risk. Charterers strike a hard bargain and the owner is subject to inflation, exchange rates, the mechanical performance of the ship and, of course, the ability of the shipper to pay his hire.

The freight market: shipowners take the 'shipping risk'

In some circumstances the shippers prefer to leave independent shipowners to take the shipping risk and to rely on hiring ships from the market when they are needed. There are many industries, notably agricultural cargoes such as grain and sugar, where shippers never know how many cargoes they will have in future or how many ships will be needed. So they go to the freight market and hire transport when they need it. They pay a price for this. Sometimes the freight is cheap and sometimes it is expensive, but at least the ships are available.

Shipowners trading on the spot market make their living by taking a 'shipping risk'. They back their judgement that the ships they buy will be in demand and provide a worthwhile return on capital. With so much at stake, it is no surprise that the 'shipping cycle' occupies much the same position in the shipping market as the dealer in a poker game. It has the undivided attention of the players, dangling the prospect of riches at the turn of each card, as they struggle through the dismal recessions which have occupied much of the last century. For investors with a taste for gambling and with access to finance, it requires only an office, a telex, and a small number of buy, sell or charter decisions, to make, or lose, a substantial fortune[5]. In this chapter we will study the long and short shipping cycles over a period of more than a century, to determine their character and whether they are regular or predictable.

2.2 Characteristics of shipping market cycles

Shipping analyst's view of short cycles

Cycles are not unique to shipping. They occur in many industries and in the economy as a whole. Economic historians have devoted much effort to analysing and classifying cycles into categories, usually focusing on their length. Many different types of cycle have been identified. The *Kitchen* is a short cycle of 3–4 years; the *Juglar* lasts 6–8 years; the *Labrousse* can last 10 or 12 years; the *Kuznets* lasts 20 years, while a *Kondratieff* spreads over a half century or more.[6] In shipping the existence of cycles has long been accepted as part of the shipping business. In January 1901 a broker noted in his annual report that 'the comparison of the last four cycles (10 year periods) brings out a marked similarity in the salient features of each component year, and the course of prices'. He went on to observe that the cycles seemed to be getting longer 'a further retrospect shows that in the successive decades the periods of inflation gradually shrink, while the periods of depression correspondingly stretch out'.[7]

Although the length of cycles is of great interest, it soon became evident to observers of the shipping business that the cycles were far more complex than a sequence of regular fluctuations in freight rates. Kirkaldy (1913),[8] saw the cycle as a consequence of the market mechanism. The peaks and troughs in the cycle are signs that the market is adjusting supply to demand by regulating the cashflow:

> With the great development of ocean transport, which commenced about half a century ago, competition became very much accentuated. As the markets became increasingly normal, and trade progressively regular, there was from time to time more tonnage available at a given port than there was cargo ready for shipment. With unlimited competition this led to the cutting of rates, and at times shipping had to be run at a loss. The result was that shipping became an industry enjoying very fluctuating prosperity. Several lean years would be followed by a series of prosperous years. The

> wealthy ship-owner could afford to put the good years against the bad, and strike an average; a less fortunate colleague after perhaps enjoying a prosperous time, would be unable to face the lean years, and have to give up the struggle.

Viewed in this way, shipping market cycles have a purpose. They create the environment in which weak shipping companies are forced out, leaving the strong to survive and prosper, fostering a lean and efficient shipping business.

While Kirkaldy dwelt on the competition between owners and the part played by cashflow pressures, E.E Fayle (1933)[9] had more to say about the mechanics of the cycle. He suggested that the build-up of a cycle is triggered by the world business cycle or random events such as wars which create a shortage of ships. The resulting high freight rates attract new investors into the industry, and encourage a flood of speculative investment, thus expanding shipping capacity:

> The extreme elasticity of tramp shipping, the ease with which new-comers can establish themselves, and the very wide fluctuations of demand, make the ownership of tramp steamers one of the most speculative forms of all legitimate business. A boom in trade or a demand for shipping for military transport (as during the South African War) would quickly produce a disproportion between supply and demand; sending freight soaring upwards. In the hope of sharing the profits of the boom, owners hastened to increase their fleet and new owners come into the business. The world's tonnage was rapidly increased to a figure beyond the normal requirements, and the short boom was usually followed by a prolonged slump.

This perception of the cycle suggests a sequence of three events, a trade boom, a short shipping boom during which there is overbuilding, followed by a 'prolonged' slump. However Fayle is not confident about the sequence, since he says the boom is 'usually' followed by a prolonged slump. He thought the tendency of the cycles to overshoot the mark could be attributed to the lack of barriers to entry. Once again the cycle is more about people than statistics.

Forty years later Cufley (1972) also drew attention to the sequence of three key events common to shipping cycles. First, a shortage of ships develops, second, high freight rates stimulate over-ordering of the ships in short supply which finally leads to market collapse and recession.

> The main function of the freight market is to provide a supply of ships for that part of world trade which, for one reason or another, does not lend itself to long-term freighting practices ... In the short term this is achieved by the interplay of market forces through the familiar cycle of booms and slumps. When a shortage of ships develops rising freights lead to a massive construction of new ships. There comes a point either when demand subsides or when deliveries of new vessels overtake a still increasing demand. At this stage freights collapse, vessels are condemned to idleness in laying up berths.

An elegant definition of the cycle as the process by which the market co-ordinates supply with changes in demand by means of the familiar cycle of booms and slumps. However, Cufley is convinced that the cycle is too irregular to predict. He goes on to say:

> Any attempt to make long-term forecasts of voyage freights (as distinct from interpreting the general trend in growth of demand) is doomed to failure. It is totally impossible to predict when the open market will move upwards (or fall), to estimate the extent of the swing or the duration of the phase.[10]

Finally Hampton (1991) in his analysis of long[11] and short shipping cycles emphasizes the important part played by people and the way they respond to price signals received from the market:

> In today's modern shipping market it is easy to forget that a drama of human emotions is played out in market movements . . . In the shipping market, price movements provide the cues. Changes in freight rates or ship prices signal the next round of investment decisions. Freight rates work themselves higher and trigger orders. Eventually excess orders undermine freight rates. Lower freight rates stall orders and encourage demolition. At the low point in the cycle, reduced ordering and increased demolition shrink the supply and set the stage for a rise in freight rates. The circle revolves.[12]

Hampton goes on to argue that market sentiment plays an important part in determining the structure of cycles and that this can help to explain why the market repeatedly seems to over-react to the price signals.

> In any market including the shipping market, the participants are caught up in a struggle between fear and greed. Because we are human beings, influenced to varying degrees by those around us, the psychology of the crowd feeds upon itself until it reaches an extreme that cannot be sustained. Once the extreme has been reached, too many decisions have been made out of emotion and a blind comfort which comes from following the crowd rather than objective fact.

All these descriptions of the shipping cycle have a common theme. They describe it as a mechanism devoted to removing imbalances in the supply and demand for ships. If there is too little supply, the market rewards investors with high freight rates until more ships are ordered. When there are too many ships it squeezes the cashflow until owners give up the struggle and ships are scrapped. Looked at in this way the length of the cycles is incidental. They last as long as is necessary to do the job. It is possible to classify them by length, but this is not very helpful as a forecasting aid. If investors decide that an upturn is due and decide not to scrap their ships, the cycle just lasts longer. Since shipowners are constantly trying to second guess the cycle, crowd psychology gives each cycle a distinctive character. Yet another reason why the cycles are irregular.

Box 2.1 Stages in the shipping market cycle

Stage 1: Trough We can identify three characteristics of a trough. First, there will be evidence of surplus shipping capacity. Ships queue up at loading points and vessels at sea slow steam to save fuel and delay arrival. Secondly freight rates fall to the operating cost of the least efficient ships in the fleet which move into layup. Thirdly, sustained low freight rates and tight credit create a negative net cashflow which becomes progressively greater. Shipping companies short of cash are forced to sell ships at distress prices, since there are few buyers. The price of old ships falls to the scrap price, leading to active demolition market.
Stage 2: Recovery As supply and demand move towards balance, the first positive sign of a recovery is positive increase in freight rates above operating costs, followed by a fall in laid up tonnage. Market sentiment remains uncertain and unpredictable. Spells of optimism alternate with profound doubts about whether a recovery is really happening (sometimes the pessimists are right, as shown by the false recovery in periods 7 to 9 in Figure 2.1). As liquidity improves second-hand prices rise and sentiment firms.
Stage 3: Peak/Plateau When all the surplus has been absorbed the market enters a phase where supply and demand are in tight balance. Freight rates are high, often two or three times operating costs. The peak may last a few weeks or several years, depending on the balance of supply/demand pressures. Only untradeable ships are laid up; the fleet operates at full speed; owners become very liquid; banks are keen to lend; the press report the prosperous shipping business; there are public flotations of shipping companies. Secondhand prices move above 'book value' and prompt modern ships may sell for more than the newbuilding price. The shipbuilding orderbook expands, slowly at first, then more rapidly.
Stage 4: Collapse When supply overtakes demand the market moves into the collapse phase. Although the downturn is generally caused by fundamental factors such as the business cycle, the clearing of port congestion and the delivery of vessels ordered at the top of the market, all of which take time, sentiment can accelerate the collapse into a few weeks. Spot ships build up in key ports. Freight rates fall, ships reduce operating speed and the least attractive vessels have to wait for cargo. Liquidity remains high. Sentiment is confused, changing with each rally in rates.

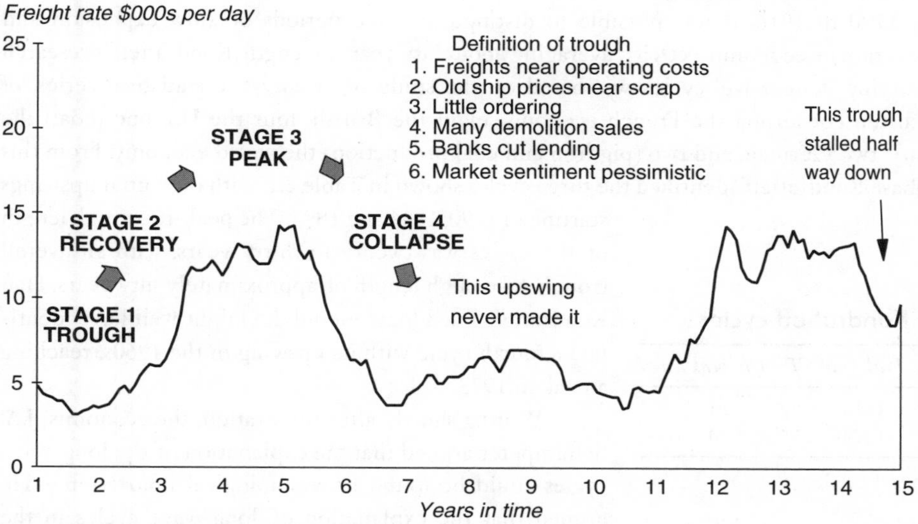

FIGURE 2.1 Stages in a dry market cargo cycle
Source: Martin Stopford, 1997

Conclusions on the short shipping cycle

There are four conclusions. *First*, the shipping cycle is a mechanism which co-ordinates supply and demand in the shipping market. A financial switchbox which regulates investment. *Second*, a complete cycle has four stages, summarized in Box 2.1. A market trough (stage 1) is followed by a recovery (stage 2), leading to a market peak (stage 3), followed by a collapse (stage 4). *Third*, the cycles are 'episodic', with no firm rules about the timing of each stage. Regularity is not a necessary part of the process. *Fourth*, there is no simple formula for predicting the 'shape' of the next cycle. Recoveries can stall half-way and slump back into recession. Market collapses may be reversed before they reach the trough. Troughs may last six months or six years. Peaks may last a month or a year. Sometimes the market gets stuck in the middle ground between trough and recession.

In short, shipping cycles, like shipowners, are unique. In each 'cycle' supply lurches after demand like a drunk walking a line that he cannot see very clearly, governed by the market fundamentals which we will examine in Chapter 3.

Long shipping cycles and the technological trend

Whilst the previous section suggests that we should not be too preoccupied with the length and regularity of shipping cycles, whether five or fifteen years, the thought that there may be a longer trend buried so deeply that we cannot easily see it deserves consideration.

The long cycle theory of the world economy was developed by the Russian economist Nikolai Kondratieff. He argued that in the major Western countries, during the 150 years from 1790 to 1916, it was possible to distinguish three periods of slow expansion and contraction of economic activity, averaging about fifty years in length. Kondratieff's research identifying 'long-wave' cycles was based on the study of twenty-five statistical series, of which ten concerned the French economy, eight the British, four the US, one (coal) the twenty-two German, and two (pig iron and coal production) the world economy. From this database Kondratieff identified the three cycles shown in Table 2.1, with the initial upswings starting in 1790, 1844 and 1895. The peak-to-trough length of the cycles was twenty to thirty years, with an overall trough-to-trough length of approximately fifty years. Had Kondratieff lived long enough he might well have identified a fourth cycle with its upswing in the 1960s, reaching a peak in 1973.

TABLE 2.1 Kondratieff cycles

Trough year	*Peak year*	*Trough–peak length*
1790	1814	24
1844	1874	20

Source: Kondratieff (1935)

Writing shortly after Kondratieff, the economist J.A. Schumpeter argued that the explanation of the long-wave cycles could be found in technological innovation.[13] He argued that the explanation of long-wave cycles in the economy at large could be found in technical innovation. He suggested that the upturn of the first Kondratieff cycle (1790–1813) was largely due to the dissemination of steam power, the second (1844–1874) to the railway boom and the third (1895–1914/16) to the joint effects of the motor car and electricity. The post-war upswing may be attributed to a combination of major innovations in the chemical industries, aircraft and the electrical/electronic industries.

By their nature these long cycles are barely visible in everyday life and a certain amount of imagination is needed to identify the cycles from the limited statistical information available. For this reason alone the long cycle theory remains controversial. What cannot be denied, and should not be ignored, is the technological trend which has done so much to shape the shipping industry over the last century.

Year by year the change is barely discernible, but over the twenty or thirty year life of a merchant ship technical obsolescence dominates shipping economics.[14] For much of the last century changing technology has set the stage for shipping cycles. In the fifty years to 1914 a downward spiral in freight rates was driven by the increasing efficiency of merchant ships and the phasing out of sail. Similarly, the fifty years from 1945 to 1995 was dominated by the mechanization of the bulk and liner shipping businesses through bigger ships and more efficient cargo handling technology. Such trends are hardly discernable as changes from year to year, but cumulatively their consequences are profound.

2.3 The frequency of shipping cycles

The vital statistics of shipping cycles

Between 1869, the beginning of modern shipping, and 1994 there were twelve dry cargo freight cycles. If we represent each cycle as the deviation from a seven year moving average in Figure 2.2 any thought of regularity is immediately dispelled. We are clearly dealing with a sequence of random fluctuations whose only common features are a beginning, a middle and an end.

Details of the length of each cycle can be found in Table 2.2 which shows the year in which each cycle peaked and its duration, measured from the peak of the previous cycle. However a word of caution is needed. Because cycles are so irrregular, identifying them is a matter of judgement. Some cycles are clearly defined, but others leave room for doubt. Does a minor improvement in a single year, as happened in 1877, 1894 or 1986, count as a cycle? There are five of these 'minicycles' where the freight rates moved slightly above trend. The definition of the twelve cycles in Table 2.2 was arrived at by checking the timing of statistical peaks and troughs shown in the freight rate statistics against comments in contemporary market reports.

The 116-year period is divided by two world wars, the first from 1914–18 and the second from 1940–45. In both cases government intervention in the shipping industry thoroughly disrupted the market mechanism, so the period during and immediately after each war is excluded from the analysis. The wars provide a convenient breaking point for subdividing the analysis of freight rates into three time periods, 1869–1914, 1920–38, and 1945–89. Each period has its own character which pervades the cyclical process.

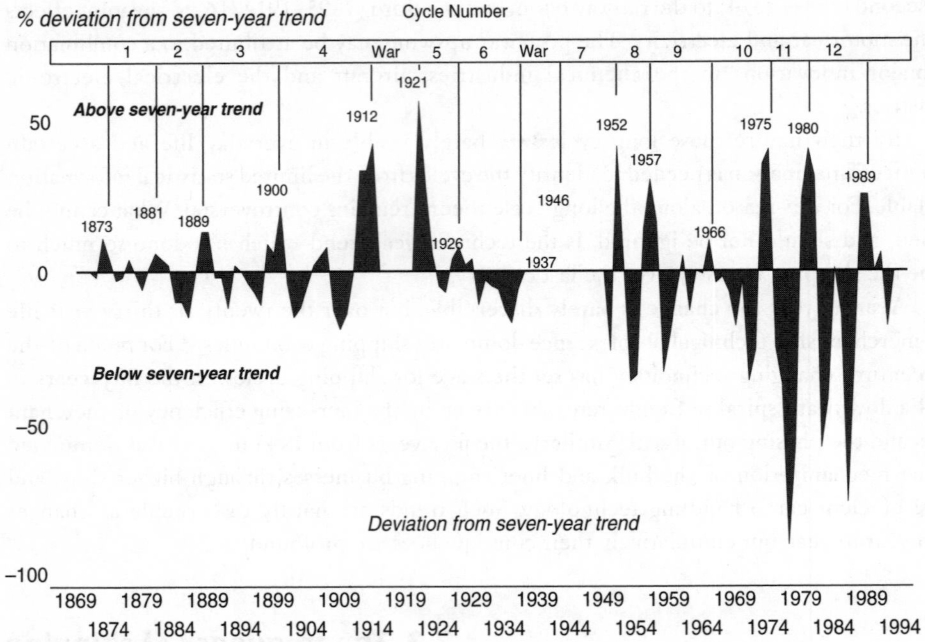

FIGURE 2.2 Twelve dry freight cycles 1869–1995
Source: Compiled by Martin Stopford from various sources

The length of shipping cycles

If we start by looking at the length of shipping cycles in Table 2.2 we find that the average between 1872 and 1989 was 8.2 years from peak to peak. The longest was 12 years (from 1900–12) and the three shortest were 5 five years. During the final period the cycles were slightly shorter. The average cycle length of 7.2 years over the period 1947–89 was 20 per cent less than the 9.2 years average between 1872 and 1936. However before jumping to the conclusion that seven years is a handy guide for predicting the length of shipping cycles, take a closer look at the individual cycles. Seven years is an average. None of the six cycles 1947–89, actually lasted seven years. Three lasted nine years, two five years and one lasted six years. In other words half the cycles were 3/4 years longer than the others. A very big difference to a business struggling to survive!

The volatility of shipping cycles

Another aspect of the cycle is the year to year volatility of freight rates. How much do freight rates change from year to year? To answer this question, Table 2.3 shows a frequency distribution of annual percentage change in freight rates 1869–1994. It seems that since 1950

TABLE 2.2 Dry cargo freight cycles 1873–1989

Cycle no	*Start peak*	*End peak*	*Length (years)*
1	1873	1881	8
2	1881	1889	8
3	1889	1900	11
4	1900	1912	12
War	1913	1919	
5	1921	1926	5
6	1926	1937	11
War	1939	1945	
7	1945	1951	6
8	1952	1957	5
9	1957	1966	9
10	1966	1975	9
11	1975	1980	5
12	1980	1989	9
Average 1873–1989			8.2
Average 1947–1989			7.2
Average 1873–1936			9.2

Source: Compiled by the author from the sources referred to in Figures 2.3, 2.6 and 2.8

TABLE 2.3 Dry cargo freight market year-by-year volatility 1869–1993

Per cent change in freight rate in year	*1869–37 Number of occurrences*	*per cent*	*1950–93 Number of occurrences*	*per cent*	*1869–93 Number of occurrences*	*per cent*
Over 100	1	1.6	3	6.5	4	2.9
50 to 99	0	0.0	2	4.3	2	1.9
25 to 49	1	1.6	5	10.9	6	5.7
20 to 24	2	3.3	0	0.0	2	1.9
15 to 19	4	6.6	1	2.2	5	4.8
10 to 14	2	3.3	4	8.7	6	5.7
5 to 9	2	3.3	5	10.9	7	6.7
0 to 4	16	26.2	6	13.0	22	21.0
−1 to −5	14	23.0	2	4.3	16	14.3
−6 to −10	10	16.4	4	8.7	14	13.3
−11 to −15	5	8.2	3	6.5	6	5.7
−16 to −20	2	3.3	3	6.5	8	7.6
−21 to −25	2	3.3	4	8.7	5	4.8
−26 to −50		0.0	2	4.3	3	2.9
Over −50		0.0	2	4.3	1	1.0
Total	61	100	46	100	107	100

Source: Calculated from the freight statistics in Figures 2.3, 2.6 and 2.8

freight rates have become more volatile. In the earlier period 1869–1937 annual changes were concentrated in the 4 per cent to −10 per cent range. About two-thirds of all years fell into this category. In the later period 1950–93 the growth was much more widely distributed. Only 25 per cent of years fell into the 4 per cent to −10 per cent range. The frequency distribution is very evenly distributed with roughly the same number of observations falling into each interval. Since there is no 'most likely' range, this is not a great deal of help in forecasting. Taken at face value, it is equally likely that freight rates next year will increase by 100 per cent, fall by 50 per cent, or anything in between.

2.4 Freight market cycles, 1869–1914

The forty-five years before 1914 provide a fascinating example of the interplay between short-term cycles and long-term trends. The pattern of freight rates in Figure 2.3 shows a long-term downward trend during which the freight index fell from 100 in 1869 to 45 in 1908.[15] Onto this long-term trend was superimposed a series of four shorter cycles of about ten years in length.

The technological trend in freight rates 1869–1913

The fall in freight rates between 1969 and 1913, which coincided with the tail end of the third Kondratieff cycle, was driven by technical change which steadily reduced costs. This trend is well documented in both academic and shipping literature. Lecturing at Oxford in 1888 Professor James Rogers commented:

> There is perhaps no branch of human industry in which the economy of cost has been so obviously exhibited as in the supply of transit. The voyage across the Atlantic is completed in less than half the time it took forty years ago, a great saving in motive power and labour. The same is true on voyages to and from India, China and other distant places. The process of loading and unloading ships does not take a third of the time, a third of the labour and a third of the cost which it did a few years ago.

Shipyards were gaining confidence in steel shipbuilding and production grew rapidly. Between 1868 and 1912 shipbuilding output of the shipyards on the Wear, shown in Figure 2.4, trebled from 100,000 grt to 320,000 grt. The ships became bigger and more efficient. In 1871 the largest transatlantic liner was the *Oceanic*, a 3,800 gt vessel with a 3,000 horsepower engine capable of 14.75 knots. It completed the transatlantic voyage in 9½ days. By 1913 the largest vessel was the 47,000 gt *Aquatanai*. Its 60,000 horsepower engines drove it at 23 knots. The transatlantic voyage time had fallen to under five days. These vessels were comparable in length with a 280,000 dwt tanker and vastly more complex in terms of mechanical and outfitting structure.

Perhaps the most important technical improvement was in the efficiency of steam

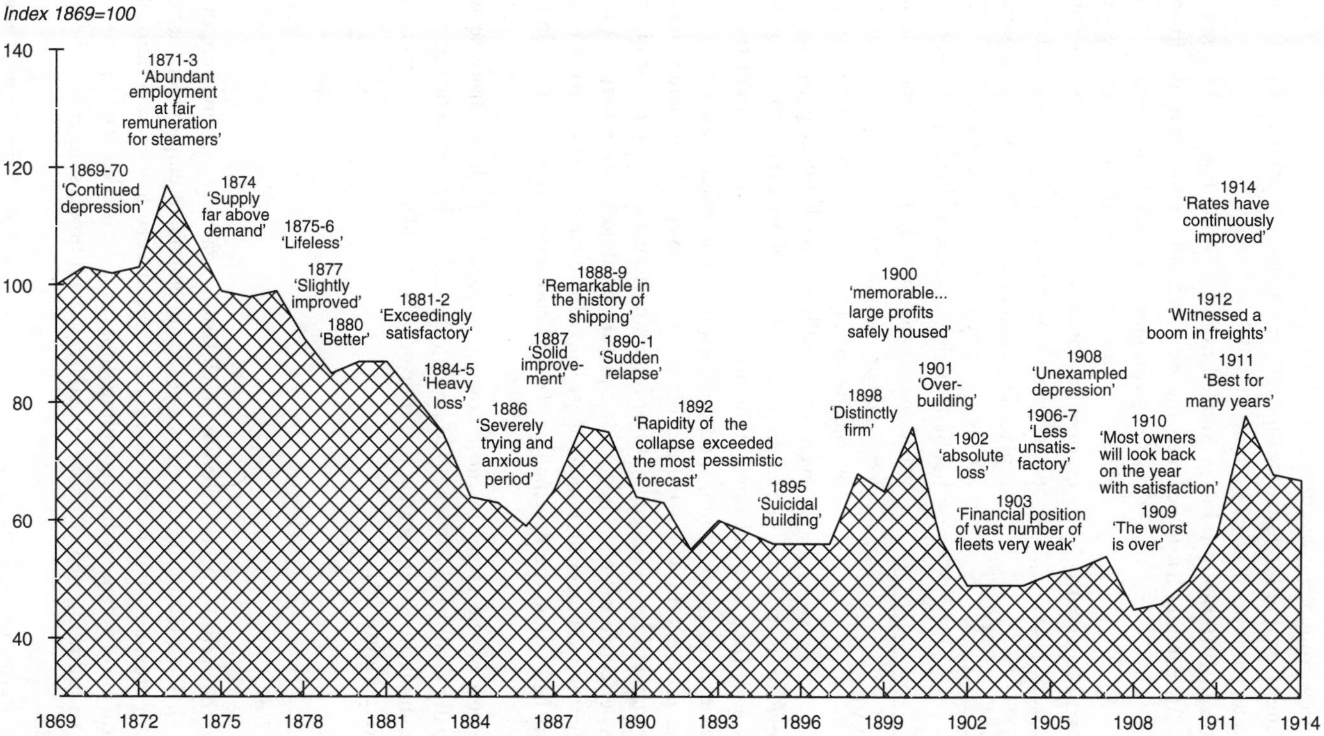

FIGURE 2.3 Dry cargo freight rates and market cycles 1869–1914

Source: Isserlis (1936) and contemporary brokers reports

Note: During the forty years from 1870–1914 freight rates fell by about 50 per cent in response to the rapid advances in shipping (especially bigger ships and improved cargo handling) and shipbuilders technology. The freight rates shown above and contemporary records suggest that this downward trend was driven by four cycles, 1987–81, 1881–89, 1889–1900 and 1900–12

engines. With the introduction of the triple expansion system and higher pressure boilers the cargo payload of the steamships increased rapidly.[16] The economic advantage of steam ships was compounded by economies of scale. The average size of merchant ship launched on the River Wear grew from 509 gross tons in 1869 to 4,324 gross tons in 1913.[17] Finally, the opening of the Suez Canal in 1869 gave steamships the economic advantage they needed to oust sail as the preferred type of new building.

Between 1870 and 1910 the world fleet doubled from 16.7 million grt to 34.6 million grt and the continuous running battle between the new and old technologies dominated market economics as each generation of more efficient steamers pushed out the previous generation of obsolete vessels. The first to come under pressure were the sailing ships, which were replaced by steamers. In 1870 steamers accounted for only 15 per cent of the tonnage (Table 2.4) but by 1910 they accounted for 75 per cent of the world merchant fleet.[18] The competition was long and hard fought. Sailing ships with their low overheads managed to survive recessions and even occasionally win back a little ground.

TABLE 2.4 Transition from sail to steam

	World Merchant Fleet		
	Steam (GRT)	*Sail (GRT)*	*Total (GRT)*
1870	2.6	14.1	16.7
1910	26.1	8.4	34.5

Source: Kirkaldy (1914) Appendix XVII

Change is never easy and the market used a series of short cycles to alternately draw in new ships and drive out old ones. At a time when the shipping industry was growing rapidly and making great technical strides forward, shipbrokers saw little of the current of technical progress on which the market was being swept along. Their reports focus on the charter market where each generation of marginal tonnage struggled for survival against the new cost-effective vessels. They paint a picture of almost continuous gloom as year after year the better and bigger high technology ships drove out the obsolete tonnage.[19] Yet by the end costs had fallen, the fleet had grown and enormous volumes of cargo had been shipped.

The brief review of the cycles in the following paragraphs is drawn from several sources, but principally Gould and Angier (1920), supplemented by the details of the cycles in shipbuilding output on the River Wear, at that time one the world's most active merchant shipbuilding areas (see Figure 2.4).

Cycle 1: 1873–81

Our review starts in the early 1870s with a cycle which lasted eight years. There were three good years in 1871–3. The first was described as a year with 'abundant employment at very fair remuneration for steamers, but restricted employment at very low remuneration for sailing ships'. This theme of steamers driving sailing ships from the market was to persist for the next decade. The following two years were patchy, though brokers described them as better than expected.

The recession started in 1874 and lasted five years until 1879. By 1876 the market was

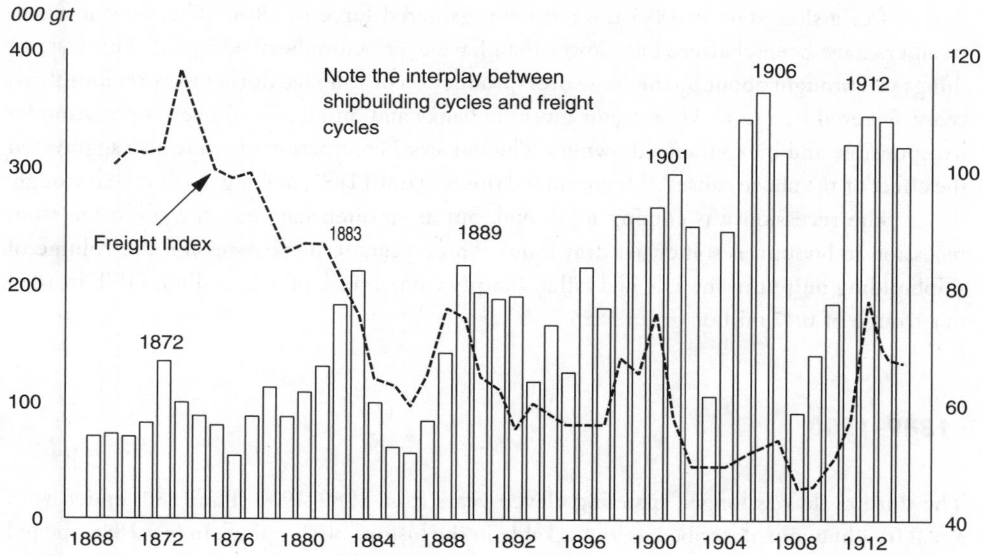

FIGURE 2.4 Ships launched on the Wear
Source: Smith and Holden (1946), statistical annex, Isserlis (1936)

'still stagnant', but started improving in 1877, a trend that is clear from the pick up in shipbuilding output on the River Wear (Figure 2.4). Steamers were gradually winning the battle with sail. According to MacGregor '1878 can be regarded as the last year in which sail figured at the same equality as steam in the China trade'.[20]

Although the market was weak, it was not a particularly severe recession. Rates were seasonal, and the words 'dull', 'lifeless' and 'stagnant' were repeatedly used in contemporary reports to describe business. Shipbuilding deliveries were running well below the peak of 1872. On the Wear launches fell from a peak of 134,825 gt in 1872 to 54,041 gt in 1876, after which it picked up to 112,000 gt in 1878 and reached 205,000 grt in 1881.

Cycle 2: 1881–89

The next cycle also lasted eight years, spanning most of the 1880s. The boom started in the Autumn of 1879 when rates showed 'considerable firmness' and 'in almost every trade a fair amount of business is doing which leaves more or less profit, and there is a better state of things than could be noted during several winters past'. Firm rates continued until 1882, driven by an expanding trade cycle. The strength of this boom is apparent from the sharp rise in shipbuilding launches (Figure 2.4). This was a real shipbuilding boom. Output on the Wear passed 100,000 gt in 1880 and, following heavy ordering in 1880/81, rose to a peak of 200,000 gt in 1883.

After a slow start in 1883 the recession gathered force in 1884. 'The rates at which steamers have been chartered are lower than have ever before been accepted. This state of things was brought about by the large over-production of tonnage during the previous three years, fostered by the reckless credit given by banks and builders, and over-speculation by irresponsible and inexperienced owners. The universal contraction of trade also aggravated the effect of the above causes'.[21] It continued this way until 1887, making it a four year trough. In fact, the recession was coming to an end, but as so often happens, the transition from recession to boom was somewhat drawn out. Three years into the recession the volume of shipbuilding output in the UK had fallen sharply from a peak of 1.25 million GRT in 1883 to a trough of 0.47 million grt in 1886.

Cycle 3: 1889–1900

The third cycle was longer, spanning eleven years from 1889–1900. The 1880s ended with a real freight boom, described as 'remarkable in the history of shipping'. In fact 1888 opened quietly, but in the autumn the freight index, which had fallen to 59 in 1886, peaked at 76, a 29 per cent increase. In 1889 freights remained at this level and prices for completed cargo steamers rose by 50 per cent from £6.7 to £9.9 per ton. Shipbuilding output continued to grow and launches on the Wear in 1889 reaching 217,000 gt, higher than the previous peak of 212,000 gt in 1883. In total the peak lasted a little over eighteen months.

In 1890 the market moved sharply into recession. By the end of the year observers commented on 'The sudden relapse of all freights and all values of steam property from the high points reached in 1889 to about the lowest figures touched during the long recession from 1883 to 1887 . . . The rates now ruling leave a heavy loss in working for all but cheaply-bought new steamers . . . The only sure means of improving the position was a wholesale laying-up of steamers in order to reduce the amount of trading tonnage by 25 per cent.'

The recession which followed lasted most of the decade. There was a modest recovery in 1895 and the market progressively improved during the next three years. Once again attention is focused on the shipbuilding scene, where the level of production had not fallen as sharply as in the previous recession. Launches on the Wear reached 215,887 gt in 1896, almost back to the 1889 peak.

Cycle 4: 1900–12

The fourth and last cycle before the 1914 war was also the longest, lasting twelve years. After the protracted recession of the early 1890s, there was a three-year freight market boom, starting in 1898. That year opened with a distinctly firm market as 'the effect of the long stoppage of work in the engine shops and shipyards caused by the engineers' strike of 1897, and a general awakening of trade, but the actual advance in prices was so gradual that purchasers were able to get in contracts for an immense amount of tonnage at cheap rates'.

The year 1899 proved less profitable than expected, but far from unsatisfactory. Bad crops in India and Russia meant that exports from these areas were lower than expected, undermining the anticipated boom. Nineteen hundred was a memorable year for the shipping industry. 'It would be hard to find any year during the century which could compare in respect of the vast trade done and the large profits safely housed.' The freight index reached the highest level since 1880 and as a result of orders placed during this period, in 1901 shipbuilding launches on the Wear were close to 300,000 gt.

A major factor during 1900 was the large amount of government transport taken for the South African war, and also for India and China. By the last quarter the market was starting to run out of steam. 'The last quarter witnessed a general sobering down, showing distinctly that the flood tide was spent, and a gradual ebb commenced. The general conditions of the world's trade point to no sudden contraction or slump, but to a continuance of steady and widespread business for some time to come, though at gradually reducing margins of profit.'

Things did not work out quite so well. By 1901 the market was back into recession. Starting from a decline of 20–30 per cent from the best rates fixed in 1900, there was a further fall of 20–30 per cent. By the Autumn of 1901 rates were 50 per cent below the peak levels in 1900. 1901 was poor and in 1902 'the result of the year's trade, as far as the 80 per cent of British shipping is concerned, was an absolute loss to the vast majority of ships, or at best the bare covering of out-of-pocket expenses. Of the remaining 20 per cent of tonnage, consisting of 'liners' proper, only the few most favoured companies have done well, viz. those with good mail contracts'. The market remained more or less in depression until 1909.

Despite the recession, by 1906 shipbuilding launches on the Wear reached 360,000 gt, an all time record. Considering the level of freight rates the newbuilding boom is difficult to explain. It may have been triggered by the large cash reserves built up during the previous market boom and anticipation of a market upturn. Shipbuilders trying to maintain their business volume may also have contributed. Angier thought so, commenting that in 1906 'The knowledge that many fleets of steamers were owned far more by the builders than by the registered owners has become a commonplace, but this year we have seen a shipbuilder's syndicate entering directly into competition with shipowners and securing a mail contract from Australia. This action was received with natural annoyance on the part of the established lines.'

Finally in 1910 the industry moved into a period of better trading conditions during which most owners made modest profits. This improvement was 'contributed to by the general improvement in the trade of the world, the cessation of building brought about by the lockout of the boiler makers by the shipbuilders, and the removal from freight markets of a number of obsolete steamers which their owners have been driven, by the prohibitive premiums demanded by underwriters, to sell for breaking up'. In 1911 freights were higher than in any year since 1900, though returns on capital were not much more than 'would have been made by the investing of a like amount in first class securities, involving no labour or retention'. Nineteen twelve witnessed a 'boom' in freights which enabled shipowners to make a real profit. The freight market collapse started again in 1913 but was interrupted by the war.

2.5 Market cycles, 1919–38

The period between the First and Second World Wars had a very different character. It was not a particularly prosperous period for shipowners, and Jones (1957) comments 'For most of the period between the wars it appears from the statistics of laid up tonnage that the world was over-stocked with shipping.' In fact the period falls into two separate decades, the first poor and the second disastrous. The first, 1922–26, was volatile and from time to time shipping was modestly profitable. The second, 1927–1938, was dominated by the great shipping depression of the 1930s.

Cycle 5: 1921–1926

The 1920s started with a boom and in 1921 *The Economist* freight index shown in Figure 2.5 reached 200. After this spectacular start to the decade, the market was never really strong. By 1922 the freight index had fallen to 110. From then onwards freights fluctuated throughout the 1920s, creating conditions which, though not wildly profitable for shipowners, provided a modest living when one year was taken with another.[22] There was a brief recession in 1924–5 followed by a brief 'boom' when freight rates touched 170 in 1926. This is taken as the end of the fifth cycle, though the precise timing is debatable. After a spectacular start to the decade, second-hand prices were relatively stable, offering no opportunity for asset play profits. The Fairplay price index for a standard 7,500 dwt vessel opened at £258,000 in the first quarter of 1920. By spring 1921 it had fallen to £63,750, where it stayed, with the exception of a brief fall to £53,000 in 1925, until December 1929.

There were three developments which gave this period its character. One was the rapid trade growth. Between 1920 and 1929 (Figure 2.6), the volume of seaborne trade increased by more than 50 per cent from 300 mt to 470 mt in 1929. The second was the more than adequate shipbuilding capacity available to meet this demand. The shipbuilding industry emerged from the war with greatly increased capacity. The annual merchant tonnage launched during the war was 3.9 million gross tons, 62 per cent greater than the average launchings 1906–13.[23] After record output of 4.45 million grt in 1921, output fluctuated between 2 million grt and 3 million grt. The lowest year was 1926, when production fell to 1.9 million grt. This was the best year of the decade for freight rates. Third, this was a period of technical change. There were several changes going on simultaneously. Internal combustion engines were replacing steam engines, oil was replacing coal as a primary fuel, there was great expansion of the tanker fleet and ships continued to get bigger.

Cycle 6: 1926–37 (The great depression)

A patchy market in the 1920s turned into the great shipping depression in the 1930s. Ironically in 1929 some shipowners were predicting a return to more favourable market conditions, but the Wall Street Crash of October 1929 and the subsequent recession in world

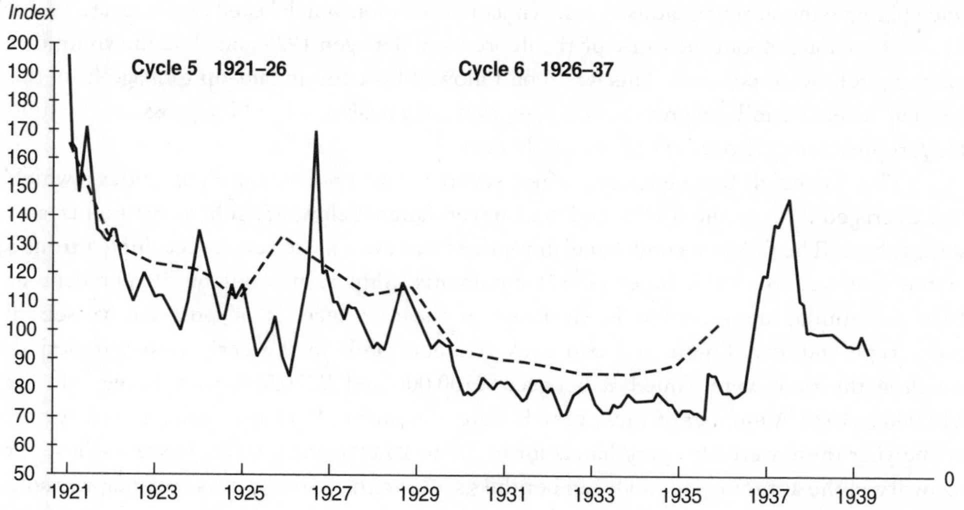

FIGURE 2.5 Freight rates 1921–40

Source: *Economist* freight index (solid line) and Isserlis, 1936 (dotted line)

Note: It is difficult to identify the cycles clearly in the period 1921–40. Cycle 5 started with a strong peak in 1921 and, arguably, ended with the short peak in 1926. On this interpretation cycle 6, which included the shipping depression of the 1930s, lasted eleven years. An alternative interpretation would be to count the period 1926–29 as a separate cycle.

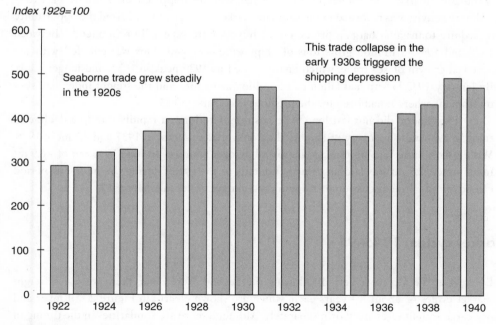

FIGURE 2.6 Seaborne trade 1922–40

Source: Sturmey (1962)

trade plunged the shipping industry into a major depression which lasted until the late 1930s. There is no doubt about the cause of the depression. Between 1929 and 1932 the volume of sea trade fell by 26 per cent. This was soon followed by a rise in laid-up tonnage from the 'normal' level of 3 million gross tons in June 1930, to a peak of 14 million gross tons by June 1932, representing 21 per cent of the world fleet.

The financial consequences were severe. *The Economist* freight index, which had averaged 110 in the 1920s and had never fallen below 85, fell to 80 points and stayed there. The fall in second-hand ship prices was even more severe, reaching a trough in the first half of 1933. Jones (1957) comments 'Ship values fell by 50 per cent in 1930 ... Similar depreciation is disclosed in the sale records of post-war vessels of every type and size. Single-and two-deck steamers built in the early post-war period, which at the time were valued at between £200,000 and £280,000, were being sold for £14,000 in 1930. A number of these vessels were sold during 1933 and during the early part of the year these were changing hands for between £5,000 and £6,000. There was a slight recovery in the autumn, and in December the s.s. *Taransay*, a single-deck steamer, was sold for £11,500.'

By 1933 financial pressures had become so great, and market sentiment so adverse, that financially weak owners were forced to sell their ships at the distress prices which distinguish a depression from a recession. The banks played a leading role in forcing down prices and 'the market was hammered into insensibility by the ruthless and incredible course pursued by British banks in 1931 and thereafter'.[24] This trough in prices created an active speculative market and 'values having reached such an unprecedented low level, extraordinary activity was recorded in the ship sale market. Foreign buyers seized the opportunity to acquire tonnage at bargain prices. Greek buyers were especially prominent'[25] Between 1935 and 1937, 5 million gross tons of ships were scrapped. This was coupled with the renewed growth of sea trade, which finally passed its 1929 peak in 1937, and longer hauls. By January 1938 lay-up had fallen to 1.3 million gross tons and the freight index had shot up from 80, where it had been for the previous five years, to 145.

This 'boom' did not last long. The position deteriorated rapidly due to a decline in trade in 1938 and a recovery of shipbuilding deliveries to 2.9 mt in 1937 and 2.7 mt in 1938. Within six months laid-up tonnage increased by over a mt (on 30 June 1938 out of 66.9 mt in existence, 2.5 mt was laid up). Further details of the cycles during the inter-war period can be found in the discussion of shipbuilding market cycles in Chapter 13.

2.6 Market cycles, 1945–95

Looking at the fifty-year period following the Second World War, there were five freight market cycles of about 7.4 years each, which are shown clearly in Figure 2.7. Tanker and dry cargo freight rates are shown separately. Although there are similarities in the timing of cycles, the shape is different. The dry cargo cycles are more clearly defined and the peaks are longer, while the tanker cycles are more 'spiky'. Since freight rates do not tell the whole story, the graphs are annotated to show the terms in which shipbrokers were describing the market at each point.

The technological trend 1945–95

The first twenty-five years after the Second World War was dominated by an extraordinary growth in sea trade (Figure 2.8) which increased from 500 mt in 1950 to 3.2 bt in 1973. Once again this was a period of great technical change in the shipping industry, though the emphasis was on organization as much as hardware. Major shippers in the energy and metal industries took the initiative in developing integrated transport operations designed to reduce their transport costs. The trend towards specialization was continuous and pervasive. In 1945 the world merchant fleet consisted of passenger ships, liners, tramps and a small number of tankers. Few vessels used for cargo transport were larger than 20,000 dwt. By 1975 the fleet had changed out of all recognition and all the major trades had been taken over by specialized ships. Dry bulks were carried by a fleet of bulk carriers, oil by crude tanker, and general cargo for the most part by container ships, vehicles in car carriers, forest products in open hatch lumber carriers and chemicals in chemical parcel tankers. Specialization allowed the size of ship to increase. The largest cargo ships in 1945 were not much more than 20,000 dwt. By the mid 1990s the specialist bulk fleets contained many ships over 100,000 dwt and in the liner trades the largest container ships were four or five times the capacity of their multi-deck ancestors. Thus the familiar theme of large modern ships forcing out small obsolete vessels continued just as it had in the nineteenth century.

In addition the market was disrupted by a series of political developments. The Korean War which started in 1950; the Nationalization and subsequent closure of the Suez Canal in 1956; the second Suez closure in 1967; and the Yom Kippur War in 1973. Although the pattern of freight peaks and troughs coincided with fluctuations in the OECD industrial trade cycle, the effect of these political influences were also apparent.

In the mid-1970s the shipping environment changed. There was a fall in sea trade in the mid-1970s, followed by a major dip in the early 1980s. The scale of this downturn in trade rivalled the 1930s in its severity. In the tanker market the sprint for size lost momentum and the fleet, which had previously been young and dynamic, grew old and sluggish. Shippers became less confident about their future transport requirements, and the role of tanker owners as subcontractors gave way to an enlarged role as risk takers. In other parts of the shipping market the technical evolution continued. Bulk carriers continued to increase in size, with volume cargoes like iron ore and coal moving up into Capesize vessels of over 100,000 dwt. A fleet of car carriers was built, with the largest able to carry 6,000 vehicles. Chemical parcel tankers grew in size to 55,000 dwt. Container ships increased from 2,000 TEU in the early 1970s to 6,500 TEU in the mid-1990s. Ship technology improved with the unmanned engine room, satellite navigation, anti-fouling paint finishes, more efficient diesel engines, vastly improved hatch covers and a host of other technical improvements in the design and construction of merchant ships.

a Dry cargo time charter rates

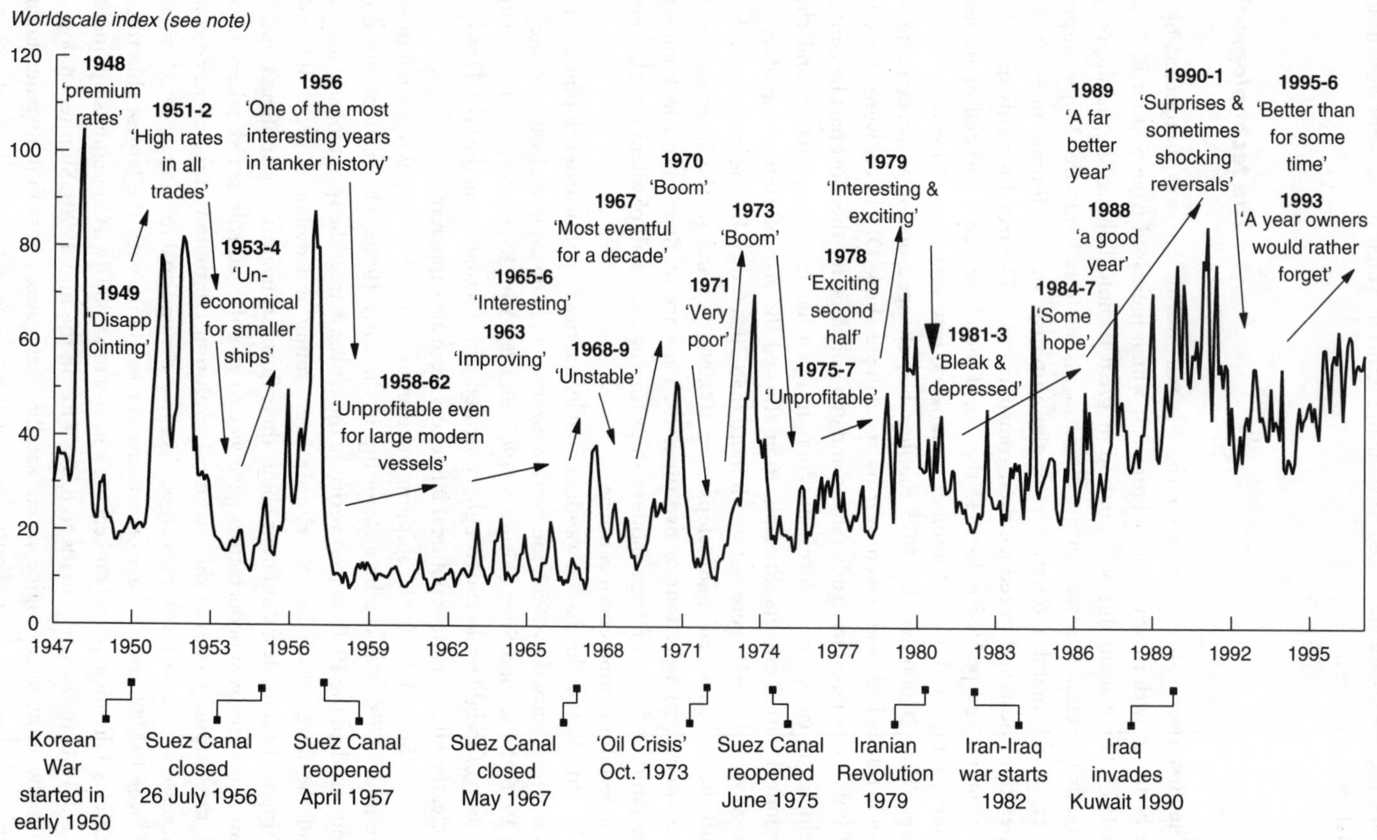

Worldscale index (see note)
120
100
80
60
40
20
0
1947
1950
1953
1956
1959
1962
1965
1968
1971
1974
1977
1980
1983
1986
1989
1992
1995
1948 'premium rates'
1949 'Disappointing'
1951-2 'High rates in all trades'
1953-4 'Un-economical for smaller ships'
1956 'One of the most interesting years in tanker history'
1958-62 'Unprofitable even for large modern vessels'
1963 'Improving'
1965-6 'Interesting'
1967 'Most eventful for a decade'
1968-9 'Unstable'
1970 'Boom'
1971 'Very poor'
1973 'Boom'
1975-7 'Unprofitable'
1978 'Exciting second half'
1979 'Interesting & exciting'
1981-3 'Bleak & depressed'
1984-7 'Some hope'
1988 'a good year'
1989 'A far better year'
1990-1 'Surprises & sometimes shocking reversals'
1993 'A year owners would rather forget'
1995-6 'Better than for some time'
Korean War started in early 1950
Suez Canal closed 26 July 1956
Suez Canal reopened April 1957
Suez Canal closed May 1967
'Oil Crisis' Oct. 1973
Suez Canal reopened June 1975
Iranian Revolution 1979
Iran-Iraq war starts 1982
Iraq invades Kuwait 1990

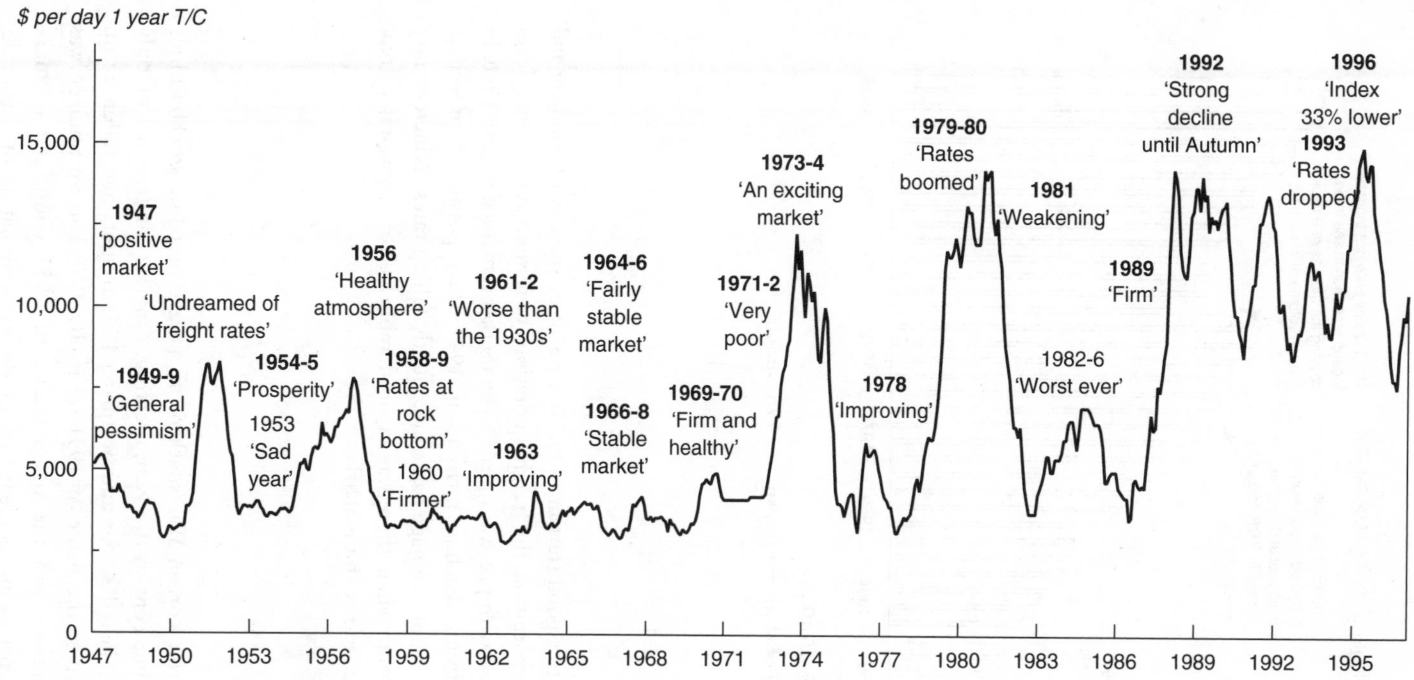

b Tanker single voyage rates

FIGURE 2.7 Freight rates 1947–97

Source: Compiled by Martin Stopford from various sources

Note: In order to produce the long time-series of tanker freight rates shown in this figure, it was necessary to combine several different series of data. The first was an MOT index covering the period 1947–49; the second was an INTASCALE index, running from 1949–69; and the third was a Worldscale index of a VLCC trading AG/West. The earlier indices were used to extrapolate the W/S index back to 1947. Although the graph provides an accurate account of year-to-year movements in freight rates, it does not necessarily accurately reflect movements in rates over long periods.

To produce the long time-series of dry cargo freight rates shown in this figure, it was necessary to combine three series. A monthly dry cargo index 1947=100, covering the period 1947 to 1959; a monthly index 1966=100, running from 1959 to 1975; and a one-year T/C rate for a 60/65,000 dwt bulk carrier. The indices were used to extrapolate the one-year T/C rates back to 1947. Although the graph provides an accurate account of year-to-year movements in freight rates, it does not necessarily accurately reflect movements in rates over long periods.

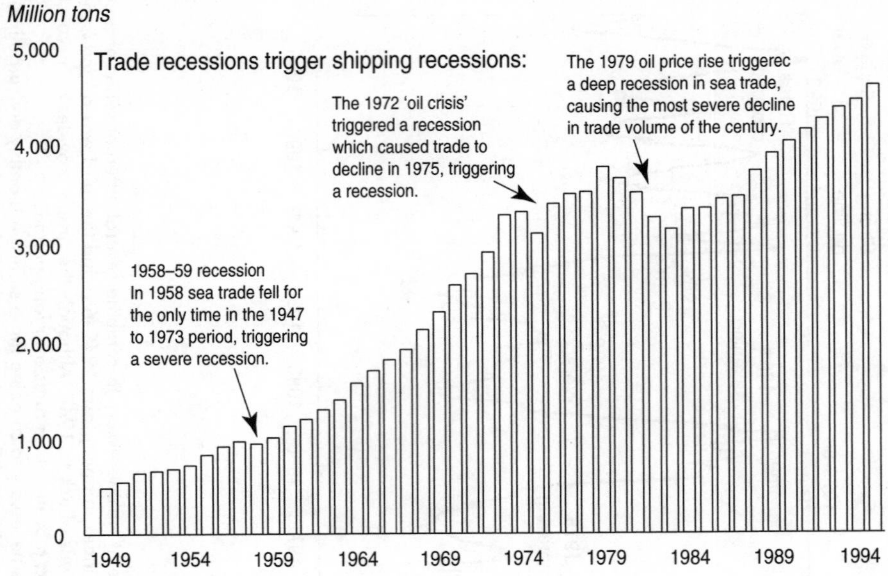

FIGURE 2.8 Seaborne trade 1949–94
Source: United Nations 'Review of Maritime Transport' 1995, various

Cycle 7: 1945–1951

The post-war market got off to a good start in 1945. 'As a result of scarcity of tonnage and the tremendous need for transportation, the freight quotations were soon at a sky high level and seemed fantastic compared with pre-war rates'.[26] The market remained firm in 1946. In 1947 it started a downward trend, reaching a trough in 1949 when 'pessimism prevailed. Generally speaking there was ample tonnage and consequently falling rates'. Nineteen fifty was a quiet year until the Autumn when 'there was a considerable lack of tonnage in a great many trades resulting in a sudden rise in the market'.[27]

Cycle 8: 1951–57

In 1951 anxieties raised by the Korean War sparked off a wave of panic stockbuilding. Seaborne trade grew by 16 per cent in the year, creating a market 'undreamed of only one year ago'. The peak only lasted a year and by spring 1952 freights had fallen by up to 70 per cent as the reaction to the panic of 1951 set in. By 1953 laid up tonnage was increasing as import restrictions and the overstocking of 1951 continued to make themselves felt. Secondhand prices give a clear idea of the extreme nature of this cycle.

The price of a reasonably prompt Liberty ship built in 1944 increased from £110,000 in June 1950 to £500,000 in December 1951. By December 1952 it was back down to £230,000.[28]

Nineteen fifty-four was a year which showed how unpredictable the shipping industry can be. 'The freight market went from bad (1953) to worse (in the first half of 1954) and then to a considerable improvement in the last half of 1954.' In the Autumn of 1954 the market started to tighten and by year end rates were up 30 per cent. The improving trend continued through 1955 and when the Suez Canal closed in November 1956, diverting Suez traffic to the longer journey round the Cape, there was a tremendous boom in rates and time charter activity.

Cycle 9: 1957–66

The events which followed the Suez crisis provide a case study of the 'shipping game' at its most exciting. Platou (1970) comments:

> The year 1957 shows how almost impossible it is to predict the future of the shipping industry. The forecasts made at the end of 1956 by leading shipping personalities were fairly optimistic. Nobody seemed to expect the recession which subsequently occurred, a depression which must be considered the worst since the middle thirties. From sky high rates at the end of 1956 they fell throughout 1957 to what can only be termed an almost rock bottom level . . . There were few people, if any, who imagined that, with small changes, it would turn out to be a ten year depression only relieved by a second and more lasting closure of the Suez Canal in 1967.

A complex range of economic and political variables conspired to produce the lengthy recession. Tugenhadt (1968) describes the part which the oil companies played in creating a tanker investment boom which drove the market down:

> It was during the 1956 Suez crisis that owners made their biggest killings. When the canal was closed and tankers had to be rerouted round the Cape of Good Hope there were not enough available to carry the oil that was needed, and charter rates rose astronomically. The companies, believing like everybody else that the Egyptians would be incapable of running the canal after it had been cleared, thought the shortage would last well into the 1960s until new ships had been built. They therefore signed contracts in which they not only hired tankers for immediate work at the high prevailing rate but also agreed to terms for chartering ships which had not yet been built for work in the 1960s. . . . When the Egyptians showed they could operate the canal efficiently the bottom fell out of the tanker market, but the companies were stuck with the contracts.[29]

Several other factors contributed to the over-capacity which developed in dry cargo in 1958. Platou (1970) singles out stockbuilding, overbuilding, more efficient ships and the world economy:

> The reasons for this decline were many. Stockpiles in Europe at the end of 1956 made it possible to slightly reduce the demand for tramp tonnage in the early months of 1957. The rate of completion of new tramps had increased enormously and these were rapidly replacing the Liberty vessels. These new tramps, averaging 3,000 tons higher capacity than the war-built ships, and faster by four knots, were carrying considerably more cargo than the Libertys they were designed to replace. Also contributing to the decline were the restrictions on trade imposed in a number of countries caused by shortage of foreign exchange. Other contributory causes were the accelerating tendency towards self-sufficiency in shipowning, chartering, and shipbuilding in hitherto nonmaritime countries, and the fact that Japan suddenly became an important supplier of tramp tonnage to the world's merchant fleet. Last, but not least, the recession in world trade helped to force rates down to well below operating levels.

The severe recession in the world economy certainly played a major part. OECD industrial production fell by 4 per cent in 1958, producing the first decline in seaborne trade since 1932 (Figure 2.6). The reopening of Suez reduced tanker demand and coincided with record deliveries of new buildings ordered during the strong market of 1955–6. However the cause of this long recession was not primarily a lack of demand. After the setback in 1958, seaborne trade grew from 990 mt in 1959 to 1,790 mt in 1966, an increase of 80 per cent in seven years. The real problem was on the supply side. After the shortages of the 1950s, shipbuilding output more than doubled, and an expanding flow of large modern vessels was largely responsible for keeping charter rates down. It was not until the closure of the Suez Canal in 1967 that tanker freight rates returned to really profitable levels. However, this second Suez crisis was not really a re-run of its predecessor because supply had become more flexible:

> So many ships were ordered in the aftermath of the 1956 crisis that for several years before the canal closed again in 1967 there was a considerable surplus of tankers, and many of them had to be converted into grain carriers to find employment. As a result, the shipowners were unable to repeat their coup. Within a few weeks of the closure some 200 tankers totalling 5m. tons had been brought back into oil carrying, and Europe's supplies were assured. The companies therefore refused to charter vessels for more than two or three voyages at a time, instead of for several years ahead. Nevertheless, the crisis was highly profitable for owners... The Norwegian Sigval Bergeson showed what this meant in overall terms when he chartered the 80,000 ton *RINFORM* to Shell for two voyages that brought in £1m.[30]

In short, the decade following the 1956 Suez boom was less prosperous for the shipping industry. Sizeable losses were made by owners trading on the spot market during the first half and, although in the second half the market improved, demand never got sufficiently far ahead of supply to push rates to acceptably profitable levels.

Cycle 10: 1966–75

The Six Day War between Israel and Egypt in 1967 and the subsequent closure of the Suez Canal marked the start of seven prosperous years for shipowners in the charter market. There were three freight market booms, and many owners were able to fix time charters at highly profitable rates. Since oil was the largest cargo moving through the Suez Canal at this time, the main impact of its closure was felt in the tanker market.

The dry cargo market benefited indirectly from improved rates for ore carriers owing to combined carriers switching into oil trading but, in general, the increase in rates was less noticeable than in the tanker market. The booms of 1970 and 1973 both coincided with exceptional peaks in the industrial trade cycle, reinforced by political events such as the closure in May 1970 of Tap Line, the oil pipeline running from the Arabian Gulf to the Mediterranean, which cut back the availability of oil from Sidon by 15 mt. Later in the year the restrictions on Libyan oil production by the new regime gave a further boost to the market. A similar pattern occurred when the nationalization of Libyan oil supplies in August 1973 made their oil companies cut back their take-up of Libyan oil in favour of the more distant Middle East sources.

However, the real cause of the buoyant market was an unprecedented growth of trade. Seaborne trade increased from 1,807 mt in 1966 to 3,233 mt in 1973, a 78 per cent increase. The increased requirement for ships during this seven-year period was greater than in the previous sixteen years. Despite rapidly expanding shipbuilding capacity, the shipyards had difficulty keeping pace with demand. There was a recession in 1971 but it proved short-lived, and many owners were covered by profitable time charters contracted in 1970. It was, therefore, a period of great prosperity and expansion in the shipping industry.

The year 1973 was one of the great years in shipping, comparable with the 1900 boom triggered by the South African boom. During the summer the time charter rate for a VLCC doubled from \$2.5 dwt/month (\$22,000 per day) to \$5 dwt/month (\$50,000 per day). The extremity of conditions sowed the seeds for a spectacular bubble in ship prices. Hill and Vielvoye (1974) describe the price spiral in the following terms:

> The upward movement in ship prices began at the end of 1972, and during 1973 the price of all types of ships rose by between 40 and 60 per cent compared with the previous year, with the most significant increase being paid for tanker tonnage. Owners were prepared to pay vastly inflated prices as a result of premiums on ships with an early delivery . . . In this situation a very large crude carrier which had been ordered in 1970 or 1971 at a cost of about £11 million could realise a price of between £25m and £30m.[31]

The tanker market collapsed following the Yom Kippur War in 1973, but the dry cargo market held up through 1974 and for small bulk carriers into 1995, spurred on by buoyant economic growth, a phase of stockbuilding in the world economy as a result of commodity price inflation and the heavy congestion in the Middle East and Nigeria resulting from the oil lead boom in these areas.

Cycle 11 (tankers): 1975–88

In the tanker market, the October 1973 Yom Kippur War ushered in a structural depression which lasted until 1988, relieved by only a brief market improvement in 1979. There were essentially three problems which contributed to the depth of this recession. The first was the oversupply of tankers resulting from the speculative investment in the early 1970s. During the peak year of 1973, the operational tanker fleet was 225 m.dwt, but so many new tanker orders were placed that, despite the decline in tanker demand during the next two years, the fleet actually increased to 320 m.dwt, creating surplus tanker capacity of 100 m.dwt. Second, the world shipbuilding industry was now able to build 60 m.dwt of merchant ships each year. This was far more than was required to meet the demand for new ships even if the trend of the 1960s had continued. Shipyard capacity was not easily reduced and it took a decade of over-production to cut capacity to a level more in line with demand. Third, the oil price rises in 1973 and 1979 dramatically reduced the demand for oil imports. By 1985, the tonnage of crude oil shipped by sea had fallen by 30 per cent.

The result was a severe depression as the market squeezed cashflow until sufficient tankers had been scrapped to restore market balance. This took fourteen years to achieve. In 1974 tanker freight rates fell sharply. A 270,000 dwt tanker was reported fixed in March on a three-year time charter for $28,000 per day, but a similar fixture was reported in November at only $11,000 per day.[32] There was little sale and purchase activity, but by year end prices had already fallen by more than 50 per cent. For example, the second-hand price of a 1970 built 200,000 dwt VLCC fell from $52 million in 1973 to $23 million in 1974. This proved to be only the beginning. In 1975 the price fell to $10 million, $9 million in 1976 and $5 million in mid-1977.

There followed a modest recovery in the tanker market. Laid up tonnage fell from 13.4 m.dwt to 8.6 m.dwt in 1979 and the tanker freight rates increased. However this was a poor sort of recovery and VLCC rates did little more than cover voyage expenses. Second-hand prices also edged up, and the price of a 200,000 dwt VLCC rose to $11 million. An intermission in a long recession rather than a market peak. By 1981 brokers commented:

> the tanker freight market in 1981 could very well be described by two words, bleak and depressed. The previous 5 years gave an acceptable return to owners of tonnage up to 80,000 dwt, and even occasionally some encouragement to larger tankers through periodic increases in demand. However 1981 cannot have given any tanker owners with vessels on the spot market anything but net losses. The rates for VLCC and ULCC tonnage showed an overall slide. At rates hovering around W 20 the transport of crude oil is virtually subsidised by the tanker owners by hundreds of thousands of dollars per voyage.

Laid up tonnage increased to 40 m.dwt in 1982 and 52 m.dwt in 1983. By this time tanker prices were back to scrap levels and even at these prices, ships of five or six years old could not always attract a bidder. In the autumn VLCCs were sold for little over $3 million. The statistics do not do justice to the difficulties faced by tanker owners trading on the charter market during this period. In 1985 sentiment hit 'rock bottom' as reflected in the 1985 Fearnleys Annual Review.

> The last ten years of capital drain in the tanker industry have no historical precedent and we have witnessed a decimation of shipping companies which has probably no parallel in modern economic history, even taking into account the depression of the 1930s. The surviving members of the Independent tanker fleets must be akin to those of the world's endangered species whose survival appeared questionable in a changing and hostile environment, but have instead shown a remarkable ability to adapt.

If nothing else, this demonstrates that in a free shipping market the adjustment of supply is a long-drawn-out, uncomfortable and expensive business, however simple it may look in theory. In 1986 the market showed the first signs of starting to pick up. Over the year freight rates increased by 70 per cent and the price of an eight-year old 250,000 dwt VLCC doubled from $5 million to $10 million. This was the start of a spiral of asset price appreciation and by 1989 the vessel was worth $38 million, despite being three years older. Inevitably this triggered heavy investment in new tankers and the great tanker depression 1974–88 ended as it had begun with a phase of speculative building.

Cycle 11 (dry bulk carriers): 1975–80

Over the twenty years 1975 to 1995 the dry cargo market followed a different pattern from tankers. For bulk carriers cycle eleven only lasted six years from 1975 to 1980. The very firm market in 1973–4 allowed owners to fix time charters that yielded profits for several years after. However the spot market moved into recession in 1975 and the three years from 1975 to 1978 were very depressed for all sizes of vessels. Although there were showing some seasonal fluctuation, on average freight rates were not sufficient to cover running costs. By 1977 many owners were experiencing severe liquidity problems.[33]

In the autumn of 1978 the recovery started, leading to a very firm market in 1979–80. By year end 1978 freight rates had risen 30 per cent and continued their climb through 1979 to a higher level than the 1974 peak. There were several reasons for the strength of the recovery. The stage was set by a sharp improvement in the fundamentals. Trade in the major bulk commodities grew by 7.5 per cent in 1979, but supply increased by only 2.5 per cent due to the low ordering during the previous recession. On top of this came the knock-on effect of the 1989 oil price increase. Power utilities around the world switched from oil to coal, giving a major boost to the thermal coal trade. This effect was reinforced by congestion. According to Fearnleys:

> the backbone of the freight market in 1980 was the heavy congestion in important port areas. In the last quarter of the year the waiting time for coal carriers in US ports soared up to 100 days which in fact trebled the need for tonnage in these trades.

The congestion was widespread, particularly in the Middle East and West Africa where traditional port facilities could not cope with the flood of trade. Rates climbed further in 1980 and at the end of December were 50 per cent over the good average reached in 1979.

Cycle 12: (bulk carriers): 1980

The freight boom lasted until March 1981 when a sharp fall set in and cycle 12 started. The daily earnings of a Panamax fell from $14,000 per day in January to $8,500 per day in December. The initial trigger of the fall was a US coal miners' strike which caused a decline in the Atlantic market.[34] The more fundamental problem was the start of a severe recession in the world economy. Falling oil prices, a stagnant coal trade and elimination of congestion pushed rates down to levels that by 1983–4 some brokers were describing as the worst ever experienced.

The following year, 1982, brought a further halving of freight rates. By December 1982 the earnings of a Panamax bulk carrier were down to $4,200 per day. In the time charter market a great number of time charters negotiated in the previous year had to be renegotiated to allow the charterers to survive and many charterers failed to meet their commitments altogether, which resulted in premature redeliveries and further difficulties for shipowners.[35] Nineteen eighty-three was a bleak year. Freight rates improved slightly in the spring, but fell to the bottom level in the summer and stayed there. Although freight rates were very depressed, in 1983–4 large numbers of orders were placed for bulk carriers. The whole process was started by Sanko Steamship, a Japanese shipping company, which secretly placed orders for 120 ships. Their example was soon followed by a flood of orders from international shipowners, particularly Greeks and Norwegians. The explanation of this counter-cyclical ordering, which resembles a similar event in 1905–6, is complex. Shipowners had accumulated large cash reserves during the 1980 boom and banks, who had large deposits of petrodollars, were keen to lend more. Ships were cheap because the shipyards still had overcapacity and no tankers were being ordered. The new generation of bulk carriers were much more fuel efficient. Finally, owners ordering in 1983 expected cycle 12 to last six years as its prececessor had done, so they would take delivery in the next cyclical upswing which was due in 1985.

If so many owners had not had the same idea this would have been a succesful strategy. Expectations that trade would improve were fulfilled. In 1984 the business cycle turned up and there was a considerable increase in world trade. However, the combination of heavy deliveries of bulk carrier newbuildings, many ordered speculatively in the previous two years, and the fact that the combined carrier fleet could find little employment in the tanker market ensured that the increase in rates was very limited. The freight statistics in Figure 2.7 show that the recovery tried to happen but failed. Panamax bulk carrier freight rates struggled up to $6,500 per day in 1985, then collapsed under a flood of deliveries. As a result Fearnleys commented: 'generally shipowners lived through another year without being able to cover their costs'. Many shipowners who had borrowed heavily to invest in newbuildings now faced acute financial problems. Bank foreclosures and distress sales were common.

In financial terms the market trough was reached in mid-1986 when a five-year-old Panamax bulk carrier could be purchased for $6 million, compared with a newbuilding price of $28 million in 1980, identifying this as a depression rather than a recession.[36] As trade started to grow and scrapping increased, the dry market moved into balance, with freight rates in both markets reaching a peak in 1989–90. Freight rates for a Panamax bulk carrier increased from $4,400 per day in 1986 to $13,200 per day in 1989. This stimulated one of the most profitable asset play markets in the history of the bulk carrier market. The five-year-old Panamax which sold for $6.2 million in 1986 was worth $12 million in 1987, 17.2 million in 1988 and $23 million in 1989.

Cycle 13: 1989 onwards

After the market bottomed out for tankers in 1985 and bulk carriers in 1986, rates rose steadily to a new market peak which was reached in 1989, coinciding with a peak in the world business cycle. During the next five years the tanker and bulk carrier markets developed very differently, due mainly to the different attitudes of investors in the two markets.

In the tanker market the freight peak was accompanied by three years on heavy ordering 1988 to 1991, during which 55 million dwt of new tankers were ordered. This rush of investment was based on three expected developments in the tanker market. First, the fleet of ageing tankers built in the 1970s construction boom was expected to be scrapped at twenty years of age, creating heavy replacement demand in the mid-1990s. Second, shipbuilding capacity had shrunk so much in the 1980s that a shortage seemed likely when the replacement cycle started, leading to very high tanker newbuilding prices. Rapidly increasing newbuilding prices seemed to support this view. In 1986 a new VLCC had cost less than $40 million but by 1990 the price was over $90 million. Third, growing oil demand was expected to be met from long haul Middle East exports, creating rapidly increasing demand for tankers, especially VLCCs. As it turned out none of these expectations were realized. Most of the 1970s built tankers continued to trade beyond twenty years; by the mid-1990s shipbuilding output had more than doubled from 15 m.dwt to 33 m.dwt; and Middle East exports stagnated as technical innovation allowed oil production from short haul sources to increase faster than expected. Delivery of the tanker order book pushed the market into a recession which lasted from early 1992 to the middle of 1995 when a recovery finally started and freight rates moved on to a steady improving path.

Conditions in the dry bulk market took the opposite path. This was one of the rare periods when there was no clear cycle. Dry bulk freight rates peaked along with tankers in 1989, but over the three years 1988 to 1991 when tanker investors ordered 55 m.dwt, only 24 m.dwt of bulk carriers were ordered. When the world economy moved into recession in 1992 bulk carrier deliveries had fallen to only 4 m.dwt per annum, compared with 16 m.dwt of tanker deliveries. This tonnage was easily absorbed and after a brief dip in 1992, dry bulk freight rates recovered, reaching a new peak in 1995. By this time five years of relatively strong earnings had triggered heavy investment in bulk carriers and in the three years 1993 to 1995 55 m.dwt of bulk carriers were ordered. As deliveries built up in 1996 the dry bulk market moved into recession.

2.7 The return on investment in shipping

Definition of return on capital (ROI) in shipping

Before we leave this chapter on the commercial environment in which shipowners operate, something must be said about the return on capital. In shipping, as in other industries, the return on investment (ROI) is the remuneration the investor receives in return for committing his funds to the enterprise. This is usually defined as net income, after depreciation, divided by the capital employed in the business. However, shipowners earn profits by buying and selling (or just owning) ships as well as by trading cargo, so from an economic viewpoint it is useful to define the return on capital in a way which recognizes this. Thus, we define the return on investment for a shipping company in the following way:

$$ROI = \frac{(R_1 - DP_1) + (MV_1 - MV_0)}{MV_0} = \frac{\textit{Trading Profit} + \textit{Asset Play}}{\textit{Value of Fleet}} \qquad E2(1)$$

Where R represents the trading cash receipts during the investment period, DP represents depreciation of the vessel; and MV represents the market value of the fleet of ships. Using this definition we can subdivide the return on investment into three component parts, each of which contributes significantly to the final result.

Trading profit (Loss) is the revenue earned by trading the ship on the spot or time charter markets (R), less the depreciation of the ship during the year (DP). Since we are concerned with the true return on trading the ship, depreciation (DP) must be deducted because the ship is a year older at the end of the accounting period. Shipowners often ignore this item, preferring to focus on the market value of the ship, but eventually the ship will wear out so, when discussing trading returns, we must take account of depreciation.
Asset play profit (Loss) The second item is the change in the market value of the ship (MV1–MV0) during the accounting period. This is the famous 'asset play' profit which has played such a prominent part in the investment strategy of the bulk shipping industry in the last decade. It is calculated by subtracting the value of the ship at the beginning of the period from its value at the end. Many shipowners consider this to be the most important source of profit for an independent shipowner.
Assets employed (MV) Total profits must be divided by the value of assete, i.e. the value of the fleet, to give the return on investment over the period.

One of the advantages of representing the return on investment in this way is that it clearly identifies the three components on which the success of a shipping investment depends – the return from trading the ships, the return from asset appreciation and, most importantly, how much capital it has tied up in the fleet. Obviously the freight market plays an important part in determining the results on the top line of the equation, but the way the shipping company sets up its fleet 'portfolio' which appears on the bottom line is equally important. For example, investing in a fleet of sophisticated new ships may generate more trading revenue due to its lower costs (see chapter 5, section 5.2), but it has high capital costs which dilutes the ROI. Conversely an old fleet is expensive to run, but the bottom line cost is low. This is the component of the ROI equation over which the shipping company has most control, so finding the right balance is one of the key variables in shipping strategy.

Comparison of shipping ROI and other investments

So what returns have shipowners actually earned from trudging through this minefield of booms and recessions? For some shipowners the rewards are very great. Few businesses have such a reputation for producing fabulously rich men. The phrase 'shipping tycoon' instantly conjures up the image of great wealth. This reputation is well deserved. Successful shipowners are among the world's richest men. Stories of Greeks or Norwegians who, in the space of fifteen or twenty years have accumulated fortunes of $1 billion liquid assets, are quite true. This is a business where the fruits of success are spectacular. However this facet of the business sits uncomfortably with the accountant's analysis of the aggregate return on investment in shipping. In the past the return on capital earned by shipowners has not been particularly high. Even before the First World War we find brokers complaining that in 1911, the best year for a decade, the returns were no better than could be obtained by investing in first class securities. Admittedly this is anecdotal evidence, but the statistical data available for later periods says much the same thing. Table 2.5 shows a selection of 'return on investment' calculations. The table also shows the return available from the stock market during the same period. Even allowing a wide margin for the inevitable shortcomings of ROI calculations of this sort, there is not much doubt that shipping is a low-return business.[37]

The first period reported from 1930–1935 covers the 1930s shipping depression. A UK government study published in 1936[38] collected financial information on two hundred

TABLE 2.5 Return on capital in dry cargo shipping

Period	*Return on investment (ROI) per cent per annun*		
	Shipping market	*UK stock market*	*Ratio*
1930–35	1.45	N	
1950–57	10.3	17.2	60 per cent
1958–69	3.5	13.6	26 per cent
1970–90	9	11.2	80 per cent

Source: 1930–45 – Jones (1957) Table VI
1950–57 – Rochdale Report (1970) Table 18.3
1958–69 – Rochdale Report (1970) Appendix 13, Table 1.
1970–79 – Stopford (1991) Table 2

and fourteen tramp shipping companies. They found that between 1930 and 1935 on average paid up capital of £25,849, the companies paid cumulative dividends from voyage profits of £592,000. An annual return on capital of 0.05 per cent per annum. In addition they were only able to provide £8.7 million of depreciation against a requirement at cost of £18.6 million.

The next decade from 1950–57 was substantially better, but the ROI was still much lower than other industries.[39] Figures for the return on capital by shipping companies published by *The Economist* show a return of 10.3 per cent per annum compared with a 17.2 per cent return shown by *The Economist's* 'all companies' index. Between 1958 and 1969, which was a poor decade in the shipping market, *The Economist* shipping return fell to 3.2 per cent per annum, compared with 13.6 per cent for all companies. A more detailed analysis published by the Rochdale Committee (1970) based on a detailed study of private and public shipping companies in the UK produced similar result. Their study produced an average return for the period 1958–69 of 3.6 per cent. By sector the return was 4.1 per cent for cargo liners, 3.3 per cent for bulk carriers, 18.7 per cent for ore carriers and 4.2 per cent for tankers. The exceptionally high return for ore carriers was explained by the fact that most of the vessels were on long-term charters designed to produce a reasonable return on capital. The tankers were also mainly on long-term charter to international oil companies, suggesting that time charters were not a guarantee of high returns.[40]

An analysis of the return on the investment on a fleet of bulk carriers over the period 1970 to 1990 shows a slightly better return. During the twenty-year period an investment of $96.2 million in a fleet of twenty bulk carriers increased to $562 million. This represents an average return of 9.2 per cent per annum, of which 4.4 per cent was derived from the trading cashflow and the balance from capital appreciation. In other words shipowners benefited during a period of high inflation, but the underlying return on trading remained below 5 per cent. However this performance was better in relation to other industries. During the same period the US stock market as measured by the S&P 500 produced a return of 11.2 per cent pa. Shipping investment kept up with equities in the 1970s, then in the mid-1980s recession shipping earnings fell below the equities investment index and never made up this shortfall.[41]

Measuring shipping risk

It does not make sense to talk about the *return* on investment in shipping without also referring to the *risk* which the investor takes. Investors do not take risks for fun. They are playing with real money. Therefore they generally require a higher return from a portfolio of risky stocks than from a safe investment such as treasury bills. In the stock market this is just what they get. The higher return required by investors to put their money in risky investments is referred to as the *risk premium.* Over the last 60 years the *risk premium* earned on US stocks compared with Treasury bills has been 8.4 per cent per year[42].

High risk investment requires a higher level of return and the financial markets have become extremely adept at measuring these differences. In practical terms, the risk taken by the equity investor is the uncertainty about what it will be worth at any point in time, combined with the risk that he will lose his investment. In the securities market this risk is measured by the standard deviation of the year on year return, since this gives an indication of the variability of the return. The standard deviation of the various types of investment are summarized in Table 2.6. Treasury bills, which are the safest investment, have a long-term standard deviation of 3.4 per cent, compared with Common Stocks which have a standard deviation of 17 per cent. Bulk shipping is more than twice as volatile as stocks with a standard deviation of 35 per cent. This means that the year on year return may vary by 70 per cent or more.

TABLE 2.6 Volatility of bulk shipping and other types of investment

Portfolio	*Period*	*Average ROI per cent per annum*	*Standard Deviation per cent per annum*
Treasury bills	1926–85	3.5	3.4
Long term govt bonds	1926–85	4.4	8.2
Corporate bonds	1926–85	5.1	8.3
Common stock	1971–90	11.0	17.0
Bulk shipping	1971–90	9.0	35.0
Tanker shipping	1980–94	5.2	30.0

Source: Brealey and Myers (1988) p. 131
Stopford (1995) Table 1

So it appears that the shipping industry is a high risk business which, on the basis of the available information in Table 2.6 offers little risk premium. Although surprising, the existence of high risk, low return businesses is well known to economists, particularly in businesses where individuals can become very rich. Adam Smith pointed out that where the potential rewards are very great 'the chance of loss by most men is under-valued'.[43] He offers the success of lotteries as evidence 'that the soberest people scarce look upon it as folly to pay a small sum for the chance of gaining ten or twenty thousand pounds; though they know that the small sum is perhaps twenty or thirty per cent more than the chance is worth'. Risky trades in which there is an element of romance often become so overcrowded that the average earnings in it are lower than if there were no risks to be run. Sopranos work for years to become opera singers, with only the slimmest hope of success and for lower wages than they could earn as waitresses.

Shipping is a romantic business. It is also a business in which the lucky few can accumulate wealth beyond the dreams of even lottery winners. With the market cycle to add the speculative excitement of the poker table, it is not surprising that investors are easily hooked and competition continually drives down the average return on capital. Since the end product is cheap transport, consumers should not complain.

2.8 The prediction of shipping cycles

So it looks as though the investor who wants to make a return of more than 4–5 per cent per annum must be prepared to take 'shipping risk' – or, if we put it in simple terms, to take a gamble. The problem is to find a decision strategy for dealing with the cycles we have discussed at such length. One obvious strategy is to exploit the volatility of freight rates by taking a position based on the expected development of the cycle. The strategy described, for example, by Alderton[44] is to spot charter on a rising market and, when the peak is reached, to sell or take a time charter long enough to carry the vessel through the trough. Ship acquisitions are made at the bottom of the market when ships are 'cheap'.[45] Few would argue with the principle of buying low and selling high. The skill lies in the execution. Most analysts have been caught out too often to believe they can forecast accurately. However there is some middle ground.

First we must restate the truth so evident from shipping history, that cycles are not 'cyclical' if by this we mean 'regular'.[46] In the real world shipping cycles are a loose sequence of peaks and troughs. Because the timing of each stage in the cycle is irregular, simple rules like the 'seven year cycle', although statistically correct over a very long period, are far too unreliable to be a worthwhile decision criteria. However, the cycles are not random and Cufley's conclusion that 'it is totally impossible to predict when the market will move upwards (or fall)' is probably too extreme. Our review in this chapter of the last twelve cycles demonstrates that the same explanations of cyclical peaks and troughs appear again and again. Economic conditions, the 'business cycle', trade growth and the ordering and scrapping of ships are the fundamental variables which can be analysed, modelled and extrapolated. Careful analysis of these variables removes some, but not all, of the uncertainty and reduces the risk. To these must be added the 'wild cards' which triggered the spectacular markets. The South African War in 1900, closure of the Suez Canal, stockbuilding, congestion, strikes in the shipyards have all played a part.

The difficulty of analysing these factors is daunting. The world economy is complex and we often have to wait years for the detailed statistics which tell us precisely what happened. Many of the variables and relationships in the model are highly unpredictable, so the prediction process should be seen as reducing risk rather than creating certainty. In this respect shipowners are in much the same position as other specialist commodity markets traders. Those playing the market must try to understand the cycles and take a risk. That is what they are paid for. An essential part of weighing up this risk is to form a realistic view of what is driving each stage in the cycle. Reading the signs as the market progresses through the stages in the cycle, extrapolating the consequences and, when the facts support it, being prepared to act against market sentiment. It is not necessary to be completely right. What matters is being more right than other traders. There is a long history of ill-advised shipping investments which, over the years, have provided a welcome source of income for more experienced investors who buy ships cheap during recessions and sell expensively during booms.

The importance of market intelligence

The whole thrust of this argument is to direct our attention towards the process of obtaining information about what is going on in the shipping market and understanding the implications of any actions we take. Research suggests that successful business decisions are based upon careful consideration of all the *relevant* facts, while bad decisions often flow from inadequate consideration of the facts. For example, Kepner and Tregoe, in their study of business decisions, made the following comments:

> In the course of our work, we witnessed a number of decisions in government agencies and private industry that ranged in quality from questionable to catastrophic. Wondering how such poor decisions ever came to be made, we decided to look into their history. We found that most of these decisions were bad because certain important pieces of available information had been ignored, discounted or given insufficient attention. We concluded that the process of gathering and organising information for decision making needed improvement.[47]

These observations, which can hardly be at variance with most people's practical experience, emphasize the importance of collecting and interpreting information.

The challenge of successful risk management

So where does this leave us in terms of predicting freight cycles? There are three conclusions to be drawn. First, in shipping cycles, as in a poker game, for every winner there must be a loser. This aspect of the business is about risk management, not carrying cargo. Shipping is not quite a zero sum game, but as we have seen, when we look at the financial returns, it comes pretty close. Second, shipping cycles are not random. The economic and political forces which drive them, although highly complex, can be analysed, and the information used to improve the odds in the player's favour. But remember that if everyone has the same idea, it will not work. Third, like poker, each player must assess his opponents, take a view on how they will play the game, and work out who will be the loser this time. In the end no loser means no winner.

We should not be surprised that this makes shipping sound more like a gambling game than a sober transport business. It is a gambling game. Shippers turn to the shipping market because they do not know how much shipping capacity they will need in future. Nobody does. The job of the shipowner is to make the best estimate he can and take a gamble. If he is wrong he loses. These decisions are complex and often require decisive action which flies in the face of market sentiment. That is why individuals are often more successful than large companies. Imagine playing poker under the direction of a board. For shipowners with many years in the business, the instinct that drives their decisions probably derives from the experience of past cycles reinforced by an understanding of the international economy and up-to-date information obtained from the international grapevine. For those without a lifetime of experience, either newcomers to the industry or outsiders the problems of decision-making are daunting. Many bad decisions have been made because of a misunderstanding of the market mechanism. Our aim in the following three chapters is to examine the economic structure of the markets in which sea transport is traded and the fundamentals which drive them.

2.9 Summary

In this chapter we have discussed the economic environment in which the shipping industry operates. We started by defining *shipping risk.* This is the risk that the investment in the hull of a merchant ship, including a return on the capital employed, is not recovered during a period of ownership. Shipping risk can be taken by the shipper (*industrial shipping*) or the shipowner (*shipping market risk*).

The market cycle dominates shipping risk. Although the existence of cycles is undisputed, their character is 'episodic' rather than regular. We identified four stages (i.e. episodes) in a cycle, a trough, a recovery, a peak, and a collapse. There are no firm rules about the length or timing of these stages. The cyclical mechanism must be flexible to do its job of managing shipping investment. The short term cyclical model is well defined. When ships are in short supply freight rates shoot up and stimulate ordering. When there is a surplus, rates fall and remain low until enough ships have been scrapped to bring the market into balance. Each stage continues until its work is completed.

There is also a longer term 'technology cycle' driven by technology. Technical developments such as the triple expansion engine or containerization stimulate investment in new ships. As the new ships are delivered they set a new standard for efficiency. The more there are, the bigger the commercial impact. The transition from one technology to another can take twenty years to complete, during which time it affects the economics of the business. Over the last century there have been a succession of these cycles – steam replacing sail, diesel replacing steam, better boilers, containerization, the bulk shipping revolution.

Analysis of short cycles over the period 1872–1989 illustrates the 'work pattern' of the shipping cycle. There were twelve cycles, averaging 7.2 years each. Four cycles lasted only 5–6 years from peak to peak, two lasted 8 years, and six lasted 9 years or more. Each cycle developed within a framework of supply and demand, so common features such as business cycles and over-ordering of ships crop up again and again. As a rule supply has no difficulty keeping up with demand, so the big freight 'booms' are often the result of unexpected events, such as the closing of the Suez Canal, stockpiling or congestion. Recessions tend to be driven by economic shocks which cause an unexpected decline in trade (as in 1930, 1958, 1973 and 1982). Over-investment also plays a part. Like a game of cards, the same pack can be dealt in many different ways.

The return on investment in shipping is lower than in other industries, averaging less than 10 per cent per annum. The returns are, however, twice as volatile as the US stock market, contradicting the widely held view that high risk industries should produce above average returns. The most likely explanation is that investors are attracted to the volatility of shipping. When combined with the large, liquid asset base and the ease of entry and exit, shipping is an industry where the winners can become very wealthy. The prospect of great gain dulls, or compensates for, the low average return.

Against this background, predicting cycles is difficult, but not impossible for a skilled player. The framework of each cycle is set by economic fundamentals. Within this framwork it is left to shipowners to 'play the game'. In a low return industry, one investor's fortune is another investor's loss, so the stakes are high. When outsiders look at the low average returns, they often ask: 'Why would anyone want to invest in shipping?', But the shrewdest and most adaptable owners know that they will survive to make massive profits the next time some unforeseen event turns the market on its head – a case of 'devil take the hindmost'.

Chapter 3

The four shipping markets

Economists understand by the term Market, not any particular market place in which things are bought and sold, but the whole of any region in which buyers and sellers are in such free intercourse with one another that the prices of the same goods tend to equality easily and quickly.

(Antoine-Augustin Cournot *Researches Into the Mathematical Principles of the Theory of Wealth* 1838 (Trans. N.T. Bacon 1897))

3.1 The decisions facing shipowners

A shipowner had a difficult decision to make. He had ordered two 280,000 dwt VLCCs which an oil company was prepared to charter for five years at $33,000 per day. This would guarantee revenue to cover his finance costs for the first five years of the ship's life, but the return on his equity worked out at only 6 per cent per annum. Not much for the risk he had taken in ordering the ships. In addition, the time charter would shut him out from the tanker boom he felt sure would happen in the next few years.

He decided to wait and trade the ships on the spot market. To begin with this looked like a good decision, since the ships were delivered into a rising market. Unfortunately the next three years proved to be very poor and the vessels earned only $15,000 per day each. To meet bank payments the owner was forced to sell three old combined carriers. Since there were no offers from trading buyers he eventually sold them to a breaker for $5 million each. Two years earlier they had been valued at $23 million each.

In this example the shipowner trades in four different markets:

1 The *newbuilding market* where he ordered the ships;
2 The *freight market* where he chartered them;
3 The *sale and purchase market* where he tried to sell the combined carriers; and
4 The *demolition market* where he finally sold them.

The aim of this chapter is to explain how the four markets work from a practical viewpoint and to identify the differences between them. How are ships chartered? How does the sale and purchase market operate and what determines the value of a ship? What is the difference between buying a new ship and buying a second-hand one? How did selling the ship for scrap differ from selling it for continued trading? An understanding of these practical questions lays the foundation for our discussion of the economic principles in chapter 4.

3.2 The four shipping markets

Jevons, the nineteenth century economist provided a definition of a 'market' which, a century later, still serves very well for shipping. He says:

> Originally a market was a public place in a town where provisions and other objects were exposed for sale; but the word has been generalized, so as to mean any body of persons who are in intimate business relations and carry on extensive transactions in any commodity. A great city may contain as many markets as there are important branches of trade, and these markets may or may not be localized. The central point of a market is the central exchange, mart or auction rooms where traders agree to meet and transact business . . . But this distinction of locality is not necessary. The traders may be spread over a whole town, or region of country and yet make a market if they are . . . in close communication with each other[1]

In shipping there are four shipping markets trading in different commodities. The freight market trades sea transport, the sale and purchase market trades second-hand ships, the newbuilding market trades new ships and the demolition market deals in scrap ships. Beyond this there is no formal structure. This is an important point which calls for a warning. In the next two chapters we will discuss the economics of the shipping markets. While this analysis provides guidance on how the markets operate, we are not dealing with immutable laws. The fact that market traders have behaved in a particular way in the past is no guarantee that they will do so in future. Because markets consist of people going about their business, the best commercial opportunities often arise when the market behaves inconsistently. For example, ordering ships at the top of the market cycle is usually bad business, but if for some reason few ships are ordered, the rule will not apply. Commercial judgements must be based on an understanding of market dynamics, not economic principles taken out of context.

Because the same shipowners are trading in all four shipping markets their activities are closely correlated. When freight rates rise or fall the changing sentiment ripples through into the sale and purchase market and from there into the newbuilding market. The markets are also linked by cash. The relationship is shown graphically in Figure 3.1. Cash flows back and forth between the industry's bank account (represented by the circle) and the four shipping markets (represented by the squares). The cashflow *into* the shipping companies' bank account is shown by the light shaded bars, while the black bars show *outflows*. The hatched bars indicate cash which *changes hands* from one shipowner to another, but does not change the cash balance of the industry as a whole.

The main cash inflow is *freight revenue*. This goes up and down with freight rates and is the primary mechanism driving the activities of shipping investors. The other cash inflow comes from the *demolition market*. Old or obsolete vessels sold to scrap dealers provide a useful source of cash, especially during recessions. The *sale and purchase (S&P) market* has a more subtle role. Investing in a second-hand ship involves a transaction between a shipowner and an investor. Because the investor is usually another shipowner money changes hands, but the transaction does not affect the amount of cash held by the industry. The sale of a tanker for $20 million just transfers $20 million cash from one shipping bank account to another, leaving the aggregate cash balance unchanged.[2] In this sense the sale and purchase market is a zero sum game. For every winner there is a loser. The only real source of wealth is trading cargo in the freight market.[3] In the case of the *newbuilding market* the cashflow (shown in black) is in the opposite direction. Cash spent on new ships flows out of the shipping industry because the shipyard uses it to pay for materials, labour and profit.

Waves of cash flowing between the four markets drive the shipping market cycle. At the beginning of the cycle freight rates rise and cash starts to pour in, allowing shipowners to pay higher prices for second-hand ships. As prices are bid up investors turn to the newbuilding market which now looks better value. With the confidence created by bulging wallets they order many new ships. A couple of years later the ships arrive on the market and the whole process goes into reverse. Falling freight rates squeeze the cash inflow just as investors start paying for their newbuildings. Financially weak owners who cannot meet their day-to-day obligations are forced to sell ships on the second-hand market. This is the point

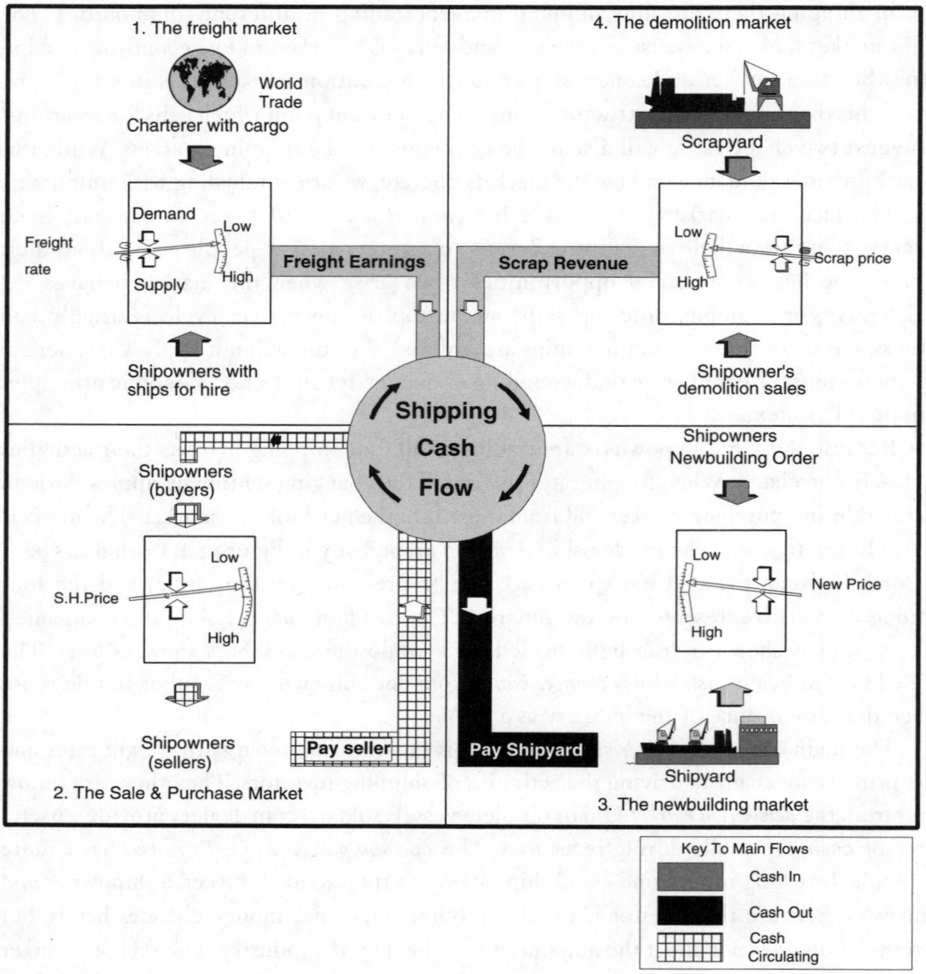

FIGURE 3.1 The four markets which control shipping

Source: Martin Stopford *Maritime Economics*, 2nd edn, 1997

Note: **This diagram shows the cashflow in the shipping market. It involves three markets, the Freight Market, the Sale and Purchase Market and the Newbuilding Market. Note that cash invested in newbuildings shows OUT of the industry, while the main inflows come from freight earnings and scrap.**

at which the asset play market starts for those shipowners with strong balance sheets. In extreme circumstances like 1932 or 1986 modern ships change hands at bargain prices. For older ships there will be no offers from trading buyers, so hard pressed owners are obliged to sell for demolition. As more ships are scrapped the supply falls, freight rates are bid up and the whole process starts again.

The whole commercial process is controlled and co-ordinated by cashflow between markets. Cash is the 'stick and carrot' which the market uses to drive activity in the required direction. Whether they like it or not, shipowners are part of a process which controls the price of the ships they trade and the revenue they earn.

3.3 The freight market

What is the freight market?

The freight market is one of the markets Jevons must have had in mind when he wrote the definition cited in the previous section. The original freight market, the Baltic Shipping Exchange, was opened in London in 1883, though its functions had long been performed, in a less organized way, by the Baltic Coffee House. The Baltic operates in exactly the way Jevons described. At this institution merchants looking for transport met ships' Captains looking for cargo. The freight market today remains a marketplace in which sea transport is bought and sold, though the business is mainly transacted by telephone and telex rather than on the floor of the Baltic. Nowadays there is a single international freight market but, just as there are separate sections for cows and pigs in the country market, there are separate markets for different ships in the freight market. In the short term the freight rates for tankers, bulk carriers, container ships behave quite differently, but because it is the same group of traders, what happens in one sector eventually ripples through into the others. Also, because it takes time for ships to move around the world, there are separate regional markets which are only accessible to ships ready to load cargo in that area. This becomes important when we discuss the theory of short term and long-term freight rate determination in section 4 of the next chapter.

The freight market has two different types of transaction, the *freight contract* in which the shipper buys transport from the shipowner at a fixed price per ton of cargo and the *time charter* under which the ship is hired by the day. The freight contract suits shippers who prefer to pay an agreed sum and leave the management of the transport to the shipowner, while the time charter is for experienced ship operators who prefer to manage the transport themselves.

Fixing a ship

When a ship is chartered or a freight rate is agreed, the ship is said to be 'fixed'. Fixtures are arranged in much the same way as any major international hiring or subcontracting operation. Shipowners have vessels for hire, charterers have cargo to transport, and brokers puts the deal together. Let us briefly consider the part played by each of these:

The *shipowner* comes to the market with a ship available, free of cargo. The ship has a particular speed, cargo capacity, dimensions and cargo handling gear. Existing contractual commitments will determine the date and location at which it will become available. For example, it may be a Panamax bulk carrier currently on a voyage from the US Gulf to deliver grain to Japan, so it will be 'open' (available for hire) in Japan from the anticipated date at

BOX 3.1 Glossary of chartering terms

Shipper Individual or company with cargo to transport.

Charterer Individual or company who hires a ship.

Charter-party Contract setting out the terms on which the shipper contracts for the transportation of his cargo or the charterer contracts for the hire of a ship.

Voyage charter Ship earns freight per ton of cargo transported on terms set out in the charter-party which specifies the precise nature and volume of cargo, the port(s) of loading and discharge and the laytime and demurrage. All costs paid by the shipowner.

Consecutive voyage charter Vessel hired to perform a series of consecutive voyages between A and B.

Contract of Affreightment (COA) Shipowner undertakes to carry quantities of a specific cargo on a particular route or routes over a given period of time using ships of his choice within specified restrictions.

Period charter The vessels is hired for a specified period of time for payment of a daily, monthly or annual fee. There are three types, time charter, trip charter and consecutive voyage charter.

Time charter Ship earns hire, monthly or semi-monthly. The shipowner retains possession and mans and operates ship under instructions from charterer who pays voyage costs (see chapter 3 for definition).

Trip charter Fixed on a time charter basis for the period of a specific voyage and for the carriage of a specific cargo. Shipowner earns 'hire' per day for the period determined by the voyage.

Bare boat charter The owner of the ship contracts (for a fee, usually long-term) to another party for its operation. The ship is then operated by the second party as if he owned it.

Laytime The period of time agreed between the party to a voyage charter during which the owner will make ship available for loading/discharging of cargo.

Demurrage The money payable to the shipowner for delay for which he is not responsible in loading and/or discharging beyond the laytime.

Despatch Means the money which the owner agreed to repay if the ship is loaded or discharged in less than the laytime allowed in the charter-party (customarily demurrage).

Common abbreviations

c.i.f. The purchase price of the goods (by importer) include payment of insurance and freight which is arranged by the exporter.

f.o.b. Goods are purchased at cost and the importer makes his own arrangement for insurance and freight.

which the coal has been discharged, say 12 May. Depending upon his 'chartering strategy', the shipowner may be looking for a short charter for the vessel or a long charter.

The *shipper or charterer* may be someone with a volume of cargo to transport from one location to another or a company that needs an extra ship for a period of time. The quantity, timing and physical characteristics of the cargo will determine the type of shipping contract required. For example, the shipper may have a cargo of 50,000 tons of coal to ship from Newcastle, New South Wales, to Rotterdam. Such a cargo might be very attractive to a bulk carrier operator discharging coal in Japan and looking for a cargo to reposition into the North Atlantic, because he has only a short ballast leg from Japan to Australia and then a full cargo back to Europe. The question is, how does the shipper contact the shipowner?

Often the principal (i.e. the owner or charterer) will appoint a *shipbroker* to act for him. The broker's task is to discover what cargoes or ships are available; what the owners/ charterers want to be paid; and what is reasonable given the state of the market. With this information they negotiate the deal for their client, often in tense competition with other brokers. Brokers provide other services including post fixture processing, dealing with disputes, and providing accounting services in respect of freight, demurrage, etc. Some owners or shippers carry out these tasks themselves. However, this requires a staff and management structure which only very large companies can justify. For this reason most owners and charterers use one or more brokers. Since broking is all about information, brokers tend to gather in shipping centres. London remains the biggest, with other major centres in New York, Tokyo, Hong Kong, Singapore, Piraeus, Oslo, Hamburg, etc.

Four types of contractual arrangement are commonly used. Under a *voyage charter*, the shipowner contracts to carry a specific cargo in a specific ship for a negotiated price per ton. A variant on the same theme is the *contract of affreightment*, in which the shipowner contracts to carry regular tonnages of cargo for an agreed price per ton. The *time charter* is an agreement between owner and charterer to hire the ship, complete with crew, for a fee per day, month or year. Finally the *bare boat charter* hires out the ship without crew or any operational responsibilities.

The voyage charter

A voyage charter provides transport for a specific cargo from port A to port B for a fixed price per ton. For example, a grain trader may have 25,000 tons of grain to transport from Port Cartier in Canada to Tilbury in the UK. So what does he do? He calls his broker and tells him that he needs transport for the cargo. The broker will 'fix' (i.e. charter) a ship for the voyage at a negotiated freight rate per ton of cargo, e.g. $5.20. The terms will be set out in a charter-party and, if all goes well, the ship arrives on the due date, loads the cargo, transports it to Tilbury, discharges and the transaction is complete.

If the voyage is not completed within the terms of charter-party then there will be a claim. For example, if laytime (i.e. port time) at Tilbury is specified at seven days and the time counted in port is ten days, the owner submits a claim for three days *demurrage* to the charterer. Conversely, if the ship spends only five days in port, the charterer will submit a claim for two days *despatch* to the owner. The rates for demurrage and despatch are stated in dollars per day in the charter-party.

The calculation of demurrage and despatch does not normally present problems, but cases do arise where the charterer disputes the owner's right to demurrage. Demurrage becomes particularly important when there is port congestion. During the 1970s there were delays of up to six months in discharging cargo in the Middle East and Lagos, while during the coal boom of 1979–80 bulk carriers had to wait several months to load coal at Baltimore and Hampton Roads. In cases where the demurrage cannot be accurately predicted it is important to the charterer that he receives a demurrage payment equivalent to his daily hire charge.

The contract of affreightment

The Contract of Affreightment (COA) is a little more complicated. The shipowner agrees to carry a series of cargo parcels for a fixed price per ton. For example, the shipper may have a contract to supply ten consignments of 50,000 tons of coal from Colombia to Rotterdam at two-monthly intervals. He would like to arrange for the shipment in a single contract at an agreed price per ton and leave the details of each voyage to the shipowner. This allows the shipowner to plan the use of his ships in the most efficient manner. He can switch cargo between vessels to give the best possible operating pattern and consequently a lower charter rate. He may also be able to arrange backhaul cargoes which improve the utilization of the ship. Companies who specialize in COAs sometimes describe their business as 'industrial shipping' because their aim is to provide a service. Since a long-term contract is involved, COAs involve a greater commitment to marketing the service to the shipper and providing an efficient service.

Most COA business is in the major dry bulk cargoes of iron ore and coal and the major customers are the steel mills of Europe and the Far East. The problem in negotiating COAs is that the precise volume and timing of cargo shipments is not generally known in advance. Cargo volume may be specified as a range (e.g. 'minimum x and maximum y tons') while timing may rely on generalizations such as 'The shipments under the contract shall be evenly spread over the contract period.'

The time charter

A time charter gives the charterer operational control of the ships carrying his cargo, while leaving ownership and management of the vessel in the hands of the shipowner. The length of the charter may be the time taken to complete a single voyage (trip charter) or a period of months or years (period charter). When on charter, the shipowner continues to pay the operating costs of the vessel (i.e. the crew, maintenance and repair as detailed in Chapter 4), but the charterer directs the commercial operations of the vessel and pays all voyage expenses (i.e. bunkers, port charges and canal dues) and cargo handling costs. With a time charter, the shipowner has a clear basis for preparing the ship budget, since he knows the ship operating costs from experience and is in receipt of a fixed daily or monthly charter rate (e.g. $5,000 per day). Often the shipowner will use a long time charter from a major corporation such as a steel mill or an oil company, as security for a loan to purchase the ship needed for the trade.

Although simple in principle, in practice time charters are complex and involve risks for both parties. Details of the contractual agreement are set out in the 'charter-party'. The shipowner must state the vessel's speed, fuel consumption and cargo capacity. The terms of hire will be adjusted if the ship does not perform to these standards. The charter-party will also set out the conditions under which the vessel is regarded as 'off hire', for example during emergency repairs, when the charterer does not pay the charter hire. Long time charters also deal with such matters as the adjustment to the hire charge in the event of the vessel being laid up, and will set out certain conditions under which the charterer is entitled to terminate the arrangement, for example if the owner fails to run the ship efficiently.

There are three reasons why subcontracting may be attractive. First, the shipper may not wish to become a shipowner, but his business requires the use of a ship under his control. Second, the time charter may work out cheaper than buying, especially if the owner has lower costs, due to lower overheads and larger fleet. This seems to have been one of the reasons that oil companies subcontracted so much of their transport in the 1960s. Third, the charterer may be a speculator taking a position in anticipation of a change in the market.

Timechartering to industrial clients is a prime source of revenue for the shipowner. The availability of time charters varies from cargo to cargo and with business circumstances. In the early 1970s about 80 per cent of oil tankers owned by independent shipowners were on time charter to oil companies. Figure 3.2 shows that twenty years later the position had reversed and only about 20 per cent were on time charter. In short there had been a major change of policy by the oil companies, in response to changing circumstances in the tanker market and the oil industry. About 30 per cent of iron ore is carried on the spot market but a larger proportion of grain.

The bare boat charter

Finally, if a company wishes to have full operational control of the ship, but does not wish to own it, a bare boat charter is arranged. Under this arrangement the investor, not necessarily a professional shipowner, purchases the vessel and hands it over to the charterer for a specified period, usually ten to twenty years. The charterer manages the vessel and pays all operating and voyage costs. The owner, who is often a financial institution such as a life insurance company, is not active in the operation of a vessel and does not require any specific maritime skills. It is just an investment. The advantages are that the shipping company does not tie up its capital and the nominal owner of the ship may obtain a tax benefit. This arrangement is often used in the leasing deals discussed in Chapter 6.

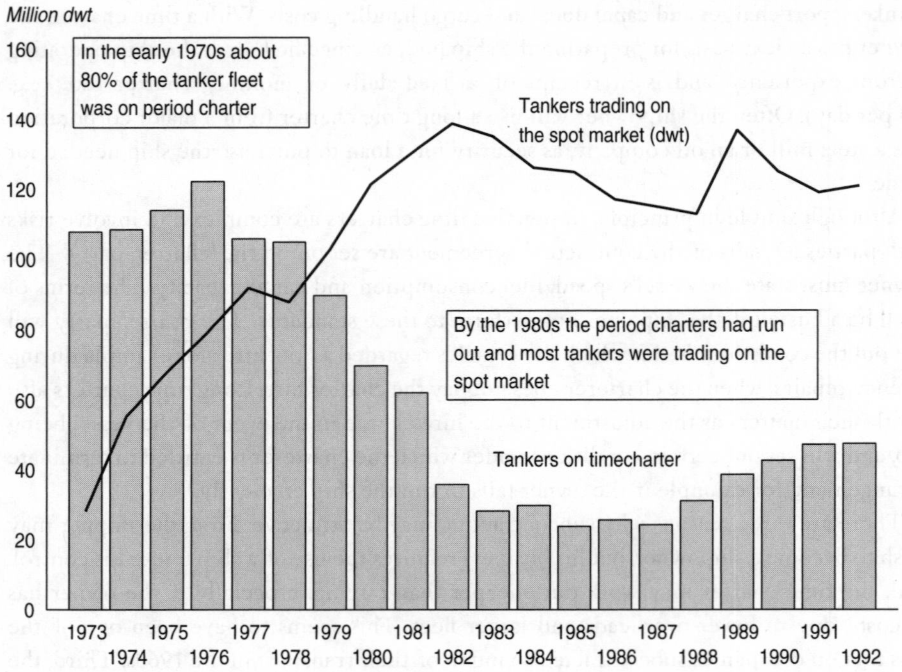

FIGURE 3.2 Oil time charter market
Source: Compiled by Martin Stopford from various sources

The charter-party

Once a deal has been 'fixed', a charter-party is prepared setting out the terms on which the business is to be done. Hiring a ship or contracting for the carriage of cargo is complicated and the charter-party must anticipate the problems that are likely to arise. Even on a single voyage with grain from the US Gulf to Rotterdam any number of mishaps may occur. The ship may not arrive to load at the time indicated, there may be a port strike or the ship may break down in mid-Atlantic. A good charter-party will provide clear guidance on precisely who is legally responsible for the costs in each of these events, whereas a poor charter-party may force either the shipowner, the charterer or the shipper to spend large sums on lawyers to argue a case for compensation.

For the above reasons the charter-party or cargo contract is an important document in the shipping industry and must be expertly drawn up in a way that protects the position of the contracting parties. It would be too time consuming to develop a new charter-party for every contract, particularly voyage charters, and the shipping industry uses standard charter-parties that apply to the main trades, routes and types of chartering arrangement. By using one of these standard contracts, proven in practice, both shipper and shipowner know that the contractual terms will cover most of the eventualities that are likely to arise in that particular trade.

An example of a basic general charter-party is the BIMCO 'Gencon'. This consists of two parts, a schedule (Part 1) setting out details of the charter, shown in Figure 3.3, and notes (Part 11) setting out the standard terms, shown at the end of the chapter. It is usual to specify the standard charter-party to be used at the time when the order is quoted – this avoids subsequent disputes over contractual terms, a very important point in a market where freight rates can change substantially over a short period and one of the contracting parties may look for a legitimate loophole. Because there are so many variants there is no definitive list of charter-party clauses.[4] Taking the 'Gencon' charter-party as an example, the principal sections in the charter-party can be subdivided into six major components:

1 Details of the ship and the contracting parties. The charter-party specifies:

- The name of the shipowner/charterer and broker;
- Details of the ship – including its name, size and cargo capacity;
- The ship's position;
- The brokerage fee, stating who is to pay.

2 A description of cargo to be carried, drawing attention to any special features. The name and address of the shipper is also given, so that the shipowner knows whom to contact when he arrives at the port to load cargo.

3 The terms on which the cargo is to be carried. This important part of the voyage charter-party defines the commitments of the shipper and shipowner under the contract. This covers:

- The dates on which the vessel will be available for loading;
- The loading port or area (for example, US Gulf);
- The discharging port including details of multi port discharge where appropriate;
- Laytime, i.e. time allowed for loading and discharge of cargo;
- Demurrage rate per day in US dollars;
- Payment of loading and discharge expenses.

If loading or discharge is not completed within the time specified the shipowner will be entitled to the payment of liquidated damages (demurrage) and the amount per day is specified in the charter-party (e.g. $5,000/day).

4 The terms of payment. This is important because very large sums of money are involved. The charter-party will specify:

- The freight to be paid;
- The terms on which payment is to be made;

1. Shipbroker	RECOMMENDED THE BALTIC AND INTERNATIONAL MARITIME CONFERENCE UNIFORM GENERAL CHARTER (AS REVISED 1922 and 1976) INCLUDING "F.I.O." ALTERNATIVE, ETC. (To be used for trades for which no approved form is in force) CODE NAME: "GENCON" Part I
	2. Place and date
3. Owners/Place of business (Cl. 1)	4. Charterers/Place of business (Cl. 1)
5. Vessel's name (Cl. 1)	6. GRT/NRT (Cl. 1)
7. Deadweight cargo carrying capacity in tons (abt.) (Cl. 1)	8. Present position (Cl. 1)
9. Expected ready to load (abt.) (Cl. 1)	
10. Loading port or place (Cl. 1)	11. Discharging port or place (Cl. 1)
12. Cargo (also state quantity and margin in Owners' option, if agreed; if full and complete cargo not agreed state "part cargo") (Cl. 1)	
13. Freight rate (also state if payable on delivered or intaken quantity) (Cl. 1)	14. Freight payment (state currency and method of payment; also beneficiary and bank account) (Cl. 4)
15. Loading and discharging costs (state alternative (a) or (b) of Cl. 5; also indicate if vessel is gearless)	16. Laytime (if separate laytime for load. and disch. is agreed, fill in a) and b). If total laytime for load. and disch., fill in c) only) (Cl. 6) a) Laytime for loading
17. Shippers (state name and address) (Cl. 6)	b) Laytime for discharging c) Total laytime for loading and discharging
18. Demurrage rate (loading and discharging) (Cl. 7)	19. Cancelling date (Cl. 10)
20. Brokerage commission and to whom payable (Cl. 14)	
21. Additional clauses covering special provisions, if agreed.	

It is mutually agreed that this Contract shall be performed subject to the conditions contained in this Charter which shall include Part I as well as Part II. In the event of a conflict of conditions, the provisions of Part I shall prevail over those of Part II to the extent of such conflict.

Signature (Owners)	Signature (Charterers)

Printed and sold by Fr. G. Knudtzon Ltd., 55, Toldbodgade, Copenhagen, by authority of The Baltic and International Maritime Conference (BIMCO), Copenhagen.

FIGURE 3.3 BIMCO 'Gencon' Charter, Part I

There is no set rule about this – payment may be made in advance, on discharge of cargo or as instalments during the tenure of the contract. Currency and payment details are also specified.

5 Penalties for non-performance – the notes in Part 11 contain clauses setting out the terms on which penalties will be payable, in the event of either party failing to discharge its responsibilities.

6 Administrative clauses, covering matters that may give rise to difficulties if not clarified in advance. These include the appointment of agents and stevedores, bills of lading, provisions for dealing with strikes, wars, ice, etc.

Time charter-parties follow the same general principles, but include boxes to specify the ship's performance (i.e. fuel consumption, speed, quantity and prices of bunkers on delivery and redelivery) and equipment, and may exclude the items dealing with the cargo.

Efficient business depends upon shippers and shipowners concluding the business quickly and fairly without resorting to legal disputes. In view of the very large sums of money involved in shipping cargo, this goal can be achieved only by detailed charter-parties that provide clear guidance on the allocation of liability in the event of many thousands of possible mishaps occurring during the transport of cargo across the world.

Freight market reporting

The rates at which charters are fixed depend on market conditions and the free flow of information reporting latest developments plays a vital part in the market. Since the starting point for the charter negotiations is 'last done', shipowners and charterers take an active interest in reports of recent transactions. In this section we shall review the way in which charter rates are reported. As an example we will take the daily freight market report published in Lloyd's List. Figure 3.4 shows a typical dry cargo market report, while Figure 3.5 shows a typical tanker chartering report.

Dry cargo market report

The report consists of a commentary on market conditions followed by a list of reported charters under the headings: grain, coal and time charters. Not all charters will be reported. On this particular day the report comments: 'Panamax freight rates continued to edge lower, while capesize levels moved higher due to the volume of forward coal cargoes.' In the fixture report, the details of the charter are generally summarized in a specific order. For voyage charters we can illustrate this point by referring to the first example of a grain charter as follows:

> US Gulf to Japan – *Tai Zhou Hai*, 52,000–54,000 t heavy grains, $24.25 fio, basis no combination, 11 days, Mid-Mar, (Korea Line)

Coal cargoes lift capesize levels

By Anthony Poole

DRY BULK **Tone: mixed**

PANAMAX freight rates conti-nued to edge lower, while cape- size levels moved higher, due to the volume of forward coal cargoes.

The drop in panamax rates was reflected in an 11 point fall in the Baltic Freight Index to 1,443. The largely panamax-dominated index was influenced heavily by lower grain freight rates, as well as softer time charter rates, leading some to say that it was not accurately reflecting the state of the dry bulk market as a whiole. The three capesize routes were stea- dy or moved higher.

In the coal market a 115,000 tonnes cargo was fixed for the first half of April from Richards Bay to Rotterdam at a reported level of $6.95 com- pared with previous business on the route at $6.85.

In the time charter market a newbuilding capesize was re- ported fixed for delivery in Japan at the end of March for a Pacific round voyage at a firm level of £18,000 per day. This compares with recent business on modern tonnage at around $16,000 per day.

Elsewhere in the market, modern panamax tonnage was typically being fixed in the Pacific for steady levels of around £12,000 per day.

The handymax market was generally steady, with vessels fixed in the Pacific for around $10,000 per day. The 1994-built *Parisian Trader* was fixed for prompt delivery in the Far East for two laden legs at a firm level of $10,200 per day.

Smaller handysize vessels did not do so well, with the ex- ception of the *Olympian Merit*, which was widely reported fixed by Pearl for prompt delivery in Hong Kong for a trip via Thailand, redelivery Japan-South Korea range at $7,500 per day.

Other vessels in this size range were generally commanding lower rates, but they were also older vessels.

The mixed trend in the dry bulk market was clearly reflec- ted in estimates for average worldwide earnings. In its weekly report Clarkson Re- search Studies estimated worldwide average daily capesize earnings had risen to $14,753 this week compared with $14,743 a week ago. Panamax earnings fell to $9,975 per day from $10,177.

GRAINS

US Gulf to Japan – *Tai Zhou Hai*, 52,000-54,000t heavy grains, $24.25 fio, basis no combination, 11 days, mid-Mar. (Korea Line)*

North Pacific to Taiwan – vessel to be nominated, 54,000t heavy grains, $13.75–14 fio, 10,000t/4,000t, mid-Marh, (Continental Grain)*

COAL

Richards Bay to Rotterdam – *Protector 2*, 115,000t ±10%, $6.95 fio, scale load/25,000t SHinc, April 1–15. (Cobelfret)

Hampton Roads to Con- stantza – *Royal Clipper*, 105,000t ±10%, $7.50 fio, 30,000t SHinc/15,000t SHinc, end-Mar. (AMCI)*

TIME CHARTER

Cape Jupiter (170,000 dwt, built 1977) delivery Japan, end March, Pacific round voyage, $18,000/day. (K Line)

Hellas (139,000 dwt, built 1982) delivery Continent, end-Mar, trip via Brazil, redelivery China, $13,300/day. (Pan Ocean)

Koula L (71,730 dwt, 13k on 38t + 2.8t mdo, built 1977) de- livery Shanghai Mar 1-10, trip via Australia, redelivery Visk- hapatnan, $8,950 / day (charterer not reported)

Tomis Spirit (65,330 dwt, 13.5k on 38t + 2.75t mdo, built 1986) delivery Black Sea, early Mar, trip to China, $14,000/day. (UBT)

FIGURE 3.4 A dry cargo market report
Source: Lloyd's List, 28 February 1997

The vessel *Tai Zhou Hai* has been chartered to load cargo in the US Gulf and transport it to Japan. The cargo consists of 52–54,000 tons of heavy grains, at a freight rate of $24.25 per ton. According to the *Clarkson Bulk Carrier Register* the *Tai Zhou Hai* is 64,170 dwt, so this is a part cargo, loading the ship to the maximum draft for Panama Canal transit. 'No combination' means it will be a single port discharge (many cargoes have two or three port discharge). Eleven days are allowed for loading and discharge. The vessel must present itself ready to load in mid-March, though the charter-party will certainly be more specific, naming the precise dates. The charterers are Korea Line.

The layout for time charters is slightly different, as we can see taking the first example:

> *Cape Jupiter* (170,000 dwt, built 1997) delivery Japan, end March, Pacific round voyage, $18,000 per day. (K Line)

Demand starts to pick up in Caribbean Sea area

By our Markets Staff

Tone: steady

TANKERS

ACTIVITY was picking up in the Caribbean Sea yesterday with tankers in the 50–70,000 tonne range very much in demand.

World rates for a 70,000-tonne cargo had risen from W115 earlier in the week to W125 yesterday. All were bound for the US – the Gulf coast in particular – where a holiday period recently came to an end.

For example, the *Bona Skipper* was chartered by Clark Oil for the US Gulf Coast at for W124 while an Amoco vessel was fixed for the same run for W125.

Persian Gulf rates were holding quite steady with rates for ULCCs such as the *Jahre Viking* being maintained at around W42.5. However, the *Tina* was fixed at W45 for the Iraq to the US Gulf route. The Persian Gulf VLCC market was said to be stable with rates in the $47.5–50 range.

Rates for Aframax tankers from West Africa to the US had risen slightly from around W90 to W92.5–W95. The North Sea suezmax market was reported to be stable.

A number of rates were not reported, including the *Kandilousa* chartered by shell for Scandinavia to Italy in March, *Amity* (Hess) from St Croix to the US Atlantic coast in Febr- uary, *Jahre Trader* (Elf) from West Africa to Mohammedia on March 11, *Kirsten* (Glencore) from Sullom Voe to Saldanha on March 1 and *BT Stream* (BP) from Hamble to UK-Continent on March 1.

Meanwhile, the inquiries market was said to be gradually improving and was expected to pick up by the end of the day.

Petron was open with a 250,000-tonne cargo from Taz Tanua to Bataan in the Phillip- pines for March 11–12.

In its latest weekly review, Galbraith's said that next week should be the busiest of the month in the ULCC and VLCC market with charterers giving their stem calculations for the month ahead.

CLEAN

Aden to Presian Gulg and Japan - *Sponsalis*, 55,000t, W205, Mar 2. (SSS)

Persian Gulf to East coast India - *Hope* - 49,000t, W165, Feb 25. (US Titan)

Persian Gulf to East coast India - *Four Rays*, 40,000t, W185, option West coast India, W190, Mar 1. (Shell)

Persian Gulf to West coast India - *Tomis North*, 33,000t, W230. Feb. (Shell)

Persian Gulf to Colombo - *Al Dhabiyyah*, 28,000t, W250, Feb. (Total)

DIRTY

Al Bakr to US Gulf - *Tina*, 350,000t, W45, Mar 3. (Exxon)

Karg Island to UK/Continent/ Mediterranean - Vessel to be nominated, 285,000t, W50, option to Red Sea, W52.5, Mar 10. (NITC)

Persian Gulf to Brazil - *Tijuca*, 270,000t, cost of affreightment, Mar 12. (Petrobras)

Persian Gulf to Japan - *Helios Breeze*, 250,000t, W59.5, Mar 10. (Tonen)

FIGURE 3.5 A tanker market report
Source: Lloyd's List, 28 February 1997

The ship details are given in brackets after its name, and in this case the vessel is a brand new 170,000 dwt bulk carrier delivered 1997, so it is almost certainly on its maiden voyage. Sometimes the speed and fuel consumption are quoted, since these are significant in determining the charter rate. The vessel is to be delivered to charterers in Japan at the end of March, to undertake a Pacific round voyage at a charter rate of $18,000 per day and is chartered by K Line. Often the location of redelivery is specified. For example, the next time charter for the *Hellas* specifies 'redelivery China'. Note that the daily charter rate for the *Hellas*, a 139,000 dwt vessel built 1982, is $13,300 per day, about 26 per cent below the charter rate for the *Cape Jupiter*. All of the time charters reported in Figure 3.4. are for a single round voyage or a six-month period, emphasizing the fact that the time charter is not exclusively a means of fixing vessels for long periods.

Tanker market report

The tanker charter report in Figure 3.5 follows a similar pattern to the dry cargo market, though in this case the main division in the reported charter is between 'clean' and 'dirty'. The clean charters refer to products tankers carrying clean oil products, while the dirty charters refer to crude oil and black products. Tanker fixtures are generally in Worldscale, an index based on the cost of operating a standard tanker on the route. The first item reported in the commentary is the firming of rates for tankers of 50–70,000 dwt in the Caribbean from W115 to W125. Also the report notes that rates for ULCCs like the *Jahre Viking*, the world's biggest tanker of 564,763 dwt, were quite steady at about W42.5 (the vessel had been fixed to Exxon two days earlier). The details reported for each charter follow a similar pattern to dry cargo. For example:

Aden to Persian Gulf and Japan – *Sponsalis*, 55,000 t, Worldscale 205, Mar 2.(SSS)

This means that the motorship *Sponsalis* has been fixed for a voyage charter from Aden to Japan via the Persian Gulf. The cargo is 55,000 tons, which is a part cargo – checking in the *Clarkson Tanker Register*, we see that *Sponsalis* is a 1986-built epoxy coated products tanker of 87,000 dwt. The charter rate is Worldscale 205 and commences on 2 March. The charterer is SSS, which is the designation of Showa Shell. Note that the charter rate for the 87,000 dwt products tanker is almost four times higher than for the 564,763 dwt ULCC, reflecting the smaller cargo size and indirect voyage undertaken on the products fixture.

Liner and specialist ship chartering

The biggest international charter market is in tanker and dry bulk tonnage. There is also a significant market for liner and specialist vessels. Liner companies from time to time need to charter in additional ships to meet the requirements of an upswing in trade or to service the trade while their own vessels are undergoing major repairs. For this reason there is an active charter market in 'tweendeckers, roll on, roll off vessels (ro-ros) and container ships.

Freight rate statistics

Shipowners, shippers and charterers take great interest in statistics showing trends in freight rates and charter rates. Three different units of measurement are commonly used. *Voyage rate statistics* for dry cargo commodities are generally reported in $/ton for a standard voyage. By convention this is a negotiated rate covering the total transport costs. This measurement is commonly used in the dry cargo trades where, for example, brokers such as Clarksons report average rates on 26 routes each week. For example, $12 per tonne for grain from the US Gulf to Rotterdam or $5.50 per tonne for coal to Queensland to Japan. In contrast *time charter rates* are generally measured in $000s per day. Time charterer rates are commonly reported for 'trip' (i.e. round voyage), 6 months, 12 months and 3 years.

The Worldscale Index (W/S)

The third and most complex measure of freight rates is *Worldscale.* The tanker industry uses this freight rates index as a more convenient way of negotiating the freight rate per barrel of oil on many different routes. The concept was developed during the Second World War when the British Government introduced a schedule of official freight rates as a basis for paying the owners of requisitioned tankers. The schedule showed the cost of transporting a cargo of oil on each of the main routes using a standard 12,000 dwt tanker. Owners were paid the rate shown in the schedule or some fraction of it. The system was adopted by the tanker industry after the war and has been progressively revised over the years, the last amendment being in January 1989 when 'New Worldscale' was introduced.

The Worldscale index is published in a book which is used as the basis for calculating tanker spot rates. The book shows, for each tanker route, the cost of transporting a metric tonne of cargo using the standard vessel on a round voyage. This cost is known as 'Worldscale 100'. Each year the Worldscale Panel meet in London and updates the book. The standard vessel has, from time to time, been updated. The one in use in 1997 is shown in Table 3.1. The Worldscale system makes it easier for shipowners and charterers to compare the earnings of their vessels on different routes. Suppose a tanker is available spot in The Gulf and the owner agrees a rate of Worldscale 50 for a voyage from Jubail to Rotterdam. To calculate how much money he will earn he first looks up the rate per metric tonne for Worldscale 100 from Rotterdam to Jubail. Consulting the appropriate entry he finds that it is $17.30 per metric tonne. Since he has settled at Worldscale 50 he will receive half of this amount, i.e. $8.65 per metric tonne. If his ship carries 250,000 metric tonnes, the revenue from the voyage will be $2,162,500. It is an equally simple matter to make the same calculation for a voyage to Japan.

TABLE 3.1 Worldscale basis tanker

Total capacity	75,000 tonnes
Average service speed	14.5 knots
Bunker consumption	
steaming	55 tonnes per day
other	100 tonnes per round voyage
in port	5 tonnes per port
Grade of fuel oil	380 cst
Port time	4 days for a voyage from one loading port to another discharging port
Fixed hire element	$12,000 per day
Bunker price	US$ 116.75 per tonne
Port costs	Most recent available
Canal transit time	30 hours per Suez transit

Source: Worldscale Association, London

The Baltic Freight Index (BFI)

The volatility of the charter market creates uncertainty over future freight charges that may be unwelcome to many businessmen. Consider the case of a European grain merchant who in February purchases 55,000 tons of maize to be shipped from the US Gulf to Rotterdam in July. Since he is obliged to wait until July before chartering a vessel, there is a risk that the freight rate will increase, wiping out his profit on the deal.

The Baltic International Freight Futures Exchange (BIFFEX) was opened in January 1985 to enable shippers, owners and charterers to hedge against sudden changes in the freight rate. The freight future market is based on the Baltic Freight Index (BFI), a statistical index covering freight rates on eleven different trade routes (grain (four routes), coal (three routes), iron ore, and trip charter (three routes)). The index is calculated each day as the weighted average of actual rates on the thirteen routes. If there are no charters, a panel of brokers independently submit their estimates of what the charter rate would have been and these are averaged. In addition to providing a settlement index for hodging, the Baltic Freight Index (BFI) is the most widely used market indicator in dry bulk shipping. The path which the index has followed since it was set up in 1985 is shown in Figure 3.6. Also shown on this graph are brief notes recording key events which influenced the market. Over the decade 1987 to 1997 there were thirteen occasions on which the index moved several hundred points up or down in a period of a few months. This is the volatility which hedging markets are designed to deal with.

The hedging operation is achieved by trading units on the freight futures exchange. Like any futures market, the price at which individuals are prepared to buy and sell forward depends upon their expectations of the future – if in January it is expected that freight rates will have risen by April, then the price of contract units for settlement at end April will be higher than the current BIFFEX Index and vice versa. Contract units can be bought and sold at a rate of $10 per BIFFEX index point, with units traded ahead for settlement at three-monthly intervals. A typical broker's report of trading on 11 February 1997 is illustrated in Table 3.2. This shows that on the day in question the actual value of the index was 1,435 but contract units for settlement at the end of February were being traded at $15,100, while contract units for settlement at the end of July were being traded at $13,050 suggesting that traders expected freight rates to fall during the next six months.

A shipper who purchased a contract unit for $13,050 on 11 February for settlement at the end of July would be entitled to receive on the last day of July a payment of $10 for each point in the actual BIFFEX Index at the end of July (in practice the settlement price is calculated by taking the average of the index for each of the last five trading days

TABLE 3.2 Example of BIFFEX trading report

Data	*Baltic Freight Index closing trade Index Jan 85=100*	*Trading price of contract unit at $10 per index point*
Actual 11 February 1997	1,435	
Forward Rates (distant)		
end February settlement	1510	15,100
end April Settlement	1,565	15,650
end July settlement	1,305	13,050
end October settlement	1,420	14,200

Source: Lloyd's List, 11 February, 1997

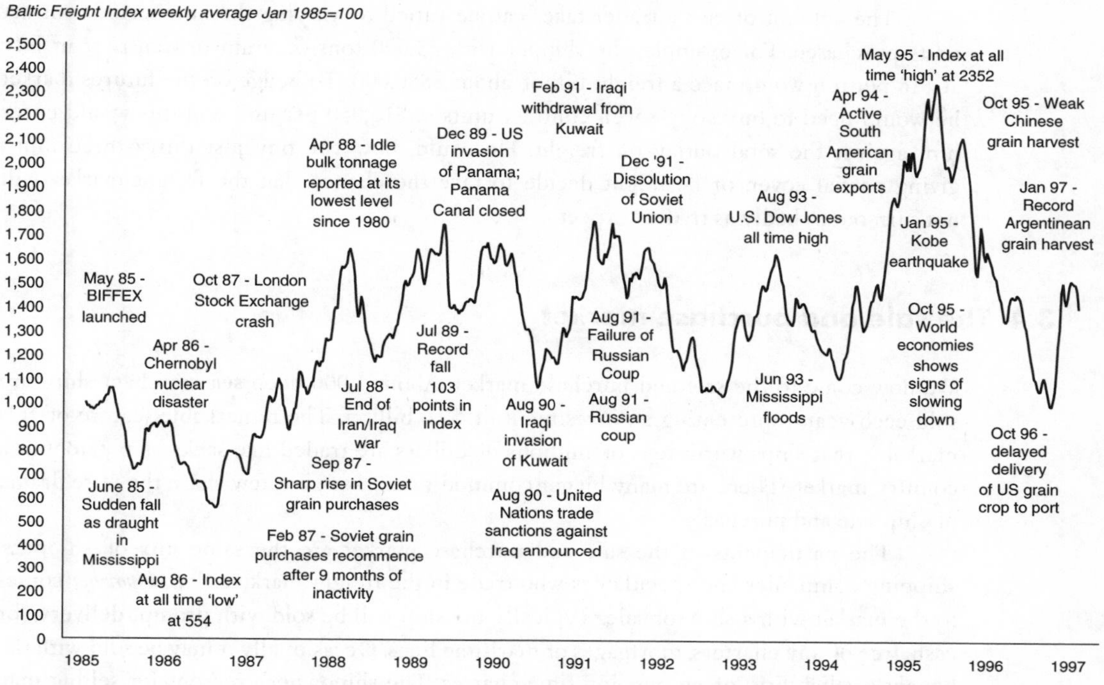

FIGURE 3.6 The Baltic freight index (BFI 1985–97 and significant events)
Source: Clarkson Research Studies

in the month of settlement). If, for example, the BIFFEX Index had risen to 1,500 at the end of July then the holder of a July contract unit would receive $15,000, giving a gross profit of $1,950 over the original purchase price. Out of this he must pay a commission to the broker who carried out the transaction for him. Conversely, the trader who sold the contract unit for $13,050 in January would have to settle at $15,000 at the end of July, incurring a loss on the transaction.

From the shipowner's point of view, if he sells contract units for settlement in July at $13,050 and by July the BIFFEX Index has fallen below 13,050, then he will make a profit on the transaction that will compensate him for the losses he will be making on chartering his ship at the lower freight rate. Conversely, if the index rises to 1,500 then he will make a sizeable loss, but he should be able to recoup this loss from the additional profits made by chartering his ships at the higher rate. In short, by using the futures market he is able to hedge his future income.

On the other side of the deal, the shipper has also secured his future financial position. If he buys forward and the outturn BIFFEX rate is higher than the purchase price, he makes a profit that compensates him for the higher freight rate he will have to pay to charter a ship. Conversely, if BIFFEX falls below the rate at which he bought forward, he will make a loss that he will recoup by chartering a ship at less than the anticipated rate.

The amount of risk a trader takes can be varied by varying the number of contract units purchased. For example, the shipper with 55,000 tons of grain to transport in July at $16 per ton would face a freight bill of about $880,000. To hedge on the futures market he would need to buy sixty-seven contract units at $13,050 per unit and this would cover him against the total outlay on freight. He could, however, buy just thirty-three units, giving partial cover, or he might decide to take the chance that the freight market will not turn out as badly as traders expect.

3.4 The sale and purchase market

We now come to the sale and purchase market. About 1,000 deep sea merchant ships are sold each year, representing an investment of $9.6 billion. The remarkable feature of this market is that ships worth tens of millions of dollars are traded like sacks of potatoes at a country market. There are many bigger commodity markets, but few share the pure drama of ship sale and purchase.

The participants in the sale and purchase market are the same mix of shippers, shipping companies and speculators who trade in the freight market. The *shipowner* comes to the market with a ship for sale. Typically the ship will be sold with prompt delivery, for cash, free of any charters, mortgages or maritime liens. Occasionally it may be sold with the benefit (or liability) of an ongoing time charter. The shipowner's reasons for selling may vary. He may have a policy of replacing vessels at a certain age, which this ship may have reached; the ship may no longer suit his trade; or he may think prices are about to fall. Finally there is the 'distress sale' in which the owner sells the ship to raise cash to meet his day-to-day commitments. The *purchaser* may have equally diverse objectives. He may need a ship of a specific type and capacity to meet some business commitment, for example a contract to carry coal from Australia to Japan. Or he may be an investor who feels that it is the right time to acquire a ship of a particular type. In the latter case his requirements may be more flexible, in the sense that he is more interested in the investment potential than the ship itself.

Most sale and purchase transactions are carried out through *shipbrokers*. The shipowner instructs his broker to find a buyer for the vessel. Sometimes the ship will be given exclusively to a single broker, but it is common to offer the vessel through several broking companies. On receipt of the instruction the broker will telephone or fax any client he knows who is looking for a vessel of this type. If the instruction is exclusive, he will call up other brokers in order to market the ship through their client list. Full details of the ship are drawn up, including the specification of the hull, machinery, equipment, class, survey status and general equipment. Simultaneously the broking house will be receiving enquiries from potential purchasers. For example an owner may be seeking a 'modern' 65,000 dwt bulk carrier. The broker may have suitable vessels for sale on his own list, and would not pursue enquiries through other brokers. If no suitable candidates can be found, he may look for suitable candidates and approach their owners to see if there is any interest in selling.

The sales procedure

Broadly speaking the procedure for buying/selling a ship can be sub-divided into the following five stages:

1 *Putting the ship on the market.* The first step is for the buyer or seller to appoint a broker – or he may decide to handle the transaction himself. Particulars of the ship for sale are circulated to interested parties in the market.

2 *Negotiation of price and conditions.* Once a prospective buyer has been found the negotiation begins. There are no hard and fast rules. In a buoyant market the buyer may have to make a quick decision on very limited information. Alternatively during a weak market, he can take his time, inspecting large numbers of ships and seeking detailed information from the owners. When agreement has been reached in principle, the brokers may draw up a 'recap telex' summarizing the key details about the ship and the transaction, before proceeding to the formal stage of preparing a sale contract.

3 *Memorandum of Agreement.* Once an offer has been accepted a Memorandum of Agreement is drawn up setting out the terms on which the sale will take place. A commonly used pro forma for the Memorandum of Agreement is the Norwegian Sales Form (1987).[5] The memorandum sets out the administrative details for the sale (i.e. where, when and on what terms) and lays down certain contractual rights, such as the right of the buyer to inspect Class Society records. A summary of the key points covered in sales form documents are listed in Box 3.2. At this stage the memorandum is not generally legally binding, since it will include a phrase to the effect that it is 'subject to . . .'.

4 *Inspections.* The buyer, or his surveyor make any inspections which are permitted in the sales contract. There will probably be a physical inspection of the ship, possibly including an underwater inspection by divers. There will also be an inspection of the Classification Society records for information about the mechanical and structural history of the ship. Sales often fail at this stage if the buyer is not happy with the results of the inspections.

5 *The closing.* Finally the ship is delivered to its new owners who simultaneously transfer the balance of funds to the seller's bank. At the closing meeting representatives of the buyer and seller on board ship are in telephone contact with a meeting ashore of representatives of sellers, buyers, current and prospective mortgagees and the ship's existing registry.

How ship prices are determined

The sale and purchase market thrives on price volatility. 'Asset play' profits earned from well-timed buying and selling activity are an important source of income for shipping investors. Bankers are just as interested in ship values because a mortgage on the hull is the primary collateral for their loans.

BOX 3.2 Sale and purchase Memorandum of Agreement (MOA): example: Norwegian sales form 1987

This four page pro-forma contract has 15 clauses covering the issues which can be problematic in selling a ship. The following summary refers to the MOA as drafted. Individual clauses are generally modified during the negotiation, with terms added or removed.

Preamble: At the top of the form are spaces to enter the date, the seller, the buyer and details of the ship, including the classification society, year of build, shipyard, flag, etc.

1 **Price**: The price to be paid for the vessel.

2 **Deposit**: States the deposit paid by the purchaser, when it must be paid and where.

3 **Payments**: The purchase money (amount and bank details stated) must be paid on delivery of the vessel, but not later than three banking days after the buyer has been notified that the vessel is ready for delivery.

4 **Inspections**: The buyer can inspect the vessel and its class records. The clause states where and when the vessel will be available and restricts the scope of the inspection (no 'opening up'). After inspection the buyer has 48 hours to accept in writing, after which the contract is null and void. (N.B. In practice buyers generally inspect the ship before the MOA is drawn up, in which case this clause does not apply).

5 **Place and time of delivery**: States where the vessel will be delivered and when, usually a range of ports over a period of time. The buyer can cancel the purchase if the ship is not delivered by the stated date.

6 **Drydocking**: The seller is to drydock the vessel at the port of delivery for the bottom inspection. Any defects which affect the vessel's class must be rectified. It states who is responsible for the various expenses. (N.B. Nowadays it is more common to use divers.)

7 **Spares/Bunkers etc**: Names moveable items included in the sale of those which the seller can take ashore. Bunkers and lubricating oils are handed over at the market price.

8 **Documentation**: The seller must provide a notarially attested bill of sale; a certificate stating that the vessel is free from registered encumbrances; a certificate demonstrating that the vessel has been deleted from its current registry; and all class papers

9 **Encumbrances**: The seller warrants that the vessel is free from any third party claims which could damage its commercial value. Any claim arising subsequently but incurred before delivery, must be paid by the buyer.

10 **Taxes**: Buyers and sellers are responsible for their own costs of registration etc.

11 **Condition on delivery**: The ship must be delivered in the condition in which it was inspected; it must be in class, and the class society must have been notified of anything which could affect its class status.

12 **Name/Markings**: On delivery the buyer must change the name of the vessel and all funnel markings (i.e. so that it is clear that it is not still trading under the previous owner).

13 **Buyer's default**: If the buyer defaults and the deposit has not been paid, the seller can claim his costs from the buyer. If the deposit has been paid, but the purchase money is not paid, the seller can retain the deposit and claim compensation for losses, with interest.

14 **Seller's default**: If the seller fails to deliver the vessel with everything belonging to her by the agreed date, the buyer can cancel the contract and receive interest and compensation for expenses.

15 **Arbitration**: Sets out the terms under which arbitration will be carried out.

There has always been plenty of volatility to attract investors and worry bankers. Early in the twentieth century Fairplay monitored the price of a 'new, ready 7,500 ton cargo steamer'. The price of this vessel increased from £48,000 in 1898 to £60,750 in December 1900, and then fell by one-third to £39,250 in December 1903.[6] The same vessel was worth £232,000 in 1919, £52,000 in 1925 and £48,750 in 1930. In the 1970s and 1980s we find much the same pattern. For example the price of a 60,000 dwt bulk carrier, shown in Figure 3.7, fell to $6 million in December 1977. Three years later December 1980 the price had increased by 60 per cent to $22 million. Within two years the price was down to $7 million, and did not reach $22 million again until late 1989, after which it was steady for several years.

If we express the price of a 30,000 dwt bulk carrier as a percentage deviation from a linear regression trend fitted over the period 1976–94, the extent of the volatility becomes clear. In 1980 the price reached a peak 70 per cent above the trend, while in 1986 it fell 70 per cent below trend (Figure 3.8). Obviously selling a ship at the bottom of a market cycle is disastrous, and a great bargain for the buyer. No shipping company follows this suicidal course of action by choice. 'Distress' sales during market troughs are generally driven by cashflow pressures. The seller might be a shipowner who cannot pay his bunker bill, or a banker who has foreclosed on his client and taken posession of the fleet. Fortunately the extreme price fluctuations shown in Figure 3.8 are relatively uncommon and the more limited volatility which occurred between 1987 and 1997 is more common. It all depends on the underlying cashflow of the industry.

Movements in the price of different ship types tend to be closely synchronized. Over the twenty-year period shown in Figure 3.7, 89 per cent of the price movements of a 65,000

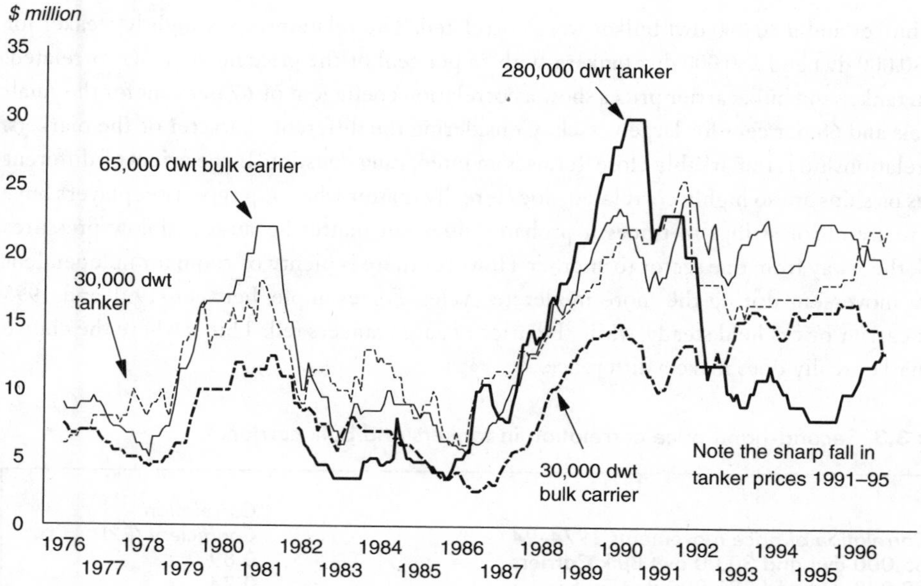

FIGURE 3.7 Price cycles for tankers and bulk carriers (five-year-old ships)
Source: Clarkson Research Studies

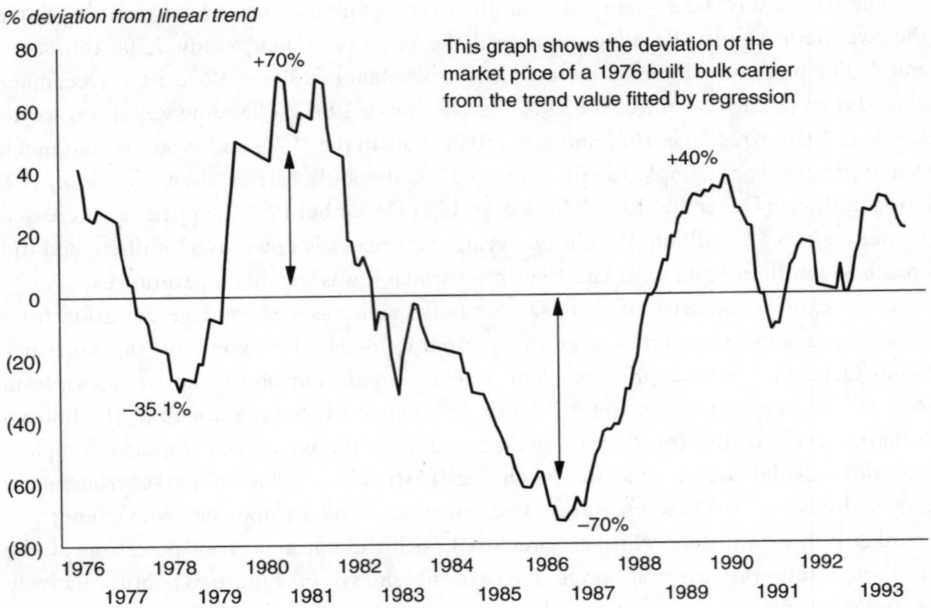

FIGURE 3.8 Bulk carrier price volatility 1976–93 (30,000 dwt bulk carrier)
Source: Figure 3.7

dwt bulker and a 30,000 dwt bulker were correlated. The relationship is slightly weaker for the 30,000 dwt and 280,000 dwt tankers, with 75 per cent of the price movements correlated. Even tanker and bulk carrier prices show a correlation coefficient of 67 per cent for the small vessels and 68 per cent for large vessels. Considering the different character of the markets, the relationship is remarkably close. It raises an interesting question. If the prices of different types of ships are so highly correlated, does it really matter what ship type asset players buy? For really major swings in prices it probably does not matter because cashflow pressures work their way from one sector to another. However there is plenty of room for independent price movement during the more moderate cycles. For example, between 1991 and 1995 bulk carrier prices held steady, while the price of large tankers fell. This is where the choice of market really does make a difference.

Box 3.3 Second-hand price correlation in tankers and bulk carriers

Correlation of price movements 1974–94	*Correlation Coefficient (R2)*
65,000 dwt and 30,00 dwt Bulk Carriers	0.89
30,000 dwt and 280,000 dwt Tanker	0.74
65,000 dwt Bulk Carrier and 280,000 dwt Tanker	0.68
30,000 dwt Bulk Carrier and 30,000 dwt Products Tanker	0.67

Price dynamics of merchant ships

In the circumstances outlined above it is natural that second-hand prices play a major part in the commercial decisions of shipowners – very large sums of money are involved. What determines the value of a ship at a particular point in time? There are four factors which are influential: freight rates, age, inflation and shipowners' expectations for the future.

Freight rates are the primary influence on ship prices. Peaks and troughs in the freight market are transmitted through into the sale and purchase market, as can be seen in Figure 3.9 which traces price movements from 1976–93 for a five-year-old bulk carrier, comparing the market price with the one-year time charter rate. The relationship is very close, especially as the market moves from trough to peak. When the freight rate fell from $8,500 per day in 1981 to $3,600 per day in 1985, the price fell from $12 million to $3 million. Conversely, when the freight recovered to $8,500 per day, the price increased to $15 million. This correlation provides some guidance on valuing ships using the gross earnings method. Analysis of the past relationship between price and freight rates suggests that when freight rates are high the S&P market values a five-year-old ship at about six times its current annual earnings, based on the one year time charter rate. For example if it is earning $4 million per annum it will value the ship at $24 million. When the market drops, so does the earnings multiple. In recessions the value may fall as low as three time earnings.

The second influence on a ship's value is *age*. A ten-year-old ship is worth less than a five-year-old ship. The normal accountancy practice is to depreciate merchant ships

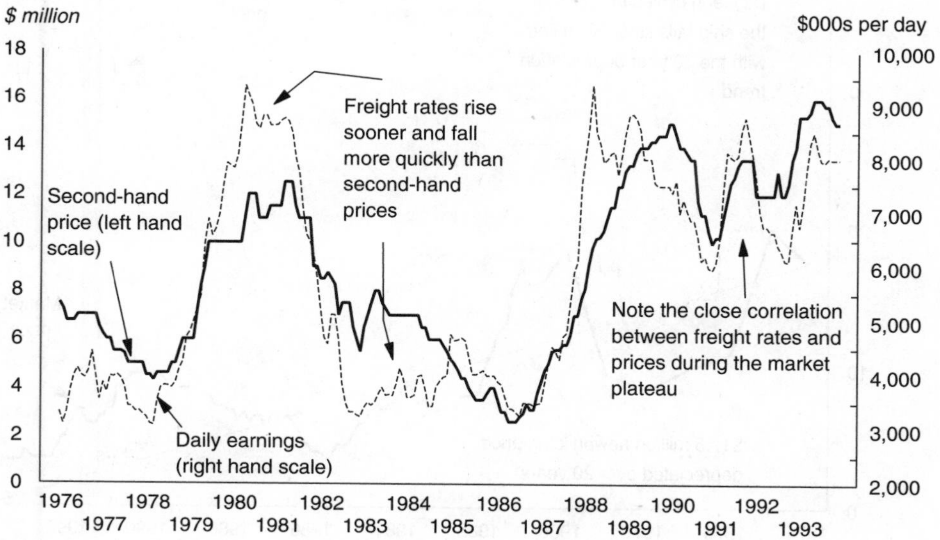

FIGURE 3.9 Correlation of second-hand price and freight rate (five-year-old bulk carrier)

Source: Clarkson Research Studies

down to scrap over 15 or 20 years. Brokers who value ships take much the same view, generally using the 'rule of thumb' that a ship loses 5 or 6 per cent of its value each year. As an example of how this works out in practice, Figure 3.10 shows the price of a 1974 built products tanker over the 20 years to 1994. The slope of the depreciation curve reflects the loss of performance due to age, higher maintenance costs, a degree of technical obsolescence and expectations about the economic life of the vessel. For a specific ship the economic life may be reduced by the carriage of corrosive cargoes, poor design, or inadequate maintenance. When the market value eventually falls below the scrap value the ship is likely to be sold for scrapping. The average age of tankers and bulk carriers scrapped in 1995 was 23–25 years, but in protected trades, such as the US domestic trades, the average scrapping age in the mid-1990s was about 35 years.[7] Ships operating in fresh water environments such as the Great Lakes last much longer.

In the longer term, *inflation* affects ship prices. Inflation of asset values accounted for about half the return on bulk shipping in the 1970s and 1980s. To illustrate the effects discussed above we can look at past behaviour of the price of a second-hand bulk carrier as the ship grows older. The development of a second-hand price for a 35,000 dwt bulk carrier built in 1965 is shown in Figure 3.11. The graph was calculated by taking the reported resale price of the ship in dollars, deflating it to remove the effects of inflation using the OECD consumer price index and fitting a linear trend to the deflated data. The trend line thus

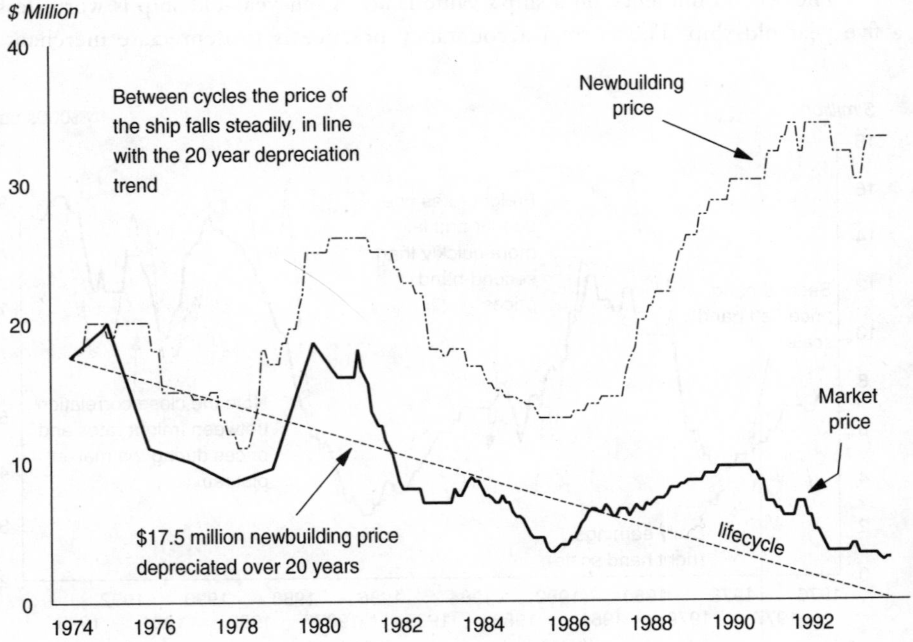

FIGURE 3.10 **Price life cycle and depreciated trend (30,000 dwt products tanker built 1974)**

Source: Clarkson Research Studies

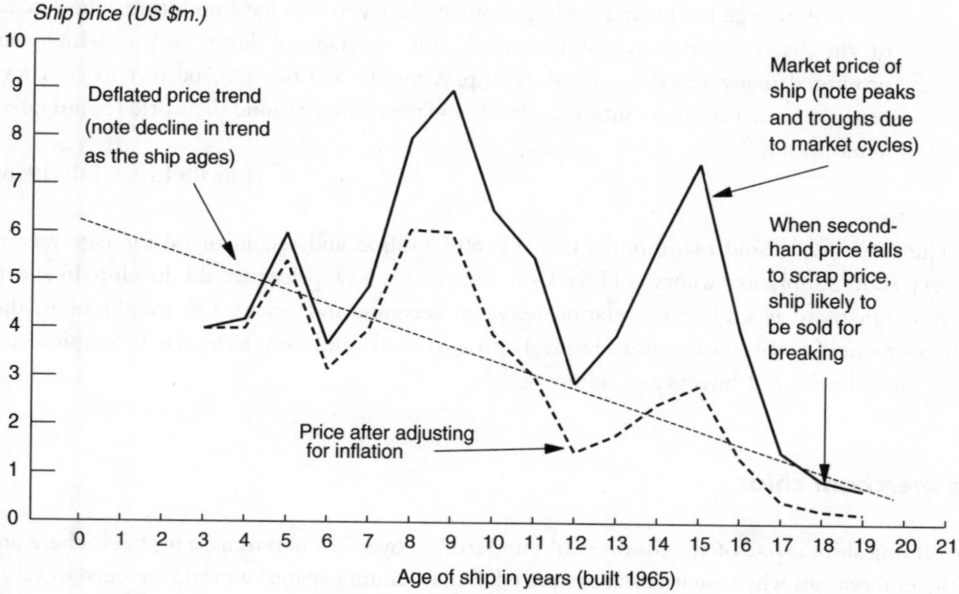

FIGURE 3.11 The effects of age, market cycles and inflation on a bulk carrier (35,000 dwt)

Source: Compiled by Martin Stopford from various sources

presents a rough estimate of what the resale price of the ship would have been if there had been no market cycles and no inflation during the life of the vessel.

After 10 years the trend resale value of the 35,000 dwt vessel has fallen by 49 per cent relative to its new value. This suggests that, if this vessel is typical, leaving aside the effects of market cycles and inflation, we would expect that after 10 years the vessel would have a market resale value of about 50 per cent less than the original newbuilding value. However, inflation seems to have a very significant effect and, as time passes, the market price line moves progressively further above the deflated price line. After a few years, even during depressions the market price does not fall below the trend value.

The fourth and in some ways most important influence on second-hand prices is *expectations.* This accelerates the speed of change at market turning points. For example buyers or sellers may first hold back to see what will happen, then suddenly rush to trade once they believe the market is 'on the move'. The market can swing from deep depression to intensive activity in the space of only a few weeks, as the following newspaper report demonstrates:

> A very large crude carrier damaged in a Persian Gulf missile attack and destined to be broken up has become the subject of one of the year's most remarkable sales deals. Market sources believe that the buyer has paid $7 million for the tanker which, until

> the recent surge in demand for large tonnage, appeared to have no future. The rescue of the *Volere* is indicative of the continuing shortage of large tankers which has prompted many vessels to break lay-up. A month ago the 423,700 dwt *Empress* was brought from Taiwanese interests after being towed half around the world for intended demolition.
>
> (Lloyd's List, 4 July 1986)

The *Volere* was resold two months later for $9.5 million and second-hand tonnage was in very short supply as owners held back on sales to see how prices would develop. In short, although there is a clear correlation between second-hand prices and freight rates, the movement of prices is often not a leisurely process. Peaks and troughs tend to be emphasized by the behaviour of buyers and sellers.

Valuing merchant ships

Valuing ships is one of the routine tasks undertaken by sale and purchase brokers. There are several reasons why valuations are required. Banks lending against a mortgage need to value the collateral and will probably continue to monitor the ship's value over the term of the loan. Prospectuses for public offerings of equity generally include a valuation of the company's fleet, as do the annual accounts of public companies. Finally, leases often require a view on the 'residual value' of the ship at the end of the loan period. This is a much more complex and difficult task than simply appraising the current value.

Valuing a merchant ship involves a mixture of procedure, market knowledge and judgement. First the broker consults his records to check the physical characteristics of the ship and recent sales of similar vessels. He will pay particular attention to the ship type, size, age, yard of build, survey status, equipment and specification. Most of these are self evident, but some deserve comment. Bigger ships are generally worth more than smaller ships, but the relationship varies with the freight cycle. For example, in the distressed market of the 1980s a 250,000 dwt tanker could be bought for the same price as an 80,000 dwt vessel, whereas at the market peak in 1989 the 250,000 dwt vessel was worth twice as much. We have already discussed age and the 'rule of thumb' that ships lose about 5 per cent of their value each year. This is a useful guideline, but it is not always reliable, especially for very new or very old ships. The yard of build is important because ships built in some marginal yards sell at a discount, so care is needed.

Equipment is sometimes important. Shipowners prefer ships with standard machinery, so any ship with an unusual engine or auxiliary equipment is likely to be discounted. Some ships are better specified than others and owners are keen to see this reflected in the valuation. A double hull tanker, above average cargo handling gear, tank coatings, good fuel economy, high speed, pallet capability (in reefers), automated engine room all make the ship more desirable. However, like 'extras' on motor cars, these features make the ship easier to sell but do not always increase its value. Sometimes an 'extra' is not an advantage. For example, small bulk carriers frequently require cargo handling gear, and a geared ship is worth more.

In contrast Panamax bulk carriers are not generally geared, so a geared Panamax may not attract a premium.

Physical condition certainly affects the price of a ship, but this is something which brokers are not in a position to evaluate. For valuation purposes the ship is generally assumed to be 'in good and seaworthy condition'. *The responsibility for establishing the physical condition of the ship lies entirely with the purchaser/owner/banker.* Survey status is another matter. If the ship is old and a special survey is imminent, this will be taken into account. Although the valuer does not know how much the ship will need spending on it, he knows how the market treats ships in this situation, and will take that into account.

Ultimately the valuation is the broker's judgement of what the vessel would fetch if put on the market on a 'willing buyer, willing seller' basis. This qualification is important, because if no 'willing buyer' is available, normal prices may be heavily discounted. Although the broker will take into account 'last done', the ship is normally valued at what it would sell for today. In a rising market, the valuation will be above recent reported sales and lower in a falling market. Sometimes a broker may be asked to value a ship of a type for which there has been no recent sale. In this case the valuation is entirely judgemental. Three brokers may arrive at three different prices, depending on how they feel the market would respond to the sale of a ship of this type.

TABLE 3.3 Example of residual value calculation

	Value $ mill
Initial cost of the ship	28
Depreciation rate (per cent per annum)	5 per cent
Book value after 10 years	14
Inflation rate (per cent per annum)	3 per cent
Replacement cost after 10 years	18.8
Value at cyclical trough:	
Cyclical trough margin, say	−70 per cent
Resale price at trough	5.6
Value at market peak:	
Cyclical peak margin, say	70 per cent
Resale price at peak	32

In view of the large sums of money involved, it is to be expected that there will be disputes over what a ship is really worth. For example a bank may produce a valuation showing that the collateral cover on a loan is inadequate due to the falling value of the mortgaged ships, but the borrower produces his own higher valuations. When prices are falling there is often little business transacted, so the valuation is particularly subjective, with the result that different brokers take different views. A panel of valuers is the usual solution to this difficulty.

Another common problem is the charter status of the ship. What happens if the ship has a time charter? One possibility is to carry out a present value calculation, based on the charter revenue and projected operating costs, but this raises the difficult question of whether the charterer is creditworthy and how to value the ship at the end of the charter. Most brokers value vessels charter free.There may also be problems valuing ship types that are rarely sold. This is often a problem with specialized ships such as chemical parcel tankers, LNG tankers, big container ships, etc. Because the market for these vessels is so thin, brokers find it very difficult to value them. To deal with this problem more than one shipbroker may be asked to value the vessel.

Finally, there is the question of quality. Owners often argue that their ships are of superior quality and should be valued above the average market rate. In general valuers are unwilling to fall in with this line of thought. Quality ships sell more easily, but this is not something which can be quantified accurately. For this reason most valuers still insist on the 'average market condition' clause, despite today's quality consciousness in the shipping industry.

Valuing a ship for scrap starts with the lwt tonnage of the ship. This is the physical weight of the vessel (i.e. the amount of water it displaces). Scrap prices are quoted in $/lwt ton. for example a VLCC might have a lwt of 36,000 tons. At $180 per ton its scrap value is $6.48m. In practice scrap prices are almost as volatile as second-hand ship prices. During the last 10 years the scrap price of tankers has swung between $100/lwt and $240/lwt.

Calculating the residual value of ships

So much for the current value of a ship, but what will it be worth in future, for example at the end of a 10-year lease? The basic methodology is to use the three determinants of a ship's price: the depreciation rate, the rate of inflation and the market cycle. Take as an example a new bulk carrier costing $28 million in 1996 (see Table 3.3). If we assume that vessel depreciates at 5 per cent per annum on a straight line basis during the first 10 years of its life, by the end of 10 years its book value will have fallen to $14 million. However, during this time we assume that shipbuilding prices have increased by 3 per cent per annum, so the replacement cost after 10 years would be $18.8 million. This is the most likely value. However, we need to take account of the market cycle, which we have seen can affect the resale price by plus or minus 70 per cent, if we take the most extreme price movements in Figure 3.9. A sale at the top of the market could bring a price of $32 million, which is higher than the initial purchase price of the ship. If, however, the sale occurs at the bottom of a trough and we allow for a price 70 per cent below the trend value, the minimum resale value would fall to US$5.6 million, which is 20 per cent of the initial cost.

This approach has many pitfalls. Depreciation rates and inflation are difficult enough to predict, but the market cycle is the real challenge. The cyclical value range of $5.6 million to $32 million is so wide that a view has to be taken on what intensity of cycles might lie ahead. This is pure shipping risk and it is up to the investor to decide what level of risk he is prepared to accept. For example the analysis in Table 3.3 is based on one of the most extreme market cycles of the century. The view might be taken that this is unlikely to happen in the period under consideration, so a smaller residual value range would be appropriate.

Study of the market cycles discussed in chapter 2 and the market fundamentals in chapter 4 can help to narrow the range, but will never entirely remove it. That is the judgement that no amount of statistical analysis will remove. Someone has to take a risk. That, after all, is what the shipping market is all about.

3.5 The newbuilding market

Although the shipbuilding market is closely related to the sale and purchase market, its character is quite different. Both markets deal in ships, but the newbuilding market trades in ships which do not exist. They must be built. This has several consequences. First, the specification of the ship must be determined. A few shipyards sell standard vessels, but most merchant ships are designed, at least to a certain extent, to the buyer's specification. Second, the contractual process for such a major undertaking is more complex. Third, the ship will not be available for 2 or 3 years from the contract date, by which time conditions may have changed.

The *purchaser* entering the newbuilding market may have several different motives. He may need a vessel of a certain size and specification and nothing suitable is available on the second-hand market. This often happens when market conditions are firm and the supply of good quality ships is restricted. Second hand prices may even be higher than the price of a newbuilding. Another possibility is that the ships are needed for an industrial project. Steel mills, power stations, LNG schemes and other major industrial projects are generally developed with specific transportation requirements met by newbuildings. Some large shipping companies have a policy of regular replacement of vessels but this is less common than it used to be years ago when British shipping companies would replace their fleets at 10 or 15 years of age. Finally, speculators may be attracted by incentives offered by shipbuilders short of work – low prices and favourable credit are examples.

The shipyards form a large and diverse group. There are about 250 major shipyards in the world. Their size and technical capability ranges from the small yards with a workforce of less than 200 employees building tugs and fishing boats to the major South Korean yards employing 15,000 workers building container ships and gas tankers. Although some shipyards specialize in one particular type of ship, most are extremely flexible and will bid for a wide range of business. In adverse markets major shipyards have been known to bid for anything from floating production platforms to research vessels.

The negotiation is complex. Occasionally an owner will appoint a broker to handle the newbuilding, but many owners deal direct. The buyer may approach the shipbuilding market from several different directions. One common procedure is to invite tenders from a selection of suitable yards. The tender documentation is often very extensive, setting out a precise specification for the ship. Once tenders have been received the most competitive yards are selected and, following a detailed discussion of the design, specification and terms, a final selection is made. This whole process may take anything from six months to a year. In a sellers market the tender procedure may not be possible. Buyers compete fiercely for the few available berths and shipyards set their own terms and conditions. Often shipyards take advantage of a firm market to insist upon the sale of a standard design.

The contract negotiation can be divided into four areas on which negotiations focus, the price, the specification of the vessel, the terms and conditions of the contract, and the newbuilding finance offered by the shipbuilder. In a weak market buyers will seek to extract the maximum benefit from their negotiating position in each area. Conversely in a strong market the shipbuilder will negotiate for the maximum price possible on a standard vessel, with favourable stage payments.

Price is the most important. Usually ships are contracted for a fixed price, payable in a series of 'stage payments', which spread payment over the construction of the vessel. The shipbuilder's aim is to be paid as he builds the ship, so that he does not need working capital and will aim for stage payments along the lines shown in Box 3.4.

BOX 3.4 Typical pattern of shipyard stage payments

Stage in production	***Payment due***
Signing of contract	5 per cent
1,000 tons steel delivered	5 per cent
Commencement of steel fabrication	15 per cent
25 per cent steel erected	20 per cent
75 per cent steel erected	20 per cent
Steel erection complete	15 per cent
Launch	5 per cent
Delivery	15 per cent

The pattern varies. In a seller's market the builder may demand 50 per cent on contract signing. In a weak market the buyer may insist on payment on delivery. The specification of the vessel is also important, because modifications to the design may add 10–15 per cent to the cost. There are many negotiable elements in the contract, as discussed below. Finally, the provision of finance by the shipbuilders is a long established way of securing business, especially by shipyards who are uncompetitive on price, or during recessions when customers find it difficult to raise finance. This is discussed in Chapter 6.

The shipbuilding contract

Once the preliminary negotiations are complete, a 'letter of intent' is often drawn up as a basis for developing the details of the design and the construction contract. At this stage the letter of intent is not generally legally binding, though this can become a delicate issue if the shipyard is devoting significant resources to working up the design. The cost of developing a detailed design for a ferry or a containership can exceed $1 million.

The shipyard contract is often drawn up on a standard form. Two commonly used forms are the AWES form and the SAJ form. These are much more detailed than the sales for used for second-hand transactions. The AWES form runs to thirty pages containing a preamble and nineteen articles. The brief summary in Box 3.5 provides an insight into the problems which can arise during the construction of a merchant ship.

BOX 3.5 Articles in the AWES shipbuilding contract

Article 1: Subject contract A detailed description of the ship, it's yard number, registration and classification.

Article 2: Inspection and approval Important section covers the rights of the purchaser to inspect the vessel during construction. The purchaser is required to approve three copies of the drawings and technical information for machinery and equipment to which the vessel must be built. The shipyard may sub-contract work subject to the purchaser's approval.

Article 3: Modifications Lays down the rules for any modifications to the design requested by the purchaser after the contract date, or to meet changing regulatory requirements. It gives the builder the right to charge for any changes and modify the building programme if necessary.

Article 4: Trials Specifies the terms under which sea trials will be carried out, including the conditions under which tests will be carried out and the right of the contractor to repeat trials or postpone them if necessary.

Article 5: Guarantee for speed, cargo carrying capacity and fuel consumption Sets out the compensation which will be paid if the speed, deadweight, cargo capacity and fuel consumption measured on the sea trials do not exactly comply with the terms of the contract.

Article 6: Delivery of the vessel States where the vessel will be delivered, sets out the liquidated damages and premiums for late/early delivery and defines 'force majeure' which may be acceptable reasons for late delivery. The latter include strikes, extreme weather conditions, shortage of materials, etc.

Article 7: Price Specifies the contract price, the instalments and the method of payment for modifications, liquidated damages and premiums.

Article 8: Property Defines who owns the plans, the working drawings and the vessel itself during construction. Three alternative formats are offered. The first specifies that the vessel belongs to the contractor until delivery; the second makes it the property of the purchaser, but gives the contractor a lien for any unpaid portion of the price; the third lays out a procedure for marking parts which become the purchaser's property held as secturity against instalments paid.

Article 9: Insurance The builder is responsible for insuring the vessel and all associated components.

Article 10: Defaults by the purchaser Defines the interest rate at which late payments will be charged and defines the terms under which the contractor can rescind the contract and sell the vessel. Four alternative clauses are offered.

Article 11: Defaults by the contractor Defines the rights of the purchaser to be repaid with interest if the contractor defaults. Two alternatives are offered.

Article 12: Guarantee Sets out the terms and period over which the vessel is guaranteed against defects due to bad workmanship or defective materials.

Article 13: Contract expenses Allocates payment of taxes, duties, stamps and fees between the contractor and the purchaser.

Article 14: Patents Makes the contractor liable for any infringements of patent on his own work, but not on the work of suppliers.

Article 15: Arbitration Nominates the legal regime, and sets the conditions for appointing a technical expert to resolve any disputes over the construction of the vessel and the arbitration regime for any contract disputes.

Articles 16–19 Deals with various technicalities, including the terms on which the contract becomes binding, legal domicile of the purchaser and contractor, the purchaser's right to assign the contract to a third party, and addresses for correspondance.

Shipbuilding prices

Shipbuilding prices are just as volatile as second-hand prices and are closely correlated with them, as can be seen in Figure 3.12. Like second-hand prices they are determined by supply and demand. However, in this case the sellers are not other shipowners, but shipyards. On the demand side, the key factors are freight rates, the price of modern second-hand ships, financial liquidity of buyers, the availability of credit and, most importantly, expectations. From the shipyard supply viewpoint the key issues are the number of berths available and the size of the orderbook. A yard with three years' work cannot offer a realistic delivery, while another yard with only the ships under construction on order will be desperately keen to find new business. This balance is what drives shipyard prices. During booms when the yards have built up long orderbooks and many owners are competing for the few berths available, prices rise sharply. In a recession the opposite happens. Shipyards are short of work and there are fewer buyers, so the yards have to drop their prices to tempt in buyers.

3.6 The demolition market

The fourth market is demolition. This is a less glamorous but essential part of the business. The mechanics are simple enough. The procedure is broadly similar to the second-hand market, but the customers are the scrap yards (see Chapter 13) rather than shipowners. An owner has a ship which he cannot sell for continued trading, so he offers it on the demolition

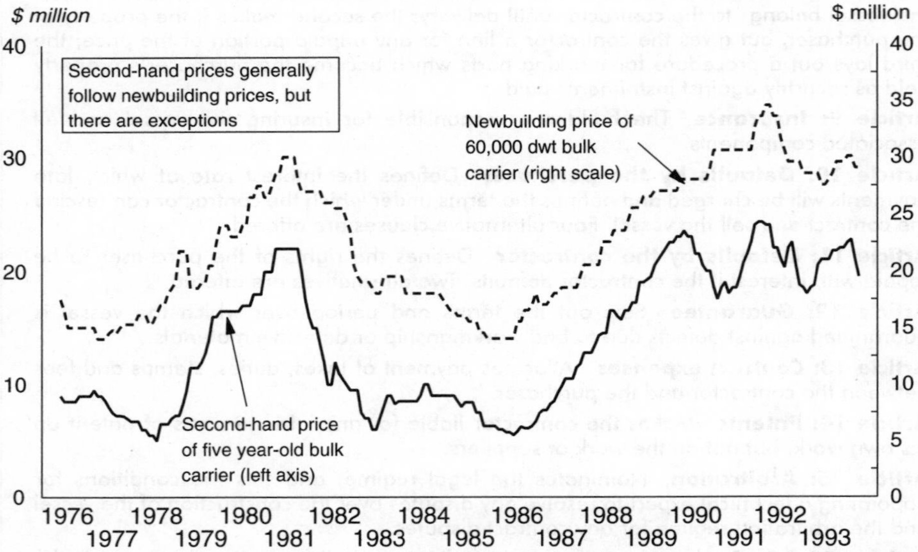

FIGURE 3.12 Correlation of new and second-hand prices (five-year-old 60,000 dwt bulk carrier)

Source: Clarkson Research Studies

market. Usually the sale is handled by a broker and large broking companies have a 'demolition desk' specializing in this market. These brokers keep records of recent sales and, because they are 'in the market', they know who is buying at any point in time. When he receives instructions from the owner the broker circulates details of the ship, including its lightweight, location and availability to interested parties.

The ultimate buyers are the demolition yards, most of which are located in the Far East, for example in India, Pakistan, Bangladesh and China. However the buying is usually done by cash speculators who act as intermediaries, buying the ships for cash and selling them on to the demolition yards. Prices are determined by negotiation and depend on the availability of ships for scrap and the demand for scrap metal. In Asia much of the scrap is used in local markets where it provides a convenient supply of raw materials for mini-mills, or cold rolled for use in construction. Thus, demand depends on the state of the local steel market, though availability of scrapping facilities is sometimes a consideration. Thus prices can be very volatile, fluctuating from a trough of $100/lwt in the 1980s to more than $200/lwt in the 1990s. The price also varies from ship to ship, depending its suitability for scrapping.

As offers are received, the price firms up and eventually a deal is made. Although a standard contract such as the Norwegian Sales Form is sometimes used, so few of the clauses are relevant to a demolition sale that brokers tend to use their own simplified contract. On completion the purchaser takes delivery of the ship and, if he is an intermediary, makes the arrangements for delivering the ship to the demolition yard.

3.7 Summary

In this chapter we have looked at the four shipping markets, the freight market, the sale and purchase market, the newbuilding market and the demolition market. Since markets are practical places, economists who want to understand how they work must study what actually happens, and this is what we did. Starting from the definition of a market place, we examined how the four shipping markets go about the business of managing the supply of ships.

The *freight market* consists of shipowners, charterers and brokers. There are four types of contractual arrangement, the voyage charter, the contract of affreightment, the time charter, and the bare boat charter. The owners trading in the voyage market contract to carry cargo for an agreed price per ton while the charter market involves hiring out the ships on a daily basis (time charter). The charter is legally agreed in a charter-party which sets out the terms of the deal. Freight rate statistics show the movement of prices over time, recorded in dollars per ton, worldscale, or time charter. Finally the Baltic International Freight Futures Exchange (BIFFEX) allows charterers and shipowners to hedge their freight risk.

Second-hand ships are traded in the *sale and purchase market.* The buyers and sellers are shipowners. Broadly speaking the administrative procedures are similar to real estate, using a standard contract such as the Norwegian Sales Form. Ship prices are very volatile and this makes trading ships an important source of revenue for shipowners, though these transactions do not affect the cashflow of the industry as a whole. The second-hand value of merchant ships depends on the freight rates, age, inflation and expectations.

The *newbuilding market* is quite different. The participants are shipowners and shipbuilders. Because the ship has to be built the contract negotiations are more complex than the sale and purchase market, extending beyond price to such factors as specification, delivery date, stage payments and finance. Prices are just as volatile as second-hand prices and sometimes follow the same pattern.

Finally we looked at the *demolition market.* Old or obsolete ships are sold for scrap, often with speculators acting as intermediaries between the shipowners and the demolition merchants.

These four markets work together, linked by cashflow. The 'players' are jostled in the direction the market wants them to go by a combination of cashflow and market sentiment, but the market does not have complete control. Ultimately what happens tomorrow depends on what people do today. In this respect shipping is just like the country market. By the time the farmer arrives at market with his pig and finds that all the other farmers have bred pigs, it is too late. Prices will fall, and the farmer, who has feed bills to pay, must accept the price on offer. But this situation was created a year earlier when prices were high and everyone started breeding pigs. The smart farmers saw what other farmers were doing and switched to chickens. This has nothing to do with the demand for pigs or chickens. It is a supply side management. Like the farmer, the successful shipping company must know when to steer clear of pigs!

Chapter 4

Supply, demand and freight rates

One complexity is ever-present in every management problem, every decision, every action – not, properly speaking a fourth task of management, and yet an additional dimension: time. Management always has to consider both the present and the future; both the short run and the long.

(Peter Drucker, 'Management: Tasks, Responsibilities, Practices' 1977)

4.1 The shipping market model

The search for signposts

Now it is time to look in greater detail at the economic mechanisms which the shipping market uses to regulate supply and demand. Each twist of the cycle brings a new opportunity or threat. In the space of a few months a shipowner's cashflow can swell from a trickle to a flood, and the market value of his fleet may change by millions of dollars. This is certainly a good way of catching the attention of shipping company management, but what should they do?

The usual advice is to take advantage of the cycles to buy low and sell high. This is fair enough, as far as it goes, but shipping is a game of skill and playing the cycles depends on being able to recognize, or better still predict, the peaks and troughs on the freight chart. Just being right is not enough. An investor may correctly predict a market peak, but if the charterers take the same view there will be no long-term contracts. Similarly, in market troughs owners may be ready to buy cheap ships, but who is willing to sell for a loss? As Michael Hampton pointed out, consensus is generally not a good signpost. The best opportunities go to those who can judge when the other players in the market are wrong.

From an economic viewpoint each shipping cycle is unique. If we are to improve our understanding of what is going on in the market, we must now develop a systematic explanation of how the freight market cycles are generated. To do this we will use the supply and demand model, a technique often used by economists to analyse commodity markets. The term model is used here in just the same way as when we talk about a model ship – it is a smaller version of the real thing, leaving out those details that are not relevant to the present subject. The aim is to explain the mechanisms which determine freight rates in a consistent way.

Key influences on supply and demand

The maritime economy is enormously complex, so the first task is to simplify the model by singling out those factors that are most important. This is not to suggest that detail should be ignored, but rather to accept that too much detail can hinder a clear analysis. In the initial stages at least we must generalize. From the many influences on the shipping market we can select ten as being particularly important, five affecting the demand for sea transport and five affecting the supply. These are summarized in Table 4.1.

As far as the demand for sea transport is concerned (the 'demand function'), the five variables are the world economy, seaborne commodity trades, average haul, political events and transport costs. To explain the supply of shipping services (the 'supply function'), we have identified the world fleet, fleet productivity, shipbuilding deliveries, scrapping and the freight rates. The way in which these variables fit together into a simple model of the shipping market is shown in Figure 4.1. This model has three components, demand (module a), supply (module b) and the freight market (module c) which links the two by regulating the cashflow from one sector to another.

TABLE 4.1 Ten variables in the shipping market model

Demand	*Supply*
1. The world economy	1. World fleet
2. Seaborne commodity trades	2. Fleet productivity
3. Average haul	3. Shipbuilding production
4. Political events	4. Scrapping and losses
5. Transport costs	5. Freight rates

How does the model work? The mechanics are very simple. On the demand side, the world economy, through the activity of various industries, generates the goods which require sea transport. Developments in particular industrial sectors may modify the general growth trend (e.g. a change in the oil price, which influences oil demand), as may changes in the distance over which the cargo is transported, giving a final demand for shipping services measured in ton miles. The use of ton miles as a measure of demand is technically more correct than simply using the deadweight of cargo ships required, since it avoids making a judgement about the efficiency with which ships are used. That belongs more properly to the supply side of the model.

On the supply side, in the short term, the merchant fleet represents the fixed stock of shipping capacity. At a point in time only part of this fleet may be trading. Some ships may be laid up, or used for storage. The fleet can be expanded by new building and reduced by scrapping. The amount of transport this fleet provides also depends on the efficiency with which ships are operated, in particular speed and waiting time (see para below). For example a fleet of tankers steaming at 11 knots and returning from each cargo voyage in ballast carries less cargo in a year than the same size fleet of bulk carriers steaming at 14 knots and carrying a backhaul for all or part of its journey. This efficiency variable is generally referred to as fleet productivity and is expressed in ton miles per dwt per annum. Finally, the policies of shippers, banks and regulators all have an impact on how the supply side of the market develops.

Dynamic links in the model

The fulcrum pointer in the centre of the diagram in Figure 4.1 represents the balance of supply and demand. Any imbalance feeds through into the third part of the model, the freight market, which links supply and demand. In effect the freight rate mechanism is the 'switchbox' which controls the amount of money paid by shippers to shipowners for the transport they supply. When ships are in short supply, freight rates are bid up and cash flows into the bank accounts of shipowners. Eventually the increased cashflow starts to affect the behaviour of both the shippers and shipowners. This is the behavioural part of the model. The shipowners will probably start ordering new ships, while the shippers look for ways to

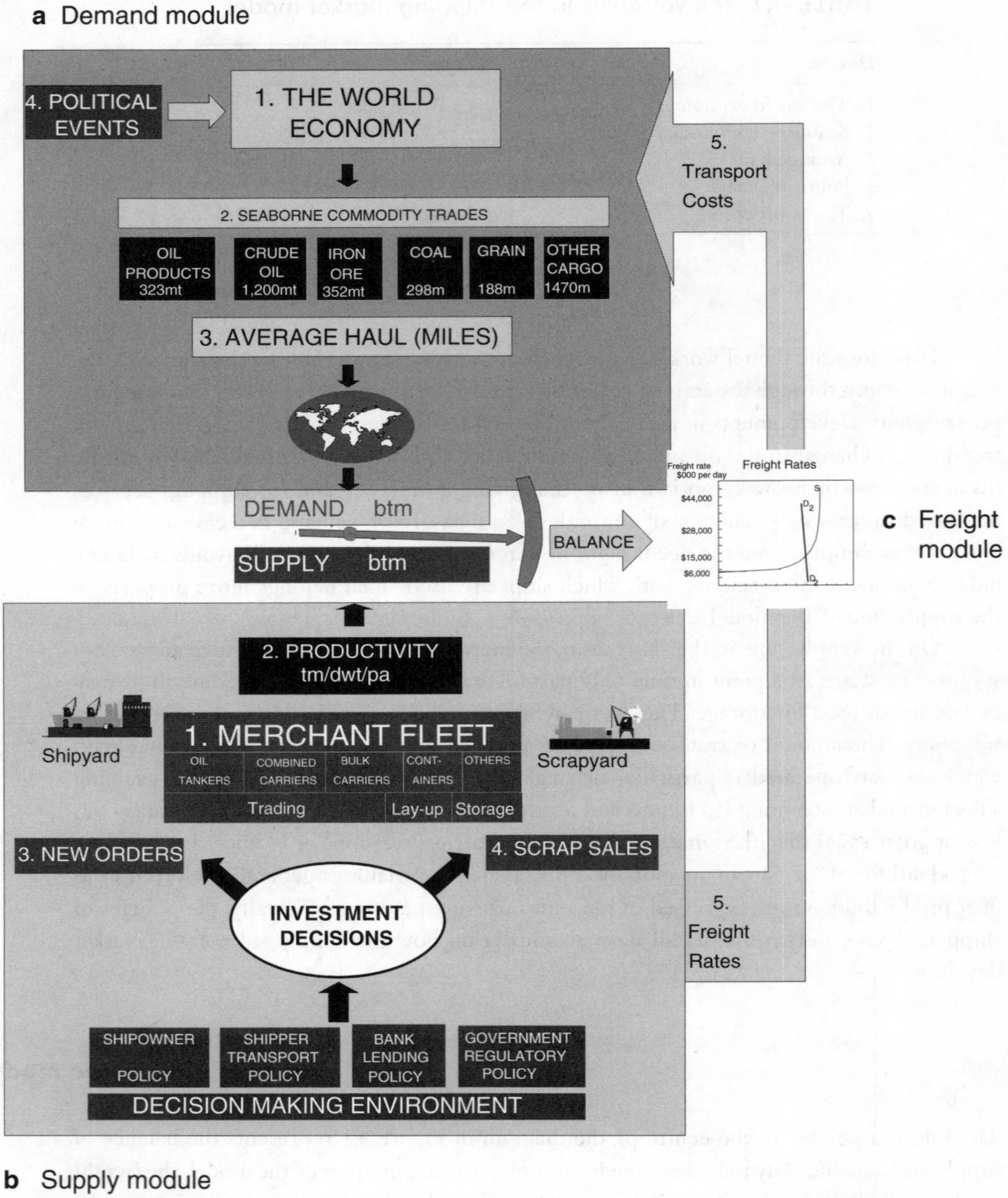

FIGURE 4.1 The shipping market model
Source: Martin Stopford, 1997

cut their transport costs by delaying cargoes, switching to closer suppliers or using bigger ships. When there are too many ships, rates are bid down and shipowners have to draw on reserves to pay fixed costs such as repairs and interest on loans. As reserves diminish some owners are forced to sell ships to raise cash. Prices of ships fall to a level where shipbreakers offer the best price for the older ships, reducing supply. Changes in freight rates may also trigger a change in the performance of the fleet, through adjustments to speed and layup. This link between market balance and freight rates is one of the most important economic relationships in the model and it is controlled by shipowners who decide how to respond. Because of this behaviourial element mathematical models can never be totally relied upon to simulate the freight market.

This model gives shipping market cycles their characteristic pattern of irregular peaks and troughs. Demand is volatile, quick to change and unpredictable; supply is ponderous and slow to change; and the freight mechanism amplifies even small inbalances at the margin. Thus the 'tortoise' of supply chases the 'hare' of demand across the freight chart, but hardly ever catches him. In a market with these dynamic we must expect 'balance', in the sense of steady earnings over several years, to be quite rare. As we saw in Chapter 2, such periods have been few and far between during the last century.

This is the market model which controls shipping investment. In the remainder of this chapter we will examine the three sections of the model. Our main interest is not in the value of the variables themselves – we discuss this extensively in later parts of the book – but rather to answer the questions:'Why does each variable change?' 'What are the relationships between them?'. The model is dynamic in the sense that supply and demand are determined separately, but linked by freight rates. In principle, supply will follow demand if decision-makers are successful in judging what the future level of demand will be and take the necessary actions to adjust the available supply.

4.2 The demand for sea transport

We have suggested that ship demand, measured in ton miles of cargo, is mercurial and quick to change, sometimes by as much as 10–20 per cent in a year. Ship demand is also subject to longer-term changes of trend. Looking back over the last two or three decades, there have been occasions when ship demand has grown rapidly over a sustained period, as happened in the 1960s, and others when ship demand stagnated and declined – notably, for example, the decade following the 1973 oil crisis.

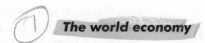

(1)

The world economy

Undoubtedly, the most important single influence on ship demand is the world economy. It came up repeatedly in our discussion of shipping cycles in Chapter 2. Fifty years ago, in his review of the tramp market, Isserlis[1] commented on the similar timing of fluctuations in freight rates and cycles in the world economy. That there should be a close relationship is

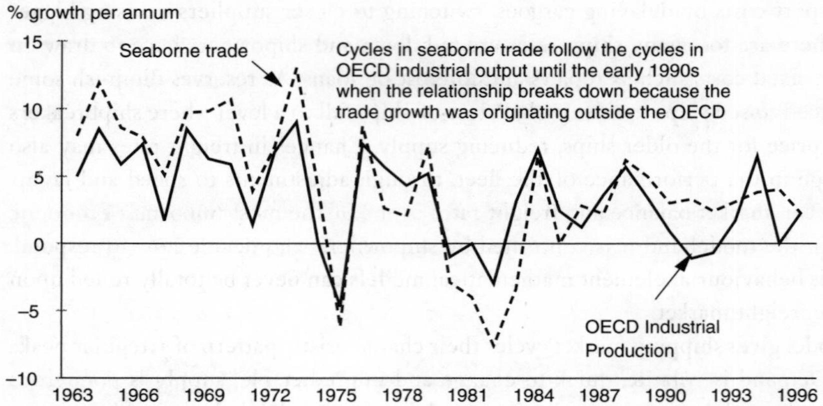

FIGURE 4.2 Industrial cycles and sea trade
Source: OECD and Fearnleys Annual Review

only to be expected, since the world economy generates most of the demand for sea transport, through either the import of raw materials for manufacturing industry, or the trade in manufactured products. It follows that judging trends in the shipping market requires up-to-date knowledge of developments in the world economy. The relationship between sea trade and world industry is not, however, simple or direct. There are three different aspects of the world economy that may bring about change in the demand for sea transport, the business cycle, the 'trade elasticity' and the trade development cycle.

The *business cycle* lays the foundation for freight cycles. Fluctuations in the rate of economic growth work through into seaborne trade, creating a cyclical pattern of demand for ships. The recent history of these trade cycles is evident from Figure 4.2 which shows the close relationship between the growth rate of sea trade and industrial production over the thirty years 1963–95. Invariably the cycles in the OECD economy were mirrored by cycles in sea trade. Note in particular the two deep recessions in sea trade in 1975 and 1981–83 which coincided with recessions in the world economy. Since world industrial production creates most of the demand for commodities traded by sea, this is hardly surprising. Clearly the business cycle is of major importance to anyone analysing the demand side of the shipping market model.

Nowadays most economists accept that these economic cycles arise from a combination of external and internal factors. The external factors include events such as wars or sudden changes in commodity prices such as crude oil, which cause a sudden change in demand. Internal factors refer to the dynamic structure of the world economy itself, which, it is argued, leads naturally to a cyclical rather than a linear growth path. Five of the more commonly quoted causes of business cycles are:

- *The multiplier and accelerator.* The main internal mechanism which creates cycles is the interplay between consumption and investment. Income (GNP) may be spent on investment goods or consumption goods. An increase in investment (e.g. road building) creates new consumer demand from the workers hired. They spend their wages, creating even more demand (the investment multiplier). As the extra consumer expenditure trickles through the economy, growth picks up (the income accelerator), generating demand for even more investment goods. Eventually labour and capital become fully utilized and the economy over-heats. Expansion is sharply halted, throwing the whole process into reverse. Investment orders fall off, jobs are lost and the multiplier and accelerator go into reverse. This creates a basic instability in the economic 'machine'.[2]

- *Time-lags.* The delays between economic decisions and their implementation can make cyclical fluctuations more extreme. The shipping market provides an excellent example. During a shipping market boom, shipowners order ships that are not delivered until the market has gone into recession, when the arrival of the new ships at a time when there is already a surplus further discourages new ordering just at the time when shipbuilders are running out of work. The result of these time-lags is to make booms and recessions more extreme and cyclical.
- *Stockbuilding* has the opposite short-term effect. It produces sudden bursts of demand as industries adjust their stocks during the business cycle. The typical stock cycle, if such a thing exists, goes something like this. During recessions financially hard pressed manufacturers run down stocks, intensifying the downturn in demand for sea transport. When the economy recovers, there is a sudden rush to rebuild stocks, leading to a sudden burst of demand which takes the shipping industry by surprise. Fear of supply shortages or rising commodity prices during the recovery may encourage high stock levels, reinforcing the process. On several occasions shipping booms have been driven by short-term stockbuilding by industry in anticipation of future shortages or price rises. Examples are the Korean War in 1952–3, the dry cargo boom of 1974–5, and the mini tanker booms in 1979 and summer 1986, both of which were caused by temporary stockbuilding by the world oil industry.
- Some economists argue that cycles are intensified by *mass psychology.* Professor Pigou put forward the theory of 'non-compensated errors.[3] If people act independently, their errors cancel out, but if they act in an imitative manner a particular trend will build up to a level where they can affect the whole economic system. Thus periods of optimism or pessimism become self-fulfilling through the medium of stock exchanges, financial booms and the behaviour of investors.
- *Random shocks* which upset the stability of the economic system may contribute to the cyclical process. Weather changes, wars, new resources, commodity price changes, are all candidates. These differ from cycles because they are unique, often precipitated by some particular event, and their impact on the shipping market is often very severe. One of the most prominent examples was the 1930s depression, which followed the Wall Street crash of 1929. More recently examples, the effects of which are clearly visbible in Figure 4.2 are the two oil price shocks which happened in 1973 and 1979. On both occasions, industrial output and seaborne trade suddenly declined, setting off a shipping depression. Some economists think the whole cyclical process can be

explained by a stream of random shocks which make the economy oscillate at its 'resonant frequency'.

To help in predicting business cycles, statisticians have developed 'leading indicators' which provide advance warning of turning points in the economy. For example, the OECD publishes an index based on orders, stocks, the amount of overtime worked and the number of workers laid off, in addition to financial statistics such as money supply, company profits and stock market prices. It is suggested that the turning point in the lead index will anticipate a similar turning point in the industrial production index by about six months. To the analyst of short-term market trends such information is useful, though few believe that business cycles are reliably predictable. Two quotations serve to illustrate the point:

> No two business cycles are quite the same; yet they have much in common. They are not identical twins, but they are recognisable as belonging to the same family. No exact formula, such as might apply to the motions of the moon or of a simple pendulum, can be used to predict the timing of future (or past) business cycles. Rather, in their rough appearance and irregularities, they more closely resemble the fluctuations of disease epidemics, the vagaries of the weather, or variations in a child's temperature.[4]
>
> A remark that can perhaps be made about industrial cycles in general is certainly applicable to the shipping industry:
>
> - it is certain that these cycles exist;
> - their periodicity – the interval from peak to peak – is variable; and their amplitude is variable;
> - the position of the peak or of the trough of a cycle in progress is not predictable.
>
> An *ad hoc* explanation can usually be found for each period of prosperity and for each phase of the cycle if sufficient knowledge is available of the conditions at the time . . . but it is impossible to predict the occurrence of the successive phases of a cycle which is in progress, and still more so in the case of a cycle which has not yet commenced.[5]

In conclusion, the 'business cycle' in world industry is the most important cause of short-term fluctuations in seaborne trade and ship demand. However business cycles, like the shipping cycles to which they contribute, do not follow in an orderly progression. We must take many other factors into account before drawing such a conclusion.

The trade elasticity of the world economy

We now turn to the long-term relationship between seaborne trade and the world economy. Over a period of years does sea trade grow faster, slower, or at the same rate as industrial output? Economists use the concept of 'elasticity' to describe this relationship. The *trade elasticity* is the percentage growth of sea trade divided by the percentage growth in industrial production. For most of the last 30 years the trade elasticity has been positive, averaging 1.4. In other words, sea trade grew 40 per cent faster than world industry. However, if we study the year-by-year pattern in Figure 4.3, we detect a change, starting in about 1975. Until the early 1970s, the elasticity was fairly steady at about 1.6, but during the next period 1976–90 the average fell to 1.4, and in the early 1990s it became highly volatile.[6] It is important to be aware that such changes are possible. There are two reasons why, over long periods, the trade elasticity of individual regions will probably change.

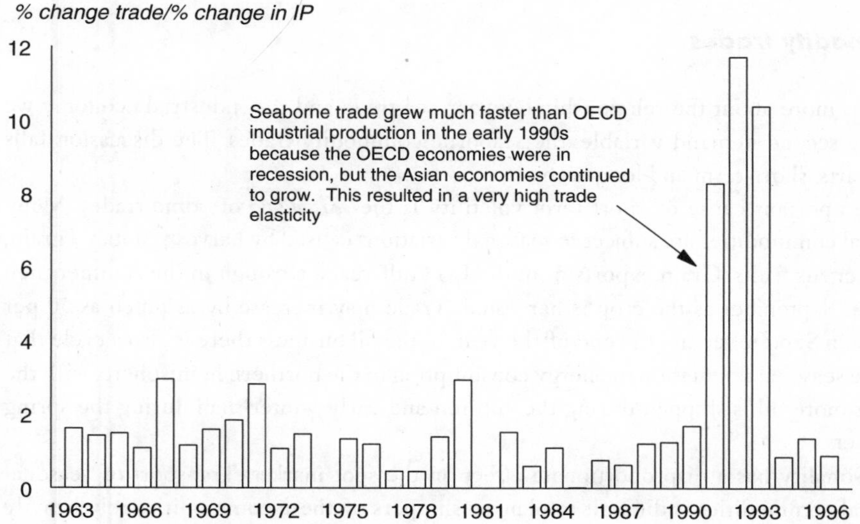
% change trade/% change in IP
12
10
8
6
4
2
0
Seaborne trade grew much faster than OECD industrial production in the early 1990s because the OECD economies were in recession, but the Asian economies continued to grow. This resulted in a very high trade elasticity
1963
1966
1969
1972
1975
1978
1981
1984
1987
1990
1993
1996

FIGURE 4.3 Sea trade elasticity
Source: Calculated from the data contained in Figure 4.2

The first is that balance of demand to available local resources of food and raw materials is likely to change over time. This happens when domestic raw materials are depleted, forcing users to turn to foreign suppliers – for example iron ore for the European steel industry during the 1960s and crude oil for the USA market during the 1970s and 1980s. Or the cause may be the superior quality of foreign supplies, and the availability of cheap sea transport. Secondly, industrial development brings changes in demand for bulk commodities such as iron ore, which make up a large part of seaborne trade. As industrial economies mature, economic activity tends to become less resource intensive, and the emphasis switches from construction and stockbuilding of durables such as motor cars to services such as medical care and recreation, with the result that there is a lower requirement for imported raw materials.[7] This contributed to the slower import growth of Europe and Japan during the 1970s and 1980s.

Another reason is that the mix of countries generating industrial growth may change – new countries emerge or others decline in importance. For example, the industrial growth of Japan in the 1960s had an impact upon sea trade that greatly exceeded its importance as an industrial nation. Japanese imports generated 54 per cent of the growth of the world deep sea seaborne dry cargo trade between 1965 and 1972.[8] An even more extreme pattern was seen in the early 1990s, as South Korea and other Asian countries moved along the industrial path, producing the very high trade elasticities. This accounts for the very high trade elasticity in 1991–3. As the world economy grows and develops, the value of the trade elasticity will change.

Seaborne commodity trades

To find out more about the relationship between sea trade and the industrial economy we turn to the second demand variable, the seaborne commodity trades. The discussion falls into two parts, short-term and long-term.

An important cause of short term volatility is the *seasonality* of some trades. Many agricultural commodities are subject to seasonal variations caused by harvests, notably grain, sugar and citrus fruits. Grain exports from the US Gulf reach a trough in the summer then build up in September as the crop is harvested. Trade may increase by as much as 50 per cent between September and the end of the year. In the oil business there is also a cycle that reflects the seasonal fluctuation in energy consumption in the northern hemisphere, with the result that more oil is shipped during the autumn and early winter than during the spring and summer.

Seasonality has a disproportionate effect on the spot market. Transport of seasonal agricultural commodities is difficult to plan, so shippers of these commodities rely heavily on the spot charter market to meet their tonnage requirements. As a result, fluctuations in the grain market have more influence on the charter market than some much larger trades such as iron ore where tonnage requirements are largely met through long-term contracts. Some agricultural produce, such as fruit, meat and dairy produce, require refrigeration. For this trade, special 'reefer' ships and reefer containers are required.

Long-term trends in commodity trade are best identified by studying the economic characteristics of the industries which produce and consume the traded commodities. This is a topic we will examine in chapter 7. Although every business is different, there are four types of change to look out for; changes in the demand for that particular commodity (or the product into which it is manufactured); changes in the source from which supplies of the commodity are obtained; changes due to a relocation of processing plant which changes the trade pattern; and finally changes in the shipper's transport policy.

A classic example of *changes in demand* is the crude oil trade, which Figure 4.4 shows is the largest individual commodity traded by sea. During the 1960s, crude oil demand grew two or three times as fast as the general rate of economic growth because oil was cheap and the economies of Western Europe and Japan switched from coal to oil as their primary energy source. Imported oil replaced domestic coal, and the trade elasticity was very high. However, with the increase in oil prices during the 1970s, this trend was reversed and the demand for crude oil first stagnated and then declined. Coal regained some of its original market share and the oil trade elasticity fell.

The same trade illustrates the importance of *changes in supply sources*. In the 1960s the main source of crude oil was the Middle East. However in the 1970s new oil reserves near to the market, such as the North Sea and Alaska, came on stream, reducing the need for deep sea imports. These developments had a major impact upon the volume of seaborne trade, as can be seen from Figure 4.4 which shows how the growth trend of crude oil changed in 1973 and again in 1980. Depletion of local resources provides another example of how changing supply sources affects seaborne trade. An example is provided by European iron ore imports.

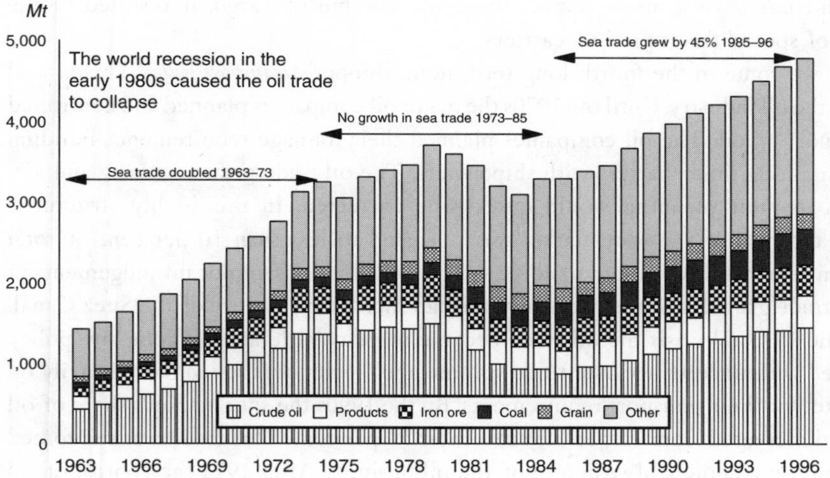

FIGURE 4.4 Major seaborne trades by commodity 1963–96
Source: Fearnleys, Annual Review

During the first century after the industrial revolution, Western Europe relied on iron ore produced locally in Europe and Scandinavia. However, with the expansion of the steel industry in the 1960s it became increasingly difficult to meet demand from this source and, as new high-grade iron ore mines were developed in Brazil, Australia and West Africa, domestic supplies were progressively replaced by imports. As a result of the rundown of local supplies, iron ore imports into Western Europe during the 1960s grew faster than steel production, boosting the demand for sea transport.

A third factor to consider is that, for industrial raw materials, *relocation of processing* can have a direct effect on the volume of cargo shipped by sea and the type of ship required. Take, for example, the aluminium industry. The raw material of aluminium production is bauxite. It takes about 3 tons of bauxite to produce 1 ton of alumina and 2 tons of alumina to produce 1 ton of aluminium. Consequently a commercial decision to refine bauxite to alumina before shipment reduces the volume of cargo shipped by sea by two-thirds. Alumina has a higher value and is used in smaller quantities than bauxite so the transport requirement switches from larger vessels suitable for the bauxite trade to smaller bulk carriers suitable for alumina.

Sometimes processing does not actually reduce the volume of cargo but changes the shipping requirement. In the early days of the oil trade, crude oil was refined at source and transported as oil products in products carriers. In the early 1950s, the oil companies moved towards the transport of crude oil, locating their refineries at the market. This led to the construction of very large crude carriers (VLCCs). Similarly, forest products were originally shipped as logs, but with developing sophistication in the industry there has been a trend towards processing logs into sawn lumber, woodchips, panels or wood pulp prior to shipment. While this did not have a major impact upon the volume of cargo, it resulted in the construction of special forest product carriers.

Finally we come to the fourth long-term item, shipper's *transport policy*. This is well illustrated by the oil industry. Until the 1970s the major oil companies planned and controlled the sea transport of oil. The oil companies planned their tonnage requirements, building ships or signing long time charters with shipowners. The oil trade grew regularly and any minor errors in their planning would quickly be corrected. In this highly structured environment the role of the spot market was relegated to less than 10 per cent of total transport requirements. It was there to cover seasonal fluctuations, minor misjudgements in the speed of trade growth and the occasional mishap such as the closure of the Suez Canal.

After the 1973 oil crisis the oil trade became more volatile and oil company policy changed. Faced with uncertainty over trade volume, the oil shippers relied more heavily on the spot market for their transport requirements. By the 1990s the spot market's share of oil shipments had increased from 10 per cent to almost 50 per cent. This trend was reinforced by a change in the commercial structure of the oil business. After 1973 the control of oil transport changed. Producers, oil companies in industrializing areas like South Korea and oil traders, who had less incentive to become directly involved in oil transport, started to play a bigger part.

The commodity developments outlined above are not of major significance when considering short-term cycles in ship demand, since changes of this type do not take place overnight. They are, however, of considerable importance when judging the medium-term growth of demand and the employment prospects for particular ship types. As a result, any thorough medium-term analysis of the demand for sea transport needs to consider carefully the development of the commodity trades. Further discussion of the major commodity trades can be found in Chapter 6.

Average haul and ton miles

The demand for sea transport depends upon the distance over which the cargo is shipped. A ton of oil transported from the Middle East to Western Europe via the Cape generates two or three times as much demand for sea transport as the same tonnage of oil shipped from

Libya to Marseilles. This distance effect is generally referred to as the 'average haul' of the trade. To take account of average haul, it is usual to measure sea transport demand in terms of 'ton miles', which can be defined as the tonnage of cargo shipped, multiplied by the average distance over which it is transported.

The effect on ship demand of changing the average haul has been dramatically illustrated several times in recent years by the closure of the Suez Canal, which increased the average distance by sea from the Arabian Gulf to Europe from 6,000 miles to 11,000 miles. As a result of the sudden increase in ship demand there was a freight market boom on each occasion. Another example was the closure of the Dortyol pipeline from Iraq to Turkey when Iraq invaded Kuwait in 1990. As a result 1.5 million barrels per day of oil which had previously been shipped from the East Mediterranean had to be shipped from the Arabian Gulf.

In most trades we find that the average haul has changed over the last few decades. Figure 4.5 shows the average haul of crude oil, oil products, iron ore, coal and grain during the period 1963–94. In the crude oil trade, the average haul jumped from 4,500 miles in 1963 to over 7,000 miles a decade later, fell precipitately back to 4,500 in 1985 and then increased to 5,400 miles. The products trade was stable at about 3,800 miles until the early 1980s when long haul exports from Middle East refineries pushed the average up to 5,000 miles. There was also rapid growth in the average haul in the iron ore and coal trades, both of which increased steadily from about 3,000 miles in 1963 to over 5,000 by the early 1980s.

Analysing changes in the average haul of a commodity trade can be extremely complex, requiring information in the form of detailed trade matrices, but very often the key issue is simply the balance between long haul and short haul suppliers. For example, in

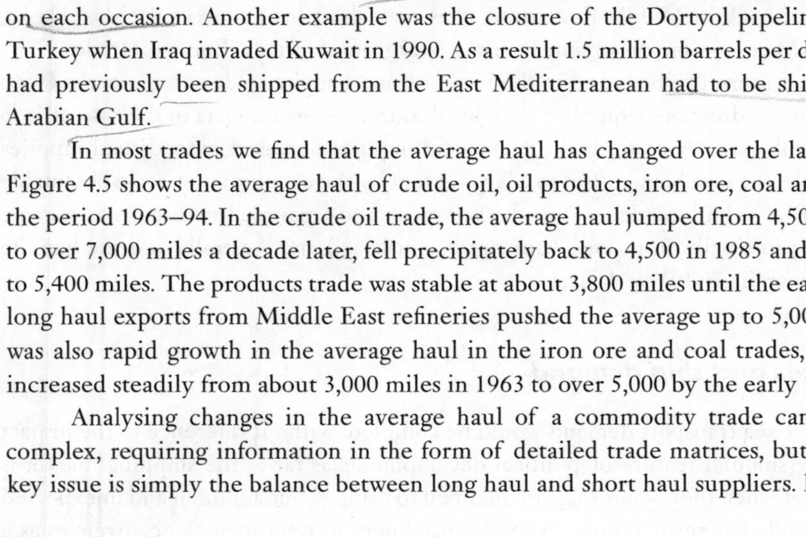

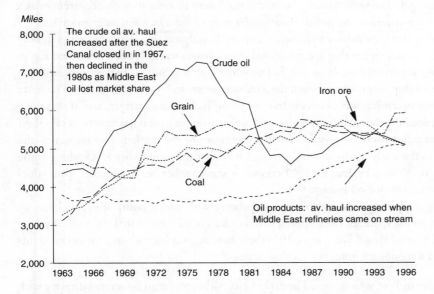

FIGURE 4.5 Average haul of commodity trades 1963–96

Source: Fearnleys, Work Bulk Trades

the oil trade some oil producers are located close to the major consuming markets: Libya, North Africa, the North Sea, Mexico, Venezuela and Indonesia are all located close to their principal markets in Western Europe, Japan and the United States. Oil not obtained from these sources is, of necessity, shipped from the Middle East, which is about 11,000 miles from Western Europe and the USA and about 6,500 miles from Japan. Consequently, the average haul in the oil trade depends upon the balance of output from these two groups of suppliers. The rapidly increasing haul during the 1960s can be explained by the growing share of the Middle East in total oil exports, while the declining haul during the mid-1970s reflected the cut-back in Middle East supplies as new short haul sources such as Alaska, North Sea and Mexico came on stream against a background of a declining oil trade.

A similar pattern can be found in the iron ore, and bauxite trades. In the early 1960s the major importers drew their supplies from local sources – Scandinavia in the case of iron ore and the Caribbean for bauxite. As the demand for imports increased, more distant supplies became available, the cost being offset to a large extent by the economies of scale obtainable from the use of large bulk carriers. Thus the European and Japanese iron ore markets came to be supplied principally from long haul sources in Brazil and Australia and the bauxite market from Australia and West Africa.

Political disturbances and ship demand

No discussion of sea transport demand would be complete without reference to the impact of politics. The singular feature of political developments as far as the shipping market is concerned is that when they occur they are inclined to bring about a sudden and unexpected change in demand. The term 'political event' is used here to refer to such occurrences as a localized war, a revolution, the political nationalization of foreign assets or even strikes.

Events of this type do not necessarily impact directly on ship demand; it is generally their indirect consequences that are significant. The various wars between Israel and Egypt had important repercussions, owing to the proximity of the Suez Canal and its strategic importance as a shipping route between the Mediterranean and the Indian Ocean. The more protracted and extensive war between Iran and Iraq had no such effect, and if anything probably reduced the demand for sea transport by encouraging oil importers to obtain their supplies from other sources, most of which were closer to the market. The impact of the Korean war in the early 1950s was felt through its effect on commodity stockpiling, while the invasion of Kuwait by Iraq in 1990 created a short tanker boom because speculators started to use tankers for oil storage.

Having made these reservations, the regularity with which political events have, by one means or another, turned the shipping market on its head is quite striking. Leaving aside the First and Second World Wars, since 1945 there have been at least seven political incidents that have had a significant influence on ship demand:

- The Korean War, which started in early 1950. Although cargo associated directly with the war was mainly transported by ships of the US reserve fleet, political uncertainty sparked off a stockbuilding boom in Western countries;

- The Suez crisis and the nationalization of the Suez Canal by the Egyptian government in July 1956. Oil tankers trading to Europe were diverted round the Cape and this created a sudden increase in ship demand;
- The Six Day War between Israel and Egypt in May 1967 resulted in the closure of the Canal. European oil imports were again diverted round the Cape;
- The closure of the Tap Line oil pipeline between Saudi Arabia and the Mediterranean in 1970 redirected crude oil previously shipped through the pipeline around the Cape;
- The nationalization of Libyan oil assets in August 1973 resulted in the oil companies turning to the more distant Middle East producers for oil supplies;
- The Yom Kippur War in October 1973 and the OPEC production cut-back triggered the collapse of the tanker market. The associated oil price rise had an effect on the world economy and the shipping market that was to last more than a decade.
- The 1979 Iran Revolution and the temporary cessation of Iranian oil exports precipitated a major increase in the price of crude oil, with significant repercussions for the world economy and the shipping market.
- The 1990/1 Gulf War which resulted in the closure of the Dortyol pipeline and a phase of short term oil stockbuilding. Both increased tanker demand.

Other political events have had a more localized effect on the shipping market. For example, the Falklands War in 1982 resulted in the British government chartering ships from UK owners. In the early 1960s, the Cuban crisis resulted in Cuban sugar exports being diverted to the USSR and China, while US importers obtained their supplies from other sources, again causing some disruption of the shipping market. The Iran–Iraq War of 1982 had localized effects on the tanker market.

On this evidence it is clear that any balanced view of the development of the shipping market must take account of potentially important facts of a political nature. Information of this type is often outside the experience of market analysts, with the result that few market forecasts take very much account of such factors. However, in this case, the facts speak for themselves in emphasizing the importance of this topic as a regular contributor to the mercurial behaviour of ship demand.

Transport costs and the long run demand function

Finally we come to the cost of sea transport. Many of the developments in sea trade of the type discussed in the previous section depend on the economics of the shipping operation. Raw materials will only be transported from distant sources if the cost of the shipping operation can be reduced to an acceptable level or some major benefit is obtained in quality of product. This makes transport costs a significant factor for industry – according to an EEC study, in the early 1980s transport costs accounted for 20 per cent of the cost of dry bulk cargo delivered to countries within the Community.[9]

Over the last century, improved efficiency, bigger ships and more effective organization of the shipping operation have brought about a steady reduction in transport costs

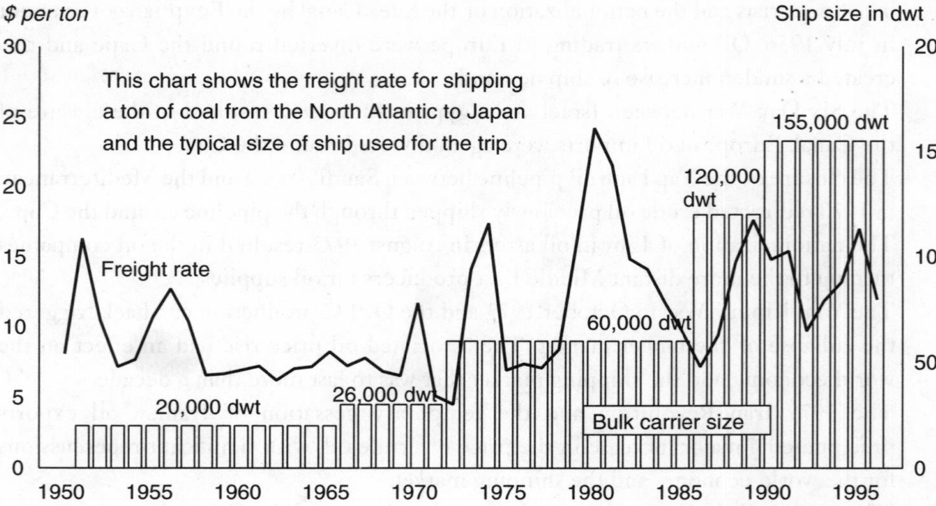

FIGURE 4.6 Coal transport costs Hampton Roads/Japan 1950–96

Source: Fearnleys, various brokers' reports

and higher quality of service. In fact the cost of shipping a ton of coal from the Atlantic to the Pacific hardly changed between 1950 and 1994 (Figure 4.6). This was achieved by using bigger ships. In 1950 the coal would have travelled in a 20,000 dwt vessel at a cost of $10–15 per ton. Forty years later a 150,000 dwt bulker would be used, still at $10–15 per ton. There can be little doubt that this has contributed materially to the growth of international trade. Developing this point, Kindleberger comments: 'what the railway did for the development of national markets in England and France the development of cheap ocean shipping has done for world trade. New channels of trade have been opened up, new links forged.'[10] Although transport costs may not appear to be such a dramatic influence upon seaborne trade as the world economy, their long-term effect on trade development should not be underrated.

4.3 The supply of sea transport

In the introduction to this chapter we characterized the supply of shipping services as being slow and ponderous in its response to changes in demand. Merchant ships take several years to build and this in itself introduces a time-lag into the response to an upsurge in demand. Once built, the ships have a physical life of 15–30 years, so responding to a fall in demand is a lengthy business, particularly when there is a large surplus to be removed. Our aim in this section is to explain how this adjustment process is controlled.

The decision-makers who control supply

We start with the decision-makers. The supply of ships controlled, or influenced, by four groups of decision-makers, shipowners, shippers/charterers, the bankers who finance shipping and the various regulatory authorities who make rules for safety. Shipowners are the primary decision-makers, ordering new ships, scrapping old ones and deciding when to lay up tonnage. Shippers may become shipowners themselves or influence shipowners by issuing time charters. Bank lending influences investment and it is often banks who exert the financial pressure that leads to scrapping in a weak market. Regulators affect supply through safety or environmental legislation which affects the transport capacity of the fleet. For example, IMO Regulation 13G introduced in 1992 requires large tankers to fit a double hull at 30 years of age, a modification no shipowner is likely to comply with on economic grounds.[11]

At this point, a warning is needed. Because the supply of shipping capacity is controlled by this small group of decision-makers, the supply side relationships in the shipping model are behavioural. If we draw an analogy with a poker game, there are many ways of playing a particular hand. The player may be cautious, or he may decide to bluff. All his opponent can do is make the best judgement he can based on an assessment of character and how he played previous hands. Exactly the same problem faces the shipping analyst trying to judge the relationship between, for example, freight rates and newbuilding orders. The fact that high freight rates have stimulated orders in the past is no guarantee that the relationship will hold in future. Market behaviour cannot be explained in purely economic terms. In 1973, when freight rates were very high, shipowners ordered more tankers than could possibly have been required to meet even the most optimistic forecast of oil trade growth. Similarly, in 1982–3 when freight rates were low, there was an ordering boom for bulk carriers. It is in situations like this that clear sighted analysts have something to say.

The merchant fleet

The starting point for a discussion of the supply of sea transport is the merchant fleet. The development of the fleet over the three decades 1963 to 1993 is shown in Figure 4.7. This was a period of great change, comprising periods of rapid growth, stagnation, decline and more gradual growth.

In the long run scrapping and deliveries determine the rate of fleet growth. Since the average economic life of a ship is about 25 years, only a small proportion of the fleet is scrapped each year, so the pace of adjustment to changes in the market is measured in years not months. A key feature of the shipping market model is the mechanism by which supply adjusts when ship demand does not turn out as expected. Looking back over the last three decades we find examples of the merchant fleet in both expansion and contraction phases. It can be seen in Figure 4.7 that the adjustment process involved changes in the type of ship within the fleet.

Starting in the early 1960s, the oil *tanker* fleet went through a cycle of growth and

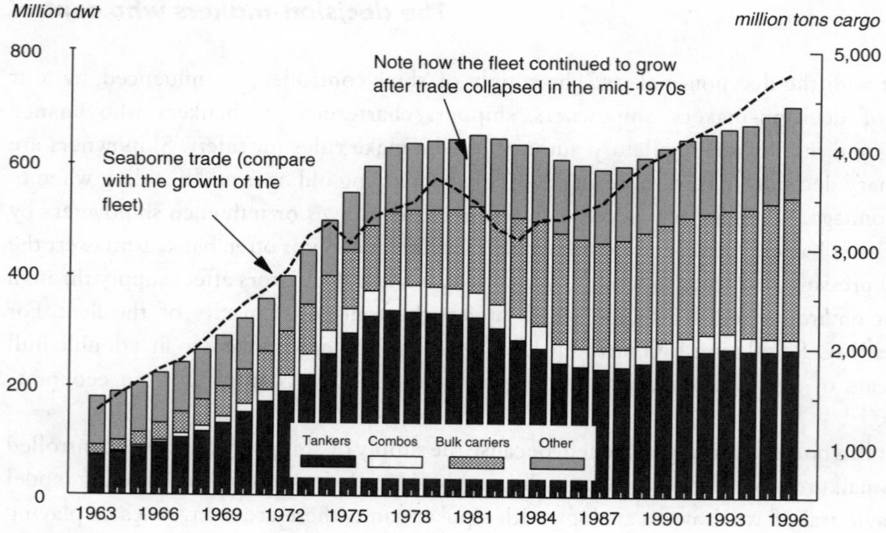

FIGURE 4.7 World fleet by ship type 1963–96
Source: Fearnleys, Annual Review

contraction that took over 20 years to achieve. Between 1962 and 1974 the demand for seaborne oil transport measured in ton miles almost quadrupled and, despite the expansion of shipyard capacity, by the late 1960s supply could not keep up with demand (compare sea trade growth with fleet growth in Figure 4.7). As a result, there was an acute shortage of tanker capacity; in the early 1970s tankers were in such short supply that ships were sold 'off the stocks' for twice their original contract price – in the peak freight market of 1973 the profits on a few voyages were sufficient to pay off the investment in the ship. This led to record orders for new ships.

In the mid-1970s the whole process was thrown into reverse. Over the next decade tanker demand fell by 60 per cent and the tanker market was confronted with the problem of bringing supply and demand into balance. It took about 10 years for supply to adjust to such a major change in demand. The fleet statistics in Figure 4.7 show what happened. After the collapse of the trade in 1975, the fleet continued to grow as the orders placed in 1973 were delivered, reaching a peak of 332 m.dwt in 1977. Scrapping did not start until the owners of the vessels became convinced that there was no future for them. This position was reached in the early 1980s when the second-hand price of VLCCs, some of which had cost $50–60 million to build in the mid-1970s, fell to $3 million. There was so little demand that sometimes ships put to auction did not attract a bid. The only buyers were shipbreakers. As scrap sales increased the fleet started to decline, reaching a trough in 1985. When the oil trade recovered in the late 1980s, supply and demand grew closer together, and freight rates increased. The whole cycle took about 14 years.

The *combined carrier fleet* links the wet and dry markets. Combination tonnage was pioneering in the early 1950s to obtain high cargo performance by carrying oil in one direction with a return load of dry cargo. However, real growth of the fleet was sparked off by the closure of the Suez Canal in 1967, when combined carrier owners, who had previously traded mainly in dry cargo, were able to take advantage of the very favourable oil freight market. Many orders were placed in the next few years and the fleet reached a peak of 48.7 m.dwt in 1978 and then declined to below 20 m.dwt in the 1990s. Most of the fleet is in the 80,000–200,000 dwt size group, which limits its activities in dry bulk to the larger bulk cargoes such as iron ore, or part cargoes of grain and coal.

Dry *bulk carriers* started to appear in the shipping market in the late 1950s and between 1963 and 1996 the bulk fleet grew from 17 m.dwt to 237 m.dwt. The use of large bulk carriers played an integral part in the growth of major deep sea bulk trades such as iron ore and coal, because economies of scale allowed these raw materials to be imported at very low cost. During the same period, there was a progressive switch of cargoes such as grain, sugar, minor ores, and steel products, which had previously been carried in 'tweendeckers or as bottom cargo in liners, into dry bulk carriers. The market widening meant that the market share of bulk tonnage grew steadily during the 1960s and 1970s at the expense of the multi-deck fleet, with a progressive upward movement in ship size and none of the chronic overcapacity problems encountered in the oil market.

In recent years the major change in the deep sea liner trades was the replacement of traditional liners by cellular container ships. The first containership went into service in 1966. By 1995 the fleet had grown to 43.4 m.dwt, averaging 13 per cent per annum growth during the previous 5 years (Table 4.2). In contrast, the general cargo fleet of 81.9 m.dwt grew at only 2 per cent per annum. This fleet is composed of multi-deck general cargo ships, purpose-built deep sea liners, and 'tweendeckers. The size of the 'tweendecker fleet is not known precisely, but it is probably about 10–15 million grt – there are, 4 million grt of SD14s and Freedoms. Finally, there are specialist fleets of chemical and specialist tankers (19.9 m dwt), gas tankers (22 million cubic meters), ro-ros and refrigerated vessels.

In practice, the different ship types discussed above do not operate in separate and self-contained markets. Although there is much specialization in the shipping market, there is

TABLE 4.2 The world fleet (m.dwt)

	1990	*1995*	*Per cent growth per annum*
Oil tankers	247	265.8	2
Bulk carriers	201	227	3
General cargo	75.3	81.9	2
Container	26.1	43.4	13
Chemical	16.5	19.9	4
Liquified gas	10.9	14.7	7
Ro-ro cargo	10.4	11.3	2
Refrigerated cargo	7.5	7.6	0
Total	594.7	671.6	3

Source: Lloyd's Register of Shipping Statistical Tables 1996

also a high degree of substitution between ship types. In a volatile market, flexibility is desirable and some ships, such as 'tweendeckers and combined carriers, are built with the objective of being flexible. This leads us to the important Principle of Lateral Mobility (which is discussed further in Chapter 11, section 11.4): shipowners redeploy surplus vessels into more profitable applications in other sectors of the market. An example of the way this works in practice is provided by the following extract from a broker's report:

> Larger vessels of 40,000 dwt and above were particularly economical on the long hauls, and charterers now quoted substantially reduced rates for such trades. This pressed medium-sized bulk carriers of about 30,000 dwt into finding employment in trades previously serviced by vessels of 10–20,000 dwt and in the scrap trade from US to Japan units of 25–35,000 dwt were successfully introduced . . . with tankers and large dry cargo vessels taking care of the main part of the grain movements a new market was created for Liberty type vessels as barges in India and Pakistan where ports cannot accommodate large vessels.[12]

Thus ships move freely from one market sector to another. As we have noted, combined carriers are built for this purpose and were used very successfully in 1967 when the Suez Canal was closed, as the following quotation suggests:

> The improvement in freights was mainly brought about by the many combined carriers which switched to oil transportation as did the majority of tankers employed in the grain trades. Heavy demand for large conventional bulk carriers to replace the combined carriers caused a considerable number of this kind of newbuilding in the 50–100,000 dwt class to find a very favourable market when commissioned.[13]

Perhaps the most striking feature of the world merchant fleet during the last 30 years has been the rapid escalation of ship sizes, particularly in the bulk sector of the fleet. In the tanker market there was a steady increase in the average size of tankers until the early 1980s when the size structure stabilized. In bulk carriers there was a similar upward movement in ship size, but the pattern was more evenly spread between the different ship size groups with the fleets of 'handy' vessels (20,000–40,000 dwt), Panamax (40,000–80,000 dwt) and large bulk carriers over 80,000 dwt all expanding. Larger and more efficient ships have progressively pushed their way into the market and depressed rates for smaller sizes. At the same time investment for specialization, as in the case of car carriers, and chemical tankers played an important part in the development of the fleet. These apparently conflicting objectives emphasize the complexity of the investment decisions facing the modern shipowner.

Fleet productivity

Although the fleet is fixed in size, the *productivity* with which the ships are used adds an element of flexibility.[14] Past productivity statistics in Figure 4.8 shows how much the productivity of the various sections of the fleet has changed over the past decade. For example, crude oil tankers reached a peak productivity of 44,000 ton miles per deadweight in 1972, but by 1985 this had fallen to 24,000 ton miles per deadweight; in other words, productivity had halved. A few years later it had increased by 40 per cent to 33,000 ton miles per deadweight. The productivity of dry cargo ships was more stable at around 20,000–25,000 ton miles per deadweight.

The nature of these productivity changes becomes more apparent when we look in detail at what merchant ships actually do. Carrying cargo is just one small part of the story. As an illustration Figure 4.9 shows what the 'average' VLCC was doing during the year. Surprisingly, it spent only 137 days carrying cargo – little more than one-third of its time. What happened to the rest? Ballast time accounted for 111 days and cargo handling for 40 days. The remaining 21 per cent of the time was spent in non-trading activities. This included incidents (i.e. accidents), repair, lay-up, waiting, short-term storage and long-term storage. When we analyse these activities more systematically, it becomes apparent that some are determined by both the physical performance of the fleet, and market forces.

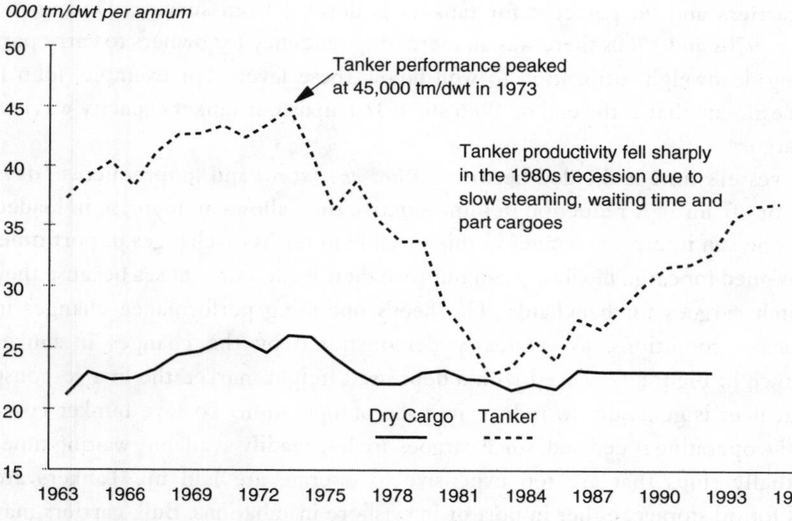

FIGURE 4.8 Performance of the tanker and dry cargo fleets 1963–95
Source: Fearnleys, Annual Review

The productivity (P) of a fleet of ships measured in ton miles per dwt depends upon four main factors, speed, port time, deadweight utilization and loaded days at sea (see chapter 5, section 5.4 for a more detailed discussion of productivity).

First, *speed* determines the time a vessel takes on a voyage. Tracking surveys show that, owing to a combination of operational factors, even in good markets ships generally operate at average speeds well below their design speed. For example, in 1991 the fleet of tankers over 200,000 dwt had an average design speed of 15.1 knots, but the average operating speed between ports was 11.5 knots.[15] The speed of the fleet will change with time. If new ships are delivered with a lower design speed, this will progressively reduce the transport capacity of the fleet. Similarly, as ships age, unless exceptionally well maintained, hull fouling will gradually reduce the maximum operating speed.

Second, *port time* plays an important part in the productivity equation. The physical performance of the ships and terminals sets the upper limit. For example, the introduction of containerization dramatically reduced port time for liners. Organization of the transport operation also plays a part. After the oil crisis in 1973 changes in the oil industry reduced the opportunities for maximizing the efficiency of tanker operations by the transport planning departments of the major oil companies. Congestion produces temporary reductions in performance. Middle East port congestion absorbed large amounts of shipping in the mid-1970s, and in 1980 there was heavy congestion at Hampton Roads, USA, with queues of over 100 bulk carriers waiting to load coal. This congestion reduced the supply of ships available for trading.

Third, *deadweight utilization (DWU)* refers to the cargo capacity lost owing to bunkers, stores, etc. which prevent a full load from being carried. A rule of thumb estimate of 95 per cent for bulk carriers and 96 per cent for tankers is derived from surveys. During the recessions of the 1970s and 1980s there was an increasing tendency for owners to carry part cargoes, reducing deadweight utilization to well below these levels. For example, John I. Jacobs' statistics estimate that at the end of 1986 about 16.6 m.dwt of tanker capacity was lost owing to part cargoes.

Finally, a vessel's time is divided between *loaded days at sea* and 'unproductive' days (in ballast, port, or off hire). A reduction in unproductive time allows an increase in loaded days at sea, and one can interpret changes in this variable in terms of changes in port time, etc.[16] Vessels designed for cargo flexibility can improve their loaded time at sea because they are able to switch cargoes for backhauls. The fleet's operating performance changes in response to market conditions, as is clearly demonstrated by the changes in tanker productivity shown in Figure 4.8. Faced with a depressed freight market, the first response of the merchant fleet is generally to reduce its pace of operation. To save bunker costs, owners reduce the operating speed and, since cargoes are less readily available, waiting times increase. Eventually ships that are too expensive to operate are laid up. Tankers are frequently used for oil storage, either in port or in offshore installations. Bulk carriers may be used to store coal or grain. Some tankers in storage are on contracts lasting only a few months, after which they will become available for trading. Others used in offshore oil production may be employed on long contracts, so for practical purposes they are no longer part of the trading fleet.

Shipbuilding production

The shipbuilding industry plays an active part in the fleet adjustment process described in the previous paragraphs. In principle, the level of output should adjust to changes in demand, and over long periods this does happen. Thus, in 1974, shipbuilding output accounted for

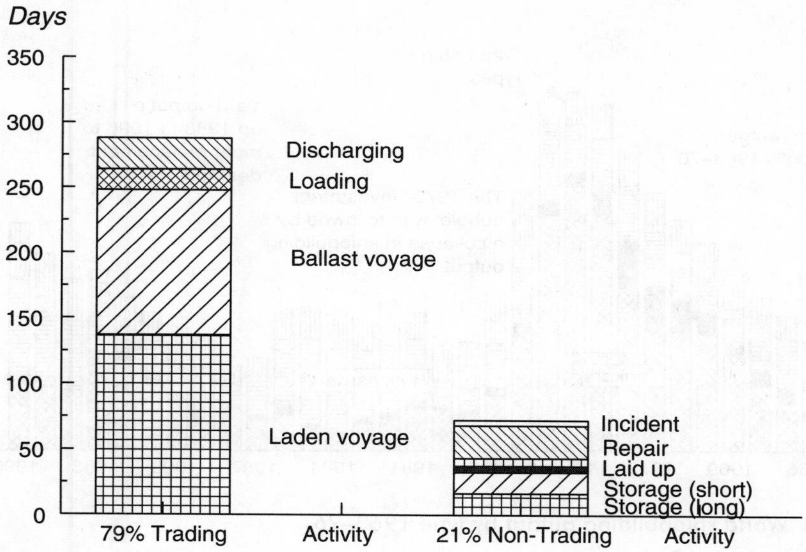

FIGURE 4.9 **VLCC operating performance: use of the 'average' VLCC 1991**
Source: VLCC Quality Survey (1991), Clarkson Research Studies

about 12 per cent of the merchant fleet, whereas in 1996 it had fallen to 4.7 per cent. Adjustments in the level of shipbuilding output on this scale do not take place quickly or easily. Shipbuilding is a long-cycle business, and the time-lag between ordering and delivering a ship is between 1 and 4 years, depending on the size of orderbook held by the shipbuilders. Orders must be placed on the basis of an estimate of future demand and in the past these estimates have often proved to be wrong, most dramatically in the mid-1970s when deliveries of VLCCs continued for several years after demand had gone into decline. In addition, downward adjustments in shipbuilding supply may be seriously hampered by political intervention to prevent job losses.

From the point of view of the shipping industry, the type of ship built is important because peaks and troughs in the deliveries of specific ship types have an impact on their market prospects. In recent years there have been major changes in the product range of ships built by the merchant shipbuilding industry. These are illustrated graphically in Figure 4.10.

Tanker production illustrates the extreme swings which can occur in shipping investment. Tanker newbuilding dominated the period 1963–75, increasing from 5 m.dwt in 1963 to 45 m.dwt in 1975, when it accounted for 75 per cent of shipbuilding output. The collapse of the tanker market after the 1973 oil crisis reversed this trend and tanker output fell to a trough of 3.6 m.dwt in 1984, accounting for only 1 per cent of the tanker fleet. In the absence of VLCC orders, the tanker deliveries during the period 1978–84 were principally products tankers or 80,000–120,000 dwt crude oil tankers. As the tanker

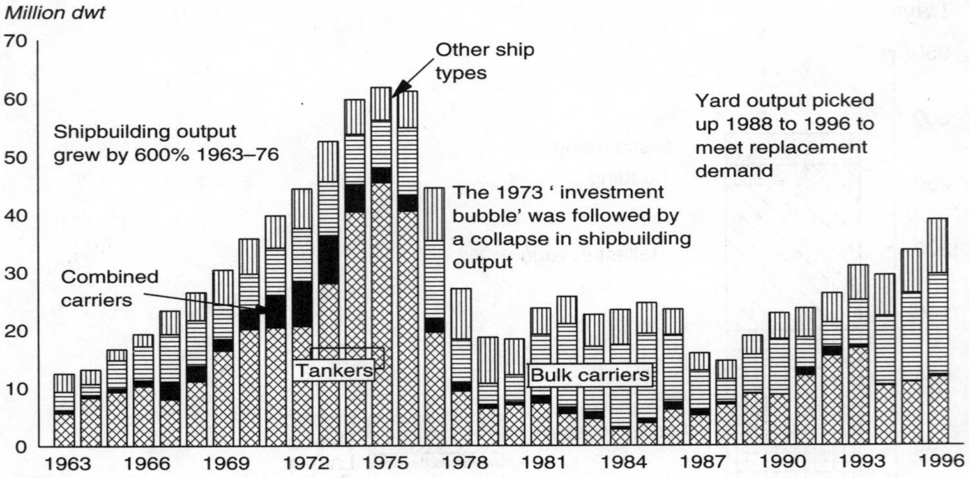

FIGURE 4.10 World shipbuilding output by type 1963–96
Source: Fearnley's Annual Review

fleet built in the 1970s needed to be replaced the trend was again reversed and by 1993 tanker production had increased to 17.3 m.dwt.

Compared with oil tankers, the dry bulk carrier newbuilding market has been comparatively stable since the mid-1960s. However, investment has been very cyclical with deliveries fluctuating between 5 and 15 m.dwt per annum. A very low output of 4 m.dwt in 1979 was followed by the 'mini boom' in the dry cargo market during 1979–80. Heavy ordering resulted in peak deliveries of 14.7 m.dwt in 1985, accounting for 59 per cent of total world shipbuilding output in deadweight tonnage terms. In a very real sense bulk carriers took over the dominant role in the shipbuilding market previously occupied by VLCCs, and by the mid-1980s were facing the same problems of overproduction and chronic surplus. One consequence of this heavy investment was a deep recession in the mid-1980s. Ordering stopped and deliveries of bulk carriers fell to 3.2 m.dwt in 1988. By 1990 deliveries were back up to 9.2 m.dwt, and so the cycles continued.

The remaining category of shipbuilding output comprises an enormous range of merchant cargo and service vessels – ro-ros, container ships, conventional general cargo vessels, fishing boats, ferries, cruise liners, tugs, etc. The total tonnage of deliveries in 1996 was 7.3 m.dwt, accounting for 22 per cent of total output, and the newbuilding trend in this sector has been comparatively stable over the last two decades at about this level. Although these ship types account for only a fifth of the total merchant shipbuilding output in deadweight terms, in terms of work content they are much more important – for example, a deadweight ton of ferry tonnage may contain four or five times as much work as a deadweight ton of tanker tonnage. For this reason, the various ship types in this category are substantially more important to the shipbuilding industry than might appear at first sight.

Scrapping and losses

The rate of growth of the merchant fleet depends on the balance between deliveries of new ships and deletions from the fleet in the form of ships scrapped or lost at sea. This balance changed radically during the late 1970s, as can be seen from Figure 4.11. In 1973, only about 5 m.dwt of vessels were scrapped, compared with deliveries of over 50 m.dwt, with the result that the fleet grew rapidly. By 1982, scrapping had overtaken deliveries for the first time since the Second World War, accounting for 30 m.dwt compared with 26 m.dwt of deliveries. Thus scrapping, which appeared to be of little significance in 1973, was of major importance by the early 1980s.

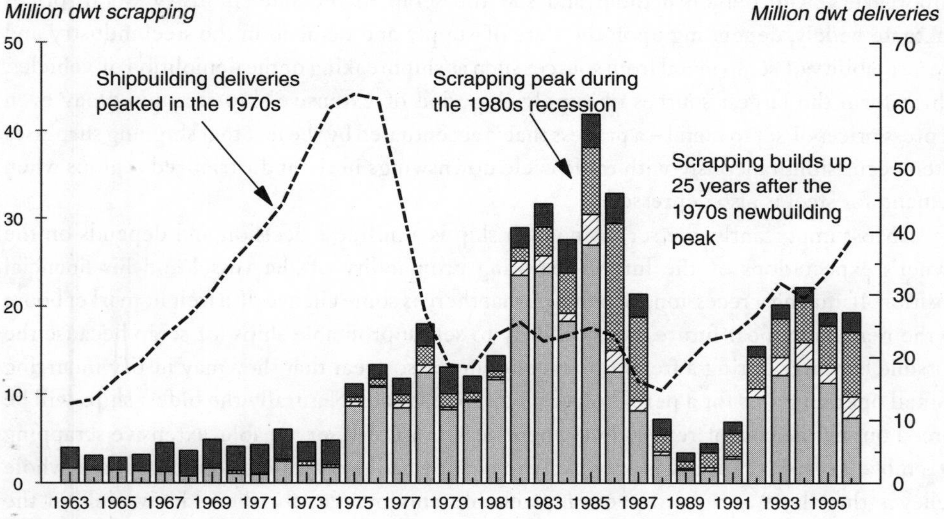

FIGURE 4.11 World ship scrapping by type 1963–96
Source: Fearnleys, Annual Review

Whilst it is clear that scrapping has a significant part to play in removing ships from the market, explaining or predicting the age at which a ship will actually be scrapped is an extremely complex subject, and one that causes considerable difficulties in judging the development of shipping capacity. The reason is that scrapping depends on the balance of a number of factors that can interact in many different ways. The main ones are age, technical obsolescence, scrap prices, current earnings and market expectations.

Age is the primary factor determining the tonnage of vessels scrapped. Ships deteriorate as they grow older and the cost of routine repairs and maintenance increases; thus the owners of elderly vessels face the combination of heavier costs and more time off hire for planned and unplanned maintenance. Because physical deterioration is a gradual process, there is no specific age at which a ship is scrapped; a look through Lloyd's Demolition

Register generally reveals a few examples of vessels scrapped with an age of over 60 or 70 years, or at the other extreme tankers sold for demolition at as little as 10 years. In 1996 when 217 bulk vessels were scrapped the average scrapping age was 25 years for both tankers and dry cargo vessels. In each case there was a wide spread.

Technical obsolescence may reduce the age at which a particular type of vessel is scrapped because it is superseded by a more efficient ship type. For example, the high scrapping rate of multi-deckers in the late 1960s is attributable to these vessels being made obsolete by containerization. Obsolescence also extends to the ship's machinery and gear – tankers fitted with inefficient steam turbines were among the first to go to the scrapyard when prices rose in the 1970s.

The decision to scrap is also influenced by the scrap prices. Scrap ships are sold to shipbreakers, who demolish them and sell the scrap to the steel industry. Scrap prices fluctuate widely, depending upon the state of supply and demand in the steel industry and the availability of scrap metal from sources such as shipbreaking or the demolition of vehicles, which form the largest sources of supply. A period of extensive ship scrapping may even depress prices of scrap metal – a process that is accentuated by the fact that shipping surpluses often occur simultaneously with trade cycle downswings in the industrialized regions when demand for steel is also depressed.

Most importantly, the scrapping of a ship is a business decision and depends on the owner's expectations of the future operating profitability of the vessel and his financial position. If, during a recession, he believes that there is some chance of a freight market boom in the reasonably near future, he is unlikely to sell unprofitable ships for scrap because the possible earnings during a freight market boom are so great that they may justify incurring a small operating loss for a period of years up to that date. Naturally the oldest ships will be forced out by the cost of repairs but, where vessels are still serviceable, extensive scrapping to remove a surplus capacity is only likely to occur when the shipping community as a whole believes that there is no prospect of profitable employment for the older vessels in the foreseeable future, or when companies need the cash so urgently that they are forced into 'distress' sales to shipbreakers. It follows that scrapping will occur only when the industry's reserves of cash and optimism have been run down.

Freight rates

Finally the supply of sea transport is influenced by freight rates. This is the ultimate regulator which the market uses to motivate decision-makers to adjust capacity in the short term, and to find ways of reducing their costs in the long-term. In the shipping industry there are two main pricing regimes, the freight market and the liner market. Liner shipping provides transport for small quantities of cargo for many customers and is a essentially a retail shipping business.[17] The liner company is a common carrier, accepting cargo from any customer at prices set out in the rate book. That is not to suggest that the business is not competitive. On the contrary, as we will see in chapter 10, it has spent most of its 125-year history in deep competition. In contrast bulk shipping is a wholesale operation. It sells its services in large quantities, by contract to a much smaller number of industrial customers at individually negotiated prices. In both cases the pricing system is central to the supply of transport. In the short run supply responds to prices as ships change their operation speed and move to and from layup, while liner operators adjust their services. In the longer term freight rates contribute to the investment decisions which result in scrapping and ordering of ships. How this works in the bulk market is the subject of the next section. Liner pricing, which has a different economic structure, is discussed in chapter 10.

4.4. The freight rate mechanism

The third part of the shipping market model, labelled C in Figure 4.1, is the freight market. This is the adjustment mechanism linking supply and demand. The way it operates is simple enough. Shipowners and shippers negotiate to establish a freight rate which reflects the balance of ships and cargoes available in the market. If there are too many ships the freight rate is low while if there are too few ships it will be high. Once this freight rate is established, shippers and shipowners adjust to it and eventually this brings supply and demand into balance. The three key economic concepts we will use to analyse this process more formally are the supply function, the demand function and the equilibrium price.[18]

The supply and demand functions

The *supply function* for an individual ship, shown in Figure 4.12a is a hockey stick shaped curve describing the amount of transport the owner provides at each level of freight rates. The ship in this example is a 280,000 dwt VLCC. When the freight rate falls below $155 per mtm the owner puts it into layup, offering no transport. As freight rates rise past $155 per mtm he breaks layup but, to save fuel, steams at the lowest viable speed of 11 knots per hour. If he trades loaded with cargo at this speed for 137 days per annum (see Figure 4.9), he will supply 10.1 btm of transport in a year (i.e. 11*24*137*280,000). At higher freight rates he speeds up until at about $220 per mtm the ship is at full speed of 15 knots and supplying 13.8 btm of sea transport per year (a lot of transport for just one ship!). Thus by increasing freight rates the market has obtained an extra 38 per cent supply. Evidence of this process at work can be seen in Figure 4.8 which shows how the productivity of the tanker fleet peaked in 1973 when freight rates were very high and fell in the early 1980s when freight rates were very low.

Economic theory can help to define the shape of the supply curve. Provided the market is perfectly competitive, the shipowner maximizes his profit by operating his ship at the speed at which marginal cost (i.e. the cost of providing an additional tonmile of transport) equals the freight rate. The relationship between speed and freight rates can be defined as follows:[19]

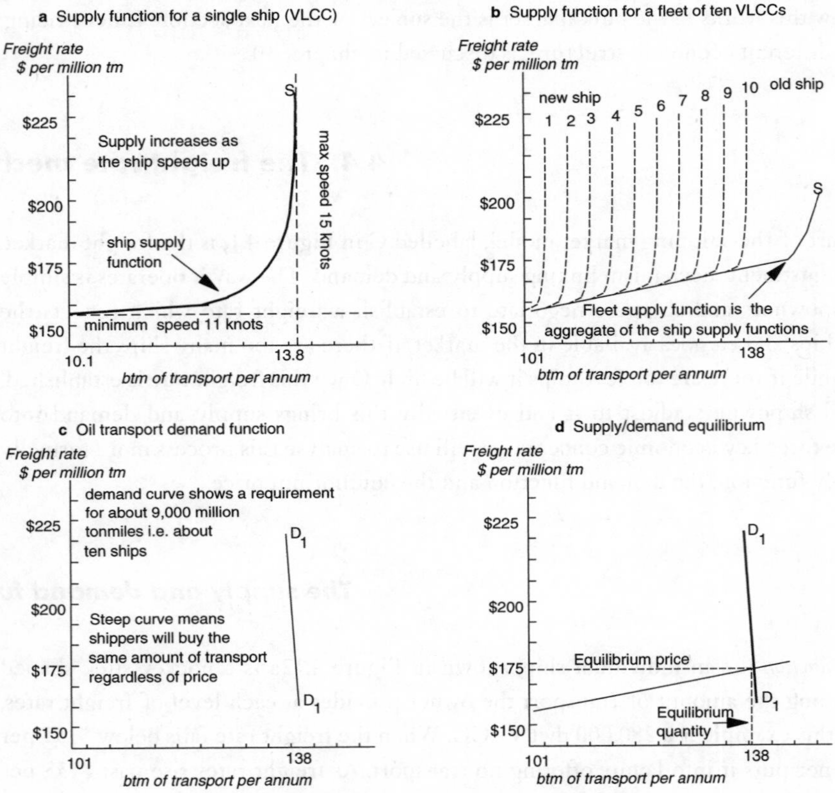

FIGURE 4.12 Shipping supply and demand functions
Source: Martin Stopford, 1997

$$s = \sqrt{\frac{R}{3pkd}} \qquad \text{E4(1)}$$

Where s = optimum speed in miles per day
R = voyage freight rate
p = price of fuel
k = the ship's fuel constant
d = distance

This equation defines the shape of the supply curve. In addition to freight rates the optimum speed depends on the price of fuel, the efficiency of the ship and the length of the voyage. We will discuss these costs in Chapter 5.

In reality the supply function is more complex than the simple speed–freight rates relationship described in the previous paragraphs. Speed is not the only way supply responds to freight rates. The owner may take advantage of a spell of low freight rates to put his ship into dry dock, or fix a short-term storage contract. At higher rates he may decide to ballast back to the Arabian Gulf through the shorter Suez Canal route rather than taking the longer 'free passage' round the Cape. All of these decisions affect supply. Similarly freight rates are not the only way the market adjusts shipowners' revenue. During periods of surplus ships have to wait for cargo or accept small cargo parcels. This reduces the operating revenue in just the same way as a fall in freight rates, a factor often forgotten by owners and bankers doing cashflow forecasts on old ships. They may predict freight rates correctly but end up with an embarrassing cash deficit due to waiting time and part cargoes.

The next step is to show how the market adjusts the supply provided by a *fleet of ships*. To illustrate this process the supply function for a fleet of 10 VLCCs is shown in Figure 4.12b. The fleet supply curve (S) is built up from the supply curves of individual ships of varying age and efficiency. In this example the age distribution of the fleet ranges from two years old to twenty years old in intervals of two years. Ship 1 (newest ship) has low daily operating costs and its layup point is $155 per mtm. Ship 10 (oldest ship) has high operating costs and its layup point is $165 per mtm.

The *fleet supply function* works by moving ships in and out of service in response to freight rates. If freight rates fall below the operating costs of ship 10, it goes into layup and supply is reduced by one ship. Ship 9 breaks even and the other eight ships make a margin over their fixed expenses, depending on how efficient they are. If shippers only need five ships they can drop their offer to $160 per mtm, the layup point of ship 5. In this way supply responds to movements in freight rates. Over a longer period the supply can be increased by building new more efficient ships and reduced by scrapping old ones.

The slope of the short term supply curve depends on three factors which determine the layup cost of the marginal ship. First, old ships generally have higher operating costs so the layup point will occur at a higher freight rate. We discuss this in chapter 5. Second, bigger ships have lower transport costs per ton of cargo than small ships, so if big and small ships are competing for the same cargo, the bigger ship will have a lower layup point and will generally drive the smaller ships into layup during recessions. If the size of ships has been increasing over time, as has happened for most of the last century, the size and age will be correlated and there will be quite a steep slope to the supply curve which becomes very apparent during recessions. Third, the relationship between speed and freight rates discussed in E4(1) above.

The *demand function* shows how charterers adjust to changes in price. The demand curve (D) in Figure 4.12c is almost vertical. This is mainly supposition, but there are several reasons why this shape is likely for most bulk commodities. The most convincing is the lack of any competing transport mode. Shippers need the cargo and, until they have time to make alternative arrangements, must ship it regardless of cost. Conversely cheap rates will not tempt shippers to take an extra ship. The fact that freight generally accounts for only a small proportion of material costs, reinforces this argument.[20]

Equilibrium and the importance of time

The supply and demand curves intersect at the equilibrium price. At this point buyers and sellers have found a mutually acceptable price. In Figure 4.12d the equilibrium price is $170 per mtm. At this price buyers are willing to hire ten ships and owners are prepared to make ten ships available. The equation balances.

However that is not the end of the story. If our aim is to understand why freight rates behave the way they do, it is just the beginning. We must be precise about *time frame.* In the real world the price at which buyers and sellers are prepared to trade depends on how much time they have to adjust their positions. There are three time periods to consider; the *momentary* equilibrium when the deal must be done immediately; the *short run*, when there is time to adjust supply by short-term measures such as layup, reactivation, combined carriers switching markets or operating ships at a faster speed; and there is the *long run*, when shipowners have time to take delivery of new ships and shippers have time to rearrange their supply sources. We will look at each of these in turn.

Momentary equilibrium

Momentary equilibrium describes the freight rate negotiated for 'prompt' ships and cargoes. The ships are ready to load, the cargoes are awaiting transport and a deal must be done. The shipowner is in the same position as the farmer when he arrives at market with his pig (see Chapter 3, section 3.2). Within this time frame the shipping market is highly fragmented, falling into the regions so familiar in brokers' reports – the Arabian Gulf, the Caribbean, USAC (United Stated Atlantic Coast), etc. Local shortages and surpluses build up, creating temporary peaks and troughs which show up as spikes on the freight chart. This is the market owners constantly trying to anticipate when selecting their next cargo, or deciding whether to risk a ballast voyage to a better loading point.

Once these decisions are taken and the ship is in position, the options are very limited. The owner can 'fix' at the rate on offer, or sit and lose money. Charterers with cargoes face the same choice. The two parties negotiate to find a price at which supply equals demand. Figure 4.13 illustrates how this works out in practice. Suppose there are about 75 cargoes on offer during the month. The demand curve, marked D1, intercepts the horizontal axis at 75 cargoes, but at freight rises it curves to the left because at very high freight rates some cargoes will be withdrawn.

The supply curve S shows there are 83 ships available to load, so there are more ships than cargoes. Since the alternative to fixing is earning nothing, rates fall to operating costs which equates to 18 cents a barrel, shown by the intersection of S and D1. If the number of cargoes increases to 85 (D2) there are more cargoes than ships. Charterers bid desperately to find a ship and freight rate shoots up to almost $1 per barrel. A swing of 10 cargoes is quite common, but the effect on rates is dramatic.

In this very short-term situation market sentiment can make rates very volatile. If there are more ships than cargoes, but owners believe that rates are rising, they may decide to wait

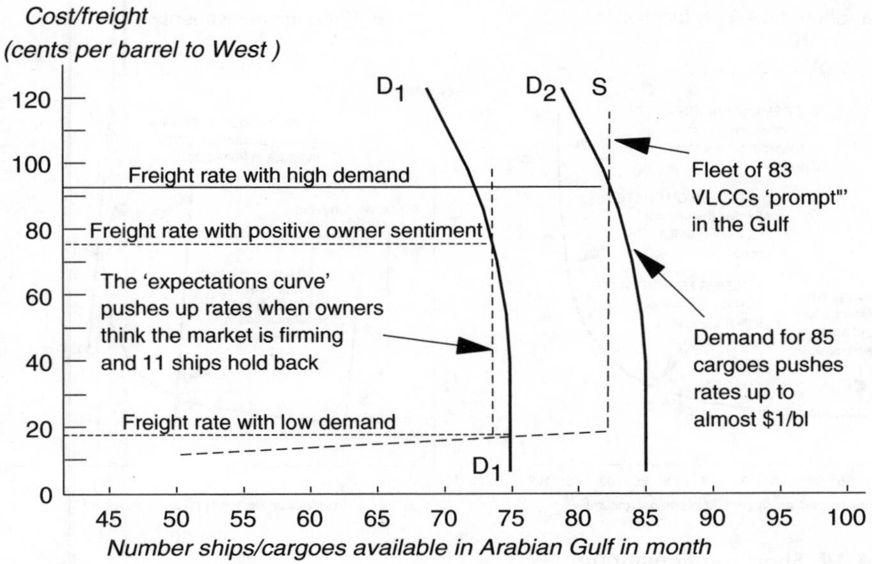

FIGURE 4.13 Momentary equilibrium in the VLCC market
Source: Martin Stopford, 1997

(sometimes owners attempt to hide their ships from charterers by reporting the presence of only one ship in their fleet, or waiting outside the loading area). Suddenly there are more cargoes than ships and rates rise, at which point the reticent owners enter the market and fix at 'last done'. This is shown by the 'expectation curve' in Figure 4.13. If the surplus of ships persists, the ships which hold back may be unable to fix at all and rates quickly collapse.

The short run equilibrium

In the 'short run' there is more time for owners and charterers to respond to price changes by moving ships in and out of lay-up, so the analysis is a little different.

The short run supply curve shown in Figure 4.14a plots, for a given size of fleet, the ton miles of transport available at each level of freight rates. The transport supply is measured in thousand btm per annum and the freight rate in dollars per thousand ton miles of cargo transported.

At point A, the supply offered is only 5,000 btm per annum because the least efficient ships are laid up; at point B, all ships are back in operation and the supply has risen to about 8,500 btm per annum; at point C, the fleet is at maximum speed and the whole fleet is at sea; finally, at point D, no further supply is obtained by increasing freight rates and the supply curve becomes almost vertical. Very high freight rates may tempt out a few remaining unutilized ships. For example, during the 1956 boom 'A number of vessels half a century old and barely seaworthy obtained freights of up to five times the rate obtained a year earlier.'

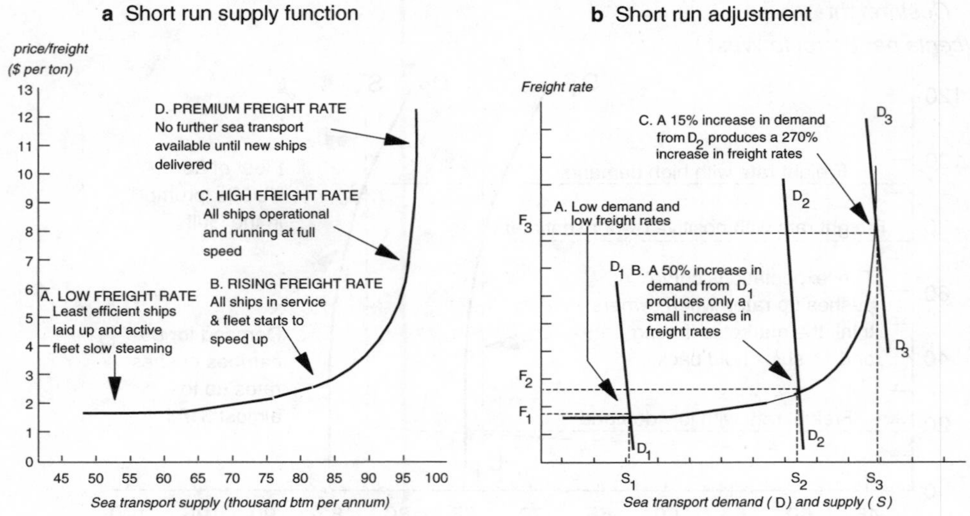

FIGURE 4.14 Short run equilibrium

Source: Martin Stopford, 1997

Note: The supply function shows the amount of sea transport offered at each freight rate.

If we now bring the *short run demand curve* into the picture we can explain how freight rates are determined. The market settles at the freight rate at which supply equals demand. Consider the three different equilibrium points marked A, B, and C in Figure 4.14b. At point A demand is low and the freight rate settles at point F1. A major increase in demand to point B only pushes the freight rate up slightly because ships immediately come out of lay up to meet increasing demand.[21] However a small increase in demand to point C is sufficient to treble the level of freight rates because the market rate is now set by the oldest and least efficient ships which need very high freight rates to tempt them into service. Finally, with no more ships available charterers bid against each other for the available capacity. Depending on how badly they need transport, rates can go to any level. However this is an unstable situation. Shippers look for cheaper supply sources and the high freight rates almost always trigger frenzied investment activity by owners and shippers.

The long run

Finally, we must consider the the long run during which the size of the fleet can be adjusted by ordering new ships and scrapping old ones. The longer-term adjustment mechanism balances supply and demand through the three other markets we discussed in chapter 3, the sale and purchase market, the newbuilding market and the demolition market. As freight rates fall during a recession, the profitability of ships and, consequently, their second-hand value also falls. Eventually the price of the least efficient ships falls to the scrap price. Ships are scrapped, removing them permanently from the market and reducing the surplus. Falling second-hand prices also make new uses of the surplus tonnage financially viable; the use of supertankers for oil storage or bulk carriers as trans-shipment facilities are examples. In these ways the price mechanism gradually reduces the supply of ships to the market. Conversely, when a shortage of ships pushes up freight rates this works through to the sale and purchase market. Shipowners are keen to add to their fleets and, because there is a shortage of ships, shippers may decide to expand their own shipping operations. With more buyers than sellers, second-hand prices rise until used ships become more expensive than newbuildings. Frustrated shipowners turn to the newbuilding market and the orderbook expands rapidly. Two or three years later the fleet starts to grow.

To illustrate this process we can take the example of the adjustment of the tanker market over the period 1980 and 1991. Figure 4.15 shows four charts, illustrating the position of the supply demand chart in a different year, 1980 (chart a), 1985 (chart b), 1991 (chart c) and 1992 (chart d). The freight rate is shown on the vertical axis measured in $000s per day and as an indicator of transport supply the tanker fleet is shown on the horizontal axis, measured in m.dwt. Neither of these units of measurement is strictly correct[22] but they are are adequate for an illustration. In the centre of Figure 4.15 is a freight chart (chart e) which shows the level of freight rates in each of the four years. Our aim is to explain how the supply and demand curves moved between the 4 years. In 1980 (chart a) freight rates were moderately high at $15,000 per day, with the demand curve intersecting the 'kink' of the supply curve. By 1985 (chart b) the supply curve has moved to the left as heavy scrapping reduced the tanker fleet from 320 m.dwt to 251 m.dwt, but demand had fallen even more to below 150 m.dwt due to the collapse in the crude oil trade after the oil price rises in 1979. This left 60 m.dwt of tankers laid up, extensive slow steaming, and the demand curve intersecting the supply curve way down its span at D85. Freight rates averaged about $7,000 per day, close to operating costs.

Between 1985 and 1991 (chart c), despite heavy scrapping, the tanker fleet fell by only 7 m.dwt, due to increased newbuilding in the late 1980s. As a result the supply curve moved very slightly to the left to S91, but a growing oil trade increased demand by 30 per cent to D91, suggesting an equilibrium freight rate of about $15,000 per day. However, in 1991 another factor intervened. After the invasion of Kuwait in August 1990 oil traders used tankers as temporary storage, moving the demand curve temporarily to the right, shown by the dotted line in Figure 4.15c. Freight rates increased to $29,000 per day. Then in 1992 supply increased due to heavy deliveries and the demand curve moved back to its 'normal' position as the temporary storage market disappeared. This was enough to drive freight rates down to $15,000 per day (chart d).

It is the combination of volatile demand and a significant time-lag before supply adjusts to demand which creates the framework for shipping market cycles. Shipowners tend to base investment on the current state of the market – they order more ships when freight rates are high and fewer when freight rates are low. The delay in delivering these ships means, however, that demand may have changed by the time the ships are delivered so any cyclical tendency is amplified.[23] Our analysis of the length of shipping cycles in Chapter 2 showed

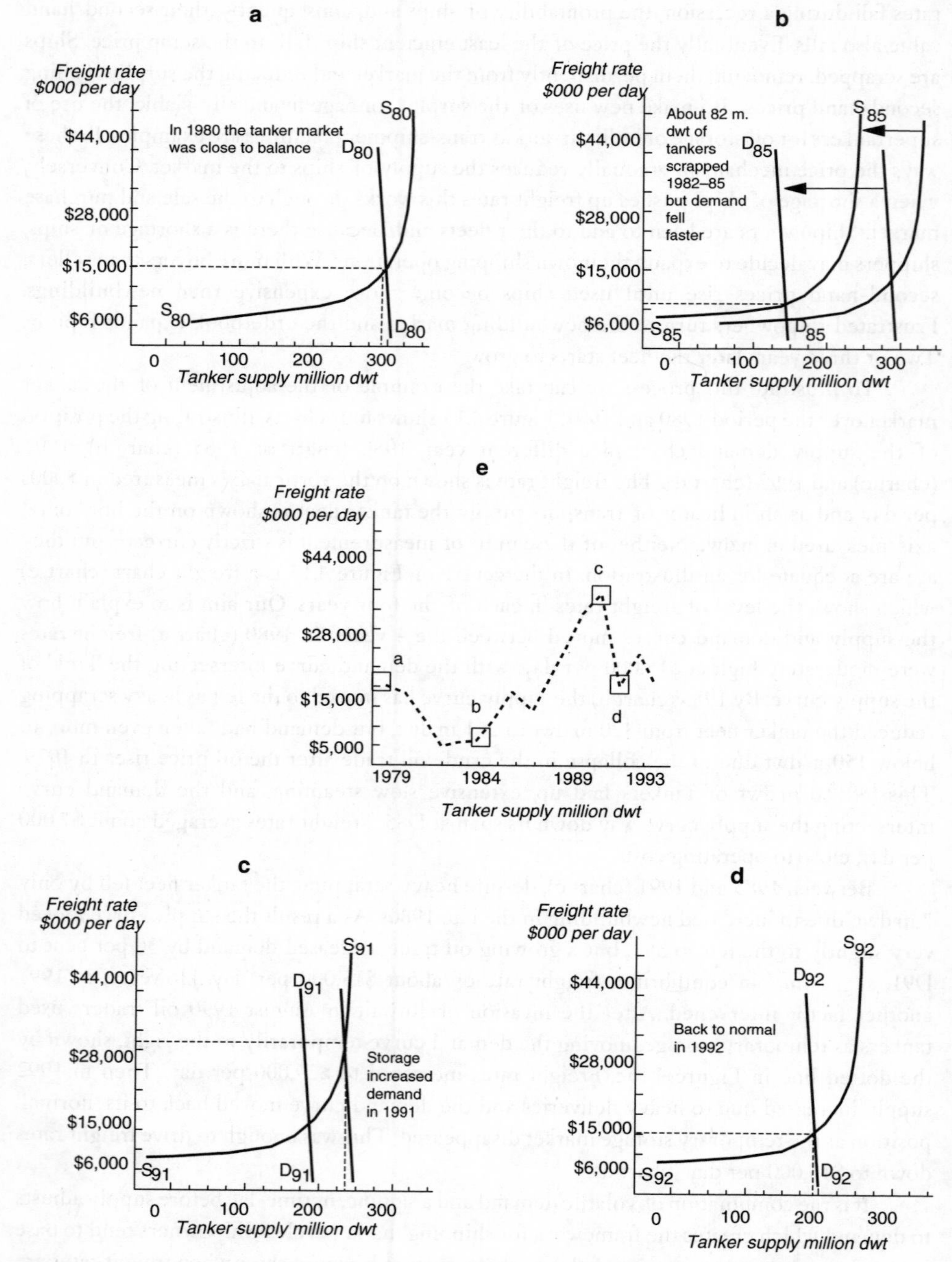

FIGURE 4.15 Long-term adjustment of supply and demand 1980–92
Source: Martin Stopford, 1997

that over a century the average cycle was about seven years long, which is about the length you would expect in a market with the adjustment mechanism we have discussed. It takes two or three years for new orders to be delivered, two or three years for scrapping to catch up, and two or three years for the market to build up a head of steam for the next round of ordering. Of course it never happens exactly this way, but it makes a neat generalization.

Long run prices and costs

What determines the long-run freight rate in the shipping market? Where will earnings average out? Will the average be high enough to pay for a new ship? This is a matter of great interest to investors who, quite reasonably, want to know what return they can expect in the long-term, taking one cycle with another.

The early economists argued that there is a built-in tendency for prices to cover costs. For example Adam Smith distinguished between the *market price*, which could be very variable, and the *natural price* which just covered the cost of production. He argued that the natural price is *the central price towards which the prices of all commodities are continually gravitating.*[24] This is a comforting idea for investors, since it suggests that if they wait long enough the market will ensure that they will earn a proper return. It is, however, a very dangerous concept.

Marshall warned against placing too much faith in the idea of a 'natural' price which, in the long run, covers costs. It is not that the theory is wrong, but that it only works *if the general conditions of life were stationary for a run of time long enough to enable {economic forces} to work out to their full effect.*[25] The natural price is unlikely to prevail because the world is constantly changing. Demand and supply schedules are constantly on the move as technology and events change. Every change alters the equilibrium amount and the equilibrium price. The unexpected intervenes long before the 'natural' price has been achieved. This is the common sense view which every shipping investor knows only too well. The world is far too mercurial for the concept of a *long run equilibrium price* to be significant in an industry where the product has a life of twenty years or more. Investors cannot expect any comfort from this quarter. They must back their judgement that on this occasion prices will cover their real costs. Economic theory offers no guarantees, and as we saw in Chapter 2, the returns have, on average, tended to be rather low.

4.5 Summary

We started this chapter with the idea that shipping companies should approach the shipping market from a competitive viewpoint, i.e. playing other players. The rules of the shipping market game are set by the economic relationships which create freight cycles. To explain them we discussed the economic 'model' of the shipping market. This model has two main components, supply and demand, linked by freight rates which, through their influence on the actions of shippers and shipowners, bring supply and demand into balance. Because the demand for ships changes rapidly but supply is slow and ponderous, freight cycles are irregular.

We identified five key demand variables, the world economy, commodity trades, average haul, political events and transport costs. The demand for ships starts with the world economy. We found that there is a close relationship between industrial production and sea trade, so close scrutiny of the latest trends and lead indicators for the world economy provide some warning of changes in the demand for ships. The second important demand variable is the structure of the commodity trades, which can lead to changes in ship demand. For example a change in the oil price in the 1970s had a major impact on the oil trade. Distance (average haul) is the third demand variable and here again we found that there have been substantial changes in the past. Political events were the fourth variable, since wars and disturbances often have repercussions for trade. Finally transport costs play an important part in determining the long-term demand.

On the supply side we also singled out five variables, the world fleet, productivity, shipbuilding production, scrapping and freight rates. The size of the world fleet is controlled by shipowners who respond to the freight rates by scrapping, newbuilding and adjusting the performance of the fleet. Because the variables in this part of the model are behavioural, the relationships are not always predictable. Market turning points depend crucially on how owners manage supply. Although the orderbook provides a guide to the size of the world fleet twelve to eighteen months ahead, future ordering and scrapping are influenced by market sentiment, and are very unpredictable. Sometimes shipowners do things which economists find difficult to understand, so relying too much on economic logic can be dangerous.

Freight rates link supply and demand. When supply is tight freight rates rise, stimulating shipowners to provide more transport. When they fall it has the opposite effect. We looked in detail at the dynamics of the mechanism by which freight rates are determined and found that timescale is important in reaching an equilibrium price. Momentary equilibrium describes the day-to-day position as 'prompt' ships in a particular loading area compete for the available cargoes. Short run equilibrium describes what happens when ships have time to move around the world, adjust their operating speed or layup. In shipping the long-term is set by the time taken to deliver new ships – say two or three years. This characteristic certainly influences the 7–8 year duration of freight cycles.

Our analysis of supply–demand charts showed that the short term supply function has a characteristic 'hockey stick' shape, while in the short term demand is inelastic. Freight cycle peaks and troughs are produced by the demand curve moving along the supply curve. When the demand curve moves into the 'kink' of the supply curve, freight rates move above operating costs and become very volatile. In the long-term the volatile freight cycles ought to average out at a 'natural' freight rate which gives investors a fair return on capital. Although this is true in theory, Alfred Marshall warned that we should not to rely on it. In a constantly changing world long-term average earnings are not subject to rules. In the past the over-eagerness of shipping investors has tended to keep market returns low, as we saw in chapter 2. Despite this, enough shipping fortunes have been made to encourage a steady flow of hopeful investors and equally hopeful bankers.

No amount of statistical analysis can reduce this complex economic structure to a simple predictive 'rule of thumb'. The requirements of success in the shipping cycle game are a lifetime's experience in the shipping industry, a direct line to the world economic and political grapevine, and a sharp eye for a bargain. Decision-makers without the advantage of experience must rely on what they can glean from books.

Chapter 5

Costs, revenue and financial performance

Annual income twenty pounds, annual expenditure nineteen nineteen six, result happiness. Annual income twenty pounds, annual expenditure twenty pounds ought and six, result misery.

(Mr Micawber in *David Copperfield*)

5.1 Cashflow and the art of survival

The impact of financial pressures on shipowners' decisions

In this chapter we look at shipping economics from the perspective of the individual shipping company. Every company faces the challenge of navigating its way through the succession of booms, recessions and depressions which characterize the shipping market. During prosperous periods when funds flood in it must meet the challenge of investing wisely for future growth and a commercial return on capital. The seeds of future problems are often sown under the heady influence of market sentiment at the peak of a cycle. In recessions the challenge is to keep control of the business when the market is trying to force surplus capacity out of the system by squeezing cashflow. During these periods the shipping market is like a marathon race in which only a limited number of entrants are allowed to finish. The race has no fixed length, it goes on lap after lap until enough competitors drop out from exhaustion, leaving the surviving runners to pick up the prizes.

In the last resort what sorts out the winners from the losers is financial performance. The risks faced by shipping companies are illustrated by a ship sale decision reported in Lloyd's List during the 1980s recession (Figure 5.1). This was at a time when the freight market was very depressed and the article reviews the considerations that entered into the decision by a shipping company to sell a VLCC from its fleet.

The circumstances are very familiar in shipping boardrooms during depressions. The company was losing money – $14.5 million in the previous year – and the ship was laid up and generating a negative cashflow. For several years the company had accepted this drain on its cashflow, in the hope that the market would improve, but the board had now decided that 'with the benefit of hindsight it is evident that our hopes for the future of the VLCC were ill founded' and had decided to sell the vessel. Its sale would mean writing off as a loss the remainder of its 'book value' not covered by the selling price, so the company would have to announce a large loss, but the proceeds from the sale would improve the cashflow.

Since the vessel was turbine powered and had been laid up for several years it was considered likely that at prevailing market prices the vessel would be sold for scrapping. In the final paragraph the article discusses a further significant decision by the group to sell its dry bulk fleet and concentrate entirely on the tanker market – a strategic decision to sacrifice one part of the business to provide cash to allow the remainder to continue, based on a belief that the prospects for the tanker market were better than those for the dry cargo market.

On the basis of this example, the challenge is to create sufficient financial strength when times are good to avoid unwelcome decisions such as selling ships for scrap when times are bad. It is the company with a weak cashflow and no reserves that gets pushed out during depressions and the company with a strong cashflow that buys the ships cheap and survives to make profits in the next shipping boom. It is not therefore the ship, the administration, or the method of financing that determines success or failure, but the way in which these are blended to combine profitability with a cashflow sufficiently robust to survive the depressions that lie in wait to trap unwary investors.

Lofs is poised to sell 'London Pride'

By Tony Gray, Business Editor

FLEET pruning looks set to continue
1 at London & Overseas Freighters, the
UK tanker owner which suffered a
loss of £14.5 million last year.

After yesterday's annual meeting,
Lof's managing director Mr Miles
Kulundis disclosed that the group
was actively considering the sale of
the VLCC *London Pride*.

This 12-year old 259,182-tonnes
2 deadweight tanker is the group's
largest and oldest vessel, and has
been a drain on the group's financial
performance.

For some years, Lofs harboured the belief that it would be able to cash in on the *London Pride's* earning potential once the market picked up. But, the depression in the tanker market has persisted, and the heavily over- tonnaged VLCC size range has been the worst affected.

A hint that the *London Pride's* future in the Lofs fleet was in doubt came in the recent annual report.

The chairman's statement disclosed
3 the group's disenchantment with the
vessel: "Our VLCC *London Pride*, is
still laid-up and, with the benefit of
hindsight, it is evident that our hopes
for the future of the VLCC were ill-
founded."

The *London Pride* has, in fact, been
4 laid-up since December 1981. As she
is turbine-powered, it seems likely
that the vessel will be scrapped if
Lofs proceeds with a sale. In current
market conditions, a demolition sale
5 may bring in around £4m for Lofs.

A sale for further trading could
6 involve an additional $0.5m.
Whatever the price achieved, it is
likely to be below the sterling book
7 value – of £3.56m at Mar 31 1983 –
and a loss being carried into the
current year's accounts.

However, the sale would have a
8 beneficial impact on the group's cash
flow.

The departure of the *London Pride* would leave Lofs with a fleet comprising five tankers: the two 61,000-tonnes general purpose tankers *London Spirit* and *London Glory*; and the three 138,000-tonners – one of which is jointly owned – *London Glory*, *London Enterprise*, and *Overseas Argonaut*.

Lofs hopes that this will remain its
core fleet for the anticipated recovery in
freight rates later this year and next
9 as oil re-stocking takes effect. The
group placed all its eggs in one
basket through the sale earlier this
year of its dry bulk fleet to the
Onassis group for $20.55m.

Lofs is not alone in discerning a more imminent recovery in the tanker market rather than for bulk carriers. Some fear the dry bulk market could be facing problems of a similar scale to those that have plagued tanker owners for so long.

It is vital for Lofs, after many years of losses and strain on the company's cash resources, that the tanker market does improve this winter.

Lofs has a versatile fleet that should be able to capitalise quickly on a rise in freight rates. A phase of oil re-stocking is expected to particularly benefit medium-sized tankers, and the group's 61,000 and 138,000-tonne vessels fit the bill.

FIGURE 5.1 Newspaper report illustrating the commercial influences on a scrapping decision

Source: Lloyd's List, July 1983

Notes: Influence on scrapping decision: 1 financial performance of the owner, 2 age and size of vessel, 3 market expectations, 4 operating costs (turbines use a lot of fuel), 5 scrap prices, 6 state of second-hand market, 7 book value of vessel in relation to its scrap or resale price, 8 cashflow of company, 9 management policies and attitudes

Financial performance and investment strategy

If financial performance is the key to survival in the shipping market, the next question is: 'How is it achieved?' The three key variables with which shipowners have to work with are:

1 The revenue received from chartering/operating the ship;
2 The cost of running the ship;
3 The method of financing the business.

The relationship between these cashflow items is shown diagramatically in Figure 5.2. *Revenue*, represented by the box on the left, is received from trading the ship. Although shipowners do not generally control the price they receive per ton of cargo, there are various ways of squeezing more revenue out of the ship. Increasing cargo capacity to achieve economies of scale is one solution. A few thousand tons of revenue earning capacity can make all the difference. Increased productivity by operational planning, reducing backhauls, minimizing time off hire, improved dwt utilization and cutting cargo handling time are other possibilities. From the revenue earned by the ship must be deducted *running costs and capital payments* shown by the boxes in the centre section of Figure 5.2. The costs include operating, voyage and cargo handling costs, while capital repayments cover interest and periodic maintenance of the ship. What is left after these charges may be subject to taxes, though few shipowners are subject to this particular cost. The residual is paid out in dividends or retained within the business.

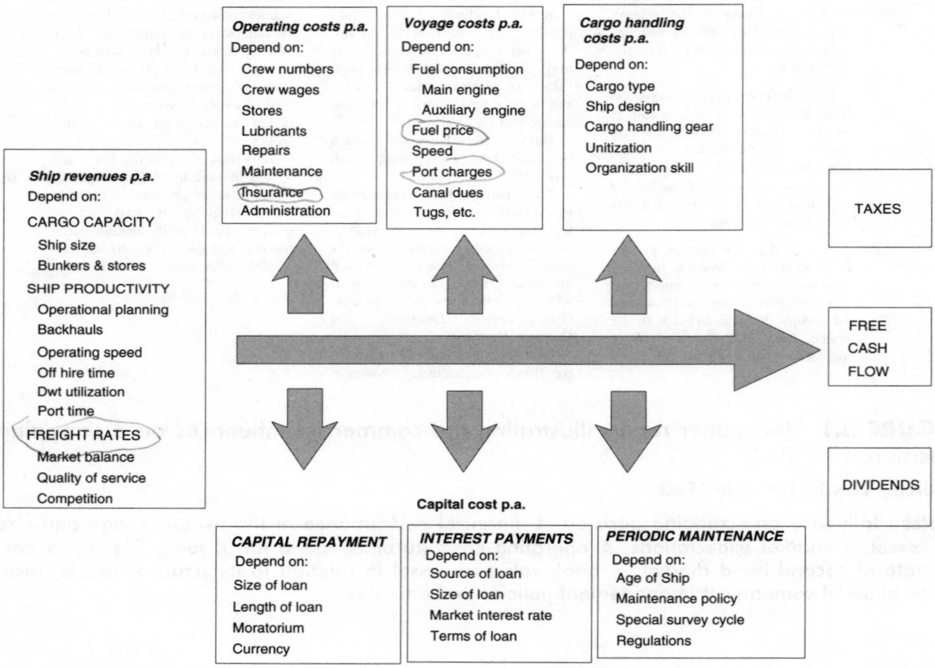

FIGURE 5.2 Cashflow model

Source: Martin Stopford, 1997

As we shall see, the way shipping companies manage these cost and revenue variables has great influence on the financial performance of the business. More specifically:

- The choice of ship influences the running cost. Day-to-day cash costs are higher for old ships with ageing machinery requiring constant maintenance, a rusty hull requiring regular steel replacement and high fuel consumption. Modern vessels with lower crew costs, reliable fuel-efficient machinery and negligible maintenance cost less to run.

- Running a successful shipping operation is not just a matter of cutting costs. It also involves squeezing as much revenue as possible out of the ship. Revenue may be steady on a long time charter or irregular on the spot market. It may be increased by careful management, clever chartering and flexible ship design to minimize time in ballast and ensure that the vessel is earning revenue for a high proportion of its time at sea.
- Financing strategy is crucial. If the vessel is financed with debt, the company is committed to a schedule of capital repayments, regardless of market conditions. If the ship is financed from the owners's cash reserves or outside equity finance there are no fixed payments to capital. In practice if a shipping company has only limited equity capital, the choice is often between an old ship with high running costs but no debt and a new ship with low running costs and a mortgage.

The trade-off between new and old tonnage, single-purpose or sophisticated multi-purpose tonnage, and debt or equity financing offers an enormous range of possible ship investment strategies. Each shipping company makes its own choice, giving it a distinctive style of operation which soon becomes well known in the shipping market. However, once a fleet has been purchased and financed, many of these parameters are fixed and the options open to shipowners become more restricted.

A good example of two very different investment strategies is provided by the Greek and Norwegian merchant marines. After the Second World War many Greek shipowners specialized in operating older tonnage with low debt and high equity. The low fixed capital cost made it possible to lay the ships up during depressions with minimum cashflow and make good profits during booms, often by the sale of the ship itself. Conversely, Scandinavian operators tended to invest in modern, highly sophisticated ships, which gave the maximum revenue-earning potential through their high flexibility and ability to carry special cargoes. This strategy was capital intensive and often involved a high degree of debt financing, with the result that the ships had to be operated continuously throughout a depression. In this sense, the Scandinavian strategy depended on minimizing unit costs on a continuous basis, whereas the Greek approach was much more concerned with skipping between market peaks. Both proved very successful for some shipowners.

The classification of costs

If we start with the basics, the cost of running a shipping company depends on a combination of three factors. First, the ship sets the broad framework of costs through its fuel consumption, the number of crew required to operate it, and its physical condition, which dictates the requirement for repairs and maintenance. Second, inflation in the cost of bought-in items, particularly bunkers, consumables, crew wages, ship repair costs and the interest rates, all of which are subject to economic trends outside the shipowners's control. Third, costs depend on how efficiently the owner manages the company, including the administrative overhead and operational efficiency.

Unfortunately the shipping industry has no internationally accepted standard cost classification, which often leads to confusion over terminology. The approach used in the present volume is to classify costs into five categories:

- Operating costs, which constitute the expenses involved in the day-to-day running of the ship – essentially those costs such as crew, stores and maintenance that will be incurred whatever trade the ship is engaged in.
- Periodic maintenance costs, which are incurred when the ship is dry-docked for major repairs, usually at the time of its special survey. In older ships this may involve considerable expenditure, so shipping companies often include a 'dry-docking provision' in their operating costs. Since this is a provision rather than a cash item it is better treated separately from operating costs.
- Voyage costs are variable costs associated with a specific voyage and include such items as fuel, port charges and canal dues.
- Capital costs depend on the way the ship has been financed. They may take the form of dividends to equity, which are discretionary, or interest and capital payments on debt finance which are not.
- Cargo handling costs, represent the expense of loading, stowing and discharging cargo. They are particularly important in the liner trades.

By analysing these different categories of costs we can develop a more thorough understanding of the market economics discussed in Chapter 4. In particular they provide an important insight into the shape of the short run supply curve and decision process which drives the adjustment of supply and demand. There are two important cost-related principles which we must explore, first the relationship between cost and age, and second the relationship between cost and size.

Ship age and the supply price of freight

Within a fleet of similar sized ships, it is usual to find that the old ships have a completely different cost structure from the new ones. Indeed, this relationship between cost and age is one of the central issues in shipping market economics, since it defines the slope of the short run supply curve shown in Figure 4.12 in the previous chapter. As the ship ages its capital cost reduces, but its operating and voyage costs increase relative to newer ships which are more efficient due to a combination of technical improvement since the ship was built (for example more efficient engines) and the effect of ageing.

An illustration of the way the cost profile changes with age is provided by the comparison of the annual costs of three Capesize bulk carriers, one five years old, one ten years and one twenty years, shown in Figure 5.3.[1] All three ships are trading under the Liberian flag using the same crewing arrangements and charging capital at 8 per cent per annum. The overall cost works out at about $24,171 per day for the 5-year-old ship, $24,165 per day for the 10-year-old ship and $20,942 per day for the twenty-year-old ship. However, the structure of costs of the new and old ships is quite different. If we consider only the direct

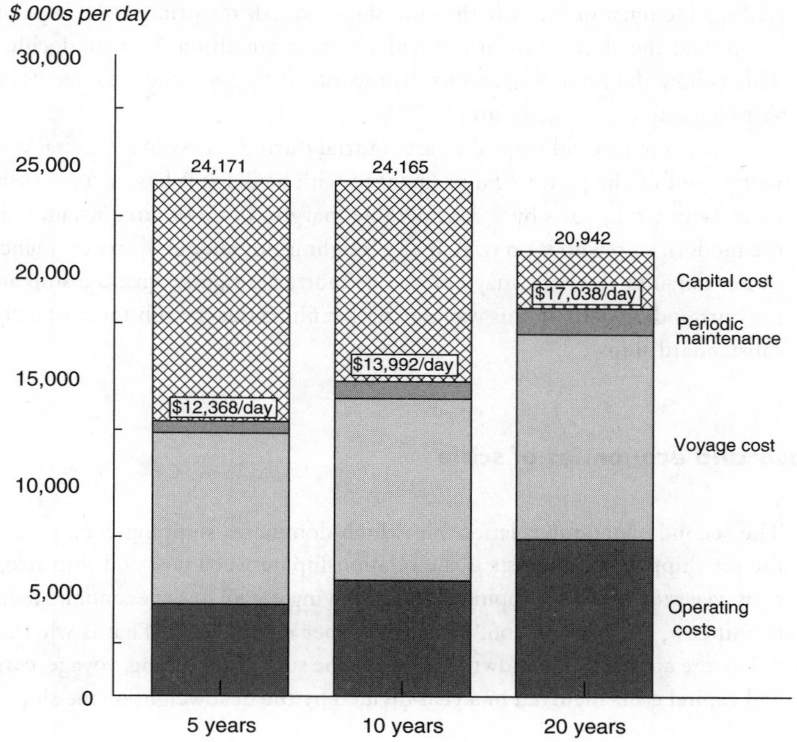

FIGURE 5.3 Capesize bulk carrier costs and age
Source: Capesize Quality Survey (1993) Clarkson Research Studies

cash costs and exclude capital costs and periodic maintenance the modern ship costs only $12,038 per day to run compared with $17,038 per day for the 20-year-old ship. This differential is due to a higher operating costs, larger crew, more routine maintenance and lower fuel efficiency (remember the owner trading spot gets paid per ton of cargo, so fuel is an out-of-pocket expense).

This cost differential plays an important part in the cashflow 'race'. If we ignore capital costs and periodic maintenance, the modern vessel can survive at freights which are way below the layup point for older ships. It is this differential which determines the slope of the supply curve. Because spot earnings have to cover operating and fuel costs, for any given spot rate the old ship generates less cash than the new ship. If *gross* earnings for a capesize (i.e. before bunker costs) fall below $17,000 per day for any length of time, the owner of the 20-year-old ship will probably lay it up, since revenue does not cover operating and voyage costs.[2] Will the ship come out of layup? This is where periodic maintenance costs come into play. Although these costs are postponable, they cannot be deferred indefinitely. In this example, when the fourth special survey arrives at about twenty years, the owner of the average ship is faced with a bill for $2.2 million, which he must pay if the ship is to continue trading. He must decide whether the ship is worth repairing. If he is pessimistic about the future and the ship is not in particularly good condition, he may decide to sell for scrap. This is how the scrapping mechanism works. It forces owners to decide whether their old ships have an economic future.

It is not just old ships that are on trial during recessions. Capital costs cannot just be written out of the picture. Ships financed with bank loans have a fixed cash flow which may exceed operating costs by a considerable margin. In these circumstances it is the owner of the modern ship who is on trial. If the freight is not enough to cover financing costs and the owner defaults, the bank may enforce its mortgage rights, seize the ship and sell it to cover the outstanding debt. In this way the market filters out the substandard owners as well as the substandard ships.

Unit costs and economies of scale

The second economic relationship which dominates shipping economics and complicates life for shipping economists is the relationship between cost and ship size, usually referred to as *economies of scale*. Shipping is about moving cargo, so the economic focus of the business is unit cost, the cost per ton, per TEU or per cubic metre. That is where we will start. We define the annual cost per dwt of a ship as the sum of operating, voyage, cargo handling costs and capital costs incurred in a year divided by the deadweight of the ship.

$$C_{tm} = \frac{OC_{tm} + PM_{tm} + VC_{tm} + CHC_{tm} + K_{tm}}{DWT_{tm}} \qquad \text{E5(1)}$$

where: C = cost per dwt per annum
OC = operating cost per annum
PM = periodic maintenance provision per annum
VC = voyage costs per annum
CHC = cargo handling costs per annum
K = capital cost per annum
DWT = ship deadweight
t = year
m = m^{th} ship

From the many factors that have influenced unit costs during the twentieth century, this has been particularly important. Because operating, voyage and capital costs do not increase in proportion to the deadweight of the vessel, using a bigger ship reduces the unit freight cost. For example, a VLCC of 280,000 dwt requires only the same number of crew as a 29,000 dwt products tanker, and uses only a quarter as much fuel per deadweight ton. Similarly, for dry bulk carriers the annual running cost per deadweight for a ship of 170,000 dwt is about one third that of a 30,000 dwt vessel, as can be seen in Table 5.1. Provided the cargo volume

TABLE 5.1 Economies of scale in bulk shipping

Ship size dwt	*Operating cost* $'000*	*Bunker cost $'000*	*Total cost $'000*	*Cost per dwt $ per annum*
30,000	1,414	680	2,095	70
40,000	1,476	778	2,254	56
65,000	1,633	972	2,605	40
150,000	1,940	1,458	3,398	23
170,000	2,120	1,620	3,740	22

Source: Drewry Shipping Consultants (1997), various
* Assuming 270 days at sea per annum at 14 knots

and port facilities are available, the owner of a large ship has a substantial cost advantage, which enables him to generate a positive cashflow at rates that are uneconomic for smaller ships. In this particular example, at a hire of $70 per deadweight per annum, the owner of a 30,000 dwt bulk carrier would just cover his operating and bunker costs, whereas the owner of 65,000 dwt vessel would generate a positive cashflow of $30 per deadweight.

This explains why, over the last century, ships have got bigger. In 1870 brokers talked about a 'handy' (i.e. flexible) vessel of 2,000 tons. In the 1990s a 'handy' vessel is over 40,000 tons. Since ships have grown steadily bigger over the years, in practice age/cost differentials and economies of scale have worked together. The penalty of size is the loss of flexibility, which impacts on the revenue side of the equation by limiting the ports that can be entered and making it more difficult to reduce ballast time by obtaining backhaul cargoes. Investors in the next generation of bigger ships always face the risk that they have overstepped the mark.

The history of freight cycles is an economic struggle between the big modern ships and earlier generations of smaller ships with outdated technology. Usually the combination of size and efficiency becomes devastating when ships reach twenty to twenty-five years old, forcing them from the market. However when the size of ships stops growing, as happened in the tanker market during the 1980s and 1990s, the economic advantage of the modern ships becomes less clearly defined, extending the economic life of ships.[3]

5.2 The cost of running ships

The costs we discussed in the last section are just examples which illustrate the general principles involved. In practice all costs are variable, depending on external developments such as changes in oil prices and on the way the shipowner manages and finances the business. To understand ship investment economics we must look in much greater detail at the structure of costs. Figure 5.4 summarizes the key points we shall consider. Each box in the diagram lists a major cost category, the variables which determine its value, and the per cent

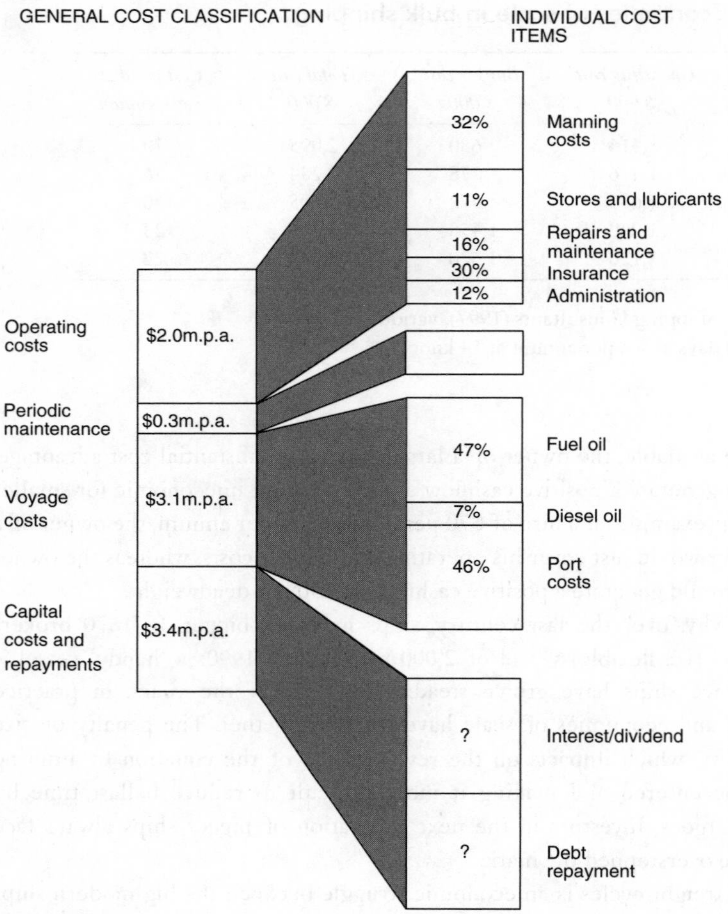

FIGURE 5.4 Analysis of the major costs of running a bulk carrier

Source: Compiled by Martin Stopford from various sources

Note: This analysis is for a ten-year-old Capesize bulk carrier under a Liberian flag at 1993 prices. Relative costs depend on many factors that may change over time.

cost for a ten-year-old ship. In the remainder of this section we examine how operating costs, periodic maintenance, voyage costs and capital costs are built up to determine an overall financial performance of the ship.

Operating costs

Operating costs are the ongoing expenses connected with the day-to-day running of the vessel (excluding fuel, which is included in voyage costs), together with an allowance for day-to-day repairs and maintenance (but not major dry dockings which are dealt with separately). They account for about 25 per cent of total costs. The principal components of operating costs are:

$$OC_{tm} = M_{tm} + ST_{tm} + MN_{tm} + I_{tm} + AD_{tm} \qquad \text{E5(2)}$$

where: M = manning cost
ST = stores
MN = routine repair and maintenance
I = insurance
AD = administration

An example of the operating cost structure of a Capesize bulk carrier is shown in Table 5.2, subdivided into these categories. In summary, the operating cost structure depends on the size and nationality of the crew, maintenance policy and the age and insured value of the ship, and the administrative efficiency of the owner. Table 5.2 shows the relative importance of each of these components in operating costs and compares them for ships of three different ages, a 5-year-old ship, a 10-year-old and a 20-year-old. It also shows an average column which, for convenience, we will refer as 'operating costs' in the following discussion.

Crew costs

Crew costs include all direct and indirect charges incurred by the crewing of the vessel, including basic salaries and wages, social insurance, pensions, victuals and repatriation expenses. The level of manning costs for a particular ship is detemined by two factors, the size of the crew and the employment policies adopted by the owner and the ship's flag state. In total manning costs may account for up to half of operating costs, for the Capesize bulk carrier shown in Table 5.2 they account for 26 per cent to 32 per cent.

The minimum number of crew on a merchant ship is specified in regulations laid down by the flag of registration. However, it also depends on commercial factors such as the degree of automation of mechanical operations, particularly the engine room, catering and cargo handling; the skill of the crew; and the amount of on-board maintenance undertaken. The reduction of crew numbers by automation and reliable monitoring systems has played a particularly important part in reducing crew numbers.[4] It is now common practice for the engine room to be unmanned at night and various other systems have been introduced such as remote control ballast, single-man bunkering and rationalized catering. As a result crew numbers declined from about forty to fifty in the early 1950s to an average of twenty-eight in the early 1980s. Current levels of technology on modern ships allow a basic crew of seventeen in a deep sea vessel, while experimental vessels have been operated with a crew of ten. Under some flags manning scales govern the numbers of personnel required on the various types and sizes of vessels, and any reductions must be agreed between the shipowner's organization and the seamen's unions.

TABLE 5.2 Operating costs of Capesize bulk carriers

	$000s			
Age of ship	*5 years*	*10 years*	*20 years*	*Average*
Crew cost				
Crew cost	445	524	575	515
Travel	48	58	62	56
Manning and support	20	20	20	20
Medical Insurance	6	6	6	6
Victualling	40	47	56	48
Total	559	655	719	645
per cent	32	31	26	29
Stores and consumables				
General stores	80	100	80	87
Cabin stores and water	11	11	11	11
Lubricants	125	115	170	137
Total	216	226	261	235
per cent	12	11	9	11
Maintenance and repairs				
Maintenance	80	150	180	137
Spares	60	140	170	123
Navigation and comms service	10	20	10	13
Total	150	310	360	273
per cent:	9	15	13	12
Insurance				
Hull and machinery and war risks	440	490	1,000	643
P&I	120	180	230	177
Total	560	670	1,230	820
per cent	32	32	44	36
General costs				
Overheads	90	90	90	90
Communications	80	70	80	77
Miscellaneous	30	30	30	30
Owner's port charges	50	50	50	50
Total	250	240	250	247
per cent	14	11	9	11
Total per annum	1,735	2,101	2,820	2,220
Daily costs (365 days)	4,754	5,756	7,727	6,079

Source: Capesize Quality Survey (1993), Clarkson Research

An idea of the basic manning cost in 1993 is provided by the budget in Table 5.2. The crew cost of $445,125 for a 5-year-old ship covers direct wages, and employment related costs. An additional $114,000 per annum is required to cover travel; manning and support; medical insurance and victualling. The manning and support item covers the basic management costs that apply to crewing – crew selection, rotation, making travel arrangements, purchase of victuals and ship supplies. In total these add 25 per cent to the crew bill for a 5-year-old ship, bringing the total crew cost to about twice the basic wages. This may seem high, but it is very much in line with overhead rates in land based industry.

A more detailed account of the crewing arrangements of three Capesize bulk carriers, one 5 years old, one 10 years old and one 20 years old is provided in Table 5.3. The modern vessel has a crew of twenty, comprising the Master, four officers, three engineers, a Bosun, eight seamen and three catering staff. The 10-year-old ship, where the maintenance workload is beginning to increase, might require a crew of twenty-four, while a 20-year-old ship might have a crew of twenty-eight. The extra crew includes an additional engineer, an electrician, four seamen and one messman. They are needed to handle the repair and maintenance workload which is a continuous cycle on an old ship and which can be carried out more cheaply at sea.

The wages paid to the crews of merchant ships have always been controversial.

TABLE 5.3 Crew cost 160,000 dwt bulk carrier (1993)

				$ p.a.		
Rank	*Source*	*Basic*	*Leave*	*Overtime*	*Provident fund / Social security*	*Totals*
Master	India	26,500	5,300	7,950	3,975	43,725
Ch officer		22,000	4,400	6,600	3,300	36,300
2nd officer		17,000	3,400	5,100	2,550	28,050
3rd officer		12,000	2,400	3,600	1,800	19,800
Radio officer		12,000	2,400	3,600	1,800	19,800
Ch engineer		26,000	5,200	7,800	3,900	42,900
1st asst engr		22,000	4,400	6,600	3,300	36,300
2nd asst engr		17,000	3,400	5,100	2,550	28,050
Bosun	Philippines	10,000	2,000	6,000	250	18,250
5AB		42,500	8,500	25,500	1,250	77,750
3 Oiler		25,500	5,100	15,300	750	46,650
Cook/std		10,500	2,100	6,300	250	19,150
Std		8,500	1,700	5,100	250	15,550
Messman		7,000	1,400	4,200	250	12,850
20		258,500	51,700	108,750	26,175	445,125
Additional						
3rd asst engr	India	12,000	2,400	3,600	1,800	19,800
Electrician		17,000	3,400	5,100	2,550	28,050
AB	Philippines	8,500	1,700	5,100	250	15,550
1 oiler		8,500	1,700	5,100	250	15,550
24		304,500	60,900	127,650	31,025	524,075
Additional						
2 OS	Philippines	14,000	2,800	8,400	500	25,700
1 oiler		7,000	1,400	4,200	250	12,850
1 messman		7,000	1,400	4,200	250	12,850
28		332,500	66,500	144,450	32,025	575,475

Source: Capesize Quality Survey (1993), Clarkson Research

The International Transport Workers' Federation (ITF) lays down minimum basic monthly wages for all ranks, as well as rates and leave as part of its world-wide and Far East wage scale, but these are not universally accepted. There are, in fact, wide disparities in the rates of pay received by crews of different nationalities. The nationality of the crew is often governed by national statute of the country of registration and under some flags shipowners are prevented from employing non-nationals on their vessels. The cost per crew member may be 50 per cent higher for a vessel registered under a European flag than for a comparable vessel 'flagged out' to one of the countries of open registration such as Liberia, Panama and Singapore, where employment regulations are less stringent. As the practice of flagging out became more widely accepted in the 1990s, the cost differentials narrowed and quality became as much an issue as cost.

These costs are certainly not standards. Shipowners have far more opportunity than land based businesses to determine manning costs by operating under a flag that allows the use of a low-wage crew and by shopping around the world for the cheapest crews available. Exchange rates will be an important factor here if wages are paid in a currency other than the one in which revenue is earned. Although shipping is a dollar-based business, shipping companies typically find themselves handling cashflows in many different currencies.

Stores and consumables

Another significant cost of operating a vessel, accounting for about 11 per cent of operating costs, is expenditure on consumable supplies. These fall into three categories listed in Table 5.2. General stores such as spare parts, deck and engineroom equipment; cabin stores cover the various domestic items used on board ship, while the largest is lubrication oil. Most modern vessels have diesel engines and may consume several hundred litres of lube oil a day while at sea. Expenditure on spare parts and replacement equipment is likely to increase with age.

Repairs and maintenance

This item, which accounts for 12 per cent of operating costs, covers all outside charges associated with maintaining the vessel to the standard required by company policy, the classification society and the charterers of the vessel who choose to inspect it. Broadly speaking this cost can be subdivided into two categories:

- *Routine maintenance.* Includes maintaining the main engine and auxiliary equipment, painting the superstructure and carrying out steel renewal in those holds and cargo tanks which can be safely accessed while the ship is at sea. As with any capital equipment, the maintenance costs of merchant ships tend to increase with age.
- *Breakdowns.* Mechanical failure may result in additional costs outside those covered by routine maintenance. Work of this type is often taken by ship repair yards on 'open order' and is therefore likely to be expensive. Additional costs are incurred owing to loss of trading time.

The typical maintenance costs for a Capesize bulk carrier listed in Table 5.2 cover visits to repair yards, plus the cost of riding crews and work carried out on board. All items of maintenance costs increase substantially with age, and a 20-year-old vessel may incur twice the costs of a more modern one.

Insurance

Insurance accounts for 37 per cent of the operating costs of a Capesize bulk carrier, though this is the cost item which is likely to vary most from ship to ship. A more appropriate range might be 15–40 per cent. A high proportion of marine insurance costs is determined by the insurance of the Hull and Machinery (H&M), which protects the owner of the vessel against physical loss or damage, and Protection and Indemnity (P&I) insurance, which provides cover against third party liabilities such as damaging a jetty or oil pollution. Additional voluntary insurance may be taken out to cover against war risks, strikes and loss of earnings.

Hull and machinery insurance is obtained from a marine insurance company or through a broker who will use a policy backed by Lloyd's Underwriters. Two important contributory factors in determining the level of H&M insurance are the owner's claims record and the claimed value of the vessel. Ship values fluctuate with the freight market and the age and condition of the vessel. Protection and Indemnity insurance is obtained through P&I clubs, which insure shipowners against injury or death of crew members, passengers or third parties, pilferage or damage to cargo, collision damage, pollution and other matters that cannot be covered in the open insurance market. The level of premium will be determined by the shipowner's claims record and other factors such as the intended trading area, the cargo to be carried, the flag of registry and the nationality of the crew. In the early 1990s insurance costs rose very sharply and now account for 20–40 per cent of operating costs. They account for 32 per cent of the operating cost of the modern Capesize bulk carrier in Table 5.2 and 44 per cent of the costs of the 20-year-old vessel.

General costs

Included within the annual operating budget for the ship is a charge to recover shore-based administrative and management charges, communications, owners' port charges, and miscellaneous costs. The overheads cover liaison with port agents and general supervision. The level of these charges depends on the type of operation. For a small tramping company operating two or three ships they may be minimal, whereas a large liner company will carry a substantial administrative overhead. With improved communications, many of these functions can now be undertaken by shipboard personnel in tramping companies. It is also an increasingly common practice for day-to-day management to be sub-contracted to specialists for a predetermined fee.

Periodic maintenance

Periodic maintenance is a provision set aside to cover the cost of interim dry-docking and special surveys. To maintain class for insurance purposes, all merchant ships must undergo regular surveys. The ship must be dry-docked every two years and every four years must have a special survey, approving its seaworthiness. At its special survey the vessel is dry-docked, all machinery is inspected and the thickness of the steel in certain areas of the hull is measured and compared with acceptable standards. The extent of these measurements increases with age. All defects must be remedied before a certificate of seaworthiness is issued. In older ships these surveys often necessitate considerable expense, for example in replacing steelwork that, owing to corrosion, no longer meets the required standards. In addition dry-docking allows hull maintenance to remove marine growth, which would otherwise reduce the operating efficiency of the ship.

Table 5.4 shows a typical periodic maintenance schedule for a standard Capesize bulk carrier. It covers the interim dry dockings and the special surveys. In total eighteen cost areas are covered. Some, such as the cost of using the dry dock ($35,000) do not vary with age, but others such as steel replacement, work on the hatch covers and the main engines increase very rapidly as the ship gets older. In this example the periodic cost increases from $586,000 at 5-years old to $1,579,000 at 20-years. Naturally this depends on the ship. Owners who operate preventive maintenance policies may incur lower costs, while for ships in poor condition the cost may be much higher.

Voyage costs

We now turn to voyage costs, which can be defined as the variable costs incurred in undertaking a particular voyage. The main items are fuel costs, port dues, tugs and pilotage, and canal charges.

$$VC_{tm} = FC_{tm} + PD_{tm} + TP_{tm} + CD_{tm} \qquad \text{E5(3)}$$

where: VC = voyage costs
FC = fuel costs for main engines and auxiliaries
PD = port and light dues. etc.
TP = tugs and pilotage, etc
CD = canal dues

Fuel costs

Fuel is the single most important item in voyage costs, accounting for 47 per cent of the total. In the early 1970s when oil prices were low, little attention was paid to fuel costs in ship design and many large vessels were fitted with turbines, since the benefits of higher

TABLE 5.4 Standard Capesize, lifetime periodic maintenance costs

Time and costs of drydocking	*Drydock age*							
	2.5	5	7.5	10	12.5	15	17.5	20
Time out of service (days)	10	10	10	13	10	30	10	30
Time in drydock (days)	4	6	6	8	8	15	6	12
Cost items (USD)								
Drydock charges	29,500	32,500	32,500	35,500	35,500	46,000	32,500	41,500
Port charges, tugs, agency	35,000	35,000	35,000	38,300	35,000	57,000	35,000	57,000
General services	40,000	40,000	40,000	52,000	40,000	120,000	40,000	120,000
Hull blast, clean and painting	44,200	58,600	58,600	70,200	70,200	113,400	38,600	60,400
All drydock paint	82,500	81,600	81,600	93,900	93,900	113,100	84,750	109,350
All steel replacement	0	70,000	140,000	210,000	140,000	1,050,000	140,000	700,000
Cargo spaces	0	22,200	47,400	16,800	20,000	106,000	20,000	130,000
Ballast spaces	20,000	16,400	12,400	10,800	16,400	9,600	16,400	31,000
Hatch covers and deck fittings	10,000	18,000	10,760	45,560	15,000	45,560	15,000	45,560
Main engine and propulsion	15,000	31,000	18,000	24,000	24,000	24,000	24,000	24,000
Auxiliaries	8,000	19,000	14,000	20,000	20,000	114,000	20,000	24,000
Piping and valves	4,000	14,000	13,000	24,000	14,000	36,000	14,000	20,000
Navigation and communications	2,000	7,000	4,000	7,000	4,000	7,000	4,000	7,000
Accommodation	3,000	3,000	4,000	4,000	3,000	4,000	3,000	4,000
Surveys and surveyors	34,000	36,000	36,000	42,500	38,000	75,000	36,000	72,000
Miscellaneous	50,000	50,000	50,000	50,000	50,000	50,000	50,000	50,000
Spare parts and subcontractors	30,000	40,000	40,000	60,000	40,000	60,000	60,000	60,000
Owner's attendance	11,900	11,900	11,900	13,700	11,900	23,900	11,900	23,900
Estimated Total (USD)	419,100	586,200	649,160	818,260	670,900	2,054,560	645,150	1,579,710
Averaged annual cost	167,640	234,480	259,664	327,304	268,360	821,824	258,060	631,884
Averaged daily cost	459	624	711	897	735	2,252	707	1,731

Source: Capeside Quality Survey (1993) Clarkson Research

power output and lower maintenance costs appeared to far outweigh their high fuel consumption. However, when oil prices rose during the 1970s, the whole balance of costs changed. During the period 1970–85, fuel prices increased by 950 per cent (Figure 5.5). Leaving aside changes in the fuel efficiency of vessels, this meant that, if fuel accounted for about 13 per cent of total ship costs in 1970, by 1985 it had increased to 34 per cent, more than any other individual item. As a result, resources were poured into designing more fuel-efficient ships and operating practices were adjusted, so that bunker consumption by the shipping industry fell sharply. In 1986 the price of bunkers fell and the level of interest in this aspect of ship design reduced.

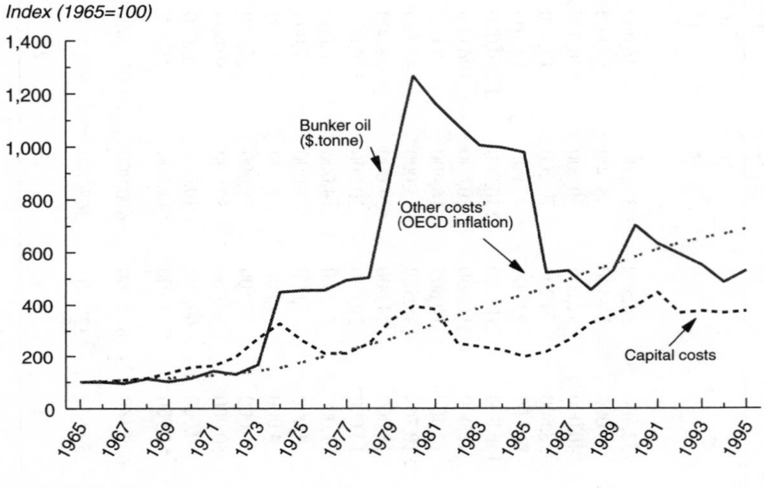

FIGURE 5.5 Shipping cost inflation (1965–95)

Source: Marine fuel oil prices from *Petroleum Economist*; other costs based on OECD consumer price index, capital costs from Fearnleys contracting price for a 70,000 dwt bulk carrier (in $)

The shipping industry's response to changing bunker prices provides a good example of how the design of ships responds to changes in costs. Although the shipowner cannot influence fuel prices, he does control the level of fuel consumption. Like any other piece of complex machinery, the amount of fuel burnt in a ship depends upon the way it is designed and the care with which it is operated. To appreciate the opportunities for improving the fuel efficiency of ships it is necessary to identify the way in which energy is actually used. Take, for example, a typical bulk carrier Panamax illustrated in Figure 5.6. At a speed of 14 knots it consumes 30 tons of bunker oil and 2 tons of diesel oil in a day. Approximately 27 per cent of this energy is lost in cooling the engine, 30 per cent is lost as exhaust emission, 10 per cent is lost at the propeller, and hull friction accounts for an additional 10 per cent. Only a residual 23 per cent of the energy consumed is actually applied to propelling the vessel through the waves. Whilst this is a highly simplified view of a complex process, it serves to focus attention on the areas where technical improvements can, and have, been made – the main engine, the hull and the propeller. The extent of the improvement can be

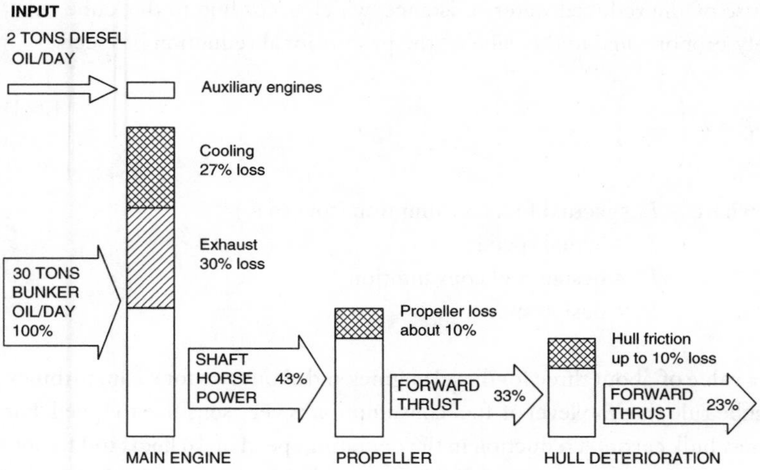

FIGURE 5.6 Energy loss in a typical 1990s built Panamax bulk carrier, 14 knots design speed
Source: **Compiled by Martin Stopford from various sources**

judged from the fact that ships built in the 1970s typically consumed 10 tons per day more fuel to achieve the same speed.

The design of the main engine is the single most important influence on fuel consumption. Following the 1973 oil price rises, and particularly since 1979, there were major improvements in the thermal efficiency of marine diesel engines. Between 1979 and 1983 the efficiency of energy conversion in slow-speed marine diesel engines improved from about 150 grammes per brake horsepower/hour to around 127 grammes per brake horsepower/hour. In addition to lower fuel consumption, engine operating speeds were reduced to below 100 rpm, making it possible to use more efficient large-diameter, slow-speed propellers without installing a gear box. The ability to burn low-quality fuel was also improved. In some cases the fuel savings achieved were quite spectacular. Diesel powered VLCCs built in the 1990s consumed 60 tons of bunkers a day, compared with fuel consumption of 130–150 tons per day by turbine powered vessels built in the 1970s.

It is also possible to improve the fuel efficiency of a ship by fitting auxiliary equipment. One method is to install waste heat systems, which use some of the heat from the exhaust of the main engines to power a boiler that drives the auxiliary engines when the main engine is running, thus saving diesel oil. An alternative method is to use generators driven direct from the main engine while the vessel is at sea. This means that auxiliary power is obtained from the more efficient main engine rather than a small auxiliary engine burning expensive diesel fuel.

In operation, the amount of fuel actually used by the ship depends on its hull condition and the speed at which it is operated. When a ship is designed, naval architects optimize the hull and power plant to a prescribed design speed which may be, for example, 15 knots for a bulk carrier or 18 knots for a container ship. Operation of the vessel at lower speeds results in fuel savings because of the reduced water resistance, which according to the 'cube rule', will be approximately proportional to the cube of the proportional reduction in speed.

$$F = F^* \left(\frac{S}{S^*} \right)^a \qquad \text{E5(4)}$$

where: F = actual fuel consumption (tons/day)
S = actual speed
F^* = design fuel consumption
S^* = design speed

The exponent a has a value of about three for diesel engines and about two for steam turbines. It follows from the cube rule that the level of fuel consumption is very sensitive to speed. For example, for a Panamax bulk carrier a reduction in the operating speed of 16 knots to 11 knots results in a two-thirds saving in the tonnage of fuel burnt per day, as shown in Table 5.5.

For any given speed, fuel consumption depends on hull design and hull smoothness. Between dry docking, marine growth on the hull of the ship increases its water resistance, reducing the achievable speed by 2 or 3 knots in extreme cases. Even after dry docking, the hull becomes increasingly rough as the ship grows older and the surface has been scraped and repainted many times. The development of self-polishing paints (SPCs), which also release a poison to kill marine growth, reduces the incidence of hull fouling between dry dockings. According to work carried out by the British Ship Research Association (now British Maritime Technology), a reduction in hull roughness from 300 microns to 50 microns can save 13 per cent on the fuel bill.

Taken together, these variables mean that there can be a very wide disparity between the fuel consumption of vessels of a similar size and speed. For example, the fuel consumption of two Panamax bulk carriers could differ by 20–30 per cent depending on age, machinery and hull condition. Obviously the cost importance of this difference in efficiency depends on the price of fuel.

TABLE 5.5 How speed affects fuel consumption for a Panamax bulk carrier

Speed knots	*Main engine fuel consumption tons/day*
16	44
15	36
14	30
13	24
12	19
11	14

Source: Sample of bulk carriers

Port charges

Port-related charges represent a major component in voyage costs and include various fees levied against the vessel and/or cargo for the use of the facilities and services provided by the port. Charging practices vary considerably from one area to another, but broadly speaking they fall into two components – port dues and service charges. Port dues are levied on the vessel for the general use of port facilities, including docking and wharfage charges, and the provision of the basic port infrastructure. The actual charges may be calculated in four different ways, based on: the volume of cargo; the weight of cargo, the gross registered tonnage of vessel; or the net registered tonnage of vessel. The service charge covers the various services that the vessel uses in port, including pilotage, towage and cargo handling.

The actual level of port costs depends on the pricing policy of the port authority, the size of the vessel, the time spent in port and the type of cargo loaded/discharged. For example, a typical port cost for a Panamax bulk carrier loading 63,000 tons of coal in Australia in 1995 was about $44,600, while discharging in Rotterdam would cost about $80,000. By convention, the allocation of port charges differs for different types of charter. Under a voyage charter, all port dues and charges related to the vessel are charged to the shipowner, while all charges on the cargo are generally paid for by the charterers, except for cargo handling charges, which are generally agreed under the charter terms. Under a trip charter or time charter, all port charges are carried by the charterer.

Canal dues

The main canal dues payable are for transiting the Suez and Panama canals. The toll structure of the Suez Canal is complicated since it is based on two little-known units of measurement, the Suez Canal Net Ton (SCNT) and Special Drawing Rights (SDRs). Tariffs are calculated in terms of the SDRs/SCNT. The Suez Canal Net Tonnage of a vessel is a measurement based on late nineteenth-century rules that were intended to represent the revenue-earning capacity of a vessel. It broadly corresponds to the cargo-carrying space below deck, though it is not directly comparable to the more normal measurement of cargo capacity (net tonnage).

The SCNT of a vessel is calculated either by the classification society or by an official trade organization, which issues a Suez Canal Special Tonnage Certificate. For vessels wishing to transit the canal that do not have a certificate, the SCNT is provisionally calculated by adding together the gross and net tonnage, dividing by two and adding 10 per cent. Tariff are then calculated on the basis of SDRs per SCNT. Special Drawing Rights were chosen as the currency unit in an attempt to avoid losses owing to fluctuations in exchange rates, as their value is linked to a number of major national currencies. Suez Canal toll charges per Suez net ton vary for different types and sizes of ships. For the Panama Canal a flat rate charge per Panama Canal Net Ton (PCNT) is used (see chapter 8 for more details of the Suez and Panama Canals).

Cargo handling costs

Finally we come to cargo handling costs. The cost of loading and discharging cargo represents a significant component in the total cost equation, and one to which considerable attention has been paid by shipowners, particularly in the liner business. A traditional cargo liner can easily spend half its time in port. The relationship is specified in equation E5(5) as representing the sum of loading costs, discharging costs and an allowance for the cost of any claims that may arise.

$$CHC_{tm} = L_{tm} + DIS_{tm} + CL_{tm} \qquad \text{E5(5)}$$

where: CHC = cargo handling costs
L = cargo loading charges
DIS = cargo discharge costs
CL = cargo claims

The level of these costs may be reduced by investment in improved ship design – to facilitate rapid cargo handling, along with advanced shipboard cargo handling gear. For example, a forest products carrier with open holds and four cranes per hold can achieve faster and more economical, cargo handling than a conventional bulk carrier relying on shore-based cranes.

5.3 The capital cost and financial performance

The third component in the cost equation is the cost of capital. In our 'typical' ship in Figure 5.4 capital costs account for 39 per cent of total costs. In cash terms capital behaves very differently from other costs. Crew costs, bunkers, insurance and the other cost items are paid for as they are used. Capital costs may appear in the cashflow in three ways. First, there is the initial purchase; second, cash payments to banks or equity investors who put up the capital to purchase the vessel; and third, cash received from the sale of the vessel.

The distinction between profit and cash

Before discussing this process in detail we need to be quite clear about the distinction between cash and profit. 'Profit' is a concept used by accountants and investment analysts to measure the financial return from a business. It is calculated by taking the total revenue earned by the business during an accounting period (e.g. a year) and deducting the costs which the accounting authorities consider were incurred in generating that revenue. The cashflow of a company, in contrast, represents the difference between cash payments and receipts in the accounting period. In surviving shipping recessions cash is what matters, while for companies with investors providing a commercial return on assets is equally important. The main reason cashflow differs from profit in a particular year is that some costs are not paid in cash at the time when the accountant considers them to have been incurred. In shipping the best example is the timing of payment for the ship. The cash transaction takes place when the ship is built. However each year the ship grows older and loses value.

To give investors a fair account of whether the business is making money, accountants have developed procedures for reporting large capital items in the profit and loss account. When a capital item is purchased, its full cost does not appear in the P&L account. If it did shipping companies would report a massive loss whenever they bought a new ship. Instead the cost of the ship is recorded in the company's balance sheet as a 'fixed asset' and each year a percentage of its value (e.g. 5 per cent) is charged as a cost in the profit and loss account to reflect the loss of value during the accounting period. This charge is known as 'depreciation' and is not a cash charge. The ship was paid for in cash long ago. It is just bookkeeping, so profit will be lower than cashflow by that amount.

To illustrate this point, if a merchant ship is depreciated (or written off) over 20 years on a linear basis (and there are many different methods), it means one-twentieth of its original cost is included in the company's overhead costs each year for 20 years. For example, if the ship was purchased for $10 million cash and depreciated at the rate of $1 million per annum, the position might be as shown in Table 5.6. In each of the first two years the company has the same profit of $1 million (line 3), which is calculated by deducting costs, including depreciation, from the total revenue earned. However, the cashflow profile is quite different. The operating cashflow at line 3 is $2 million in each year because depreciation is not a cash item – it is simply a book-keeping entry, so it does not appear in the cashflow calculation. From this is deducted the cash payment for the ship in year 1 giving a negative cashflow of $8 million in year 1 and a positive cashflow of $2 million in year 2.

However this is not the whole story. Not many shipping companies can afford to buy their ships for cash. A particularly important aspect of cashflow is the method used to pay for the ship. In Table 5.6 the company pays cash on delivery. If the ship is purchased with a loan, the whole cashflow profile changes because the cashflow now includes

TABLE 5.6 Example of profit (loss) account and cashflow for shipping company purchasing vessel for cash (equity) ($ million)

	Profit (loss) account		*Cashflow*	
	Year 1	*Year 2*	*Year 1*	*Year 2*
Freight revenue	10	10	10	10
Less: operating costs	5	5	5	5
voyage costs	3	3	3	3
depreciation*	1	1	0	0
Total operating profit/cashflow	1	1	2	2
Less capital expenditure on ship	None *	None*	20	0
Total profit/cashflow	1	1	(8)	2

* Capital expenditure is covered by the depreciation item – see text

payment of interest and repayment of the loan. This situation is illustrated in Table 5.7, which shows what happens if, instead of paying cash, the ship is financed with a five-year loan. Although the company generates a positive operating cashflow of $2 million (line 3), after deducting interest (line 4) and capital repayments (line 6) it has a net cash outflow in both years. If the company has sufficient funds available, this negative cashflow required to meet finance payments may not present a serious problem. The problems arise if there is a negative cashflow but no cash reserves to meet it.

TABLE 5.7 Example of profit (loss) and cashflow for shipping company purchasing vessel on five-year loan ($ million)

	Profit (loss) account		*Cashflow*	
	Year 1	*Year 2*	*Year 1*	*Year 2*
Freight revenue	10	10	10	10
Less: operating costs	5	5	5	5
voyage costs	3	3	3	3
depreciation*	1	1	0	0
Total operating profit/cashflow	1	1	2	2
Less interest at 10 per cent	1	0.8	1	0.8
Profit/cashflow after interest	0	0.2	1	1.2
Less capital repayment	None	None	2	2
Total profit/cashflow	0	0.2	(1)	(0.8)

* Capital expenditure is covered by the depreciation item – see text

Cashflow costs and 'gearing'

Capital is the cashflow item over which the owner has the most control at the outset. Operating and voyage costs can be adjusted marginally, depending on the ship he buys, but capital costs are completely variable. In cashflow terms they can be very high or non-existent, depending on how the ship is financed. The initial purchase of the ship may be paid for with cash, either from reserves or, in the case of very large companies, from cashflow. In that case there is a one-off capital payment and no further cashflow relating to capital until the ship is sold. Thus a shipowner purchasing a new ship for cash will have no further cash costs and can survive on a freight rate equal to operating and voyage costs. For the 5-year-old Capesize bulk carrier quoted in section 5.1 this 'fixed cost' is $12,300 per day. An alternative to paying cash is to borrow part of the purchase price from a bank. The owner puts up some 'equity', for example 30 per cent of the purchase price, and the bank provides a loan for the remaining 70 per cent. This commits him to regular capital repayments, the size of which will depend on the size of the loan, the repayment period and the interest rate. A 10 year loan could easily increase the owner's 'fixed cost' from $12,300 per day to $25,000 per day. The ratio of debt to equity is referred to as 'gearing'.

Security and bank lending policy

The terms on which bank loans are made available, and in particular the gearing they permit, is very important. We will discuss debt finance in Chapter 6, but it is worth previewing the way in which banks approach the repayment of interest and principal on a shipping loan. Since most commercial banks lend money at only 1 or 2 per cent above the rate at which they borrow, there is little margin for risk – the bank must be sure before it lends that it will receive repayment of capital and interest in full. For this reason a major consideration in ship finance is the security against the loan. A shipowner borrowing money must be able to satisfy the lender that if he defaults the loan can be recovered. The following methods are used to provide security:

- Assignment of earnings, insurances etc.
- The lender takes a first mortgage on the ship being purchased, giving him the first claim on the proceeds of the sale should the borrower default.
- A mortgage on other ships or assets may be offered. As with any security the bank must be convinced that in a forced sale the assets will realize sufficient cash to cover the outstanding debt.
- The income from a long charter with a 'blue chip' company is assigned to the lender and provides assurance that the cashflow will be available to service the loan.
- A guarantee of the loan may be given by the owner, shipping company, the shipbuilding company constructing the vessel or a government agency such as the UK's Export Credit Guarantee Department (ECGD).

The choice of finance thus has a tremendous impact on the shipowner's cashflow commitments. During recessions shipowners who fund investment with equity are safe so long as freight revenue is sufficient to cover operating and voyage costs. The ship may not be profitable but at least the owner remains in control. The shipowner who has financed his investment from debt faces a very different situation. He must make regular payments to his banker to cover interest and capital repayments. If the freight rate only covers operating and voyage costs, as often happens during depressions, he must meet his financing costs from elsewhere or lose control of the business to his bankers. Thus two shipowners running identical vessels with similar operating and voyage costs face radically different cashflows during a depression if one has financed his fleet on an equity basis and the other using debt.

Taxation

Taxation does not figure prominently in the accounts of most bulk shipping companies. The international nature of the business provides shipowners with the opportunity to avoid tax by making use of the many flags of registration which exempt shipping companies from taxation. In general the only companies that pay tax are those who have some specific reason for doing so. Liner companies whose business involves large staff departments often take this route. The other main reason is to take advantage of investment incentives available to local businesses.

5.4 The revenue calculation

The classification of revenue

Before discussing revenue, something must be said about the way revenue is received. As we saw in chapter 3, there are several different ways a shipowner can earn revenue, each of which brings a different distribution of risk between the shipowner and the charterer and a different apportionment of costs. The risks are shipping market risk, which concerns the availability of cargo and the freight rate paid and operational risk arising from the ability of the ship to perform the transport. The costs are those discussed in the previous section. Each of the revenue arrangements deals with these items differently:

- *Voyage charter.* This system is used in the voyage charter market, the specialist bulk market and in a rather different way in the liner trades. The freight rate is paid per unit of cargo transported, for example $20 per ton. Under this arrangement, the shipowner generally pays all the costs, except possibly cargo handling, and is responsible both for managing the running of the ship and for the planning and execution of the voyage. He takes both the operational and the shipping market risk. If no cargo is available; if the ship breaks down; or if it has to wait for cargo he loses out.
- *Time charter.* The charter hire is specified as a fixed daily or monthly payment for the hire of the vessel, for example $5,000 per day. Under this arrangement, the owner still takes the operational risk, since if the ship breaks down he does not get paid. The charterer pays fuel, port charges, stevedoring and other cargo-related costs. He takes the market risk, paying the agreed daily hire regardless of market conditions (unless the charter rate is linked to the market in some way).
- *Bareboat charter.* This is essentially a financial arrangement in which the charter hire only covers the financing cost of the ship. The owner finances the vessel and receives a charter payment to cover expenses. All operating costs, voyage costs and cargo-related costs are covered by the charterer, who takes both the operational and the shipping market risk.

A further discussion of these revenue concepts can be found in chapter 3. For simplicity the discussion in this chapter assumes that revenue is earned as a unit freight rate per ton mile of cargo carried.

Freight revenue and ship productivity

The basic revenue calculation involves two steps: first, determining how much cargo the vessel can carry in the financial period, measured in whatever units are appropriate (tons, ton miles, cubic metres, etc.), and, second, establishing what price or freight rate the owner will receive per unit transported. In more technical terms, the revenue per deadweight of shipping capacity can be viewed as the product of the ship's productivity, measured in ton miles of cargo transported per annum, and the freight rate per ton mile, divided by the ship's deadweight, thus:

$$R_{tm} = \frac{P_{tm} \cdot FR_{tm}}{DWT_{tm}} \qquad \text{E5(6)}$$

where: R = revenue per dwt per annum
P = productivity in ton miles of cargo per annum
FR = freight rate per ton mile of cargo transported
t = time period
m = ship type

The concept of a ship's 'productivity' is useful because it measures overall cargo-carrying performance, encompassing both operating performance in terms of speed and cargo deadweight and flexibility in terms of obtaining backhaul cargoes. For example, a combined carrier potentially has a much higher productivity than a tanker because it can carry a backhaul of dry cargo if one is available. The analysis of productivity can be carried further by subdividing into its component parts as follows:

$$P_{tm} = 24 \cdot S_{tm} \cdot LD_{tm} \cdot DWU_{tm} \qquad \text{E5(7)}$$

where: S = average operating speed per hour
LD = loaded days at sea per annum
DWU = deadweight utilization

This definition states that ship productivity, measured in terms of ton miles of cargo transported in year t, is determined by the distance the vessel actually travels in 24 hours, the number of days it spends loaded at sea in a year, and the extent to which it travels with a full deadweight of cargo. By further examination of each of these components a precise definition of productivity can be obtained.

Optimizing the operating speed

When a vessel is earning unit freight revenue, the mean operating speed of the ship is important because it determines the amount of cargo that can be delivered during a fixed period and hence the revenue earned.

In a high freight market it pays to steam at full speed, whereas at low freight rates a reduced speed may be more economic because the fuel cost saving may be greater than the loss of revenue. This certainly happens in practice. For example, in early 1986 the VLCC fleet was operating at a speed of around 10 knots, but when freight rates rose in 1988–9 it speeded up to almost 12 knots. For the same reasons, a substantial increase in bunker prices will change the optimum operating speed for a particular level of freight rates because it increases the cost saving for a given reduction in fuel consumption.

The financial logic behind the optimum operating speed calculation can be illustrated with a simple example in Table 5.8 which shows the effect of speed on the cashflow of a ship for different fuel prices and freight rates. By slowing down from 14 knots to 11 knots, the amount of fuel used in a year is almost halved, bringing a saving in bunker costs that depends

TABLE 5.8 The effect on speed on operating cashflow

		Fuel cost saving by slowing down at. . . .		Revenue loss by slowing down at. . . .	
Speed (knots)	*Fuel consumption per annum tons*	*Fuel oil $200/ton $'000*	*Fuel oil $100/ton $'000*	*Low freight rate $'000*	*High freight rate $'000*
14	10,176	—	—	—	—
13	8,184	398	199	224	448
12	6,546	726	363	455	910
11	5,156	1,004	502	692	1,384

on the level of fuel prices. There is, however, a corresponding loss of revenue, because at the low speed less cargo is delivered. The size of this loss depends on the level of freight rates. As a result the shipowner is confronted by a trade-off between lower costs and lower income, and the balance will determine his decision.

To illustrate this point we can examine the circumstances under which it would pay the shipowner to slow down to 11 knots:

- *Case 1*: fuel cost $100/ton and low freight rates – he would save $502,000 costs but would lose $692,000 revenue, so it is not worth slowing down.
- *Case 2*: fuel cost $200/ton and low freight rates – he would save $1,004,000 and lose $692,000, so it is worth slowing down.
- *Case 3*: fuel cost $200/ton and high freight rates – he would save $1,004,000 costs but would lose $1,384,000 revenue, so it is not worth slowing down.

In fact, for any level of freight rates and fuel costs there is an optimum speed.

Maximizing loaded days at sea

A ship's time is divided between 'productive' loaded days at sea and unproductive days spent in ballast, in port, or off hire. A change in any of these variables will affect the loaded days at sea, as follows:,

$$LD_{tm} = 365 - OH_{tm} - DP_{tm} - BAL_{tm} \qquad \text{E5(8)}$$

where: LD = loaded days at sea
OH = days off hire per annum
DP = days in port per annum
BAL = days in ballast per annum

Days off hire reflect time spent for repairs, breakdowns, holidays, etc. A survey of bulk carriers showed an average of twenty-four days per annum off hire, though this figure can be expected to vary with conditions in the freight market. Owners will always attempt to minimize the time the vessel is not earning, but during periods of low freight market activity the ship may spend substantial time waiting for cargo, this being one of the major costs incurred during a market recession. For example, a ship that waits twelve days for a cargo with daily operating costs of $6,000 will have lost $72,000.

Port days depend upon the type of ship, the loading facilities available and the cargo being loaded. The more time the ship spends in port the less it spends carrying cargo. Homogeneous cargoes such as iron ore and grain can load very quickly where good facilities are available – iron ore loading rates of 6,000 tons per hour are common. Difficult cargoes such as forest products and general cargo may take weeks rather than days to load under some circumstances. Ships handling bagged sugar can spend a month loading or discharging.

Days spent in ballast is the third and most important determinant of loaded days at sea. For tankers and other single cargo ships it is a simple calculation, since backhauls are not generally available and the ship spends half its sea time in ballast. For combined carriers, most bulk carriers, reefers and liners the calculation is more difficult because these vessels can carry a wide range of different cargo types, and are often able to pick up backhaul cargo. Relatively little statistical information is available about the average time spent in ballast. A rule of thumb is 'the bigger the ship, the more time in ballast'. For example, a 30,000 dwt bulk carrier is always better placed to obtain a backhaul than a 160,000 dwt vessel since draught restrictions may limit the larger vessel's ability to pick up part cargoes.

The financial impact of obtaining a backhaul cargo can be illustrated by the example in Table 5.9 of a Panamax bulk carrier operating in the coal trade from Hampton Roads, USA, to Japan during the shipping depression in 1985. At a freight rate of $15 per ton this vessel would have a negative cashflow of $500,000 per annum when operating on a 50 per cent ballast basis. However, by picking up a backhaul of coal from Newcastle, New South Wales, to Norway at a rate of $15 per ton, the vessel would generate a positive cashflow of $19,000 per annum.

Deadweight utilization

This refers to the extent to which the vessel travels with a full payload of cargo. In other words, it is the ton mileage of cargo carried divided by the ton milage of cargo that the vessel

TABLE 5.9 The effect of the backhaul on cashflow

	Cargo 000 tons per annum	*Freight per ton $*	*Annual revenue $million*	*Annual cost* $million*	*Cashflow $'000*
Backhaul	308	15	4.62	4.43	19
No backhaul	252	15	3.78	4.28	(500)

could actually have carried if it had always obtained a full payload. In practice, the deadweight cargo capacity of a vessel represents a physical maximum, and it is a commercial decision whether this capacity is fully utilized. The shipowner always has the option to accept a part cargo and during the difficult market conditions of the 1980s this became an increasingly common practice in both the dry bulk and the tanker markets. The change was particularly noticeable in the tanker market after the 1973 oil crisis, when the oil companies were no longer able to match cargo parcels to ships.

In conclusion, the shipowner making ship investment decisions faces a trade-off between revenue and cost variables. For example, a continuous self-discharging bulk carrier may be capable of unloading cargo at a rate of 6,000 tons per hour, but at the cost of higher initial investment and a loss of cargo deadweight owing to the weight of the cargo handling gear. Similarly, a combined carrier offers the shipowner the option to obtain a very high deadweight utilization by carrying alternate cargoes of oil and dry cargo, while incurring higher capital and operating costs. Containerization involves heavy investment in cargo handling efficiency, whereas the ro-ro combines some of the benefits of containerization with a higher degree of cargo flexibility. A discussion of the roll on, roll off and lift on, lift off vessels may be found in Chapter 11.

5.5 Computing the cashflow

At the beginning of this chapter we discussed the crucial role of cashflow in determining the ability of a shipping business to survive the long depressions that are such a feature of the shipping market. We then examined the cost and revenue items that underlie a shipping business's cashflow, with a view to understanding how costs can be controlled and how revenue can be increased within the overall constraints imposed by the ship, the business organization and the legal framework within which the vessel is operating. It now remains to discuss the techniques for preparing cashflow calculations that can be used as a basis for decision making.

Four methods of cashflow analysis are widely used in the shipping industry, each of which approaches the cashflow from a different perspective:

1. *The voyage cashflow (VCF) analysis* is the technique used to make day-to-day chartering decisions. It computes the cashflow on a particular ship voyage or combination of voyages. This provides the financial basis for operational decisions such as choosing between alternative charter opportunities where there are several options, or in a recession deciding whether to lay up the ship or fix it.
2. *The annual cashflow (ACF) analysis* calculates the cashflow of a ship, or a fleet of ships on a year-by-year basis. It is the format generally used for cashflow forecasting. By projecting the total cashflow for the business unit during a full financial year, it shows whether, on specific assumptions, the business as a whole will generate enough cash to fund its operations after taking account of complicating factors such as tax liabilities, capital repayments and periodic maintenance.

3 *The required freight rate (RFR) analysis* is a variant on the annual cashflow analysis. It focuses exclusively on the cost side of the equation, calculating the revenue the ship needs to earn to cover its costs. This is useful for shipowners calculating whether a ship investment will be profitable and bankers carrying out credit analysis to decide how much to lend. It can also be used to compare alternative ship designs.

4 *The discounted cashflow (DCF) analysis* is concerned with the time value of money. It is used for comparing investment options where the cashflows differ significantly over time. For example, a new ship involves a large initial investment but is cheap to run, whereas an old ship is cheap to buy but has higher costs later in its life. DCF provides a structured way of comparing the two investments.

These methods are complementary and each approaches the cashflow in a different way appropriate to the needs of different decisions.

The voyage cashflow (VCF) analysis

The VCF analysis provides information about the cash that will be generated by undertaking a particular voyage or sequence of voyages. Typically the owner with a ship which is 'open' on a particular date will have brokers' lists showing cargoes available in the relevant loading area. Sometimes there will be one obvious cargo, so the decision is easy. In most cases, however, there will be several alternatives, all possible but none ideal. He has to decide which cargo to take. This means answering questions like: 'Should I accept the grain cargo from US Gulf to Japan, or from US Gulf to Rotterdam?' 'Should I fix now or wait a few days to see if the rates improve?' 'Should I lay up the vessel or continue to trade?' By providing an estimate of the profitability of a particular voyage the VCF analysis plays an essential part in making operating decisions.

An example of a voyage cashflow analysis is shown in Table 5.10. A Panamax bulk carrier is on a multi-leg voyage from the US Gulf to Japan with grain, then ballasting down to Australia, where it picks up another cargo of coal to deliver to Europe before returning in ballast to East Coast North America to reload grain. The aim is to estimate how much cash the voyage will actually generate.

Inevitably this table is in a summarized form. In practice, a more detailed voyage estimating programme would be used. The five sections of the table are reviewed below:

- *Section 1: Ship information.* Details of the ship size, speed fuel consumption, etc. In this case the speed is the same on the loaded and ballast voyage. The ship, which is relatively modern, burns 33 tons per day on the laden voyage and 31 tons on the ballast voyage. The bunker price is $109 per ton for bunker oil and $169 per ton for diesel oil for the auxiliaries. Bunker prices vary around the world and a bunkering plan will be considered, to ensure that the ship bunkers in the cheapest location.
- *Section 2: Voyage information.* Details of the voyage including cargo, distances, port days and freight rates. In this case the cargo is 54,500 tons of grain and 62,375 tons of coal.

A ship of this type would probably carry about 3,500 tons of bunkers and stores, leaving an available cargo capacity of 62,500 tons, so the vessel is not fully loaded on the first leg. On this voyage the ballast legs are much shorter than the cargo legs. Both cargo legs involve lengthy port calls.

- *Section 3: Days on voyage.* The time taken to complete the round voyage is calculated from the average speed, the voyage distance on loaded and ballast legs, and the port times. The speed is lower than the ordered speed due to the need to allow a 'sea margin' for weather.[5] This is an operational decision. In a firm market the owner might take the ballast leg and a faster speed to save time. For the reasons discussed earlier in the chapter, the cashflow may be improved by changing the speed. The port time includes time taken waiting for a berth, documentation, loading/discharging cargo, bunkering and a day for transiting the Panama Canal. It is not always easy to estimate port times precisely.
- *Section 4: Voyage cashflow.* The freight earnings are shown in line 4.1. From this is deducted the broker's commission and voyage costs to calculate the contribution to operating costs (line 4.4). This represents the cash generated by the voyage towards paying the ongoing cost of running and financing the vessel. Finally, the operating costs are deducted at line 4.4 to give the net cashflow for the voyage (line 4.5).

- *Section 5: Operating costs.* These are calculated for the vessel on an annual basis and reduced to a daily rate using the assumption that the vessel is available for hire 350 days a year. The daily rate is used to calculate the operating costs attributable to the voyage in the voyage cashflow calculation in Section 4. Since this is concerned with annual cash costs, the actual cashflow attributable to operating costs will not necessarily fall within the time-scale of the voyage.

In this example the freight rates are taken from a period of recession in August 1992. The ship would earn just enough to cover its full operating and voyage costs, leaving a surplus of $64,290 as a contribution to capital costs, an average of $509 per day. A modern ship of this type financed by debt may incur debt repayments equivalent to $10–12,000 per day, so the charter would make no contribution to finance costs.

So what does the owner do in this situation? He will not actually lose money if he accepts the voyage at this level of freight rates. If there is a mortgage on the vessel, he has a cashflow problem because the voyage will make little contribution to meeting these costs. He will have to meet mortgage interest and capital repayments from other income, or ask his bankers to defer payment until the market improves. He will certainly consider other voyage options, but if nothing else turns up it is not a difficult decision. He must take the voyage and invite his bank manager to lunch.

For an older ship with higher voyage costs the decision is more difficult. If we re-run the voyage estimate for a vessel which, because of its age, takes the voyage a knot slower at 13 knots, but burns 35 tons a day loaded and 33 tons a day in ballast, we estimate a loss of $28,432 for the voyage. This puts him in a very difficult position. If he accepts the charter

TABLE 5.10 Voyage cashflow analysis

1	SHIP INFORMATION					
	Ship type	*dwt*	*Speed*	*Bunkers (tons/day)* *Knots*	*Main*	*Auxiliary*
	Bulk carrier	66,000	Design	15.0		
			Laden	14.0	33	1
			Ballast	14.0	31	1
			In port	0	3	2
			Bunker price $/ton		109	169

2	VOYAGE INFORMATION					
	Route	*Distance (miles)*	*Days at sea*	*Days in port*	*Cargo*	*Freight $/ton*
Leg 1	US Gulf–Japan	9,123	28.6	19	54,500	19.5
Leg 2	Japan–Australia	4,740	14.8	0	Ballast	0
Leg 3	Australia–Europe	12,726	39.9	10	62,375	10
Leg 4	Europe–ECNA	4,500	14.1	0	Ballast	0
		31,089	97.4	29	116,875	1,686,500

Rates shown are at 21st August 1992

3	DAYS ON VOYAGE CALCULATION		
3.1	Charter party speed	14.0	Average for trip
3.2	less sea margin	5%	Allowance for weather etc
3.3	Actual average speed	13.3	
3.4	Voyage distance	31,089	From section 2 above
3.5	Loaded days at sea	97.4	31,089/ /(12.5*24)
3.6	Port time/canal transit	29	From section 2
3.7	TOTAL	126	Line 3.3 + Line 3.4
4	VOYAGE CASHFLOW		
4.1	Freight earnings $	1,686,500	From section 2 above
4.2	less broker's commission	33,730	At 2 per cent
4.3	less voyage costs		
	Bunker oil for main engine	353,508	At consumption in section 1
	Diesel oil for auxiliaries	26,262	At consumption in section 1
	Port costs	418,000	Cost of four port calls
	Canal dues	80,000	One Panama canal transit
	TOTAL	877,770	
4.4	Net earnings $	775,000	
	memo; Daily earnings	*6,131*	
4.4	less operating costs	710,710	116 days at $5,623/day
4.5	Net voyage cashflow	64,290	
4.6	Contribution to capital ($/day)	509	
5	OPERATING COSTS		
5.1	Manning costs $	1,068,000	Crew of 30 at $35,600 per annum
5.2	Stores	195,000	
5.3	Maintenance	270,000	
5.4	Insurance	220,000	
5.5	Administration	215,000	
5.6	TOTAL ANNUAL COST	1,968,000	
5.7	Cost per day	5,623	At 350 days on hire per annum

he will not earn enough to recover his voyage costs, even if things go as planned. With old ships he knows that things do not always go as planned. However if refuses the cargo he will be even worse off. The operating costs of $5,392 per day must be paid whether the ship has a cargo or not. One option is to send the ship to layup, saving a large part of operating costs, but unless the vessel is carefully maintained during layup its future value can be badly affected.

In these circumstances it is easy to see how during recessions the business becomes totally preoccupied with the problem of obtaining enough cash to pay each day's bills as they come in and with cutting costs wherever possible. The lesson re-learned by each generation of over-leveraged shipowners and their bankers is that once the recession has started it is too late. There are no real options. With a real effort the owner might cut his annual operating costs to, say, $4,500 per day using a cheaper crew, defer all but the most essential repairs and tightening up on administration costs. However if he is highly leveraged, whether the ship is new or old, the extra $1,500 per day will not make much difference to his cashflow. Indeed, if he cuts costs too much it could lead to expensive operational problems.

If he cannot obtain sufficient cash from elsewhere, and if his bankers press for payment, then the only option may be to sell assets to raise cash. This usually means selling a ship, and brings us back to the sale and purchase decision that we discussed at the beginning of the chapter in Figure 5.1. The problem is that a ship that cannot generate a positive cashflow, even when well managed, will not command a high price on the market. As desperate owners are driven to sell their ships in order to raise cash, and as few potential purchasers can be found, the price falls. For newer vessels, a speculative investor will almost always be found, but for old ships whose economic life may not span the depression the scrapyard may be the only willing purchaser.

The moral is that surviving depressions depends upon being able to generate cash when other shipowners are losing money, and having enough cash reserves to survive the recessions which, as we saw in Chapter 2, are a regular feature of the shipping market. By the time the voyage decision arrives, it is too late. Banks rarely lend money to customers who are in financial difficulties and if they do, it is usually on very disadvantageous terms. Financial planning for such contingencies must be undertaken before the ship is purchased, when rates are high, and the shipowner still has some room for manoeuvre. Cashlow planning is the technique to use.

The annual cashflow (ACF) analysis

Annual cashflow analysis is concerned with calculating the cashflow generated by the business as a whole over a period of time. In this sense it is less concerned with the ship as an operating unit than with the total cashflow that the business must finance over a period of time, either months or years.

There are several different methods of calculating the annual cashflow, but the simplest is the receipts and payments method shown in Table 3.11. The top of the table shows cash revenue, the lower half of the table shows cash costs, and the bottom line indicates the cashbook balance carried forward from one year to the next in the company's bank account. This simple example illustrates the ACF technique for a one-ship company trading over a four-year period. The figures are loosely based on actual market conditions between 1990 and 1995, and the freight rates, prices, operating costs and the outstanding loan are shown as a memo item at the bottom of Table 5.11. For simplicity, inflation and bunker price changes have not been included in the analysis.

TABLE 5.11 Example of annual cashflow analysis for 280,000 dwt tanker built 1976 scrapped at fourth survey

	$000s					
	Year 0 (1990)	*Year 1 (1991)*	*Year 2 (1992)*	*Year 3 (1993)*	*Year 4 (1994)*	*Year 5 (1995)*
1 Opening balance	8,500	1,900	4,450	815	(798)	(1,488)
2 Cash receipts						
2.1 Operating revenue (gross)	0	10,820	4,327	6,041	3,436	
2.2 Capital receipts	15,400					
2.3 Revenue from ship sale					6,300	
3 TOTAL RECEIPTS	15,400	10,820	4,327	6,041	9,736	
4 Cash payments						
4.1 Operating costs		3,650	3,650	3,650	3,650	
4.2 Drydocking						
4.3 Voyage costs						
4.4 Purchase of ship	22,000					
4.5 Loan repayments		3,080	3,080	3,080	6,160	
4.6 Interest		1,540	1,232	924	616	
4.7 Tax payments						
5 TOTAL COSTS	22,000	8,270	7,962	7,654	10,426	
6 CASHBOOK BALANCE AT YEAR END	1,900	4,450	815	(798)	(1,488)	(1,488)
memo						
Charter rate/day	22,883	31,824	12,727	17,768	10,107	15,789
Days trading		340	340	340	340	340
Second-hand price of ship	22,000	20,000	9,500	11,000	8,000	10,000
Operating costs $/day	10,000	10,000	10,000	10,000	10,000	10,000
Outstanding loan (year end)	15,400	12,320	9,240	6,160	0	0
Asset cover	1.4286	1.6234	1.0281	1.7857		

The shipping company has an opening balance of $8.5 million (line 1). On the last day of year 0 it purchases a 1975 built tanker of 280,000 dwt for $22 million. A bank loan is used to finance 70 per cent of the purchase price, to be paid back in equal annual instalments of $3.08 million per annum over five years. The remainder of the purchase price is paid from the company's own cash reserve. Receipt of the loan from the bank is shown at line 2.2 as a capital receipt of $15.4 million, while the payment for the ship is shown at line 4.4 as $22 million. In year 1, freight rates are running at $31,824 per day and the ship generates total revenue of $10.8 million, more than enough to cover operating costs, voyage costs and capital charges, so the company ends year 1 with a positive bank balance of $4.45 million. In each of the following years, however, freight rates fall to $12,727 per day in year 2, $17,768 per day in year 3 and $10,107 per day in year 4. Each year the company's bank balance is slowly eroded, so that by the end of year 3 the strong positive balance has disappeared and the company needs to raise an additional $798,000 in cash just to meet day-to-day commitments.

At the end of year 4 the negative cashflow would force the company to make some major decisions of the type discussed at the beginning of the chapter. To make matters worse, in year 4 the ship faces its fourth special survey and the estimate is $5 million. One option, shown in Table 5.11, would be to avoid the survey by selling the ship. During the recession the market price reported by brokers for an average 280,000 dwt VLCC built in 1975 has fallen to $8 million. However a ship due for its fourth special survey is not in average condition and would not attract even that price – a scrap sale at $6.3 would be more likely. With $3.08 million of the original loan still outstanding and debts of $798,000, a sale for $6.3 million would leave the shipping company with a loss of $1.487 million, compared with an opening balance of $8.5 million. Obviously this option would suit the bank, which would be repaid in full, but the shipping company would have lost heavily on the deal. By selling the ship any hope of recovering the losses would be gone.

The second option is to put the ship through survey and trade on. The cashflow in Table 5.12 shows what would happen. First, the owner would have to raise an overdraft of $10.5 million cash to meet his negative cashflow in years 3 and 4. This will be very difficult. Few bankers are willing to lend to a business with no assets and a negative cashflow. There is little he can do to raise money within the business. Cost economies might be possible if the company is paying top rates to the crew and maintaining the vessel to a very high standard. Closing expensive offices is another source of economy. If rigorous cost-cutting saves $1,500 per day, that is worth $0.5 million in a full year. This might convince his bankers that he is determined to tackle the problem, but would not even pay the interest on his overdraft. All he can offer his bankers is a straight gamble on the market and bankers do not like to gamble. Bankers do not generally gamble, but they might not be willing to take the unrecoverable write-off of $1.5 million which would accompany foreclosure (see option 1). Choosing between foreclosing or providing a $10.5 million overdraft is a decision most bankers would rather avoid. Such decisions test the concept of 'relationship banking' which we discuss in Chapter 6.

On this occasion the bank's decision to back the owner would pay off. The out-turn in year 5 (Table 5.12) shows how quickly a company's financial position can change in shipping. Freight rates increase to $15,789 per day in year 5 which brings in an extra $2 million income. In response to higher freights the market price of the ship goes up to $11 million. Since the ship has now passed survey, it would probably fetch this price if sold, so its real asset value has increased by 66 per cent from $6.3 million to $11 million in a year, adding $4.7 million to the net worth of the company. Lower operating costs contribute an extra $0.5 million. In total the company's financial position has improved by

TABLE 5.12 Example of annual cashflow analysis for 280,000 dwt tanker built 1976 traded through fourth survey

	$000					
	Year 0 (1990)	*Year 1 (1991)*	*Year 2 (1992)*	*Year 3 (1993)*	*Year 4 (1994)*	*Year 5 (1995)*
1 Opening balance	8,500	1,900	4,450	815	(798)	(9,707)
2 Cash receipts						
2.1 Operating revenue (gross)	0	10,820	4,327	6,041	3,436	5,368
2.2 Capital receipts	15,400					
2.3 Revenue from ship sale						11,000
3 TOTAL RECEIPTS	15,400	10,820	4,327	6,041	3,436	16,368
4 Cash payments						
4.1 Operating costs		3,650	3,650	3,650	3,650	3,103
4.2 Drydocking					5,000	
4.3 Voyage costs						
4.4 Purchase of ship	22,000					
4.5 Loan repayments		3,080	3,080	3,080	3,080	3,080
4.6 Interest		1,540	1,232	924	616	308
4.7 Tax payments						
5 TOTAL COSTS	22,000	8,270	7,962	7,654	12,346	6,491
6 CASHBOOK BALANCE AT YEAR END	1,900	4,450	815	(798)	(9,707)	171
memo Current account interest	190	445	82	(80)	(971)	17
memo						
Charter rate/day	22,883	31,824	12,727	17,768	10,107	15,789
Days trading	340	340	340	340	340	
Second-hand price of ship	22,000	20,000	9,500	11,000	8,000	11,000
Operating costs $/day	10,000	10,000	10,000	10,000	10,000	8,500
Outstanding loan (year end)	15,400	12,320	9,240	6,160	3,080	0
Asset cover	1.4285	1.6233	1.0281	1.7857	2.5974	

$7.2 million. At the end of that year the last instalment on the loan is paid off, so there will be no more repayments. If he sells the ship he would end the year with a negative balance of $.17 million, and he still has to pay interest on his current account. However he has no debt and the ship has passed its survey. He has survived and by taking a gamble he and his bankers have avoided taking a loss. If all goes well he will soon be a very rich man.

As always in recessions, the crucial issue is survival. By the time the unpaid bills start to pile up in year 4 it is too late to do very much – the right time to raise questions about costs, efficiency and working capital is before the ship is purchased. The example discussed in the preceding paragraphs shows how a realistic annual cashflow analysis can provide the framework for thinking ahead and planning financial strategy in the shipping market. If the shipowner had borrowed less, or borrowed more and provided for emergency working capital at the outset the problem would never have arisen. Or would it? We started this chapter by likening competition in a depressed shipping market to a marathon race with only a few prizes. Someone has to lose. It is through annual cashflow analysis that shipping companies can measure their fitness to finish the race, and identify those actions that can enhance their chances of future survival.

The discounted cashflow (DCF) analysis

So far we have concentrated on cashflow analysis which helps management to think through the implications of certain decisions in terms of the future cashflow of the business. However, business is not just about surviving recessions. Staying in business also depends on making a commercial return on capital and that calls for sound investment decisions. Often the decision facing management is a choice between two different investment projects where the future cashflows are well established, but different. For example, consider a shipowner who purchases a tanker for $45 million and is offered two different deals by oil companies, Big Petroleum and Superoil Transport & Trading:

- *Contract 1*: Big Petroleum offers to charter the ship for $18,000 per day for seven years, trading 355 days a year. At the end of the charter the oil company guarantees to buy the ship for $35 million.
- *Contract 2*: Superoil Transport & Trading's proposal is a little more complex. To fit its trading patterns the company wants the owner to have the cargo tanks epoxy coated. This will cost $3 million, bringing the total price up to $48 million. However, Smartoil is willing to buy the ship at the end of the charter for $45 million. Also, they want to escalate the charter rate by $2,000 per day from $12,000 per day in year 1 to $24,000 per day in year 7.

The owner is particularly impressed by Superoil's contract. The charter revenue over the 7 years of $44.3 million is exactly the same as for the Big Petroleum deal. However the buyback terms are far better. He loses only $3 million on the ship with Superoil, compared with a loss of $10 million in the Big Petroleum deal. It seems he will be $8 million better off with Superoil. Although this seems obvious, Superoil has a reputation for driving a hard bargain and the owner is worried. So he should be. He has ignored the time value of money.

If we take the time value of money into account, we find that there is less difference between the two offers than appears at first sight. The technique we will use is known as discounted cashflow (DCF) analysis. The rationale behind this approach is very simple. Investors can earn a return on their money, so cash promised in the future is worth less than money in the bank today. For example if the interest rate is 10 per cent per annum, $1,000 received today can be invested and in a year's time is worth $1,100. In contrast $1,000 to be paid in a year's time is only worth $1,000. It other words the $1,000 receivable in a year's time is worth $100 less than $1,000 received today, so we say that the 'present value' of $1,100 receivable in a year's time is $1,000. The 'discount rate' is 10 per cent.

Net present value (NPV)

The net present value method of discounting the cashflow uses a discount rate to convert each cash payment receivable in the future into a 'present value', i.e. the amount it is worth today. The method is as follows. The first step is to determine the discount rate which represents the time value of money to the company. There are several ways of determining which discount rate is appropriate. The simplest way, if the company has a cash surplus, is to use the interest rate which the company would receive if it invested the cash in a bank deposit. Or the discount rate might be set at a level which reflects the average return on capital obtained from investments in other parts of the business. Many businesses use 15 per cent per year. Finally, if the company has to borrow to finance the project, the marginal cost of debt might be more appropriate.

Once the discount rate has been agreed it is a simple matter of arithmetic to calculate the discount factor which applies to each year in the calculation. In the examples in Table 5.13 we use 12 per cent as the discount rate, since this is what the owner expects to earn if he invested the money in the US stock market. A 'discount factor' is calculated for each year, as shown in row 4 of the table. Row 5 shows the discounted cashflow, calculated by multiplying the cashflow in each year by the discount factor for that year. The discounted cashflow in row 5 is summed over all years to produce the Net Present Value (NPV) of each project shown in row 6. In effect the NPV shows how much better off the shipowner is in putting his money into this project rather than the US Stock Market.

For Contract 1 the NPV is −$5,000. It seems he would be better off investing in stocks, though not by very much. However the real surprise comes when we look at Contract 2. The $8 million extra return from this project has completely disappeared. The NPV is $58,000, which on a $45 million project is insignificant. The reason this project looked so good is that all the extra revenue was received towards the end of the project and was heavily discounted. In financial terms Superoil's offer is not significantly better than the Big Petroleum deal.

The internal rate of return (IRR)

An alternative approach to calculating the return on investment projects is the internal rate of return. Whereas the net present value method starts from a net cashflow in current terms and calculates the value today, the internal rate of return technique works out the discount rate which gives a net present value of zero. The internal rate of return in the two examples works out at 12 per cent for both projects. This is exactly what we would expect since the NPV is close to zero in both cases using a 12 per cent discount rate.

The calculation of the internal rate of return is an iterative process, and rather more time-consuming than the NPV. Fortunately most computer spreadsheet programs now have IRR functions which provide estimates quickly and easily.

TABLE 5.13 Example of discounted cashflow (DCF) analysis for tanker charter options ($ million)

			Year 0 (*1998*)	*Year 1* (*1999*)	*Year 2* (*2000*)	*Year 3* (*2001*)	*Year 4* (*2002*)	*Year 5* (*2003*)	*Year 6* (*2004*)	*Year 7* (2005)
	Contract 1									
1	Ship purchase/sale		(45,000)							35,000
	Timecharter rate			18,000	18,000	18,000	18,000	18,000	18,000	18,000
2	Timecharter at $27,000 pd	44,730		6,390	6,390	6,390	6,390	6,390	6,390	6,390
3	Cashflow	79,730	(45,000)	6,390	6,390	6,390	6,390	6,390	6,390	41,390
4	Discount rate	12.0%	0.89	0.80	0.71	0.64	0.57	0.51	0.45	0.40
5	Discounted cash flow		(40,179)	5,094	4,548	4,061	3,626	3,237	2,891	16,717
6	Net Present Value (npv)		(5)			Internal Rate of Return (IRR)			12.0%	
	Contract 2									
1	Ship purchase/sale		(48,000)							45,000
	Timecharter rate $000s per day			12,000	14,000	16,000	18,000	20,000	22,000	24,000
2	Timecharter revenue	44,730		4,260	4,970	5,680	6,390	7,100	7,810	8,520
3	Cashflow	89,730	(48,000)	4,260	4,970	5,680	6,390	7,100	7,810	53,520
4	Discount rate	12.0%	0.89	0.80	0.71	0.64	0.57	0.51	0.45	0.40
5	Discounted cash flow	(42,857)		3,396	3,538	3,610	3,626	3,597	3,533	21,616
6	Net Present Value (npv)		58			Internal Rate of Return (IRR)			12.0%	

5.6 Summary

In this chapter we have reviewed the shipowner's financial performance. We started by observing that shipping companies have a great deal of influence on their future cashflow when they frame their strategy. The choice between new ships and old, flexible ships or specialized and debt or equity finance all make a difference. Once these major decisions are made an owner may use his management skills to optimize cashflow on a day-to-day basis through efficient ship management and resourceful chartering, but major cost and revenue items are beyond his control. They have already been determined by the initial investment decision. Once these particular decisions have been made, the owner is very much at the mercy of the market and his bankers.

Cash is the difference between receipts and payments. Costs are subdivided into operating costs (which represent the fixed costs of running a ship), voyage costs (which are variable, depending upon the way in which the ship is employed) and capital costs. Crew costs account for almost half of operating costs and the shipowner can reduce these by purchasing a highly automated ship, which reduces the number of crew required, or operating under a flag that allows the use of a low-cost Third World crew. Voyage costs are dominated by bunker prices which can be controlled or reduced by investing in modern tonnage with the latest fuel-efficient machinery. Both operating and voyage costs are likely to be substantially higher for an old ship than a new ship, while economies of scale lead to lower unit costs for bigger ships.

On the revenue side the owner can play the spot market, in which he accepts full market risk, or time charter which shifts that risk to the charterer. Earnings also depend on the 'productivity' of the ship, i.e. the number of tons of cargo it can carry in a year. Again we find that the initial investment decision has a part to play in determining productivity by investment for rapid cargo handling, greater cargo flexibility to enable the ship to pick up backhauls, and high speed. Drawing these factors together with the influences on cost, we can deduce that in terms of the trading cashflow there are many options. Age, size, technical flexibility and cargo management all play a part in generating more revenue and cutting costs.

When we turn to the capital account, the picture changes substantially. The large modern ship financed by debt carries an annual cashflow for interest and debt repayment in excess of its operating costs, whereas the small old vessel financed on equity would have no cashflow obligations on the capital account. As a result, during a depression the owner of a small, old vessel can afford to withdraw from the market and leave his vessel in layup until conditions improve, whereas the owner of the large, modern, debt-financed vessel faces a fixed capital charge that must be paid even if the ship is laid up. If, however, he is registered under a national flag he has little capital to depreciate against profits, and he will pay high taxes.

All of these problems and opportunities associated with cashflow can be brought into focus by cashflow analysis. Three techniques were discussed, voyage cashflow (VCF) analysis which addresses voyage decisions, annual cashflow (ACF) analysis for longer term planning and discounted cashflow (DCF) analysis for comparing projects when the timing of payments is an issue.

In the last resort it is for the shipowner to use the system that suits him best. The trade-off between cost minimization, revenue maximization and the approach to ship finance gives each shipping venture its own particular characteristics.

Chapter 6

Financing ships and shipping companies

For the ordinary investor, the tramp company remains a form of investment to be avoided. It is a very special business and at its best financed and managed by those who are versed in its difficulties

(A.W. Kirkaldie *British Shipping* 1913)

6.1 Ship finance and shipping economics

Shipping is one of the world's most capital intensive industries. Container ships and tankers can cost up to $125 million each, about the same as a Jumbo Jet. LNG tankers, the most expensive ships, cost $250 million each. The tankers carrying the oil imported by the United States alone have a replacement cost of $150 billion. In the early 1990s the bulk shipping industry invested about $20 billion each year on new and second-hand ships.[1] Capital payments dominate shipping companies' cashflow and decisions about financial strategy are among the most important that their executives have to make. For this reason alone ship finance deserves a special place in the study of shipping economics.

Unfortunately some of the characteristics of the shipping business do not fit easily with the financial community's requirements. Prudent bankers like predictable earnings, clearly defined financial structures, high levels of disclosure and well-defined ownership. Shipping companies do not always satisfy these criteria. Revenues are volatile, the assets are mobile, financial structures often lack transparency and audited financial information is not always available. For many shipowners investment in a ship is more than the acquisition of a transportation vehicle. It is a speculation. Ship values change by up to 60 per cent in a few months. The owner can make, or lose, millions of dollars and so can his bankers if things go badly wrong. The history of volatility described in Chapter 2 is not likely to inspire confidence in potential lenders, while the return on capital can hardly be attractive to investors. Despite recent efforts by shipping companies to adopt more conventional financial structures, shipping remains an idiosyncratic business to finance.

This brings us face to face with one of the paradoxes of the shipping business. Raising finance should be difficult, but historically the shipping industry has often suffered from too much finance. In 1844 George Young complained to a House of Commons Select Committee that during the period 1836–41 mortgages for the purchase of ships had led to an increase in the supply of shipping 'inducing persons without capital or with inadequate capital to press into shipowning, to the injury of shipowners in general'.[2] One hundred and fifty years later the same complaint can still be heard. In the mid-1990s even the bankers were complaining about the intense competition, with more than 150 banks targeting the ship finance market. In the equity markets ship funds, K/S companies and public offerings have appeared and disappeared in succession. There have been times when the industry has indulged in phases of wild speculation, mainly using borrowed money. Whilst it would be wrong to say that ship finance drives the market – that responsibility lies firmly with the shipowners – it has certainly helped to grease the tracks of the shipping roller-coaster.

Our aim in this chapter is to explain the role of ship finance in the shipping market from the shipowner and the shipping companies' point of view. First, we will see how ships have been financed in the past and how ship finance has participated in the successes and problems of the industry. Second, we will explain how ship finance fits into the world financial system alongside other forms of investment. Third, we will examine the different options open to shipping companies wishing to raise finance. Finally we will draw some conclusions about the interplay between the activities of bankers on the four shipping markets discussed in chapter 4 and the way in which bankers should approach this form of lending.

6.2 How ships have been financed in the past

Ship finance in the pre-steam era

Although the history of ship finance can be traced back to the joint stock companies of the sixteenth century, the logical starting point for this discussion is the 1850s when steam ships started to appear in significant numbers. A widely used technique was the 'sixty fourth' company. In the United Kingdom a ship is registered as sixty-four shares, so an investor could buy part of a ship as a stand alone investment. An investor who bought thirty-two sixty-fourths owned half the ship, while to hold sixty-four equal shares was to be a sole owner. Legally shareholders were tenants in common, each having a separate interest which could be sold or mortgaged without reference to other owners of the vessel.[3]

There were three ownership structures. Shares could be held by individuals on their own account, by individuals organized into partnerships, or by investors in a joint stock enterprise. However, most ships were owned by one person. According to records for ships registered in the City of London in 1848, out of 554 vessels, 89 per cent were owned by individuals and 8 per cent by trading partnerships. The remaining 3 per cent were owned by joint stock companies. Only 18 per cent of the vessels were mortgaged, mainly to cover the cost of repairs.[4] Where partnerships were used, they were generally limited to only two or three partners, possibly reflecting the difficulty of managing larger groups.

The evolution of the shipping corporation

As ships grew in size during the second half of the century, the joint stock company rapidly became the preferred financial vehicle for raising the large sums of money required. A major factor in this development was the UK Companies 'Limited Liability' Act 1862 which protected investors from liability claims by company creditors. This opened the way for small investors whose other assets were now protected, though share ownership in such a risky and individualistic business tended to be restricted to family and friends.

A good example is the Tyne Steam Shipping Company which was formed as a joint stock company with limited liability on 1 July 1864. The company was to carry the growing bulk export trade of bulk coal from Newcastle on Tyne. It owned the first bulk carrier the John Bowes (see Chapter 10). The nominal capital was set at £300,000 in 12,000 shares of £25 each. Initially 10,100 shares were issued on which £18 was paid up, raising £181,800. This was used to purchase 10 vessels for £150,000, leaving £30,000 working capital. Approximately one quarter of the shares were taken by previous owners of the new company's steamers and the rest were sold, as far as possible, to the public locally because 'a shareholder at London, Liverpool or Manchester brings little business to the company'.[5] This company is typical of many others in the international shipping industry at this time. Some such as Cunard, P&O, and Hapag–Lloyd are still in operation.

Although these companies were capitalized with equity raised from the public, share ownership was often closely controlled and many companies relied on self-financing or borrowing rather than share capital to finance expansion. For example share ownership in the Charante Shipping Company Ltd which was set up in 1884 with share capital of £512,000, and a fleet of 22 vessels, was 'limited to a small and closely-knit family group'.[6] In each subsequent year, with only two exceptions, the company ordered at least two new ships, and by 1914 the fleet had increased from twenty-two ships to fifty-seven. No further capital was raised and investment was paid for from cashflow. Figure 6.1 compares the cost of the investment programme with the company's charter revenue, showing that adequate investment funds were available, despite the many freight recessions (see chapter 3 which reviews these cycles). Majority ownership remained with three families, the Harrisons, the Hughes and the Williamsons.

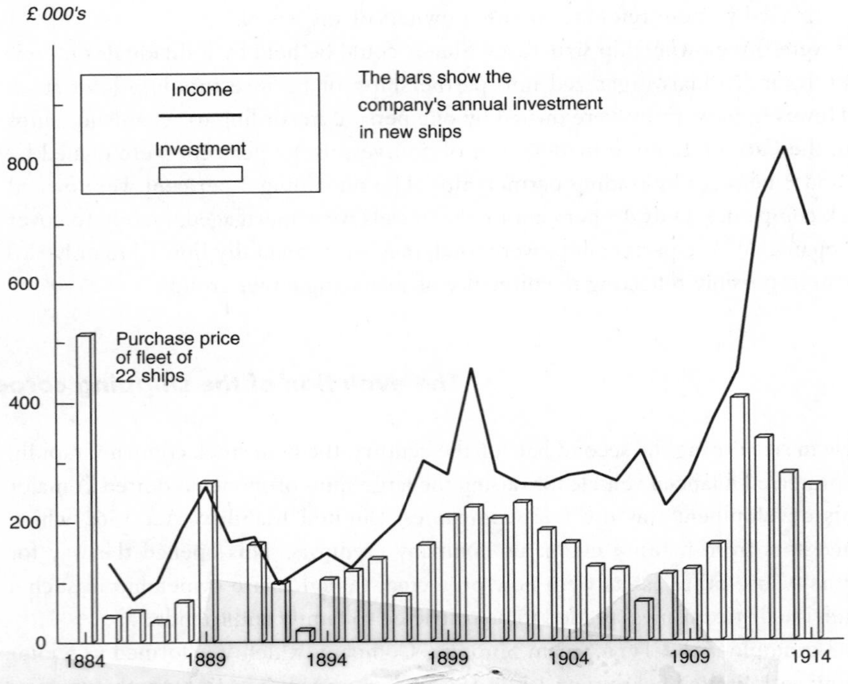

FIGURE 6.1 **Charante Shipping Company: investment and charter income 1885–1914**
Source: Hyde (1967), Appendix 1

Other companies were less conservative. In the nineteenth century borrowing was common. According to Sturmey (1962), during the long recession of 1904–11 many heavily indebted lines failed and 'the financially conservative men who controlled the major shipping lines observed the failure and took the lesson to heart'. For the next 50 years British shipowners stuck firmly to the policy of financing investment from accumulated depreciation reserves. 'Borrowing became anathema'[7] In 1969 the Rochdale Committee on Shipping found that only £160 million out of over £1,000 million capital employed by British owners was represented by loans, a 16 per cent gearing rate.[8] The same financial conservatism was shared by many of the older established Greek names.

Although this policy provided protection against recessions, earnings were never strong enough to fund expansion or attract external equity. Between 1950 and 1970 the return on British shipping shares averaged only 6 per cent per annum compared with 15 per cent per annum for all companies. As a result, although most of the larger shipping companies were publicly listed, no cash was raised by issuing equity capital to the public[9] and the British fleet played little part in the post-war bulk shipping boom.

Charter backed finance in the 1950s and 1960s

In the 1950s the balance of financial conservatism, with its protection from market cycles and high leverage which boosts the return on equity, took a new turn. The rapidly growing industrial economies in Europe and Japan needed cheap raw materials. Industrial shippers, particularly oil companies and steelmakers, started to look abroad for new supply sources. As a result an important new player entered the ship financing game, the industrial shipper. Prior to this development merchant ships were mainly liners or tramps. Shipping was not part of an integrated industrial operation. As more materials were sourced abroad shippers had a vested interest in the shipping operation – if oil companies were to obtain the cheapest possible transport, it was in their interest to encourage economies of scale. This led to the practice of *charter backed finance*. Oil companies and steel mills offered shipowners time charters as an incentive to order large vessels which were too specialized in their trading opportunities to make attractive speculative investments. The owner would then use the time charter as cashflow collateral for a loan to buy the ship.

Charter backed financing seems to have originated in the 1920s when the Norwegians started to build up a tanker fleet, most of which was on charter to major oil companies. In 1927, as part of their fleet replacement programme, Anglo Saxon Petroleum Ltd offered 37 ten-year-old tankers for £60–70,000 each with ten year time charters. The financing terms were 20 per cent cash down and the balance over five years at 5 per cent interest.[10] Twenty-six were bought by Norwegians, mostly newcomers to the business, and they turned out to be very profitable. After the war licences allowing Norwegian owners to order ships abroad were only awarded if the vessel was 100 per cent financed abroad. Soon adept Norwegian brokers perfected borrowing techniques based on pre-construction time charters. This initiated the great expansion of the Norwegian fleet which, during the 1950s, almost trebled in size, drawing heavily on finance raised from American banks.[11] The Greeks were also quick to exploit this opportunity. A high proportion of tanker construction was financed with American loan capital and 'Greek owners appear to have operated largely on the basis of securing a time charter for 7 or even 15 years from an oil company, a 95 per cent mortgage from American financiers on the security of the time charter, then building to fit the charter and finally sitting back to enjoy the profits'.[12] US shipowners were equally active, though the charter back system was refined to its most sophisticated form in the 'Shikumi-Sen' arrangements developed between Japanese charterers and Hong Kong shipping entrepreneurs.

The new form of financing called for a different form of legal and business organization. The result was the 'single ship company'. Using the Flags of Convenience developed for this purpose (see chapter 12), these one-ship companies were built into complex business empires. The individual ships were registered offshore using one-ship companies. Ownership was vested in the group, with management often handled through agencies. For financing purposes the ships could be treated as self-contained units secured by their time charters. Organization structures were loose with few published financial accounts, little regulation and no taxation.

This phase lasted about 20 years, but during the 1970s and 1980s gradually shrank in importance. There seem to have been three reasons. First, the charters had been made available during a period of structural change when it was in the interests of charterers to encourage owners to take the risk of ordering ever larger vessels. By the early 1970s economies of scale had been pushed to their limit and it was no longer necessary for shippers to make this onerous commitment in order to secure the ships they needed. Second, after two decades of headlong growth in the bulk trades, there was a change of trend and the crude oil and iron ore trades stopped growing (see chapter 4). Third, some shipowners who had expected to 'sit back and enjoy the profits' found themselves locked into contracts whose small profit margins were eaten away by inflation. Worse still was the failure of several charterers to honour their commitments, notably Sanko in the mid-1980s.

Asset backed finance in the 1970s

As a result, in the early 1970s, after two decades of highly leveraged charter-backed finance, shipping bankers started to revise their lending policies. Instead of securing the loan against a long-term contract, for a brief, but disastrous spell in the early 1970s the financiers became prepared to rely on the first mortgage on the hull, with little additional security. A prominent banker summarized the reasons for this change as follows. 'A long-term charter-party with no or few escalation clauses built into it can be disastrous to the shipowner . . . Inflation, engine breakdowns and other accidents as well as changes in currencies can very quickly alter or wipe out the best planned cash flows . . . On the other hand, shipowners who run vessels on the spot market have recently been better off . . . Many bankers have objected to a gearing of 1 to 5, or lending of up to 80 per cent of the cost price or market value of the vessel . . . I believe that from a commercial bank's point of view this form of lending has caused no major disasters, and the main reason is perhaps that good, well maintained modern ships have retained their value or even appreciated'.[13] In short, bankers started to see shipping as a form of 'floating real estate'.

This was a very fundamental change of policy because it removed the link between supply and demand. During the period of charter backed finance, newbuilding was restricted by the availability of charters. If the hull was regarded as acceptable collateral, there was no limit to the number of ships which could be ordered from the slimmest equity base. When, in 1973, petrodollars flooded into the world capital markets, shipping seemed an obvious target. The tanker industry was swept away on a tidal wave of credit which allowed 105 million deadweight of tankers, representing 55 per cent of the fleet, to be ordered in a single year. In the stampede for business, financing standards became so casual that loan syndications could be arranged by telephone with little documentation and few questions asked.[14] It took the tanker market 15 years to recover.

Unfortunately that was not the end of the story. In the early 1980s the money markets were again awash with petrodollars, generated by $40 per barrel oil and, to make matters worse, desperate shipbuilders started to use credit as a thinly disguised way of building for stock. Mortgage backed debt underpinned orders for 40 mt deadweight of bulk carriers in 1983/4 when freight rates were at rock bottom. The rationale was counter-cyclical ordering, but the volume of orders was so great that the cycle did not turn. With so many deliveries, the recession dragged on through 1986 and the owners could not service their debt, causing many defaults and reducing second-hand ship prices to distress levels as owners were forced to sell ships to raise cash.

Financing asset play in the 1980s

As the shipping market cycle bottomed out in the mid-1980s, the distress sales created opportunities for 'asset play' (i.e. buying ships cheaply and selling them at higher prices). The problem was that conventional sources of equity and debt had no interest in additional shipping exposure, so new sources of finance were required. One of the first devices to emerge was the self-liquidating ship fund. 'Bulk Transport', the first of these schemes, was set up in February 1984 and proved very successful, with assets appreciating to four times their purchase price during the following 4 years (see page 208). As the success of the early schemes filtered into the market place, imitators appeared, using the same basic structure and offering equity to non-shipping investors. Ironically, as the asset values increased it became progressively easier to place the equity. Eventually, a total of about $5–600 million was raised. Very few investors made a commercial return and some lost their money.

A parallel development was the re-emergence of the Norwegian KS Limited Partnership. Much has been made of the impact of the KS market on second-hand ship prices during the 1980s, and rightly so. KS partnership structures were similar to ship funds, or indeed the trading partnerships of the 1840s, but had the added advantage that profits earned by investors were tax free, provided they were re-invested within a specified period. At a time of very high tax rates in Norway this was very attractive to private investors, many of whom invested in K/S companies set up to buy ships. Perhaps the most significant development was not so much the KS structure, which had been available for many years, but the growth of the Norwegian banks during this period. At the beginning of the 1980s the Norwegian banks carried a shipping portfolio, variously estimated at around $1 billion. During the 1980s it grew to a peak of around $6–7 billion in 1989. The availability of this finance and the willingness of Norwegian banks to make advances to the KS companies, despite their unconventional structure, must surely be one of the key factors in determining the phenomenal success of this market (see page 207 below for more details of the K/S structure).

Shipbuilding credit

A source of ship finance available throughout the period was shipbuilding credit. During each of the recessions reviewed in Chapter 2 shipyards would compete by offering shipowners favourable credit. This practice was already common in the nineteenth century when some UK shipbuilders would, out of their own funds, allow a reliable client 25–30 per cent credit for 3–5 years to tide them over a period of low freight rates. By the early twentieth century governments had decided that shipbuilding was an important strategic industry and became involved in the provision of subsidised credit. In the 1920s the German and French Governments offered favourable credit terms to help their yards win business against the then dominant British shipbuilding industry. During the recession of the 1930s, the Danish, French and German Governments all offered government credit schemes to owners. The practice of subsidizing credit reappeared in the first major post-Second World War recession 1958–63 and was regulated by the OECD understanding on export credit in 1969. The provision of credit is generally co-ordinated by a government controlled credit agency (ECGD in UK, Hermes in Germany, COFACE in France, KEXIM in Korea, Exim Bank in Japan etc). These agencies are responsible for co-ordinating the credit on behalf of the government and providing financial guarantees and interest rate support when appropriate.

6.3. The world financial system and types of finance

Where does the money to finance ships come from?

This brief historical review has touched on many ways of financing shipping, showing how the financial techniques employed have changed from one decade to another. We now turn to a more rigorous discussion of the financial structures currently in use. Raising ship finance is essentially a matter of persuasion, so a good starting point is to return to two basic questions. First, 'where does the money to finance ships come from' and, second, 'what do businessmen have to do to get it?'

To answer these questions we need to look at the world financial system as a whole. The flow chart in Figure 6.2 shows how the different parts of the system fit together. Column 3 on the right shows the *source* investment funds; column 2 shows the markets where these funds are traded, while column 1 shows the '*arrangers*' who act as intermediaries and risk-takers in providing the shipping business with access to the pool of funds in columns 2 and 3.

Investment funds come from savings

First the source: the money comes from corporate or personal 'savings' which need to be invested. Some corporations and individuals handle the investment themselves. For example, an individual might buy a house as an investment and let it out. However this is much less

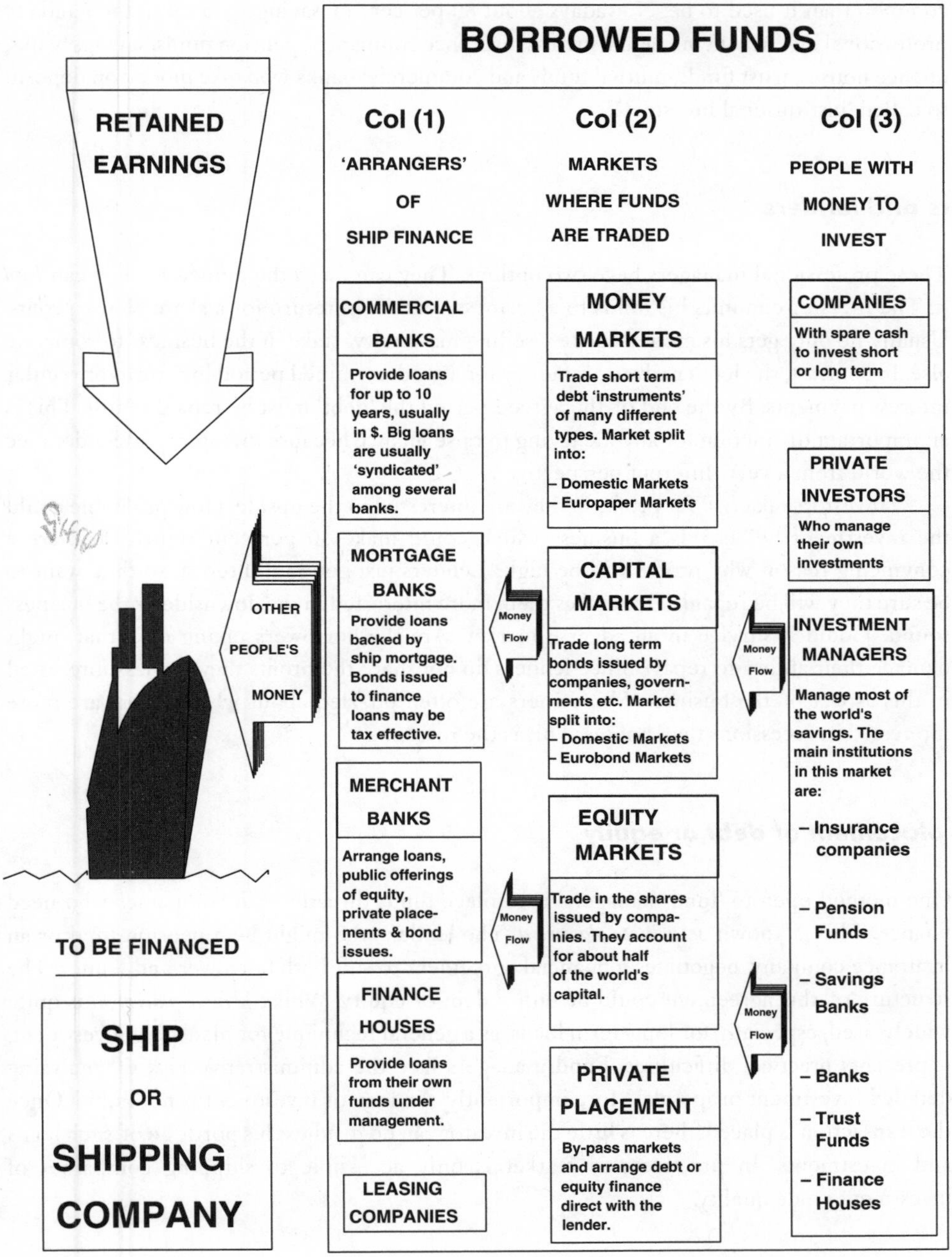

FIGURE 6.2 Where the money comes from to finance ships
Source: Martin Stopford, 1997

common than it used to be. Nowadays about 80 per cent of savings end up in the hands of professional investment managers such as insurance companies, pension funds, savings banks, finance houses, trust funds, mutual funds and commercial banks who take money on deposit, so called 'institutional investors'.[15]

Investors and lenders

These professional managers have two options. They can *invest* the money, or they can *lend* it. The investor commits his funds to a business venture in return for a share of the profits. Usually he only gets his money back by selling his 'equity' stake in the business to someone else. In contrast, the lender advances money for a predetermined period in return for regular interest payments. By the end of the agreed period the 'debt' must be repaid in full. This is an important distinction for anyone trying to raise finance because investors and lenders see the world from a very different perspective.

Investors take risk for profit, so they are interested in the upside. How profitable could the investment be? Is this a business which could make 30 per cent return? Is there a convincing reason why profits will be high? Lenders just get paid interest, so they want to be sure they will be repaid. This makes them more interested in the downside. Is the business sound? Could it survive in an adverse market? Are the borrowers taking risks that might damage their ability to repay? Since lenders do not share the profits they are less interested in this aspect of the business. Shipowners are often puzzled about why bankers are more interested in recessions than booms. This is the reason.

Private placement of debt or equity

One method open to 'fund managers' is to place funds directly with companies who need finance. This is known as *private placement.* The lender, who might be a pension fund or an insurance company, negotiates a financial agreement to suit both borrower and lender. The structure of this agreement could be either debt or equity. Whilst *private placement* is quite widely used, especially for long-term loans, as a general technique for managing investment, it presents practical difficulties. Fund managers face the administrative task of analysing detailed investment proposals. More importantly, the loan or investment is not liquid. Once the transaction is placed, there is little the investor can do to adjust his portfolio of such loans and investments. In practice this market is only accessible to shipping companies of investment grade quality.

The financial markets buy and sell packaged investment funds

An alternative is to use the financial markets. Ingeniously, the world financial system has succeeded in developing markets which trade investments as commodities. In these markets investment 'packages' are bought and sold in a standardized form called 'securities'. Securitizing investment is rather like containerizing cargo. It takes a unique investment packages and processes it into a unit which conforms to rigid standards and is thus easy to buy and sell. Securities markets are strictly regulated to ensure that the rules are followed. There are three different markets trading in different types of security:

1 *Money Markets*: trade in short-term debt (less than a year). The 'market' consists of a loose network of banks and dealers linked by telex, telephones and computers (rather like the voyage charter market) who deal in anything which is sufficiently standardized and credit-worthy to be traded.[16] For example, a shipowner with spare cash who wants to keep his funds liquid can purchase 'commercial' paper which gives him a slightly better return than he would get on deposit. The markets trade funds held in local currency by local investors (the domestic market) and funds held outside the issuing country (the 'eurocurrency' market. These markets have a different interest rates structure,[17] the Eurodollar interest rate being the London Interbank Offer Rate (LIBOR).

2 *Capital Markets*: trade in longer term debt finance instruments known as 'bonds' or 'debentures'. Borrowers issue bonds, via a dealer, which repay the holder a specified sum of money on a prescribed maturity date, e.g. in 10 years. Interest is payable by redeeming coupons attached to the bonds and reflects the credit rating of the issuer (less than BBB are known as 'high yield bonds'). In order to make them readily tradable, publicly issued bonds have to be highly standardized.[18] Dealings in off-shore funds are referred to as the 'Eurobond' market.

3 *Equity Markets*: trade in equity shares (also known as securities or stocks). This allows credit-worthy companies to raise capital by means of a 'public offering' on the stock market. To raise capital in this way a company must follow regulations (for example, laid down by the SEC in the United States) and convince the shareholder that the investment will be a good one.[19] Issues are made through an investment bank and the cost of underwriting, legal and auditing fees is usually about 5 per cent of the sum raised.

Considerable sums of money are traded in the securities markets. In 1996 total world securities market totalled $13.5 trillion, of which transport accounted for 0.18 per cent.[20]

To put the annual borrowing of the shipping industry into context, if the total world capital was US$100, the transport industry, which includes airlines, shipping, ports, etc. would need to raise 18 cents. Obtaining even such a small sum is not easy. The job of the markets is to channel funds to where they can be used most productively. There are many other industries fishing in the same pool so borrowers must offer a competitive rate of return. Nor is raising money just a matter of satisfying investors. The markets are highly regulated. To raise capital a shipping company must achieve recognized standards of 'credit-worthiness'. Companies who wish to borrow money in the Money and Capital markets must first obtain a credit rating. *Credit rating agencies* such as Standard & Poors and Moodys

BOX 6.1 Institutions providing or arranging ship finance

Commercial banks. These are the most important source of debt finance for the bulk shipping industry. Many have dedicated ship finance departments. They offer term loans of 2–10 years which they finance by borrowing from the capital and money markets. The short term funding limits the tenor of loans commercial banks are willing to take on to their balance sheet and most are uncomfortable lending for more than 5/8 years possibly with a 'balloon' (i.e. a proportion of the loan repaid at the end of the term). Borrowers who want 12 years must look elsewhere such as ship mortgage banks or leasing companies.

Loans are generally quoted at a margin over LIBOR. Typical spreads range from 0.5 per cent for an exceptionally strong account to 2 per cent for a more risky transaction. Sums of more than $50 million are generally syndicated between several banks (see para below). In addition to loans, banks now offer many other services, including risk management products, M&A, financial advisory services, etc.

Ship mortgage banks. In some countries credit is provided by specialist ship mortgage banks which either obtain their funds in the market or issue bonds which have tax concessions for local investors (for example, in Germany and Denmark). In Germany loans may not exceed three-fifths of the value of the ship and 12 years in tenor.

Investment and merchant banks. These arrange and underwrite finance but do not generally make loans themselves. They will arrange loan syndications, public offerings of equity, bond issues in the capital market and the private placement of debt or equity with financial institutions or private investors. Because so few shipping companies have the right organizational structure for raising equity and the associated services, merchant banks who specialize in shipping are comparatively rare.

Finance houses and brokers. Some financial institutions like GE Capital, Fidelity Capital etc. which have substantial funds under management have specialist shipping departments which lend direct to the industry. In addition there are a number of organizers and brokers of ship finance who specialize in putting together inventive financing packages.

Leasing companies. These specialize in leasing assets and some will arrange long-term leasing of ships. In addition, in Japan, leasing companies are significant lenders. Since they are subject to different regulations they can offer long-term finance which commercial banks could not take on to their balance sheets.

Shipbuilding credit schemes. Most countries offer shipbuilding credit to domestic and foreign owners. The terms of export credit are agreed under the OECD Understanding on Export Credit and currently are set at 80 per cent advance of 8.5 years at 8 per cent per annum interest. With the exception of South Korea this credit is generally offered in domestic currency. The funds are provided either by a government bank or a commercial bank which receives a government guarantee and a subsidy covering the difference between the pricing of the loan and the rate they borrow at in the local Money Market.

regularly monitor the performance of companies and publish a rating of their credit worthiness. This means that purchasers of bonds and commercial paper have a guide to the company's credit worthiness. They look up the issuing company's credit rating. In short, the markets act as a sophisticated 'risk filter'.

The role of financial institutions

To access these markets to borrow or invest, businesses have to work through intermediaries who provide a range of services (see column 1 of Figure 6.2). The commercial and mortgage banks borrow in the financial markets and lend on to shipowners at a profit ('spread'). In doing this they use their specialist knowledge to identify those shipping investment opportunities which offer an acceptable risk. The Merchant banks (known as Investment Banks in the USA) help companies which have a sufficiently strong credit rating to issue bonds, equity and private placements. There are at least 200 institutions world-wide who have specialist expertise in some aspect of ship finance, usually through shipping departments. A brief description of the main ones and their activities is listed in Box 6.1. In the following paragraphs we will go through the different ways a shipping company can raise finance, following the structure set out in Figure 6.3. We start with equity, then discuss mezzanine finance, senior debt and finally leasing.

6.4 Financing ships with equity

We start with equity. In this case the shipping company is seeking *investors* who will take a stake in the company, sharing the risks and receiving the rewards. Currently there are four main types of financial structure used for raising equity. These are summarized in Figure 6.3 and include owner equity, limited partnerships, ship funds and public offerings.

Owner equity and cashflow finance

The first and most obvious way of financing ships is with equity derived from the owner's private resources, the earnings of other ships he owns, or possibly direct investment by close friends or members of the family. Most shipping companies finance at least part of their activities from internally generated equity, though the proportion varies enormously.

Public offering of equity

Shipping companies can also raise equity by arranging a public offering on one of the stock exchanges around the world. New York, Oslo, Hong Kong, Singapore and Stockholm are all used for public offerings of shipping stock. A prospectus is drawn up offering shares in

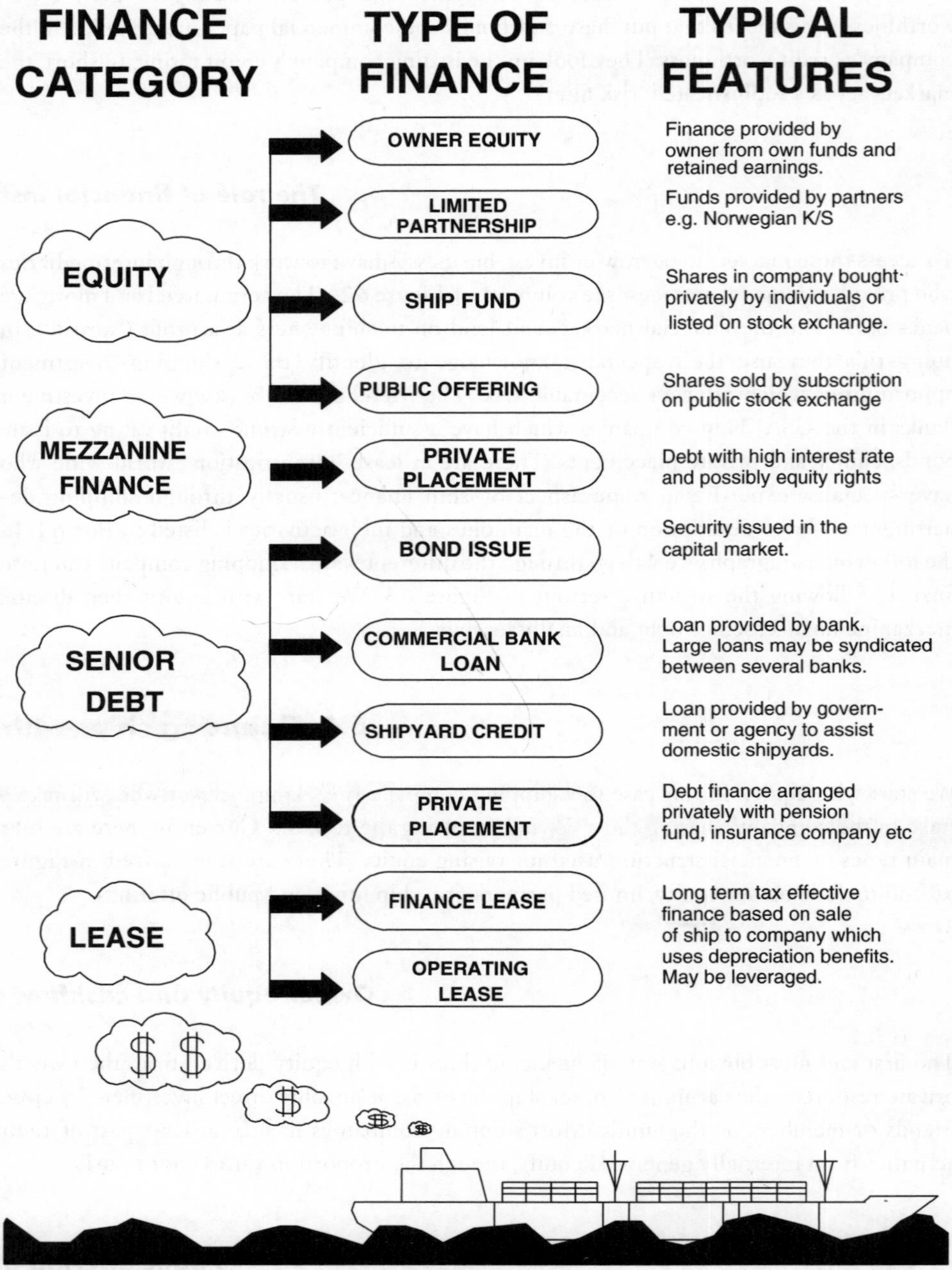
FINANCE CATEGORY
TYPE OF FINANCE
TYPICAL FEATURES
OWNER EQUITY
Finance provided by owner from own funds and retained earnings.
LIMITED PARTNERSHIP
Funds provided by partners e.g. Norwegian K/S
EQUITY
SHIP FUND
Shares in company bought privately by individuals or listed on stock exchange.
PUBLIC OFFERING
Shares sold by subscription on public stock exchange
MEZZANINE FINANCE
PRIVATE PLACEMENT
Debt with high interest rate and possibly equity rights
BOND ISSUE
Security issued in the capital market.
SENIOR DEBT
COMMERCIAL BANK LOAN
Loan provided by bank. Large loans may be syndicated between several banks.
SHIPYARD CREDIT
Loan provided by government or agency to assist domestic shipyards.
PRIVATE PLACEMENT
Debt finance arranged privately with pension fund, insurance company etc
LEASE
FINANCE LEASE
Long term tax effective finance based on sale of ship to company which uses depreciation benefits. May be leveraged.
OPERATING LEASE
$ $
$

FIGURE 6.3 Options for financing merchant ships

Source: Martin Stopford, 1997

the company, to be listed on a specified stock exchange. For example, in 1993 Bona Shipholding Ltd issued a prospectus offering 11 million shares at $9 per share, to be listed on the Oslo Stock Exchange from 17 December 1993. Once the issue is made and trading starts, the price is determined by market supply and demand. By 1996 the Stock in Bona Shipholdings Ltd was trading at $11.79, so investors had made a 'paper' profit of $2.79 per share. The listing of equity is very important because it gives investors liquidity in the sense that they can buy or sell shares at any time. For this to work the offering must be big enough to allow reasonable trading volume.

Public stock issues are handled by investment banks who prepare the prospectus, submit it to the stock exchange authorities, gain approval for the issue and place the shares with investors. The whole process takes about 10–15 weeks and costs about 5 per cent of the funds raised. If enough investors are willing to purchase the stock at the offer price, the offering is a success. If not, it may be withdrawn. Successful listings depend on convincing investors that the company is sound. This in turn depends on their perception of the shipping industry and partly on whether the company looks well managed. A clear corporate structure, a well defined strategy, a credible management track record, and plenty of information are helpful.

Raising equity through the stock markets has a mixed history in shipping and the suitability of this form of finance remains controversial. There are surprisingly few successful public shipping companies outside the liner trades. Stokes (1992) thinks that the volatility of the shipping market is one of the fundamental problems, since 'the essentially opportunistic nature of the tramp shipowning business somehow appears incongruous in the context of the stock market, where highly rated companies are those which are able to achieve consistent profit growth year after year. Even the liner companies, which conform more to the stock market's idea of a reasonably stable investment, have been guilty of sharp swings in profitability'.[21] Possibly the corporate structures expected by the equity markets are less well suited to exploiting the volatile market. Entrepreneurial flare and contrarian decision-making can be difficult in a structured corporate environment where major decisions must wait for a consensus. There are also cultural issues to consider. The fact that throughout this book the terms 'shipowner' and 'shipping company' are used interchangeably says a great deal about the industry's priorities in this context. If a shipowner has the skill to become very wealthy, why should he share his success with equity investors?

Despite these reservations, shipping is a key business in the world economy and financial institutions have a place in their investment portfolios for the equity of well-managed transport companies. From this perspective there is no doubt that the equity markets have a part to play in financing liner, bulk and specialist shipping.

Partnership structures

During the late 1980s substantial amounts of partnership capital were raised through the Norwegian K/S limited partnerships. It is estimated that during this period about half of the Norwegian shipping industry operated through K/S companies and during 1987/9 investors in K/S partnerships committed equity of $3 billion.

The K/S partnership, a standard form of Norwegian company, offered investors tax advantages. The K/S's were usually set up on a one ship basis with management subcontracted. The organizer appointed a 'general partner' and invited equity partners to commit capital.[22] To obtain the tax advantages, under Norwegian law at that time, committed equity capital was required to equal 70 per cent of the cost of the project (i.e. purchase price of the ship plus working capital), of which the general partner provided 10 per cent.[23] At least 20 per cent of the committed capital had to be available in cash at the time of incorporation and another 20 per cent within two years. The remainder was only called if needed.

As a rule 80 per cent of the purchase price was raised as a bank loan and the remainder with cash drawn against the committed equity. For example the purchase of a $10 million ship requiring $.5 million working capital might be financed as follows:

	$ million
Mortgage loan (80 per cent)	8.00
Called equity capital	2.50
Uncalled capital	4.85

For tax purposes the committed capital could be depreciated at an annual rate of 25 per cent on a declining balance basis. In addition provisions could be made for classification costs, though allowable depreciation could not exceed the total capital committed.[24] The K/S shares could be sold and there was a limited market within Norway through brokers or advertisements in Norwegian newspapers.

In the early 1990s these tax benefits were much reduced and the K/Ss, which had obtained a mixed reputation after a series of losses, fell out of favour. They remain a fascinating example of opportunism in ship finance. The speed, flexibility, and relatively low cost of the K/S system were ideally suited to financing asset play during the period of escalating ship values in the late 1980s, allowing many small investors to become involved in shipping. Their weakness, from the investors' point of view, was the lack of the rigorous regulation which plays such an important part in protecting investors in the stock market.

'Ship Funds' and private placement of equity

A third way of raising equity is by setting up a *Ship Fund.* A ship fund is an investment vehicle designed for the specific purpose of allowing equity investors to invest in merchant ships. The first modern shipping fund was Bulk Transport which was set up during the tanker depression in 1984/5 to purchase four ULCCs at prices just above scrap.[25] As an investment it proved extremely successful, with the assets appreciating to five times their purchase cost during the following 4 years. Between 1987 and 1989 a succession of funds were organized by US commercial and investment banks. In most cases the equity raised has been between $30 and $50 million, often topped up with 40–60 per cent debt in order to improve the return to the investor. In total these funds raised about $500 million of equity capital.

The procedure for structuring a ship fund is roughly as follows. A *registered company* is set up in a tax efficient location (e.g. The Bahamas, Cayman Islands, etc.) and a general manager is appointed to handle the buying, selling and operating of the company's ships. For this service he is paid a management fee – for example one fund with four ships paid $100,000 plus 1.25 per cent of revenue earned. Because ship funds are investment vehicles rather than shipping companies, in most cases the shareholders have the option to wind up the company after 5–7 years, thus ensuring liquidity if the shares prove not to be tradable. To improve the return to the equity investor, many funds raised debt finance, ranging from 50–75 per cent of the purchase price of the ships. Obviously, the higher the gearing, the greater the risk/reward ratio for the equity investor.

A *prospectus* is drawn up setting out the terms on which shares are offered for sale. This document may range in size from a few pages of typescript to a large glossy brochure. It sets out the business in which the company is to operate, its strategy, the market prospects, the terms on which shares can be purchased, administrative arrangements, control mechanisms and winding up arrangements. On the basis of this prospectus shares are sold by private placement to wealthy individuals or institutions, or in a few cases by public offering (see section 5.4). Investment institutions have limited funds for high risk ventures of this type, so ship funds depended heavily on wealthy individuals who appreciate a good sales story – in this case the fact that ships were undervalued. When sufficient funds have been raised, management purchases ships and operates the company according to the terms set out in the prospectus.

As a 'pure' investment vehicle ship funds face two problems. First, the equity must be raised before the ships can be purchased, facing the organizers with the difficult task of finding good quality ships at very short notice. Second, their commercial and management structure is ambiguous. They are not shipping companies because they have a limited life, but they are charged with running ships over a fairly long period. Both these problems arise from the perception of ships as commodities. Although ships are traded on the sale and purchase market as commodities, in terms of ongoing management they are complex engineering structures. Efforts to 'package' them as commodities brought a whole range of risks which neither the organizers nor the investors in ship funds had anticipated. Only two or three of the ship funds produced a commercial return for investors.

Mezzanine finance structures

Between debt and equity there is a half-way house which is known as *Mezzanine Finance.* This is a loosely defined term which usually refers to high yielding debt, typically priced at several percentage points above LIBOR, often with some form of equity 'Kicker' attached – for example equity warrants. One such structure involved $40 million of senior debt, topped by $26 million of Mezzanine finance in the form of cumulative participating *preference shares.* These preference shares, redeemable after five years, paid a basic 10 per cent per annum dividend plus an additional 20 per cent of cashflow after interest and principal repayment. They also included detachable 5-year warrants for 25 per cent of the company at original cost. Despite the apparent generosity of this offer it was never placed and the company resorted to more conventional financing. Mezzanine has not been widely used in shipping and is not easy to place.

6.5 Financing ships with debt

Debt has been the favoured way of financing shipping in the last 30 years. It is attractive to borrowers as a flexible way of financing a shipping company, while retaining full ownership of the business. There are four types of debt structure: bonds, commercial bank loans, shipyard credit and private placements.

Bonds and fixed term securities

As already mentioned, borrowers with an acceptable credit rating can raise money by issuing bonds in the capital market. First the company must obtain a credit rating from Moodys or Standard and Poors (see the discussion of capital markets above). The rating awarded determines whether the bonds can be issued at all and the level of interest. Although there are no clear guidelines, the requirement is for a credit rating, a sound management team with a good track record, a clear corporate structure which analysts can understand and a convincing strategy. An investment bank handles the deal, drawing up the offer document and handling the placement. A list of shipping companies which have used this method of raising finance, as shown in Table 6.1. The sums involved were $1–200 million and are all 'high yield' rather than 'investment grade' issues. The procedure is relatively time-consuming, taking several months to develop a prospectus and place the bonds in the market.

TABLE 6.1 Companies raising high yield debt

Company	*Security*	*Amount $ million*	*Coupon*
Eletson Holdings	1st mortgage	140	9.25
Gearbulk Holdings	Senior notes	175	11.25
ISC	Senior notes	100	9.00
OMI Corporation	Senior notes	170	10.25
OSG	Debentures	100	8.75
	Notes	100	8.00
TMM	Notes	200	9.25
	Notes	150	8.50
TeeKay	1st Mortgage	175	9.63

Source: Hayalidis & Cotsoradis (1995) *High Yield Debt as a Source of Capital for Shipping Companies*

Commercial bank loans

By far the most common way of financing ships and shipping companies is the term loan. There are at least twenty major banks who consistently offer ship finance and have dedicated shipping departments, though sometimes the number swells to over a hundred. The procedure for raising a shipping loan is relatively simple. The shipowner or shipping company approaches a shipping bank and explains his requirements. If, after reviewing the case, the bank officer feels that the bank may be interested in making a loan, he draws up a proposal, discusses it with the borrower and negotiates any points which are not acceptable. The five key aspects of a shipping loan are the *tenor* (i.e. the period of the loan, 5 years, 7 years, etc.); *interest rate* (loans are generally made at a fixed spread over the bank's funding cost, e.g. the London Inter Bank Offer Rate, LIBOR); *fees* (the charges for arranging and administering the loan); *collateral* (the assets or funds to which the bank has legal access if the borrower defaults); and the *covenants* (the security conditions imposed by the lender setting out the conditions that the owner must satisfy and the rights of the bank if he defaults). A more detailed definition of some of the terms and concepts discussed in this section is shown in Box 6.2. Negotiating these terms is, of course, the most important part of the lending process.

Before the loan can be made it must be approved by the bank's credit system. For a client well known to the bank, this will only take a few days, but difficult or risky loans obtaining credit approval can be a lengthy process. The job of the credit officers is to judge whether the borrower will be able to service the loan in all foreseeable circumstances and to ensure that sufficient security is available to compensate the bank if he defaults. Cashflow projections will be prepared to allow the credit officers to review debt service. If a time charter is available, this part of the analysis is greatly simplified, provided the bank is convinced that the charterer is sound. A valuation of the ship is obtained to establish its current market value, and the value of other security is reviewed, along with the covenants which ensure that the bank has a degree of legal control if things start to go wrong. Sometimes the bank credit committee will ask for the terms to be revised and this will need to be agreed with the borrower. When approval is obtained a closing is arranged at which the papers are signed and the funds transferred. Repayment then proceeds in accordance with the loan agreement, generally at six-monthly intervals.

When structuring the loan, the usual practice for an owner is to establish a *one ship company* for each vessel financed and assign the first mortgage on the ship to the lender as security.[26] This structure, which has been standard practice over the last 20 or 30 years, lies at the heart of ship finance as a specialist sector of banking. By creating a stand-alone company in an acceptable legal jurisdiction (e.g. Liberia), legal access to the ship's earnings and insurances is assured and the ship becomes immune from arrest for claims against other ships in the borrower's fleet. This is important because shipowners are often secretive and the banker may not feel confident that he can keep track of his business activities. It also means that the bank is lending to a company with no assets other than the ship and its earnings, so security becomes a crucial issue in structuring the loan. First, the banker must decide what proportion of the ship's current market value can safely be advanced. This will depend on

BOX 6.2 Eleven key points in a commercial 'term loan' facility

1 **Tenor**: The length of the loan. The loan may be offered for anything from 3 to 15 years, depending on circumstances.

2 **Gearing**: The ratio of the loan to the asset value (e.g. ship value). Varies from 40–80 per cent depending on the ship type, employment, collateral, age, competition from other banks and general lending policy. Unless exceptionally well secured, loans of more than 50 per cent can be regarded as containing a 'neo-equity' component.

3 **Repayment schedule**: Usually equal instalments over the period of the loan. In the London or Eurodollar market, instalments are usually every six months. If lending policy does not allow a loan over a sufficient period of time necessary for the vessel to repay its debt, a 'balloon' repayment may be used as a way of keeping annual principal repayments to a manageable level. For example, a newbuilding might be paid off over 8 years, but with a 30 per cent 'balloon' payment at the end. This reflects the banker's confidence that the ship will have a significant asset value at the end of its tenor. For older vessels the balloon is often related to the predicted scrap value.

4 **Currency**: Most commercial banks lend in Dollars. However, credit provided by shipyards may be in the domestic currency – for example, Yen, Pounds Sterling, Deutschmarks, etc. This presents the borrower with a major currency risk which must often be hedged against.

5 **Interest rates**: Most financing by commercial banks is done on a floating rate basis. Two exceptions are the ship mortgage banks (primarily German) and government subsidized interest rate schemes. In the former, the banks fund themselves through the issues of ship mortgage bonds, while in the latter, the financing bank is usually paid the difference between the fixed rate to the agencies. Commercial banks generally lend at a spread over the rate at which they borrow, six month LIBOR being the most common. Typical spreads range from 0.5 per cent to 2.0 per cent, according to the standing of the borrower, maturity, etc.

6 **Fees**: Where a standby period or an extensive drawdown period is involved, the bank will customarily charge the borrower a commitment fee of about 0.5 per cent per annum on the unused portion of the commitment. In certain circumstances, a management fee or arrangement fee of up to 1 per cent is charged as a front-end payment, to cover the costs of processing and administering a complex transaction or where syndication is involved.

7 **Syndication of shipping loans**: May be used to spread the risk of a large loan among several participating banks. One bank leads the syndicate and others participate.

8 **Interest rates and currency hedging**: To reduce risk, interest rates can be fixed, capped (i.e. subjected to a ceiling) or even inverted. Currencies can be hedged forward by using swaps, options or even compound options. These techniques enable the borrower to remove much of the risk of currency and interest rate fluctuation from the finance.

9 **Security**: The security sought against the loan may include the following: a first mortgage on the ship financed, mortgages on other ships, assignment of time charter earnings and other assignment of insurances, a corporate guarantee or a personal guarantee of the shipowner.

10 **Covenants**: The documentation of the financial agreement will generally include a range of covenants, some of which may be major issues in the negotiation. These covenants may include the provision of regular financial information, maintenance of working capital and net worth, and a minimum value clause which requires additional collateral to be provided if the value of the asset falls below a certain multiple of the amount owed.

11 **Documentation**: The documentation will be tailored to fit each case, and contains details of the loan interest rate, repayment terms, fees, prepayment conditions. The collateral is described in detail and if charter money is being assigned, the arrangement is spelled out in detail.

the age of the ship and the state of the market. Some bankers consider that the loan should not exceed 50 per cent of the market value of the vessel unless additional security is available. With a time charter, mortgages on other ships, a personal guarantee from the owner, or a history of successful business with the owner, the advance may be increased to 60–80 per cent. In some exceptional circumstances bankers may lend 100 per cent. However there are no firm rules. Banking, like shipping, is a competitive market. If another bank offers 80 per cent against a first mortgage, that is the market rate. A credit judgement must be made on whether the risk is acceptable. It is here that the real skill of ship finance lies.

This credit judgement is also reflected in the interest rate on the loan. *Spreads* (i.e. the margin over the bank's borrowing rate) vary from 0.5 per cent and 2 per cent per annum over LIBOR, depending on the borrower and the banking market. This spread has to cover the bank's overheads, administrative expenses, return on equity and any losses on loans which are not repaid. The covenants will probably include a requirement that the borrower maintains the collateral at a certain ratio to the loan, say 150 per cent (the 'minimum value clause'). If the value of the ship falls below this level the borrower will be expected to provide additional collateral. There will also be covenants assigning insurance to the banker and probably others placing restrictions on the movement of funds and the payment of dividends.

For large shipping companies, borrowing against individual ships is inconvenient because any change in the fleet involves a time-consuming loan transaction. For this reason companies with well defined corporate structures often prefer to borrow as a company, using their corporate balance sheet as collateral. Most liner companies and a few bulk shipping companies are able to access this type of finance. Sealand, APL, Mitsui OSK, OSG, OMI, Bergesen, A.P. Moller, Stolt Neilsen and Argonaut are names that come to mind. For example in 1996 Bergesen AS, a Norwegian company with forty-five tankers, borrowed $500 million over 7 years, at a pricing of twenty basis points in the first 5 years.[27] The loan was secured against the company balance sheet and structured as a *revolving credit*, allowing them to draw on the loan up to the limit as required by the business. Large loans are almost always syndicated among several banks and usually incorporate covenants to ensure that the company maintains a strong balance sheet. Typically these covenants cover the leverage rate, the earnings to interest ratio and the asset cover.

Loan syndications and asset sales

Lenders like to diversify their risk and are generally unwilling to keep more than, say, $25–50 million of a particular transaction on their books. For larger loans the usual practice is to spread the risk by sharing the loan among a syndication of several banks . Asset 'distribution', as this is known, is thus used to split large loans into small packages which can be distributed around many banks. In addition to spreading the risk, it allows banks without the expertise to appraise shipping loans to participate in the business under the guidance of a lead bank who does.

Setting up a syndication for a large shipping loan of, say, $200 million is a complex task. In addition to the normal credit appraisal process, the lead bank must manage the relationship with the borrower, whilst organizing a syndicate of banks to provide the loan. The simplest way to explain the process is to work through an example of a typical syndication timetable, focusing on the key areas. The main items are as follows:

1 *Getting a mandate.* First the lead bank meets the client to discuss his financing needs. For example a loan of $500 million might be required to finance a newbuilding programme. The bank's syndication department will be consulted about the terms on which the loan could be syndicated to other banks and unofficial enquiries will be made to discover how difficult the loan will be to place and what particular features in terms of pricing, etc. will be necessary. If the bankers are sure the loan can be placed they will offer to underwrite it. Otherwise the offer will be on a 'best efforts' basis. When the client is satisfied with the terms and conditions, he will issue a mandate letter.

2 *Preparation for syndication.* Next, documentation is prepared and the whole package is agreed with the client. Again this is a complex exercise involving the Syndications Department, the Shipping Department and the bank's Credit Control officers. It also requires skills in drafting documentation and preparing an Information Memorandum designed to answer the questions likely to be raised by participating banks.

3 *Syndicating the loan.* When the preparations are complete the terms will be circulated to those banks which the Syndication Department believes may be interested in participating. For a specialized business like shipping the list may extend to 20 or 30 banks who will be asked to respond by a given date, indicating their interest. In the meantime the lead bank will visit interested banks to discuss the proposal and the participating banks carry out their own enquiries, since they will have to process the loan through their own credit control system. Those banks who are prepared to participate will indicate the sum they are willing to take and when sufficient commitments have been obtained a closing is arranged at which all banks and the owner sign the necessary documents.

4 *Administration, fees, etc.* The loan documentation sets out the procedures for administering the loan. As a rule the lead bank acts as agent and charges a fee for doing so. For large syndications a management group may be set up. Their task is to handle ongoing problems without the necessity for approaching every participant. The pricing of the loan and the split of fees, etc. between the lead bank and participants will form a key part of the offer documentation.

The time taken to arrange a syndication depends on its complexity. Some loans can be placed very quickly because they are readily acceptable in the market. Others may require many months to line up the full subscription. Obviously one problem to be faced is that the shipowner may not be in a position to wait many months.

Widely syndicated shipping loans can sometimes be difficult to manage. If the borrower runs into difficulties, the lead bank and management group may find it difficult to control a diverse group of participating banks, some of whom know nothing about the shipping market and its cycles. This makes borrowers uncomfortable and it is often argued that it is better if syndication is restricted to *club* deals between banks who combine to offer joint financing. For example five banks may join to finance a $150 million newbuilding programme, each taking $30 million.

Asset sales (Participation Agreement)

A third form of 'distribution' commonly used by banks is asset sales. The bank goes ahead and books the loan in the normal way, placing it on its balance sheet. For example, it may lend $50 million to a shipowner to purchase an $80 million tanker. If at some later date the bank decides to reduce its exposure to shipping risk, it may sell the loan to another bank which has room on its balance sheet for shipping risk. Large banks have an Asset Sales Department which arranges the sale of loans. The bank officer in the Asset Sales Department approaches banks that he knows are interested in taking shipping loans. When a buyer has been found the two banks sign a joint participation agreement, transferring a specified proportion of the loan, say $5 million to the buyer, on agreed terms of interest and capital repayment. Naturally the bank which booked the loan will aim to sell it on favourable terms, retaining a margin for itself. The originating bank will continue to manage the loan in the normal way. In some cases the shipowner may not even be aware that his loan is now held by another bank.

Private placement of debt

Instead of borrowing from a bank it may be possible to arrange a private placement of debt with a pension fund, insurance company or leasing company. Since this involves a one-off deal it can be expensive, but well structured and credit-worthy companies with a good story to tell can achieve good results. Stolt Neilsen placed $100 million debt by this method in the US in 1989. The placement was arranged by Furman Selz and involved fixed interest notes. In April, 1991 a second placement was made of $175 million unsecured *fixed interest* notes.[28] The advantages of this form of finance are the fixed interest rate, long tenor and the *corporate* obligation which leaves individual assets unencumbered.

6.6 Finance for newbuildings

Now we come to debt finance for newbuildings. Although the principles of financing a new ship are generally the same as for second-hand ships, there are two additional problems to overcome. First, the capital cost of a new ship is generally too high relative to its likely spot market earnings to be financed from cashflow, especially if the loan is amortized over the short periods of 5–8 years favoured by commercial banks. Unless a time charter is available, arranging security can be difficult, especially if a one-ship company structure is used. Second, the finance is needed before the ship is built, so there is a period before delivery when part of the loan is drawn but the hull is not available as collateral.

Because these problems make it difficult to raise newbuilding finance from commercial banks, especially during recessions when shipyards are keen to win orders, there is a long tradition of shipbuilders offering finance to their customers, often with the support of their governments. This practice stretches back to the 1930s, but the modern shipbuilding credit regime developed in the 1960s. In 1962 the Japanese shipyards took the first step by launching an export credit scheme offering customers 80 per cent over 8 years at 5½ per cent interest. This started a period of fierce credit competition between Japanese and European shipyards, leading eventually to the OECD Understanding on Export Credit for Ships in 1969 (see chapter 13) in an effort to regulate intercountry competition shipbuilding credit terms.

The OECD Understanding is a 'gentleman's agreement' which sets out the most favourable terms a signatory government is entitled to offer on a shipbuilding credit. It defines a 'ship' as any seagoing vessel of 100 grt and above used for the transportation of goods or persons, or for the performance of a specialized service (for example fishing, ice-breakers, dredgers, etc.). In 1995 the terms were 80 per cent loan over 8 years at 8.5 per cent interest. However the terms vary. Japan offers export finance in Yen through the EXIM bank on OECD terms. South Korea provides through the KO-EXIM bank. Terms on offer are up to 68 per cent of the purchase price at 8 per cent per annum interest amortized over 8.5 years after a two-year holiday. Loans are generally in dollars and a first class bank guarantee is required. Most European shipyards offer OECD terms, though with some local variations for domestic customers.

In the 1990s this long established practice is under pressure along with other shipyard subsidies. At the same time commercial bankers have become much more sophisticated in structuring shipyard finance. A shipowner may accept the shipbuilding credit, but ask a commercial bank to enhance it by extending the repayment period, capitalizing the interest rate subsidy through a SWAP, converting the fixed rate interest to floating rate or converting the whole loan into Dollars rather than the domestic shipbuilding currency. Any of these transformations are easily achievable by a sophisticated shipping bank.

Pre-delivery finance can sometimes be a problem. Shipyards generally require their customers to make 'stage payments' to the shipyard on a sufficient scale to pay for the material and labour required to build the ship. This generally involves a down payment to the builder for the purchase of materials on signing the contract, with the balance being paid in roughly equal instalments on keel laying, engine delivery, launching and delivery (see Chapter 3, section 3.5 for a discussion of this practice).

The pattern of stage payments is negotiable. If pre-delivery credit has been arranged, the purchaser meets the first payment from his own equity and the bank pays the remaining stage payments. The risk for the lender is that stage payments are made, but the ship is not completed, either because the shipyard goes bankrupt with a partly finished ship in the yard, or there is some form of civil or political disturbance which prevents completion or delivery. With no ship to act as collateral, some other form of security has to be found. In most cases stage payments are covered by a 'refund guarantee' issued by the shipyard's bank. However, problems may arise when dealing with shipyards where bankruptcy is a risk, or are located in politically unstable areas. This is where a government guarantee is particularly valuable, or possibly the purchaser can arrange political risk insurance.

Post-delivery finance is generally drawn on delivery of the vessel. It may be obtained from three sources, a Shipyard Credit Scheme, Commercial Bank Credit or leasing. Bank credit and leasing are discussed elsewhere, so here we will focus on the shipbuilding credit schemes. There are three ways in which governments may intervene to make shipbuilding credit more attractive to the shipowner than commercial bank credit, they are:

1 *Government guarantee.* By obtaining a Government guarantee of the loan the shipowner may be able to raise credit with a commercial bank. The value of this guarantee to the borrower depends on the credit standards which the government agency applies in issuing the guarantee. Sometimes the standards are the same as those applied by commercial banks, so the guarantee has little value. If, however, the government is keen to help the shipyard win the order, it may be prepared to guarantee credit terms which the owner would otherwise have no hope of obtaining from a commercial bank. In doing this the government takes a credit risk, which is in effect a subsidy.

2 *Interest rates subsidy.* Some government agencies offer subsidized interest. For example, in the UK a loan is raised from a UK commercial bank, which receives an interest rate make-up from the Government to cover the difference between the agreed rate on the loan (i.e. 8 per cent) and the current market rate.

3 *Moratorium.* In difficult circumstances the Government may agree to a one or two year moratorium on interest or principal repayments.

Governments have different ways of handling shipyard credit. In some cases there is a government bank which carries out credit analysis and makes the loan. For example, the Export Credit Bank of Japan carries out this function. Other governments have an agency which performs the credit analysis, but the loan is provided by local commercial banks. For example, the Export Credit Guarantee department in the UK performs in this way.

6.7 Leasing ships

Finally we come to leasing ships. This is a device originally developed in the property business where land and buildings are very commonly leased. Essentially the owner of the property (the lessor) hands it over to the lessee who, in return for a rental stream, is free to use it as though it were his own. At the end of the lease the property reverts to the lessor. This technique is widely used for leasing mechanical equipment with a long working life, including ships. In transactions of this sort there are three main risks to consider, the revenue risk (will the lessor be paid in full for the asset he has purchased), the operating risk (who will pay if it breaks down?) and the residual value risk (who gets the benefit if it goes up in value?).

The two common types of leasing structures, the *operating lease* and the *finance lease*, deal with these risks in different ways. The operating lease, which is widely used for hiring equipment and consumer durables, is generally a rather short-term arrangement which leaves most of the risk to the lessor. The lease can usually be terminated at the lessee's discretion, maintenance is carried out by the lessor and at the end of the lease the equipment reverts to the lessor. Finance leases are generally longer, covering a substantial part of the assets's life. The lessor, whose main role is as financier, has little involvement with the asset beyond ownership. All operating responsibilities fall on the lessee who, in the event of early termination, must fully compensate the lessor.

Shipping leases usually fall into the second category because finance leases often bring a tax benefit. Governments in some countries encourage investment by providing tax incentives such as accelerated depreciation. Companies with high profits but no suitable investment of their own can obtain tax relief by purchasing a ship which they lease to a shipowner who operates the ship as his own until the end of the lease. The lessor does not have to get his hands dirty, but, hopefully, he collects a tax benefit some of which is passed on to the lessee. Obviously this depends on the good will of the tax authorities.

A simple lease structure is shown in Figure 6.4. The ship, built to the lessee's specification, is purchased by the company providing the finance (the lessor) – a bank, large corporation or insurance company – and leased under a long-term agreement (e.g. a bare boat charter) to the shipping company (lessee). The lease gives the shipping company (the lessee) complete control to operate the asset but leaves the ownership vested in the finance company who can obtain tax benefits by depreciating the ship against profits. Some of this benefit is passed on to the operator in lower rent (charter) payments. A variant is the leverage lease which raises most of the cost of the ship in bank debt (e.g. 90 per cent) and the lessor buys the equity at a price which reflects the tax benefits he gets from depreciating the whole ship.

This type of finance has several advantages. It provides funding for longer periods than is available from commercial banks, possibly as much as 15 years or even 25 years. Capital costs are reduced to the extent that any tax benefits are reflected in the charter back arrangement and since the company does not actually purchase the ship, the liability does not appear on the balance sheet, though nowadays there is generally a requirement for published accounts to reveal such liabilities.

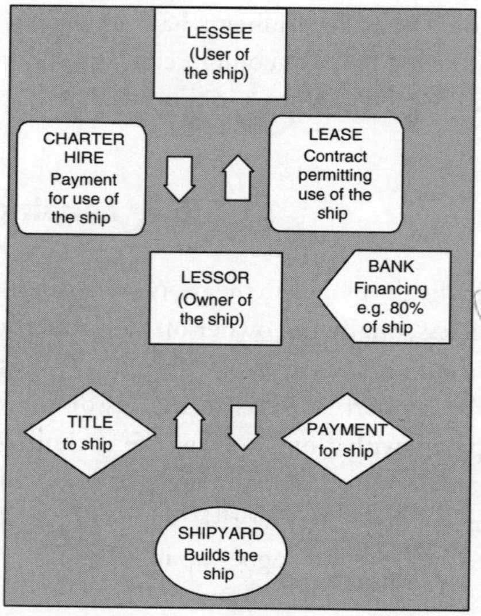

FIGURE 6.4 Leasing structure
Source: Martin Stopford, 1997

There are several drawbacks. The lessor, who usually has no interest in the ship, must be satisfied that the lessee will meet its obligations under the lease. Only financially sound shipping companies are likely to qualify. The lessee is tied into a long-term transaction. If he decides to sell the ship he must go through the complex business of unwinding the lease. Another problem is that, since tax laws may change, the tax benefit is never quite certain and this must be covered in the documentation. With so many eventualities to cover, the paperwork on leasing transactions can be prodigious. For this reason leasing works best where there is a well defined long-term requirement for the ship and a well established shipping corporate.

6.8 Appraising risk on shipping investment

Throughout this chapter we have repeatedly referred to the evaluation of credit risk in the shipping market. In chapter 2 we discussed shipping risk in terms of the shipping cycle and drew attention to the history of generally low returns compared with other forms of investment. Now it is appropriate to say something more about the risks involved. The risk of an investment is usually measured by the standard deviation of the year-on-year return, since this gives an indication of the variability of the return.[29] In these terms shipping is a high risk industry with a standard deviation of bulk shipping revenues roughly twice as high as the US stock market (see Table 2.5).

A good starting point is to divide the risk faced by a shipping company and its bankers into three parts. *Economic risk* occurs because shipping companies are exposed to a world economy which is itself extremely volatile and risky. All industries face this risk to some extent, but we saw in our discussion of the shipping market model in chapter 4 that ship demand is particularly closely linked to the world industrial economy. The two deep recessions which hit the shipping market in the 1970s and 1980s were partly caused by recession in the world economy. Other capital goods industries encountered much the same problems. *Operating risk* arises from the performance of the ship and the shipping company which manages it. The most common problem here is that the ship or fleet are in poor condition and break down frequently or need large amounts of unplanned maintenance. Finally there is *shipping market risk*, the risk specific to the shipping industry itself, particularly the market cycle. As we have seen, the shape of each cycle is uniquely moulded by supply side factors. Over-ordering of ships by shipowners; over capacity in shipbuilding or any of the other factors which uniquely affect the shipping industry, are risks which must be taken into account in the credit appraisal.

It is with the shipping risk that we are particularly concerned in this book. This risk, which often seems to arise from the lack of foresight and market discipline by shipowners, lies at the heart of the shipping business. It poses a particular problem because any view of the future depends on the expectation of whether past mistakes will be repeated. If shipowners become wiser and better informed, it is a small step to the expectation that past mistakes will not be repeated in future, making shipping less cyclical. Readers of previous chapters in this book know that this view misses the point of shipping cycles. Shipping cycles have a purpose. The shipping market uses them to control supply and demand in an unpredictable world. From this perspective the guiding light for financiers is 'know the enemy'. Each shipping cycle, like each shipowner client, has its own character. Shipping banks place great value on 'name lending', in which they get to know and trust the clients they lend to. It is a logical step to apply the same principle to shipping cycles. Just as familiarity with the client reduces risk, so does familiarity with shipping cycles. As they progress through each cycle, lenders (and investors) must ask 'what is its character?' 'Is it trustworthy?' This approach leads to an understanding of the unique character of each cycle as it unfolds, and an opinion on how risky that particular cycle really is. Sometimes the opinion will be wrong – it happens with people as well.

Implications of volatility for portfolio management

The implication of the shipping volatility for bankers is rather substantial. It has been the tradition in recent years for large banks to set up shipping departments which operate large portfolios of shipping assets – $3–5 billion was by no means exceptional in the 1980s. Whilst this is an understandable response to an industry which clearly requires specialist skills, it is precisely the opposite of the strategy adopted by investment managers in handling high volatility shares. The accepted practice is to use a well-diversified portfolio of high risk shares to remove the 'unique risk' attached to individual shares.

The strategy of consolidating shipping assets in a single portfolio leaves the management of the 'shipping division' with the problem of managing a portfolio whose main source of security, the ship itself, is both volatile and highly correlated. If we accept the close correlation between the prices of different types of ships discussed in chapter 3, then the management of the portfolio will sometimes be extremely difficult. The ship banking executive with a large portfolio of assets whose collateral sudden halves in value is immediately at a disadvantage within the bank, unless the corporate policy has been set up in advance to accommodate often large and often prolonged fluctuations in the return on investments.

One solution is the wider distribution of shipping assets discussed in section 6.5. Asset distribution has the advantage that the concentration of shipping assets in the bank's balance sheet is greatly diluted, removing them from the focus of corporate attention. Portfolio theory is the way that the equity market deals with high risk stocks, and exactly the same principals apply in shipping.

6.9 Ship finance and shipping market dynamics

Finally we should say something about the way the activities of bankers feeds back into the shipping market. In Chapter 4 we likened the mechanism which drives investment in the shipping market to a switchbox directing cash between the four shipping markets. During cyclical upswings cash is sucked into the market and increasing liquidity encourages shipowners to order new ships. As these vessels are delivered supply overtakes demand, freight rates fall and cash is pumped out of the market, forcing owners to sell ships for scrap in order to raise funds.

Banks play an important part in the 'pumping' process. Figure 6.5 which is a development of Figure 3.1, shows the cash flows which underlie this market mechanism. The focus of the diagram is the circle showing the shipping cash flow, with net payments into the shipping industry's bank account shown by the square-hatched bars and payments out by the black bars. As before there are four markets involved, each of which plays an important part in the 'financial pumping' mechanism. However we have now introduced shipping banks who are prepared to lend on new and second-hand transactions. They are shown in the centre of the diagram. Their loans to second-hand buyers are shown as a square-hatched bar because the cash they advance is paid to a shipowner. However loans on newbuildings are

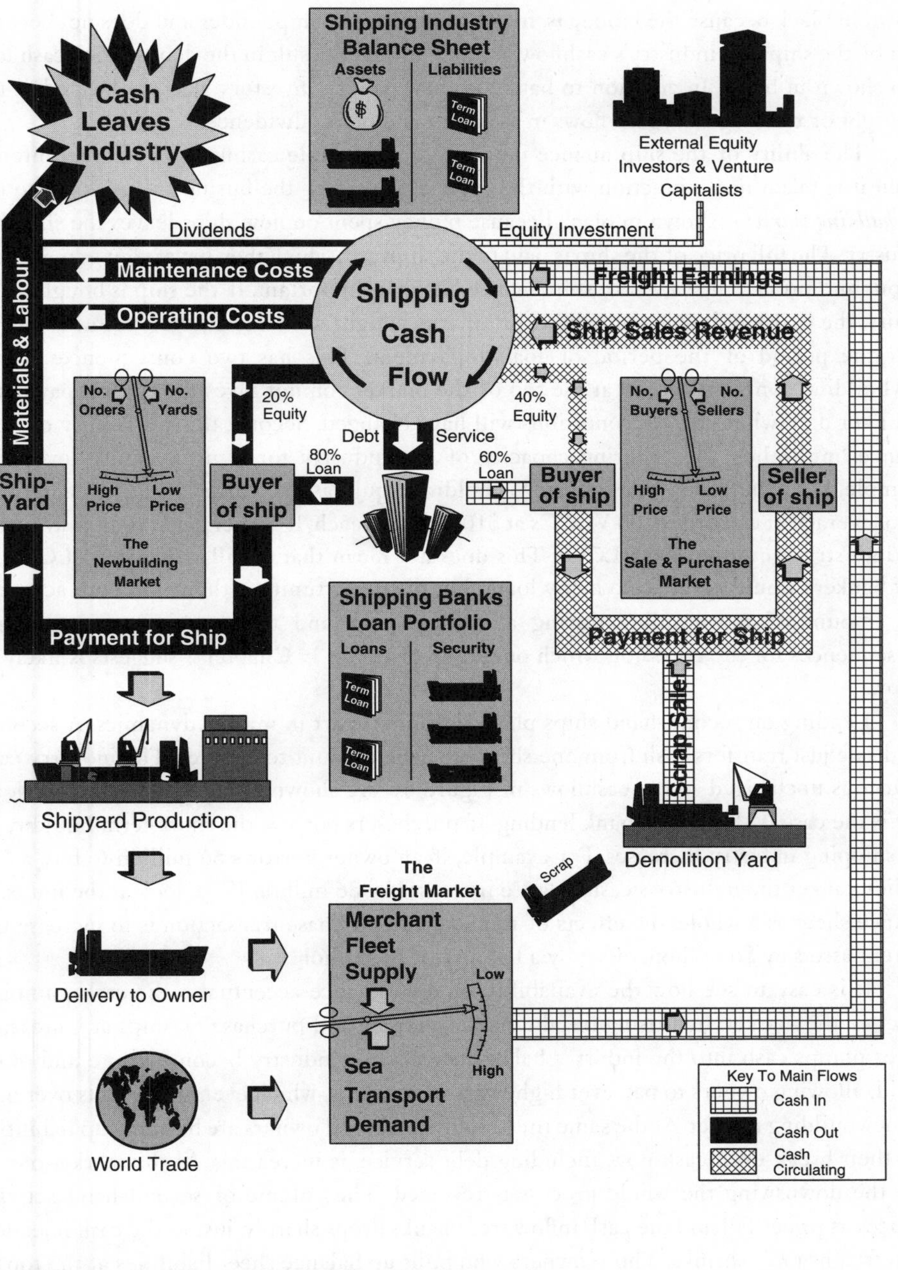

FIGURE 6.5 Cashflow model of the shipping market

Source: Martin Stopford, 1997

Note: This diagram shows the cashflow in the shipping market. It involves three markets, the freight market, the sales and purchase market and the newbuilding market. Note that cash invested in newbuildings flows *out* of the industry, while the main inflows come from freight earnings, bank loans and scrap

shown in black because the money is, in effect, paid to the shipbuilder and does not become part of the shipping industry's cashflow. It does, however, result in the debt service cashflow, also shown in black. In addition to banks we have equity investors who are located at the top right of the diagram. Cash flows in as equity and out as dividends.

The ability of the ship finance industry to reschedule cashflows is of great interest when it is taken in conjunction with the cyclical nature of the business. Cash paid to the *newbuilding market* is shown in black because money spent on new ships leaves the shipping industry. The full price of the ship is paid to the shipyard, which then pays it out as materials, labour and profit. This is where ship finance becomes important. If the ship is bought from equity, the cash outflow is immediate, but if it is bought with a loan, the outflow is spread over the period of the period of loan repayment. This has two consequences. First, newbuilding contracts placed at the top of the market commit investors to cash payments at a later date when market conditions will have changed. Second, the availability of debt finance 'multiplies' the ordering capacity of the industry for a given equity level. For example, if the bulk shipping industry is holding liquid assets worth $10 billion and there is no leverage, it can order 100 VLCCs at $100 million each. If 80 per cent credit is available the industry can order 500 VLCCs. This does not mean that it will order 500 VLCCs, or that bankers would agree to so many loans, but the opportunity is there. On both accounts the amount of newbuilding during a cyclical peak and the way it is financed has consequences for the recession which our study of cycles in Chapter 2 suggests is likely to follow.

Lending on second-hand ships plays a different part in market dynamics. A second-hand sale just transfers cash from one shipping bank account to another. The industry cash balance is unchanged so the cashflows in Figure 6.5 are shown as hatched bars. Or at least that is the case if there is no bank lending. If purchasers borrow, the short-term liquidity of the shipping industry increases. For example, if an owner borrows $6 million to buy a $10 million tanker the industry's cash balance increases by $6 million If we look at the industry balance sheet as a whole, the effects of this sale and purchase transaction is to increase the current assets by $6 million, offset by a liability of $6 million.

It is easy to see how the availability of debt finance accentuates the cash pumping effect of the market. In a rising freight market the sale and purchase of ships at increasing prices pumps cash into the industry balance sheet. The industry becomes more and more liquid, allowing owners to pay ever higher prices for ships, which eventually spills over into the newbuilding market. At the same time highly leveraged owners are building up liabilities and their break-even cash flow, including debt service, is increasing. As the market moves into the downswing the whole process is reversed. The volume of second-hand activity reduces as prices fall and the cash inflow from banks drops sharply, just as the cash injection from freight rates shrinks. Those owners who built up balance sheet liabilities at the top of the cycle now find that the incoming cash flow is inadequate to meet their day-to-day obligations. They are forced to sell ships on the second-hand market. This is the point at which the asset play market starts for those shipowners with strong balance sheets, or external investors. Buying ships cheap in recessions is one of the ways that shipowners top up the poor returns from carrying cargo. Some of the best bargains are to be had when bankers foreclose and force distress sales. In the right hands ship finance is a valuable service which spreads the substantial cash cost of investment in ships over a period of time. For bankers, the trick is to back the winners.

6.10 Summary

In this chapter we have discussed how the shipping industry finances its massive requirement for capital in a business which is volatile and historically has offered low returns. We started by reviewing the history of ship finance. This revealed that the type of finance available to the shipping industry has gone through distinct phases. As the world economy grew in the 1950s and 1960s there was a long phase of charter-backed investment, mainly initiated by the shippers. This was followed by new forms of asset-backed finance during the very volatile markets of the 1980s, notably ship funds and K/S companies. Finally, in the 1990s, shipping companies have shown more interest in corporate structures, with public offerings and corporate lending.

The money to finance ships comes from the pool of savings which are mainly held in three markets, the money markets (short term debt), the capital markets (long-term debt) and the stock market (equity). Nowadays most of the investment is carried out by institutions such as pension funds and insurance companies, though there are a few private investors. Accessing these financial markets can be done directly by the shipping company, or indirectly through an intermediary such as a commercial bank. Direct access requires well defined corporate structures which are less widely used in shipping than elsewhere. Shipping has traditionally relied heavily on bank debt, particularly bulk shipping.

There are four different financial structures which can be adopted for raising ship finance, equity, mezzanine finance, debt and leasing. In recent years the shipping industry has experimented with raising equity through ship funds, K/S partnerships and public offerings. The sums of money raised are small relative to the industry's total requirements. Mezzanine finance, a half way house between debt and equity, is even more rare. Debt, the most widely used form of ship finance, is available in several forms. Bonds have attractions, but are restricted to shipping companies able to obtain a credit rating to issue them. Commercial bank loans are by far the most popular form of finance. There are more than 100 banks offering loans for ship purchase. For large loans a syndication will be arranged. Shipyard finance is a widely used way of financing new ships, since it addresses the difficult question of the pre-delivery guarantee, and credit terms are often subsidized. Finally, leasing offers the opportunity to reduce finance costs by transferring ownership of the vessel to a company which can use its depreciation to obtain a tax break.

The conclusion must be that ship finance, like everything else in shipping, moves with the times. Each phase in the industry's history has its own character. The common theme which runs through each period is the shipping cycle.

Chapter 7

The economic principles of maritime trade

A kingdom, that has a large import and export, must abound more with industry, and that employed upon delicacies and luxuries, than a kingdom that rests contented with its native commodities. It is, therefore, more powerful as well as richer and happier

(David Hume, *Essay of Commerce*, 1752)

7.1 Why study seaborne trade?

Sea trade is one of the great economic success stories of the last 50 years. Between 1950 to 1995 it grew from 0.55 bt to 4.3 bt, making shipping one of the fastest growing sectors of the post-war economy. Although this trend looks simple, it conceals a trading world seething with change. The growth path was irregular. Trade grew rapidly in the 1950s and 1960s, but there were two deep recessions in the 1970s and 1980s. Regional trade was constantly on the move. Two of the biggest trading regions, Western Europe and Japan, went through a cycle of growth until the early 1970s and stagnation for the next two decades. New high growth economies emerged in other areas, notably Asia and North America. The commodities trade changed. Some trades grew rapidly, many stagnated and some declined. A few new trades such as steam coal appeared and others like asbestos disappeared.

Businesses with a long-term commitment to sea transport need to understanding these changes. Liner companies planning new services, shipowners specializing in industrial shipping, shipbuilders planning capacity, and bankers financing fleet expansion all have an interest in understanding why trade changes. Shipping is derived demand, so we must delve into the world economy for the explanation.

There are several different ways in which we can analyse trade. First there is trade by country. We can study why countries trade and how their trade fits in with the growth of their economies. Second, we can look at trade from a geographical viewpoint and study the regional distribution of maritime trade and the trade flows between the trading regions of the world. Third, we can view trade as a collection of commodities such as iron ore, coal, oil, etc. and study the economic characteristics of each commodity. In this chapter we are mainly concerned with the country structure of trade. In chapter 8 we look at regional trade and in chapter 9 we study commodity trade economics as part of our analysis of bulk shipping.

7.2 The countries that trade by sea

Although countries are very diverse there are compelling reasons for selecting the nation state as the basic unit for analysing sea trade. It is the obvious economic and political unit with common policies, separated from other countries by their currency. Government policy affects free trade, tariffs and even the participation in trade. These policies can be very important. Many countries have restrictive trade policies such as tariffs. In the fifteenth century the Chinese introduced laws prohibiting sea trade. More recently the policies of the European Union (EU) have had a significant impact on the size and direction of trade. There are many other examples. Even if these reasons are not persuasive, the fact that most trade statistics are collected by governments on a national basis is a practical reason why we should analyse trade in this way.

There are currently about 100 countries which trade by sea. If every single country is included, down to the smallest Pacific island, there are many more, possibly as many as 170. However we are concerned with the larger countries whose trade exceeds 100,000 tons a year. There is tremendous diversity in the volume of cargo shipped, as can be seen in Figure

7.1 which plots the imports and exports of the major trading countries (note that a log scale is used). Trade volume varies from a few hundred thousand tons at one extreme to hundreds of millions of tons at the other, showing some correlation between the volume of imports and exports. This chart offers an important insight into seaborne trade from the viewpoint of the trade analyst. Every one of the one hundred dots in Figure 7.1 represents a country with its own unique geographical position, economic infrastructure, and political policies. To be aware of each country's circumstances in a general way is difficult enough; to follow these circumstances in sufficient detail to forecast their future trade flows calls for a research team of a size rarely found in the shipping industry. If nothing else, this shows what a complex task trade analysts face. Clearly a short cut is needed. We must look for a theory which will allow us to generalize about the factors which determine a country's trade. Armed with this theory we can reduce the task to more manageable proportions.

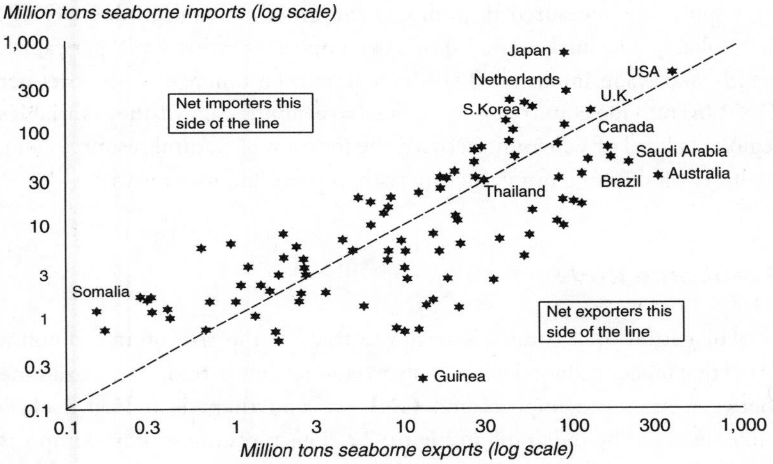

FIGURE 7.1 Seaborne imports and exports 1991

Source: United Nations *Monthly Bulletin of Statistics*

The starting point is to look more closely at the economic differences between the trading countries. Table 7.4 (at the end of this chapter) ranks the countries by their tonnage of total trade in 1990/1. The first two columns show the imports and exports of each country, column 3 shows total trade, which has been used for the ranking exercise, while the remaining columns show a selection of economic variables for each country.

The biggest trading country is the United States with 838 mt of trade, followed by Japan with trade of 815 mt and Netherlands with trade of 373 mt. Whilst it is hardly surprising that the United States, the world's largest economy, should appear at the top of the list, it is more surprising that the Netherlands, a tiny country, should appear in third place. This provides a first glimpse of the type of questions that need to be answered. Moving to the bottom of the list, we find some countries with very little trade. Lebanon

TABLE 7.1 Analysis of trade relationships

	R sq.	*Constant*	*Regression coefficient*
GNP and imports	0.69	17,562	0.1157
Area and trade	0.22	40,432	0.328
Population and trade	0.04	76,310	195.9
Resources and trade	0.24	45,197	251.4

Source: Figures 7.2–7.4

with trade of 1.3 mt, Haiti with trade of 874,000 tons and Cambodia with trade of 106,000 tons.[1]

Also shown in the table are three indicators of economic size, land area (measured in thousand hectares), population (measured in millions) and gross national product (GNP) (measured in million dollars). The final column shows two important ratios, GNP per capita, an indicator of wealth, and trade intensity (TI) which shows the tonnage of imports per billion dollars of GNP. In studying country trade we need to examine each of these variables – the size of the region, its level of economic activity, the location of natural resources and, of course, the availability of shipping infrastructure such as ports and waterways.

Economic activity and seaborne trade

The most obvious explanation of a country's seaborne trade is the size of its economy. Common sense tells us that bigger economies are likely to generate more trade. If we examine the relationship between seaborne imports and GNP we find there is indeed a close relationship, as is demonstrated by the graph in Figure 7.2. This plots the seaborne imports of 94 countries in 1990/1 against their GNP, using a logarithmic scale. As the level of GNP increases, so do imports. For example the USA has a GNP of $5,610 billion and imports of 449 mt, whereas the GNP of Gabon is only $4.8 billion and it has sea imports of 212,000 tons.

Taking the analysis a stage further and fitting a linear regression model of seaborne imports on GNP (see graph inset) we find that 69 per cent of the variation in seaborne imports is explained by variations in GNP. The model implies that trade starts when GNP reaches $17.5 billion and increases by 116,000 tons for each $1 billion increase in GNP. The relationship is not perfect, but it is clearly significant and follows the sort of pattern we would expect. There are three reasons why rich countries with a high GNP might be expected to have a higher level of imports than a poor country with low GNP. First, a larger economy has greater needs in terms of the raw materials and manufactured goods which are shipped by sea. By the law of averages some of these will not be available locally. Second, along the long road to economic development, local resources are likely to become depleted, leading to the need for imports. Third, a country with high GNP can afford to purchase imports and has more to export in return.

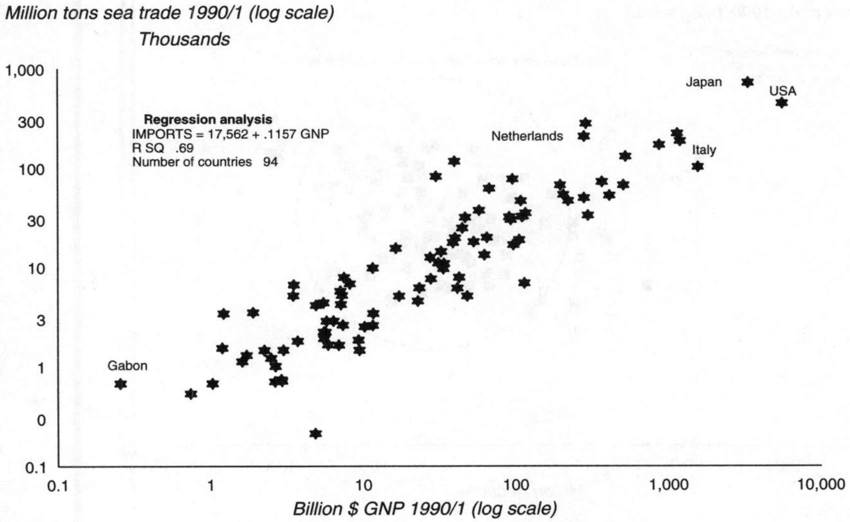

FIGURE 7.2 Seaborne imports and GNP
Source: United Nations *Monthly Bulletin of Statistics*

Size, natural resources and seaborne trade

When considering the trade of a country, the next factor to consider is its physical size. We might expect the size of a country in terms of its land area to influence trade because it determines the amount of physical resources available locally. After all, reserves of energy, minerals and the production of agriculture and forestry are all likely to be greater in a large land mass than a smaller one. When we examine the correlation between sea trade and land area, measured in million hectares, shown in Figure 7.3, we find that there is indeed a relationship. The correlation coefficient is 0.22, suggesting that 22 per cent of the variation in trade is explained by a country's area. However, the relationship is much weaker that the relationship with GNP and there are many countries that very obviously do not fit the model. Of the countries shown in Table 7.4, Canada has the largest land mass with 997 million hectares, but ranks fourteenth in terms of trade. Singapore, a country with only 62,000 hectares has roughly the same trade volume as Canada. Land area obviously plays a far smaller part in determining trade volume than economic activity. On reflection this is not really such a surprising result. It reinforces the point that trade is about economic growth, not physical size. A country may be very large, but if it is mainly empty, there will not be very much trade.

Much the same result is obtained when we examine the relationship between natural resources and trade. Obviously seaborne trade, particularly bulk trade, must be influenced by the availability of raw materials, particularly cereals, oil, coal, gas and iron ore. These

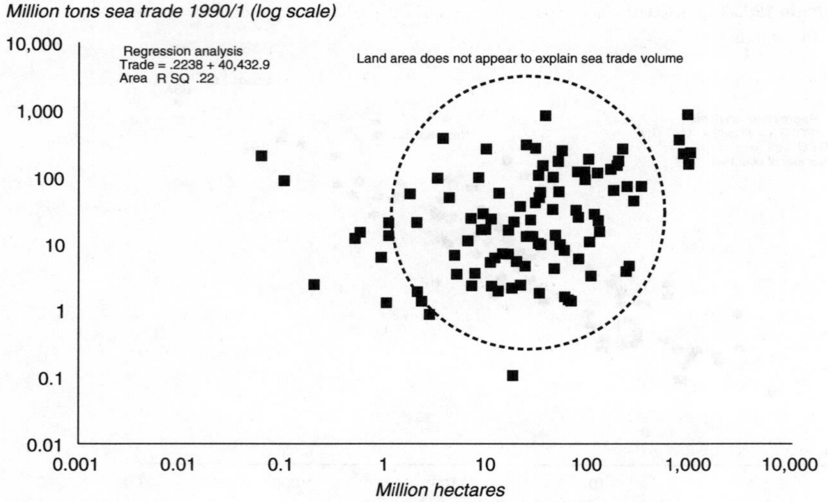

FIGURE 7.3 Sea trade and land area

Source: United Nations *Monthly Bulletin of Statistics*

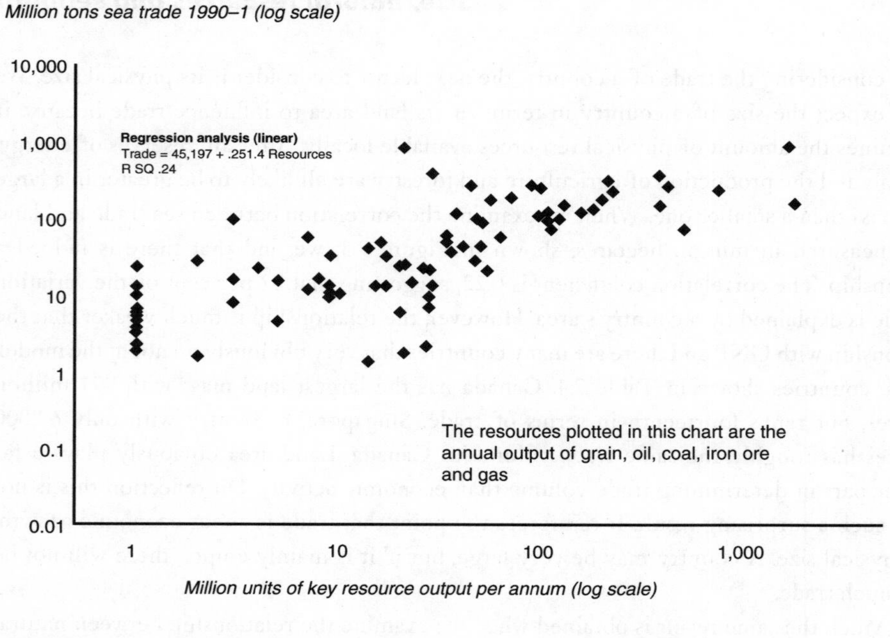

FIGURE 7.4 Seaborne trade and resources

Source: United Nations *Monthly Bulletin of Statistics*

are the essential inputs to a modern industrial society. The statistical evidence confirms the existence of this link, but also demonstrates that the relationship is not sufficiently consistent to show up in a simple regression analysis. A regression of trade volume on the total tonnage production of cereals, oil, coal and iron ore listed for each country produces a correlation coefficient of 0.24. In other words about one quarter of the variation in trade can be explained by resources. The relationship is shown graphically in Figure 7.4.

It is not difficult to account for the weakness of this relationship. The precise amount of trade arising from natural resources in a matter of supply/demand economics. Where demand is high and no local reserves are available, as in the case of iron ore used by the Japanese steel industry or oil used by France and Germany, trade is directly related to demand. More often there is an economic choice between domestic and imported resources. For example, Europe has extensive coal deposits, but recently preferred to import cheaper foreign coal. In the United States oil imports are influenced by decisions taken about the depletion of domestic oil fields. In large economies domestic resources are diverted to the domestic market, whereas in small economies they are available for export. As we shall see when we study trade theory, factor endowments play a vital part in explaining trade, but this does not allow us to generalize about the relationship between resources and trade. The results of the regression analysis is a reminder of this fact.

Population and sea trade

Finally there is population. The idea that population and trade go hand in hand stretches back to the nineteenth century trader's dream of 'oil for the lamps of China'. If there are enough people, it was argued, there is great trading potential. Much the same hopes were extended to South American countries like Brazil. In both cases the expectations were disappointed and trade was slow to develop, despite the size of the population. For example, Brazil has a population of 150 million, considerably larger than Japan's 124 million, but generates only one quarter as much trade. A statistical analysis of the relationship between population and trade, shows virtually no correlation. The coefficient of correlation is 0.04. If nothing else this demonstrates that sea trade is primarily an economic phenomenon. Economic activity creates the demand for imports and the supply of exports, not numbers of people.

7.3 An explanation of trade theory

This discussion of the causes of trade naturally leads on to the question of trade theory. Why do some countries trade more than others? In a general way we have seen that this can be explained by the level of economic activity and, to a lesser extent, by land area and natural resources. A theoretical framework would be useful, however, to explain these relationships. We have shown empirically that the most important single cause of trade growth is GNP, but these are just statistical relationships. Every economist is taught that statistical relationships can change. It would be reassuring to know why trade increases with GNP and, more importantly, the circumstances under which this important relationship might break down. To answer these questions we must turn to trade theory. Although there is no single theory of trade because in reality countries trade for a variety of reasons, economists have come up with some principles which are useful in explaining the basic principles which govern trade. In the following sections we review trade theory, to establish the theories developed by economists to show why trade is so beneficial. We then review the economic relationship between economic growth and seaborne trade. Finally we examine the dynamic relationships involved, to establish why regions differ in their trading patterns.

The reason why countries trade

We start with the question 'why do countries trade?' At first sight this seems too obvious to deserve very much attention, but in a world of politically motivated nation states, trade cannot be taken for granted. If countries do not believe that trade is in their interest they can close their borders. China, the USSR, and Japan have all followed this policy in recent history. A policy of not trading, or limiting trade by tariffs or quotas, is known as 'protectionism', or in its extreme form 'isolationism'. It seeks to exclude the goods produced by foreigners from local markets in order to protect the livelihood of local producers. Protectionism can look very attractive to a community which feels that its livelihood is under threat. One reason for adopting these policies is to protect local resources. It may seem that valuable raw materials are being exported by unprincipled traders, leaving nothing for the local inhabitants. When the reserves are all gone, the country will be left in poverty.[2] Another is to protect local jobs and skills which have been developed over many years. If the local shipyard or car plant, on which thousands of jobs depend, is about to close because it cannot compete with foreign yards, offering subsidies or passing laws preventing imports is a natural response. After all, this could be just the beginning. Soon other industries will be under attack and then how will the country earn its living? Currency reserves will drain away and the country will be left in poverty. Or will it?

Three hundred years ago David Hume addressed this question in his *Discourse on the Balance of Trade* (1752) (see Meek, 1973). Hume did not think much of this line of protectionism, commenting:

> It is very usual in nations ignorant of the nature of commerce, to prohibit the exportation of commodities, and to preserve among themselves whatever they think valuable and useful ... There still prevails, even in nations well acquainted with commerce, a strong jealousy with regard to the balance of trade, and a fear, that gold and silver may be leaving them.

In nineteenth-century Britain, as in many developing economies, free trade became a major political issues, centring on the question of whether the import of cheap grain should be permitted. Manufacturers in the towns were in favour because they wanted cheap food for their workers, but the domestic landowners, who stood to lose their protected market, were opposed. The issue split the country. Eventually free trade prevailed and in 1847 the 'Corn Laws', which prohibited imports, were repealed allowing Britain to develop as an industrial economy. Today the principles of free trade are broadly accepted through the General Agreement on Trade and Tariffs (GATT), but protectionism remains a live issue. In the West there are still concerns that developing economies in Asia will put the older industrial countries out of business, as demonstrated by the difficulties faced by the GATT negotiations over ten years. Apart from any personal considerations for the inhabitants of the developed countries, this would be very bad for shipping. Even where trade is relatively open, many countries protect inefficient industries whose output, in a free market would be replaced by trade.

In the face of these often strongly held views, one of the challenges facing economists is to show that free trade is always in the interest of the trading parties. This is one area where the early nineteenth century economists were very successful. They came up with a very convincing proof that trade is beneficial. Since this theory also provides some useful insights into the causes of trade and guidance in developing trade models, the study of trade theory is doubly useful.

The theory of absolute advantage

The first step in developing a proof that trade is beneficial was made by Adam Smith and is referred to as the 'theory of absolute advantage'. He argued that countries are better off if they specialize, trading their surplus production for the other goods they need. Specialization allows them to become more productive and everyone benefits because the world's limited economic resources (factors of production) are used more efficiently. To illustrate the point he drew an analogy with tradesmen who are better off if they specialize,

> It is the maxim of every prudent master of a family, never to attempt to make at home what it will cost him more to make than to buy. The tailor does not attempt to make his own shoes, but buys them from the shoemaker. The shoemaker does not attempt to make his own clothes, but employs a tailor. What is prudence in the conduct of every private family, can scarce be folly in that of a great kingdom. If a foreign country can supply us with a commodity cheaper than we ourselves can make it, better buy of them with some part of the produce of our own industry, employed in a way in which we have some advantage.[3]

Goods are cheaper because trade permits greater division of labour, allowing more to be produced with the same resources. So long as transport costs do not exceed the cost saving in production, trade is bound to be beneficial.

The point is easily demonstrated. Consider two countries, Britain and the US, who produce two goods, food and cloth. Both have sixty labourers. US labour is more efficient at producing food, but UK workers are more productive at making cloth. Assume that there are constant costs (i.e. it requires the same amount of labour to produce a unit of output, regardless of volume) and the labour requirements are as follows:

Labour requirement per unit of output	*UK*	*US*
Food (tons)	4	3
Cloth (bales)	2	6
Production possibilities		
Available labour	60	60
Food production (tons)	15	20
Cloth production (bales)	30	10

The UK can produce 15 tons of food, 30 bales of cloth, or any combination. Write this as (15,30). Similarly the US can produce 20 tons of food or 10 bales of cloth, so the production possibility is (20,10). Now suppose the population of each country needs 12 tons of food to live on. Without trade Britain would need 48 units of labour to produce 12 tons of food. With the remaining 12 units of labour it could produce 6 bales of cloth, so its output would be (12,6). The US would only need 36 units of labour to produce the 12 tons of food. With the remaining 24 units of labour they could produce 6 units of cloth (12,6). In other words both countries are equally well off, being able to feed themselves and produce 6 bales of cloth.

Now we introduce trade and allow the two countries to specialize in their best products. The US switches all its labour into food. It produces 20 tons, of which it consumes 12 and exports 8 units to the UK. Thanks to the imports the UK only needs to produce 4 tons of food, which requires 16 units of labour. With the remaining 44 units of labour it can produce 22 bales of cloth. It consumes 11 bales of cloth itself and exports 11 bales to the US in return for the food. Thus with trade both countries consume (12,11). Thanks to trade they each have the food they need and almost twice as much cloth. They are rich.

The theory of comparative advantage

This theory leaves a crucial question unanswered. In the example one country is more efficient at producing each commodity – the US is better at food and the UK at cloth. Suppose one country is better at producing all goods? Surely free trade would be a threat to the less efficient country whose food and textile businesses would be driven out of business, leaving them in poverty? If this is true, inefficient countries must avoid trade at all costs. The *Theory of Comparative Advantage*, published by David Ricardo in 1817, demonstrated that this was not the case. He proved that trade is beneficial, even if one country is more efficient than its trading partners at producing all goods. If we rerun the example, but make the US better at producing both food and cloth, the countries are still richer with trade than without.

Labour requirement per unit of output	*UK*	*US*
Food	4	3
Cloth	2	1

The US now requires less labour than the UK to produce both food and cloth. If there is no trade it can produce the 12 tons of food it needs and 24 bales of cloth (12,24). Britain would produce 12 tons of food, but only six bales of cloth (12,6). However if the countries specialize in the product in which they are relatively more efficient, their production increases. The UK is now relatively more efficient at food production, because British food requires only twice as much labour as cloth, whereas in the US food requires three times as much labour. So the UK specializes in food, producing 15 tons, consuming 12 and leaving a surplus of 3 to export. With imports of 3 tons of food, the US would now only have to produce 9 tons of food, requiring 27 units of labour. With the remaining 33 units of labour it could produce 33 bales of cloth. This compares with the total world cloth production before trade of 30 units (i.e. 24 plus 6). Trade has increased output by 3 bales of cloth. Not much, but better than nothing.

The heart of the theory is that provided each country is more efficient at producing some goods than others, trade will be beneficial if each country specializes in the products at which it is relatively most efficient. More wealth is created by trade because limited 'factors of production' are used more efficiently and all participants are better off than they would be without trade.[4] This has important implications for trade. The appearance of new competitors in the international market does not put existing traders out of business. Provided there are relative differences in efficiency it leads to more trade and greater wealth, though it does leave some difficult questions about how the gains from trade are distributed between the participating countries.

Of course free trade it is not all good news. Changes in trading patterns as the comparative advantage alters are often painful for the interest groups concerned. The landowners who resisted the repeal of the Corn Laws in nineteenth century Britain were right in thinking that they would suffer from free trade. After the industrial interests won and the Corn Laws were repealed in 1847, cheap imported corn impoverished the countryside and many workers migrated to the towns helping Britain to become even more successful as an exporter of manufactures. In the end Britain as a whole was better off for free trade, but the process of change left some individuals, particularly landowners worse off. There are parallels with the competition between European and Far East heavy industry in the 1970s and 1980s. Much European heavy industry was driven out of business by Far East competition. It is not much compensation to the redundant shipyard worker that he has lost his job because the country now has a comparative advantage in financial services, a business that has no call for welders.

7.4 Theories about the pattern of trade

So far we have concentrated on the general principles which explain trade. The next step is to consider which countries trade in what commodities. Why does the US, a major oil producer, import oil? What determines the goods which countries like Greece or the UK export? Why did China suddenly import 34 mt of steel products in 1994. Why is the Japanese export trade in manufactures so high? Why does Europe import so many Japanese motor cars when it has a car industry of its own? There are many explanations of trade, but we will focus on four, resource based trade, technology based trade, trade based on differences in consumer tastes, and cyclical trade.

Resource based trade and the Heckscher–Ohlin theory

One of the most important causes of trade from the shipping industry's point of view is the fact that different countries are endowed with different natural resources. The importance of resources was first recognized by trade economists who were looking for an explanation of what determines the comparative advantage of a country. This was an issue which Ricardo did not address and it was more than a century before that economists came up with a theoretical explanation. The key issue turned out to be the assumption of constant costs, which is one of the basic building blocks of Ricardo's model.

The theory of comparative advantage assumes that resources can be freely switched between the manufacture of different products without any loss of productivity. Even in the abstract world of economic theory this is clearly not realistic. In the 1920s two Swedish economists, Eli Heckscher and Bent Ohlin, concluded that productivity differences occur because countries have different endowments of factors of production, and there is limited factor substitution. For example, America with its great prairies can expand grain production, but if the UK tries to do the same thing, as we assumed in the example on page (235), by switching its abundant labour into agriculture, yields start to fall as the land is farmed more intensively. Conversely, although the UK with its abundant skilled labour can easily expand cloth production, the US runs into diminishing returns due to the lack of suitable labour. Thus the Heckscher–Ohlin theory argues that the explanation of comparative advantage lies in differences in the factors of production between countries. All we need for trade to be beneficial is that economic resources are unevenly distributed between countries. Winters (1991)[5] summarizes these minimum conditions as follows:

1. The production functions for the two products give constant returns to scale if both factors are applied proportionally, but diminishing returns to any individual factor (i.e. if a country runs out of land, but keeps applying more labour, fertilizers, machinery, etc., marginal returns fall).
2. Goods differ in their requirements of different factor inputs (e.g. food production needs more land than textile manufacture).
3. The countries have different relative factor endowments.

As an illustration, imagine the 'no trade' situation on two islands. Each relies on its domestic resources. Island A struggles to feed a large population by intensive agriculture on the limited land available. It mines coal from a few deep mines and manufactures a whole range of products, mainly on a small scale. In agriculture and labour they face sharply increasing costs as they try to maintain growth by pouring more labour into fixed physical resources. Island B is the same but has open cast coal mines and better land. If trade is opened up the islands specialize. Because Island A has few natural resources, its comparative advantage is in manufacturing. It imports coal and food from Island B and switches the labour into relatively more productive manufacturing industry. In other words they export those goods whose production is relatively intensive in the factors with which they are well endowed. Island B opens more coal mines and switches labour into them, exporting coal. It all depends on their relative factor endowment. The precise definition of 'natural resources' raises all sorts of questions. In chapter 8 we show that the trading world is constantly on the move, so we should not rely too heavily on static models. However the Heckscher–Ohlin theory suggests that in a free world market countries must make the best of whatever resources they have.

Trade based on technology differences

A very different reason for trade is technical innovation. Manufactured goods often require specialist investment and expertise. Once a particular company or country has become established in this area, it is difficult for others to build up sufficient volume of sales to break into that market. In the nineteenth century Britain developed mechanized textile manufacturing, and for some years gained a great benefit from this. Eventually other countries caught up. Today technical advance is continuous. The manufacture of medical equipment, the production of a particular type of rubber belt drive, or the manufacture of complex products such as cruise ships and aircraft are all examples where one country has developed a competitive advantage based on technical innovation and is protected by barriers such as the high cost of entry. In the case of particular inventions the manufacturing rights may even be covered by a patent.

Trade based on differences in tastes

Anyone studying trade statistics will soon notice another type of trade, called inter-industry trade where countries import and export the same products. Motor cars are a classic example, but petroleum products, electronic equipment and a whole range of consumer goods also qualify. In these cases the cause of trade is usually differences in tastes between countries. For example, motor car manufacturers face economies of scale, so low volume production is expensive. If most Americans like to drive very big motor cars, while most Europeans prefer to drive small motor cars, then the minority in Europe who wish to purchase large motor cars can benefit from importing American cars and vice versa. This has had a tremendous impact on trade. In most countries consumers can now choose from twenty or thirty different brands of motor car, each sold at a highly competitive price. The production economics of car manufacture is such that if the market were fully supplied by UK manufacturers, there could only be a small number of different designs, and costs would almost certainly be higher. Similarly if oil refineries are technically restricted to producing a mix of petroleum products which does not exactly match local demand, they will seek to export the products not needed locally.

Cyclical trade

In a world economy where demand is constantly changing, an important source of sea trade is the temporary local shortage of a product or commodity which could normally be obtained locally at a competitive price. Temporary shortages may arise from business cycles in demand, mechanical failure, disasters (e.g. the Kobe earthquake in 1994), poor planning or a sudden burst of commodity inflation which encourages manufacturers to build stocks of raw materials. In these circumstances the pattern of trade suddenly changes. For example chemical manufacturers produce many different compounds and much of the seaborne chemicals trade is to supply temporary shortages for a particular compound or feedstock.

7.5 Economic growth and sea trade

Growth and trade

Now it is time to expolore the relationship between economic growth and sea trade. Our analysis of the 'causes' of sea trade at the start of this chapter identified economic activity (GNP) as by far the most important. We showed that trade increases with GNP at an average rate of 116,000 tons for each $1 billion of GNP. One of the important lessons to be learnt is that the relationship between trade and GNP is not static. It is dynamic. When countries grow their economies change and so does their trade. One of the most fundamental principles of trade forecasting is to recognize the potential for change and build it into the forecast. To do this we must question the relationship between trade and GNP.

The key to this particular issue is the way different parts of the economy respond to growth. If we look more closely at the structure of world economic activity we can immediately see why trade is likely to change as a country grows. Gross National Product (GNP), a measure of the total economic output, can be divided into the nine different sectors shown in the table below, which follow the 'International Standard Industrial Classification' (ISIC).

ISIC	*Sector*	*% Total GNP*	*Maritime intensity*
1	Agriculture	8	High
2–3	Mining and utilities	4	High
4	Manufacturing	28	High
5	Construction	6	High
6	Wholesale and retail	16	None
7	Transport and communications	7	None
8–9	Other (services)	31	Very low
	TOTAL	100	

Each sector has a different propensity for maritime transport. Agriculture, mining and manufacturing are directly involved with trade, either through imports or exports, and growth in these sectors usually generates trade. In contrast businesses in the wholesale, retail, transport and 'service' sectors generate little cargo. The 'service' sector has a particularly low propensity to trade. It consists of activities such as banking and insurance, public administration, social services, education, medicine, recreation facilities, and household services (repair, laundry) which have little if any impact on maritime transport. A thriving industrial economy is good for the shipping industry, but any trend towards services or 'hi-tech' is bad news.

When we examine the growth of modern economies we find that economic activity shifts away from the trade intensive activities towards the service sector. It follows that we must expect the pattern of trade growth to change as the country grows and develops. To illustrate the nature of this change, Table 7.2 shows how the GDP of South Korea, Japan and the United States changed over a twenty-five-year period from 1965 to 1989. In all three countries trade intensive activities like manufacturing lost share, while services gained. In South Korea, a country in the early stages of industrialization, agriculture fell sharply by 28 per cent, while mining, utilities, construction, manufacturing and the service sector all increased. In other words South Korea changed from a rural society to a modern industrial economy and seaborne imports grow very rapidly at 11 per cent per annum. Japan was already industrialized in 1965 with a very small agricultural sector and very well developed manufacturing sector, so we see a very different pattern of development. Agriculture, mining, utilities, construction and manufacturing all lost ground, but services increased by 10 per cent. In the US we see yet another pattern, with services taking a dominant position in the economy. In 1965 the share of service was already very high at 59 per cent, but in the next 24 years it increased to 69 per cent of GDP. Agriculture, traditionally a major US business, fell to 2 per cent. Mining, utilities and construction fell by 9 per cent and manufacturing by

TABLE 7.2 **Changes in the structure of GNP 1965–89 for S. Korea, Japan and USA**

ISIC	*Sector*	*Country*	*1965–70 %*	*1989 %*	*Trend %*
0–1	Agriculture	S. Korea	38	10	−28
		Japan	10	3	−7
		USA	3	2	−1
2,3,5	Mining utilities and construction	S. Korea	25	44	19
		Japan	44	41	−3
		USA	38	29	−9
4,6,7	Manufacturing, wholesale and transport	S. Korea	18	26	8
		Japan	34	30	−4
		USA	28	17	−11
7–9	Services	S. Korea	37	46	9
		Japan	46	56	10
		USA	59	69	10

Source: World Development Report 1991, World Bank

11 per cent. The contrast between the South Korean economy with its growing industrial sector and the US with its dominant service economy is very apparent.

However this is not the whole story. As manufacturing industry loses market share, there is also a change in the type of goods manufactured. An analysis carried out by Maizels (1971) to establish a typical pattern of expansion of manufacturing industry, shown in Table 7.3, illustrates the point. At low income levels food manufacturing and textile industries are the most important when, in accordance with Engel's Law, these products make up a large part of demand. Their share then declines rapidly, to be taken over by metals, metal products and chemical. At a certain income level the share of metals stabilizes, while the share of metal products continues to grow as more value is added to the basic materials. This implies that output becomes less resource intensive at high income levels, being directed towards value added products. For example, motor car production progresses from economy models to executive limousines. Again we see evidence that we must expect the structure of economic activity to change with growth, bringing consequences for trade.

TABLE 7.3 Pattern of manufacturing production changes in the pattern of manufacturing production per head at 1955 prices and percentages

	$100	*$250*	*$500*	*$750*	*$1,000*
Food and beverages	40	33	26	21	18
Metals	4	5	7	7	8
Metal products	4	10	18	24	29
Chemicals	0	2	4	7	9
Textiles	26	18	13	10	8
Other manufactures	27	32	32	31	29
Total	100	100	100	100	100

Source: A. Maizels *Growth and Trade* (1971)

The stages of economic development

Academics have spent much time discussing these changes to see if there is a consistent pattern of development. The 'stages of growth' theory developed by Professor W.W. Rostow provides a useful starting point.[6] He argued that as economies grow they go through a series of different phases which he put into 5 categories according to the stage of economic development they had reached. The 5 stages are shown in Box 7.1.

There has been a good deal of discussion of Rostow's work. Like so many economic theories, Rostow's theory is based in a simple common sense idea. As economies grow they start by producing necessities like infrastructure which are resource intensive, then progressively turn to the finer things of life ('value added products') as they become wealthier.

BOX 7.1 Rostow's five stages of economic development

Stage 1 *The traditional society.* This is a predominantly agricultural economy. Unchanging technology places a ceiling on the level of attainable output per head. This ceiling results from the fact that 'the potentialities which flow from modern science and technology are either not available or not regularly and systematically applied'. These societies devote a very high proportion of their resources to agriculture. They hardly trade by sea except for food aid and the export of a few cash crops.

Stage 2 *The pre-conditions of take-off established.* The second stage requires a surplus above subsistence, the development of education and a degree of capital accumulation to provide the foundation for economic growth. For example, in seventeenth century England these conditions were established by a change in attitudes to investment, the emergence of banks and other institutions for mobilizing capital, etc. Sea trade is small but very active and growing fast.

Stage 3 *The take-off.* In Rostow's analysis this stage is followed by a long interval of sustained but fluctuating progress as modern technology is extended over the whole front of economic activities. Increased investment permits output regularly to outstrip the increase in national population. New industries appear, older ones level off and decline. Changes take place in the external trade of the country, goods formerly imported are produced at home, new import requirements develop and new commodities are made for export.

Stage 4 *Maturity.* After a period which Rostow placed at 60 years after the beginning of take-off, maturity sets in. By this stage the economy has extended its range into more refined and complex processes, with a shift in focus from coal, steel and heavy engineering industries to machine tools, chemicals and electrical equipment. He thought Germany, Britain, France and the United States passed through this phase by the end of the nineteenth century or shortly afterwards. Depletion of raw materials may boost the import trade, while manufacture will dominate exports.

Stage 5 *Mass Consumption.* The fifth stage sees a movement of the leading sectors of industry towards durable consumer goods and services. A large proportion of the population can afford to consume much more than basic food, shelter and clothing and this brings about changes in the structure of the working population, including a progressive movement into office and service work.

Maizels (1971), who made a very long-term study of this hypothesis, explained it in the following terms:

> as a country becomes progressively more industrialised the proportion of the occupied population engaged in manufacturing does not rise indefinitely – there is an effective limit which may have been reached in a number of countries. This limit comes into operation for two reasons. Firstly as the economy grows and income rises the demand for workers in service operations such as doctors, typists, government officials increases as fast or faster than the demand for manufactured goods. Secondly as productivity increases in manufacturing tend to outstrip the productivity increase in the distribution of goods from factory to the consumer, these workers tend to be absorbed in distribution to match the increased flow of industrial products.[7]

This reasoning suggests that the progress of economic growth will be associated with an increasing share for services and a corresponding decline in the growth rate of manufacturing industry and seaborne trade. Whilst it is not possible to set precise limits on the duration of a stage, or even to be sure when a new stage is about to begin, the concept of a progression is helpful.

The trade development cycle (TDC)

If we apply the 'stages of growth' concept to trade it is clear that, over a period of years, we must expect the trade of a country to change. How it changes depends on what stage the economy has reached in the economic growth cycle. The early stages of growth involve the import of all but the most simple items such as food and textiles paid for by the export of whatever 'cash crops' are available – sugar, tropical fruit, oil, copper, jute, hardwood logs are typical examples. The availability of foreign exchange is the main constraint on trade and generally keeps trade at a low level. Countries such as Guinea, Togo and Cameroon in West Africa currently fall into this category.

As the economy develops through stages 2 and 3, the demand for raw materials such as iron ore, coal, non-ferrous metal ores and forest products increases as the industrial infrastructure is built up. If raw materials are not available locally they must be imported, as must the more sophisticated machinery, and paid for by exports of semi-manufactures and any primary exports which are available. The reconciliation of domestic and foreign markets thus forms a basic requirement of growth at this stage. Industries such as shipbuilding and automobiles are frequently developed as lead export earners, a pattern set by Japan in the 1950s and subsequently followed by South Korea, Poland and several other countries.

When the economy matures, the rate of growth of seaborne trade changes again. In the course of time, possibly 20 years or 50, the building blocks of a capitalist economy are in place. Industrial infrastructure, housing, roads, railways and stocks of consumer durables such as motor vehicles and washing machines have reached a mature level. Industries such as steel, construction and vehicle manufacture, which underpinned the growth during stage 2, stop growing and economic activity gravitates towards less material intensive activities. Manufacturing gravitates towards the higher value added end of the product range. How this affects trade depends on domestic resources. If the economy has always relied on imported raw materials, the growth rate of bulk imports slows, though the trade in manufacture shipped by liner and air freight will continue to grow. Typically this produces a trade development cycle of the type shown by curve A in Figure 7.5. However the sea trade of countries with extensive natural resources is likely to follow a different growth path. Growth consumes resources and as domestic supplies become depleted, or better quality materials become available abroad, bulk imports may start to increase. This happened in the US in the 1970s when oil demand drew ahead of domestic production and imports started to grow rapidly. In such cases the trade development cycle may follow a path more like curve B in Figure 7.5.

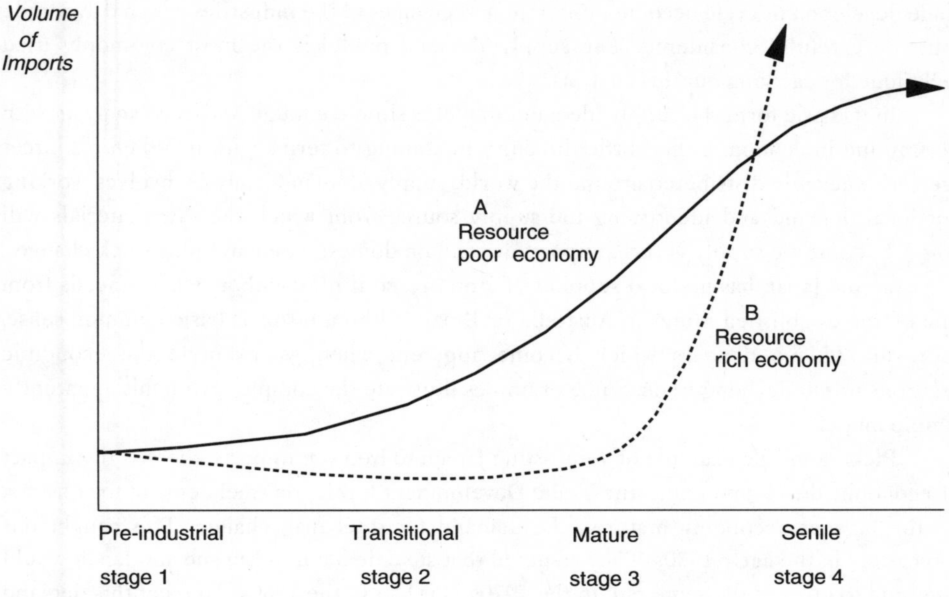

FIGURE 7.5 Seaborne trade development cycle
Source: Martin Stopford, 1997

Ultimately the seaborne trade development cycle is just a convenient way of summarizing certain common patterns which appear to occur in the world economy – it is not a law, nor does it apply in every case. Since economic development draws heavily on natural resources which are unevenly distributed between countries, we must expect each country to have a unique TDC, determined by its factor endowments or other unique political and cultural characteristics. Thus the TDC of a resource rich economy which can draw on local raw materials in the early stages of growth, possibly with an exportable surplus, will be completely different from the TDC of a country without raw materials. What we can be sure of is that economies are constantly changing and these changes have a major impact on the international transport industry.

7.6 Trade forecasting and the commodity trade model

The problems of forecasting commodity trade

Modern industrial economies need energy commodities such as coal and oil, mineral resources such as iron ore, non-ferrous metal ores, and agricultural products such as grain and other foodstuffs. One of the main tasks of the bulk shipping industry is to anticipate future trade, so that efficient transport can be planned. This is where the dynamics of the trade development cycle become important and changes in the industries which drive trade must be carefully considered. The supply/demand model is the most commonly used technique for carrying out this analysis.

In its basic form the supply/demand model is simple enough and even analysts with no training in economics find little difficulty in coming to terms with it. When resources are very unevenly distributed around the world, supply/demand analysis involves working out local demand and identifying the supply source from which the raw materials will come. If domestic supply is zero, imports depend on domestic demand plus stock changes. For example Japan has no local supplies of iron ore, so it must import what it needs from one of the established mines in Australia or Brazil. Although this is basic common sense, there are hidden dangers which become apparent when we examine the economic relationships underlying trade. Some examples illustrate the complexity of this apparently simple model.

Picking up the example of forecasting Japanese iron ore imports, there is the impact of economic development (i.e. the Trade Development Cycle) on steel demand to consider. As the Japanese economy matures, the demand for steel may change. This caught out forecasters in the early 1970s. They assumed that steel demand in Europe and Japan would continue to grow at the same rate in the 1970s as it had in the 1960s. To meet this demand steelmakers planned to expand output from 110 mt to 180 mt. As the economy matured demand stopped growing and Japanese steel production never exceeded 120 mt. A more carefully structured forecasting model would have shown that demand growth in the 1960s was driven by stockbuilding of steel intensive products like buildings and motor vehicles and that the trend was likely to change as the economy matured.

Another potential trap for unwary forecasters is *factor substitution*. Japan has no reserves of iron ore, but there are other materials such as steel scrap which will do the same job. If the supply of steel scrap increases, this can be used instead of ore. Suddenly the iron ore demand forecast becomes more complex. Or consider the coal trade for use in power stations. There may be no local coal, but power stations might start to use oil or gas in place of coal. The substitution of coal for oil in power stations was one of the major causes of the long tanker depression in the 1980s. Oil trade models at the time did not consider this possibility. Another possibility is the competition between domestic and foreign supplies. The slow rundown of European iron ore production in the 1960s was the result of price competition between high cost domestic mines and foreign suppliers with low cost but greater transport costs. Cheap transport made the trade viable. Sometimes technology changes alter the domestic or foreign production functions, with major consequences for trade. For example, the rise of 'mini mills' using cheap scrap in Asia provides direct competition for blast furnace steel, changing the pattern of the iron ore trade. Similarly new technology which reduced the cost of offshore production enabled Europe to increase its domestic oil production in the 1990s. Whilst these relationships are not easy to quantify, forecasters should at least be aware that they exist. Although the detailed discussion of the commodity trades must wait until chapter 9, in this chapter we take a closer look at the economic model which underlies most commodity trades.

Economic principles of analysing commodity trades

The starting point for the commodity trade model is price. Commodities are traded when it is cheaper to import than to use the locally available substitutes. Thus the model consists of a demand function for the commodity, showing the relationship between demand for the commodity and its price, and a supply function which shows the price at which the commodity is available. This means that we are concerned with the balance of supply, demand and prices.

The demand function describes the relationship between per capita income, commodity prices, and the consumption of the product is generally referred to as the Consumer Demand Function.

$$q_{it} = (p_{1it}, p_{2it}, y_{it}) \qquad \text{E7(1)}$$

where q is per capita consumption of the commodity, p_1 is its price in domestic currency, p_2 is the price of other commodities and y is per capita income for the i th country in year t.[8] This function suggests that the demand for a commodity responds to changes in relative prices and income. To explain how demand responds to a change in price we need to introduce two economic concepts, the income elasticity and the price elasticity.

The income elasticity shows how consumers adjust their consumption of a commodity in response to a change in income. It is defined as the proportionate change in the purchase of the commodity such as energy for a change in income, with prices constant.

$$e_i = \frac{d\,(\log q)}{d\,(\log y)} \qquad \text{E7(2)}$$

In other words the income elasticity is the percentage change in demand divided by the percentage change in income. The nature of this relationship varies from one commodity to another, with important consequences for trade. We can use the income elasticity to classify commodities into three different groups. *Inferior goods* have a negative income elasticity (i.e. less than 0), so when income rises, demand falls. For example, at higher incomes people typically consume less of basic foods such as bread and potatoes, switching their demand to other foodstuffs such as meat. *Necessities* are goods whose demand increases as income rises, but more slowly than income (i.e. the income elasticity is in the range 0–1). Finally, *luxuries* are goods for which demand grows faster as income rises (i.e. the income elasticity is over 1). These differences are important because they warn us to expect demand relationships to change as income rises (or falls). For example, the income elasticity of motor cars could be very high at low income levels because buying a motor car is a priority. When most people have a car the demand continues to rise with income as a few buy second cars, but the rate of increase slows and car demand eventually stagnates, or switches to higher value added vehicles. For anyone modelling the demand for steel, much of which is used in motor vehicle production, it is vital to model these relationships correctly. The important point is that demand for commodities changes with income.

The 'Price Elasticity' shows how demand responds to a change in prices. It is derived from the demand function and represents the percentage change of consumption for a one per cent change in prices. In mathematical terms the price elasticity can be expressed as follows:

$$e_p = \frac{d(\log q)}{d(\log p)} = \frac{p\,dg}{q\,dp} \qquad \text{E7(3)}$$

where e_p is the price elasticity, p is the price of the commodity and q the quantity consumed. It is possible to sub-divide the price elasticity into two components, the substitution effect and the income effect.

$$\frac{dq}{dp} = \left(\frac{dq}{dp}\right)^{*} - \left(\frac{dq}{dp}\right)^{**} \qquad \text{E7(4)}$$

* Utility constant ** Prices constant

Equation E7(4) is known as the Slutsky equation. The first term on the right hand side represents the substitution effect and the second the income effect. The 'substitution effect' measures the extent to which a change in the price of a commodity results in the substitution (negative or positive) of other commodities in the total budget. The 'income effect' measures the change in the level of consumption due to the change in real disposable income as a result of the price change. This relationship proved to be of crucial importance in explaining the crude oil trade during the two oil crises in 1973 and 1979. When the price of oil increased sharply in 1973, because oil was a necessity consumers were forced to spend more on oil and had less income left to buy other goods. This slump in demand for other goods triggered a deep recession in the OECD economies, which in turn produced a fall in the demand for oil. This is an extreme example of the 'income effect' of a change in the price of a commodity. In addition there was a substitution effect as consumers replaced high price oil with coal and gas whose prices had not changed. Oil fired central heating suddenly became much less desirable than it was previously (for a discussion of the substitution effect in industry, see the discussion in the next paragraph). As a result the crude oil trade fell sharply (see Figure 4.4 which shows how the oil trade declined).

Derived demand for a commodity

The next step in the raw materials trade model is to reproduce the relationship between the demand for raw materials in an industry, and demand for the products of that industry which are sold to the final consumer. Industrial users often have a choice in sourcing their raw materials, raising the possibility that manufacturers will substitute one raw material for another. Heavy industries such as steel production and motor manufacturing are major users of raw materials, as is the transport industry (for example ships' bunkers). These industries will be concerned with minimizing their costs and their demand for raw materials is derived from the underlying demand for the commodities the industry produces. The starting point is the cost function. For a given output level the cost function is:

$$C = P_1 X_1 + P_2 X_2 + b \qquad \text{E7(5)}$$

where C is the cost of production, P is the price of each commodity, X represents the quantities of factor inputs required at that price level and b is capital cost which is assumed to be fixed. Faced with a change in the price of raw material (P_1) and a fixed capital stock, the key issue for the industrialist will be 'is it cheaper to use less (X_1) and more of some other input (X_2)?' The answer to this question is provided by the 'Rate of Technical Substitution' (RTS) which represents the extent to which factor inputs can be substituted for each other. It can be defined:

$$RTS = -\frac{d\,X_2}{d\,X_1} \qquad \text{E7(6)}$$

We have already mentioned the example power stations which can use oil, coal or gas. In 1973 when the oil price increased sharply, most power stations used oil and were not equipped to burn other fuels, so the substitution effect (RTS) was small. By 1979 when the price of oil rose to over $30 per barrel most power stations had invested to allow other fuels like coal or gas to be burned. As a result the RTS was very high and oil consumption fell sharply. Thus the RTS shows how the manufacturers respond to a change in the relative price of their raw materials. The RTS relationship outlined above is subject to the influence of technical development and change, which may significantly influence the amount of primary energy required to achieve a given effect – for example as a result of an improvement in the fuel conversion rate in marine diesel engines.

7.7 Summary

In this chapter we have looked at sea trade from the viewpoint of the countries which trade. There are 100 countries that trade by sea, but some are much bigger than others. In 1991 the USA headed the list with 838 mt of imports and exports, while Cambodia, the smallest, reported trade of only 106,000 tons. When we looked for an explanation of the volume of a country's trade it was clear that the level of economic activity, measured by GNP, was by far the most important. Two other explanatory variables, the size (area) of the country, and its natural resources make a small contribution, explaining about a quarter of the variation in trade volume. This does not mean they are unimportant, but rather that their impact on trade cannot be reduced to a simple general rule. Population size, it seems, has no explanatory value whatsoever. In conclusion, we must expect sea trade to go hand in hand with economic growth, but modified by the availability of natural resources.

We then turned to trade theory for an explanation of why countries trade. The theory of Absolute Advantage shows that countries enjoy a higher living standard if they trade because it allows them to focus their scarce resources in the products which they are most efficient at producing. Trade increases efficiency and everyone is better off. Taking this explanation a step further, the theory of Comparative Advantage, shows that countries are better off with trade even if their competitors are more efficient at producing everything. All that is needed for trade to be beneficial is that they are relatively better at producing some goods than their competitors. Countries who fear that they will be reduced to poverty by foreign competition are wrong, though in a changing world adjusting to new competitors can be painful and expensive for some parts of the economy.

This leads on to the question: 'what determines the comparative advantage of a particular country?' There are several different explanations. The Heckscher–Ohlin theorem argues that if goods require different factor inputs and there are diminishing returns when factors are substituted for each other, the comparative advantage is determined by the distribution of factors of production. Thus countries specialize in the goods which make the best use of their most abundant resources. Differences in technology, tastes, transport costs and cyclical surpluses and shortages are other reasons why countries trade.

We should expect the trade of a country is likely to change over time. Starting from the proposition that GNP drives trade, we looked at the composition of GNP. The International Standard Industrial Classification (ISIC) splits it into nine categories, agriculture, manufacturing, services, etc. Some of these activities, especially manufacturing, make extensive use of sea transport, while others such as services do not. In practice we find that as a country grows, the structure of its economy changes. The early stages of growth tend to use large quantities of physical materials – infrastructure developments such as roads, railways, ports, stock of cars, ships and industrial plant. Consequently there is a rapid expansion of import trade, matched by a corresponding export trade in primary produce or simple manufactures to pay for the imports. Whilst the early stages favour the bulk shipping business, when the economy reaches maturity, the liner business gains from the almost unlimited potential for shipping components and finished goods between developed markets.

The Trade Development Cycle (TDC) summarizes this dynamic relationship between the sea trade and economic growth. Each country has its own unique TDC which depends on its factors of production as well as cultural and commercial considerations. At the earliest stages of development imports of manufactures are paid for by 'cash crop' exports. As industry expands, raw materials generate demand for sea transport. The imports of countries with few natural resources slow, but in countries which were initially resource rich, the depletion of domestic supplies may lead to growing imports of some commodities. Imports and exports of manufactures continue to grow as domestic import and export markets widen. Thus the TDC has different implications for the bulk and liner businesses.

Finally we discussed the implications for the analysis and forecasting of sea trade. The basic tool is supply/demand analysis, but we must be very careful to consider the role of price and substitution in this model, and to recognize the importance of timescale and the TDC. This model incorporates demand functions which recognize the impact of price changes on consumer demand and income (the Slutsky equation) and on the factor substitution by manufacturers.

TABLE 7.4 Seaborne trade of 100 countries, ranked by trade volume

		Sea trade 1990/91(*)			*Size 1991*		*Wealth 1991*		*Natural Resources Output 1991*					
Country	*Rank*	*Exp mt*	*Imp mt*	*Total*	*Area m HA*	*Pop. m*	*GNP US$ bn*	*kt Import /$ bn(1)*	*Cereals mt*	*Oil mt*	*Coal mt*	*Gas bcm*	*Iron ore mt*	*Total*
USA	1	390	449	838	937	253	5,611	80	280	427	904	510	57	2,178
Japan	2	90	725	815	38	124	3,362	216	13		8	0		21
Netherlands	3	92	281	373	4	15	291	967	1			69		70
Australia	4	319	33	352	771	17	300	110	19	27	220	22	118	405
U.K.	5	128	172	300	24	58	877	196	23	91	91	51	0	256
Italy	6	42	224	266	30	58	1,151	195	19		1	0		20
Saudi Ar.	7	214	46	261	215	15	109	427	4	420		32		457
S. Korea	8	52	208	260	10	43	283	737	8		15	0	0	23
France	9	58	187	245	55	57	1,199	156	60		13	0	7	81
Canada	10	161	67	228	998	27	511	131	54	94	66	105	36	355
Brazil	11	168	53	221	851	151	414	127	37	33	5	4	150	228
Singapore	12	90	116	206	0	3	40	2,913	0			0	0	0
Mexico	13	123	50	173	196	83	283	176	24	155	12	28	10	228
Spain	14	40	130	171	50	39	527	247	19		34	0	3	56
China	15	82	72	154	960	1150	370	196	395	140	1,063	15	191	1,803
Indonesia	16	113	35	148	190	181	116	300	51	77		52	0	179
Germany	17	45	102	147	36	80	1,574	65	39		346	15	0	400
Iran	18	113	17	130	165	58	97	172	14	162		26	4	206
Venezuela	19	101	18	119	91	20	53	336	2	129		22	20	173
Turkey	20	42	77	119	78	57	96	803	31		53	0	5	89
South Africa	21	83	32	114	122	39	91	349	11			0	27	38
Norway	22	87	19	106	32	4	106	177	1	93		27	2	124
Sweden	23	45	53	99	45	9	206	259	5			0	43	48
UAE	24	88	10	98	8	2	34	284	0	123		24	0	147
Belgium	25	29	67	96	3	10	197	340	2		1	0	0	3
Nigeria	26	81	11	91	92	99	34	317	13	94		4	0	111
Hong Kong	27	26	62	88	0	6	68	917	0			0	0	0
India	28	26	46	73	329	867	222	209	194	32	229	14	57	526
Algeria	29	58	14	72	238	26	33	437	4	56		53	2	115
Libya	30	55	8	63	176	5	28	271	0			6	0	7
Thailand	31	30	30	60	51	57	93	322	24			7	0	31
Finland	32	27	32	59	34	5	110	293	4			0	0	4
Greece	33	20	37	57	13	10	58	641	6		57	0	0	63
Kuwait	34	51	5	56	2	2	23	198	0	7		1	0	7
Malaysia	35	18	32	50	33	18	47	672	2	32		20	0	55
Denmark	36	16	32	49	4	5	112	290	9	7		4	0	20
Argentina	37	37	7	44	277	33	114	60	21	26		20	0	67
Philippines	38	17	25	41	30	63	45	549	14			0	0	14
Oman	39	34	2	36	21	2	10	243	0	36		3	0	39
Egypt	40	12	22	35	100	54	30	735	14	45		8	2	69
Morocco	41	20	12	33	45	26	28	450	9				0	9
Chile	42	21	11	32	76	13	31	350	3				8	11
Portugal	43	8	20	28	9	10	65	305	2				0	2
Colombia	44	22	6	28	114	33	42	147	4	22	21		1	47
Pakistan	45	5	20	25	80	116	40	488	21			12	0	33
Ireland	46	6	18	24	7	4	39	452	2				0	2
Cuba	47	8	15	24	11	11	16	942	1				0	1
N. Zealand	48	15	8	23	27	3	43	183	1		1		2	4
Angola	49	21	1	22	125	10	40	31	0	26			0	26
Syria	50	16	5	21	19	13	17	294	3	25			0	28
Israel	51	8	13	21	2	5	63	211	0				0	0
Qatar	52	18	3	21	1	0	7	351	0	21		8	0	28
Liberia	53	15	2	16	10	3	1	1,273	0				1	1
Jordan	54	10	7	16	9	4	4	1,872	0				0	0

TABLE 7.4 cont'd

		Sea trade 1990/91(*)			*Size 1991*		*Wealth 1991*		*Natural Resources Output 1991*					
Country	*Rank*	*Exp mt*	*Imp mt*	*Total*	*Area m HA*	*Pop. m*	*GNP US$ bn*	*kt import /$ bn (1)*	*Cereals mt*	*Oil mt*	*Coal mt*	*Gas bcm*	*Iron ore mt*	*Total*
Tunisia	55	6	10	16	16	8	12	839	3				0	3
Peru	56	10	5	15	129	22	48	105	2				4	5
Brunei	57	14	1	15	1	0	4	379	8			9	0	17
Cameroon	58	10	3	13	48	12	12	291	1	8			0	9
Jamaica	59	8	5	13	1	2	3	1,464	0				0	0
Gabon	60	13	0	13	27	1	5	44	0	15			0	15
Ecuador	61	10	3	13	28	11	12	221	1	16			0	17
Guinea	62	12	1	13	25	6	3	242	1				0	1
Trini. & Tob.	63	8	4	12	1	1	5	832	0	7		6	0	13
Sri Lanka	64	4	7	11	7	17	8	824	2				0	2
Mauritania	65	10	1	11	103	2	1	654	0				10	10
Cote d'Ivoire	66	5	5	10	32	12	7	710	1				0	1
Yemen, Rep.	67	2	8	10	53	13	8	1,041	0				0	0
Congo	68	9	1	10	34	2	3	253	1	8			0	9
Kenya	69	2	6	8	58	25	7	798	3				0	3
Bangladesh	70	1	6	7	14	111	23	263	28				0	28
Suriname	71	6	1	7	16	0	2	746	0				0	0
Domini. Rep.	72	3	4	7	5	7	7	583	1				0	1
Cyprus	73	2	4	6	1	1	6	788	0				0	0
Korea, PDR	74	1	6	6	12	22	0	0	0				0	
Mozambique	75	3	3	6	80	16	1	2,772	1				0	1
Senegal	76	3	3	5	20	8	6	491	1				0	1
Guatemala	77	3	2	5	11	10	9	195	1				0	1
Sudan	78	1	3	5	251	26	2	1,824	5				0	5
Ghana	79	2	3	5	24	15	6	443	1				0	1
Papua N. G.	80	2	2	4	46	4	4	478	0				0	0
Zaire	81	2	1	4	235	39	3	483	1				0	1
Panama	82	1	2	4	8	3	6	397	0				0	0
Costa Rica	83	2	2	3	5	3	6	340	0				0	0
Other W. Africa	84	1	2	3	106	12	6	386	1	0	0	0	0	1
Mauritius	85	1	1	2	0	1	2	641	0				0	0
Guyana	86	2	1	2	21	1	0	2,629	0				0	0
Sierra Leone	87	2	1	2	7	4	1	717	0				0	0
Honduras	88	1	1	2	11	5	3	377	1				0	1
Uruguay	89	1	1	2	18	3	9	153	1				0	1
Nicaragua	90	0	2	2	13	4	7	234	0				0	0
El Salvador	91	0	2	2	2	5	6	277	1				0	1
Vietnam	93	0	2	2	33	68		0	21				0	21
Madagascar	94	0	1	2	59	12	2	484	2				0	2
Somalia	95	0	1	1	64	9	2	694	0				0	0
Myanmar	96	1	1	1	68	43		0	14				0	14
Djibouti	97	0	1	1	2	1		0	0				0	0
Lebanon	98	0	1	1	1	3		0	0				0	0
Haiti	99	0	1	1	3	7	3	267	0				0	0
Cambodia	100	0	0	0	18	9	0	0	0				0	
TOTAL		3,664	3,871	7,535	9,593	4,705	19,619	197	1,564	2,459	3,138	1,174	763	9,098

Source: Compiled from various sources

Notes:

* as available

(1) Import intensity in kt imports per $ billion

Chapter 8

The global pattern of maritime trade

Such therefore are the advantages of water carriage, it is natural that the first improvements of art and industry should be made where this convenience opens the whole world for a market to the produce of every sort of labor

(Adam Smith 'Inquiry Into The Wealth of Nations' 1776)

8.1. Introduction

Shipping is first and foremost an international business, so we must be aware of how the different parts of the trading world fit together. When we delve into history it turns out that the pattern of trade, which to contemporary observers looks so firmly established, is in fact constantly changing. Today's economic geography is just a snapshot taken at a point in time as the world economy creeps along its evolutionary path. The pace is so slow that we can hardly see the motion but, viewed from a historical perspective, the progress is evident. Although economic textbooks sometimes give the impression that the evolution of trade has been one of harmonious economic development, it can equally well be seen as a continuous struggle of power politics for control of trade.[1]

Today's 'snapshot' features the 100 trading countries we discussed in Chapter 7. Our aim in this chapter is to take the analysis of trade a step further and build up the bigger picture of how these 100 trading countries fit together into the maritime trading world. We found that a country's pattern of sea trade depends on three variables, GNP, the stage of development and natural resources, and concluded that the character of trade changes as the country develops. This is the Trade Development Cycle. Just as the trade of a country changes as it grows, so does the pattern of world seaborne trade. Starting with a brief review of the history of sea trade, we discuss the current regional pattern of trade, taking the Atlantic, Pacific and Indian Oceans as the framework. We review the countries that lie on their shores, the goods that they trade and the trading routes between them.

In discussing the geography of sea trade we face a lack of detailed and accurate information. Although there is no shortage of international trade statistics, most report the value of trade and few pay much attention to where the cargo came from. A few tonnage statistics are published by the United Nations and specialist organizations, but there is no recent matrix of the distribution of trade. For this we must fall back on the United Nations 'Maritime Transport Study' which was discontinued in 1986. If some of the statistics look very out of date, that is the reason.

8.2 The Westline theory

When we examine the history of the trading world we find that over 5,000 years, whether by chance or some deeply hidden economic force, the commercial centre of shipping has followed a path westward, shown in Figure 8.1. This 'Westline' started in the Lebanon in 3000 BC, taking small steps west to Rhodes, Crete, the Greek mainland, Rome and Northern Italy. About a thousand years ago a bigger step brought NW Europe into the picture and in turn the Hanseatic towns, Antwerp/Amsterdam, London and East Coast North America became the leading centre of sea trade. Finally in the twentieth century a giant step took the centre of trade into the Pacific as Japan, South Korea, and China have picked up the baton of growth.

Each step along the Westline was accompanied by an economic struggle between adjacent states as the old centre declined and the new centre of growth emerged. In this sense

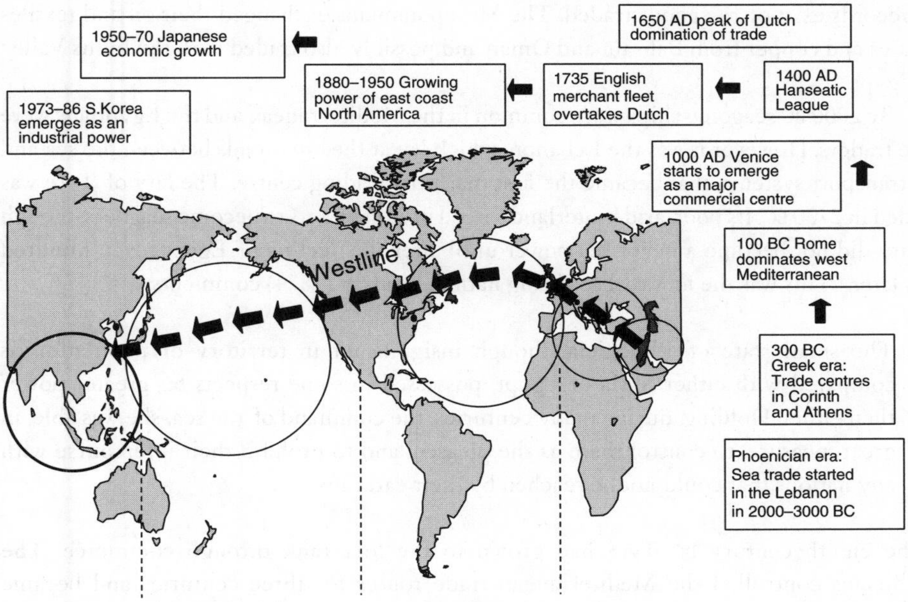

FIGURE 8.1 The Westline – 5,000 years of maritime trading centres
Source: Martin Stopford, 1997

the modern trading world is like the wake of a ship that has circumnavigated the world. The maritime tradition, political alignments, ports, and even the economic wealth of the different regions are the product of centuries of economic evolution in which merchant shipping has played a major part. In addition to offering a longer-term perspective on the world of maritime trade, this history offers a lesson is the long-term dynamics of the economic environment in which the shipping industry operates.

Mediterranean and Indian Ocean trade before 1000 AD

The earliest known illustration of a ship is a river craft drawn on the walls of an Egyptian tomb built in about 3100 BC[2] Over the next thousand years there is fragmentary evidence of developing coastal sea trade in the Arabian Gulf and the East Mediterranean. At that time there were three civilizations located in the valleys of the River Nile (Egypt), the Tigris and Euphrates rivers (Mesopotamia) and the Indus river (Harapa). Each river system probably had a population of about three quarters of a million, more than ten times as great as the population density in Northern Europe at that time.[3] These areas were linked by land, but sheltered coastal sea routes provided an environment in which maritime trade could develop.

Few records exist of the goods traded. The Mesopotamians exchanged their oil and textiles for dates and copper from Bahrain and Oman and possibly also traded with the Indus Valley and Egypt.

By 2000 BC seagoing ships were common in the Mediterranean and the Egyptians were active traders. However it was the Lebanon, which lay at the crossroads between the sea and land transport systems, that became the first maritime trading centre. The city of Tyre was founded in 2700 BC. Its poor, arid hinterland forced its inhabitants to become seagoers, though the city did not become a major sea power until after the decline of Egypt seven hundred years later.[4] This was the first real seafaring nation. Lindsay (1874) comments:

> The small state of Phoenicia, though insignificant in territory or population as compared with either Syria or Egypt, possessed in some respects far greater power than either. Holding, during many centuries, the command of the sea, she was able, in great measure, to control them as she pleased, and to prohibit their intercourse with any nations that could not be reached by their caravans.[5]

By the eighth century BC Tyre had grown to the first rank through commerce. The Phoenicians controlled the Mediterranean trade routes for three centuries and became shipbuilders and cross traders (carriers of other people's merchandise) to the world. They traded manufactures – glass, textiles, metal work – and produce – timber, wine and oil – for Egyptian linen, gold and ivory, Anatolian wool, Cypriot copper and Arabian resins.[6] Trade grew as urbanization and industry developed around the Mediterranean sea.

After the discovery of Spain and the settlement of Sades (Cadiz) about 1000 BC, the Iberian Peninsula emerged as the major source of metal for the 'developed' economies of the East Mediterranean, providing the silver, copper, and tin that guaranteed Phoenician, and in particular Tyrean, commercial domination in the Orient. On land, the domestication of camels made it possible to establish trade routes between the Mediterranean and the Arabian Gulf and Red Sea, linking with the sea trade between the Ganges and the Persian Gulf.

The rise of Greek shipping

When Tyre fell to the Assyrians in 666 BC, Phoenician domination of the Eastern Mediterranean came to an end and the centre of sea trade moved west. The growth of sizable towns in the middle of the Mediterranean at Carthage and Syracuse in North Africa, at Athens in Greece and at Memphis in Egypt meant that the East Mediterranean was ringed by major towns. As the Phoenician merchants declined, the more centrally placed Greeks with their market-based economy took their place as the leading maritime traders. As Athens expanded, the city had to import food to feed the population.[7] For the next thousand years to 400 AD, the East Mediterranean became an active trading area dominated by the four principal towns of Athens, Rhodes, Antioch and Alexandria. The latter two grew particularly strong thanks to their trading links to the East through the Red Sea and the Arabian Gulf.

The Greeks traded their wine, oil and manufactures (mostly pottery) for Carthaginian and Etruscan metals and the traditional products of Egypt and the East. Initially Corinth was the leading town, benefiting from its position on the Isthmus, but subsequently Athens became more prominent. Because the rapidly growing Greek city states were not self-sufficient, grain and fish were shipped in from the Black Sea where by 500 BC Greece had founded more than 100 colonies. Carthage held most of the West Mediterranean, including the coast of North Africa, Southern Spain, Corsica and Western Sicily. However this was not a developed area and there was little trade compared with the East Mediterranean.

Roman trade and the Pax Romana

As Rome grew in economic and political importance, the centre of trade moved to Italy. Rome imported minerals from Spain, wheat from North Africa and the Black Sea and manufactures from the East Mediterranean. Over the next 200 years the Roman Empire controlled the coast of the Mediterranean and Black Sea, and also that of Britain. Under the *Pax Romana* Mediterranean trade expanded, though the number of towns and trade routes were far greater in the east than in the west. The conurbations of the east imported minerals from the 'developing' countries of Spain and Britain, corn from North Africa, Egypt and the Black Sea, and manufactures from the still thriving commercial centres of the Lebanon and Egypt, where the eastern trade routes entered the Mediterranean.

Towards the end of the third century AD the Roman Empire started to disintegrate and split for administrative purposes into the Western Roman Empire and the Eastern Roman Empire. In modern day jargon the Eastern Roman Empire contained the economically 'developed' world while the Western Roman Empire consisted mainly of 'underdeveloped' territories. The Eastern Roman Empire with its new capital of Constantinople grew into the Byzantine Empire while the Western Roman Empire slowly declined. For the 500 years after the collapse of the Roman Empire the frontiers of trade contracted and by 700 AD sea trade centred on Constantinople with shipping routes to Rome, Venice and the Black Sea. The Islamic Empire controlled the whole of the southern coast of the Mediterranean and made very little use of sea transport, preferring to transport goods by camel trains.

Beginnings of North European sea trade

During the middle ages the economy of North Europe began to grow, based particularly upon the wool industry in England and the textile industry of Flanders. The Vikings had opened up the trade between the Baltic and North Europe, shipping out fish, wool, wine and corn. Cologne grew into a major town. As a result the 'developed' world now had two economic centres, one in the East Mediterranean, and the other in Northern Europe. In the absence of a sea route connecting the two, the shortest and cheapest route for cargo trade between these two centres was to ship cargo up to Venice or Genoa and carry it over the

Alps to be taken down river on the Rhine to North Europe. Venice had a head start in this trade due to its strength in the Byzantine trade, but Genoa was always a major rival.

The Venetian era

The Venetian Republic, a small city state positioned strategically at the crossroads of East–West trade, became the next maritime centre. During the 500 years to 1200 AD Venice emerged as the major trading, shipping and shipbuilding centre. It was helped by the economic decline of the Byzantine Empire. State legislation enforcing low interest rates for agricultural reasons discouraged the Byzantines from entering such a high risk business as long-distance trading. Carrying the overhead burden of the Empire, the Byzantine seafarers could not compete with the Venetians even on internal routes, and a Venetian network began to replace the native Byzantine one, an early example of 'flagging out'.[8] By accepting Byzantine suzerainty Venice was able to monopolize the east–west trade. In return for the shipping services they procured preferential tax rates, and in 1081 they extracted from the collapsing empire the right to trade anywhere within its boundaries without restriction or taxation of any kind. This is a development which will sound familiar to many western national flag shipowners.

Venetian sea power reached its peak in the twelfth century as North Italy became a trading 'hub'. The imports from North Europe were principally textiles, while North Italy exported high grade textiles, manufactures, and re-exported eastern produce, brought over land by camel train, to North Europe. However over the next century Venice gradually lost its 'hub' position. There were several reasons. One was the speed of growth in the West. By 1400 AD the towns of the 'Hanseatic League', an organization of North European towns, particularly, Lubeck and Hamburg which controlled the trade between North Europe and the Baltic had became very powerful. The other was the fall of Constantinople to the Ottomans in 1453. By closing the trade routes from the East, it removed Venice's jealously guarded monopoly on the trade with India.[9] More importantly the loss of the spice trade, and the potential profits from finding a new supply source, stimulated West European traders to venture into the hostile Atlantic to search for new routes to the spice islands. In doing so the centre of trade took another step west.

The voyages of discovery in the fifteenth and sixteenth centuries

The 'Voyages of Discovery' in the late fifteenth century, turned shipping into a global business. The new trading world incorporated the Mediterranean, the North Sea, the Baltic, the North Atlantic, the Indian Ocean and the Pacific. Spain and Portugal, who were already trading with Africa,[10] led the way. In 1487 the Portugese Bartholomew Diaz tried to reach the Spice Islands by sailing round the coast of Africa. He rounded the Cape of Good Hope but the storms were so severe that after making a landfall just beyond the Cape he turned back. Three years later Christopher Columbus set out to reach Japan by sailing West into the unexplored waters of the Atlantic. In three voyages 1492, 1493 and 1498 he crossed the Atlantic to discover the West Indies. Then in 1497 Vasco da Gama successfully rounded the Cape, arriving in Southern India ten months after he left Portugal. Finally, in 1520, Magellan rounded Cape Horn, establishing a route into the Pacific and demonstrating the possibility of round the world navigation. In 33 years Europe had discovered the world.

As a result of these voyages major new trading areas were opened up including Hudsons Bay and the Gulf in North America; the West Indies; South America; and the Spice Islands of the Far East, including India and China. The Cape route to the Spice Islands had the most immediate commercial value because it established a sea transport route to an area with which Europe already had a substantial trade. In addition the quality of Far East produce and spices shipped by sea was much better than by the traditional land route through the East Mediterranean. But the colonists in the New World needed manufactures and there was a steadily growing trade in produce to pay for them.

The rise of Dutch shipping

Situated at the heart of the new trading network, the Dutch sea ports of Antwerp and Amsterdam were ideally located to benefit from this trend. They were at the crossroads of Europe where the main inland waterway systems which carried much of the trade from North Italy met the incoming cargoes from East, West and the Baltic. It was the Dutch who took over from Venice as the merchants, bankers and shipping 'cross traders' of the newly emerging global trading system. Just as the Byzantine merchants had been priced out of the market by their high costs, so the North Italian merchants were pushed out by the costs of their goods and services and the loss of their strategic position.[11] By the middle of the sixteenth century Venetian ships had stopped sailing to the Netherlands and 50 years later the Mediterranean to North Europe trade was being serviced by English and Dutch vessels and more than half the Venetian fleet was built in Dutch shipyards.

Between 1520 and 1576 Antwerp was the *emporeum mercatorium*, the warehouse and market of world trade. In Antwerp the English merchant adventurers traded English cloth and wool; the south German bankers (Fuggers, Welsers, Paumgartners) traded cloth, spices and metals with Germany and Italy; great cargoes of Indian pepper, nutmeg, cinnamon and cloves were brought by agents of the kings of Portugal; Spanish merchant ships from Cadiz brought cargoes of wool, wine and silver, with backhaul cargoes of cloth, iron, coal and glass. Antwerp also became the centre of finance. The merchants evolved into capitalists, conscious of costs as well as profits, of turnover as well as mark up. The efficiency of this new society was apparent in its most essential aspect – shipping. Luigi Guicciardini counted 500 vessels moored before the roadstead in Antwerp.[12]

Antwerp's dominant position came to an end in 1585 when the city was sacked by Spanish troops and the Scheldt river, upon which Antwerp was located, was blocked by the Dutch. Many of the merchants fled to Amsterdam which rapidly took over as the leading maritime city. Between 1585 and 1620 it became the centre of a network of world trade stretching from Germany to India. To exploit the global trade network required access to risk capital. Large ships were needed for the long voyages; the resources to construct fortified trading posts; and the military strength to deal with local opposition either from natives or from competing traders. Individuals could not capitalize ventures on this scale, leading to the creation in 1602 of the Dutch East India Company. Previously merchants had often banded together for a voyage, but the capital in these new companies was permanent in the sense that a participant could only recoup his capital by selling his stockholdings. The Dutch East India Company was by far the largest with a capitalization of 6,500,000 florins, raised from the public in 3,000 florin shares. The area of the company's sphere of operation was 'westward into the Pacific from the Straits of Magellan to the Cape of Good Hope' in which it was to have total administrative and judicial authority.[13] The company was very successful and obtained a monopoly in the trade with Malaysia, Japan and China.

To carry the growing trade the Dutch developed the first ocean-going merchantman, the 'Flyboat', which was unarmed and cheap to build and operate. With the cheap freight rates provided by the flyboat, the Dutch captured the bulk trades in corn, timber, salt and sugar. Both the initial price and the operating costs of Dutch ships were a good third lower than anyone else.[14] Their biggest success was the Baltic grain trade which increased rapidly as the growing population of NW Europe created a demand for imports.

British shipping 1660–1940

During the 1600s the Industrial Revolution was starting in England and English merchants became serious competitors with the Dutch in seaborne trade. The west coast ports of Bristol, Whitehaven, Liverpool and Glasgow grew rich on the profits of the Atlantic trade in sugar, cotton, tobacco and slaves. Exports of textiles, ironware, nails and glass also grew rapidly. In the 1650s and 1660s the English parliament enacted a series of protectionist shipping laws (The Navigation Act) designed to exclude the Dutch from these profitable trades. The laws stated that no goods could be imported into England or any of the plantations of Great Britain except in British-built ships, owned by British subjects, and of which the master and three quarters of the crew were English.[15] They backed them up by building up their navy, shutting the Dutch merchants out.

This started the decline of the Dutch maritime supremacy and the rise of the English merchant marine, though Rogers (1898) argues that the Navigation Acts had little effect and the real reason for the decline of Dutch trade was that they became involved in European wars.[16] On the east coast the coal trade from Newcastle to London began to develop and the English merchant fleet grew rapidly. By the late seventeenth century English economic and naval strength shifted the centre of gravity of seaborne trade from Amsterdam to London and, by the 1870s, London lay at the centre of a maritime empire spanning the globe and controlling half of the world's deep sea shipping and three quarters of its shipbuilding.

East Coast North America was not far behind Europe in terms of economic development. Steel and heavy industry developed on the North East United States around Pittsburgh, Chicago, and Detroit on the Great Lakes and down to New York and Baltimore on the East Coast. Rapid population growth was supplemented by mass emigration from Western Europe and the East Coast became a mass market.

In the mid-nineteenth century railways and steel steamships reduced transport costs so much that geographical proximity to raw materials and markets was no longer a key issue in manufacturing economics. Raw materials and foodstuffs could be sourced world-wide and manufactures shipped almost anywhere at a cost which was rarely more than a few per cent of their value. Between 1840 and 1890 the grainlands of the United States were opened up, providing cheap grain for export to the industrial towns of the East coast USA and Western Europe. Thus by the late nineteenth century the North Atlantic was ringed by industry and had become the centre of seaborne trade, just as the East Mediterranean had done 2,000 years earlier. This phase reached its peak in the early decades of the twentieth century when high speed ocean liners linked the major ports of North Europe and North America, carrying passengers and cargo.

For most of the century prior to 1950 Western Europe dominated the international maritime scene. During this period Europe controlled most of the world's shipping, shipbuilding and liner conferences, a situation founded on the economic lead gained during the Industrial Revolution and reinforced by the extensive network of trade with the colonies acquired during the nineteenth century. The world maritime transport network that emerged was built around the colonial system – carrying outward cargoes of manufactures and returning with primary commodities.

Liberalization of shipping in the 1950s and 1960s

The decades after the Second World War saw a change in this established pattern of shipping and trade that had profound effects for the maritime industry. Many of the most important colonies were given independence, starting a process of devolution that undermined the secure economic and political framework within which the European shipping companies had previously operated. Five years after the end of the Second World War, with the exception of a few enclaves in Asia and the Caribbean area, only Africa south of the Sahara remained under foreign domination. By the late 1950s and early 1960s most of Africa had become independent. At a stroke this development shook up the established pattern of maritime trade, creating a new independent force in the shipping market, namely the developing countries, while forcing Western Europe into a different economic mould.

As the economic world moved away from the colonial pattern towards one where the developing countries were taking their place as equal partners, there was a realignment in trade.[17] Although the colonial system had disappeared, the trading links survived and Europe continued to obtain primary commodities from the developing countries and to supply manufactures such as steel, motor cars and capital equipment, though increasingly against competition from the more competitive exports of the rapidly expanding Asian economies.

At first these developments had little impact on Europe's dominant position in the shipping business. Released from their colonial empires, the West European economies embarked on a period of post-war reconstruction. Expansion of heavy industries such as steel and aluminium, combined with the substitution of imported oil for domestic coal, produced rapidly growing imports, particularly of bulk commodities. This growth persisted through the 1960s and the upward trend in imports was reinforced by the switch from domestic to imported sources for key raw materials such as iron ore, coal and oil. By the early 1970s the European economy was maturing and demand for raw material intensive goods such as steel, aluminium and electricity stabilized. As a result imports stagnated, following a cyclical path, but without the upward growth trend of previous decades.

US shipping in the twentieth century

North America, located across the busy North Atlantic, has played a more subtle part in maritime trade during the twentieth century. Much of the technology for bulk shipping, integrated cargo handling, containerization and the mass production of merchant ships originated in the USA. It was also the US which took the first step in developing international shipping regulations by calling the international maritime conference in 1889. US shipowners developed open registries in the 1930s, and it was the US which initiated tighter anti-pollution regulations in the 1990s.

In the early nineteenth century the USA held a strong position in shipping and shipbuilding, but the disruptions of the American Civil War coincided with the steel shipbuilding revolution in the 1860s. There was a rapid and largely unopposed expansion of European domination, and the USA's involvement in the international maritime scene gradually faded. By the early twentieth century the USA had only a small fleet trading overseas and depended heavily on the fleets of other nations to carry its foreign commerce. There was, however, a considerable fleet serving the domestic trades, sailing along the coastal and inland waterways, between the Pacific and Atlantic coasts, and between the mainland and distant territories and possessions.

The First World War brought home the dangers of relying heavily on the shipping services provided by cross traders. With the onset of the war foreign vessels were withdrawn and this had the dual effect of disrupting US trade and showing the nation's vulnerability, should it become involved in the war. As a result of this experience, in June 1920 the Merchant Marine Act, commonly known as the Jones Act, was introduced. This act had the aim of maintaining a merchant marine of the best-equipped and most suitable types of vessels sufficient to carry the greater portion of American commerce and, ultimately, to be owned and operated by citizens of the United States. The whole operation was controlled by the US Shipping Board, which was given wide regulatory powers. These included the number of liner services to be established, the type of vessels used, the frequency of sailings, and the activities of liner conferences.

During the First World War the United States had run a major shipbuilding programme, though most of the ships were not actually delivered until the war was over. Faced with the problem of disposing of the surplus ships, the Shipping Board offered them for sale to private owners; in so doing it became involved in a shipping subsidy programme that was to persist for much of the next 50 years. By the mid-1920s it had become apparent that, because operating and construction costs were so much higher in the US than in Europe, the aim of near self-sufficiency could not be achieved without extensive subsidy. To deal with this problem, the US Merchant Marine Act (1928) provided the Shipping Board with the means to offer loans for constructing new vessels.

This was followed eight years later by the famous Merchant Marine Act (1936), which aimed to compensate for the uncompetitiveness of US shipping through a system of direct public construction and operating subsidies. The Act made every effort to protect the jobs of American seamen by severely limiting the number of aliens who could be employed in US flag vessels and regulating the hours, conditions of work and the minimum wages of the crews. It also legislated the practice that all American exports financed in whole, or part, by any instrument of government should be carried in US flag vessels.[18] As a result of this programme, by 1939 the US fleet was, according to Lloyd's Register, the second largest in the world, with 13.9 per cent of the gross registered tonnage.[19]

The period after the Second World War saw a revival of American maritime activity.[20] For a few years the US merchant marine carried a large part of the world's commerce and a much larger share of US exports and imports than it had since the earliest years of the Republic. However, by the mid-1950s the European nations had rebuilt their merchant fleets, a process that the United States aided by selling abroad at bargain prices many of the vessels that had been built during the war. High American labour costs, the tax laws and the restrictive maritime legislation encouraged US owners to register their ships outside the US, making the US the first major maritime region to 'flag out' on a major scale (see chapter 12). Over the next 20 years the US registered fleet steadily contracted, falling to 13.6 m.dwt in 1995, less than 2 per cent of the world merchant fleet while the US owned foreign flag fleet was 36.6 m.dwt, giving the US a total fleet of 50.2 m.dwt, and a 7.5 per cent share of the world fleet.[21] This left the US a significant shipowner, but still a net importer of shipping services.

The Pacific trade 1945–75

As the twentieth century progressed the Atlantic trading economy started to mature and the centre of economic growth moved into the Pacific and Indian Oceans. Although the industrial growth of Japan started in the late nineteenth century, it was not until the 1950s and 1960s that the growing importance of Japanese maritime trade became evident. After 1946 the Japanese economy was reorganized and the 'Trading Houses' took over the traditional coordinating role of the Zaibatsu. Lead industries such as shipbuilding, motor vehicles, steel and shipping were selected for development and during the 1960s the Japanese economy embarked upon a programme of growth which made it the world's leading maritime nation. Between 1965 and 1972 Japan generated 80 per cent of the growth of the deep sea dry cargo trade.[22] By the early 1970s Japan had half the world shipbuilding industry and, taking account of open registry vessels, controlled the world's largest merchant shipping fleet.

During the 1970s the Japanese economy moved into a more mature phase and trade switched away from raw materials trade towards higher value added products. The next move west was across the Sea of Japan to South Korea which, during the late 1970s emerged as an aggressive new entrant to the maritime league table, making a bid for a major share of the world shipbuilding market, and emulating Japan in the rapid expansion of its heavy industries such as steel and motor vehicles. It is apparent that the process will not stop here. After two decades of total isolation and many centuries of restricted contact with the West, in the mid-1970s the Chinese economy started to 'open its doors' to capitalism. There followed a period of remarkable economic growth, coupled with a move towards a more westernized capitalist economic system. In the general cargo trades two trading centres were battling for regional supremacy, Hong Kong and Singapore and the countries clustering in the area between Singapore and Japan became the new commercial centre of Maritime trade.

8.3 Geographical distribution of seaborne trade

In the 1990s the volume of cargo traded by sea each year reached 4 bt, distributed around the world in the manner shown in Figure 8.2. The history of sea trade is very apparent in the geographical pattern shown in this map. The Atlantic, especially the North Atlantic, remains the largest trading area with over 50 per cent of trade (imports and exports), with the main cargo movements generated by the economies ringing the North Atlantic. However these are mature economies and the rate of growth is generally rather slow. The Pacific and Indian Oceans have a slightly smaller volume, accounting for 38 per cent of trade, but are growing very rapidly, with much of the trade clustered in the Singapore–Hong Kong–Japan triangle.

In Table 8.1 the trading world is subdivided into fourteen areas. Six in the Atlantic,

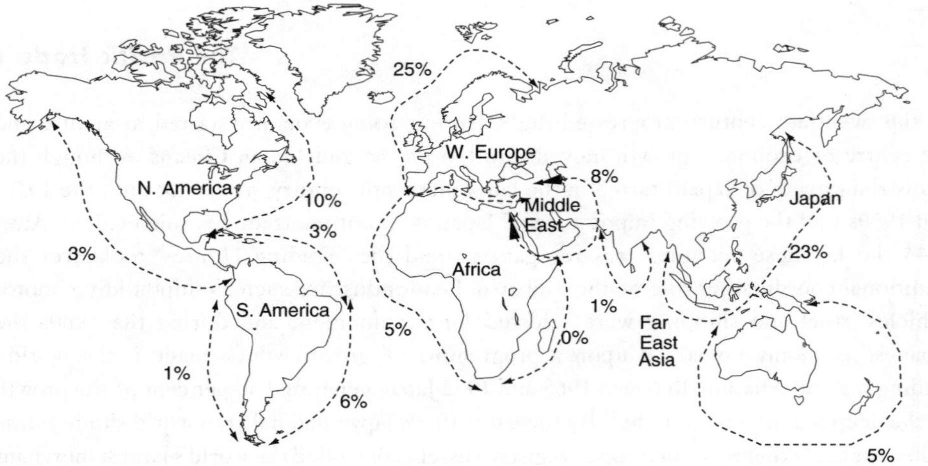

FIGURE 8.2 World seaborne trade by region 1991
Source: United Nations *Monthly Bulletin of Statistics*

seven in the Pacific and Indian Oceans and the fourteenth consisting of Russia and E. Europe. Unfortunately these regional trade statistics, which are produced annually by the United Nations, only show the total trade of the country. Several countries, notably USA and South Africa, have coastlines in two different oceans, so it is not possible to calculate the exact trade volume in each ocean. In Table 8.1 the Pacific trade of North America is included in the Atlantic, since this coastline accounts for the greater part of US trade.[23] South African trade is also included in the Atlantic region, so the totals overstate the Atlantic's importance by about 3–4 per cent, perhaps more.

TABLE 8.1 International seaborne imports and exports, by region

Region	*Exports*	*Imports*	*Total*	*%*
Trade of the Atlantic				
North America (inc. Pacific)	550.7	515.9	1,066.6	13%
Caribbean and Central America	158.5	89.4	247.9	3%
East Coast S. America	358.2	108.2	466.4	6%
Western Europe	624.9	1,337.7	1,962.6	25%
Mediterranean (excluding W. Europe)	319.5	256.6	576.1	7%
West Africa	288.2	78.6	366.8	5%
Total	2,300.0	2,386.4	4,686.4	59%
Trade of the Pacific and Indian Oceans				
Japan	89.8	725.1	814.9	10%
S.E. Asia	442.6	589.6	1,032.2	13%
South Asia	36.8	79.0	115.8	1%
Oceania	342.2	46.8	389.0	5%
Middle East	520.9	91.3	612.2	8%
East Africa	8.2	17.3	25.5	0%
West Coast S. America	41.5	18.6	60.1	1%
Total	1,482.0	1,567.7	3,049.7	38%
E. Europe and Russia	162.8	96.6	259.4	3%
Total Sea Trade	3,945	4,051	7,996	100%

Source: United Nations Monthly Bulletin of Statistics (1994)
Note: Trade data refer to 1990/91

The countries included in each region are defined in Table 8.3 for the Atlantic trading area and Table 8.4 for the Pacific and Indian Ocean trading area (see the end of this chapter). These tables show the trade of each country alongside the various economic statistics of size, economic activity and natural resources we discussed in Chapter 7. To supplement this cross section data the growth trend in the imports and exports of each region in shown in Figures 8.4 to 8.11. Although these statistics are also compiled by the United Nations, they are published as regional totals which do not exactly match Tables 8.3 and 8.4. This is not ideal, but it illustrates one point. Seaborne trade the statistics are often incomplete or inconsistent, so we must learn make the best of what is available.

8.4 Maritime trade of the Atlantic and East Pacific

Geography of the Atlantic maritime area (AMA)

For a century the Atlantic has been at the centre of world shipping, with major maritime economies spread around its rim, particularly in the North Atlantic. It is well suited to sea trade. The distance between the major industrial economies on either side is little more than 3,000 miles or about 10 days steaming for a merchant ship. W. Europe is still the largest trading region, accounting for 25 per cent of world seaborne trade, while North America accounts for 13 per cent of trade (including West coast trade). Together, these regions generate enormous trade in raw materials and manufactures. The four other Atlantic trading areas are much smaller. The ten non-European countries in the Mediterranean generate 7 per cent of world trade, the Caribbean and Central America 3 per cent, E. Coast South America 6 per cent, and West Africa 5 per cent. The trading pattern which has developed in the Atlantic consists of heavy traffic in both directions across the North Atlantic, with smaller North-South trades.

In terms of its physical geography the Atlantic is 'S' shaped and is narrow in relation to its length. Within the Atlantic region as a whole, there are 18 principal oceans, seas, and gulfs which make up the AMA, as shown in Box 8.1. The location of the larger seas and oceans is shown in the map in Figure 8.3, along with the more important ports.

BOX 8.1 Principal oceans and seas of the Atlantic maritime area

1 North Atlantic Ocean	10 Labrador Sea
2 South Atlantic Ocean	11 English Channel
3 Gulf of Mexico	12 Baltic Sea
4 Caribbean Sea	13 North Sea
5 Mediterranean Sea	14 Black Sea
6 Bering Sea	15 Great Lakes
7 Norwegian Sea	16 Hudson Bay
8 Greenland Sea	17 Gulf of St Lawrence
9 Baffin Sea	18 Arctic Ocean

The Atlantic is particularly good for shipping because the continents on its East and West coasts tend to slope towards it, so it receives a large proportion of the great rivers of the world. This is important for shipping and for the development of trade because these rivers provide cheap transport into the interior of the continents. In fact the total area of land draining into the Atlantic and Arctic Seas is nearly 17m square miles, almost four times the area draining into the Pacific Ocean and four times the area draining into the Indian Ocean. The ten Great Rivers of the Atlantic ocean are shown in Box 8.2.

FIGURE 8.3 The Atlantic maritime areas

Source: Martin Stopford, 1997

BOX 8.2 Major rivers of the Atlantic

River	*Importance to Shipping*
St Lawrence	Very Important
Mississippi	Very Important
Orinoco	Minor
Amazon	Minor
Rio de la Plata	Important
Congo	Minor
Niger	Minor
Loire	Moderate
Rhine	Very Important
Elb	Moderate

The St Lawrence, Mississippi, River Plate and Rhine, are major trading highways and act as interfaces with sea trade.

The Atlantic is linked to the Pacific and Indian oceans by four shipping routes. The two sea routes are the Drake Passage around Cape Horn, which connects the South Atlantic and the South Pacific Ocean and the Cape of Good Hope connecting the South Atlantic with the Indian Ocean. Both routes represent a considerable detour for ships trading between the major industrial economies of the North Atlantic and the economies of Asia. Two man made waterways, the Suez Canal connecting the Mediterranean Sea to the Red Sea and the Indian Ocean and the Panama Canal which links the Atlantic and the Pacific shorten the distance considerably.

The Suez Canal

The Suez Canal, opened in 1869, runs from Suez in Egypt to the Mediterranean. It is 100 miles long, linking the Red Sea at Suez with the Mediterranean at Port Said, via three natural lakes, Lake Menzala, Lake Timseh and the Bitter Lakes. Unlike the St Lawrence Seaway and the Panama Canal there are no locks. The canal reduces the transit distance from Kuwait to Rotterdam by 42 per cent, with similar savings in other Far East transits as shown in Table 8.2. A convoy system is used with two southbound convoys and one northbound each day. On entering at Port Said or Suez a ship is assessed for tonnage and cargo. During transit it is handled by three pilots, one for the approach roadstead and two for canal transit. Transit time generally takes 13–15 hours.

In 1980 the Suez Canal was deepened and widened to accommodate vessels with a maximum beam of 64 metres and draft of 16.2 metres, which in practice means up to 150,000 dwt fully loaded and 370,000 dwt in ballast. As far as the shipowner is concerned the economics of using the canal is a trade-off between operating costs, principally fuel costs and canal charges, and the cost of taking the longer route round the Cape. The toll structure of the Suez Canal is based on the Suez Canal Net Tonnage (SCNT) of the ship. Tariffs are calculated in terms of the US$/SCNT, with separate rates for laden and ballast voyages.

TABLE 8.2 Distances between selected ports (miles)

	By Cape	*By Canal*	*Saving per cent*
Rotterdam to:			
Bombay	10,800	6,300	42
Kuwait	11,300	6,500	42
Melbourne	12,200	11,000	10
Calcutta	11,700	7,900	32
Singapore	11,800	8,300	30
Marseilles to:			
Bombay	10,400	4,600	56
Melbourne	11,900	9,400	21
New York to:			
Bombay	11,800	8,200	31
Singapore	12,500	10,200	18
Ras Tanura	11,900	8,300	30

The SCNT of a vessel roughly corresponds to the cargo carrying below deck space, though it is not directly comparable with the gross or deadweight tonnage. It is calculated by either the classification society or by an official trade organization who issue a Suez Canal Special Tonnage Certificate.

The Panama Canal

The Panama Canal was opened in 1914. It shortened the distance from the Atlantic to Pacific by 7,000–9,000 miles (11,000–14,000 kilometres) and had as great an effect as Suez on world trade routes. The canal, which is about 83 kilometres long, is entered from the Atlantic at Cristobal and the Pacific at Balboa (see Figure 8.3) and has a series of locks, the maximum dimensions of which are as follows:

	Overall dimensions (metres)	*Maximum ship size (metres)*
Length	304.8	274.3
Beam	33.53	32.3
Depth	12.4	11.28

Although the nominal draft restriction is 11.28 metres (37 feet), the water level varies from 35 feet during droughts to 39 feet during wet spells. This means that a 65,000 dwt 'Panamax' beam bulk carrier with a 43 feet draft cannot transit the canal fully loaded – the average bulk carrier with a draft of 37 feet is 40,000 dwt. Bigger ships often load part cargoes.

Transiting the Panama Canal involves crossing a series of locks and lakes. Ships entering from the Atlantic terminal sail down a channel to Gatun Locks where the ship is lifted to Gatun Lake. After crossing this lake the ship enters Gaillard Cut and runs about 13 kilometres to Pedro Miguel where another lock lowers it to a small lake. Across this lake at Mira Flores are two locks which lower the vessel to sea level. It passes through a channel and enters the Pacific. Vessels are towed through the locks by electric locomotives assisted by ship's engines and rudder. A vessel of medium size can pass through the canal in about nine hours. The convoy system is not employed, but a transit booking system allows transit slots to be reserved.

The transit charges for the Panama Canal is based on a fixed tariff per net ton (PCNT) for vessels transiting laden and in ballast. Taking into account additional charges for winch operation and pilotage in 1996 the rate was $3.97 per ton loaded and $1.76 per PCNT in ballast.

In 1991 99.5 mt of cargo was transported through the canal to the Pacific, of which one-fifth was petroleum products, coal, and coke and one-third was grains. Of the 63.2 mt traversing the canal in the other direction, ores and lumber constituted about one-quarter of the total, with a great miscellany of commodities making up the other three-quarters. Asian bound traffic accounted for the greater part with Japan the predominant destination, whereas the second largest tonnage was carried from the west coast of South America to the east coast of the United States and the third largest amount was destined for Europe from South America.

Western Europe's seaborne trade

Western Europe remains the world's biggest trading region, accounting for 25 per cent of imports and exports, though this premier position is gradually being eroded. It generates a quarter of the Atlantic's export trade and more than half of its imports. In 1991 the Western European countries listed in Table 8.3 imported 1.3 bt of cargo and exported 624 mt. However the long-term trends in Figure 8.4 show that over the last 40 years export growth has been more consistent than imports which peaked out in the early 1970s and have grown little since then.

Europe's seaborne trade is carried on by thirteen countries, the largest importers being Netherlands (373 mt, though a sizable proportion of the Netherlands trade was in transit for West Germany), United Kingdom (299 mt), Italy (266 mt) and France (244 mt). Two others had seaborne imports of around 150 mt – West Germany (146 mt), and Spain (170 mt). The imports of the mature industrial economies of the EEC and Scandinavia fell during the 1970s. The decline of the United Kingdom from 200 mt of imports to 136 mt was particularly sharp, reflecting the development of North Sea oil. In contrast, the imports of the less developed countries within Europe, particularly Spain, Portugal, and Yugoslavia, showed some growth.

A mature, relatively high income, economy, Europe's resources are fully stretched, which explains the high import trade. Although Europe has a population of 353 million, a

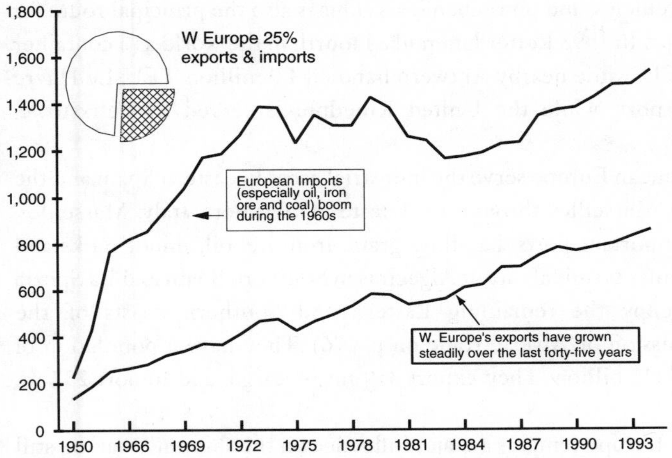

FIGURE 8.4 Western Europe's seaborne trade
Source: United Nations *Monthly Bulletin of Statistics*

third bigger than North America, and a similar GNP of $6.4 trillion as compared with 6.1 trillion, it has only 17 per cent the land mass (see Table 8.3). This explains its heavy import trade which is more than twice the size of North America's. The cereals crop is typically about 188 mt, compared with North American production of 334 mt. By intensive agriculture and the protectionist policies of the European Union the region manages self-sufficiency, with a small exportable surplus. Raw materials are a different story. Although Europe is well endowed with all the major raw materials except bauxite, reserves are now depleted and expensive to produce.

Europe is well served by rivers and ports. Narvik, the most northerly port, exports iron ore, while various ports in the Baltic handle the trade of Finland, Russia, the Baltic States, Poland, Northern Germany and Sweden. Forest products, oil, coal and general cargo are shipped through the ports of St Petersburg, Ventspils, Gdansk, Rostock, Swinoujscie, Stockholm and Malmo. Moving south, Hamburg and Bremen, located on the rivers Elbe and Weser serve Germany and its hinterland. These are important bulk ports, handling grain, fertilizers, steel and motor cars, but in recent years their real prominence has been in the container trade. In 1993 Hamburg handled 2.5 million TEU and Bremerhaven 1.35 million TEU, placing them among the ten most important container ports in the world.

Further south the river Rhine, Europe's most important inland waterway, enters the North Sea at the Port of Rotterdam. The Rhine, which is linked to various other rivers by canals, handles approximately 500 mt of cargo a year. Rotterdam is Europe's largest port and one of the busiest in the world. It is located on the New Rotterdam Waterway and the New Meuse which are open connections to the North Sea and the Rhine. The port is subdivided into three main areas, Maasvlakte, Europort and The Botlek. These areas are in turn subdivided into harbours, each containing deep water specialist terminals handling oil, grain, coal, forest products, motor vehicles, and petrochemicals. This is also the principal route for containers moving into Europe. In 1993 Rotterdam ranked fourth in the world as a container port, handling 4.2 million TEU, while nearby Antwerp handled 1.9 million TEU. Le Havre is France's main Northern port, while the United Kingdom is served by Felixstowe, Southampton and Tilbury.

The ports of Mediterranean Europe serve the industrial areas in eastern Spain and the industrial belt running from Marseilles through to Trieste in Northern Italy. Marseilles, Genoa and Trieste are all important ports, handling grain, iron ore, oil, minor bulks and containers. The biggest container terminals are at Algeciras in Southern Spain and La Spezia in Italy. Ten countries occupy the remaining Eastern and Southern coasts of the Mediterranean (see the discussion of African trade on p. 276). They have a population of 181 million and a GNP of $345 billion. They export 319 mt of cargo, and import 257 mt (see Table 8.3).

In conclusion, Western Europe remains a major influence on the shipping market, still generating the largest volume of seaborne trade. With the maturing of the economy the growth has moved from raw materials imports to a more balanced trade in manufactures and semi-manufactures.

North American trade

North America accounts for 13 per cent of world seaborne trade. It is the world's largest economic region with a population of 280 million and a GNP in excess of $6.1 trillion, one-third of the world's wealth (Table 8.3). With 1.9 billion hectares of arable land, it is six times the size of Western Europe. Cereals are grown in the centre of the continent and the Middle West is the world's largest continuous region of intensively farmed cropland. It is also rich in raw materials. In 1991 it produced 92 mt of steel, 334 mt of cereals, 521 mt of oil, 969 mt of coal, 535 billion cu metres of natural gas and 95 mt of iron ore. As one of the world's richest areas it has a tremendous appetite for manufactures. For many years the North American market was satisfied almost exclusively from domestic sources, but more recently key sectors such as motor vehicles and consumer durables have increasingly been supplied by trade.

North American trade has grown substantially in recent decades. Exports, which followed a fairly steady growth path from 232 mt in 1965 to 549 mt in 1993 (Figure 8.5), are very resource intensive. Dry bulk exports, which accounts for about 85 per cent of the total, include coal, grain, forest products, iron ore, sulphur and various minor ores. North America is the world's largest grain exporter and in 1991 it exported about 100 mt of cereals. Access to export markets is helped by the water transport system, particularly the Mississippi and the Great Lakes, while the West Coast is well located for access to the rapidly growing Asian market. North America's second largest export is coal, mainly from coalfields located in the Appalachians which run parallel to the east coast and from Canadian coalfields in the west.

North America's import trade grew from 100 mt in 1950 to 550 mt in 1991. This trade is dominated by crude oil and products which account for 65 per cent of imports, and

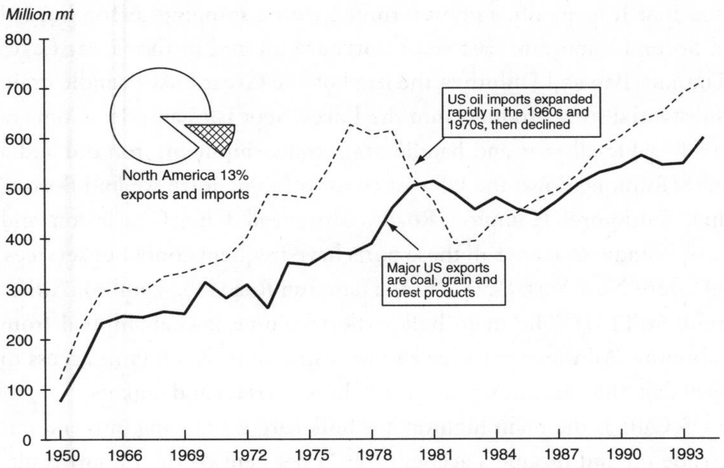

FIGURE 8.5 North America's seaborne trade
Source: United Nations *Monthly Bulletin of Statistics*

dry bulk which accounts for a further 28 per cent. Although the US is a major oil producer from oil fields located in the south, principally in Texas, domestic production is now declining and supplies are supplemented from imports. The trade in manufactures with Asia and Europe is also very important. Over the last 20 years North America has become the most important international market for motor vehicles and manufactured goods and in 1993 US and Canadian ports handled nineteen million containers, about 16 per cent of the world total.[24]

As a trading region, North America falls into three areas, a hilly east bordering the North Atlantic where much of the heavy industry is located, a flat central area given over to farming, particularly grain and a mountainous west which divides the Pacific coast from the rest of North America. The central area and east coast are served by two major waterways, the Great Lakes and the Mississippi–Missouri. In the north the St Lawrence Seaway, which stretches from Montreal to Lake Erie, gives access from the North Atlantic 2,340 miles (3,766 km) into the heartland of Canada and USA. In addition to providing an export route for grain, the lakes provide local transport for the heavy industrial belt of Pittsburgh, Chicago and Detroit. However the locks can only handle vessels of about 32,000 dwt[25] and the navigation season is limited by ice to the period April to early December, so much of the bulk cargo is trans-shipped at ports in the St Lawrence. The Mississippi and its tributaries give the central area, including most of the grain belt, water access to the US Gulf. The river system carries over 300 mt of cargo per annum. Two intracoastal waterways link the US Gulf with the east coast, extending from Boston, Massachusetts, to Key West, Florida, with many sections in tidal water or in open sea.[26]

This excellent water transport system makes the east and Gulf coasts of North America a very busy maritime area.[27] In the far north the port of Churchill lies on the remote south-western shore of Hudson Bay. It is mainly a grain terminal with a shipping season limited by ice to July–October. Several important east coast ports are located in the Great Lakes and the St Lawrence. Thunder Bay and Duluth at the head of the Great Lakes handle grain exports and there is a substantial steel products into the Lakes. Sept Isles and Bay Comeau in the St Lawrence are navigable all year and handle grain trans-shipment, iron ore and a wide range of other trades. Running down the US east coast from the north we find Boston, New York, Philadelphia, Baltimore, Hampton Roads, Morehead City, Charleston and Savannah. Since this is a busy industrial area all these ports have frequent container services. The three largest in 1993 were New York (1.97 TEU), Hampton Roads (0.87 million TEU) and Charleston (0.84 million TEU). The main bulk export volume is coal shipped from Hampton Roads and Baltimore. All these ports have draft restrictions which limit access to vessels of 60,000 to 80,000 dwt, thus excluding the largest bulk carriers and tankers.

To the south the US Gulf is the main highway for bulk cargoes moving into and out of the United States. Crude oil and products account for 76 per cent of the import trade, while over 80 per cent of the exports are dry bulk, particularly grain, oilseeds, animal feeds and coal. There is also an important refrigerated cargo trade into the Gulf. Cargo terminals along the Mississippi handle much of the export trade. There are eleven grain export elevators along the river as far inland as Baton Rouge. The US Gulf is also the largest oil importing area. For historical reasons the US refinery and distribution system centres on this area. Oil imports are brought into the Gulf, processed and distributed through the networks of rivers and pipelines. The LOOP terminal off New Orleans provides the only deep water oil terminal in the US capable of handling VLCCs. To the east of New Orleans lie Mobile and Tampa, Florida. Mobile handles coal and Tampa exports phosphate rock. To the west are Lake Charles, Beaumont, Port Arthur, Houston, Galveston and Corpus Christi all of which handle oil cargoes. Houston, the largest port, handles oil, grain, containers and chemicals. Water depth generally limits the size of tanker to below 150,000 dwt, but larger tankers carrying oil from the Middle East trade into this area by trans-shipping their cargo offshore.

The west coast of North America has a very different maritime character. It is divided from the rest of the continent by the Rocky Mountains. There are no major navigable rivers, so inland cargo mainly travels by rail or road. In the far north is Valdez, where the export terminal for Alaskan crude oil is located. Prince Rupert handles coal and grain. To the south lies Vancouver, located on the mainland opposite Vancouver island. This very large port handles Canadian raw material exports of coal, grain, forest products, potash and other minerals such as sulphur. There are major coal handling terminals at Robertsbank and Neptune Terminals and many smaller specialist terminals. Seattle, located 100 miles to the south, fulfils a similar function for the United States, with major exports of grain and forest products. It is also the largest container terminal in the area with shipments of over 1 million boxes in 1993. Tacoma, located a few miles to the south is not far behind, also lifting over 1 million TEU in 1993. Further south the ports of Portland, Oakland, San Francisco and Los Angeles (Long Beach) serve the west coast United States. There is some bulk cargo, with grain shipped out of Portland and oil into San Francisco and Los Angeles, but the main trade is container traffic. Oakland ships over 1 million TEU, but the biggest trade is through Los Angeles and Long Beach. Both ports handle over 2 million containers a year, placing them in the top ten container ports world-wide.

South America's seaborne trade

Moving down the coast to the south of the Atlantic we find a very different trading pattern. South America is still principally a primary producing area, generating about 500 mt of exports and 200 mt of imports each year, as shown by the graph in Figure 8.6. Over the last 40 years exports have followed a volatile path upwards, but since the early 1970s imports have hardly increased. For analytical purposes the area can usefully be divided into two parts, the Caribbean and Central America and East Coast South America.

The *Caribbean and Central America* covers the Caribbean islands and the coastline from Mexico in the north down to Panama, including the coastal states of Belize, Honduras, Nicaragua and Costa Rica. The economic data for the thirteen countries is listed in Table 8.3. Total population is 145 million, with a GNP of about $0.3 trillion, one twentieth the size of North America. Its area of 267 million hectares is spread among many islands and the coastal states ringing the southern shores of the Gulf of Mexico.[28]

Unfortunately several of these countries have two coastlines and the trade statistics do not distinguish between them. The trade volume is small with imports of 89 mt in 1991 and exports of 158 mt. Of the exports, almost 80 per cent is Mexican oil exported to the US Gulf and to a lesser extent Europe. The growth is explained by new oilfields developed in the 1970s and 1980s. The oil is shipped principally from the port of Coatzacoalcos

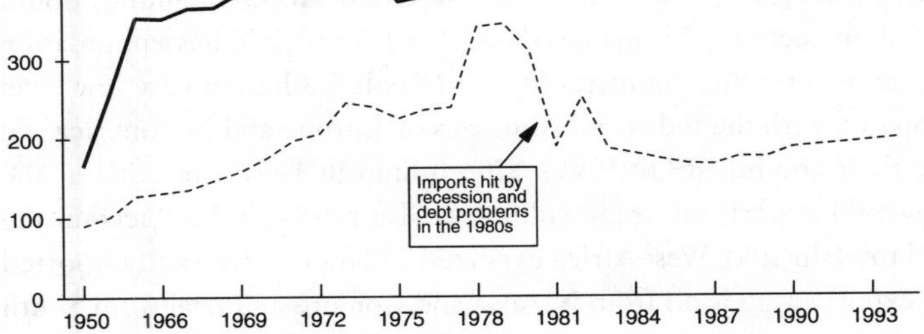

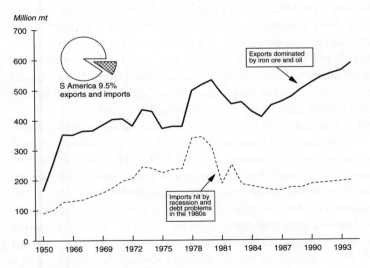

FIGURE 8.6 South America's seaborne trade
Source: United Nations *Monthly Bulletin of Statistics*

which is the focal point for the major seven oil fields of Mexico. Other Caribbean exports are bauxite from Jamaica, crude oil imported by refineries in Trinidad and Tobago and Netherlands Antilles for refining and on shipment to the United States, sugar from Cuba and bananas.

East Coast South America (ECSA) stretches along the Atlantic coast from Columbia, Venezuela, Guyana and Surinam in the north through Brazil to Argentina in the south. This region has an area of 1.8 billion hectares and a population of 240 million, making it similar in size to North America. It is, however, a much smaller economy. South America's GNP of $0.6 trillion is only 10 per cent of North America's. With so much space and so little economic activity, we would expect primary exports to predominate. This is exactly what has happened. The trade of this very long coastline is dominated by exports of raw materials and semi-manufactures.

In 1991 ECSA exported 358 mt of cargo and imported 108 mt. Dry cargo exports of 340 mt were made up of iron ore from Brazil and Venezuela, and smaller quantities of coal, crude fertilizers, forest products, minor ores and crude minerals such as salt. A declining trend in oil exports was largely offset by a moderate increase in dry cargo. Brazil is the world's premiere exporter of iron ore and during the 1960s and 1970s developed iron ore deposits served by deep water export terminals. Iron ore exports have grown from 7 mt in 1963 to 131 mt per annum in 1995, accounting for one-third of the iron ore trade. The main iron ore export ports are Tubarao, Ponta do Uba, Sepetiba Bay and Ponta da Maderia. The area is well served by liner services linking it to North America, Western Europe and Asia.

West African seaborne trade

Across the South Atlantic lies West Africa. African trade is smaller than might be expected from such a large continent. Forty countries are engaged in seaborne trade and in 1993 they imported 188 mt of cargo and exported 468 mt (see Figure 8.7), split between North Africa (60 per cent), West Africa (34 per cent) and East Africa (5 per cent). Primary commodities dominate exports and three-quarters of the export cargo is oil from Algeria, Libya, Nigeria and Cameroon. Dry cargo exports are composed principally of iron ore (Mauritania), phosphate rock (Morocco), bauxite (Guinea) and various agricultural products.

West Africa stretches from Tangiers to the Cape of Good Hope, including South Africa. The area covers 1 billion hectares, three times the size of Europe, and has a population 289 million. However the sixteen trading countries listed in Table 8.3 have a very low level of economic activity compared with the industrial countries of Europe and N. America. To put this into perspective, their combined GNP was $206 billion in 1991, the same as the GNP of Sweden. As we would expect, the trade volume is also relatively low, accounting for 5 per cent of the world total. In 1991 West Africa exported 288 mt of cargo and imported 78 mt. Two-thirds of the export cargo is oil from Nigeria and iron ore and coal from South Africa. The remainder is dry cargo exports, mainly iron ore (Mauritania), phosphate rock (Morocco), bauxite (Guinea) and various agricultural products. Since 1980 the import trade has stagnated, though there has been substantial growth of exports, as shown in Figure 8.7.

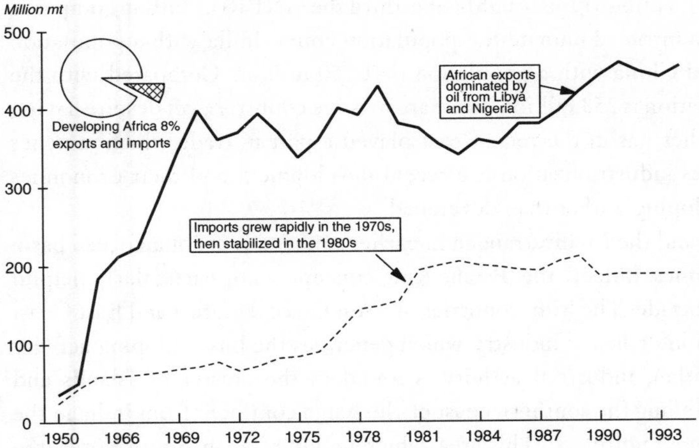

FIGURE 8.7 Developing Africa's seaborne trade
Source: United Nations *Monthly Bulletin of Statistics*

8.5 Maritime trade of the Pacific and Indian Oceans

Geography of the Pacific and Indian Oceans

The Pacific and Indian Oceans have a very different maritime character from the Atlantic. One difference is size. The Pacific Ocean occupies about one-third of the globe. It is twice the size of the Atlantic and the distances are much greater. The South China Sea, which lies at the western end of the Pacific Ocean, is over 10,000 miles, or 33.6 days steaming at 13 knots from the west coast of South America. Although there are many small islands in the Pacific, none supports sufficient population or economic infrastructure to generate significant trade.

The Indian Ocean, which merges into the Pacific, is half its size, with an area of 28.4 million square miles, compared with the Pacific's 64 million. It is bounded by India, Pakistan and Iran to the north; Africa to the west; Antarctica to the south, and the Pacific in the east. This eastern boundary with the Pacific is generally drawn through Malaya, Indonesia, Australia and the South East Cape of Tasmania to Antarctica. The six seas of the Indian Ocean, which have a long history of seaborne trade, are the Red Sea, the Arabian Gulf, the Arabian Sea (between Arabia and India); the Bay of Bengal (between India and the Thai peninsula); the Timor Sea; and the Arafura Sea (between Australia and Indonesia).

As a framework for discussing the maritime trade of the Pacific and Indian Oceans we will use the trade statistics in Table 8.4. In 1991 forty eight countries imported 1,568 mt and exported 1,482 mt. A map showing the countries and ports is contained in Figure 8.8. The countries of the Pacific and Indian Ocean which trade by sea have a smaller area than the countries of the Atlantic (4.4 billion ha compared with 6 billion ha), twice the population

(3.2 billion compared with 1.5 billion) and roughly one-third the GNP ($5.5 billion compared with $14.1 billion). Two countries dominate the population count, India with a population in 1990 of 867 million and China with a population of 1,150 million. Compared with the United States whose population is 253 million, these are massive countries, yet despite having very old civilizations, neither has in the recent past played a part in trade which matches their size. In both countries industrialization is a recent development and their economies tend to be classed as 'developing' rather than developed.

Unlike the Atlantic (and the Mediterranean in earlier times) this is not an ocean basin ringed by maritime economies. Indeed, the 'Pacific Rim' concept is not particularly helpful in a discussion of seaborne trade. The 'rim' countries of West Coast America and East Coast Africa lack the concentration of heavy industry which generates the busy shipping activity in the North Atlantic. Rather, industrial activity is found in the cluster of islands and seaboards spread in a band along the southern coast of the Asian continent from India in the east, to Japan in the west (see Figure 8.8). This area, which includes Japan, South Korea, the Chinese coastal states, Hong Kong, Indonesia, Malaysia, Taiwan, the Philippines, Singapore and India, has in the last 20 years generated seaborne inflows of energy, food and raw materials, matched by outflows of manufactured goods such as steel, vehicles, cement and general cargo. It has no geographical name, but for convenience we will refer to it as *Maritime Asia.*

Maritime Asia, which is now the world's third major seaborne trading area, comparable in scale with Western Europe and North America, falls into the three areas defined in Table 8.4. The economic centre is *Japan*, still the world's greatest concentration of maritime activity. To the west lie the economies of *S.E. Asia* including South Korea, Taiwan, mainland China, Malaysia, Singapore, Brunei, Indonesia, Philippines, Thailand, Kampuchea and South Vietnam, and *South Asia* which includes India, Pakistan and related economies. This diverse group of countries has a GNP of $4.7 trillion, representing 80 per cent of the economic activity in the Pacific–Indian Ocean area. Although this falls short of the output of Europe and America, it is growing more rapidly. S. E. Asia's cereals harvest of 543 mt in 1991 was roughly the same as USA and Europe combined.

Maritime trade matches up to expectations for an economy of this size. In 1991 the region imported 1,394 mt of cargo and exported 570 mt, much the same as Western Europe which imported 1,338 mt and exported 625 mt. It imports energy, food and raw materials, with corresponding outflows of manufactured goods such as steel, vehicles, cement and general cargo. South Korea, China, Hong Kong and Indonesia are all major importers. Containers flow in and out of the region along the trans-Pacific and Europe–Far East arterial routes, many distributed from Hong Kong and Singapore.

Japan's seaborne trade

Japan is the economic hub of maritime Asia. Its trade of 800 mt in the early 1990s (Figure 8.9) makes it the world's biggest seaborne importer. Supporting this trade is an extensive industrial base. In 1991 Japan produced 110 mt of steel compared with 136 mt in Western

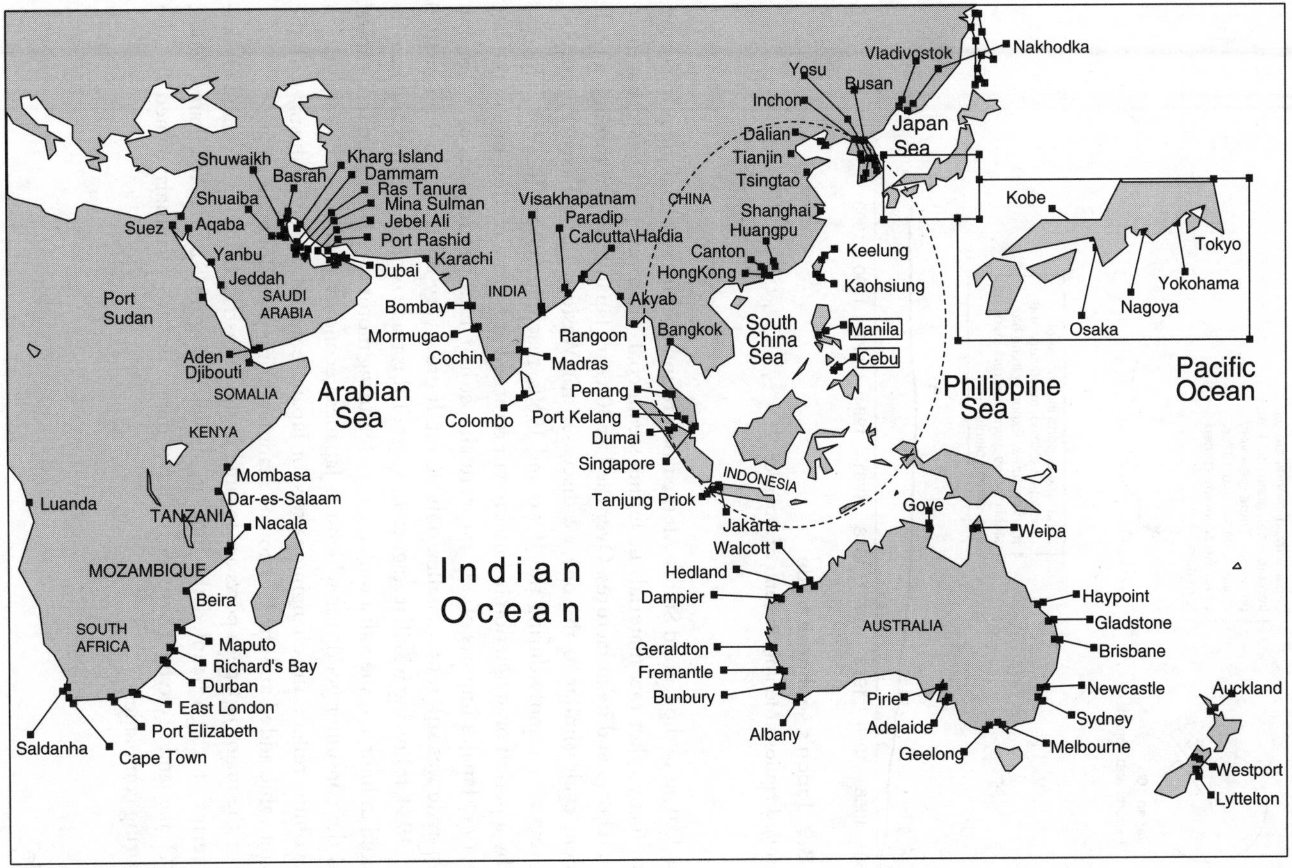

FIGURE 8.8 The Indian Ocean and South China Sea

Source: Martin Stopford, 1997

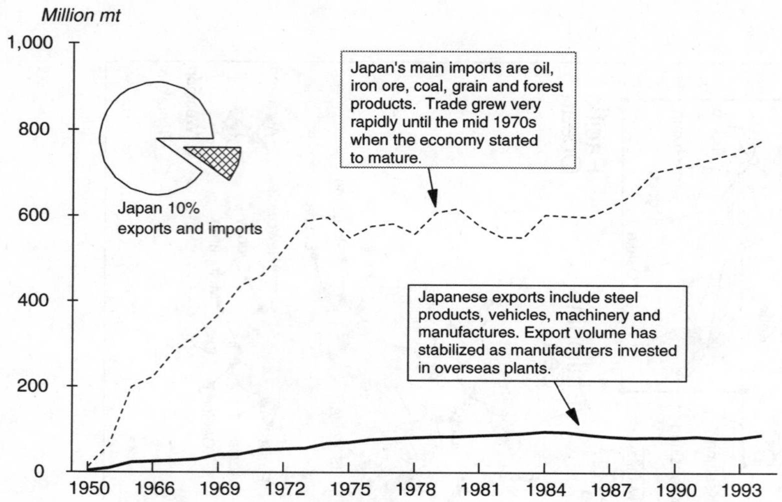
Million mt
1,000
800
600
400
200
0
Japan 10%
exports and imports
Japan's main imports are oil, iron ore, coal, grain and forest products. Trade grew very rapidly until the mid 1970s when the economy started to mature.
Japanese exports include steel products, vehicles, machinery and manufactures. Export volume has stabilized as manufacutrers invested in overseas plants.
1950
1966
1969
1972
1975
1978
1981
1984
1987
1990
1993

FIGURE 8.9 Japan's seaborne trade
Source: United Nations *Monthly Bulletin of Statistics*

Europe and 80 mt in the United States. All the iron ore and coal for steelmaking is imported, along with many other raw materials including steam coal, oil, forest products, grain, non-ferrous metal ores and manufactures. Over the last 30 years Japan has been through a trade development cycle similar to the one we discussed for Western Europe (see Figure 8.4). Imports grew very rapidly during the 1950s and 1960s, reaching 600 mt in 1971. This was followed by a period of stagnation before growth returned at a more modest rate in the late 1980s. By 1991 Japan's imports of 725 mt were almost half Europe's imports of 1.3 bt, but the export trade was still much smaller, only 90 mt. It grew very rapidly from 4 mt in 1950 to 95 mt in 1984, following which it stagnated. Most of this trade is manufactures and heavily concentrated in liner and specialist bulk cargoes, featuring motor cars, steel products, capital goods and the consumer goods for which the Japanese economy is famous. The stagnation of export volume reflects the changing pattern of Japanese manufacturing industry with the emphasis on value added and the location of manufacturing plants outside Japan.

All of the major Japanese ports are located in the industrial belt of Tokyo and Osaka-Kobe. In terms of cargo handled the biggest, shown in Figure 8.8, are Yokahama, Kobe, Nagoya, Osaka and Tokyo. These ports have many private terminals owned by the manufacturing companies.

S.E. Asia's trade

S.E. Asia handled 443 mt of exports and 590 mt of imports in 1991, roughly the same volume as Japan. This is a classic example of a maritime trading region. The trade is generated by thirteen countries (see Table 8.4) circling a 4,000 kilometres long basin stretching from South Korea in the north west to Singapore in the south east. South Korea and Japan form the boundary at one end, Singapore and Thailand the other, while Mainland Asia skirts one long side and the islands of Indonesia, Malaysia and the Philippines skirt the other. It is hard to imagine an arrangement better suited to seaborne trade. The trading countries spread around the shores of the South and East China Seas have large, often well educated, populations, but limited natural resources. Sea transport provides the coastal cities with easy access to materials and markets, without the need for major investment in transport infrastructure. The position which Singapore and Hong Kong have built up as trading and distribution centres echoes the success of the 'city states' of Antwerp and Amsterdam in the growing North Atlantic trade and Venice and Genoa in the Mediterranean.

The speed with which the trade of S.E. Asia has grown is clearly shown in Figure 8.10. Import and export volumes are closely balanced and have quadrupled during the last 20 years. This is clearly a region in the early stages of the trade development cycle, a fact which becomes more apparent when we review the individual economies. At the north-easterly end of the trading area lies South Korea, with trade of 260 mt in 1991. South Korea followed a path of development in the 1970s and 1980s which closely matched the growth of Japan twenty years earlier. Like Japan, South Korea focused on steel, shipbuilding, motor vehicles, electronics and consumer durables, relying on aggressive export marketing of these manufactures to pay for imported raw materials and energy. Also like Japan, development was controlled by a few very large corporations, with close government involvement. Although the economy is at a material intensive phase in its development and trade is growing very rapidly, South Korea is a much smaller country than Japan with only a quarter the area, half the population and one-tenth the GNP. Imports increased from 19 mt in 1970 to 208 mt in 1991, with exports of 52 mt, making Korea an important trading economy. South Korea's major ports are Busan, which ranks fifth in the world as a container terminal with 3

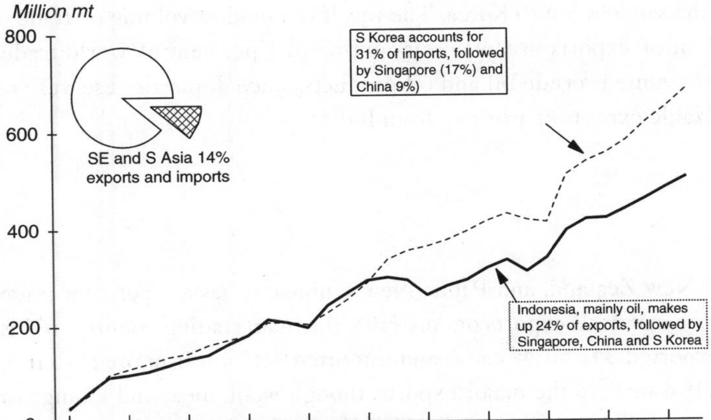

FIGURE 8.10 Other Asian seaborne trade

Source: United Nations *Monthly Bulletin of Statistics*

million lifts in 1993, Pohang where the cargo terminal of the Pohang Steelworks (POSCO) is located and Ulsan.

To the south east along the coast of the Asian continent lie North Korea, mainland China, Hong Kong, Vietnam, Thailand and, at the southerly tip, Singapore. By the mid-1990s mainland China had emerged as a major trading area, though the industrial activity remains heavily concentrated in the coastal strip, particularly around Shanghai and Canton. The major ports are Dalian and also Shanghai, which is located at the mouth of the Yangtze River. In addition to bulk cargoes Shanghai has China's main container terminal with over 1 million lifts a year. Hong Kong, essentially a trading city, lies in the heart of the maritime area. Despite its area of only 104,000 hectares it generates 26 mt of exports and 62 mt of imports. Vietnam is only just moving into the development cycle, but Thailand has a small but rapidly growing economy which generated about 60 mt of cargo in 1991. Singapore is principally a trading and distribution centre, serving the whole area. Its role in the container business is particularly prominent, in 1993 ranking alongside Hong Kong at the top of the world league table with 9 million lifts.

Strung along the south western boundary are Indonesia, Malaysia, the Philippines and Taiwan. These are all small but growing economies. There is a major crude oil export trade from Indonesia. Dry cargo exports include substantial quantities of forest products from Indonesia and the Philippines, and various manufactures and semi-manufactures.

Southern Asia

Moving east we find S. Asia Pakistan, India, Burma and various other small countries. These countries have an area of 0.5 billion hectares and a population of 1.1 billion. They produce 254 mt of cereals, much the same as the US as well as 229 mt of coal and 57 mt of iron ore. However, most of these commodities never enter trade and the GNP of $297 billion in 1991 was relatively low, about the same as South Korea. The result is a modest volume of trade – 79 mt of imports and 37 mt of exports in 1991 – amounting to 1 per cent of world trade. About half of the import volume is crude oil and oil products, since domestic reserves are very limited. There are sizable exports of iron ore from India.

Oceania

Oceania covers Australia, New Zealand, and Papua New Guinea. It has a 5 per cent trade share, due mainly to the raw materials exports of Australia, the main trading country in this group. In 1991 Oceania exported 342 mt of cargo and imported 46.7 mt. Iron ore (116 mt), coal (110 mt), and grain (10.6 mt) are the major exports, though wool, meat and a range of other primary commodities are also traded. Australia, New Zealand and the smaller countries of Oceania are rich in natural resources and it was here that Western Europe and Japan found many of the raw materials to fuel their industrial expansion in the 1960s. The bulk of the exports are to Western Europe, Japan and South Korea.

Middle East

The Middle East has a population of 113 million, more than half of which is in Iran, and a very large proportion of the world's crude oil reserves. It is the largest oil exporting area, with total exports of 520 mt in 1991 and imports totaling 91 mt, an 8 per cent trade share, mainly due to oil exports. Table 8.4 summarizes the imports and exports by the nine main countries, while Figure 8.11 shows the development of imports and exports over the last 45 years. Exports of oil grew rapidly to reach 1 bt a year in 1973. Following the 'oil crisis' in that year imports halved to a trough of 440 mt in 1985. The fall in oil prices in 1986 stimulated a recovery in export volume, though exports have still not returned to their previous peak. In contrast, the import trend has been upwards, stimulated by the sharp rise in oil revenues after the price increases in 1973 and 1979. During the decades 1973 to 1993 imports quadrupled from 44 mt to 180 mt.

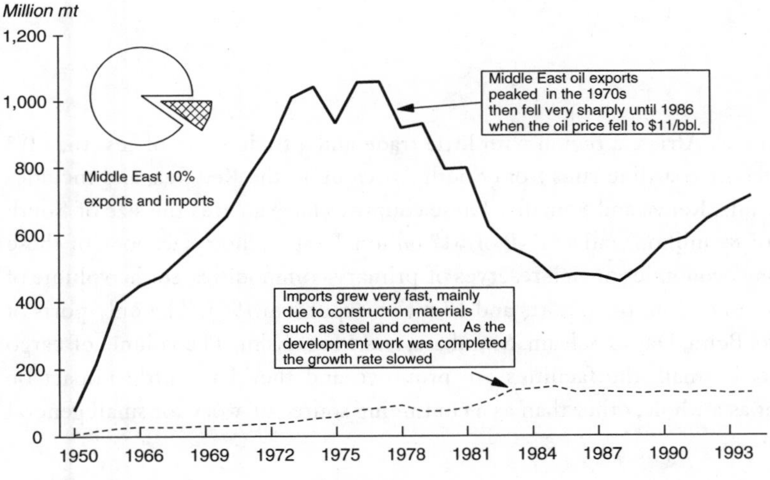

FIGURE 8.11 Middle East seaborne trade
Source: United Nations *Monthly Bulletin of Statistics*

West Coast South America

This area comprises the Pacific South America states of Chile, Bolivia, Peru, Ecuador, Mexico, Guatemala, Honduras, Nicaragua, Costa Rica, Panama and El Salvador. Unfortunately several of these countries have two coastlines and the trade statistics do not distinguish between the two. These countries have small economies and few natural resources, at least compared with the countries on the west coast of the continent. In 1991 seaborne imports were only 18.6 mt and exports were 41.5 mt.

West Coast North America

The Pacific coast of Canada and the United States, which have already been mentioned in the discussion of North American trade in the previous section, forms a modest trading region, accounting for about 3 per cent of world seaborne trade. Ports on this coast serve as an outlet for the primary products of North America, principally forest products, grain, coal from Canadian mines and minerals such as sulphur from Alberta through the terminal complex at Vancouver. There are also the major US ports of Seattle, Portland, Oakland, San Francisco and Los Angeles. These ports are shown in Figure 8.3 and the trade in Table 8.3 under the heading of North America. Container traffic now forms one of the most important forms of trade on this coast. In addition to containers shipped to local destinations, the west coast ports now handle a large proportion of the container traffic from Asia to the east coast USA. Containers are shipped to west coast ports such as Portland and Oakland and carried, usually double stacked, by rail to their final destination in the east. This is significantly faster than the 'all water' service via the Panama canal.

East Africa

Finally we come to East Africa, a region with little trade and a trade share of less than 0.5 per cent. This stretch of coastline runs from South Africa up to the Red Sea, and includes Mozambique, Tanzania, Kenya and Somalia. These countries have an area the size of South Asia, a population of 89 million, and a GNP of $17 billion. Despite their size, none of these countries have strong economies or rich reserves of primary commodities, so the volume of trade is very small – only 8 mt of imports and 17 mt of exports in 1991. The only ports of any size are Maputo, Beira, Dar es Salaam, Mombasa, and Mogadishu. The volume of cargo through these ports is small, the facilities are primitive and they have little impact on the shipping market as a whole, other than as a continuing source of work for small general cargo ships.

8.6 Eastern Europe and the former Soviet Union

The East European bloc, comprising the former USSR, and the countries of Eastern Europe generate only about 3 per cent of seaborne trade. Although the East European merchant marine has had an important impact in the liner trades, in terms of trade volume, the region still does not rank as a major maritime power, despite its geographical and economic size. That lies in the future, perhaps the next step in the Westline.

8.7 Summary

In this chapter we have built up an economic and geographical picture of the seaborne trading world. We started with the 'Westline Theory', the idea that the centre of maritime trade appeared in the East Mediterranean in 3000 BC and has moved steadily west ever since. Starting in Tyre, it moved through Greece, Rome, North Italy, Antwerp, Amsterdam, the North Atlantic and then jumped to Japan and S.E. Asia. The history of growth and competition as each new area developed has many similarities with the trade development cycle discussed in Chapter 7, though on a much bigger scale.

We then studied the geographical structure of the trading world today. The major division is between the Atlantic and the Pacific/Indian Ocean trading areas. The Atlantic remains the bigger of the two in terms of trade volume, with imports of 2.4 bt and exports of 2.3 bt. Much of the trade is generated by the mature economies ringing the North Atlantic which are exceptionally well served by rivers and ports. The Pacific and Indian Ocean area imports 1.6 bt and exports 1.5 bt. Distances in the Pacific are very large and much of the activity is clustered in the area between Singapore and Japan. This region, which covers an area about the size of the Mediterranean, has become the new centre of maritime trade.

Drawing all this together, the trading world consists of three great economic blocks strung out along the path of the Westline. Western Europe with trade (imports and exports) of 2 bt, North America with trade of 1 bt, and S.E. Asia and Japan with trade of 1.8 bt. Together these areas are responsible for about two-thirds of sea trade and arterial shipping routes run between them. That is the position today, but if there is one lesson to be learnt from this chapter, it is that trade never stands still.

TABLE 8.3 Seaborne trade and economic infrastructure of the Atlantic and maritime area 1991

	Sea trade		*Size*		*Economic activity*			*Natural resources (annual output)*				
Country	*Exp*	*Imp*	*Area*	*Pop.*	*GNP*	*GNP/Cap*	*Steel*	*Cereals*	*Oil*	*Coal*	*Gas*	*Iron ore*
	mt	*mt*	*m ha*	*million*	*US$ bn*	*US$*	*mt*	*mt*	*mt*	*mt*	*bcm*	*mt*
North America												
Canada	161	67	998	27	511	18,712	13	54	94	66	105	36
USA	390	449	937	253	5,611	22,203	80	280	427	904	510	57
Total	551	516	1935	280	6,122	21,863	93	334	521	970	615	93
Caribbean & Central America												
Haiti	0	1	3	7	3	400						
Cuba	8	15	11	11	16	1,533						
Jamaica	8	5	1	2	3	1,457						
Trinidad & Tobago	8	4	1	1	5	3,785			7		6	
Dominican Rep.	3	4	5	7	7	996		1				
Honduras	1		11	5	3	502		1				
Nicaragua	0	2	13	4	7	1,829		0				
Costa Rica	2	2	5	3	6	1,794		0				
Panama	1	2	8	3	6	2,218		0				
Puerto Rico			1	4	32	9,019		0				
Guatemala	3	2	11	10	9	985		1				
Mexico	123	50	196	83	283	3,392	8	24	155	12	28	10
El Salvador	0	2	2	5	6	1,116		1				
Total	159	89	267	145	386	2,667	9	29	162	12	34	10
E. Coast S. America								0				
Brazil	168	53	851	151	414	2,735	23	37	33	5	4	150
Venezuela	101	18	91	20	53	2,699	3	2	129		7	20
Argentina	37	7	277	33	114	3,497	3	21	26		20	
Colombia	22	6	114	33	42	1,271	1	4	22	21	4	1
Uruguay	1	1	18	3	9	3,058	0	1			0	
Suriname	6	1	16	0	1	4,901	0	0				
Guyana	2	1	21	1	0	338	0	0				
Other L.America	22	21	405	N/A		N/A		0	9	6	26	
Total	358	108	1,793	241	635	2,636	30	66	218	32	61	171
Western Europe							0	0				
Netherlands	92	281	4	15	291	19,253	5	1			69	
Italy	42	224	30	58	1,151	19,905	25	19		1		
France	58	187	55	57	1,199	21,040	18	60		13		7
United Kingdom	128	172	24	58	877	15,221	9	23	91	91	51	
Spain	40	130	50	39	527	13,516	13	19		34		3
Germany	45	102	36	80	1,574	19,654	42	39		346	15	
Belgium	29	67	3	10	197	19,687	15	2		1		
Sweden	45	53	45	9	206	24,001	4	5				43
Denmark	16	32	4	5	112	21,555	1	9	7		4	
Finland	27	32	34	5	110	22,007	2	4				
Portugal	8	20	9	10	65	6,576	1	2				
Norway	87	19	32	4	106	24,635	0	1	93		27	2
Ireland	6	18	7	4	39	11,151	0	2				
Total	625	1,338	335	353	6,454	18,279	136	188	192	486	165	56

TABLE 8.3 *continued*

Country	*Sea trade*		*Size*		*Economic activity*			*Natural resources (annual output)*				
	Exp *mt*	*Imp* *mt*	*Area* *m ha*	*Pop.* *million*	*GNP* *US$ bn*	*GNP/Cap* *US$*	*Steel* *mt*	*Cereals* *mt*	*Oil* *mt*	*Coal* *mt*	*Gas* *bcm*	*Iron ore* *mt*
Mediterranean							0	0				
Egypt	103	82	100	54	30	565	3	14	45		9	2
Turkey	42	77	78	57	96	1,671	0	31		53	19	5
Greece	20	37	13	10	58	5,621	1	6		57		
Algeria	58	14	238	26	33	1,272	1	4	56		53	2
Tunisia	6	10	16	8	12	1,414	0	3				
Israel	8	13	2	5	63	12,793	0	0				
Libya	55	8	176	5	28	5,950	1	0			8	
Jordan	10	7	9	4	4	952	0	0				
Syria	16	5	19	13	17	1,379	0	3	25			
Cyprus	2	4	1	1	6	7,873	0	0				
Total	320	257	652	182	345	1,900	6	61	126	109	89	10
West Africa							0	0				
South Africa	83	32	122	39	91	2,344	9	11				27
Nigeria	81	11	92	99	34	345	0	13	94			
Angola	21	1	125	10	N/A		0	0	26			
Morocco	20	12	45	26	28	1,076	0	9				
Liberia	15	2	10	3	1		0	0				1
Gabon	13	0	27	1	5	4,053	0	0	15			
Guinea	12	1	25	6	3	498	0	1				
Cameroon	10	3	48	12	12	980	0	1	8			
Mauritania	10	1	103	2	1	515	0	0				10
Congo	9	1	34	2	3	1,212	0	1	8			
Cote d'Ivoire	5	5	32	12	7	587	0	1				
Senegal	3	3	20	8	6	760	0	1				
Zaire	2	1	235	39	3		0	1				
Ghana	2	3	24	15	6	419	0	1				
Sierra Leone	2	1	7	4	1	177	0	0				
Other W. Africa	1	2	106	12	6	491	0	1	0	0	0	
Total	288	79	1,053	289	206	715	10	43	149	0	0	39
Total Atlantic	2,300	2,386	6,035	1,489	14,148	9,501	282	721	1,368	1,608	964	380

Source: Compiled from various sources

TABLE 8.4 Seaborne trade and economic infrastructure of the Pacific and Indian Oceans 1991

Country	Sea trade		Size			Economic activity			Natural resources (annual output)				
	Exp	*Imp*	*Area*	*Pop.*	*Arable*	*GNP*	*GNP/Cap*	*Steel*	*Cereals*	*Oil*	*Coal*	*Gas*	*Iron ore*
	mt	*mt*	*m ha*	*million*	*m ha*	*US$ bn*	*US$*	*mt*	*mt*	*mt*	*mt*	*bcm*	*mt*
Japan													
Japan	90	725	38	124	5	3,362	27,137	110	13		8		0
S.E. Asia													
Korea, Rep.	52	208	10	43	2	283	6,535	26	8		15		0
Singapore	90	116	0	3	0	40	14,280	1	–				–
China	82	72	960	1,150	97	370	322	71	395	140	1,063	15	191
Hong Kong	26	62	0	6	0	68	11,647	0	–			–	–
Indonesia	113	35	190	181	22	116	642	3	51	77		51	0
Malaysia	18	32	33	18	5	47	2,581	1	2	32		20	0
Thailand	30	30	51	57	20	93	1,631	1	24			7	0
Philippines	17	25	30	63	8	45	714	1	14				–
Korea, PDR	1	6	12	22	2	N/A	N/A	7	10				10
Vietnam	0	2	33	68	6	N/A	N/A	0	21				–
Brunei	14	1	1	0	0	N/A	N/A	–	0	8		9	–
Myanmar	1	1	68	43	10	N/A	N/A	–	14				–
Taiwan	N/A	N/A	0	N/A	N/A	N/A	N/A	11	N/A				–
Other	0	0	198	15	5	–		–	4	–	–	–	–
Total	443	590	1,586	1,669	178	1,062	636	122	543	256	1,078	102	201
S. Asia													
India	26	46	329	867	170	222	256	13	194	32	229	14	57
Pakistan	5	20	80	116	21	40	348	1	21			12	–
Sri Lanka	4	7	7	17	2	8	476	–	2				–
Bangladesh	1	6	14	111	9	23	212	0	28				–
Nepal	0	0	14	19	3	3	158	–	5				–
Afghanistan	0	0	65	18	8	N/A		–	3				–
Bhutan	0	0	5	2	0	0	160	–	0				–
Other	0	0	2		0	–		–	–				–
Total	37	79	515	1,149	213	297	259	14	254	32	229	26	57
Oceania													
Australia	319	33	771	17	47	300	17,329	6	19	27	220	22	118
New Zealand	15	8	27	3	0	43	12,606	1	1		1		2
Papua New Guinea	2	2	46	4	0	4	934	–	0				–
Other Oceania	5	4	9		1	–		–	0				–
Total	342	47	854	25	48	346	14,024	7	20	27	221	22	120
Middle East													
Iran	113	17	165	58	15	97	1,681	2	14	162		26	4
Iraq (1989)	N/A	N/A	44	19	5	64	3,443	–	3	12			–
Kuwait (1989)	51	5	2	2	0	23	10,877	–	–	7		1	–
Lebanon	0	1	1	3	0			–	0				–
Oman	34	2	21	2	0	10	6,398	–	0	36		3	–
Qatar	18	3	1	0	0	7	18,450	1	0	21		8	–
Saudi Arabia	214	46	215	15	2	109	7,055	2	4	420		32	–

TABLE 8.4 *continued*

Country	*Sea trade*		*Size*			*Economic activity*			*Natural resources (annual output)*				
	Exp *mt*	*Imp* *mt*	*Area* *m ha*	*Pop.* *million*	*Arable* *m ha*	*GNP* *US$ bn*	*GNP/Cap* *US$*	*Steel* *mt*	*Cereals* *mt*	*Oil* *mt*	*Coal* *mt*	*Gas* *bcm*	*Iron ore* *mt*
UAE	88	10	8	2	0	34	21,113	–	0	123		24	–
Yemen, Rep.	2	8	53	13	2	8	602	–	0			27	–
Other M. East	0	0	0		0	–		–	0	828	1	3	–
Total	521	91	510	113	25	352	3,119	5	22	1,609	1	123	4
East Africa													
Sudan	1	3	251	26	13	2	N/A	–	5				–
Mauritius	1	1	0	1	0	2	2,048	–	0				–
Somalia	0	1	64	9	1	2	181	–	0				–
Kenya	2	6	58	25	2	7	285	–	3				–
Madagascar	0	1	59	12	3	2	207	–	2				–
Djibouti	0	1	2	1	N/A			–	–				–
Mozambique	3	3	80	16	3	1	76	–	1				–
Total	8	17	514	89	23	17	186	–	11	–		–	–
W. Coast S. America													
Ecuador	10	3	28	11	3	12	1,074	–	1	16			–
Bolivia	N/A	N/A	110	7	2	5	688	–	1				0
Peru	10	5	129	22	4	48	2,208	0	2				4
Chile	21	11	76	13	4	31	2,337	1	3			5	8
Total	41	19	342	53	13	96	1,803	1	7	16	0	5	12
TOTAL	1,482	1,568	4,359	3,222	504	5,532	1,717	258	869	1,940	1,536	279	393

Source: Compiled from various sources

Chapter 9

Bulk cargo and the economics of bulk shipping

God must have been a shipowner. He placed the raw materials far from where they were needed and covered two thirds of the earth with water.

(Erling Naess)

9.1 The commercial origins of bulk shipping

There is nothing particularly new about bulk shipping. The idea of cutting transport costs by carrying shiploads of cargo in ships designed for efficient stowage and cargo handling has been around for centuries. Two thousand years ago Rome imported more than 30 million bushels of grain a year from the grainlands of northern Africa, Sicily and Egypt,[1] and to carry this trade a fleet of special grain ships was built. The Dutch 'fly boats', the nineteenth century tea clippers and even the slave ships of the eighteenth century are all examples.

The modern bulk shipping industry can be traced back to the coal trade between the north of England and London which started in the seventeenth century. Until mid-nineteenth century the standard 'collier' was a wooden sailing collier brig. In the 1840s, however, the rapidly growing coal trade spurred the shipbuilders on the north-east coast of England into a burst of innovation, notably the iron screw, a double bottom for the carriage of water ballast and the location of machinery fore and aft, leaving the entire hold amidships available for the carriage of cargo. The ships they built are easily recognizable as close relations of the bulk carriers used in the 1990s. Commercially the most successful of the pioneer collier designs was the John Bowes. Built at Palmer's Shipyard in Jarrow in 1852, she was iron-hulled, screw-propelled and could carry 600 tons of coal per voyage, compared with about 280 tons for a good sailing collier. Independent of weather and with much greater carrying capacity, the steam colliers could make many more round trips than a sailing vessel. These economic advantages more than cancelled out the higher capital cost.[2] Steam colliers provided the economic base for a rapidly growing coastal trade between Newcastle and London. Between 1840 and 1887 the coal trade grew from 1.4 mt to 49.3 mt.[3] A few years later in 1886 the ss *Gluckauf* was built on the Tyne creating the prototype for the modern bulk tanker fleet.

Since the nineteenth century the volume of seaborne trade has grown enormously and there has been a corresponding increase in the use of bulk shipping to exploit economies of scale and improved handling efficiency. Today there is a bulk fleet of over 9,000 bulk carriers, tankers, combined carriers and various specialist vessels. Bulk transport has been so successful at reducing costs that coal can be shipped across the world for much the same price per ton as it would have cost 125 years ago.

Our aim in this chapter is to discuss the economics of the modern bulk shipping industry, looking at the commodities traded, the particular problems they present to the bulk shipper and the way in which these problems have been resolved.

9.2 The bulk trades

The definition of 'bulk cargo'

The term 'bulk cargo' can give rise to confusion if the physical and economic aspects of bulk transport are not properly distinguished. Sometimes the term 'bulk' is used to describe commodities such as crude oil, grain, iron ore and coal whose homogeneous *physical character* lends itself to bulk handling and transport. This definition is used by the United Nations to classify commodities in the 'Maritime Transport Study'.[4] Another definition of 'bulk cargo' focuses on *transport economics* and uses the term to refer to any cargo that is transported in large quantities, usually a shipload, to reduce transport costs. Under this definition cargoes such as refrigerated meat, chilled bananas, motor cars, live animals, and logs are classified as bulk cargoes because they are transported in ship loads. Since many of these cargoes do not stow easily in bulk carriers, special ships have to be built. Both definitions highlight an important aspect of bulk cargo. The first emphasizes the physical handling characteristics of the cargo itself while the second focuses on the tailored transport operation made possible by high volume. Both are correct within their own terms of reference. Since this is an economics book, we are more interested in the economics of bulk cargo, so we will define a bulk cargo as 'any cargo that is transported by sea in large consignments in order to reduce the unit cost'. This definition helps to focus attention on the ultimate objective, which is to reduce costs, rather than the means by which that objective is achieved, i.e. the cargo handling method or the type of ship used. Since the shipowner is mainly concerned with ways of improving the service offered, it is important not to preempt his decisions by deciding, for example, that a bulk cargo must be shipped in a bulk carrier. There may be some better way of providing the same service.

The bulk commodities traded by sea are shown in Table 9.1. This table follows the physical definition, since this is the only form in which the data is available. In 1995 there were 2 bt of bulk liquids, 1.1 bt of major dry bulk commodities and 625 mt of minor bulk cargo, though not all of this travels in bulk carriers. This list of commodities is not comprehensive, but it gives a broad idea of the commodities most commonly traded in bulk carriers. As we saw in Chapter 1, each commodity has a parcel size distribution function determined by its economic and physical characteristics, and some commodities may be shipped partly in bulk and partly by liner.

The physical character of each commodity determines the type of ship used, the type of cargo handling gear required, and hence the overall structure of the sea transport system. As far as handling characteristics are concerned, the commodities shipped by sea are enormously diverse, but fall approximately into five main groups, as follows:

TABLE 9.1 Seaborne trade by commodity, 1985, 1995

	1985	*1995*	*% change*
Liquid Bulks (mt)			
Crude Oil	984	1,484	151
Oil Products	415	493	119
LPG	21	27	133
LNG	37	68	181
Chemicals	Na	Na	
Totals	1,457	2,072	
Five major Bulks (mt)			
Iron Ore	321	399	124
Coking Coal	144	167	116
Thermal Coal	132	236	179
Grain	168	196	117
Bauxite and Alumina	46	49	107
Phosphate Rock	43	28	65
Total	854	1,075	
Minor bulks (mt)			
Steel Products	170	195	115
Forest Products	133	167	126
Cement	47	53	113
Fertilizers	54	56	104
Manganese	9	5	58
Sugar	28	31	112
Soya Meal	23	28	122
Scrap	30	47	157
Coke	11	10	95
Pig Iron	11	12	113
Rice	11	19	165
Total	527	623	
Total Trade	2,838	3,770	

Source: Clarkson Research Studies, various

1 Liquid bulk cargoes which can be stored in tanks, handled by pumping and transported in tankers. Within this class there are many subdivisions. Of the liquid bulks, crude oil and oil products are the largest, while some of the others, particularly chemicals, are obscure and highly complex cargoes. Crude oil has few special requirements and can be shipped in very large quantities. Many chemical liquids are toxic and must be stored in special tanks, while others such as 'black products' must be heated if they are to remain sufficiently viscous to be handled. Liquefied gasses require vessels with refrigeration or pressurized tanks.

2 Homogeneous bulk cargoes cover a wide range of commodities which are shipped in large quantities and have a granular or lumpy composition which can be handled with automated equipment such as grabs and conveyers. For statistical purposes these commodities are generally divided into the major bulks and the minor bulks. The major bulks include commodities such as grain, iron ore, coal, bauxite and phosphate rock, while the minor bulks cover many industrial and agricultural materials. From a cargo handling viewpoint, the five major bulks are all homogeneous commodities shipped in large quantities by sea, and transport tends to focus on economies of scale using standard general-purpose bulk carriers. In contrast, the minor bulks are enormously diverse, including many unit load cargoes such as lumber, paper, steel ingots and bagged fertilizers. They present specialist shipping problems for the shipping industry, since the cargoes are often of high value, difficult to handle and the volume of individual trades is often small.

3 Unit load cargo consists of items which must be handled separately. The cargo cannot just be poured into the ship, as is the case with bulk cargoes. There are many natural unit loads, of which the most common are forest products (e.g. a tree trunk, steel products, rolls of paper, etc.) However, a major improvement in cargo handling efficiency can be achieved by packing non-standard items into standard units which give greater handling efficiency – for example, ores and fertilizers may be put in large bags, or sacks loaded on to a pallet.

4 Wheeled cargo requires special ships with access ramps and multiple deck structures. Car carriers are the main example.

5 Refrigerated cargoes present a special case because of their need for chilling or refrigerated transport. This is achieved by refrigeration of either the ship or the container. These trades cover such commodities as meat, fish, bananas, and various fruits. Some of the cargo is shipped in a fleet of refrigerated cargo ships (known as 'reefers') while the remainder is shipped by container in container ships.

9.3 The 'transport system' concept

A 'transport system' is a transport operation which has been designed so that the different parts of the system link together as efficiently as possible. Since each commodity and industry has its own particular transport requirements, there is no single system which is ideal for every situation. There are, however, certain principles which apply to most situations, and which make a useful 'checklist' when thinking about the transport system for a particular commodity.

The starting point is to view sea transport as one stage in the transport chain from origin to destination. Because cargo is transported in separate units such as shiploads, and because the production and consumption rates at either end may vary, the storage is almost as important a part of the system as the transport operation itself. In fact a transport system consists of two components, transport legs and storage areas. Cargo flows through the system as a series of discrete shipments, with the storage areas acting as buffers.

A typical bulk transport system is shown in Figure 9.1. It consists of a sea voyage and two land journeys which could be by lorry, train, conveyor, or pipeline. There are four

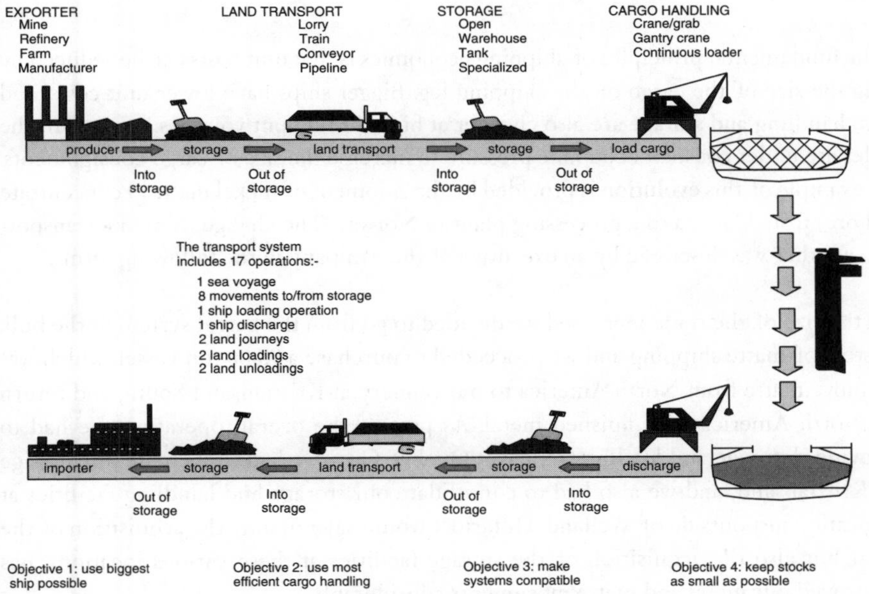

FIGURE 9.1 Elements in the bulk transport system
Source: Martin Stopford, 1997

storage areas located at the origin (e.g. mine, oilfield, factory or steel mill), the loading port, the discharging port and the destination. This creates a great deal of cargo handling. There are eight handling operations as the cargo moves in and out of the four storage areas. In addition there are four loading/unloading operations from the land transport vehicles plus the ship loading and discharge. Between the producer and the consumer, the cargo is handled fourteen times. No wonder transport system designers are so interested in finding ways to reduce this cost.

Four principles of system design

Whether transport is between a coal mine and a power station or a chemical plant and a fertilizer wholesaler, the aim is to move the cargo as cheaply and efficiently as possible. Inevitably this involves compromises. There are four ways to reduce costs. First, exploit economies of scale by using a bigger ship, second, reduce the number of times the cargo is handled, third, make the cargo handling operation more efficient, and fourth, reduce the size of stocks held. The problem for the system designer is that each of these objectives has a capital cost and some work in opposition. The challenge is to develop a system which gives the best outcome in terms of the transport user's priorities.

Objective 1: Economies of scale

One of the fundamental principles of shipping economics is that unit costs can be reduced by increasing the size of the cargo on the shipping leg. Bigger ships have lower unit costs, and unit cargo handling and storage are also cheaper at high throughput volumes. As a result the bulk trades are under constant economic pressure to increase the size of cargo consignments. A classic example of this evolution is provided by the shipment of nickel matte (a concentrate of nickel ore) from Canada to a processing plant in Norway. The change from one transport system to another was described by an executive of the company in the following terms:

> As the size of the trade increased we decided to go from the barrel system to the bulk system of matte shipping and we proceeded to purchase a 9,000 ton vessel, which was to move matte from North America to our refinery at Kristiansand South, and return to North America with finished metal. As part of the overall operation, we had to provide a storage and loading facility at Quebec City; we had to increase our storage at Kristiansand, and we also had to consolidate our storage and handling facilities at a location just outside of Welland, Ontario. I would say not only the acquisition of the ship, but also the acquisition of the storage facilities at these various locations, has improved our metal and matte movements considerably.[5]

In this case we see bulk shipping as a natural progression in the development of the business and also the importance of making bulk shipping an integral part of the whole manufacturing operation. The same process is seen in the steel industry where the size of ore carriers has increased from 24,000 dwt in the 1920s to 300,000 dwt in the 1990s. A further discussion of economies of scale in bulk carriers can be found in chapter 5.

Many of the bulk commodity trades discussed in this chapter travel partly in bulk and partly as general cargo, depending on the size of the individual trade flow. For example, 50,000 tons of wheat transported from New Orleans to Rotterdam would certainly travel in a bulk carrier, but 500 tons of malting barley shipped from Tilbury to West Africa would probably travel bagged on pallets or in containers. Because this depends on a commercial decision, there is no specific size at which a trade flow 'goes bulk'. In effect, the smallest practical bulk unit is a single bulk carrier hold; as the size of parcel falls below 3,000 tons it becomes increasingly difficult to arrange bulk transport. One expert puts the watershed at 1,000 tons.[6]

Objective 2: Efficient cargo handling

Cargo handling is a major issue. Each time the product is handled during transport it costs money. The economic costs of cargo handling can be illustrated with an example from the grain trade. A 15,000 dwt 'tweendecker discharging in a small African port might take several weeks to discharge its cargo. Typically, the grain is unloaded on to the quayside with grabs, bagged by hand and transported to the warehouse by lorry. In contrast, a large modern grain elevator can discharge barges at the rate of 2,000 tons per hour and load ships at the rate of 5,000 tons per hour. With these facilities the same vessel could be handled in a day.

A radical solution is to relocate processing plant to reduce the number of transport legs. Manufacturing plant such as steel mills can be relocated to coastal sites to avoid land transport of raw materials. Where cargo must be handled, the emphasis is on reducing cost by using specially constructed bulk handling terminals. Most large ports have specialist bulk terminals for handling crude oil, products, dry bulk and grain. The use of high-productivity cargo handling equipment contributes to the overall cost efficiency of the operation by reducing the unit cost of loading and discharging, and minimizing the time the ship spends handling cargo.

Homogeneous dry bulks such as iron ore and coal can be handled very efficiently using continuous loaders and discharged with cranes and large grabs. Cargoes such as steel or forest products, which consist of large, irregular units, benefit from packaging into standard unit loads. In some cases, such as vehicles and refrigerated cargo, bulk shipping requires the construction of special vessels. For example, importing cement in bags for onward shipment by rail involves several expensive manual handling operations. Bulk cement shipped loose in a specially designed cement carrier can be discharged mechanically into an automatic handling system, stored in silos and loaded direct into suitable bulk rail cars.

Objective 3: Integration of transport modes employed

Cargo handling can be made more efficient if care is taken to integrate the various stages in the transport system. One way to do this is to standardize cargo units. Cargo is packaged in a form that can easily be handled by all stages in the transport system, e.g. a lorry or rail truck. Containerization is a classic example of this type of development. The standard container can be lifted off the ship onto the lorry. In bulk shipping the use of intermediate units such as large bags, packaged lumber and pallets can be used to reduce handling costs.

Another is to design a system which covers all stages in the transport operation. This approach is used in many large industrial projects involving raw materials systems. Ships, terminal facilities, storage areas and land transport are integrated into a balanced system. The first integrated bulk transport system was probably in the iron ore trade. Through transport from the iron ore mine to the steel plant was planned in detail at the time the plant is built (see page 316). This approach works best where the cargo flows are regular, predictable and controlled by a single company, making it possible to justify special investment in ships and cargo handling equipment. The key word here is *integration.* What matters is that the transport system is designed as a whole.

Objective 4: Optimizing stocks for the producer and consumer

The transport system must incorporate stockpiles and parcel sizes which are acceptable to the importer and the exporter. There are two aspects to consider. One is the size of the trade flow. Although it would be cheaper to ship manganese ore in a 170,000 dwt bulk carrier, steelmakers use much smaller ships. This is partly a matter of annual throughput which does not justify investment in high volume cargo handling facilities, but there is also inventory cost to consider. Even if the storage facilities are available to handle 170,000 tons of manganese ore, the cost of holding stock for a year could well exceed the freight saving. Under 'just in time' manufacturing systems the product should arrive at the processing or sales point as close as possible to the time when it is used, minimizing the need for stocks. This approach, which calls for a transport system with many small deliveries conflicts with Objective 1 which favours a few very large deliveries.

The size of parcel in which a commodity is shipped is thus a trade-off between optimizing stockholding and economies of scale in transport. High-value cargoes, which are usually used in small quantities and incur a high inventory cost, tend to travel in small parcels. This is most noticeable in the minor bulk trades such as sugar, steel products and non-ferrous metal ores, where physical characteristics permit large bulk parcels but stockholding practices imposes a parcel size ceiling on the trade.

The combination of operational and economic factors discussed in this section can result in many different approaches to the business of shipping cargo in bulk. Each trade evolves its own distinctive style of bulk shipping operation. For regular cargo flows such as iron ore, planning the transport system is a routine matter which generally proceeds very rapidly as the cargoes grow. For cargoes that appear on the market irregularly, optimizing transport is more difficult and generally proceeds more slowly. For example, grain and shipments are seasonal; there is no regular pattern of trade since a great deal depends on each year's harvest. In this case the immediate requirement is not for an integrated shipping system, but for a chartering organization capable of obtaining the correct mix of vessels able to meet a changing pattern of trade. In the following sections we study the more important bulk commodities shipped by sea to illustrate this point.

9.4 Handling bulk cargoes

Specialized terminal facilities with deep water and capable of handling the various commodities efficiently play an essential part of the seaborne bulk transport. It is not possible for a single terminal to handle all types of cargoes efficiently because the depth of water and the cargo handling facilities, the shore based storage facilities and the through transport requirements vary from one cargo type to another. As we saw in Chapter 1, modern ports have developed into a collection of specialist terminals.

Handling liquid bulk cargoes

Crude oil and oil products require different types of handling terminals. Since the carriage of crude oils uses very large tankers, loading and discharge terminals are generally located in deep water locations with draft of up to 22 metres. Often these requirements can only be met by offshore terminals with strong fendering systems to absorb the berthing impact of large tankers. The berthing arrangements for a typical offshore oil terminal are shown in Figure 9.2.

The terminal consists of storage tanks on land linked by pipeline to the piers where tankers are berthed. These storage tanks must have enough capacity to service vessels using the port. There are two piers with four berths, one with a maximum size of 65,000 dwt, two 135,000 dwt berths and one VLCC berth. Note also the finger piers for tugs. Cargo is loaded by pumping oil from the storage tanks to the ship using the terminal's own pumping capacity. Discharge relies on the ship's pumps. Large tankers generally have four cargo pumps, located in a pump room between the engine room and the cargo tanks. Typical combined discharging rates are 6,500 cubic metres per hour for a 60,000 dwt tanker and 18,000 cubic metres per hour for a 250,000 dwt tanker.

Products terminals are generally smaller and can often be accommodated within the port complex. Handling techniques are broadly similar to crude oil, but must be capable of dealing with many small parcels of different product. These include black oils such as furnace oils and heavy diesel oils; and white oils, which include gasoline, aviation spirits, kerosene, gas oil and MTBE (a liquid petroleum feedstock).

Handling homogeneous bulk cargoes

Homogeneous dry bulks such as iron ore and coal are handled very efficiently using single purpose terminals. The iron ore loading facility shown in Figure 9.3 illustrates the way the industry tackles the problems encountered in transferring cargo to and from the ship.

Cargo arrives at the terminal railcar reception facility in railcars designed to tip or drop their cargo into a hopper below the track. From here the ore moves to the stockpile by wagon or, more usually, by conveyor. The stockpile acts as a buffer between the land and sea transport systems, ensuring the terminal has sufficient ore to load ships when they arrive. If stocks are inadequate congestion builds up as ships wait to load cargo. In the iron ore terminal shown in Figure 9.3 the stockpile consists of long rows of ore, known as 'wind-rows'. Commodities such as grain require protection and are stored in silos.

Moving material into the stockpile is known as 'spreading', while removing it is referred to as 'reclaiming'. Both processes are highly automated. The spreader moves slowly

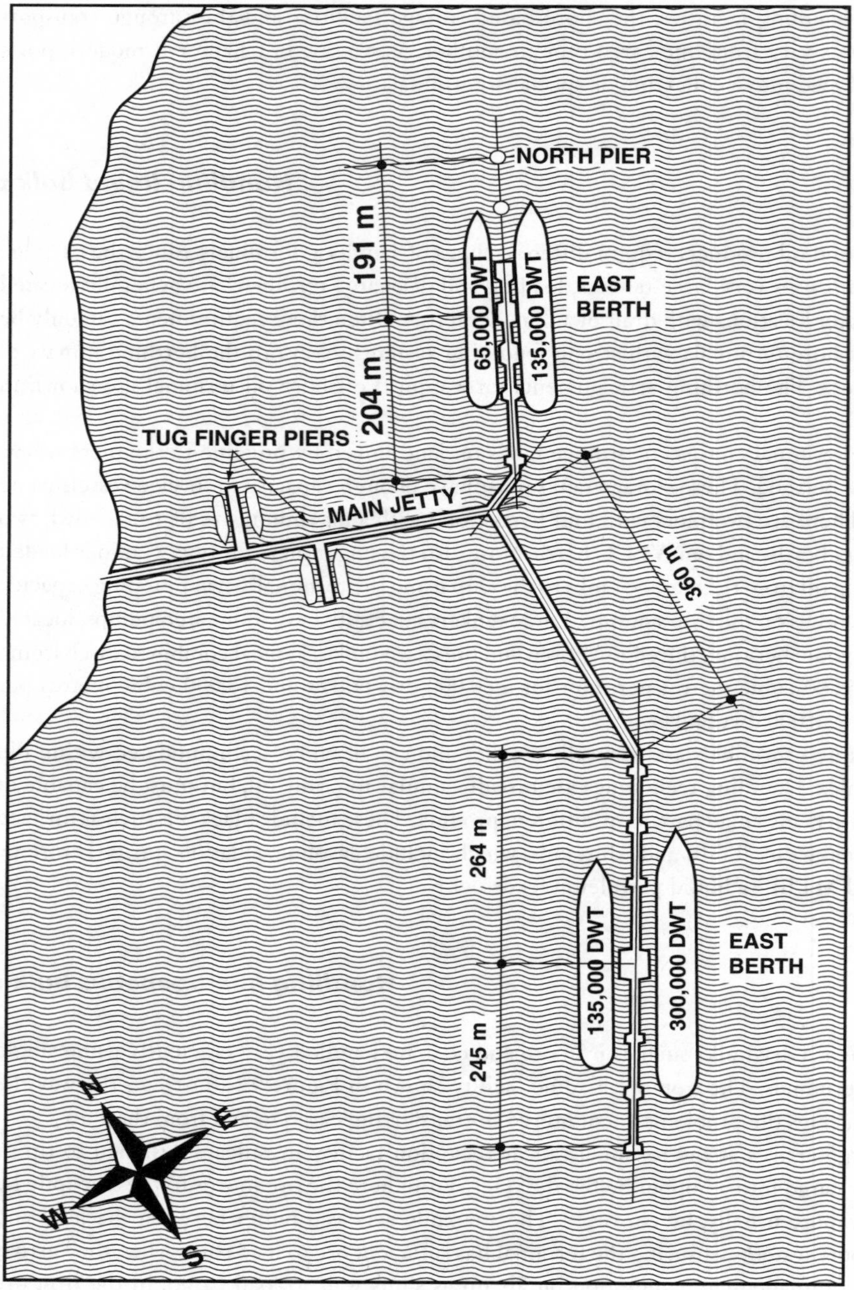

FIGURE 9.2 A crude oil terminal
Source: UNCTAD (1985)

along the stockpile rows, receiving ore from the conveyor and dropping by gravity on to the stockpile at a rate of several thousand tons an hour. When the ore is needed the reclaimer, a revolving drum with buckets, moves along the wind-row, scoops ore from the stockpile and drops it on to a belt conveyor. From the conveyor the ore is taken to the quayside where it is loaded on to the ship.

Material is weighed before loading or after unloading, to check shipping documentation, using an automatic weighing machine in the conveyor system. Sampling is also required to satisfy the purchaser that the material is in accordance with specifications.[7] The ship loader receives cargo from the conveyor and deposits it in the ship's holds in a planned sequence (the 'loading plan') which avoids putting structural stresses on the hull. Various loading systems are used. In the example illustrated a radial arm loader is used. The ship is moored alongside the loader and the two loading 'booms' (i.e. arms which extend over the ship's hatches) move from hatch to hatch, loading ore by gravity. Other designs of loader use a loading arm on rails running alongside the berth. Loading rates of 1–16,000 tons an hour may be achieved, but at higher loading speeds a limit may be imposed by the rate at which the ship can be de-ballasted. During loading the boom moves from hatch to hatch. To allow for temporary interruptions to the loading operation, for example when moving from one hatch to another, there is generally a surge hopper in the system.

At the other end of the voyage the ore is unloaded with a grab unloader which picks material from the hold and discharges it into a hopper at the quay edge, from which it is fed on to a belt conveyor. The cargo handling rate for a grab depends on the number of handling cycles per hour and the average grab payload. In practice about 60 cycles per hour is possible. Grab designs range from light grabs for animal feedstuffs and grain, to massive 50-ton lift ore handlers. The grab unloader is used mainly for iron ore, coal, bauxite, alumina and phosphate rock. Other commodities handled by smaller mobile grabbing cranes include raw sugar, bulk fertilizers, petroleum coke and various varieties of bean and nut kernels. Pneumatic systems are suitable for handling bulk cargo of low specific gravity and viscosity such as grains, cement and powdered coal. Pneumatic equipment is classified into vacuum, or suction types and pressure, or blowing types.

Handling package bulk cargoes

Handling packaged cargoes provides terminal operators with a different type of problem. The broad aims are the same, but the operational aspects are very different.

The Squamish Terminals Ltd in British Columbia provides an example of the type of terminal developed to meet these requirements in the forest products trade. The terminal handles exports of pulp from British Columbia. Pulp is shipped in bales which arrive from the pulp mill by rail. The railway line runs into the terminal alongside the warehouses. Bales of pulp are discharged from train to storage and then to the ship with a fleet of thirty-four fork lift trucks and fourteen double-wide tractor trailer units of 34 tons capacity, plus four extension trailers. Three warehouses provide covered storage for 85,000 tons of pulp, which represents two shiploads of cargo, since the vessels servicing the terminal are 40–45,000 dwt.

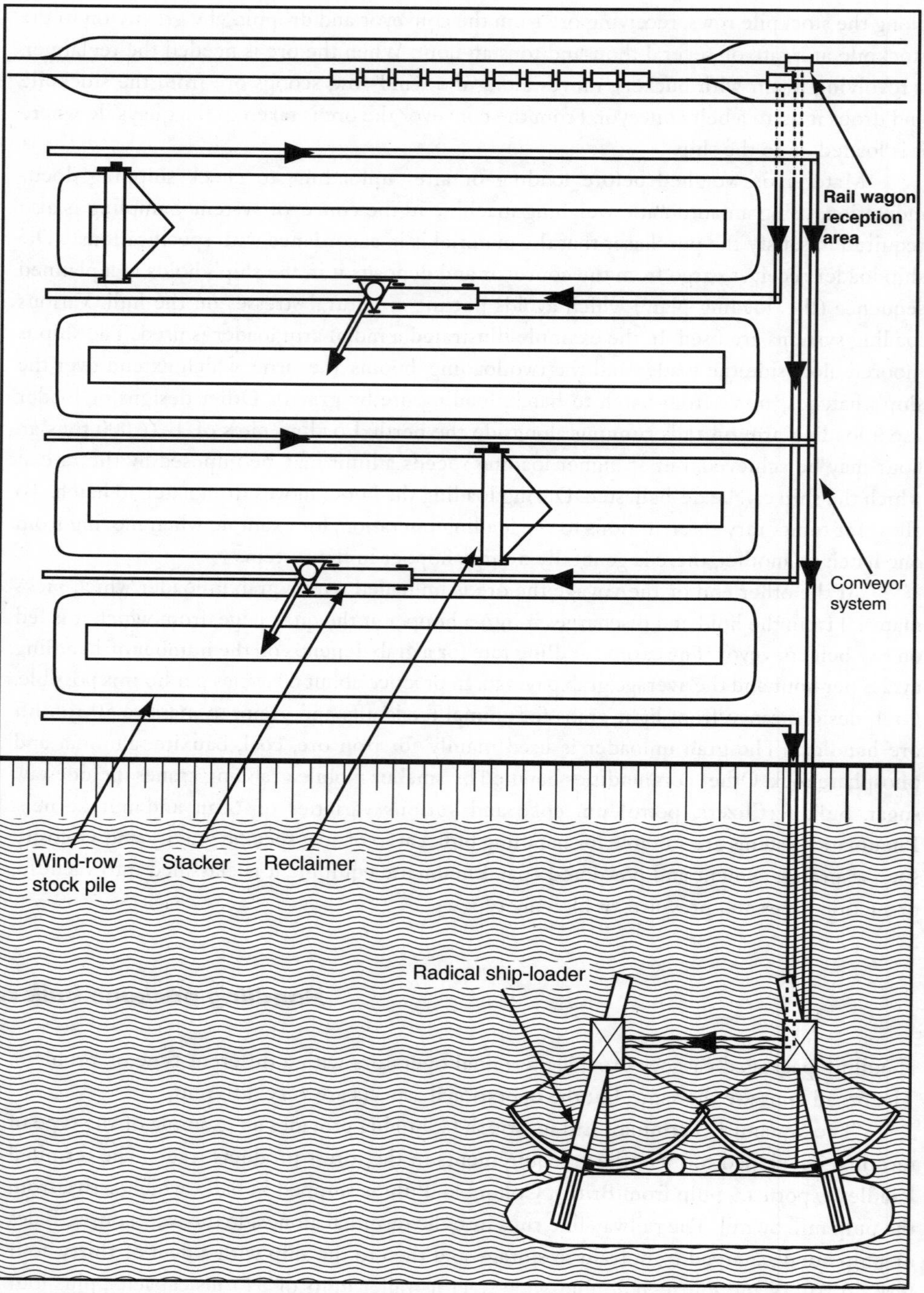

FIGURE 9.3 An iron ore export terminal
Source: UNCTAD (1985)

However the terminal operators have found that, because the pulp mills have little storage, any stockbuilding on their part ends up at the terminal. A third warehouse was built as a buffer for this purpose.

Cargo is loaded from two berths, Berth 1 of 11.6 metres and Berth 2 of 12.2 metres. Because the terminal is serviced by the Star Shipping fleet of geared bulk carriers there are no need for cranes on the quayside. Ships come alongside the apron and cargo is loaded with the ship's gantry cranes. Berth 1 can handle ships up to 195 metres, with an apron 135 metres long, which is sufficient to give access to the cargo holds. Berth 2 handles ships up to 212 metres, with an apron of 153 metres.

Cargoes such as steel products which often consist of large, irregular units, are more difficult to ship in bulk. In some cases, such as vehicles and refrigerated cargo, bulk shipping requires the construction of special vessels. For example, importing cement in bags for onward shipment by rail involves several expensive manual handling operations. Bulk cement shipped loose in a specially designed cement carrier can be discharged mechanically into an automatic handling system, stored in silos and loaded direct into suitable bulk rail cars.

9.5 Liquid bulk cargoes

The liquid cargoes shipped by sea fall into three main groups: crude oil and products; liquefied gas, principally LNG and LPG; vegetable oil and liquid chemicals such as ammonia, phosphoric acid, etc. Together these commodities account for half of world seaborne trade, with crude oil and oil products generating most of the volume. For this reason they deserve careful attention. In this section we will review the history of the bulk transport of oil by sea and the economics of the underlying commodity trade.

Origins of the seaborne oil trade

Crude oil was first produced commercially in 1859 when Colonel Edwin Drake struck oil at Titusville, Pennsylvania.[8] The first oil cargo was shipped two years later. Peter Wright & Sons of Philadelphia chartered the brig *Elizabeth Watts*, 224 tons, to load oil in barrels for London. Oil already had a reputation as a dangerous cargo and when that ship was ready for sea, her captain could not find seamen willing to sail with him. He enlisted the aid of a press gang and in November 1861 the first oil cargo sailed down the Delaware, and into history, with a drunken crew.[9]

For the next 25 years shipowners searched for better ways of transporting this disagreeable cargo.[10] Barrels, which were big and awkward to stow, were soon replaced by seven-gallon rectangular tins, packed in pairs in wooden cases. Known as 'case oil', these could be shipped as general cargo and for some years they became the standard cargo unit. As the trade grew sailing ships were fitted with tanks, and some with cargo pumps, to carry petroleum 'without the aid of casks'. A few such as the *Ramsay* (1863) and the *Charles* (1869) were built for the trade but most were converted. The *Vaderland*, built in Jarrow in 1872 for Belgian owners, was the first effort to build an ocean-going tank steamer. It was designed to carry passengers to the USA and return with oil in tanks.[11]

The first purpose-built tanker to use the outer skin as the containment vessel was the *Gluckauf*, 2,307 tons, built for the German–American Petroleum Company and launched in 1886. As a safety measure to avoid the build up of dangerous gases, the double bottom was eliminated, except under the engine room. Several similar vessels, including the *Bakuin* built for Alfred Stuart and the *Loutsch* were launched later in the year.[12] The savings by shipping bulk (four shillings a barrel) were so great that within three years half of the oil imported into the UK came in bulk.[13] Thus started the era of bulk oil transport. From twelve bulk tankers in 1886, the fleet grew to ninety tankers operating in the Atlantic in 1891.

The sea transport of oil 1890–1970

Once the ships were available the newly emerging oil companies, who were deeply involved in distribution, were quick to see the advantages of bulk transport. In the late 1880s the US Standard Oil, the world's biggest oil company, entered the tanker business.[14] They set up the Anglo-American Oil Co Ltd and, in a typical grand gesture, purchased sixteen tankers including the *Duffield* and the *Gluckauf*.[15] At about the same time Marcus Samuel, who was distributing Russian case oil in the Far East, decided to build a fleet of tankers to transport Russian oil in bulk to the Far East, thus undercutting Standard Oil.[16] The first was the Murex, delivered in 1892 and by the end of 1893 ten ships had been launched for the Samuels.[17] In 1892 the Suez Canal permitted tankers to pass through, reducing the voyage to a competitive distance. Oil was loaded at the Black Sea port of Batum and delivered by tanker to the Far East. To improve profits, the tankers carried a backhaul of general cargo. After discharging oil at Bombay, Kobe, or Batavia, the tanks were steam cleaned, whitewashed and loaded with a backhaul cargo of tea, cereals or rice. In 1897 Shell Transport & Trading was formed and in 1907 Anglo-Saxon Petroleum Co. Ltd was formed by merging the Shell and Royal Dutch fleets, creating a total fleet of thirty-four ships.

Over the next 50 years the oil trade grew steadily, reaching 35 mt in 1920 and 182 mt in 1950. Trade was controlled by the 'Oil Majors' and transport dominated oil industry economics. In 1950 the cost of a barrel of oil in the Middle East was about $1. It cost another $1 to ship it to Western Europe, so transport accounted for about half the CIF price. Every cent shaved off transport costs contributed to profitability. Shipping was a 'core' business for the oil companies, who developed a policy of balancing owned ships with time charters to independent tanker owners. In the 1950s and 1960s the growth rate of trade increased to 8.4 per cent per annum growth, compared with 5.9 per cent per annum previously and since the Middle East was the marginal supply source, ton miles grew even faster. Planning the supply of transport became a major part of the oil industry's business which they tackled it with characteristic thoroughness. In the 1950s the 'Oil Majors' set about creating a sophisticated machine for cutting the cost of oil transport. Their three guiding principles were:

1 *Economies of scale.* Throughout the 1950s and the 1960s each generation of tankers was bigger than the last. The size increased from 17,000 dwt in 1950 to the first VLCC in 1966 and the first ULCC in 1976. The economics were simple and clearcut. In 1968 an 80,000 dwt tanker such as the *Rinform* cost about 27s.5d per ton of oil to make the round trip from Rotterdam to Kuwait. On the same voyage a 200,000 dwt vessel returning via the Cape could do the voyage for 18s.1d, a 33 per cent saving.[18]

2 *Transport planning.* The majors developed a logistic network which used tankers to their maximum efficiency. They sailed with a full cargo; waiting time was negligible; regular maintenance minimized breakdown; and when problems occurred they were smoothly dealt with through inter-company cooperation. By the early 1970s the transport performance of the fleet was within a few per cent of the theoretical optimum.

3 *Subcontracting.* To avoid corporate overheads and to spread the risk, a large part of the fleet was subcontracted to independents, with Greeks and Norwegians serving the Atlantic market and Hong Kong serving Japan. To begin with in the 1950s the time charters were generally 5–7 years, but by the time VLCCs were being ordered in the 1960s 15 or even 20 year charters were not uncommon. By the end of the 1960s the oil companies owned about 36 per cent of the tanker fleet; they time-chartered another 52 per cent; and they topped up their seasonal requirements from the spot market which accounted for about 12 per cent of supply. The spot market was inhabited by the small, uneconomic elderly tankers and a few speculators trading modern tonnage through the boom and bust cycles.

This 'charter back' policy (*shikumisen* in Japan) enabled independent tanker owners to build up their tanker fleets by borrowing against the security of the oil company charter. By July 1971 there was a fleet of 178 m.dwt available for oil transport. The oil companies owned 48 m.dwt (26 per cent), with an additional 79.8 m.dwt (45 per cent) on time charter from independents. As fall back, there was 19.5 m.dwt (11 per cent) of the independent fleet trading spot, and 17 m dwt of combined carriers.

Independent tankers thus outnumbered the oil company ships by a ratio of two to one. They made their profits by careful management and asset appreciation rather than speculation.[19] However the oil companies were hard taskmasters. The charter rates they negotiated usually left little margin for error. As inflation and currency volatility developed in the late 1960s, some tanker owners became disenchanted with their role as subcontractors, especially as some owners seemed to be doing spectacularly well on the spot market.

Growth of the tanker 'spot market' 1975–95

In the 1970s the factors that had worked so positively in favour of an integrated transport operation were reversed. Everything went wrong. Demand collapsed, supply got out of control, and the oil companies decided oil transport was no longer a core business and reduced their exposure to it. In the next 20 years the transport of oil changed from carefully planned industrial shipping to a market operation. As a result the independent tanker fleet, which in 1973 was mainly trading on time charter to the oil companies, gradually transferred to the spot market. By the early 1990s over 70 per cent of this fleet was trading spot, compared with only about 20 per cent in the early 1970s (See Figure 3.2).

This fundamental change in the organisation of oil transport was precipitated by a period of volatility in the oil trade.[20] Trade had reached 300 mt in 1960, and peaked at 1,530 mt in 1978. From there it fell to 960 mt in 1983, then grew to 1,480 mt in 1995 (Figure 9.4). The fall in the oil trade in the early 1980s had three causes. First, the European and Japanese energy markets were maturing. By the 1970s the transition from coal to oil was over, and lower growth was inevitable. Second, there were two deep economic depressions, one in the mid-1970s and the other in the early 1980s. Third, higher oil prices, which reached $30 per barrel in 1980, meant that other fuels were substituted for oil and fuel-saving technology became viable. In particular, the power station market was lost to coal and technology reduced oil consumption in other areas.[21] By the end of the 1980s the oil trade had changed from a predictable trade for which transport was carefully planned by the oil companies to a volatile and risky business in which traders played a substantial part and transport was, to a large extent, left to the market-place to manage.

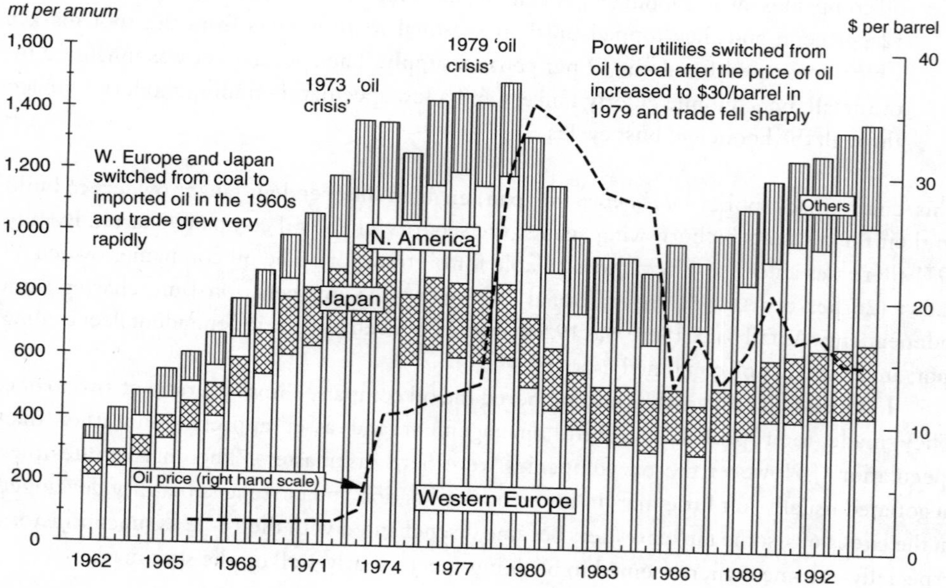

FIGURE 9.4 Crude oil imports by region 1962–96

Source: Fearnleys World Bulk Trades 1995 and earlier editions

Geographical distribution of the oil trade

The geographical location of oil supplies plays an important part in determining the number of tankers needed to carry the trade. The location of the world's major oil exporting countries is shown in Figure 9.5. The largest known source of crude oil outside the consuming areas

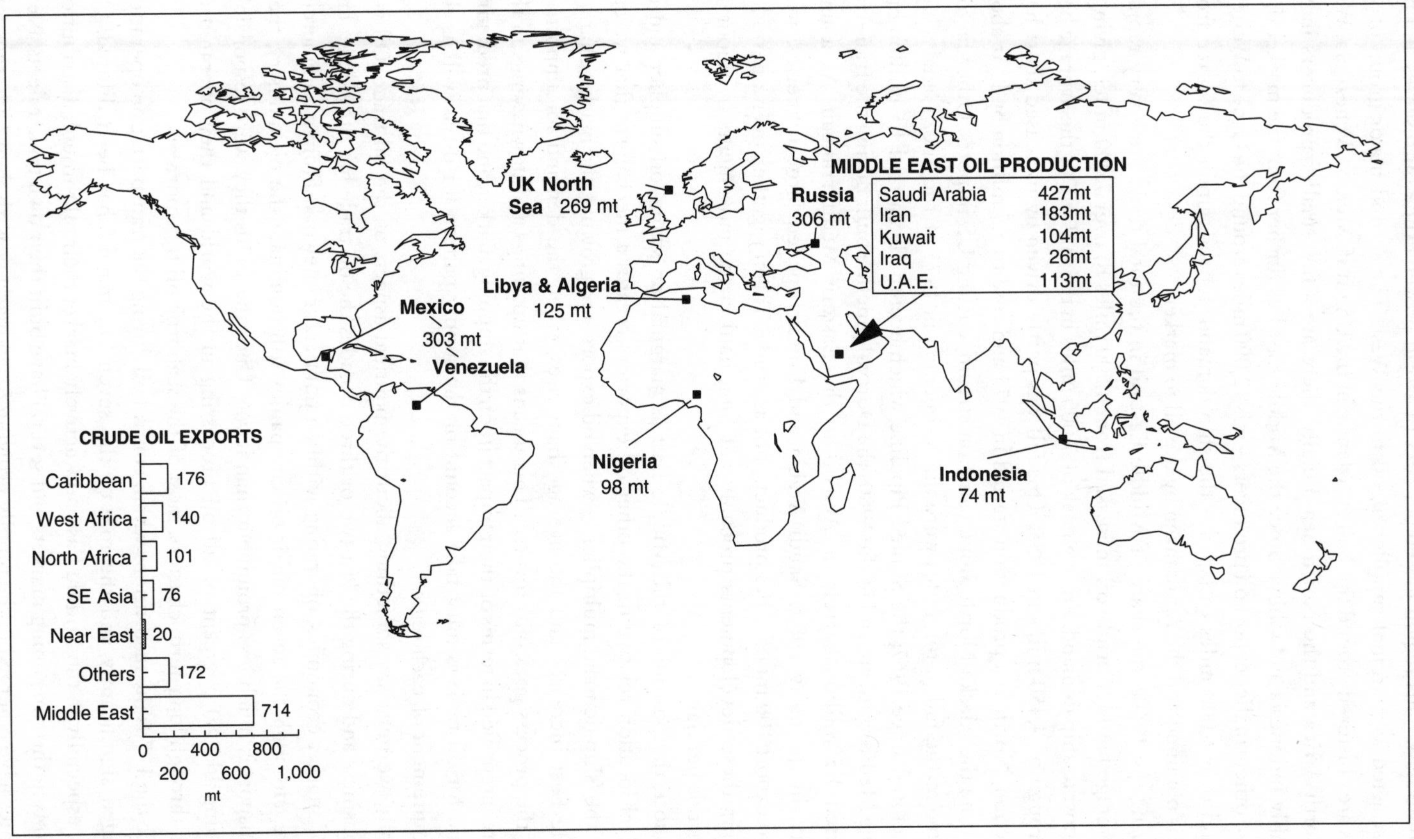

FIGURE 9.5 Major crude oil exporters 1995

Source: BP, *Statistical Review of World Energy Industry*
Note: The numbers on the graph show oil production in 1995

is the Middle East. This region has 60 per cent of world proven crude oil reserves and has in the past acted as marginal supplier of oil to the West. The second major group of oil producers are clustered around the North Atlantic in the US Gulf, Mexico, Venezuela, West Africa, North Africa and the North Sea. Finally, there are a few smaller producers in SE Asia, notably Indonesia and China. Since the Middle East lies further from the market than most of the other smaller export oil producers – it is 12,000 miles around the Cape to Western Europe and over 6,000 miles to Japan – the ship demand depends upon the source from which oil is obtained and the route taken by the oil to market.

During the 1960s, the share of Middle East oil in the total trade grew very rapidly and the average haul for crude oil increased from 4,500 miles to over 7,000 miles, giving a massive boost to ship demand. From a peak of 7,000 miles in the mid-1970s the average haul fell to a trough of 4,450 miles in 1985. This fall was partly driven by increased short haul oil production. North Sea production started in 1975 and rose to 5.5 million bpd. At about the same time the Alaska North Slope came on stream, cutting US imports. Other factors contributing to the fall in ton miles were the re-opening in 1975 of the Suez Canal which had been closed since 1967; the Sumed Pipeline which eventually carried 1.5 million bpd of oil to the Mediterranean; and in the 1980s the Dortyol pipeline built during the Iran–Iraq war diverted 1.5 million barrels of AG oil to the Eastern Mediterranean. As a final complexity, in the early 1980s Saudi Arabia and Kuwait opened large refineries, with capacity to export 100 mt of oil as products, not as crude. Taken together, over a period of fifteen years these developments probably cut long haul crude movements by about 10 million barrels per day.

In short, the position of the Middle East as marginal or 'swing' oil supplier and its geographical location relative to the other oil exporters creates a mechanism that we can refer to as the 'ship demand multiplier' – when oil exports are growing, the market share of the Middle East increases and the average haul rises; when the demand for imports is declining, the process goes into reverse. This means that upswings and downswings in the oil trade are intensified in terms of their impact upon the shipping market, and that predicting the demand for oil tankers must take account of the supply pattern for oil as well as the import requirement of each region.

Finally, we must say something about the political aspects of the oil trade. Oil is a strategic business and during the last two or three decades the oil trade has provided a fine example of market economics, operating within a political framework. From a commercial perspective, although the seven major oil companies still dominate the oil industry, their role in transport is much less prominent than it was. Until the 1970s they were responsible for something like 80 per cent of all oil processing in the world and they operated or controlled, through long-term charters, most of the seaborne oil transport.[22]

Since the 1970s the institutions which control oil during the transportation operation have changed significantly and the role of the seven 'oil majors' has been diluted. Oil producers, especially in the Middle East, now actively market their oil through distribution organizations in the consuming markets and several have built their own tanker fleets. New oil companies have emerged in the rapidly growing Asian markets, with their own transport policies. Finally, as the oil market has become more volatile the prominance of oil traders, who act as intermediary between the producer and the refinery, has become more prominent. They now often own the oil during shipment and because their interests are very different from those of the traditional oil majors, this has altered the supply side of the business.

The oil transport system

Since crude oil is by far the largest seaborne commodity trade, and practically all of it travels by tanker, a large and sophisticated industry has grown up specializing in the transportation of crude oil by sea. Crude oil for export is usually transported from the oilfield to the coast by pipeline. A pipe of small diameter is attached to each producing well and a network of these pipes connects to bulk collecting stations which feed into large terminal areas with storage tanks capable of holding hundreds of thousands of barrels. The oil is then loaded into tankers and shipped to its destination where it is off-loaded into another bulk terminal. A typical VLCC would carry about 280,000 tons of oil, at a draught of about 21 metres, a speed of 15 knots and with a pumping capacity of 18,000 tons per hour. The larger ULCC might carry 350,000 tons of oil with a loaded draught of 22 metres and a discharge pumping capacity of 22,000 tons per hour.

Such large vessels require a dedicated port infrastructure and the terminals used in the oil trade, which we discussed in section 9.4, are often in remote locations, consisting of a tank farm for temporary oil storage and a jetty or single buoy mooring projecting into deep water where large tankers can load cargo. For example, Ras Tanura the main export terminal of Saudi Arabia, has a series of jetties built offshore. From the discharge terminal the oil is delivered direct to a refinery, or to a crude oil terminal linked to refineries by a pipeline. In the early days of the oil industry much crude oil moved by rail tank car, but today pipelines, barges and ships dominate petroleum handling.

The deep draught of large tankers places restrictions on their use of key shipping lanes such as the Straits of Dover, the Straits of Malacca and the Suez Canal. The Straits of Dover, for instance, have a maximum permissible draught of around 23–25 metres, which is on the margin for larger-size ULCCs. In the Straits of Malacca, on the route between the Middle East and Japan, the maximum draught of 18 metres precludes the larger ULCCs. However, from the shipping industry's point of view, the draught restrictions on the Suez Canal were the most important. Until the mid-1950s the Suez Canal was the main route for crude oil shipped from the Middle East to Western Europe. At that time the draught was 11 metres, restricting the canal to loaded vessels of less than 50,000 dwt. The closure of the canal during the Six Day War in 1967 coincided with the trend to build VLCCs for the oil trade and as a result the imports of Western Europe and the United States from the Middle East were diverted around the Cape.

After the Suez Canal was reopened in 1975, it was deepened to 16.2 metres, allowing vessels of up to 150,000 dwt to transit full loaded, or larger vessels in ballast. As a result, shipments of oil through the canal edged up from 30 mt in 1976 to about 40 mt in 1995, but remained well below the peak of 167 mt achieved before the canal was closed in 1967. This reflects the availability of bigger ships which cannot transit the canal fully loaded. One effect of the reopening of the Suez Canal was to generate a demand for intermediate-sized tankers of 100,000–150,000 dwt.

The seaborne trade in oil products

In both economic and shipping terms the oil products trade is very different from crude oil. The trade consists of the products of the oil refining process, which in shipping terms can be loosely classified into two categories, clean and dirty products. Clean products consist of the lighter distillates, principally kerosene and gasoline, which are usually shipped in vessels with coated tanks and require care in cleanliness of storage tanks. Dirty products include the lower distillates and residual oil, which can generally be shipped in conventional tankers, though the low viscosity sometimes necessitates steam-heating coils in the cargo tanks.

In 1995, about 493 mt of oil products were shipped by sea, about half of which were clean products and the other half dirty products. In contrast to the crude oil trade, the volume of oil products trades has been fairly stable for several decades, though at regional level there has been great change (Figure 9.6). Explaining these changes is a good deal more complex than the crude oil trade. The oil products trade has a complex economic structure, arising from the fact that oil products may be traded by sea for several different reasons:

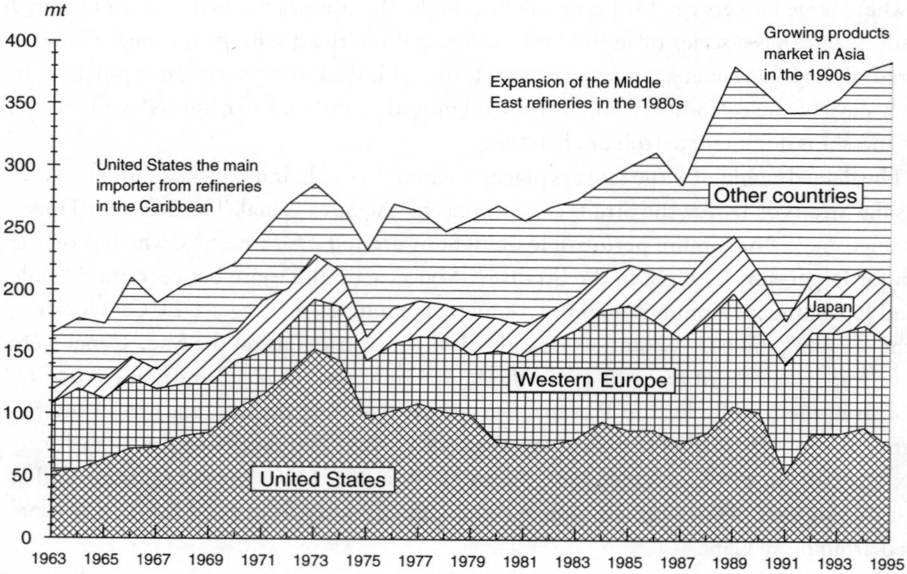

FIGURE 9.6 Oil product imports 1963–95

Source: BP, *Statistical Review of World Energy Industry*

- *Refinery location.* If the oil refinery is located at the source of the oil or some intermediate point on the sea route, then the oil products will need to be shipped on by sea to the final market.
- *Balancing trades.* The mix of products refined from a barrel of oil does not always meet the precise market structure of the market adjacent to the refinery. For this reason there is a constant movement of specific oil products from areas of surplus to areas of shortage.
- *Deficit trade.* Local shortages of refined products may occur either because demand grows faster than refining capacity can be expanded, or because the market is not sufficiently large to support a major oil refinery, as may happen in some developing countries. In these circumstances the import trade will take the form of oil products rather than crude oil.

The main importers of products are shown in Figure 9.6. Until the 1950s the two main oil trades were from refineries in Venezuela and the Caribbean to the United States and from the Middle East to Western Europe. The Caribbean to United States trade built up to a peak of 150 mt a year in the early 1970s (see Figure 9.6), then fell sharply to 80 mt as the US adjusted its domestic refining capacity. Unlike the US, European oil imports were mainly shipped as crude oil rather than products. Products imports fell to a trough of 35 mt in 1971, then revived to about 80 mt in the 1980s, compared with over 400 mt of crude imports. The explanation of this trade pattern can be found in a combination of technical, economic and political factors.

On the technical front, the 1950s brought refining techniques which enabled the mix of oil products from the refining process to be more closely linked to the local market. In addition, the amount of waste to be disposed of from the cargo of crude oil was greatly reduced, an important factor on the long sea journey from the Middle East to Western Europe. Finally, politics played a part, since nationalization of the oil refineries of the Anglo Iranian Oil Company in 1951 provided an incentive to locate refineries in the more politically secure consuming countries. As oil became more important to the economies of Western Europe, so the degree of risk that they were prepared to accept became smaller. Thus 'there was an escalating interest in the development of market-based refineries, and by the end of the 1950s Western Europe had developed sufficient refinery capacity to meet its main oil products needs'.[23]

The changing political and economic climate in the oil industry after the 1973 oil crisis brought a new dimension to the products trade. Several oil producers became interested in investing oil revenue in refineries, which would enable them to export oil products, thus increasing their value-added. The most prominent was Saudi Arabia, which in the late 1970s built two 25 million ton refineries, both aimed at the export market. In contrast, the US oil industry found itself with surplus refining capacity and started to withdraw from the refining operations in the Caribbean. The main source of trade growth came from the Asian economies whose imports grew rapidly during the decade of industrialization from 1985 to 1995 (Figure 9.6).

The transport of oil products

The transport system for products is more complex than crude oil. In the smaller high value products trades the volume of cargo is not sufficient to justify the use of very large ships or the storage and handling facilities which this would require. Petroleum products are generally shipped in tankers of 6,000–60,000 dwt, often with epoxy coated tanks. These ships are designed with cargo handling systems which enable them to carry several different types of product on the same voyage.

The transport of oil products should be distinguished from the more specialized trade in small liquid parcels such as chemical and vegetable oils. These appear on the market in quantities which are large enough to make them prohibitively expensive to ship in drums or purpose-built tankers, but not in sufficiently large packages to justify the charter of the whole ship. This led to the development of 'parcel' tankers which contain many segregated tanks, sometimes 30–40, with separate pumping arrangements, some of them with special coatings to resist toxic liquids. This enables the shipowner to load many different cargoes of liquid into a single vessel.

A transport operation of this type is highly complex, involving carefully planned investment decisions supported by a high professional operating service to schedule the cargo to ensure that high utilization levels are achieved. For this reason, the carriage of chemicals and light oils cargoes is a specialist business, and it is certainly one which requires professional skill and experience.

The liquefied natural gas (LNG) trade

A highly specialized late-comer to the bulk liquid shipping business was the liquefied natural gas (LNG) trade. LNG is mainly produced from dedicated gas fields and is transported at approximately atmospheric pressure at a temperature of −161°C.[24] The hazardous nature and the very low temperatures of LNG requires special facilities isolated from the rest of the port. Surfaces in contact with LNG must be manufactured from alloys to withstand very low temperatures, as ordinary steel would become brittle. The first commercial LNG trade started in 1964 between Algeria and Canvey Island in the UK using two specially built ships – the *Methane Princess* and the *Methane Progress*. This was followed shortly afterwards by a major scheme for the export of LNG from Brunei to Japan and a number of other schemes to export natural gas from gasfields in Algeria, Indonesia, Abu Dhabi and Malaysia. Since that time the trade has grown steadily doubling from 48 billion cubic metres in 1984 to 88 billion cubic metres in 1994 (Figure 9.7).

Special installations are required for liquefaction, storage, refrigeration, loading, unloading and regasification of LNG. Depending upon distance from the gas production area and other factors not all of these processes may be carried out at the terminal. Insulated pipelines and insulated storage tankers with refrigeration plant are required for storing LNG in the terminal. Typical export storage tanks have a capacity of 300,000 barrels, or 47,750

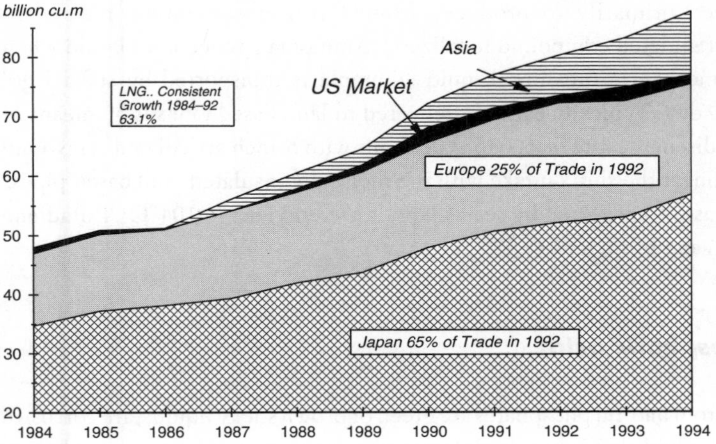

FIGURE 9.7 World LNG imports 1984–94
Source: Clarkson Research Studies

cubic metres. LNG is shipped in specially built vessels with heavily insulated cargo tanks which keeps the gas liquid during its voyage. A typical size for a large LNG carrier is 125,000 m^3.

The liquified petroleum gas trade (LPG)

LPG is mainly produced from oilfields – it is the gas that is often flared off – though small quantities are produced in the refining process. Like LNG, LPG must be liquefied for seaborne transportation; this is achieved by either cooling it to a temperature of around −50°C or subjecting it to 10–12 bar pressure. Vessels used for the carriage of LPG are also used in the chemical gas trades for the carriage of ammonia, etc.

LPG transport by sea requires a substantial investment in liquefaction and cargo handling facilities as well as the construction of specialist LPG tonnage. In economic terms, however, the trade is fundamentally different because the volume of production is linked to the volume of crude oil output. As a result, the quantities of LPG reaching the export market are not directly controlled by the supplier. The export trade is mainly from OPEC countries, particularly Kuwait and Saudi Arabia, to Japan, Western Europe and the United States.

Chemical gases (e.g. liquefied ammonia)

Ammonia is a colourless anhydrous gas, with a bitter smell. While ammonia is not easily inflammable, when mixed with air or with oxygen it can form an explosive mixture. Anhydrous ammonia contains nitrogen, which is one of the basic elements in fertilizers.

Liquid ammonia is used primarily to produce nitrate fertilizers (ammonia nitrate) or compound fertilizers (granulated compound fertilizers). Ammonia gas becomes liquid when cooled to −33°C at atmospheric pressure. Liquid ammonia is transported by special gas carriers of 3,000–40,000 dwt. Typically cargo is delivered to land based tanks is by means of the ship's pumps with a discharge rate of 600 tons per hour with 6-inch articulated arms. One or several such arms connect the ship's intake with the thermally insulated land based pipes.

Other chemical gases transported by sea as liquids are ethylene (−104°C), Butadiene (−5°C), ethane (−89°C) and propylene (−48°C).

Heavy chemicals (e.g. phosphoric acid)

Phosphoric acids made from natural phosphates are green or brown sticky liquids, are corrosive for metals such as iron, zinc and aluminium. Stainless steel, copper, bronze, brass, some plastics, rubber and acid proof paints are resistant to phosphoric acid at normal temperatures. While phosphoric acids are non-inflammable and non-explosive compounds, they react with many metals by releasing hydrogen which can result in explosions and fires. It is very dense with a specific gravity of 1.8. Other heavy inorganic mineral acids with similar properties are caustic soda liquor (SG 1.5), sulphuric acid (SG 1.7–1.8) and nitric acid (SG 1.5).

Transportation takes place in special vessels up to 45,000 dwt through stainless steel pipes. Typical handling rates are 600 tons per hour. In port the acids are stored in steel cisterns with an inner lining of rubber (self vulcanizing 4mm thick rubber sheets). The cisterns stand in watertight concrete tanks that can hold the contents of a full cistern in case of leakage or accident.

9.6 The five major dry bulks

If oil is the energy of modern industrial society, the five major bulks are the building blocks from which it is constructed. *Iron ore* and *coal* are the raw materials of steelmaking and steel is the principal material used in the construction of industrial and domestic buildings, motor cars, merchant ships, machinery and the great majority of industry products. The staple foods of the modern industrial society are bread and meat, both of which require large quantities of *grain* – for baking and as the raw material of modern factory farming for the production of meat. *Bauxite and alumina* are the raw materials of aluminium making, the second most important structural metal in modern industrial society, while *phosphate rock* is the principal bulk fertilizer used in crop production. It follows that in discussing the five major bulk trades we are concerned with the whole material development of the world economy that uses these materials.

Because of their volume, the five major bulk trades are the driving force behind the dry bulk carrier market. In 1995 the trade totalled 1 bt, accounting for more than one-quarter of total seaborne cargo, and in terms of tonnage about half the crude oil trade. The tonnage of cargo in each commodity and its historic growth are shown in Table 9.2.

TABLE 9.2 The five 'major' bulk commodities shipped by sea (mt)

Commodity	*1965*	*1975*	*1985*	*1995*
Iron ore	152	292	321	399
Coal	59	127	272	403
Grain	70	137	181	184
Bauxite and alumina	21	41	40	49
Phosphate rock	26	38	43	28
Total	328	635	857	1,063

Source: Fearnleys World Bulk Trades

It is immediately apparent from the historical trade statistics that each of these five trades followed its own distinctive growth pattern during the three decades 1965–1995. Iron ore grew rapidly until the mid-1970s, after which the trade has grown slowly. Coal followed a similar pattern until 1975, but continued to grow. It more than doubled between 1975 and 1985 and increased by 50 per cent between 1985 and 1995. Grain grew fairly steadily until 1985, then stagnated, though with substantial year-to-year fluctuations. Bauxite grew rapidly during the 1960s, but stagnated during the 1970s, then revived, increasing by 25 per cent between 1985 and 1995. Phosphate rock was unique in showing almost no growth over the 30 years. It grew, then declined.

Such major changes in the pattern of growth of the main dry bulk commodity trades are clearly of great importance to the shipping industry. One of the principal reasons for studying commodity trade economics is to explain why such changes take place. As we shall see in the following brief review of the five major bulk trades, there is no simple pattern. Each commodity has its own distinctive industrial characteristics, growth trends and impact upon the dry bulk shipping industry.

The seaborne iron ore trade

Iron ore is the largest of the five major bulk commodity trades and the principal raw material of the steel industry. Like crude oil, the iron ore trade is determined by the location of the processing plant in relation to raw material supplies. During the Industrial Revolution, steel plants were located on sites close to major sources of raw materials, notably iron ore, coal and limestone. Access to these materials was a major concern in the economics of the steel industry. However, as transport technology developed it became clear that the distance over which the materials were shipped was less important than the freight-rate structure, the transport service and the quality of the raw materials.[25]

By the early twentieth century, developments in bulk shipping technology meant that steel plants located near to raw material supplies no longer had a cost advantage, particularly when land transport was required. For example, in the United Kingdom, Northamptonshire ores were trebled in cost by transport to Middlesbrough, whereas the cost of Lorraine ores in the Ruhr was hardly more than doubled for a much longer journey owing to the availability of water transport.[26] As the demand for steel expanded in the twentieth century, the industry started to gravitate towards coastal steel plants, which could import raw materials at minimum cost by using a carefully planned integrated bulk shipping operation. This had the advantage that, with the resources of the world accessible by sea, it was possible to find higher-quality raw materials than were available locally, particularly in the traditional steelmaking areas of Western Europe where the better-quality ores were already depleted.

The prototype for the modern integrated dry bulk transport operation was probably the steel plant built by Bethlehem Steel at Sparrow's Point, Baltimore, in the early 1920s. This plant was designed specifically to import iron ore by sea from Cruz Grande in Chile, taking advantage of the newly-opened Panama Canal. To service the trade, a contract was placed with the Brostrom group, which ordered two ore carriers of 22,000 dwt. At the time these were two of the world's largest ocean-going cargo ships. Details of the shipping operation are recorded as follows:

> The contract, signed in 1922, called for two ships to carry ore from Chile through the Panama Canal to Bethlehem Steel Company's plant at Sparrow's Point, Baltimore. The ships had no conventional cargo handling gear, and hinged corrugated steel hatch covers. These were the full width of the holds, weighed 8 tons apiece and were clamped down to thick rubber gaskets. The *Sveland* was delivered on 9th April 1925 and *Americaland* on 29th June and they promptly entered their designed service between Cruz Grande and Baltimore. It was an exacting schedule and the average time spent at sea each year was 320–330 days. At Cruz Grande the 22,000 tons cargo was normally loaded in two hours, though the record was 48 minutes. Discharging at the other end required about 24 hours. Routine engine maintenance was carried out at sea, one of the two engines being shut down for eight hours per trip. Painting was also carried out while underway.[27]

This pattern of using large, specially designed ships on a shuttle service between the mine and the steel plant became standard practice for coastal steel plants. Although the size of ship used increased during the next 50 years, reaching 120,000 dwt in the 1960s and 300,000 dwt in the 1980s, the basic operational principles remain the same.

The East Coast development of the US steel industry proved something of a false start, and the major portion of US steelmaking continued to be concentrated around the Great Lakes, using locally produced ores supplemented by imports from Canada via the St Lawrence Seaway when the Labrador iron ore fields were developed. As a result, the United States did not figure prominently in the post-war overseas iron ore trade, and the principal importers of iron ore were Western Europe and Japan, as can be seen in Figure 9.8.

During the post-war period of industrial expansion, steel demand grew rapidly. In Europe and Japan this growth was met by building modern integrated coastal steel plants using imported raw materials. In Japan there was little choice since there were no domestic reserves of iron ore, but even in Europe where extensive iron ore reserves are available

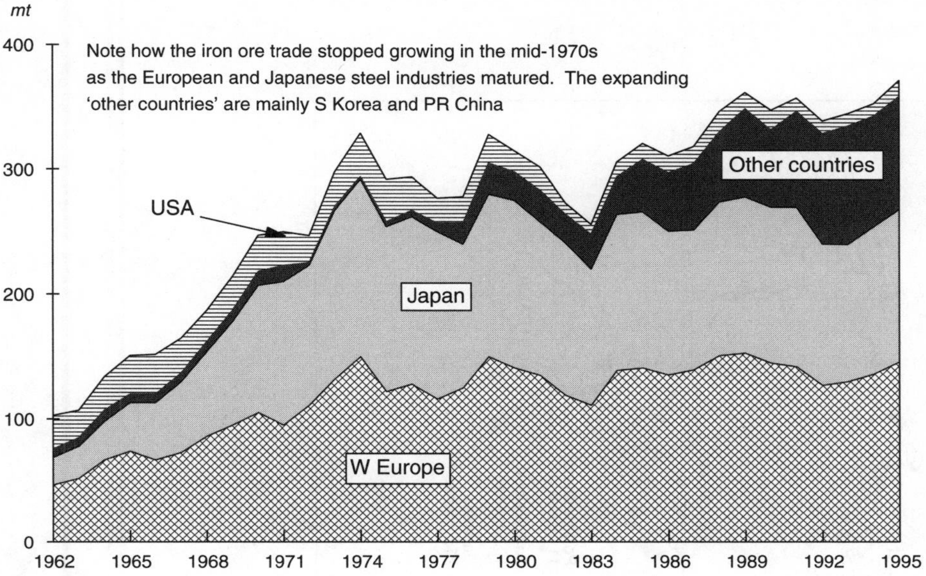
mt
400
300
200
100
0
Note how the iron ore trade stopped growing in the mid-1970s
as the European and Japanese steel industries matured. The expanding
'other countries' are mainly S Korea and PR China
USA
Other countries
Japan
W Europe
1962
1965
1968
1971
1974
1977
1980
1983
1986
1989
1992
1995

FIGURE 9.8 Iron ore imports 1962–95
Source: Clarkson Research Studies

these were of lower quality than the imported variety. For new developments, the shorter land transit leg offered little cost advantage over seaborne transport using large bulk carriers.

It was the rapid expansion of iron ore imports by the steel industry that underpinned the bulk carrier boom of the 1960s. The Japanese and European steel companies were prepared to offer long time charters to meet the regular raw material requirements of the new coastal steel plants. These charters provided many growing bulk shipping companies with the stable foundation on which to base their fleet development strategy. In the early 1970s, however, the period of growth came to an end. After a decade of steadily expanding ship demand, the steel companies found themselves facing excess capacity and 1974 proved to be a turning point for iron ore imports, as can be seen in Figure 9.8. The explanation of this change is that in these two areas steel demand had reached saturation point in the early 1970s: between 1975 and 1995, West European steel fell from 170 mt to 161 mt; during the same period Japanese production was static at 101 mt.[28]

There are many reasons for this radical change of trend, but the most important was that the industries that are intensive users of steel (principally construction, vehicles and shipbuilding) had all reached a plateau in their output.[29] As a result, the growth had been removed from the largest iron ore importers. In their place the newly industrializing countries such as South Korea started to make an impact in the 1990s, a trend that is visible in Figure 9.8.

Although we have concentrated on the demand for seaborne imports of iron ore, the

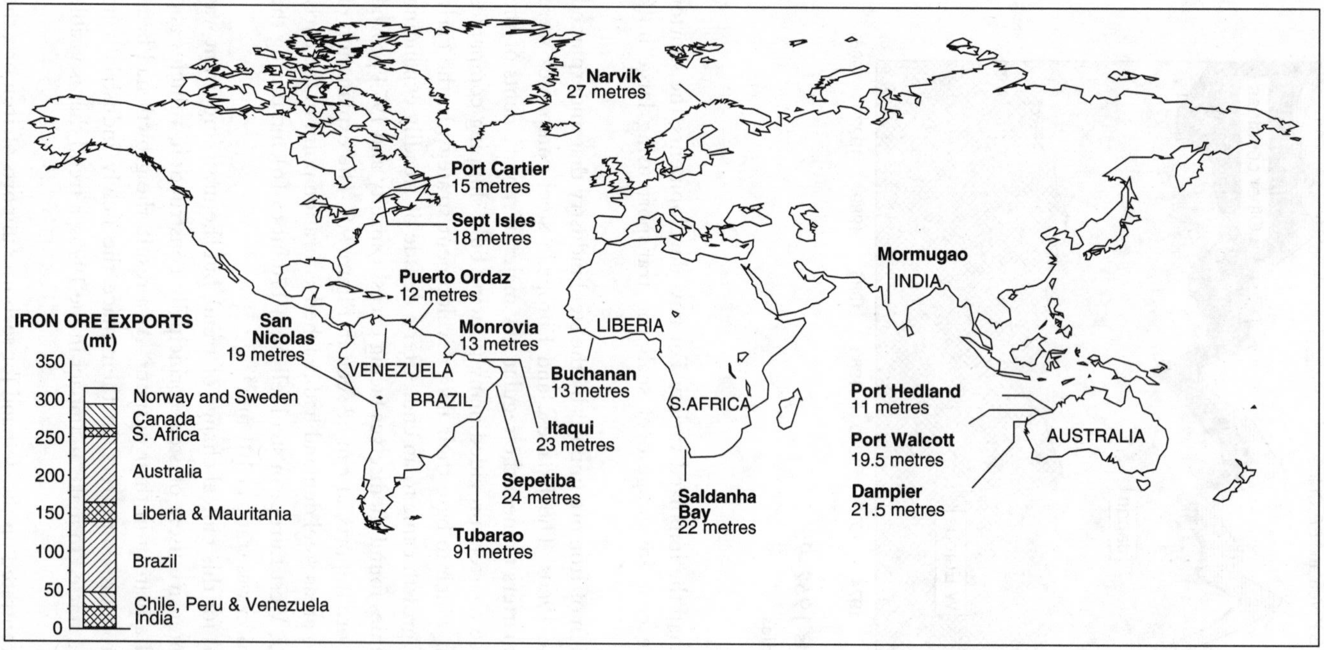

FIGURE 9.9 Major iron ore exporters and ports 1995

Source: Clarkson Research Studies

Note: Notes against each port indicate the maximum draught in Ports of the World

trade also depends crucially upon the development of a global network of iron ore supplies, and Figure 9.9 shows the pattern that developed. Generally at the initiative of the steel companies, iron ore resources were identified across the globe and the necessary capital raised to develop the mines and install the requisite transport infrastructure.

By far the largest iron ore exporters are Brazil and Australia. The first Brazilian iron ore reserves to be developed were located in the famous Iron Quadrangle of Minas Guerais and exported through the ports of Sepetiba and Tubarao. In 1986, the first cargoes were exported from Carajas, a major iron ore development in the Para region of Northern Brazil with port facilities at Itaqui geared to 300,000 dwt bulk carriers. In 1995, Brazil exported 131 mt of iron ore, accounting for almost one-third of the iron ore trade. The other major iron exporter is Australia, from mines located in Northwest Australia. In 1995, Australia exported 133 mt of iron ore, mainly through the three ports of Port Hedland, Dampier and Port Walcott. The remaining third of the iron ore trade is supplied from a variety of smaller exporters, of whom the most important are Sweden, South Africa, Liberia, India and Venezuela.

The transport system for iron ore

Iron ore transport by sea is one of the great successes of industrial bulk shipping. The iron ore generally has a stowage factor of 0.3 cubic metres per ton and is almost always transported in bulk and in full shiploads. Over the past decade there has been great competition between suppliers in the Atlantic and Pacific, leading to increasing distance between source and markets and the employment of the largest ships possible. Generally iron ore ports serve as transfer terminals linking two modes of transport, with storage areas at the port provide a surge capability between the more or less continuous overland movement and the intermittent ocean shipment.

At the mine large earth-moving equipment removes the ore from open pits and transfers it to special trains or trucks that transfer it to port, where large cranes or automatic dumping mechanisms place it in storage areas from which it is transferred by means of gravity or by cranes to the ship. The ship then steams to a port or coastal steel mill where the process is reversed. The entire system is geared to anticipate mill needs with a continuous flow of the ore from mine to mill.

Although the economies of scale which can be achieved through the use of large bulk vessels were well known in the 1950s, the transition from small vessels to the larger sizes was not immediate. In 1965 80 per cent of all iron ore was carried in vessels below 40,000 dwt, and over half the trade is still carried in ships less than 80,000 dwt. The process of introducing large ships was thus a gradual one, with the size of vessels built for use in the iron ore trade increasing steadily from around 30,000 dwt in the early 1960s to 60,000 dwt in 1965; 100,000 dwt in 1969; and 150,000 dwt plus in the early 1970s and 300,000 dwt in the 1990s. For example the *Bergeland* delivered in 1991 was a 300,000 dwt vessel designed exclusively for the carriage of iron ore. In fact the size of ship has grown with the volume of trade and the improvements in port facilities, though throughout many small vessels built in previous periods continue to be used.

The seaborne coal trade

Coal is the next largest of the dry bulk trades, with imports of 403 mt in 1995, principally into Western Europe and Japan, as can be seen in Figure 9.10. The seaborne coal trade is a good deal more complex than the iron ore trade because coal imports have two different markets. The first is as a raw material for steelmaking and the second as a fuel for the power-generating industry. This trade was important in the early twentieth century and reappeared in the late 1970s.

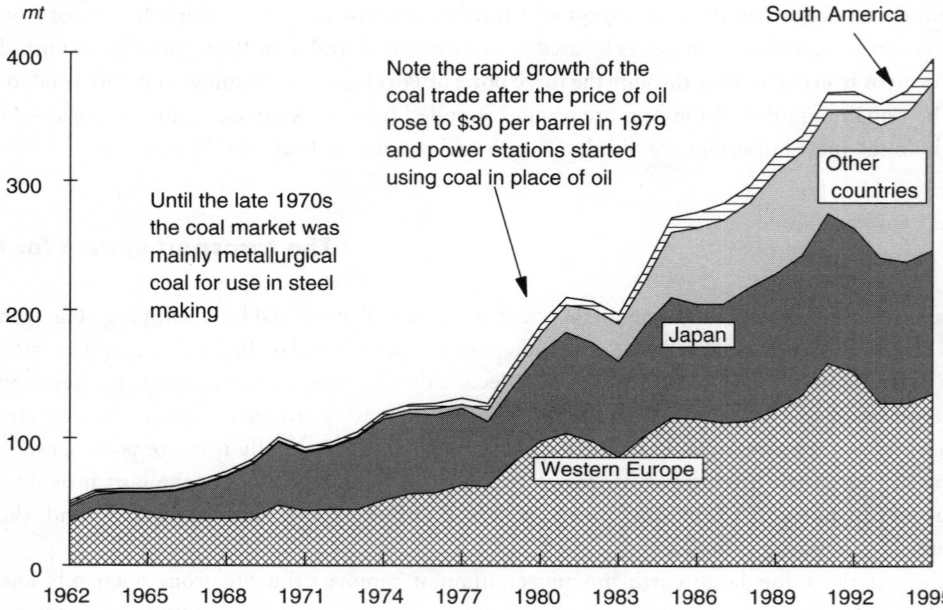

FIGURE 9.10 Coal imports 1962–95
Source: Clarkson Research Studies

The economics of the seaborne trade in metallurgical coal follows a similar pattern to that of iron ore and it was the same commercial advantages that encouraged European and Japanese steelmakers to import coal by sea. In the steel production process, coal is first converted into coke in a coke oven, and the coke is then mixed with iron ore and limestone to form a charge that is fed into the top of the blast furnace. As the charge works its way down the blast furnace, the combustion of the coke provides energy for reducing the iron ore, and at the bottom of the blast furnace pig iron is drawn off, leaving a residue of slag.

This process makes special demands upon the coal. To do its job satisfactorily the coke 'must be porous to allow air circulation, strong enough to carry the weight of the charge in the furnace without being crushed, and low in ash and sulfur.'[30] Many varieties of coal do not meet these requirements, and some grades are naturally more satisfactory than others.

In Japan the reserves of suitable coal were extremely limited, and in Europe, although coal with coking qualities is available, supplies were being depleted. The move to coastal steel plants gave steelmakers the opportunity to import the cheapest most suitable metallurgical grade coals from foreign mines and blend them to give the precise requirements for efficient steelmaking. As a result, coking coal imports grew rapidly during the 1960s, but stagnated in the 1970s in the same way as the iron ore trade and for the same reason. This trend is only partly visible in Figure 9.10 because it is overlaid by the trade in thermal coal, which grew rapidly in the late 1970s.

As a fuel, coal is extensively used in power stations, and is in competition with oil. During the 1950s, the falling price of oil undermined the commercial case for importing thermal coal by sea and by the early 1960s the thermal coal trade had disappeared. For the next decade almost the only coal moved by sea was for steelmaking. With the increase in oil prices during the 1970s, however, the relative economics of coal and oil changed, and by 1979 there was an economic case to be made for using coal as an energy source. It took several years to mobilize the necessary volume and handling infrastructure.[31] but from 1979 onwards there was a rapid increase in thermal coal imports, which is clearly visible in Figure 9.10.

Supplies of suitable coal for the seaborne export trade were met partly from established producers, and partly by developing new mines specifically for the export market. Amongst the established suppliers, by far the most important sources are North America and Australia, followed by South Africa, Canada and Columbia (Figure 9.11). There are high-grade coal deposits on the East Coast USA in the Appalachian Mountains. Coal is exported through the adjacent ports of Baltimore and Hampton Roads or from the US Gulf, making use of the inland waterway system. In 1995, about 20 per cent of world 'coal exports came from the United States.[32]

The main new mines opened to service the coal trade were in Canada, Australia South Africa, Indonesia and Columbia. In Canada, new mines were developed in British Columbia and the coal shipped 700 miles by rail for export through bulk handling terminals at Vancouver, mainly to Asian markets. In Australia, there are major coal reserves in Queensland and New South Wales. As a whole, Australia accounted for about one-third of the coal export trade in 1995. South African coal is shipped by rail to Richards Bay for export. The bulk carriers used are generally smaller than in the iron ore trade. The reasons for this appear to be the smaller volume of coking coal used, relative to iron ore, its greater volume to stockpile, the higher value and the risk of spontaneous combustion in very large units.

An example of a coal transport system is provided by the Hunter Valley/Port Of Newcastle complex in Australia. The Port of Newcastle services the export trade of over thirty coal mines located in the Hunter Valley behind Newcastle. The coal moves by rail through marshalling depots to two port stockpile areas. The port has three coal loaders loading up to four ships at once, ranging from vessels of only 10,000 dwt to coal carriers of 150,000 dwt. The water draught is maintained at 15.2 metres by a dredging programme which is paid for by the coal and steel companies, making it one of the deepest ports in Australia. The cargo handling equipment used for coal is very similar to the iron ore system described in the previous section.

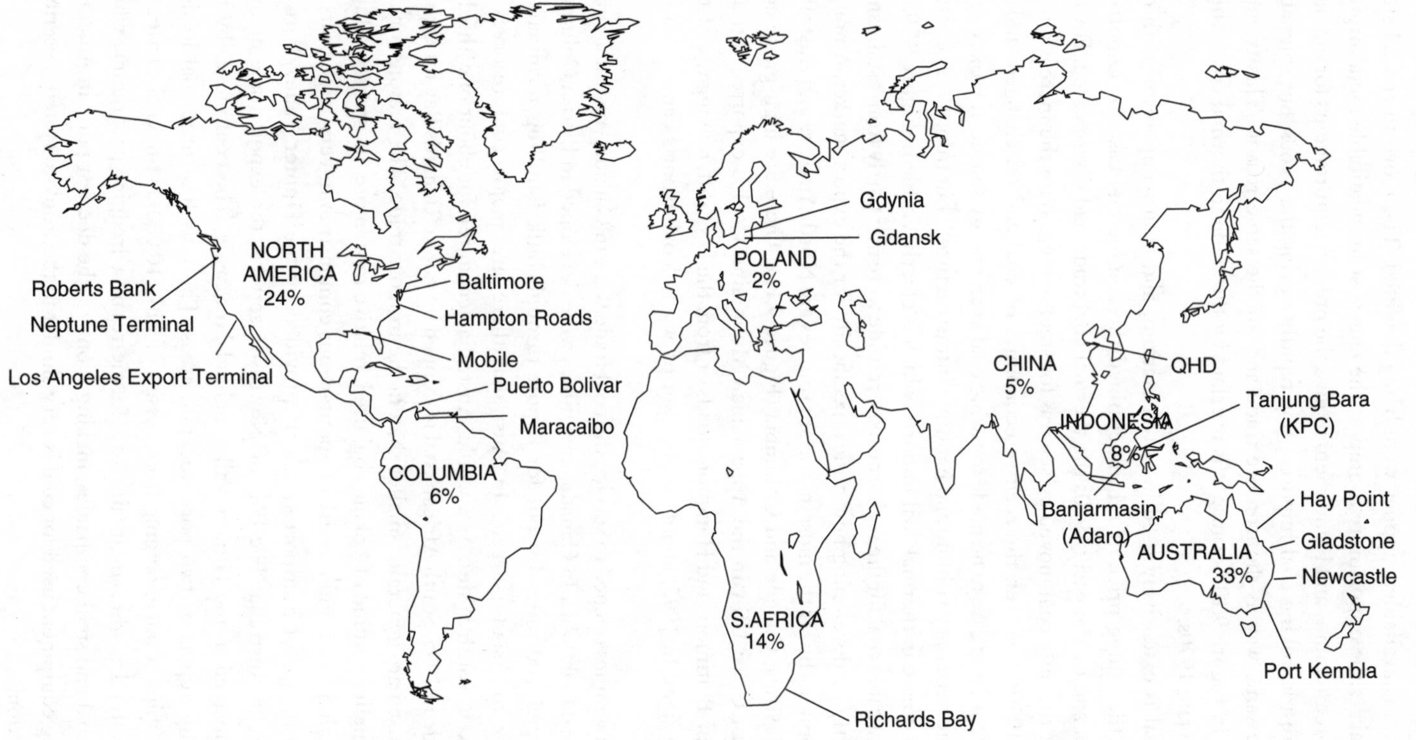

FIGURE 9.11 Major coal exporters and ports 1996

Source: Fearnleys, *World Bulk Trades*, 1995

The seaborne grain trade

Although grain is grouped with iron ore and coal as one of the five major bulks, in both economic and shipping terms it is fundamentally a different business. Whereas iron ore and coal form part of a carefully structured industrial operation, grain is an agricultural commodity, seasonal in its trade and irregular in both volume and route. Consequently it is extremely difficult to optimize, or even plan, grain shipments and the trade depends heavily on general-purpose tonnage drawn from the charter market.

In 1995, the grain trade was 184 mt. Grain is used as human food and as animal feedstuff in the production of meat. Wheat accounted for about half of the grain trade in the mid-1990s, mostly destined for human consumption; the other half consisted of maize, barley and oilseeds, mainly for use as animal feedstuff. By commodity, in 1995 the seaborne grain trade was wheat 97 mt, and course grains 91 mt.[33] Thus the grain trade is more closely linked to meat production than to direct human food.

The steady upward trend in seaborne grain imports shown in Figure 9.12 was to a large extent driven by the trend towards greater meat consumption at higher income levels. Although part of the grain trade is certainly destined to meet harvest shortfalls and relieve

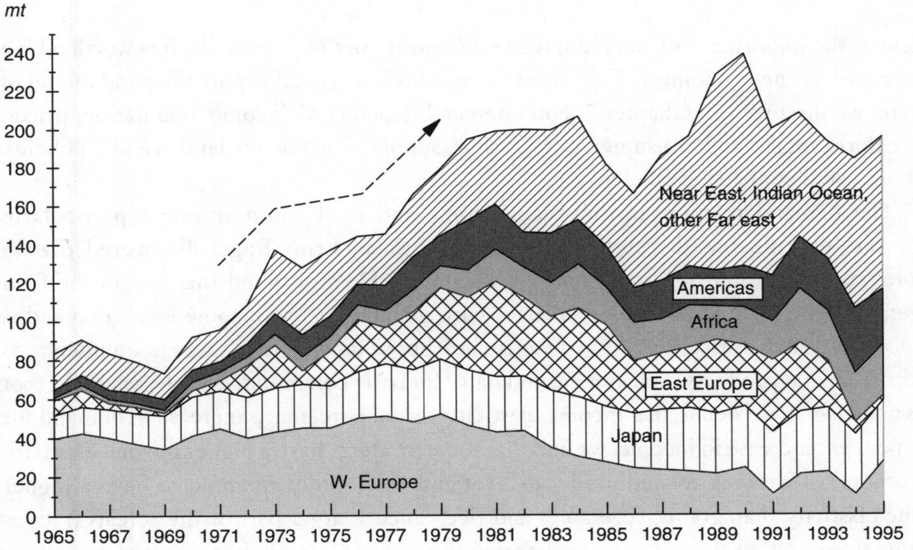

FIGURE 9.12 Grain imports 1965–95
Source: Fearnleys, *World Bulk Trades* 1995 and earlier editions

famines, the real volume is intended for feeding animals in industrial and industrializing societies where each unit of meat produced requires anything from five to fifteen units of animal feed.[34] The dietary pattern that underlies this trend, and the subsequent impact on grain demand in the post-1945 era, is described by Morgan as follows:

> Rising incomes put more money into people's pockets for buying food. Millions of families 'stepped-up' to diets that included more bread, meat and poultry. Livestock and poultry rather than people became the main market for American grain, and the soya beans and corn ranked with jet aircraft and computers as the country's major exports. As more countries aspired to this grain based diet, the need for grain increased.[35]

The pattern of trade is shown in Figure 9.12. During the 1960s the grain trade was dominated by Europe and Japan, which accounted for more than two-thirds of total grain imports. In tonnage terms this sector of the trade remained fairly static during the 1970s and early 1980s. Almost all of the growth in the volume of seaborne imports came from the entry of Eastern Europe, including the USSR, and the developing countries into the market. By 1995 the trade share of Europe had fallen to only 4 per cent and Japan had fallen to 13 per cent. Asia (29 per cent), particularly China, South America (17 per cent), and Africa (16 per cent) had all become much more important.

The grain trade model

In view of the importance of the food/feed relationship in the grain trade, it is worth taking a closer look at the economics of the food trade. This is a typical supply/demand model of the type we discussed in Chapter 7. Food demand depends on income, population, prices, daily calorie intake and consumer tastes, while supply depends on land, yields, policies, prices and feed conversion efficiency.

The demand relationship between income and food consumption is particularly important. The nineteenth-century German statistician Ernst Engel discovered that as incomes rise the proportion spent on food declines.[36] He also found that within the food budget, the type of food purchased changes with income. At low income levels demand is for necessities such as rice, cereals and vegetables, but as income rises there is a tendency to substitute animal products such as meat and dairy for basic commodities such as cereals, root crops and rice. If we define the 'income elasticity' as the percentage increase in demand for a one per cent increase in income, we find that some products have a higher income elasticity than others[37]. Livestock related food (i.e. meat and dairy products) tend to have a higher income elasticity than grains, vegetables and rice. Since a larger part of the cereals trade is for animal feed rather than direct consumption this is one of the main sources of growth.

Turning to the supply side of the food trade model, we have another set of complex relationships. Between 1980 and 1990 world output of food increased by about 26 per cent. Crop production depends upon crop yield and the area and agricultural land. Prices, political policies and stock changes are also important variables. Until the early years of the twentieth century most of the world's increase in crop production came from either an increase in land (e.g. the opening up of the North American grainlands) or from an increase in the amount of labour used. During the twentieth century these trends have been reversed. Agricultural yields have increased steadily, while the amount of arable land has remained fairly constant.

Higher yields were obtained from greater fertilizer application, improved seed varieties, mechanization, pesticides and better farming techniques. There are enormous differences in productivity around the world. For example average level of French cereal output per worker is ten times as great as Japan and forty times as great as India.

Although the analysis of the grain trade often concentrates on short term supply shortages in response to harvests, the food trade model emphasizes the importance of changing demand in response to income and prices. The rapid growth of imports by the newly industrializing countries in the 1980s and 1990s was the response to rising incomes, the high income elasticity of animal products in these countries and their need to import animal feeds. As in the oil trade, the substitution effect of prices should not be overlooked.

The transport of grain

As an example of the grain transport system we can take the processing of Canadian wheat into consumer products. The wheat is harvested by large combines in the Canadian Prairies and moved by truck from the field to a storage elevator, into which it is transferred by conveyor or by an air pressure (pneumatic) system. During high harvests or when demand is low these storage facilities may become inadequate and in the past farmers have been reduced to storing grain in sacks in any covered storage which is available. From the storage elevator the wheat is gravity fed to a railroad car and shipped to port where it is off-loaded from the rail car by opening a hopper in the bottom of the car to allow the grain to fall on to a conveyor under the rail track. From here the conveyor transfers the wheat into an elevator where it awaits transfer to a merchant ship. Naturally the elevator must hold enough grain to fill the ship.

At the other end of the voyage the process is reversed and the grain is off-loaded from the ship into a storage elevator (i.e. silo) and shipped to a flour mill or feed compounder where it is again stored in silos. From the silos it moves to the grinding facility via a conveyor or an air slide. The finished flour coming from the end of the line is either packaged for the consumer market or shipped in bulk by rail and truck to bakeries, other large industrial users, or farmers.

At the bakery the flour is again placed in a silo or hopper, conveyed to a mixing unit for dough preparation, baked into bread or other products, sent to an automatic wrapping machine, and wheeled to trucks for delivery. In many cases the first time the product is handled as a single unit is when the consumer takes it from the shelf. Such an integrated transport system is made possible by meticulous attention to required materials handling systems within each process and to the transfers of material between processes.

Despite this organization, the sea transport of grain is not managed in the same carefully planned way as the industrial commodities. Because the trade is seasonal and fluctuates with the harvest in the exporting and importing regions, shippers rely heavily on the spot market, using the ships that are available. These fluctuations are not predictable, so planning transport is very difficult and complex. To load cargoes upwards of 70,000 tons involves careful scheduling of input barges or box cars from many different sources, often at the height of the season. Discharging can be equally hazardous since there are all the problems of ensuring the prompt arrival of a multitude of barges and coasters, and penalties for faulty consignment and demurrage charges grow more rapidly with large cargoes.[38] For this reason it is more difficult to introduce large ships into the grain trade than into the iron ore and coal trades and there is often congestion.

The major grain-exporting ports are shown in Figure 9.13 in relation to the grain-producing areas from which they draw their supplies. In 1995, over 60 per cent of all grain exports were shipped out of Canada and the United States, so this is clearly the most important loading area. Essentially the US Gulf ports and the East Coast ports serve the southern end of the US grain belt, while the Great Lakes and the St Lawrence serve the northeast. Production from Saskatchewan and Alberta is shipped mainly through West Coast ports, especially Vancouver. Size limitations vary considerably, though ports on the lower St Lawrence and New Orleans can load vessels over 100,000 dwt.

The seaborne bauxite and phosphate rock trades

The two remaining major bulk trades, bauxite/alumina and phosphate rock, are a good deal smaller, together accounting for about 7 per cent of the total trade in the five major bulks in 1995. Bauxite ore is the raw material of aluminium making, while alumina is its semi-refined product. It takes about 5.4 tons of bauxite to produce 2 tons of alumina, from which 1 ton of aluminium can be smelted. Shipments of bauxite ore and the intermediate product, alumina, totalled 49 mt in 1995.

The trade in bauxite and alumina follows the familiar industrial pattern we have already discussed under the heading of oil, iron ore and coal, but with some special features. In the early 1950s the trade was dominated by North American imports from the Caribbean, but in the 1960s both Europe and Japan entered the trade on a major scale. Although aluminium is used in much smaller quantities than steel, it has been finding new markets; consequently demand grew very rapidly during the first six decades of the century. To meet this demand, during the 1960s aluminium companies in Western Europe and Japan built domestic aluminium smelters, importing bauxite from the Caribbean, the traditional producer, and also from newly developed reserves in West Africa and Australia. As a result, there was a rapid growth in the seaborne bauxite trade. This pattern changed fairly dramatically in the 1970s as the bauxite producers moved downstream into alumina refining and the aluminium smelters in Europe and Japan proved uneconomic owing to the high cost of electricity for aluminium smelting, particularly after the 1973 oil crisis. As a result, although the demand for aluminium continued to grow, the sea trade in bauxite and alumina remained at the same level of around 42–44 mt for the decade 1974–1984. After this structural adjustment growth resumed with the trade reaching 49 mt in 1995.

Aluminium production technology follows the classic pattern of industrial integration, and in principal it is generally possible to optimize the shipping operation by using vessels of Panamax size or above. The alumina trade, on the other hand, does not generally favour the use of vessels of Panamax size and over, since alumina has a high value, needs to be

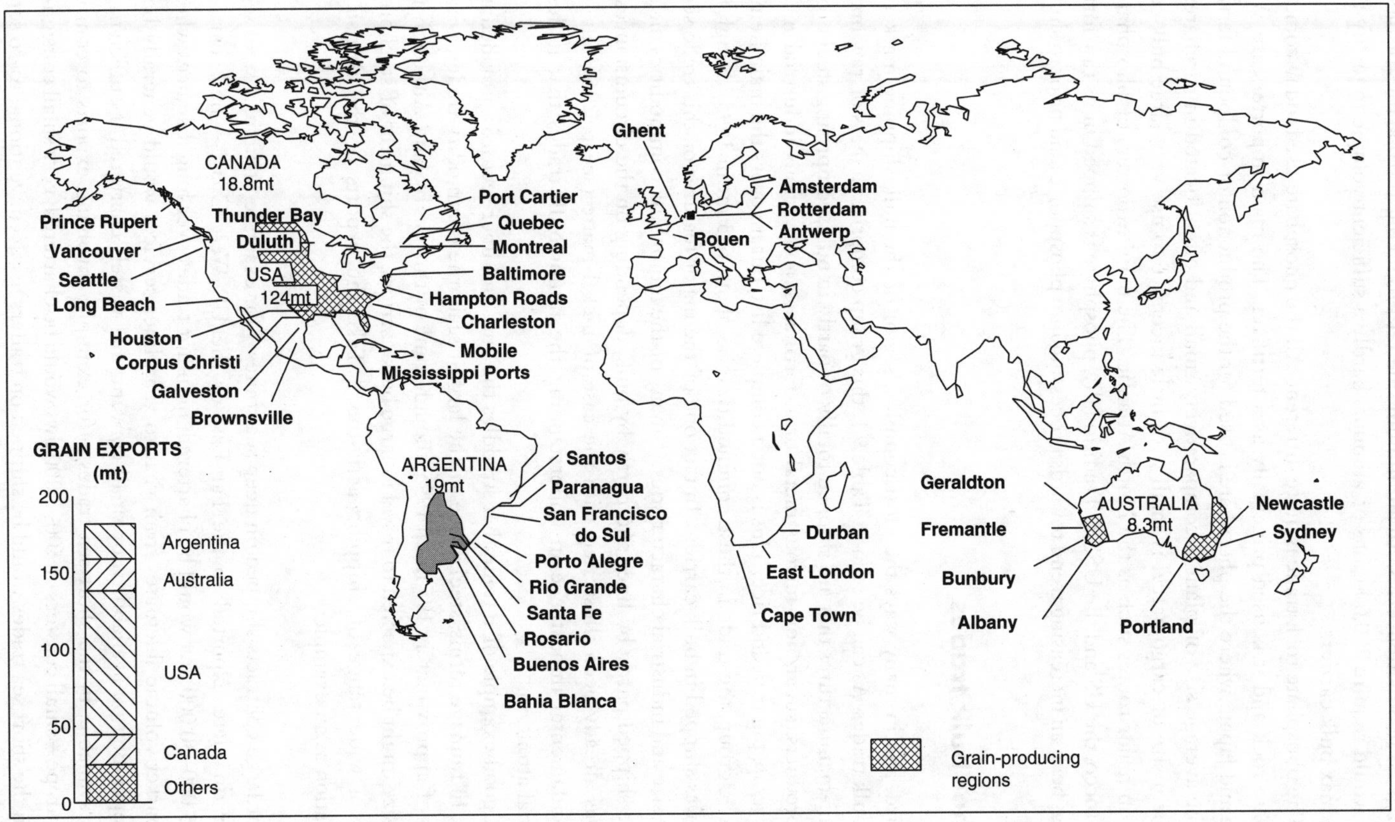

FIGURE 9.13 Major grain exporters and ports 1995

Source: Fearnleys, *World Bulk Trades*, 1995

stored under cover and the quantities of raw material required by a smelter are too small to encourage large bulk deliveries. An aluminium smelter producing 100,000 tons of metal per annum would require 200,000 tons of alumina, hardly a sufficient volume to justify the use of Panamax bulk carriers.

The phosphate rock trade is quite different. All the phosphate used today comes from phosphate rock and it is used principally as a fertilizer. The main importers are Western Europe and Japan, where the phosphate is used for the production of compound fertilizers. Since the average size of plant is comparatively small and often located in rural areas, the convenient size of cargo parcel is small with little incentive to use very large bulk carriers except on major routes such as the North Atlantic. The main exporters of phosphate rock are Morocco, the US and the USSR. Traditionally, phosphate is shipped in its raw form, but there has been an increasing trend towards processing into phosphoric acid prior to shipment.

9.7 The minor bulk trades

The third, and in many ways the most complex, sector of the bulk shipping market is the minor bulk trades. As can be seen in Table 9.1, this group comprises a mass of raw materials and semi-manufactures that are shipped totally or partly in bulk, comprising steel products, forest products, sugar, non-ferrous metal ores, fertilizers, and various industrial materials such as scrap, pig iron and rice. This is not a complete list, but it covers the main items.

As a group, the trade in these commodities was about 623 mt in 1995, though not all of this was shipped in bulk carriers. In fact one of the major features of this trade sector is that the size and industrial characteristics of many of the minor bulk commodities mean that they are shipped partly by liner and partly by bulk, depending on the circumstances. This point has already been illustrated with the case of nickel matte (see p. 296), but it is of such fundamental importance in understanding the minor bulk trades that it deserves additional attention.

A good example of a trade that straddles the bulk and liner sector is provided by *steel products*. In tonnage terms, steel is one of the largest seaborne commodity trades, with total imports of approximately 195 mt in 1995, though some of this was by land. Although a trade of this size might be expected to travel in large bulk carriers, the shipment of steel products involves a wide range of shipping activities.[39] Take the exports of the British Steel Corporation as an example:

> for large contracts shipped on deep sea routes – for example, structural steel sections or tin plate exported to the Far East or the US West Coast – bulk carriers of 25,000–30,000 dwt would be chartered; in minor trades over long distances where the market volume fluctuates from year to year, liner services would generally be used depending on availability, or small conventional vessels chartered if sufficient cargo is available; in the short sea trades – for example, involving exports to continental Europe – small coasters of 500–3,000 dwt would be chartered; very small consignments on the short sea trades would be shipped on trailers using conventional ro-ro services;

on deep sea routes, medium-size trades of, say, 50,000 tons per year may be sent by container or ro-ro service using half-size containers or other specially constructed stowage devices.

This diversity of cargo parcel sizes means that the shipper will use whatever type of shipping operation is most economic for that particular cargo; in some cases this may involve the use of a bulk carrier, but in others the use of the liner service may be more appropriate.

Another high-volume minor bulk trade is *forest products*, of which approximately 167 mt a year were shipped in 1995. Forest products share many of the bulk handling problems raised by steel products. Thomas's Stowage lists fifty-six different types of timber, all with different weights per unit volume, and twenty-six forms in which they can be shipped, ranging from logs to batons and bundles. Luan, the major export of Malaysia, has a density of about 1.25 cubic metres per ton, while Norwegian pine has a density of 1.8 cubic metres per ton. In practice, forest products stow at about 50 per cent more than the above rates due to air space, which is high for logs and bundles and lower for loose sawn timber. Sawn timber packed to length, which is the practice of Canadian exporters, has a better stowage rate than timber that has been 'truck packed', i.e. bundled together in different lengths. As a very rough guide, in purpose-built ships logs stow at 2.7 cubic metres per ton or more, bundled and sawn timber at 2.2 cubic metres per ton, and the best rate is rarely better than 1.7 cubic metres per ton.

In the 1950s the forest products trade consisted mainly of European imports, and formed a valuable backhaul cargo for liners that had discharged general cargo in Third World countries, for example West Africa. As the trade grew in the early 1960s it started to go bulk. Initially forest products shippers chartered in convention tonnage, but this proved generally unsatisfactory. Since the mid-1960s, there has been a trend towards building specialist ships, either small log carriers for use in Southeast Asia or specialized open hold bulk carriers with extensive cargo handling gear for use in long haul trades such as West Coast North America to Western Europe.

As with other primary materials, the basis of the forest products trade is supply and demand. Much the largest component of the trade is within South-east Asia, dominated by the Japanese who import logs from Malaysia, Indonesia and the Philippines. Japanese forests were depleted by over-cutting in the Second World War and the import trade developed through the established lumber mills. A trade also developed into Japan from West Coast North America, including a sizable trade in woodchips, which were also imported from Australia and Siberia. A number of special woodchips carriers were built to service this trade, which requires a very high cubic capacity compared with normal bulk carriers. In total, Japanese imports account for about half of the forest products imports.

Europe is the other major importer of forest products, though on a much smaller scale. In Europe, much of the temperate forest is already intensively used, but North Europe, particularly Scandinavia, is self-sufficient with an exportable surplus. Southern Europe has become a major importer, drawing imports from Northern Europe, the USSR and North America, though some hardwoods come from West Africa and Asia. The West Coast North America to Europe trade is mainly lumber and pulp loaded at a number of ports in the

Vancouver area and is almost entirely bulk. However, pulp, paper and logs continue to travel by liner in some cases.

Cement is another sizeable minor bulk trade and reached a record 53 mt in 1995. The trade is composed mainly of shipments to construction projects in Africa, Asia and the Middle East. By its nature the trade is volatile and ships tend to be chartered for either the carriage of bulk or bagged cement. Many small bulk carriers and 'tweendeckers are used and port restrictions often require the use of vessels over 20,000 dwt.

The minor bulk trades include various manufactured fertilizers, of which ammonium sulphate and urea are the two most important. They are generally powdered or granular in form, and can travel loose or bagged in a bulk carrier or in liners. There are few handling problems, though they usually require undercover storage, and ammonium sulphate in particular is likely to absorb water from the atmosphere if not protected. Since their final market is in agriculture, individual consignments tend to be relatively small, so this is not a commodity that is likely to be shipped in 40,000-ton lots. Many shipments are to small ports in rural areas and may be only a few thousand tons. Another factor limiting the size of vessel in the fertilizer trade is that 70 per cent of the trade is into developing countries and half is to very small importers, even the larger ones taking only a few hundred thousand tons each. This results in the trade travelling predominantly in the 10,000–18,000 dwt size group of vessels, while part still travels by container.

About 26 mt of non-ferrous metal ores are shipped by sea, including manganese ore, and nickel, zinc and copper concentrates. Manganese has a high density, with trade of about 8 mt a year shipped mainly to Europe, Japan and the US from South Africa, the CIS, Gabon and Brazil. It has a low average value and differs little from iron ore, except that it is used in much smaller quantities. Consequently manufacturers keep small stores and large shipments are inconvenient. The trades in nickel, zinc, copper and chrome concentrates generally travel in small parcels owing to their high value and the small stocks carried by refineries. Transport is by small bulk carrier, container or bags.

Sugar consists of three trades, raw sugar (which is shipped loose in bulk), refined sugar (which is generally shipped in bags) and molasses (which is a by-product of sugar refining and is shipped in tankers). The main loading areas for both raw sugar and molasses are various developing countries, South Africa and Australia. The largest producers are Cuba, Brazil, the Philippines, the Dominican Republic and Australia, but one-third of the trade is made up of very small exporters in the tropical areas. Many countries (such as Costa Rica, Pakistan, Indonesia) produce sugar as a cash crop and have exports of only a few hundred thousand tons at the most. Loading facilities in these countries are frequently very poor and, since the trade is seasonal and highly fragmented, there is little incentive to improve them. As a result the trade is still largely restricted to small ships.

The salt trade is mainly into Japan. The Mexican trade to Japan was the first to develop in the early 1960s from the Mexican solar salt plant Exportadora de Sal. The trade is something of an oddity among the minor bulks, since it is shipped in very large bulk carriers. Shortly after the Japanese started to import salt from Mexico in 1962, D.K. Ludwig, the American shipowner, realized that he could radically reduce the CIF price of salt in Japan by adopting a plan that involved building a 170,000 dwt bulk/oil vessel, the *Cedros*, which was launched in 1965, renting a small Japanese island as a bulk terminal, and obtaining a backhaul of crude oil from Indonesia to Los Angeles. The trade grew steadily throughout the 1960s. Salt is also shipped from Australia to Japan.

Sulphur is a small bulk trade. The major importers are Western Europe, various developing countries (particularly India and Brazil) and Australia, New Zealand and South Africa. Sulphur is transported either in dry form (crushed, flaked, slated or pelleted), or as a molten liquid. Although dry sulphur can be shipped in conventional bulk carriers or two-deckers, it is not an easy cargo. It ignites easily, there is a danger of explosion from sulphur dust, it is extremely corrosive and in conditions of excess moisture it may produce hydrogen sulphide gas which is poisonous. For this reason a number of special dry sulphur carriers have been built incorporating various features such as a double skin (so that the interior skin can be easily cleaned and replaced when corroded), sealed hatches, special gas monitoring equipment, intensive hold-washing equipment and mechanical ventilation. Flaking and pelleting of sulphur have brought some improvements though the commodity remains a difficult one to transport.

To ship sulphur in liquid form special tankers are required, with heating coils, stainless steel tanks, special valve gear, and inert gas systems to prevent explosions. Although these vessels can be used in other chemical trades, the reverse is not true – conventional chemical tankers are not generally suitable for sulphur transportation. In addition, special loading and discharging facilities are required, so that trade is generally conducted under long-term contract. This is, therefore, a trade for which ships must be especially built or converted.

In conclusion, the minor bulk trades form an important source of bulk carrier employment, particularly for smaller sizes of vessels. Because of the physical characteristics of some cargoes and the low volume, they offer many more opportunities for innovative shipping operations than the major bulk cargoes, and are subject to many constraints that limit them to small ships.

9.8 Refrigerated cargo

Finally we come to refrigerated cargo or 'reefer' trades. This forms an important market, but once again we find competition between the bulk and liner services for carriage of this cargo. Part of the trade is carried in reefer vessels, i.e. ships totally dedicated to the carriage of reefer cargo with insulated holds, while another part of the trade is shipped in reefer containers on liner services whose vessels are equipped to carry reefer containers. The major reefer trades are briefly summarized in Figure 9.14.

The fresh meat trade is principally from Australia, New Zealand and Argentina into the developed areas of Western Europe, the US and Japan. The trade accounts for only a very small proportion of meat consumption and growth has been more rapid into Japan and West Coast North America than elsewhere, benefiting particularly from the growth of the 'fast food' business. Fresh milk is hardly traded internationally (though there is a trade in powdered milk of over 2 mt per annum) and the main dairy trades are in butter and cheese.

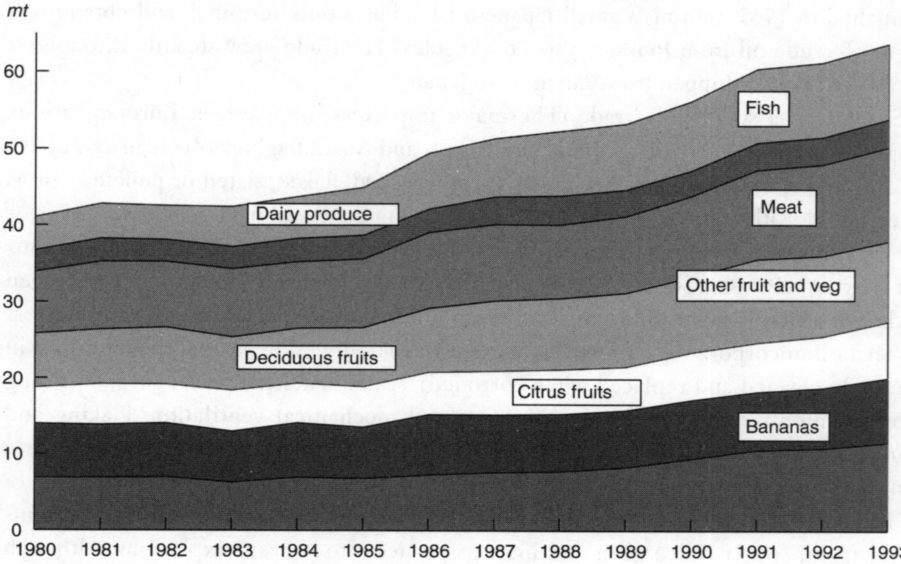

FIGURE 9.14 Trade in perishable commodities 1980–93
Source: Clarkson Research Studies

The traditional trade was from New Zealand or Australia into the UK, though this has changed in recent years as a result of the UK joining the EEC.

Finally there is the fruit and vegetable trade, which is the dominant reefer cargo. In 1993 the trade included 8.5 mt of citrus fruit, 11.6 mt of bananas, 7.4 mt of deciduous fruits and 10.5 mt of other assorted fresh fruit and vegetables. There is a major trade in oranges from the Mediterranean, especially Israel, and South Africa to Western Europe. The major exporters of bananas are the West Indies, South America and, to a lesser extent, Africa. Western Europe and the US account for about two-thirds of the imports. The 'other vegetable' trade includes a sizable trade in manioc from South-east Asia to Western Europe where it is used as an animal feed – this is not refrigerated cargo.

Food commodities transported by sea are perishable and need to be transported at carefully regulated temperatures. Broadly speaking the refrigerated cargoes can be divided into three groups:

1. *Frozen cargo.* Certain products such as meat and fish need to be fully frozen, and transported at temperatures of up to −26°C.
2. *Chilled cargo.* Dairy products and other perishables are transported at low temperatures, though above freezing point, in order to prevent decomposition.
3. *Controlled temperatures.* Fruit transported by sea is generally picked in a semi-ripe state, and allowed to finish ripening at sea at a carefully controlled temperature. For example bananas require precisely 13°C.

In all cases it is essential that temperatures are maintained consistently throughout the ship in order to prevent deterioration of the cargoes. Even quite small temperature deviations can be disastrous, especially for tropical fruit.

Because of the perishable nature of the product, a reliable transport system is essential. The key stages in the process involve harvesting, transportation to the port, where the cargo is placed in refrigerated storage facilities, transfer to the ship, the sea voyage, discharge into refrigerated storage facilities and finally distribution. In the last decade unitization has been used very extensively to improve efficiency. The degree of automation in this system varies considerably. For example, in some trades bananas are still carried on to the ship by stevedores, while in others banana conveyors are used. Palletization has also been extensively introduced into the reefer trades in order to make the transportation of refrigerated cargo more efficient.

A substantial amount of refrigerated cargo is now transported in reefer containers. These are containers which are fully insulated. Some have their own refrigeration plants which can be plugged into an electric socket on the ship, while other rely on receiving cold air from a central shipboard system in reefer container ships. The advantage of reefer containers is that temperature can be more closely and accurately regulated than is possible in the hold of refrigerated ships. In addition they facilitate transfer of refrigerated cargo through ports which have no refrigerated storage capacity.

9.9 The vehicle trade

The growth of international consumer markets in the 1970s and 1980s encouraged a rapidly growing inter-regional trade in vehicles. The trade is principally from Japan and South Korea to the United States and Europe, with a much smaller trade from Europe to North America. In 1993 the trade on the three main routes was about 3 million vehicles, 1.2 million from Japan to Europe, 1.6 million from Japan to North America and 0.3 million from Europe to North America. These deep sea trades have been static or declining for a decade because Japanese and European manufacturers are increasingly producing their car exports locally.

This is a classic industrial shipping operation. As a cargo, cars are high volume, low density, high value. Vehicles move in large numbers out of Western Europe and Japan; shipped in purpose-built vehicle carriers. When operating at full capacity, a large-scale auto assembly plan can produce about one car every 40 seconds. This means that a full 24-hour production schedule results in a maximum daily production of 2,160 cars. This level of production can be maintained for long periods despite differentiation in colour, style, accessories and trim. Materials handling to ensure that the right cars arrive at the right destination must be highly organized.

Finished cars cannot be economically stored at the plant and are moved to distribution points as quickly as possible. This extends to the carriage of export cars by sea and the shipping operation must 'fit' the overall system with storage facilities at the port, fast cargo handling, timely arrival of ships and security for the valuable product in transit. Thus the trade is carried in a fleet of 300 vehicle carriers operated to carefully scheduled timetables by professional management teams. The largest vessels carry up to 6,000 vehicles, often with hoistable decks which can be adjusted to transport trucks and earth-moving equipment, especially on the backhaul when the vessels are generally empty.

9.10 Summary

This chapter was about bulk shipping. We started by discussing two different definitions of bulk cargo. The first defines 'bulk cargo' as anything whose physical characteristics allow it to be handled in bulk. The second is just concerned with transport economics. If the trade flow is large enough almost anything can be shipped in bulk to reduce costs. The trades in motor vehicles and sheep, both shipped in specially built vessels, illustrate the point.

There are five classes of bulk cargo, liquid bulk, dry bulk, unit loads, wheeled cargo and perishable cargoes. Each needs a different bulk handling system to deal with its distinctive characteristics. We identified four principles which determine the suitability of a cargo for bulk transport: the volume of cargo, its physical handling and stowage characteristics, the value of the cargo and the regularity of the material flow. The balance of these four criteria determine the stage at which it is worth making the step from liner transport to a bulk shipping operation.

There are dozens of commodities shipped in bulk by sea. Because each has its own physical and economic characteristics it is very difficult to generalize about bulk trade. As far as commodities are concerned, crude oil and the five major bulks are shipped almost exclusively in bulk vessels. In the minor bulk trades, however, many of the commodity groups straddle liner and bulk shipment, owing to a combination of factors including low volume, irregular shipment, handling and stowage difficulties and, most importantly, the fact that manufacturing plants do not wish to receive large consignments of cargo. The shipper must select the system which gives the best commercial result for his particular industrial operation.

Many of the minor bulk trades offer opportunities for innovation and ingenuity on the part of the shipowner, and there are more novel shipping systems to be found in these trades than in the five major bulks. For this reason, minor bulk trades such as forest products, chemicals, vehicles and refrigerated cargo are dominated by a small number of shipowners who have the combined managerial skill, specialist expertise and investment in ships and terminals to provide the service required by the shipper at minimum cost.

Turning to the question of growth trends in the dry bulk trades, we found that a pattern emerged from the analysis of commodity trade growth since the Second World War. Generally the demand for imports was dominated by Western Europe and Japan, which in the period after 1945 turned to the world market for imports of bulk raw materials such as crude oil, iron ore, coking coal, bauxite, phosphate rock, forest products and non-ferrous metal ores. There was a period of rapid exponential growth during the 1960s when the industry in these areas grew rapidly, leading to rapidly expanding demand for oil tankers and dry bulk carriers.

The 1970s brought a turning point as the impetus for growth died away and the bulk trades stagnated. This change was partly due to external economic forces, particularly the dollar devaluation of September 1971 and the oil crisis of October 1973, but looking below the surface, we find that Europe and Japan were entering a more mature phase of the Trade Development Cycle. By the 1980s new countries such as South Korea, China and the 'tiger economies' of Asia had become the main source of growth in the bulk trades.

Chapter 10

The general cargo and the economics of liner shipping

The growing intricacy and variety of commerce is adding to the advantages which a large fleet of ships under one management derives from its power of delivering goods promptly, and without breach of responsibility, in many different ports; and as regards the vessels themselves time is on the side of large ships.

(Alfred Marshall, *Principles of Economics*, 8th Edition, The Macmillan Press Ltd, 1890)

10.1 Introduction

Liner services play a central part in the global trading network, carrying about 60 per cent of the value of goods shipped by sea.[1] They provide fast, frequent and reliable transport for almost any cargo to almost any foreign destination at a predictable charge. Thus, a Californian wine grower selling 2,000 cases of wine to a UK wholesaler knows that he can ship the wine by a liner service, that the journey will take twelve to fifteen days and he is quoted a through rate for the container. On this basis he can work out his profit and his cashflow and make the necessary delivery arrangements with confidence. If the destination was not Europe, but Iceland, Kenya or India, the procedure would be much the same – he could ship his wine on a regular service at a fixed tariff that may increase with inflation but will not go through the wild peaks and troughs encountered in the charter market. It is an important business for the world economy as well as the shipping industry.

This chapter examines how the liner business operates. We start with a brief review of the evolution from cargo liners to containerized transport. This is followed by a discussion of the economics of liner pricing and costs which are central to managing the business. We then look at the demand for liner services and supply in terms of ships and business organization. Finally, we examine the major liner routes, ports and terminals. Some of the technical terms used in the liner business are listed in the Glossary.

10.2 The origins of the liner service

Liners are a recent addition to the shipping business, dating from the 1870s when improving steamship technology first made it possible to offer scheduled services. Until that time a few shipowners such as the Black Ball Line had tried to run regular services with sailing ships, but most 'general cargo' was carried by 'tramps' working from port-to-port. Developments in the commercial world also made a contribution. Steamship agents became better organized, with branches at key trading points in the Far East. The banking services for day-to-day business were greatly improved and the extension of the telegraph to the Far East enabled trading houses in China to sell by telegraphic transfer in London and India.[2]

Steamships created the supply, the new commercial system stimulated demand and the shipping community was quick to seize the opportunity. The opening of the Suez Canal in 1869 demonstrated the advantages of steamships, and when this was followed by a freight market boom in 1872–3 there was a flood of orders for steamships to set up liner services on the prosperous Far East route. Once established the network of liner services grew rapidly into the comprehensive transport system which exists today.

The 'cargo liner' era 1869–1966

Until the 1960s liner companies ran fleets of multi-deck vessels known as *cargo liners*, versatile ships with their own cargo handling gear. Shipping had not subdivided into the many specialist operations we have today and the liner services had to carry a mixture of manufactures, semi-manufactures, minor bulks and passengers. The trade routes were mainly between the European countries and their colonies in Asia, Africa and South America and on many routes trade was unbalanced with an outward trade of manufactures and a home trade of minor bulks. Filling the ship was the main aim and ship designers were preoccupied with building flexible vessels which could carry all sorts of cargo – even the first oil tankers built at this time were designed to carry a general cargo backhaul. The multi-deck 'cargo liner', with its capacity to carry both general cargo and bulks, was the preferred choice.

There was another aspect of the cargo liner system which gave it great flexibility. Because the cargo liners were similar in size and design and speed to the 'tweendeckers used by tramp operators, the fleets were to a large extent interchangeable. A tramp could become a liner, and a liner could at times become a tramp.[3] This allowed liner companies to charter-in tramps to supplement their own fleets. For example, tramps returning from the UK to the River Plate to load grain would often carry a general cargo backhaul. Liner companies became charterers of tramp tonnage,[4] while tramp owners relied on the liner business as a cushion against the cycles in the bulk market and often built ships with 'tween decks and good speeds, which would fit conveniently into liner company schedules. Since the size of ships used in the bulk and liner markets was roughly the same, this system of risk management worked well for both parties.

As trade grew in the twentieth century, the system was refined and developed. To improve productivity and widen their cargo base liner companies built more sophisticated 'cargo liners', adding features such as tanks for vegetable oils, refrigerated holds, extensive cargo handling gear, ro-ro decks and much automated equipment. They became increasingly complex and expensive. The *Pointe Sans Souci* class built in the early 1970s by Compagnie Generale Maritime (CGM) for their Europe–Caribbean service illustrates the extremes to which liner companies would go in their search for a more cost-effective cargo liner. These ships of 8,000 dwt were designed to carry cargo that had previously been carried by a mixed fleet of traditional liners and reefer ships. The forward holds were insulated to carry refrigerated cargoes, with collapsible container cell guides and electrical points for refrigerated containers. Doors for banana conveyors were let into the 'tween decks in each hold and side doors allowed the 'tween decks to be worked at the same time as the lower hold. Hatch covers were strengthened to take containers, and a 35-ton crane enabled the ship to be fully self-sufficient with container loads in the smaller ports of the West Indies. Holds aft of the bridge were devoted to palletized or vehicle cargo on two decks, with access by a wide stern ramp or a side door if the port does not have facilities for stern-to-quay loading. Below were tanks for carrying bulk rum.

Although the cargo liner was flexible, it was also labour and capital intensive. In the 1950s labour became more expensive and the trading world changed in a way which made flexibility less important than productivity. As the colonies gained independence the liner companies lost many of the core trades in which the cargo liners had been most effective. At the same time many of the minor bulk backhaul trades transferred to bulk carriers at rates the liners could not possibly match. As the bulk carrier fleet grew in size the liner and bulk shipping industries grew apart. However, the most important change was in the pattern of trade. In the rapidly growing economy of the 1950s and 1960s, the real growth in trade was between the prosperous industrial centres of Europe, North America and Japan. Shippers in these trades needed fast, reliable, secure transport and the shortcomings of cargo liners became increasingly obvious. The cost, complexity and poor delivery performance of the cargo liner system became a major stumbling block. Shippers did not want to wait while their cargo made a leisurely progression round eight or ten ports, often arriving damaged.

For the liner companies, running cargo liners had become equally unrewarding. Expensive 'tailor made' ships spent up to 50 per cent of their time in port, which tied up capital, and limited the scope for economies of scale because doubling a cargo liner's capacity almost doubled its port time. There was not a great deal managers or naval architects could do to alleviate the fundamental problems of packing 10–15,000 tons of general cargo into a ship's hold.[5] By the 1960s the expense of the ships, the cargo handling problems and the segregation of their cargo from the rest of the transport system had made the cargo liners technologically obsolete.

The container era 1966–95

The solution was to unitize general cargo. Standardizing the cargo unit allowed liner companies to invest in mechanized systems and equipment which would automate the transport process and raise productivity. The whole procedure was essentially an extension of the 'production line' technology which had been applied so successfully to manufacturing industry and in many of the bulk trades. Three steps were required to implement this strategy.

- First, the product, general cargo, needed to be transformed into *standard units* so that investment could be applied to the whole transport operation. Several different systems were considered and containers were chosen by all the major operators.
- Second, components in the transport system needed to be developed into an *integrated transport system* to take advantage of the standardized unit and economies of scale. On the sea leg the investment was in purpose-built cellular container ships. On land it required investment in large numbers of road and rail vehicles capable of carrying containers efficiently.
- The third step was to build high speed *cargo handling facilities* to transfer the container between one part of the transport system and another. Container terminals, inland distribution depots and container 'stuffing' facilities all played a part in this process.

Containerization drew on the experience that already existed within the United States where, by the mid-1960s, there was a box fleet of 54,000 units (see Table 10.1).[6] For some years trucking companies and railways had adopted the concept of a single unit, detachable from its transport vehicle, which could easily be transferred from one transport mode to another (inter-modal). At sea, container tankers were introduced in the New York to Houston trade in 1956, and in 1958 the California to Hawaii trade had been containerized.

Establishing *standard containers* was crucial. Because road regulations differed across the US, various different sizes of container were in use, particularly a 35 ft box. Eventually the International Standards Organization (ISO) developed standards which applied to dimensions, corner casting strength, floor strength, racking tests and the gross weight of the container. Initially for general cargo the standard boxes were 8 ft high and 8 ft wide, with four optional lengths, 10 ft, 20 ft, 30 ft and 40 ft. In 1976, the height of standard containers was increased to 8 ft 6 ins, giving additional volume without altering the dimensions of the container. In recent years 20 ft and 40 ft containers have become the 'workhorses' of the international container business. Out of a total container stock of 9.6 million TEU (20 ft equivalent units) in 1995, 39 per cent were 20 ft units and 53 per cent were 40 ft units. About 15 per cent of the container fleet consists of special containers, including reefer containers (7.3 per cent), and special dry freight containers (5.1 per cent). The latter are mainly open top containers (Table 10.2). Containers generally have a life of 12 to 14 years. In Europe and the US about half of the container-fleet is leased.

TABLE 10.1 World container fleet 1960–95

Year-end	*Fleet (TEU)*
1960*	18,000
1965*	54,000
1970	500,000
1975	1,300,000
1980	3,150,000
1985	4,850,000
1990	6,400,000
1995	9,600,000

Sources: US Steel Commercial Research Division and CI Market Analysis

Note: Fleet sizes are in units (not TEU)

The first deep sea container service was inaugurated on the North Atlantic in April 1966 by Sea-Land, a company set up by Malcolm MacLean, who was a trucker rather than a shipowner. His experience of running trucks along the east coast of the US had convinced him of the merit of a cargo-handling system that could use all three transport modes – road, rail and sea.

TABLE 10.2 World container stock by principal type

Container type	*20-ft equivalent ur*		*Per cent change*
	1985	*1995*	
Standard	4,090	8,050	97
Open-top	221	225	2
Folding flatrack	36	42	16
Ventilated	37	39	5
Platform	38	31	−17
Bulk	27	24	−13
Other	13	19	42
Integral reefer	157	520	231
Insulated	77	72	−7
Tank	34	84	149
Total	4,776	9,194	93

Source: Containerisation International World Container Census, January 1996

The major European liner shipping companies, had by this time, also made the decision to set up their own container services. Because of the size of the investment in ships, shore-based handling facilities and of course the containers themselves, consortia were formed. For example, Overseas Containers Limited (OCL), a joint venture between P&O, Ocean Transport and Trading, British and Commonwealth and Furness Withy was set up in 1965 (in 1986 OCL was taken over by P&O and renamed P&OCL). This approach remains a feature of the container trades.

Developing a fleet of *container ships* represented a technical challenge. OCL's first order was for six 1,600 TEU Encounter Bay Class ships. The ships had open holds with cell guides which allowed the containers to be loaded without clamping. Steel hatch covers fitted flush and provided a platform on which containers could be stacked four high and clamped in place. Although the ships were not big by the standards of tankers and bulk carriers, this was a major investment in a type of vessel which had not been built previously. On land the investment in trailer friendly chassis progressed rapidly. For the first service in April 1966 Sea-Land signed up over 300 European truckers.[7]

The other link in the chain was the *container terminal*. Previously liner ports had consisted of miles of wharves backing on to warehouses where ships would sit for weeks handling cargo. The container terminals were very different. Two or three berths served by gantry cranes, backed on to open storage. To speed up the link with road transport Sea-Land stored the containers on trailers in a trailer park. Other companies preferred to stack the containers three or four high, retrieving them from storage as required. Movement within the terminals was also automated, using fork-lift trucks, straddle carriers or, in a few cases, an automated gantry system.

This system of cargo handling proved to be tremendously effective. Handling speeds vary from port-to-port, averaging about 20 lifts per crane hour, with a range from 15 lifts an hour to 30 lifts an hour. The result was a dramatic improvement in productivity. Whereas general cargo berths typically handled 100,000–150,000 tons per year, the new container terminals were able to handle 1–2,000,000 mt of cargo per berth. Inter-modal compatibility was also greatly improved because the container itself is standardized.

The consequences of containerization

Containerization of the liner trades took about 20 years, by which time all of the major liner routes and most of the minor ones had been containerized. Unitization was very successful in its main objective of reducing port time. The comparison of the operating performance of a traditional Priam class cargo liner with the Liverpool Bay container ship illustrates the change. The 22,000 dwt cargo liner spent 149 days a year in port, 40 per cent of its time. The 47,000 dwt containership spent only 64 days a year in port, 17 per cent of its time.[8]

It also had a profound effect on liner companies and other parts of the shipping business. First, and most importantly, unitization gave liner companies the opportunity to offer shippers a 'door-to-door' service. Previously most liner companies saw their responsibilities as beginning and ending at the ship's rail. In the intense competition which followed unitization, offering a complete service from origin to destination became an essential part of the product. This changed the competitive arena and the approach to pricing (see section 10.6). Second, the business consolidated into fewer companies. Hundreds of liner companies disappeared and liner shipping became the most concentrated sector of the shipping business. Third, the bustling ports of the cargo liner era disappeared, replaced by container terminals with few staff and fewer ships. Fourth, ships and shipowning slipped to the sidelines because the core business of liner companies was now through transport. Fifth, the tramp market for ships carrying containerizable cargoes disappeared. Containerships could not switch between liner charters and bulk, so liner companies had to carry the marginal capacity they needed in their own fleets. Tramp operators turned to the bulk carrier or tanker markets. Sixth, minor bulk cargoes which had occupied the deep-well tanks, lower cargo holds and ro-ro decks of cargo liners moved into specialist vessels such as 'conbulkers', parcel tankers, vehicle carriers and mini-bulkers.

10.3 Economic principles of liner operation

Economic characteristics of liner services

Now it is time to take a closer look at the economics of the liner business. We start with a definition:

> A liner service is a fleet of ships, with a common ownership or management, which provide a fixed service, at regular intervals, between named ports, and offer transport to any goods in the catchment area served by those ports and ready for transit by their sailing dates. A fixed itinerary, inclusion in a regular service, and the obligation to accept cargo from all comers and to sail, whether filled or not, on the date fixed by a published schedule are what distinguish the liner from the tramp.[9]

From an economic viewpoint, providing this service has two important differences from bulk shipping. First, transporting many small parcels requires a larger and more complex administrative overhead, and second, the obligation to sail to a timetable makes capacity inflexible. Two apparently small points, but they make a tremendous difference. Whereas tramp owners respond quickly to supply/demand imbalances by moving their least efficient ships into layup, liner companies must stick with their schedules. If it takes six ships to run a weekly service, they must operate six ships. From the outset this has created problems for liner operators, making capacity management a key feature of the business.

In addition to the usual trade cycles which affect all shipping business, there are several reasons why capacity management can be a problem. *Seasonality* occurs on many liner routes where cargo volume is higher at some times of the year than others. *Cargo imbalances* occur when there is more trade in one direction than the other, forcing ships to sail part loaded on the leg with the smaller trade flow. Finally *indivisibilities* arise because the supply of capacity is not continuous, but a series of ship-sized increments. This means that when trade is growing, new ships must be ordered in multiples dictated by the service frequency, with sufficient capacity to cater for future growth. These problems also occur in the bulk market, but they are quickly resolved by market forces as shipowners negotiate rates and move from trade to trade. Liner companies lack this flexibility. With so many customers it is not practical to negotiate a rate for every cargo. This combination of fixed prices and inflexible capacity, leaves liner companies with a pricing problem which has dominated the industry since it started.

The liner pricing problem

The principles of liner pricing can be illustrated with the supply/demand charts shown in Figures 10.1 and 10.2. Consider the case of competing liner companies, each operating a single ship, say a 4,000 TEU containership which makes five trips a year. Each ship costs $40,000 per day to run, including capital, operating costs and bunkers, and it costs $400 to handle each container. When the ship is full, no additional cargo can be shipped. The vertical axis of the graph shows the price (freight rate) or cost in $ per TEU, while the horizontal axis shows the number of boxes shipped per trip.

The liner company must charge a price that covers its costs. If this objective is not achieved, in due course it will go out of business. Costs may be fixed or variable. In this simplified case the $40,000 per day cost of the ship is a *fixed cost*[10] because the company is committed to running the service regardless of cargo volume, while the cargo handling costs can be termed *variable costs* because these are not incurred if there is no cargo. This is a great simplification, but serves to illustrate the principle (we will discuss the matter in more detail later in the chapter).

Because the company is already committed to the costs of the voyage, when the ship is part empty the only additional cost of accepting another container is the $400 per container cost of cargo handling. This is known as the *marginal cost* (MC). Once the ship is full the marginal cost rises sharply to, say, $2,500 per container, the cost of chartering another ship or hiring slots on another vessel. This is shown by the marginal cost curve (MC) in Figure 10.1. Note that the MC curve is horizontal at $400 from 1500 TEU to 4,000 TEU when the ship is fully loaded and the MC curve moves up vertically to $2,500 per TEU. Also shown in Figure 10.1 is the average cost curve (AC), which shows, at each output level, the fixed and variable costs divided by the cargo volume. At low throughput levels the average cost is very high because a small number of containers must absorb the total cost of the ship. For example when the ship is only carrying 1,500 containers the average cost is $2,400 per TEU, but as the load factor increases the average cost falls steadily to $1,150 per TEU when the ship is full.

Case 1: marginal cost prices

To make a profit, the liner company must generate enough revenue to cover the average cost. Figure 10.1 shows what happens in a free market (i.e. without conferences). When there is more shipping space than cargo, which is represented by the demand curve D1, the liner

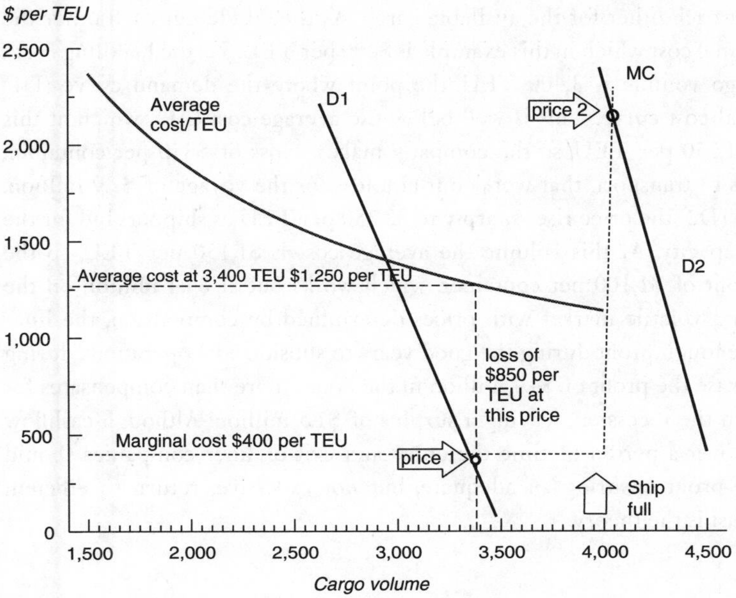

FIGURE 10.1 Liner pricing case 1: marginal cost pricing
Source: Martin Stopford, 1997

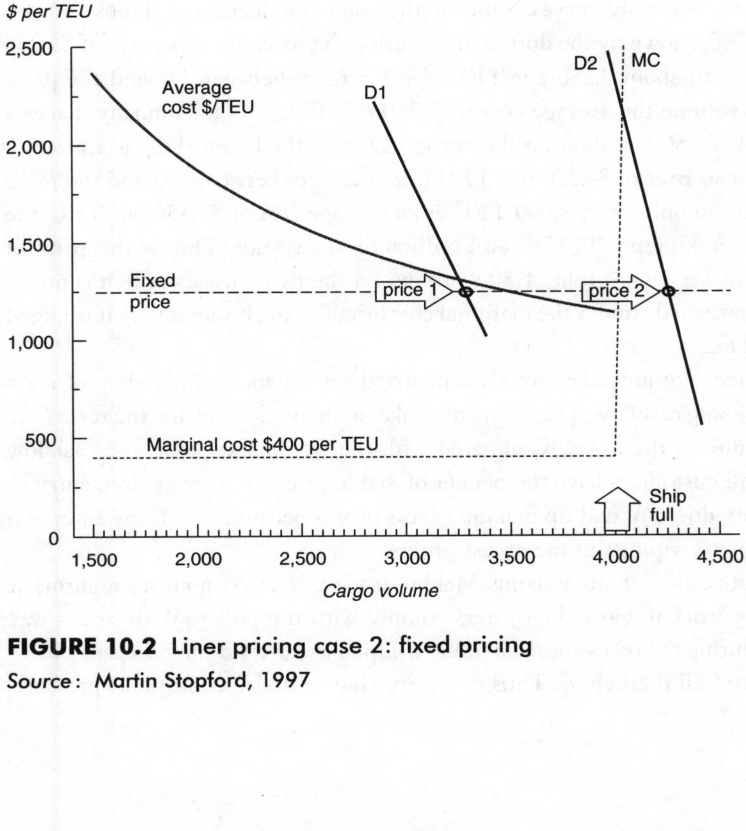

FIGURE 10.2 Liner pricing case 2: fixed pricing
Source: Martin Stopford, 1997

companies bid against each other for the available cargo. As they undercut each other the price falls to the marginal cost which in this example is $400 per TEU (i.e. the handling cost). At this price the cargo volume is 3,400 TEU, the point where the demand curve (D1) intersects the marginal cost curve. This is well below the average cost (AC) which at this throughput level is $1,250 per TEU, so the company makes a loss of $850 per container. With 3,400 containers to transport, that works out at a loss for the voyage of $2.9 million. When demand is high (D2) the price rises sharply to $2,250 per TEU as shippers bid for the limited 4,000 TEU capacity. At this volume the average cost is $1,150 per TEU, so the company makes a profit of $1,100 per container, which works out at $4.4 million on the voyage. To survive in a volatile market with prices determined by competition, the liner company must make enough profit during the good years to subsidize its operations during the bad years. In this case the profit of $4.4 million in the boom more than compensates for the $2.9 million loss in the recession, leaving a surplus of $1.5 million. Although cashflow will be very volatile, over a period of time the entry and exit of liner companies should regulate the level of profit ensuring an adequate, but not excessive, return to efficient companies. That at least is the theory.

Case 2: fixed prices

The alternative strategy is for liner companies to fix prices at a level which gives a reasonable margin over average cost. We see the consequences of this approach in Figure 10.2 which has the same demand and supply curves. Suppose the company decides to impose a fixed price of $1,250 per TEU, shown by the dotted line. During the recession at a price of $1,250 per TEU demand falls to about 3,250 per TEU (see intercept between D1 and the price curve). At this cargo volume the average cost is $1,350 per TEU, so the company makes a loss of $100 per TEU or $0.3 million on the voyage. During the boom (D2) at a price of $1,250 per TEU demand rises to $4,250 per TEU (see intercept between D2 and the price curve). Since the ship can only carry 4,000 TEU at an average cost of $1,150 per TEU, the voyage makes a profit of $100 per TEU or $0.4 million on the voyage. Thus at this price of $1,250 the company makes a net profit of $0.1 million on the two voyages, which is not as much as they would have made under the marginal cost pricing case. It seems they misjudged the price they should fix.

If the fixed prices are judged correctly and strictly maintained this policy offers a practical way of stabilizing cashflow. The company makes a smaller loss during the recession, and a smaller profit during the boom. Compared with the free market case, the cashflow cycles are reduced and customers have the benefit of stable prices. If there is free entry to the trade, the company does not end up making excess profits because new firms enter and old firms expand capacity, wiping out the excess profits.

This is the positive side of price fixing. Making it work is an economist's nightmare. Fixed prices can only work if most shipowners comply with the policy. With prices way above marginal cost during the recession, individual companies have a tremendous incentive to drop their prices and fill their ships. Thus the 'price ring' is under continuous pressure.

Even worse, during the boom there is a risk that outsiders will pile into the trade, soaking up the premium cargo at profitable prices. If strict discipline cannot be enforced, the cartel is squeezed in both directions. Because each route is just a small island in a sea of liner capacity, efforts to enforce discipline from within or without are easily frustrated.

An example puts the problem into perspective. Suppose there are three ships in a service, two in a conference (i.e. cartel) and the third an 'outsider'. Trade is depressed and there is enough cargo to load 3,000 TEU per ship. If the conference holds, each ship charges a fixed price of $1,200 per TEU and loads 3,000 TEU, making a small profit of $0.4 million on the voyage. If, however, the outsider offers a price of $1,100 per TEU, the whole picture changes. At this price he will win enough cargo to fill his 4,000 TEU ship, so his average cost falls to $800 per container and his voyage profit increases to $1.2 million. The conference members are left with only 2,500 TEU each. At this volume their average cost rises to $1,200 per TEU, so their profit is wiped out. It has been hijacked by the outsider and there is nothing they can do about it. The examples we have considered so far relate to market cycles. Exactly the same principles apply to seasonal cycles or trade imbalances.

Case 3: price discrimination

The third pricing option is *price discrimination.* One of the benefits of marginal cost pricing is that flexible prices help to co-ordinate cargo volume with the available capacity. Thus the low price during the recession in Figure 10.1 draws in marginal cargoes such as waste paper, hay or building blocks, helping to fill up empty ships and generate extra revenue. As a result the cargo volume in the recession is 3,400 TEU compared with only 3,250 when the price is fixed at $1,250 per TEU. Conversely during booms, high prices discourage cargo that will not bear the freight, rationing the scarce capacity to priority cargo, whereas the fixed price leaves the liner company with demand for 4,250 TEU of demand, but only 4,000 slots. From this viewpoint flexible prices bring a positive benefit to the shipper and the liner company. One way to get the best of both worlds is to offer different prices for each commodity. Economists refer to this approach as price discrimination and it is widely used in the transport system (e.g. business class versus economy class on the airlines). Low value cargoes are offered cheap transport to fill empty capacity, while higher value cargoes are charged a premium. Commodity price discrimination is widely used by liner companies, though it has become more difficult since containerization has standardized the physical cargo. Price discrimination can also be applied to customers. For example, special rates may be offered to customers who have large volumes of cargo. With all price discrimination the key is ensuring that the marginal revenue obtained from the cargo fully compensates the company for the cost of the service, including such hidden costs as repositioning containers. This is known as 'yield management'.

This economic analysis demonstrates the dilemma facing managers in the liner business. They are 'between a rock and a hard place'. They have a diverse customer base, regular schedules, an inflexible investment in ships, and an administrative overhead. In a free market, trade cycles, seasonal cycles and trade imbalances produce highly volatile revenues. Living with a volatile cashflow is not particularly attractive and since they are in a position to form cartels this is an obvious strategy. As we have seen, efforts to take over from the market and 'manage' prices or capacity present great problems. Economic forces do not favour stable liner price cartels. Companies which break the price ring reap such handsome profits at the expense of the cartel members that restraint never lasts long, especially in the age of containerization. With bank managers to pay, shareholder pressure for higher returns, or a government sponsor keen to see its domestic shipping company take a bigger share of the trade, there are too many temptations. In an industry where the barriers to entry are low, rate stability must be the exception rather than the rule.

Despite these difficulties the quest continues. Over the years managers in the liner business have come up with a bewildering array of solutions. Some concentrated on the revenue side, seeking to fix prices for the whole trade, often supported by a complex arrangement of loyalty rebates, commodity discounts, service agreements offering special rates to major clients and other devices designed to blend fixed pricing with a degree of flexibility. Others have tackled capacity, attempting to strike at the root of the problem by fixing trade shares so that companies cannot compete for each other's cargo. From time to time there have been inter-company agreements to share shipping space and increase flexibility. There have always been some major companies who have preferred independence and the free market, but one way or another most liner companies end up seeking ways to restrict market forces. In the next section we discuss these arrangements. Because they are constantly changing they are not easy to analyse or classify. We briefly review their history, more as an illustration of what can happen than a definitive account of the system.

10.4 Liner conferences and their regulation

The *conference system*, which was developed in the mid-1870s, was the industry's first attempt to deal with the pricing problem. The major British shipping companies such as P&O, Alfred Holt and Glen Line who set up the first liner services to the Far East in the early 1870s, found that, from the outset, competition was forcing tariffs to levels that would not cover their average costs. They faced all the problems mentioned in the previous section. There was over-capacity due to over-building; the trades were highly seasonal, particularly in agricultural products such as tea, so for part of the year the ships were only half full; and there was also an imbalance between the east-bound and the west-bound trade with the demand for shipping space to China falling short of the demand from China.[11] As a result there was often more shipping capacity than cargo. Of course none of this was new. What had changed was the organization of the business. Because the newly emerging liner companies were operating regularly in the same trades they were in a much better position to form a cartel to fix rates so that, in the words of John Swire, 'the companies may not ruin each other'.[12]

The first conference was formed in August 1875 by the lines trading between the United Kingdom and Calcutta. It was agreed to charge similar rates, to limit the number of sailings, to grant no preferences or concessions to any shippers and to sail on a given date regardless of whether they had a full load of cargo.[13] However, because of the over-tonnaging situation, this simply resulted in the major shippers, particularly the powerful Manchester merchants, threatening to use vessels outside the conference that would offer lower rates.[14] A custom already existed that the charge made for the use of ship's gear in loading and unloading was remitted to merchants who shipped regularly with the same company. In 1877 the conference developed this into the rebate system. A reduction in rates of 10 per cent was made to merchants who shipped exclusively with the conference for a period of six months, but the rebate was not paid until a further six months had elapsed, during which time the loyalty rebate was forfeit if the merchant used a ship owned by a firm not a member of the conference.[15] This meant that any shipper tempted by the cut-price rates of non-conference operators stood to lose a very substantial sum if they accepted.

This was only the beginning. Over the next century there was a constantly evolving network of agreements covering rates, the number of sailings, the ports served, the goods carried, and the sharing of freight revenues ('pool' agreements). *Closed* conferences control membership, share cargo and use price discrimination to encourage the major shippers to ship exclusively with the conference. For example, regular shippers might be charged a lower 'contract' rate, with a higher rate for shippers who sometimes used outsiders. The 'deferred rebate' developed in the Calcutta trade was also used. Loyal shippers receive a cash rebate, say 9.5 per cent. *Open* conferences allow any company to join provided they comply with the rate agreements. Members are thus guaranteed the prices set by the conference but, since there is no control on the number of ships in service, open conferences are more vulnerable to over-tonnaging. By the early 1970s there were more than 360 conferences with membership varying from 2 to 40 shipping lines.[16]

Regulatory control of liner cartels

From the outset conferences were constantly under attack. In 1879 the *China Mail*, a Hong Kong paper, set the tone for a debate which lasted a century by describing the China Conference as 'one of the most ill-advised and arbitrary attempts at monopoly which has been seen for many a year'.[17] The first legal challenge came in 1887 when the Mogul Line sought an injunction to stop the Far East Freight Conference from refusing rebates to shippers using Mogul vessels. At that time the Far East Freight Conference had seven members. In 1885 Mogul Line had applied for admission to the conference, but was refused because Mogul ships did not bear a full share of running regular services at off-peak periods. This refusal led to a rate war during which the conference's Shanghai agents issued a circular warning that any shippers using Mogul ships would forfeit their rebates. Mogul went to law and sought an injunction to stop the conference from refusing the rebates, but the application was refused, confirming the legality of the conference. Some years later, the Royal Commission on Shipping Rings was set up to investigate the rebate system. Its report in 1909 again confirmed that the commercial relationship between shippers and conferences was justified and that the possible abuses of the deferred rebate system should be tolerated in the interests of achieving a strong liner system.[18]

The conference system reached its peak during the 1950s. The prominence which the conferences had achieved by this time is demonstrated by the UNCTAD Code of Conduct for Liner Conferences which was initiated at the first UNCTAD conference in Geneva in 1964 (see Chapter 12, section 12.9). Many of the developing countries which had gained independence during the previous decade had balance of payments problems and were searching for solutions. Sea freight played an important part in the price of the primary exports on which most of them relied. In addition the freight itself was a drain on their scarce foreign currency reserves. Setting up a national shipping line seemed the obvious solution to both problems. However, the liner conferences were not generally sympathetic and the emerging nations lacked the experience in the liner business to press their case. This lead to political action by the 'Group of 77' (a pressure group of developing countries within UNCTAD). The result was the UNCTAD Code which aimed to give each country the right to participate in the liner conferences servicing its trade.

The UNCTAD Code covers four major areas of liner shipping. It provides the right to automatic conference membership for the national shipping lines of the countries served by the conference. A cargo-sharing formula gives national shipping lines equal rights to participate in the volume of traffic generated by their mutual trade with third parties carrying the residual. For example, under a 40:40:20 cargo sharing agreement the bilateral traders reserve 40 per cent of the cargo for their national vessels and 'cross traders' carry the remaining 20 per cent of the cargo. Finally, shipping conferences are required to consult shippers over rates and national lines have the right of consent on all major conference decisions affecting the countries serviced.

The Code took almost 20 years to develop and by the time it came into force in 1983 the liner business had changed out of all recognition. It has never been ratified by the United States and implementing a convention of this complexity, which involves agreeing and measuring trade shares, has proved too great a challenge. Despite this, the Code has two significant achievements to its credit. The first is that it gave rights to the Third World shipping industry at a time when this recognition was needed. Second, it was the first international attempt to regulate the extensive, and over-weighty, system of closed conferences. By opening the conferences to new participants, it weakened the tight control which had developed and set the scene for a new regulatory attitude towards the conference system.

During the next 15 years the political climate became progressively less tolerant of liner cartels. In the mid-1980s the system was examined by regulators in the US and Europe. The conference system survived, but only just. Under US anti-trust laws, agreements which restrict competition are illegal. The US Merchant Shipping Act (1984) re-affirmed that conferences were excluded from anti-trust legislation and legitimized inter-modal rate making, but placed severe limitations on their activities. Closed conferences and loyalty rebates became illegal and strict limitations were placed on price fixing. All tariffs fixed by US conferences must be filed with the Federal Maritime Commission and all service contracts made be public. In 1986 the European Commission Competition Directorate implemented EC Regulation 4056 which excluded conferences from European anti-trust law. Rebates remained legal, but by the late 1980s the system had become seriously weakened.[19]

This legislation weakened the conference system and changed its role, but efforts to resolve the pricing problem continue as actively as they did a century ago, to the general disapproval of regulatory authorities. On the Pacific route a series of stabilization agreements were developed, no longer called conferences, the first being the Trans Pacific Discussion Agreement (TPDA). On the Atlantic the Trans Atlantic Agreement (TAA) subsequently became the Trans Atlantic Conference Agreement (TACA). In the mid-1990s about 60 per cent of the liner capacity on the major routes belonged to some sort of conference system, though the modern open conferences are very different from the tightly controlled closed conferences of the 1950s. Some act mainly as secretariat to the trades, administering rate agreements and dealing with the various regulatory bodies. As containerization has weakened the industry's ability to enforce price cartels, and the regulatory environment has become less sympathetic, attention has increasingly switched to strategies for reducing unit costs through consortia, alliances, and mergers which generate economies of scale.

10.5 The components of liner service costs

Costs lie at the heart of liner service economics and now it is time to look at them from a more practical viewpoint. We will approach the task in two stages. Stage one establishes the six 'building blocks' from which liner service costs are constructed, while stage two uses these costs to construct a service cash flow model similar to the one used to analyse the bulk shipping industry in Chapter 5. This model shows how the cost and revenue elements fit together, and their implications for the business, especially economies of scale. As an example we will take a liner service operating on the North Atlantic and compare the cost structure for four different sizes of ship, 1,200 TEU, 2,600 TEU, 4,000 TEU and 6,500 TEU. The six cost building blocks are summarized in Table 10.3, while the 'service cashflow analysis' is shown in Table 10.4. Of course liner companies operate many services and their published accounts are far more complex than this simple example. However it serves the important function of identifying the key economic variables which are the basis of management decision making.

The six building blocks of line costs

The six components of liner service costs listed in Table 10.3 are the service schedule; ship costs; port charges (including cargo working); container operations; container costs; and administration. This is not a classification which appears in the accounts of any liner company, but it is a useful way of grouping cost variables to discuss their role in the business.

The logical starting point for liner cost analysis is the *service schedule* (Table 10.3, section 1), since this sets the inflexible framework of transport capacity per annum around which costs are incurred. There are three key decisions for service planners to make, the service frequency, the number of port calls and the size of the ships to be used. In the example in Table 10.3 the service frequency is weekly and there are seven port calls on the round voyage

TABLE 10.3 The six building blocks of liner costs

		Ship size (TEU)			
		1,200	2,600	4,000	6,500
1. Service schedule		1,200	2,600	4,000	6,500
Distance of round trip		8,500	8,500	8,500	8,500
Service frequency		weekly	weekly	weekly	weekly
Portcalls on round voyage		7	7	7	7
Average operating speed (knots)		19	19	19	19
Days/portcall		1.35	1.35	1.35	1.35
Days at sea		18.6	18.6	18.6	18.6
Days in port		9.5	9.5	9.5	9.5
Total voyage time		28.1	28.1	28.1	28.1
Outward capacity utilization (%)		80%	80%	80%	80%
Return capacity utilization (%)		90%	90%	90%	90%
Containers shipped outward (TEU)		960	2,080	3,200	5,200
Containers shipped back (TEU)		1,080	2,340	3,600	5,850
Annual transport capacity (TEU)		106,371	230,471	354,571	576,179
2. Ship Costs					
Operating Costs ($/day)		5,500	6,650	8,550	9,500
Capital value $mill		25	42	58	80
Depreciation period (years)		20	20	20	20
Interest rate (% pa)		8%	8%	8%	8%
Capital cost/$ day		8,904	14,959	20,658	28,493
Fuel consumption (tons/day)		50	65	80	95
Bunker price $/ton (average)		110	110	110	110
Bunker cost ($/day)		5,500	7,150	8,800	10,450
Unit cost per TEU ($/day)		16.6	11.1	9.5	7.5
3. Port charges (excluding cargo handling)					
Port Cost/$ TEU		18	11	9	7
Port Cost/$ call		22,000	29,000	35,000	43,000
4. Container operations					
Twenty ft containers (% ship capacity)		37%	37%	37%	37%
Number of units loaded		444	962	1,480	2,405
Forty ft containers (% ship capacity)		57%	57%	57%	57%
Number of units loaded		342	741	1,140	1,853
Refrigerated containers (% ship capacity load)		6%	6%	6%	6%
Number of units loaded		72	156	240	390
Number of units on full vessel		858	1,859	2,860	4,648
Container turnaround time (days/voyage)		75	75	75	75
Containers repositioned empty (%)		10%	10%	10%	10%
5. Container costs					
Container costs ($/TEU/day)	20 ft	0.9	0.9	0.9	0.9
	40 ft	1.4	1.4	1.4	1.4
	20 ft reefer	8.5	8.5	8.5	8.5
Maintenance and repair ($/box/voyage)		75.0	75.0	75.0	75.0
Terminal costs for container handling ($/lift)		200.0	200.0	200.0	200.0
Refrigeration cost for reefer containers ($/TEU)		150.0	150.0	150.0	150.0
Trans-shipment ($/TEU)		225.0	225.0	225.0	225.0
Inland intermodal transport cost ($/TEU)		150.0	150.0	150.0	150.0
Interzone Re-positioning ($/TEU)		150.0	150.0	150.0	150.0
Cargo Claims ($/box/voyage)		25	25	25	25
6. Administration Costs					
Administrative productivity (TEU/employee)		400	550	700	950
Number of employees required		266	419	507	607
Cost/employee $ per annum		40,000	40,000	40,000	40,000
Administration cost ($/TEU)		100	73	57	42

Source: Various, but particularly Drewry Shipping Consultants (1996)

TABLE 10.4 The liner service cash flow model

	Ship size (TEU)			
	1,200	*2,600*	*4,000*	*6,500*
	$ 000s	$ 000s	$ 000s	$ 000s
1. Fixed costs of the ship				
Operating costs	154	187	240	267
Capital costs	250	420	580	800
Bunkers	103	133	164	195
Ports	154	203	245	301
Total	**661**	**943**	**1,229**	**1,563**
Per cent total voyage costs	42%	33%	30%	26%
2. Costs of the containers				
Cost of supplying containers	125	272	418	679
Container maintenance & repair	90	195	300	488
Total	**215**	**467**	**718**	**1,167**
Per cent total voyage costs	14%	16%	18%	19%
3. Administration cost				
Administrative cost allocated to voyage	**120**	**189**	**229**	**274**
	8%	7%	6%	4%
4. Cargo handling and onward transport				
Terminal costs for container handling	172	372	572	930
Refrigeration cost for reefer containers	11	23	36	59
Inland intermodal transport cost	306	663	1,020	1,658
Interzone re-positioning	36	78	120	195
Cargo claims	51	111	170	276
Total	**575**	**1,247**	**1,918**	**3,117**
Per cent total voyage costs	37%	44%	47%	51%
5. Total voyage cost				
Total cost	**1,572**	**2,846**	**3,696**	**5,570**
Cost per TEU Outward Leg ($)	819	684	640	588
Cost per TEU Return Leg ($)	728	608	569	523
Average cost/TEU[1]	771	644	602	554
Per cent reduction in cost/TEU by using bigger ship		−16%	−6%	−8%
6. Total voyage revenue ($ 000s)				
Freight rate per TEU Outward Leg	820	820	820	820
Freight rate per TEU Return Leg	750	750	750	750
Revenue outward leg[1]	787	1,706	2,624	4,264
Revenue return leg[1]	810	1,755	2,700	4,388
Total revenue	**1,597**	**3,461**	**5,324**	**8,652**
7. Profit (loss) ($ 000s)				
Voyage profit (loss)	25	615	1,230	2,531
Per cent	2%	18%	23%	29%

Note: 1 based on the number of containers shipped outward and back shown in Table 10.3, section 1 (e.g. Rotterdam, Le Havre, New York, Baltimore, Norfolk, Bremerhaven, Felixstowe). The capacity calculation is repeated for four ship sizes (1,200 TEU, 2,600 TEU, 4,000 TEU, 6,500 TEU).

With a round-voyage distance of 8,500 miles a single ship can make one round voyage every 28 days if it averages 19 knots. To run a weekly service, four ships are needed. However, there are plenty of choices open to service operators if they vary the speed or the number of port calls. If only one port call is made at each end of the journey, the round trip could be reduced to 21 days, and the route can be serviced with only three ships, which would be cheaper. Alternatively, it might be argued by the marketing department that to service the trade properly ten port calls are needed rather than seven. Since each port call takes an average of 1.35 days, this would extend the round voyage time to 32.1 days, which would not fit conveniently with a weekly schedule. Increasing the speed to 24 knots would cut the voyage time back to 28 days, but that would be a punishing schedule for the ships and would incur higher capital and bunker costs. These are difficult decisions, with crucial cost implications.

Once the voyage cycle has been fixed, the remaining variable is the size of ship to be used. This depends on how much cargo the company thinks it can win, how much headroom it allows for future volume growth and any cargo imbalances on different legs of the route. In this example we assume that there is 80 per cent capacity utilization on the outward leg and 90 per cent on the return leg. At these capacity levels a weekly service could transport an annual cargo volume of 230,471 TEU using a 2,600 TEU ship and 576,179 TEU for the 6,500 TEU vessel. Which ship size should the service planners select?

This question leads on to the second building block, the *ship cost.* This variable is usually expressed in terms of the unit slot cost (i.e. the daily cost of providing one TEU of transport capacity on the route). Now we are on familiar territory. The calculation of the unit cost per TEU in dollars per day shown in Table 10.3. Section 2 is built up from operating cost, capital cost, and fuel consumption in just the same way as the costs for the bulk vessels in Chapter 5. For the new 2,600 TEU ship in this example the operating cost is $6,650 per day, the capital cost $14,959 per day and the bunker cost $7,150 per day. These costs depend substantially on the investment decisions of the shipowner. There is a trade-off between capital costs and operating costs which we discussed in detail for bulk vessels in Chapter 5. Modern ships cost less to run but more to finance, so unit slot costs depend on the age profile of the fleet as well as the size of the ships. Since bunker costs are substantially higher for container ships than bulk vessels, due to their higher speed, fuel consumption is a particularly important variable.

The impact of economies of scale is clear from the unit slot cost, expressed in $/TEU/day, shown at the end of section 2 in Table 10.3. For a 1,200 TEU vessel the daily cost is $16.6/TEU/day, but the cost falls sharply to $11.1/TEU/day for a 2,600 TEU vessel, $9.5/TEU/day for a 4,000 TEU vessel and $7.5/TEU/day for the 6,500 TEU vessel. A clear case of economies of scale, but with diminishing marginal returns. The first step up in size to 2,600 TEU cuts the slot cost by $5.5, but the same 1,400 TEU size increase to 4,000 TEU only saves $1.6/TEU.

Port charges (Table 10.3, section 3) are an item over which the shipowner has less control, since they vary considerably around the world. Since port charges are generally levied on the basis of the ship's tonnage, this introduces an additional element of economies of scale, since the port costs/teu reduces as the ship gets bigger. In Table 10.3, section 3, we assume a reduction in the port costs/teu from $18 for the 1,200 teu ship to $7 for the 6,500 TEU ship. Liner operators have a considerable incentive to develop ship designs with a low tonnage relative to their container capacity, especially for distribution trades where the vessels make many portcalls. This encourages designs with a low deadweight and gross tonnage per teu.

The fourth building block of liner costs is *container operations* (Table 10.3, section 4). To run a liner business, the service operator must supply and manage a stock of containers to support the cargo flow. The decisions taken set the framework for the container costs. There are three important issues that arise at the operational level. First, there is the question of obtaining the right mix of container types. As we saw earlier in the chapter, there are many different sizes of containers, including general purpose and specialized designs. These must be available for delivery to the customer as required. The example in Table 10.3 section 4 splits 37 per cent 20 ft containers, 57 per cent 40 ft containers and 6 per cent refrigerated units. This is fairly typical of the North Atlantic route, though the balance in other trades is different. For example on the long Pacific journey the proportion of 40 ft containers increases to 80 per cent. There may also be a requirement to supply specialized containers, for example open top containers or tanks. Most liner companies own a substantial proportion of their containers, since this is generally the cheapest option, leasing a proportion, say 20–30 per cent. Second, there is the issue of container turn-around. Between voyages the containers are delivered to the customer, following which they must be collected and repositioned for the next cargo. This calls for a container stock which is substantially greater than the container capacity of the vessels employed in the trade. In this example we assume a 75 days turn-around time for the cycle, of which 28 days are spent at sea and 47 days in transit to and from the customer. Naturally this will vary a great deal with the trade. Third, where trade imbalances exist empty containers must be repositioned inter-regionally so that they are available for loading cargo. In this example we assume that capacity utilization on the return leg is 10 per cent higher than on the outward leg, so 10 per cent of the containers must be repositioned empty. This offers a classic opportunity for marginal cost pricing. If the container is travelling empty, any cargo which will pay the handling charges is worth carrying. Hay, waste paper, building blocks, animal feeds and a host of other cargoes fall into this category. The danger arises when these marginal cargoes create hidden costs which are unseen by the salesman and end up being shipped at a loss.

When we turn to the fifth building block, *container costs* (Table 10.3, section 5), we must consider the daily cost of the containers; maintenance and repair; terminal costs for container handling (i.e. the cost of handling it on and off the vessel); various on-shipment costs, including trans-shipment by sea or inland; repositioning empty containers between zones; and cargo claims.

The cost of the container itself depends on the purchase price, its economic life and the method of finance. In the mid-1990s a 20 ft container cost about $2,400 and a 40 ft container about $3,900. Refrigerated containers are much more expensive, costing $21,000 for a 20 ft unit. In practice containers have an average life of 12–16 years, at the end of which they have a scrap value of several hundred dollars. On these parameters the daily cost of a container can be calculated, working out at about 90 cents per day for a 20 ft unit and $1.40

per day for a 40 ft unit. Like ships, containers and other equipment require continuous maintenance, for which an annual budget must be allowed.

Container handling and through transport costs vary enormously. Terminal costs differ from one region to another. For example in 1995 handling a 40 ft container in Singapore cost about $150, compared with $350 per lift in Japan. Terminals generally charge up to 50 per cent extra for handling a 40 ft box, though, for simplicity, the handling charges in Table 10.3 are limited to a single rate of $200 per lift. Refrigerated containers also require special terminal services which are costed here at $150 per unit. The on-shipment of the container is dealt with under three headings, transhipment by sea, inland inter-modal transport and inter-zone repositioning. These costs depend specifically on the trade and the method of pricing adopted by the company. Some operators charge separately for delivery, in which case the freight rate does not include the cost of on-transport. Other carriers offer 'door-to-door' rates. Since some cost will certainly be incurred, Table 10.3 assumes values of $225/TEU for transhipment, $150 for inland transport, and $150 for interzonal repositioning when regional imbalances appear and the containers have to be shipped to a different part of the world. Finally there is an item for cargo claims. Concluding the discussion on container costs, perhaps the most significant feature is that because these costs are based on the standard container, they are not subject to economies of scale. The 6,500 TEU ship faces the same unit costs as the 1,000 TEU ship.

Finally there is *administration costs* (Table 10.3, section 6). Somehow the shipping company must recover the cost of the administrative function which is required to operate a container service. A simple way to do this is to 'charge out' an administration cost to each vessel on a proportional basis which will recover the full overheads of the company. Some idea of the nature of these costs is given by the organization chart in Figure 10.3. The five main functional activities are as follows:

- *Marine Operations*: This covers the management of the ships, scheduling, cargo stowage and terminal management.
- *Logistics*: Responsible for the overall maintenance and control of the company's fleet of own and leased containers, including maintenance, repair and scheduling.
- *Finance*: A major activity including voyage accounts (e.g. booking, rating, tracking, billing, etc.) EDP, management accounts and budgeting.
- *Commercial*: This covers the booking and documentation of cargo, plus dealing with conferences where appropriate.
- *Sales*: This function sets the pricing, PR and advertising and deals with agents.

Some companies carry out all of these activities themselves, while smaller companies sub-contract. As a result the numbers on the payroll vary a great deal. For example, ACL, which in 1995 shipped 224,000 containers on the North Atlantic, employs a staff of about 380, which works out at a throughput of 588 TEU per employee. The salary cost was $91/TEU. However, the ACL traffic included ro-ro cargo, so it is not a pure container service. Typically for major liner companies with a full range of activities, the administrative cost is in the range $100–200/TEU. The example in Table 10.3, section 6, builds in an

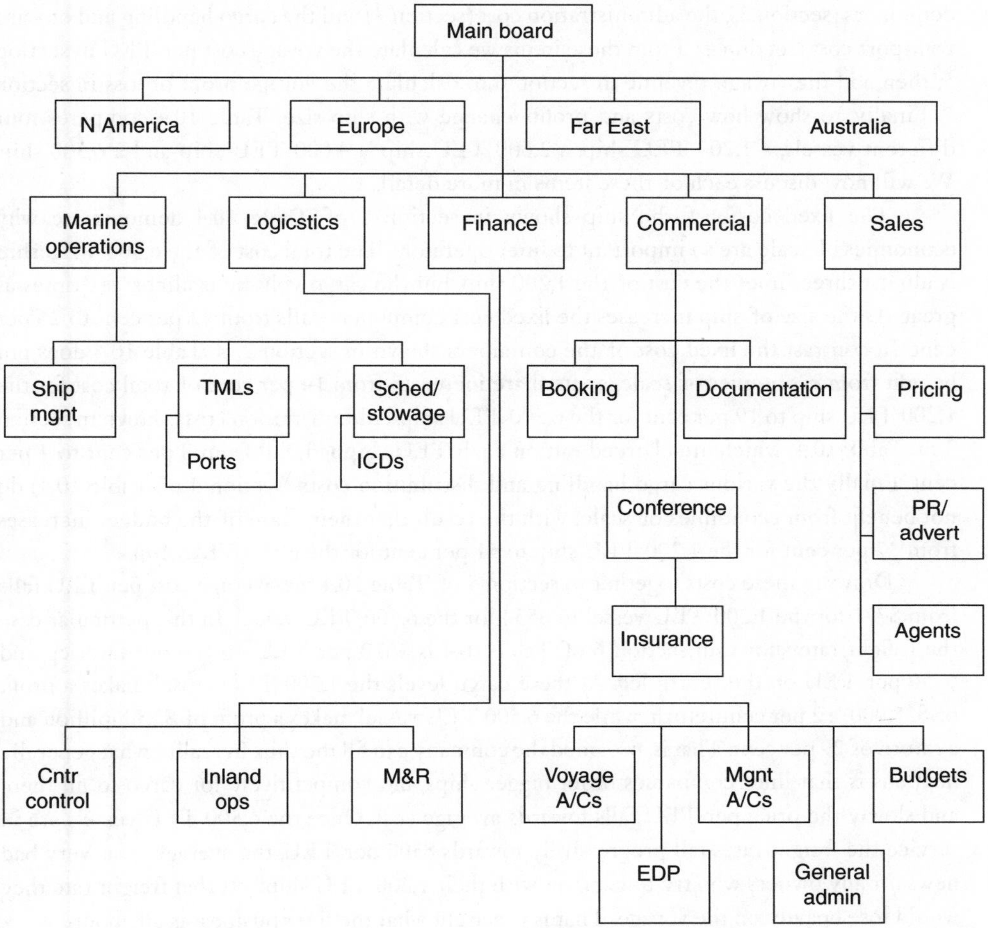

FIGURE 10.3 Liner company organization

Source: Compiled by Martin Stopford from various sources

element of economies of scale because staff levels increase less than proportionally with the service volume, resulting in a falling administration cost from $100/TEU for the 1,200 TEU ship to $42/TEU for the 6,500 TEU ship.

10.6 The liner service cashflow model

Now we come to stage 2 which involves combining the cost information with revenue to show how these determine the financial performance of a liner service. The *service cashflow model* shown in Table 10.4 takes the detailed cost information from Table 10.3 and summarizes it into four components, the fixed cost of the ships (section 1), the cost of the containers (section 2), the administration cost (section 3) and the cargo handling and onward transport cost (section 4). From these items we calculate the voyage cost per TEU in section 5, then add the voyage revenue in section 6 to calculate the voyage profit or loss in section 7. Finally, to show how costs and profits change with ship size, Table 10.4 compares four different vessels, a 1,200 TEU ship, a 2,600 TEU ship, a 4,000 TEU ship and a 6,500 ship. We will now discuss each of these items in more detail.

The fixed costs of the ship shown in section 1 of Table 10.4 demonstrate why economies of scale are so important to liner operators. The total cost of the 6,500 TEU ship is almost three times the cost of the 1,200 ship, but the cargo volume is almost six times as great. As the size of ship increases the fixed cost component falls from 42 per cent to 26 per cent. In contrast the fixed cost of the containers shown in section 2 of Table 10.4 does not benefit from economies of scale, so its share increases from 14 per cent of total cost for the 1,200 TEU ship to 19 per cent for the 6,500 TEU ship. Administration costs shown in section 3 of Table 10.4, which are charged out on each TEU shipped, fall from 8 per cent to 4 per cent. Finally the various cargo handling and distribution costs (section 4 of Table 10.4) do not benefit from economies of scale, with the result that their share of the budget increases from 37 per cent for the 1,200 TEU ship to 51 per cent for the 6,500 TEU ship.

Drawing these costs together in section 5 of Table 10.4 the average cost per TEU falls from $771 for the 1,200 TEU vessel to $554 for the 6,500 TEU vessel. In this particular case the freight rate shown in section 6 of Table 10.4 is $820 per TEU on the outward leg and $750 per TEU on the return leg. At these cargo levels the 1,200 TEU vessel makes a profit of $25,000, a 2 per cent return, while the 6,500 TEU vessel makes a profit of $2.53 million and a return of 29 per cent. That is, provided the company can fill the ship. In reality what generally happens is that liner companies order bigger ships, bid competitively for cargo to fill them and slowly the price per TEU falls towards average cost. Once the 6,500 TEU vessels are in service the freight rates fall progressively towards $500 per TEU, the average cost. Very bad news for any owners who try to hang on with their 1,200 TEU ships. At that freight rate they would lose heavily on the voyage. That is precisely what the liner business is all about.

10.7 Liner prices

Now we come to the question of pricing for liner services. Ultimately liner prices, like bulk freight rates, are determined by competition in the market-place. Shipping is a free business which companies may enter or leave as they wish. However, as we saw earlier in the chapter, the price-making process is more complex than for the bulk industry and the procedures are constantly changing in response to competitive and regulatory pressures.

During the cargo liner era a very centralized system was developed for handling pricing. Liner conferences were firmly established and in most trades they conducted the price negotiations, usually with a central body representing the shippers, for example a shippers' council. They would meet regularly to negotiate rates and agree 'General Rate Increases' (GRIs). Outsiders, accounting for a small or a large share of the trade, followed an independent pricing policy. The introduction of containerization has diluted this process.

Conferences still exist, but the price-making has become less structured, passing to a variety of discussion agreements, alliances and negotiated service agreements.

Most liner companies still build their pricing policy around the dual principles of price stability and price discrimination. The case for price stability is obvious. Liner companies have a fixed overhead, so why not fix prices? Anyway, with so many customers, negotiating every price is not practical. Ideally once prices are set, they should change only when there is some valid reason for doing so, such as an increase in the cost of providing the service or a major change in the underlying unit costs. The case for commodity price discrimination is equally obvious. Charge higher rates to commodities which can bear the cost, and discount low value commodities. This enables the liner company to attract a wider range of cargoes than would be economic if there was a single standard freight charge. By increasing the volume, the companies can use larger ships and offer more regular sailings. In this way it is argued that the pricing policy supports the provision of a better service package for all customers, though the role of cross-subsidization remains one of active debate. The second type of *price discrimination* is between customers. Large customers, with whom it is worth negotiating, can be offered special discounts (e.g. a 'service agreement') while the smaller customers continue to pay the regular tariff.

The method used to implement the commodity pricing system is the tariff which defines the price classes, typically ten to thirty in number, for which different rates are charged. Each commodity is listed in the rate book, showing the price class to which it is assigned. Thus the freight rate for a particular cargo is worked out by looking up the rate for the commodity, multiplying by the amount to be shipped, say 209.5 cubic metres, and adding any additionals. Containerization has made it much more difficult to enforce this system. If it costs $10,000 to ship a 20 ft container when the shipper knows that boxes are being shipped on the same service for $1,500, it is bound to cause price resistance.[20] Many liner companies now charge a standard box rate or apply a FAK (freight all kinds) tariff. Ultimately it is a matter of what the market will bear, though the discussion of price discrimination showed that the FAK system has disadvantages. Some shippers are more price sensitive than others. An auto parts distributor might value reliability and service, while for the shipper of a price sensitive product like cellophane rolls, the freight rate is more important. In a complex business offering a differentiated transport product there is certainly a case for a degree of price discrimination. The product and the pricing system must both be adapted to the client's needs.

Even with a FAK rate, the procedure for quoting the customer a freight charge and preparing an invoice is quite complex because liner companies charge separately for items which they regard as 'additional' to the basic transport service they provide. Typically the invoice sent to a customer will include some or all of the following items:

- *Freight charges*: The charge for transporting the box or cargo. Sometimes the customer is quoted a 'door to door' rate, but often there are separate charges for port-to-port transport, and collection or delivery.
- *Sea freight additionals*: Surcharges to cover unbudgeted costs incurred by the liner company. The *bunker adjustment factor (baf)* covers unexpected increases in the cost of

bunker fuel, which accounts for a major proportion of operating costs on long routes. *Currency adjustment factor (caf)* covers currency fluctuations. The currency adjustment factor is based on an agreed basket of costs and is designed to keep tariff revenue the same, regardless of changes between the tariff currency rates of exchange. *Port congestion surcharges* may be charged if a particular port becomes difficult to access due to congestion.

- *Terminal handling charge (THC)*: These are charged per container handled in local currency per container to cover the cost of handling the container in the port. Within a region, ports may have different charges. Some operators absorb THCs into the through freight rate.
- *Service additionals*: If the shipper undertakes additional services for the customer – for example, storage of goods, customs clearance or trans-shipment – there would be an additional charge for this.
- *Cargo additionals*: Some cargoes attract additional charges because they are difficult or expensive to transport. For example an open top container, heavy lift, etc.

To simplify the charging process some companies may negotiate special contracts with major customers, offering discounts on volume or other concessions. These are known as Service Contracts.

10.8 The demand for liner services

General cargo and container movements

So far we have concentrated on the economics of transporting general cargo. Now it is time to look more closely at the cargo liners carry. In Chapter 1 we discussed how seaborne trade splits between bulk cargo and *general cargo* which we defined as cargo parcels that are too small for bulk shipment.[21] This is a business in which the customers have widely differing transport requirements and the cargoes are tremendously varied, ranging from television sets to building blocks.

Some cargoes are high value (typically $5,000–10,000 a ton). Manufactured and semi-manufactured products – consumer goods, machinery, textiles, chemicals and vehicles fall into this category. For the most part these have too high a value and too low a volume to travel by any other service than liner, though if enough cargo is available bulk shipment may be viable. The motor vehicle trade is a classic example, and the liner business has lost much lucrative cargo to car carriers in recent decades. There is also intense competition for these cargoes from the air freight transport industry, especially on long routes where the time saving of air transport is a strong selling point. Clothing shipped from the Far East to Europe, or electrical components are the sort of cargoes that fall into this area. Sea–air services have now stripped some of the business from the Asia–Europe trade.

At the other end of the scale are the low value cargoes such as steel products, forest products, building materials, foodstuffs such as coffee or empty gas canisters. These are the cargoes for which liner companies compete with other transport operators, particularly specialist shipowners such as chemical parcel tankers, reefers, pure car carriers and open hatch bulk carriers. Although these cargoes do not support high freight rates they are a valuable source of marginal revenue for operators pursuing economies of scale, or on routes where there is an imbalance of cargo.

The growth of containerized cargo between 1966 and 1995 was spectacular. In the two decades from 1975 to 1994 the volume of containers handled by container terminals increased from 17.4 million TEUs to 126.6 million TEUs in 1994 (Figure 10.4), a seven-fold increase. Trade doubled in the 1980s and increased by 46 per cent in the first half of the 1990s. These figures cover total container movements through ports, including deep sea, feeder, local services and empties. By the mid-1980s all of the major liner routes had been containerized. However on a few of the minor routes the small volume of cargo, the extreme imbalance of containerizable trade, and the continuing availability of multi-purpose ships meant that even in the 1990s some break bulk trades continued to operate.

Analysing the general cargo trade presents difficulties. Commodity analysis is not really practical, except for a few of the larger trades. In reality the growth of liner cargo is more closely related to the general growth trend in international trade which, as we saw in Chapter 7, is driven by the search for lower costs and greater variety. The improved speed and reliability of the liner services since containerization and the downward trend in the cost of transport has certainly contributed to the speed of trade growth. Unfortunately, the statistical database for analysing these trends is rather thin but, by a process of deduction,

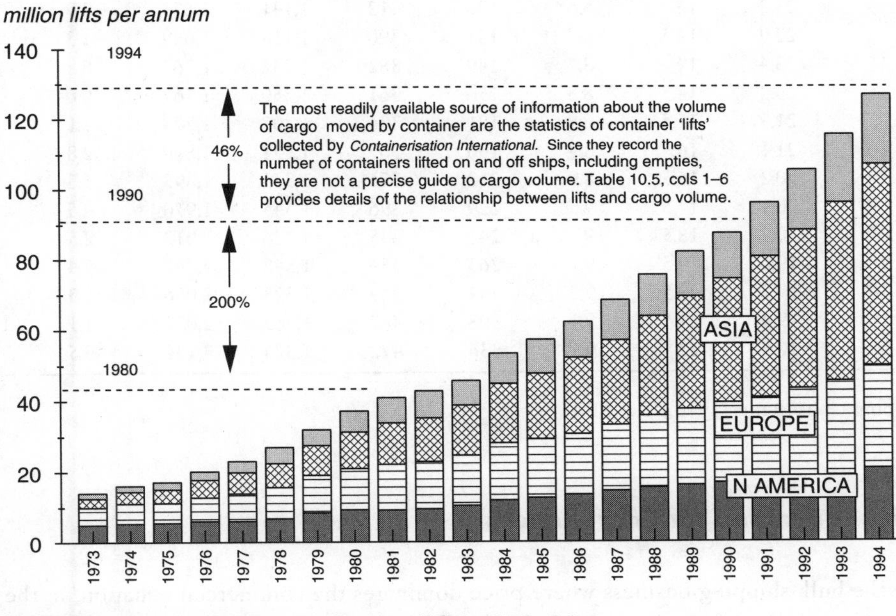

FIGURE 10.4 Container movements (lifts) 1973–94

Source: Drewry Shipping Consultants

we can piece together a broad picture of the volume of general cargo. The calculations are shown in Table 10.5. The total dry cargo trade (column 9) splits into three parts, dry bulk (column 8), break bulk (column 7) and containerized cargo (column 6). The containerized cargo, which has grown so rapidly, is estimated from the number of container lifts by deducting a percentage for empty containers (about 20 per cent shown in column 3) and for containers which are transhipped, and thus handled twice on the voyage (22 per cent in 1994, shown in column 4). The number of container journeys left after making these deductions must be divided by two, to eliminate the fact that the container is lifted on and off the ship, and multiplied by the average cargo payload (9.1 tons shown in column 5). In 1994 that gives a containerized cargo volume of 336 mt, an increase from 109 mt in 1980. In contrast break bulk cargo shown in column 7 only increased from 418 mt in 1980 to 472 mt in 1994.

TABLE 10.5 The container and break bulk trades 1980–94

	1	2	3	4	5	6	7	8	9	10
	Containerized cargo movements (moves)									
	Container lifts TEU (m)	*%*	*Empty %*	*Trans-shipment %*	*Weight/ TEU mt*	*Container cargo mt*	*Break bulk mt*	*Dry Bulk mt*	*Total mt*	*% per annum*
1980	38.7	13	21.8	12	8.5	109	418	1,306	1,833	
1981	41.9	8	22	12.5	8.6	117	449	1,183	1,749	1.8
1982	43.8	5	23.2	13	8.6	120	412	1,141	1,673	−3.9
1983	47.5	8	22.9	13.5	8.7	131	390	1,118	1,639	−1.3
1984	54.6	15	23.4	14	8.7	149	382	1,232	1,763	8
1985	57.2	5	23.3	14.5	8.8	156	361	1,250	1,767	0.6
1986	62.2	9	21.9	15.5	8.8	171	396	1,207	1,774	1.1
1987	68.3	10	21.1	16	8.9	190	367	1,252	1,809	2.8
1988	75.4	10	20.2	16.5	8.9	212	356	1,325	1,893	5.3
1989	82	9	20.1	17.5	9	229	396	1,345	1,970	4.5
1990	87.4	7	20.2	18.5	9	241	445	1,326	2,012	2.5
1991	95.8	10	19.6	19.5	9	263	456	1,348	2,067	3.4
1992	105.2	10	19.7	20.5	9	284	469	1,323	2,076	1.3
1993	115.3	10	19.4	21.5	9.1	308	467	1,302	2,077	1.1
1994	126.7	10	19.5	22	9.1	336	472	1,324	2,132	3.5

Source: Drewry Shipping Consultants (1996), Table 3.11

Characteristics of demand for liner services

Unlike the bulk shipping business where price dominates the commercial equation, in the liner business *quality* of service is often the focus of competition. In practice there are six aspects of the freight service which shippers consider to be important:

- *Freight cost.* The charge for transporting the container from origin to destination, including additionals.
- *Frequency of sailings.* Sea transport is one stage in the overall production process. Frequent sailings offer the manufacturer the opportunity to service one-off orders rapidly and enable him to reduce the level of stocks held at each end of the transport operation.
- *Transit time door-to-door.* On long voyages, particularly for high-value products, speed of transit may be a major consideration owing to the cost of inventory. In this context, air freight may be a significant competitor, particularly where a shipping time of four weeks is involved in a Far East to Europe voyage.
- *Reliability of timekeeping.* On deep sea routes the liner service is the customer's only direct link to his export market. Some customers are likely to value reliability of service. In terms of the transport service, adherence to fixed day schedules and on-time pick up and delivery are important.
- *Reliability of administration*: Customers value prompt and accurate administration. The ability to provide timely quotations, accurate bills of lading, prompt arrival notices, accurate invoices and to resolve problems when they arise all play a part in the customer's evaluation of the liner company's performance.
- *Space availability.* The ability of the service to accept cargo, even at short notice, may be valued by businesses that are not able to plan their transport requirements far in advance.

Most shippers look for a combination of these factors, though research suggests that there is no clear pattern of preferences which applies to all shippers. Surveys of shipper's attitudes produce widely differing results.

A survey of 50 shippers in the US domestic trades[22] found that timeliness of service was the most important single factor, but another study of the attitudes of shippers in North America and Europe found that cost of service and problem-solving capability were ranked most highly. Transit time, which had been placed third in an earlier survey carried out in 1982, had fallen to seventh place by 1991, suggesting that priorities change.[23] Common sense suggests that this must be the case. Price will only be a significant decision variable if different prices are quoted by different companies. More fundamentally, different shippers have different priorities, depending on the cargo and the nature of their business.

Price and liner demand

Price is particularly important for lower value commodities where the transport cost contributes to determining whether the trade is viable. For example, a company distributing large tonnages of low value cellophane rolls to processing plants in Europe might take the view that as long as they have a reasonable tonnage in the pipeline at any one time, considerations of service and claims experience are of far less importance than rate per ton.[24] For this type of commodity, prices are subject to intense competition and liner companies often discount heavily to win the business, especially where they have spare capacity on one leg of the voyage. Some examples of the price sensitive cargoes that are containerized are given below:

- *Wool.* A high proportion of the wool trade is containerized. Wool is 'dumped' (i.e. compressed) into bales which are packed into 20 ft containers, giving an average container weight of 18 tons.
- *Cotton.* US West Coast cotton exports are now containerized. A total of 82 standard dumped bales can be packed into a 40 ft container.
- *Wine* is shipped by container either in cases or in 5,000-gallon bulk container tanks. A 40 ft container can hold 972 cases of 1 litre bottles and 1,200 cases of 750 millilitre bottles.
- *Rubber* used to be shipped in bales. To facilitate containerization, some companies have now adopted standard bale sizes and pack the bales in shrink film rather than timber crates. Latex is shipped in drums packed in containers.

Service quality and liner demand

For many cargoes, particularly those of high value, the shipper may have far more to lose if the service is poor than he could possibly gain from squeezing the price down a few per cent. For example a motor cycle manufacturer exporting its products world-wide must be able to meet delivery schedules to its dealer network. Frequent services, sufficient volume of available shipping space, reliable advance information about vessel arrival and departure times, speed, and responsible management of cargo landed at the destination are all of crucial importance to a company distributing its products over a long distance.

We should not be surprised that service requirements now dominate the liner business. Over the last 30 years international businesses have systematically tightened the management of product flows and inventory costs, often using 'just in time' control systems. Containerization played a major part in this process by allowing companies to access global markets through a fast, reliable transport network. A good example of why customers are willing to pay extra for speed and reliability is illustrated by a freight forwarder dealing with the motor trade:

> We are heavily involved in spare parts traffic for the motor industry where in recent years inventory stocks have been reduced to the absolute minimum. This obviously has given quite substantial cost savings to importers and exporters. But they are prepared to spend some of this cost saving in additional freighting charges to ensure that their production lines are kept moving.[25]

Liners are part of a supply system and customers view the cost and benefits of transport in the context of the business as a whole.

Another service characteristic valued by shippers is strict timekeeping. Even if the ships are available, keeping to precise schedules is not easy. A survey of timekeeping of services in North America and the Far East found that in North America three-quarters of the vessels tracked arrived on or one day after their scheduled time. In the Far East ports 89 per cent of the vessels arrived within a day of schedule.[26] At first sight it might seem surprising that timekeeping presents such a problem. However, liners work in such diverse conditions that it is difficult to plan for every contingency. Some delays are caused by breakdowns such as engine failure, or dry dockings that over-run. Then there are accidents (e.g. a collision), natural disasters such as earthquakes, adverse weather, and congestion. Many of these are avoidable at a price. In the long-term powerful ships which can make up lost time and realistic schedules which incorporate a margin for delays are the solution. In the short-term skipping ports is a common way of catching up on schedule, or for serious delays chartering a replacement ship, if one is available.

Containerizing marginal and specialized cargoes

Containerization of low value or specialized cargoes plays an important part in helping service operators to obtain a balanced cargo payload and new types of containers have been developed to allow the transportation of *low value* or non-standard cargoes. The main types were summarized in Table 10.2. Open-top containers are used for heavy lift; reefer and ventilated containers are used for frozen and chilled cargo and various perishable agricultural crops; flat tracks are used for awkward cargoes; and tanks are used for various bulk liquids such as wine and chemicals.

Containerizing new cargoes often involves research into packing, stowage and handling methods. For this reason the speed with which containerization has penetrated some trades, particularly the minor bulks, depends upon finding practical ways to allow difficult cargoes to be containerized. Sometimes the problem is the delicate nature of the cargo. For example confectionary exports from the UK are containerized using insulated containers which need special handling to avoid condensation and tainting from previous cargoes.[27] Or it might be a matter of finding a way to reduce the cost by more effective stowage. Most of the motor cycle export trade from Japan is now containerized. By careful planning and some dis-assembly, a total of 28 large motor cycles or up to 200 small ones can be packed into a 40 ft container. This emphasis on efficient stowage led some manufacturers to take container dimensions into account in their design. However the trend is not always towards packing more cargo into a container. In the integrated transport business, what matters is the total cost. High density stowage which calls for some assembly at the destination can be expensive and difficult to control. As transport costs have fallen and labour costs have increased many manufacturers have reverted to shipping motor cycles fully assembled and carefully packed.

A good example of the practicalities of containerizing difficult cargoes is provided by the export of bulk coffee from Brazil to the US.[28] Traditionally coffee beans were shipped in 60 kg bags, loaded into the hold of a general cargo ship. When containerization was introduced, the bags were packed into a container. Problems with condensation were overcome by using 'dry bags' which absorbed the moisture released by the coffee beans and a massive improvement in efficiency was achieved. Instead of having to individually handle about 250 sacks, the single container is dropped into place in the container ship, an operation taking about one-and-a-half minutes in a purpose-built container vessel. Then in the mid-1980s importers started looking for ways to reduce the labour required to 'stuff' and 'unstuff' containers with 60 kg bags. Eventually they developed a new cargo handling system which loaded the container by gravity feed and discharged by a special chute, taking only a few minutes compared with several hours and a lot more labour for manual handling. This example illustrates the important point that containerization does not just save transport costs. It has an impact on packaging costs and cargo handling costs at either end of the cargo leg.

Finally there is *project cargo.* Some specific items shipped by liners include, for example, equipment for two cement plants, electrification projects for Singapore and Korea, a water filtration plant for Hong Kong, a textile fibre plant for the Philippines, a telecommunications project for Malaysia and equipment for a mass transit railway system in Hong Kong.

10.9 The liner shipping routes

Providing liner services that cover the globe is a daunting task. In the 'Maritime Transport Study' the United Nations identified thirty-two maritime coastal regions. There are 1,024 potential liner routes between these areas. Some of the coastal regions cover thousands of miles of coastline and all have many ports. The task of the liner market is to sort out a route network which cost-effectively meets the changing needs of the shippers in these coastal regions.

The industry generally divides the trade routes into three groups, shown in Table 10.6. The East–West trades, which account for 44 per cent of the cargo, circle the globe in the Northern Hemisphere, linking the major industrial centres of North America, Western Europe and Asia. The North–South trades which operate mainly between the three major industrial areas and the economies in the Southern Hemisphere account for another 22 per cent, while the remaining 34 per cent of the trade is intra-regional cargo, which is shorter-haul and uses smaller ships. This global network is constantly evolving to meet the changing needs of the world economy. Because liner services straddle the world in a complex network of arterial routes, spurs, and feeder services which oflen overlap, it is not possible to describe the routes in a precise way. The following paragraphs provide a broad description of the major routes as they exist in the mid-1990s.

By far the largest volume of trade is on the East–West routes. These trades dominate the liner business. Over the last 20 years they have grown enormously, underpinning the rapidly expanding trade links between these areas. The routes provide employment for 60 per cent of the container ship fleet, and for the majority of ships over 2,000 TEU.

The trans-Pacific trade

Containerization started in the Far East trade in December 1968 when Sea-Land introduced the container service from Seattle to Yokohama and the Japanese shipping companies

TABLE 10.6 Major liner routes and trade imbalances, 1996

		000 TEU per annum	*% World trade*	*Biggest trade*	*Trade imbalance*
East-West trades					
Trans Pacific		7,470	20	Eastbound	22%
Trans Atlantic		3,030	8	Westbound	18%
Europe-Far East		4,895	13	Westbound	12%
Europe-Mid East		645	2	Eastbound	88%
N. America-Mid East		205	1	Eastbound	72%
Far East-Mid East		255	1	Westbound	66%
Total		16,500	44		22%
North-South trades					
Europe to	L. America	1,150	3	Southbound	17%
	S. Asia	475	1	Northbound	27%
	Africa	950	3	Southbound	35%
	Australasia	400	1	Southbound	40%
	Total	2,975	8		28%
N.America to	L. America	2,000	5	Southbound	26%
	S. Asia	250	1	Northbound	44%
	Africa	100	0	Southbound	33%
	Australasia	275	1	Southbound	47%
	Total	2,625	7		30%
Far East to	L. America	725	2	Southbound	55%
	S. Asia	425	1	Northbound	11%
	Africa	425	1	Southbound	45%
	Australasia	875	2	Northbound	16%
	Total	2,450	7		32%
Total North-South trades		8,050	22		30%
Intra-Regional					
Asia		6,750	18		
Europe		4,250	11		
N.America		1,250	3		
Other		300	1		
Total intra regional		12,550	34		
Total container trade		37,100	100		25%

Source: Drewry Shipping Consultants (1996) various tables

introduced six 700/800 TEU container ships into a service between California and Japan. Now the biggest deep sea liner route is the trans-Pacific trade between North America and the Far East, with 7.5 million TEU of trade, representing 22 per cent of the world total. The services operate between North American ports on the East Coast, the Gulf and the West Coast, to the industrial centres of Japan and the Far East, with some services extending to the Middle East. Some of the services to the eastern USA operate direct by water, but in recent years containers to East Coast US are shipped under one bill of lading to a US West Coast port and by rail to the East Coast destination, thus avoiding the Panama transit. On the rail leg containers may be double stacked. There is a substantial cargo inbalance, with eastbound shipments exceeding westbound shipments by 22 per cent in 1994.

In 1995, there were about twenty-eight liner companies servicing the trade, including American companies such as Sea-Land, Japanese companies such as Mitsui OSK, European companies such as Maersk, and, more recently, national lines established by Singapore, Taiwan and South Korea. The round voyage for a vessel calling at four ports in South East Asia and two on the US West Coast is about 16,500 miles. At a speed of 21 knots the sea time is thirty-two days, with an additional ten days in port, giving a round journey time forty-two days, or six weeks. To provide weekly sailings in this trade requires a fleet of six ships, though some services reduce the number of port calls so as to operate to a five-week round voyage which can be operated by five ships. The 'all water' service to the US East coast requires nine vessels. Because of the long voyage time the trans-Pacific trade uses the biggest ships, with many 'post-Panamax' vessels over 4,000 TEU on this service.

The North Atlantic trade

The North Atlantic was the first route containerized in the mid-1960s, as one might expect since at that time it linked the two major industrial centres of the world, East Coast North America and Western Europe. In the mid-1990s it had a trade of 3 million TEU, accounting for 8 per cent of world container trade. There is an 18 per cent trade imbalance westbound, reflecting the greater volume of cargo to North America.

Geographically, the North Atlantic trade covers the major European ports of Gothenburg, Hamburg, Bremerhaven, Antwerp, Rotterdam, Felixstowe and Le Havre, though there are some other smaller ports included on the itineraries of certain liner companies. At the North American end of the operation it is organized into two sections covering North Europe to US Atlantic and North Europe to the St Lawrence. The principal Canadian ports serviced are Montreal and Halifax, while in the US Boston, New York, Philadelphia, Baltimore, Hampton Roads, Wilmington and Charleston are all regular port calls. Some services extend into the US Gulf.

Typically the round voyage distance is about 8,000 miles which can be completed in eighteen days at a speed of 19 knots. Allowing ten days for port time, the round trip takes about twenty-eight days. The usual pattern is for larger operators to offer weekly sailings using a fleet of four or five ships. About twenty-five companies/consortia offer scheduled services on the North Atlantic. In the North Atlantic, an open conference prevails, the Trans Atlantic Conference Agreement (TACA) which was set up in 1995 covering about 60 per cent of the capacity on the trade. Anyone can join it and there are no trade shares. Out of the twenty operators on the North Atlantic, about thirteen are conference members, and there is a strong tradition of non-conference competition in this trade.

Western Europe to the Far East trade

This route covers the trade of North Europe, stretching from Sweden down to St Nazaire in France to the Far East, comprising West Malaysia, Singapore, Thailand, Hong Kong, Philippines, Taiwan, South Korea and Japan. As we saw earlier in the chapter, it was one of the first trades to be covered by a conference system, the Far East Freight Conference (FEFC). In 1995 there were about twenty-one operators or consortiums running 200 ships on the trade, of which about half are members of the FEFC and the other half are 'outsiders'.

Three major operators in the Far East trade are the Grand Alliance composed of P&O, NYK, Neptune Orient Lines and Hapag-Lloyd; the Global Alliance consisting of MOL, Nedlloyd, OOCL, APL and MISC; and Maersk/Sea-Land. The round voyage time is sixty-three days, requiring nine ships to provide a weekly sailing. The major operators run separate weekly services direct to Japan and Korea, and to South East Asia. It is the large number of ships required to operate a regular service in this trade that necessitated the development of consortia. A typical round voyage would involve calling at four European ports (for example, Le Havre, Rotterdam, Southampton, and Hamburg), Singapore and four or five other ports in South East Asia (for example, Hong Kong, Busan, Osaka, Tokyo, Kaohsiung). Not all services call at Japan and South Korea, preferring to turn in Hong Kong or Taiwan instead.

Round the world services

A logical development was to fuse these three main liner routes into a single global service. In the early 1980s several operators took this step, of which the most important were Evergreen and United States Lines. Evergreen runs twelve vessels in each direction around the world with a round trip of eighty days, providing a ten-day service frequency in each direction. This service was initially introduced with eight ships in September 1984, but it rapidly became apparent that the ten-day service compared unfavourably with the seven-day service operated by competitors, particularly on the North Atlantic. As a result, in 1985 the number of ships was increased to eleven in each direction, and then to twelve giving a weekly service with a round trip time of seventy-seven days. The ships used on the service were G-class vessels of 2,700 TEU which have now been lengthened to 3,428 TEU. In November 1986, the United States Lines' operation was withdrawn as a result of the company's financial difficulties. For some years DSR-Senator and Cho Yang ran a round-the-world service, but with the notable exception of Evergreen this method of operation has attracted remarkably few operators.

The round-the-world service follows the three main arterial routes. Going westbound, after calling at the UK and north continent ports, vessels proceed down the East Coast of

North America through the Panama Canal to the US West Coast, Japan, the Far East and through the Suez Canal to the Mediterranean.

The North-South liner routes

The North-South liner services cover the trade between the industrial centres of Europe, North America and the Far East and the developing countries of Latin America, Africa, Far East and Australasia. There is also an extensive network of services between the smaller economies, especially those in the Southern Hemisphere. These trades, which are listed in Table 10.6, have a very different character. Cargo volumes are much lower, accounting for only 22 per cent of the container cargo volume in 1994. However, this understates the importance of these trades to the shipping business. With many more ports to visit and often less efficient port itineraries, they generate more business than the container volume suggests. Although most trades are now containerized there remains a considerable amount of break bulk cargo which cannot be handled in containers, so the liner services are more varied. These trades are too extensive to review in detail, so we will concentrate on one example, the Europe to West Africa service.

The Europe to West Africa trade operates between North West Europe and the eighteen countries of West Africa, stretching from Senegal down to Angola. Nigeria is comparatively rich, but many of the others are very poor with few ports and limited supporting transport infrastructure. European trade accounts for two-thirds of the seaborne traffic, with the remainder divided between the United States and Asia.[29]

The Europe to West Africa trade is a typical developed Third World trade with the outward cargo leg dominated by manufactures and the return cargo dominated by minor bulks. Southbound shipments include chemicals, cement, iron and steel, machinery and various foodstuffs. The return cargo is principally composed of primary products and semi-manufactures with a substantial trade in logs, coffee, cocoa, oilseeds, vegetable oil, cotton and non-ferrous metals. The volume of cargo southbound is almost twice the volume northbound, a fact that creates considerable problems in terms of obtaining full utilization for the vessels.[30]

In 1995 there were eleven services offering regular sailings between North West Europe and West Africa, with service intervals ranging from seven to twenty-one days. Only about 60 per cent of the cargo is containerized, the remainder being a mix of break bulk, wheeled and bulk cargo. The fleet of forty ships engaged in these services reflect the efforts of the companies to respond to the diversity of cargo. In January 1996 the fleet was as follows:

Ship type	*Description*	*Number*
Baco liners	Barge carrier	3
Conbulker	Open hatch bulk carrier	4
Containerships	Fully cellular	10
Multipurpose	Open hatch	11
ro-ro	700–1300 TEU	9
ro-ro/container	580 TEU	3

Only a quarter of the fleet is fully cellular, the remainder being more flexible vessels which allow general cargo, wheeled cargo, containers and bulk to be carried in the same ship.

These services do not have the regimented discipline of the deep sea container services, varying the ships and services to meet the needs of the trade. For example one service, shown in Figure 10.5, offers weekly container-ship sailings with less frequent break bulk sailings. The ships load cargo in Europe at Felixstowe, Rotterdam, Antwerp, Hamberg and Le Havre. In West Africa the line offers shipment to virtually all major ports either direct or via a feeder system. A typical itinerary might cover calling at Dakar, Freetown, Monrovia, Takoradi, Tema, Lome, Port Harcourt, Douala, and Pointe Noire. To deal with the mix of containers, break bulk and bulk cargo the service uses a fleet of six ships. Two container ships of 1,600/1,800 TEU, three multi-purpose vessels of 600/700 TEU and a Conbulker of 800 TEU. The multi-purpose ships have wide hatches and cargo handling gear

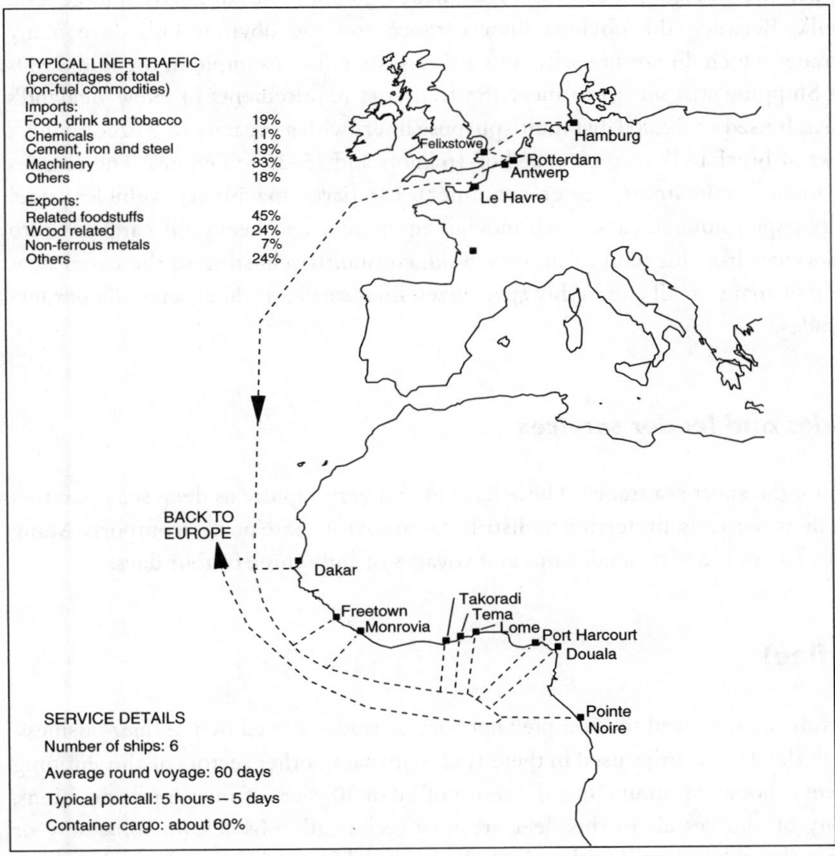

FIGURE 10.5 Typical liner route: UK–West Africa

to enable containers to be worked on all hatches even in ports where no suitable cargo handling gear is available.

The imbalance of containerized cargo leaves the shipping line with empty containers to transport back to Europe, and strenuous efforts have been made to containerize return cargoes in order to utilize the container space on ships. On the West Africa to Europe leg the following commodities were containerized: coffee (bagged in containers), empty gas cylinders (returned for refilling), high-value veneers, ginger, cotton, mail. Attempts to containerize cocoa were initially unsuccessful because the product 'sweats', while the large logs shipped from West Africa are not generally suitable for containerization. About two-thirds of the containers shipped out to West Africa thus travel back empty.

The marginal liner services

In discussing the liner trades it is easy to forget that cargo does not fall neatly into general cargo and bulk. Between the obvious liner cargoes and the obvious bulks are many 'borderline' trades which do not fit easily into either system. For example in the mid-1980s Tasman Asia Shipping was set up to meet the transport requirements of New Zealand's forestry exports. It used six 22,000 dwt multi-purpose liners with a capacity of 350 containers and 10,000 dwt of break bulk cargo, a speed of 16 knots and 25–35 ton cranes. The cargoes they carried include containers, reefer containers, car parts, machinery, vehicles, steel products, pulp, paper, lumber, cars, earth moving equipment and heavy lift cargoes up to 120 tonnes. Services like this tend to be very fluid, constantly adjusting to the cargo flow. This is just one of many small and highly specialized liner services which serve the borders of the liner trades.

Intra-regional trades and feeder services

Finally there are the short sea trades. These have grown very rapidly as deep sea operators have reduced their portcalls, preferring to distribute cargo from base ports to outports. Many of the short sea trades use very small ships and voyages of only three or four days.

10.10 The liner fleet

In the last section we reviewed the complex network of trades served by the liner business. Now we turn to the fleet of ships used in these trades. Just as in other sectors of the shipping market, the fleet is not an optimum. It is the result of 20 or 30 years of investment decisions. Although many of the vessels in this fleet are now technically obsolete in some way or another, the fact that they are still trading is evidence that they retain economic value.

The fleet of ships currently operating in the liner trades now consists of six different types of ships shown in Figure 10.6:

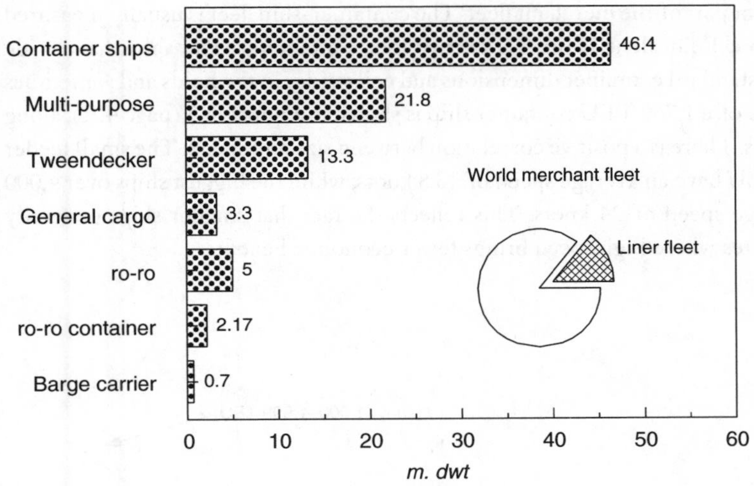

FIGURE 10.6 Liner fleet by ship type
Source: Clarkson Research Studies

- *Container ships*: Cellular 'lift on lift off' container ships are now the biggest and most modern part of the fleet. All the ships in this fleet have open holds with cell guides and are designed exclusively for the carriage of containers.
- *Multi-purpose vessels*: There is a fleet of about 22 m.dwt. These are ships designed with a fast speed, good container capacity and the ability to carry break bulk and other unitized cargo such as forest products. They were mainly built during the early years of containerization when operators were handling a mix of containerized and break bulk cargo. Most have open holds without cell guides and often incorporating a 'tween deck.
- *'Tweendeckers*: These flexible 'tramp' vessels continued to be built until the 1980s and there is still a fleet of 13 m.dwt in operation. Two standard designs, the SD14 and the Freedom were very popular. 'Tweendeckers have two decks, narrow hatches, economical speed, limited container capacity and cargo gear.
- *General cargo liners*: In the mid-1990s there were still a few of the purpose-built cargo liners still in service (the *Pointe Sans Souci*, mentioned earlier in this chapter, was scrapped in 1996). They are fast with multiple decks, extensive cargo gear but poor container capacity.
- *Ro-ros*: Multi-deck vessels in which the holds are accessed by ramps in the bow, stern or side. Although sometimes similar in design to car ferries, they have no accommodation or public areas and are designed primarily to carry cargo on deep sea routes.
- *Barge carriers*: A 1970s experiment which did not catch on. Carries 500 ton standard barges which are floated or lifted on and off the ship.

The number of container ships increased from 750 in 1980 to 2,094 in 1997, and they now dominate the liner fleet, accounting for 50 per cent of the total capacity in dwt. This compares with a tanker fleet of 3,500 vessels and a bulk carrier fleet of 5,500 vessels, making container ships a very significant part of the merchant fleet. The container-ship fleet is usually measured in TEU (Twenty foot Equivalent Units, i.e. twenty foot containers). The ships have wide hatches designed to standard container dimensions and cell guides in the holds and sometimes on deck. An example of a 1,769 TEU container ship is shown in Figure 11.3 (page 401), along with technical details. There is a positive correlation between size and speed. The small feeder ships of 100–299 TEU have an average speed of 13.8 knots, while the biggest ships over 4,000 TEU have an average speed of 24 knots. This reflects the fact that smaller ships generally operate on short routes where high speed brings fewer economic benefits.

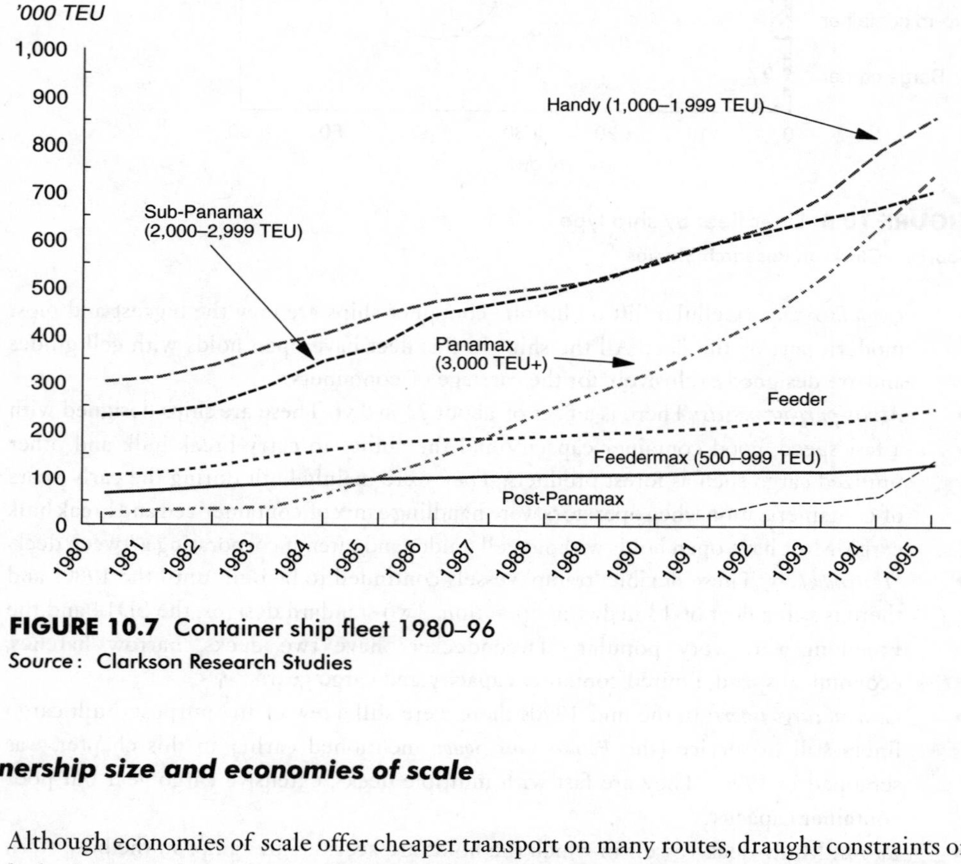

FIGURE 10.7 Container ship fleet 1980–96
Source: Clarkson Research Studies

Containership size and economies of scale

Although economies of scale offer cheaper transport on many routes, draught constraints or lack of cargo volume require the use of small ships on some routes. Since the cargo base of the container business covers a spectrum of different sized trades, this implies that liner operators require a range of different sizes of container ships. As the container business has matured the fleet has evolved into segments, each serving a different part of the market. Figure 10.6 sub-divides the fleet into six segments.[31] Three segments (Feeder, Feedermax and Handysize) are mainly concerned with the short sea and draught restricted trades particularly on the North–South routes while the larger vessels (sub-Panamax, Panamax, and post-Panamax) serve the long haul deep sea business.

In both sectors of the fleet the trend has been towards bigger ships which offer economies of scale. At the upper end the Panamax fleet (over 3,000 TEU and able to transit Panama) has grown most rapidly in recent years, with a new generation of post-Panamax vessels appearing in the 1990s. However, the fleet of smaller vessels has also been growing, notably the fleet of 'Handy' container ships. These medium sized vessels of 1–2,000 TEU are flexible enough for short sea operations, large feeder services and North–South trading.

Not all containers travel in specialist container ships – the container is part of a system that is independent of the vessel in which it is carried. Perhaps the most challenging task is welding *ad hoc* container shipments into an integrated inter-modal system, a process that by the mid-1990s had reached a very advanced stage in the developed countries, and is progressing rapidly in most Third World countries.

10.11 Container ports and terminals

Port calls and liner pricing

Containerization changed the way the liner business managed its port itineraries. Previously cargo liners operated a port-to-port service, 'equalizing' prices by charging the same rate for all ports on their itinerary. Because shippers paid for the journey to and from the port they had an incentive to use a liner service which called at the local port. Each port had its own catchment area and to win a share of this cargo, liner services had to include that port on their itinerary. This pricing system encouraged lengthy itineraries and much duplication of port calls.

When containerization was introduced, the pricing system changed. Because the liner companies now controlled the land transport they could plan and adopt the itinerary which gave the cheapest overall unit transport cost. The result was to channel trade through fewer ports, each major port having a greatly enlarged catchment area. It also led to great competition between the ports to attract liner services. Choosing a port itinerary involves a trade-off between the cost of the call, against the revenue obtained from providing a direct service to and from the port. Then there is the possibility of setting up intermediate distribution points to serve a third area. For example, the Arabian Gulf might be served by a feeder service from Jeddah in the Red Sea. In fact, we can define two levels of service:[32]

- *Load centres (base ports).* These have a regular service with frequent loading and discharge of cargoes. The shipper is guaranteed a regular service at a fixed tariff, whether they are served direct or not. For example, Antwerp will attract the same rate as Rotterdam, even if the ship does not call there.
- *Feeder ports (outports).* Some ports are not included in the normal service because they do not handle sufficient cargo to make this cost-effective. However, in order to discharge their obligation to 'meet the requirements of the trade', the company accepts cargo at outports and provides a feeder service from a direct port. These cargoes will be charged extra.

The port infrastructure

Although there are currently about 400 ports which have a significant throughput of containers, the top 60 handle 98 per cent of the throughput. Many countries now have only one or two major container ports serving the deep sea trades, supported by a range of smaller ports handling short sea and distribution trade. Table 10.7 which lists the most important container ports in 1994, organized by region. The two largest container ports, Hong Kong and Singapore, each handle over 9 million TEU per annum, acting as regional distribution centres for the predominantly maritime Asian distribution system.

Container terminals generally have several berths, each served by one or more large cranes capable of lifting 40 tons. In an adjacent storage area the containers are stored to await collection. To carry the weight of the container crane it is generally necessary to strengthen the quay to take loads of 60–80 tons. Several types of container terminal have been developed to meet differing requirements. One system is to lift the container off the ship on to a trailer chassis, which is then moved to a storage park to await collection. This has the advantage that the container is handled only once and it interfaces efficiently with the road haulage system. Its main drawback is that it uses a large amount of land and there is a significant investment in trailers. Where land is at a premium, containers may be stacked up to five high, using a system of gantry cranes which may also be used on the quayside. However, the disadvantages of this system are the difficulty of obtaining random access to containers in the stack and the cost of multiple handling of individual units. The compromise is to stack containers two or three high, using 'straddle carriers', large fork-lift trucks or low loaders to move them from the quayside to the stack and retrieve them when required. In small ports an area of the quayside is often allocated for container storage.

In the advanced industrial areas of Europe, North America and the Far East, containerization has channelled trade through a small number of ports that have invested in high-productivity container terminals of the type outlined above. In the developing countries, the problem is more complex, since the inland infrastructure is often not sufficiently developed to handle a sophisticated container network. As we saw in the example of the West Africa trade, cargo is not exclusively containerized. In such cases, even small ports need to be equipped to handle containers. This generally involves developing an existing berth for container handling, undertaking any necessary strengthening of the quay, the purchase of a suitable crane and straddle carriers or fork-lift trucks and the provision of a container-packing service for break bulk cargo not delivered to the port in a container. The containers are then stacked in a suitable location.

10.12 Liner companies, consortia and alliances

There are currently about 250 companies offering liner services of one sort or another. A list of the largest companies is shown in Figure 10.8. These are very different organizations from the bulk shipping companies. Most of the largest ones have several thousand employees to handle the administration of freight cargo scheduling and transport. Ownership in the liner business is much more highly concentrated than in bulk shipping. The ten biggest companies control 11 per cent of the dry bulk fleet, 17 per cent of the tanker fleet, but 35 per cent of the container ship fleet.

This consolidation into larger companies is a consequence of the very large amounts of capital investment required to operate a unitized general cargo transport system. Under the commercial pressure to achieve greater economies of scale through bigger ships and at the same time provide more frequent services, in the 1990s several of the major companies formed *alliances* in which they pooled their ships. The first of these, the Global Alliance was formed by APL, OOCL, MOL, and Nedlloyd in May 1994 with the intention of launching an integrated Europe–Far East service. The Alliance operators had a fleet of 187 container ships with 375,000 slots. This was followed soon afterwards by the Grand Alliance consisting of Hapag-Lloyd, NOL, NYK, and P&OCL with 182 ships and 371,000 slots capacity. In 1995 a third alliance was formed between the two largest liner companies, Maersk and Sea-Land with a total of 206 ships.

A different solution to the capital intensity problem faced by liner operators was removing the ships from the balance sheet. This was achieved by leasing the ships or chartering them from independent operators. By the mid-1990s about 40 per cent of the container ship capacity was being serviced in this way.

Despite the benefits to the customer of containerization, operating a liner service is hardly more rewarding in the 1990s than it was in the 1960s. In the 1960s British shipping companies earned a return of 6 per cent on assets, about half the industrial average at that time. By the 1990s things had not improved very much. The return on assets achieved by the major liner companies who publish accounts show that in the first half of the 1990s the average return varied between 1 per cent and 8 per cent per annum. This compares with a long-term return on the US stock market of about 11 per cent.

TABLE 10.7 World container port traffic (1994)

World rank	*Port*	*Traffic(lifts) million TEU*	*Country*	
	Asia			
1	Hong Kong	9.20	Hong Kong	
2	Singapore	9.00	Singapore	
3	Kaohsiung	4.63	Tawan	
5	Busan	3.07	S. Korea	
6	Kobe	2.67	Japan	
9	Yokohama	2.16	Japan	
13	Keelung	1.86	Taiwan	
17	Tokyo	1.54	Japan	
21	Manila	1.27	Phillipines	
20	Bangkok	1.27	Thailand	
22	Nagoya	1.15	Japan	
25	Tanjung Priok	1.00	Indonesia	
27	Shanghai	0.90	PRC	
29	Colombo	0.85	Sri Lanka	
34	Port Kelang	0.77	Malaysia	
	Total Asia	41.34		15
	W. Europe			
4	Rotterdam	4.16	Netherlands	
7	Hamburg	2.48	Germany	
12	Antwerp	1.88	Belgium	
15	Felixstowe	1.64	UK	
18	Bremerhaven	1.35	Germany	
28	Le Havre	0.89	France	
31	Algeciras	0.81	Spain	
33	La Spezia	0.78	Italy	
	Total Europe	13.99		8
	Middle East			
26	Jeddah	0.94	Saudi Arabia	
14	Dubai	1.68	UAE	
	Total Middle East	2.62		2
	North America			
8	Los Angeles	2.37	USA	
10	Long Beach	2.07	USA	
11	New York	1.97	USA	
19	Oakland	1.30	USA	
23	Seattle	1.15	USA	
24	Tacoma	1.07	USA	
30	Charleston	0.84	USA	
32	Hampton Roads	0.78	USA	
35	Honolulu	0.74	USA	
	Total N. America	12.29		9
	Other			
36	Melbourne	0.72	Australia	
16	San Juan	1.55	Puerto Rico	
	Total container lifts	72.51		

Source: Containerisation International

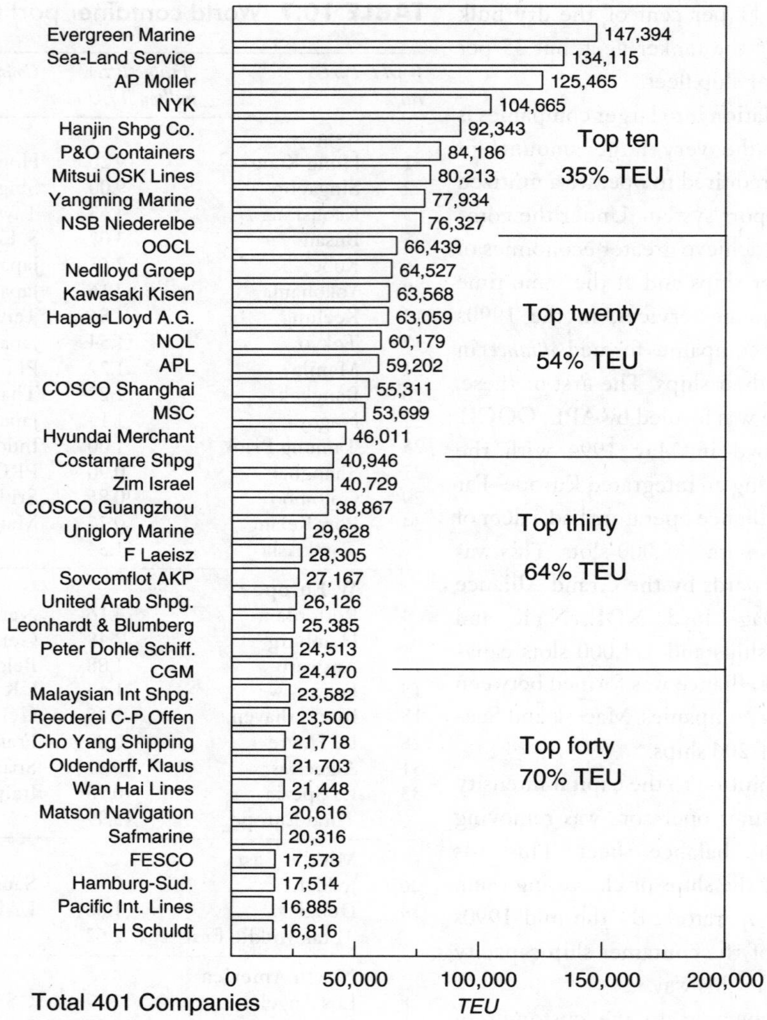

FIGURE 10.8 Container ship fleets by capacity 1996
Source: Clarkson Research Studies

10.13 Summary

As we have seen in this chapter, liner companies operate in a market which has all the competitive edge of the bulk shipping market, but two substantial differences. First, the commitment to run a regular service makes liner capacity inflexible. Second, with so many customers, price negotiation is more restricted. With these restrictions the free market mechanism which regulates the bulk shipping market takes on a very different character in the liner business. When we examine the economic principles, we find that free market pricing would lead to a highly volatile cashflow, but that a system of fixed prices is difficult to enforce. That, in essence, has been the problem faced by the liner industry throughout its 125 year history.

We examined the structure of liner costs and identified five 'building blocks', which contribute to the economics of a liner service, the *service schedule*, the *unit slot cost*, *container operations*, *container costs* and *administrative costs*. The choices made by the liner company for each of these determines the cost profile of the operation. On the revenue side the key principles are price stability and price discrimination. The published rate book sets the framework for pricing which involves differing degrees of discrimination by commodity and owner.

Our review of the demand for liner services concluded that the 'commodity analysis' used to analyse the demand for bulk carriers is less appropriate as a methodology for the liner trades. There are so many commodities and so few statistics that detailed commodity analysis can hardly be expected to succeed. More importantly, the demand for liner transport is not determined by regional imbalances in supply and demand, but by the relative price and availability of goods. If a manufacturer in England can source more cheaply from Taiwan than from Scotland, he will choose Taiwan. In this sense the growth of demand depends on cost differences within the world economy, while inter-company competition revolves around a range of factors including price, speed, reliability and the quality of service.

Liner services are constantly changing to meet the needs of the trade. The major liner routes, known as the east–west trades, operate between the three industrial centres of North America, Western Europe and Asia. These are supplemented by a complex matrix of north–south trades serving the various developing countries. At the margin are the small services designed to meet particular local needs.

The liner trade is carried by a fleet of ships comprising container ships, multi-purpose vessels, 'tweendeckers, traditional cargo liners and ro-ros. Some of these vessels are designed to meet specific trading needs, while others are left over from another shipping era, serving out their useful lives. The whole liner business is supported by an extensive network of port facilities, ranging from the 'super terminals' in Rotterdam, Hong Kong and Singapore to the many minor local ports which serve the feeder trades.

The lessons from the liner business are simple enough. By using containers to mechanize the transport of general cargo, it has, in Adam Smith's words 'opened the whole world to a market for the produce of every sort of labour'. The financial return to liner companies may not be spectacular, but their contribution to the global trading economy is beyond question.

Chapter 11

The economics of ships and ship designs

The market is as elastic as our vessel flexibility and cargo handling systems allow it to be: it is not easy to build up a market based on the ship. The name of the game is to build the ship around the market.

(Bengt Koch, Managing Director, Atlantic Container Line Services, at RoRo 83 Conference, Gothenberg, 1983)

11.1 What type of ship?

The derived demand for ships

So far we have said much about shipping economics, but little about the ships themselves. The classification systems used by statistical organizations such as Lloyd's Register of Shipping recognize literally hundreds of ship types. This wealth of different designs confronts shipowners with the difficult question 'What type of ship should I order?'. To help them in their decisions, they often ask shipping economists questions like 'What will be the future demand for container ships?'. The aim of this chapter is to discuss the different types of merchant ships and how their design features fit into the economic model discussed in Chapter 4.

First we must be clear about the meaning of *demand.* Although ships occupy the centre of the stage, the product in demand is not a ship, but transport. It is not the containership that the customer wants, it is the transport of the container. Shipowners can use whatever ships provide the transport most profitably. Unfortunately this makes the shipping economist's job much more difficult. If containers could only be carried in container ships, all the shipping economist would have to do is predict the trade in containers, and the demand for container ships is determined. With several ship types available to carry containers, and different sizes to choose from, the calculation of demand involves two additional questions. First, ''What options are open to the shipowner?' and, second, 'What economic criteria apply in choosing between them?'

The answer depends on the type of shipping venture for which the vessel is intended. Although there are many different influences to consider, the most important can be summarized under the three following headings:

1 *Cargo type.* The physical and commercial properties of the cargo to be transported set a limit on the ship types that can potentially be employed in the transport operation. In a limited number of cases, such as liquid natural gas or nuclear waste, the cargo demands a specific type of ship, and the shipowner's choice is limited to general design and operating features such as speed, crew, etc. For most cargoes, however, the shipowner can choose from several ship types. Crude oil can be carried in a specialist tanker or a combined carrier; dry bulk can be carried in a conventional bulk carrier, an open hold bulk carrier or a combined carrier; containers in a containership, a 'tweendecker, a multi-purpose vessel or a ro-ro.

2 *Type of shipping operation.* In the previous paragraph we assumed that the shipowner knows the precise type of cargo to be carried, but in practice his knowledge of both the cargo and other physical operating constraints will depend upon the type of shipping operation for which the vessel is intended. There are several different types of shipping operation. For example:

- *long-term charters* where the shipowner knows precisely the cargoes to be carried and the ports to be used;

- *spot charter market operations* where the owner has only a general idea of the type of cargo to be carried and no knowledge of the ports to be visited;
- *liner operations* where the owner has a specific knowledge of the ports to be visited and the likely cargo volume, but where both may change during the operational life of the vessel.

The design criteria for a shipowner choosing a vessel for a long-term time charter are likely to be quite different from those for the owner intending to trade on the spot market. For example, the former will be preoccupied with optimizing the ship to a specific operation, whereas the latter will be more concerned with such factors as the vessel's acceptability to charterers, and its short-term resale value.

3 *Commercial philosophy.* The way in which the shipowner or shipping company approaches the business may extend or limit the range of options. For example, one shipping company may prefer vessels that are highly flexible, servicing a number of different markets and thereby reducing the risk. This philosophy might lead the shipowner to prefer a more expensive open hold bulk carrier, which can carry both dry bulk cargo and containers. Another owner may follow a policy of specialization, preferring a vessel that is in every respect designed for the efficient carriage of a single cargo, offering greater efficiency or lower costs but at the price of less flexibility.

It follows that shipping economists cannot forecast the demand for a particular type of ship just by studying cargo movements. In the real world the choice of a particular ship type depends on all three factors – cargo type, shipping operation and commercial philosophy. This makes it difficult to predict which factors will predominate in the final decision. Market research techniques of the type discussed in chapter 14 will certainly form part of this process, as will fashion and market sentiment.

Before leaving this discussion of demand, we must also define the term *ship type.* Technical classifications start from the physical characteristics of the ship. Tankers and bulk carriers are obviously different ship types because they have different hull designs. However, as economists, we must take a broader view. Ships belong to the same ship type if, from the shipowner's point of view, they are substitutes. From this perspective size plays as great a part in determining a ship's type as its general design features. A shipowner who buys a 280,000 dwt tanker ends up trading in completely different markets from the owner who buys a 30,000 dwt tanker. They are different ship types and we must recognize this in our analysis. Sometimes there are physical limitations which draw a clear line between groups of ships, for example the Suez Canal, the Panama Canal or the St Lawrence Seaway. More often one size group merges into another. The fact that ship size groups overlap simply emphasizes the point we have already made that ship demand is not about ships, it is about transport.

Finally the detailed *design features* must also be considered. Cargo handling gear is an important issue on many ships. In tankers the pumping capacity and the segregation of individual cargo tanks must be considered. In bulk carriers and container ships the key issue is the provision of cargo handling gear, usually cranes. Coatings are another small but important item The coating of the tanks and ballast spaces is a particular issue in tankers. Bow thrusters to assist docking; the standard of accommodation; fuel saving equipment; and many other minor items contribute to the long-term efficiency of the ship. In financial terms these items may add significantly to the cost. It is not unusual for a well-specified tanker or bulk carrier to cost 5–10 per cent more than the 'basic' design offered by the shipyard. This higher initial cost is not always reflected in the resale price, so an owner ordering a ship speculatively may have a very different approach from an owner building for his own long-term business.

Comparing the options – art or science?

When the range of suitable designs has been narrowed down, the preferred design is identified by carrying out a projected cashflow analysis of the type discussed in chapter 5, reduced to a form that allows the economic performance of different ship types to be compared.[1] We shall discuss these techniques later in the chapter, but at the outset it is necessary to draw attention to the difficulty of quantifying some of the important variables in economic terms. Although some ships are ordered for specific projects where the precise operating conditions are known in advance, often the future revenue, cargo or voyage pattern is not known except in a very general way. In these cases the main consideration will be ensuring that the ship is 'marketable', in the sense of being acceptable to charterers and second-hand buyers.

Where these factors cannot be specified with precision, there is less scope for 'fine tuning' either the design or the economic analysis. In short, the process of identifying the future demand for ship types cannot be reduced to purely economic criteria. Benford develops this point in the following way:

> Whether we use computers, hand held calculators, or backs of envelopes one rule applies: the decision will be made by some person, or group of persons, and will not hinge simply on the best numerical projection of some measure of merit. Like nearly all else in our business, there is art as well as science in this. Indeed – and roughly speaking – the more important the decision the greater is the reliance upon art. That is what makes ship design so fascinating.[2]

Faced with an uncertain future and several finely balanced options, it is possible that the shipowner may take his lead from the marketplace – when 45,000 dwt products tankers are in fashion he will order them, or when Panamax bulk carriers are in fashion he may order these in preference to the 'handy-size'. Ship ordering statistics suggest that this is the case. The 'acid test' comes during depressions when a shipowner's survival depends upon maintaining a stronger cashflow than his competitors, and for companies in the liner or specialized bulk market this cannot easily be assessed on a ship-by-ship basis. Ideally each ship should be seen as part of the company's investment portfolio and the cashflow tested on a company basis, an issue we shall return to later in the chapter.

In the remainder of this chapter we first discuss in greater detail the influences that cargo type, shipping operations and commercial philosophy have on ship design. We then discuss, with examples, the various ship types used in each operating sector. Finally, we take a brief took at the economic evaluation of ship designs.

11.2 Cargo type and ship design

It was suggested in the previous section that the type of cargo to be carried does not generally restrict the shipowner to a specific type of vessel. There are, however, aspects of the ship design that can be optimized to give the best possible result for a particular cargo type. These include cargo deadweightt, tank and hold dimensions, cargo space access, speed and cargo handling gear.

These are all features of the ship design on which the naval architect needs clear guidance, and the more clearly the future cargo operations are defined the greater scope there is for developing a design that caters specifically for the requirements of that particular cargo. Three aspects of cargo are of particular significance in relation to ship design – the cargo value, its stowage factor and the cargo units in which it is shipped.

Cargo value

The value of the cargo is important because it influences the financial cost of transit time and hence the design speed of the ship. High-value cargoes incur a substantial inventory cost, so there is a financial incentive to transport and store small quantities. There is also a cost attached to time in transit. At an interest rate of 10 per cent per annum, a 10,000-ton cargo worth $4,000 per ton would incur implicit interest charges of $1 million on a three-month journey. In addition, it is in the high-value commodities that air freight becomes a significant competitor with sea transport and, although the tonnages are small, the competition is significant because it is concerned with premium cargo. Clearly, a fast transit time is important for high-value goods and, for this reason, vessels built to carry high-value cargoes generally justify a faster speed. The range of values of seaborne cargoes is extremely wide, as Table 11.1 shows.

At the lower end of the range, some bulk commodities such as iron ore and coal have very low values. These are commodities that are generally shipped in very large consignments (up to 300,000 tons) and, since they have a low inventory cost, the emphasis is upon minimizing the unit transportation cost. For such cargoes, ship designers will generally work out the optimum operating speed for the vessel, taking account of the anticipated level of operating costs, bunker costs and the amount of cargo required to be delivered in a year. An important exception to this rule arises where the vessel is to be traded on the spot charter market. In these circumstances, even though the shipowner may expect to carry iron ore, he may specify a higher design speed so that he will be able to complete more voyages during periods of high freight rates when he is making premium profits.

TABLE 11.1 Value per ton of OECD imports by commodity

Commodity	*Quantity million mt*	*Value $ million*	*$ per ton*
Stone, sand, gravel	101	888	9
Iron ore	179	3,059	17
Maize	62	8,331	134
Barley	14	1,999	142
Fresh fruit	8.5	5,765	678
Synthetic fibres	1.4	2,236	1,597
Furniture	2.12	7,920	3,735
Electrical apparatus	0.342	7,196	21,040
Clothing	0.13	3,462	26,630

Source: OECD, Series C *Trade Statistics by Commodity*, 1969

The stowage factor

The cargo stowage factor tells the ship designer how many cubic metres of hold space will be occupied by a ton of any given kind of cargo. It determines how much cargo can be fitted into the ship or, conversely, how much hold volume must be provided if the ship is to accommodate its full deadweight. The density of cargoes varies widely as shown by the figures in Table 11.2. Since the stowage factor relates to the space actually taken up by the cargo in the ship, this obviously depends on how well the ship is designed to accommodate the cargo. For example, it is possible to fit much more packaged timber into a purpose-built bulk carrier than into a general purpose bulk carrier with self trimming holds.

TABLE 11.2 Stowage factor for various commodity trades

Cargo type	*Stowage factor*	
	ft³/ton	*m³/ton*
Iron ore	18	0.5
Grain	45–50	1.3–1.4
Coal	50	1.4
Pre-slung timber	80	2.3
China clay (bagged)	80	2.3
Logs	100	2.8
Containers	120	3.4
Cars (vehicle carrier)	150	4.2
Toys, footwear	300–400	8.5–11.3

Source: Deakin and Seward (1973)

Given such a wide range of stowage factors, the ship designer must have some idea what cargoes are to be carried before he can determine the internal cubic capacity of the vessel. For example, if the ship is to be used to carry only iron ore, it can be designed with cargo spaces that will accommodate a dense commodity stowing at 0.5 cubic metres per ton, whereas if it is to be used for commodities such as coal or grain an internal cubic capacity of about 1.4 cubic metres per ton is required, and this is the capacity of the average general-purpose bulk carrier.

For ships carrying a mix of cargoes the problem is more complex since the ship designer will be concerned with the average of high- and low-density commodities. On average, containers stow at around 3 cubic metres per ton and, in order to utilize the full ship deadweight, containers are generally stacked on deck. However, this depends on what the containers are carrying, which may change. We saw in chapter 10 that the average container payload per TEU is about 9 tons, but that varies considerably from trade to trade. Where commodities with stowage factors that depart significantly from the average are shipped in large quantities, it is often economic to build specialist ships to carry them. Ore carriers, woodchip carriers and car carriers are three prominent examples, the first to deal with a high-density cargo and the latter two to deal efficiently with low density cargoes.

Cargo units

Cargo units are important because they present the ship designer with the challenge of designing a ship that can handle and stow a particular type of cargo efficiently. This is not just a matter of identifying the type of commodity being shipped, because the same commodity can be transported in many different ways. For example, china clay can be loaded into bags and the bags can be transported loose, on a pallet, or in a container. Alternatively, the china clay could be shipped loose in the hold of a bulk carrier or mixed with water to form a slurry and shipped in a special tanker. In practice we can classify these different forms of shipping commodities in terms of 'cargo units'. Ten of the cargo units that occur most commonly are summarized in Table 11.3.

The first five items on the list are 'natural' cargo units, that is, the cargo is shipped in its natural form without specialist treatment. General cargo units are loose items such as bags or boxes, without any special packing. This type of cargo is the most difficult and expensive to transport by sea. Packing it into the hold of a ship is time-consuming, requires skill, and there are associated problems of loss and damage in transit as was explained in chapter 10.

A bulk cargo unit consists of a ship or hold-size parcel of homogeneous cargo – for example, 100,000 tons of iron ore, 50,000 tons of coal, 12,000 tons of sugar or 200,000 tons of crude oil. Homogeneous bulk cargoes can be loaded and unloaded using grabs, suction or pumps as appropriate, and the aim is generally to design a ship that can load a full cargo deadweight of a single commodity. In practice, the hold is the smallest size unit for dry bulk cargo and the cargo tank the smallest unit for liquid bulk. Unit bulk cargoes consist of ship-sized parcels made up of units each of which must be handled individually – for example, steel products, forest products or bales of wool. In such cases it may be possible to design 'tailored' vessels offering improved stowage or faster cargo handling. Finally, the other natural cargo units are heavy and awkward cargoes and wheeled cargoes. Heavy and

TABLE 11.3 Cargo units in which commodities are shipped by sea

Cargo unit	*Comment/commodity*
Natural cargo units:	
General cargo	Small quantities of loose items – e.g. boxes, bags, packing cases, drums, a few cars, machines, etc.
Bulk cargo	Bulk load of cargo that is shipped without benefit of packaging and handled in bulk by, gravity/pump loading and grab/suction/pump discharging – e.g. oil, iron ore, coal, grain and cargo. Units of 3,000–200,000 tons for dry bulk and up to 500,000 tons for oil.
Unit cargo	Shipload of cargo that can be shipped in bulk but must be handled by units; e.g. steel products, forest products and wool can benefit from a special ship design for improved cargo handling or stowage.
Heavy and awkward cargo	Heavy industrial plant up to 500 tons – locomotives, yachts, etc.
Wheeled cargo	Cars, tractors, lorries, etc.
Artificial units:	
Pre-slung or banded	Usually used for sacks, bales and forest products, to speed up loading and discharge. The slings are left in place during transit.
Palletized cargo	Cargo is stacked on a pallet and usually held in place by steel or plastic bands or 'shrink fit' plastic. Can be handled by fork-lift truck. Dozens of sizes up to 6' × 4'. Palletized cargo stows at about 100 cu.ft/ton.
Flats	Normally about 15' × 8', often with corner posts to allow stacking two high. Handled by fork-lift or crane.
Containers	Standard boxes usually 8' × 8'6" in lengths of 20' and 40', each box handling 10–20 tons of cargo, typically stowing at 120 ft^3 ton.
Barges	LASH barges load about 400 tons cargo and Seabee about 600 tons. The barges are designed to be floated to the ship and loaded/discharged as a unit.

awkward cargoes are worth singling out because they present special shipping problems in terms of handling and stowing the cargo. For example, the tunnel kiln for a cement plant or a harbour ferry being shipped from Europe to the Far East both present stowage problems.

Turning to the 'artificial' units in Table 11.3 (that is, cargo specially packed for transport), we are concerned with packing cargo into easily handled units. The technique of 'unitization' has two dimensions. The first is to pack the cargo in such a way that it can be handled mechanically rather than requiring skilled manual handling and stowage. The second is to establish standardization between different transport modes of rail, road and sea so that an integrated 'door-to-door' transport service can be provided for unitized cargo. In practice, there are five main forms of artificial cargo units: pre-slung or banded; pallets; flats; containers; and barges.

The use of standard 20 ft and 40 ft containers gives the shipowner carrying general cargo a homogeneity similar to that of unit bulk cargo. This allows mechanized loading and discharging systems to be fully used, with a ship designed to make the handling system operate efficiently. The uncompromising size, shape and weight of the container require square cargo holds and wide hatches. Initially, liner companies built fleets of specialist container vessels, though it rapidly became apparent that container capacity was an important aspect of the design of conventional multi-purpose vessels or even bulk carriers.

The use of pallets and flats provides a degree of unitization without requiring the high capital costs incurred by containers and trailers, and there are fewer problems in returning the empty units. Pallets have not become established as a base unit for a sea transport system in the same way as containers except on individual routes where they meet a special need, particularly in the multi-purpose liner trades for those goods that are not containerized. The cargo is loaded on to a pallet, of which there are a variety of sizes, and secured with bands or a plastic cover shrunk to protect the cargo. Loading and discharge are still labour-intensive operations and rely on the skill of stevedores to pack the pallets into the ship efficiently. It is, however, dramatically more efficient than the handling of individual drums, sacks or bales. Standard barges were introduced in an attempt to cater for the small bulk packages of medium-value cargoes, especially where an inland waterway system allows through water transport to inland destinations. The barge system has not been adopted on any significant scale to date.

There are many ways in which a ship design can be developed to improve its efficiency in handling and stowing unitized cargo, provided the dimensions of the units are known in advance. Some of the most important are:

- *Hold dimensions.* Ships carrying containers, packaged timber or any standard unit can be designed with holds that precisely match the external dimensions of the units they are to carry. For example 'pallet friendly' reefer vessels are designed with decks tailored to accommodate the maximum payload of standard pallets.
- *Cell guides.* To speed up handling on container ships, cell guides are fitted in the holds and occasionally on deck so that containers do not need to be secured.
- *Hatch design.* Bulk carriers for the transportation of packaged lumber may be designed with hatch coamings that match the standard lumber package size, thus facilitating the efficient stacking of packages on deck. Wide (sometimes called 'open') hatches provide vertical access to all parts of the hold.
- *Cargo access ramps.* Ramps may be fitted to allow cargo to be loaded by fork-lift truck, or to be driven aboard on its own wheels. They may be located at the bow, the stern or in the side of the vessel.
- *Cargo handling gear.* Gantry cranes, heavy lift derricks, or other cargo handling gear may be fitted to speed up the loading and discharge of standard units.
- *Hoistable decks.* These may be fitted to allow the head-room to be adjusted for different cargoes.
- *Tank segregations.* For liquid cargoes the provision of 'self contained' tanks capable of handling many different liquid parcels within a single ship increases flexibility. This

generally involves the installation of separate pumping systems for each tank and often special coatings such as zinc or stainless steel to allow difficult chemicals to be carried.

This is not an exhaustive list, but it illustrates the way in which ships may be adapted to the carriage of unit cargoes.

11.3 Fitting the ship to the shipping operation

The next step is to examine the ships themselves and see how this works out in practice. In Figure 11.1, the main cargo-carrying ship types currently in use in the world merchant fleet are shown. This is not an exhaustive analysis but it shows the main categories of ship type and is the framework we will use in the remainder of this chapter. In terms of market segments, these ships can be broadly divided into liner fleet, the bulk carrier fleet, the tanker fleet, combined carriers and the fleet of ships designed for a single cargo.

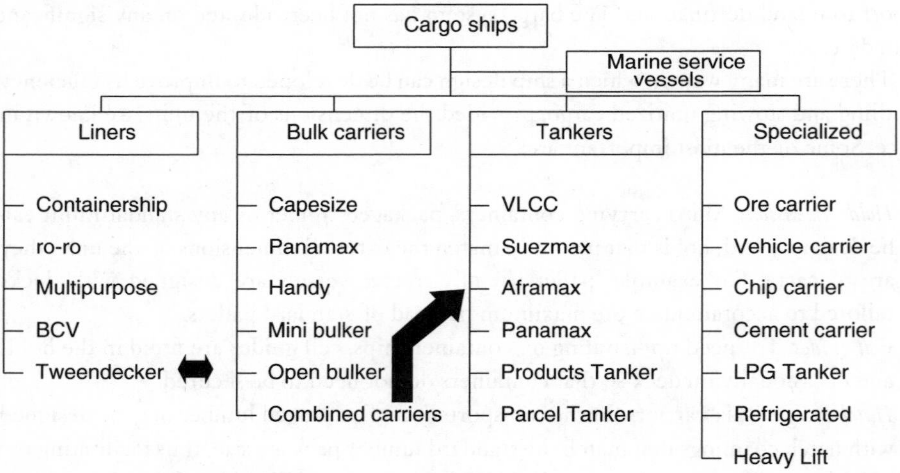

FIGURE 11.1 The merchant cargo fleet by ship type
Source: Martin Stopford, 1997

At least five different ship types are used in the liner market, their principal design features being the ability to group many small cargo units within a single vessel and usually a relatively high speed, reflecting the value of the cargo carried. Containerships now form the greater part of the fleet in terms of cargo capacity, but ro-ros, and a variety of more or less sophisticated multi-purpose vessels continue to be used. There is also a great deal of variety in the design of ships used in the bulk trades, the main ones being tankers, bulk carriers, ore carriers, combined carriers, gas tankers, chemical tankers and forest products carriers. The shipping operation can affect ship design in several different ways. This can best be illustrated by some examples:

- *Example 1.* A steel plant purchasing an iron ore carrier to service a long-term iron ore supply contract between Brazil and Japan. In this case, the cargo, the cargo volume and the trade route are all known in advance, so the ship can be designed to optimize the shipping operation in terms of the cargo to be carried, the ports to be utilized and the opportunities for exploiting economies of scale. In addition, since the vessel is to be operated over a number of years, the shipowner is likely to take a close interest in any technology that will reduce operating costs – for example, automation and fuel-saving equipment.
- *Example 2.* A dry bulk carrier operator purchasing a bulk carrier to trade on the voyage charter market. In this case, the shipowner has only a general idea of the cargoes and ports that the vessel will be required to service. Depending upon his style of operation, he may choose a small ship that can access many ports, or a larger ship that will be more competitive in some of the major bulk commodity trades. In particular, he will be concerned to ensure that the ship will be attractive to charterers and that it will have a good resale value even after a short time. For this reason, a well-established standard design may be of interest.
- *Example 3.* A bulk operator offering shipping services in specialist bulk markets such as motor vehicles or forest products. In this case, the shipowner may not have a precisely defined future operating pattern, but he will have a clear idea of the special cargo features that he wishes to build in to the vessel in order to reduce his operating costs and improve the service offered to the shipper. This may involve the design of a specialist ship such as a vehicle carrier, or a sophisticated version of a standard ship such as a forest products carrier. In such cases, the cargo figures prominently in the ship design, as do the range of ports, terminals and cargo handling facilities servicing this particular trade.

There are no hard and fast rules. Ultimately the merchant ship has to fit into the business and, as the preceding examples show, different shipowners have different requirements.

Cargo flexibility and the LCM rating

Inevitably the process of ship design involves compromise, particularly over the range of different cargoes that the vessel can carry. A shipowner who invests in specialist tonnage automatically shuts himself out from markets that could be serviced by more flexible vessels, or at least he is likely to incur a cost penalty. As a result, the question of operational flexibility is a central issue in ship design.

Looked at from the owner's viewpoint, the ship is a capital asset that will carry whatever cargo yields the greatest profit; obviously, the more different types of cargo it can carry and the more efficiently it can carry them, the more attractive the ship is in commercial terms. However, the process of designing a ship is complicated by a series of complex trade-offs between the cargo performance of the ship, its seagoing performance and its commercial performance. Buxton describes the problem in the following way:

> Merchant ships are mobile warehouses whose many different forms have evolved as a result of attempts to balance on the one hand the need for suitable storage capacity, against on the other hand the need for mobility. Thus a ship constructed as a simple rectangular box of appropriate dimensions could provide an ideal space for storing containers, but would be difficult to propel through the water, while an easily driven hull would offer relatively little useable cargo space. Ship design is largely a matter of solving such conflicts to produce vessels which are suited to the services in which they will employed.[3]

A rough idea of the degree of cargo unit flexibility of different ship types is illustrated by Figure 11.2, which lists on the left-hand side the various cargo units we have discussed and on the right-hand side a range of recognized ship types. A line links each cargo unit to the various ships that are capable of transporting it, and for each ship type the lateral cargo mobility (LCM) coefficient records the number of different cargo units that the vessel can carry.

Four ships are sufficiently specialized to have an LCM rating of 1 – the container ship, the vehicle carrier, the bulk carrier and the tanker. All these vessels are restricted to a single type of cargo unit. The combined carrier has an LCM rating of 2, reflecting its ability to switch between dry bulk and crude oil, while the open hatch bulk carrier can transport containers, pallets and pre-slung cargo in addition to dry bulk parcels. The ro-ro is even more flexible, with the ability to carry almost any cargo except bulk and barges, giving it an LCM rating of 6. However, the most flexible of all is the multi-purpose cargo liner, which can carry everything except liquid bulk parcels and barges.

This analysis reveals a surprising trend. Common sense seems to suggest that the more flexible the ship, the more successful it will be. After all, flexibility reduces risk and increases revenue earning opportunities. However, when we look at the ship types which are most in demand, the trend is decisively in favour of specialization. In the 30 years 1966 to 1996 the fastest growing sectors of the fleet were tankers, bulk carriers, container ships and vehicle carriers, all of which have an LCM ratio of 1. In contrast the fleets of highly flexible ship types such as cargo liners, ro-ros, barge carriers and combined carriers have been noticeably in retreat. This suggests that in the modern shipping industry the economic benefits of specialization outweigh the economic benefits from flexibility. A useful reminder that ultimately the KISS (Keep it Simple, Stupid) principle is the best guide to ship design. Sophisticated ships make interesting conference papers, but in the harsh commercial world simple vessels, which do one job well, do best.

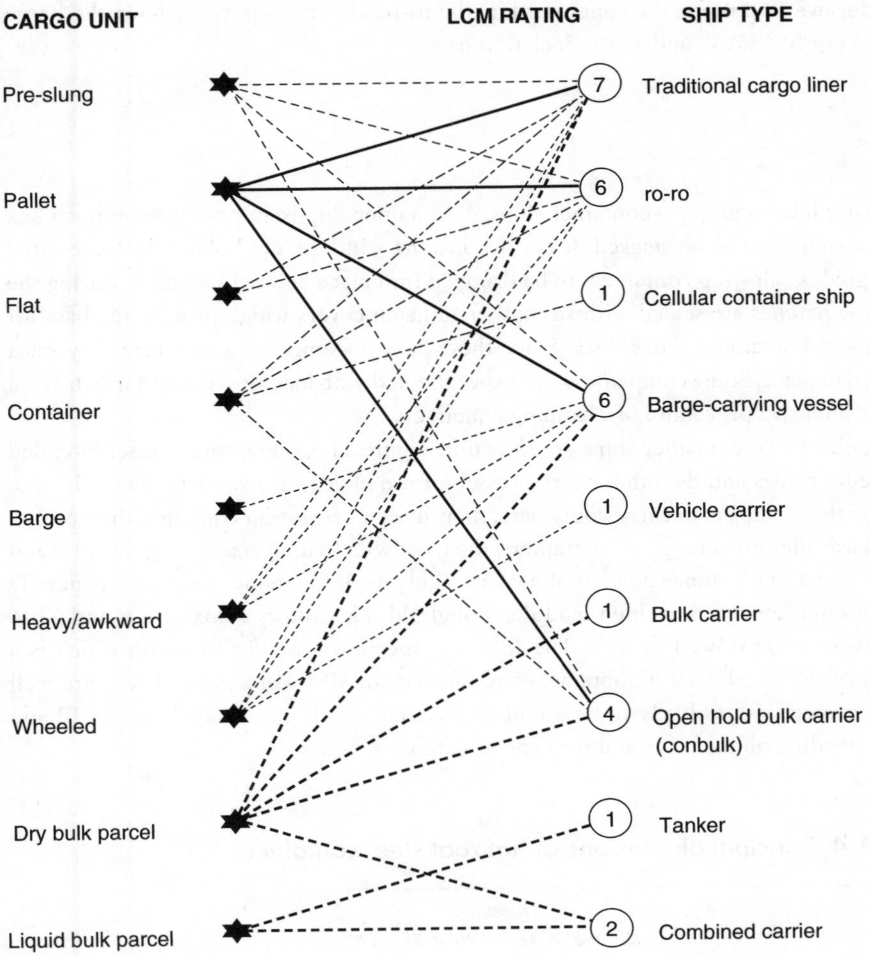

FIGURE 11.2 Analysis of flexibility

Source: Martin Stopford, 1997

Note: Lateral cargo mobility (LCM) rating reflects the number of different types of cargo units that the vessel can carry, i.e. its flexibility. The higher the number, the greater the flexibility.

11.4 Ships for the liner trades

In no sector of the shipping industry have ship designs changed so fundamentally as the liner business. As we saw in Chapter 10, in the 1960s the liner companies changed strategy, substituting specialized container ships for flexible cargo liners. Like the switch from sail to steel, the transition has taken many years and a large number of vessels left over from the cargo liner era continue to be used and in some cases are being replaced. Under this heading we consider five ship types, the containership, the ro-ro, the multi-purpose liner, the Barge Carrying Vessels (BCVs), and 'tweendeck tramps.

Container ships

All the major liner trades use container ships. A container ship is, in principle, an open box in which containers can be stacked. It has hatches the width of the holds, which are fitted with cell guides, allowing containers to be dropped into place and held securely during the voyage. The hatches are sealed with strengthened hatch covers which provide the base for stacking more containers above deck. Since these have no supporting structure they must be clamped in place. Some companies have experimented with hatchless designs which avoid the labour intensive procedure of clamping containers.

Details of two container ships are shown in Figure 11.3, one a small vessel intended for the feeder trades and the other a large vessel for use in deep sea services. Since the sole purpose of these ships is to carry containers, their design centres on container dimensions. ISO standards identify a range of containers, the most widely used sizes being the 20 ft and 40 ft containers, with dimensions as shown in Table 11.4. Container ships are generally designed around the 8 ft 6 ins high module, though this also allows a mix of 8 ft and 9 ft 6 ins containers to be stowed as well. The ISO also specifies a weight standard, which is a maximum of 24 tons for 20 ft containers and 30 tons for 40 ft containers. These are well above the average values likely to be found in practice, which may range between 10 and 15 tons depending on the trade and the type of cargo.

Table 11.4 Principal dimensions of flat roof steel containers

	Dimensions	
	20′ × 8′ × 8′6″	*40′ × 8′ × 8′6″*
Length (metres)	5.9	12.0
Width (metres)	2.4	2.4
Height (metres)	2.6	2.6
Cubic capacity (cubic metres)	32.9	67.0
Stacking capacity	9 high	9 high
Maximum weight (metric tons)	24	30

Source: UNCTAD (1985), p. 141

To begin with containership designs were categorized into 'generations', reflecting the evolving technology. As the fleet has matured and grown in size to more than 2,000 ships it has polarized into several different size categories shown by the fleet statistics in Table 11.5. Each sector has a different place in the market. Smaller container ships of less than 1,000 TEU, often referred to as 'Feeder' (0–499 TEU) and 'Feedermax' (500–999 TEU) vessels are

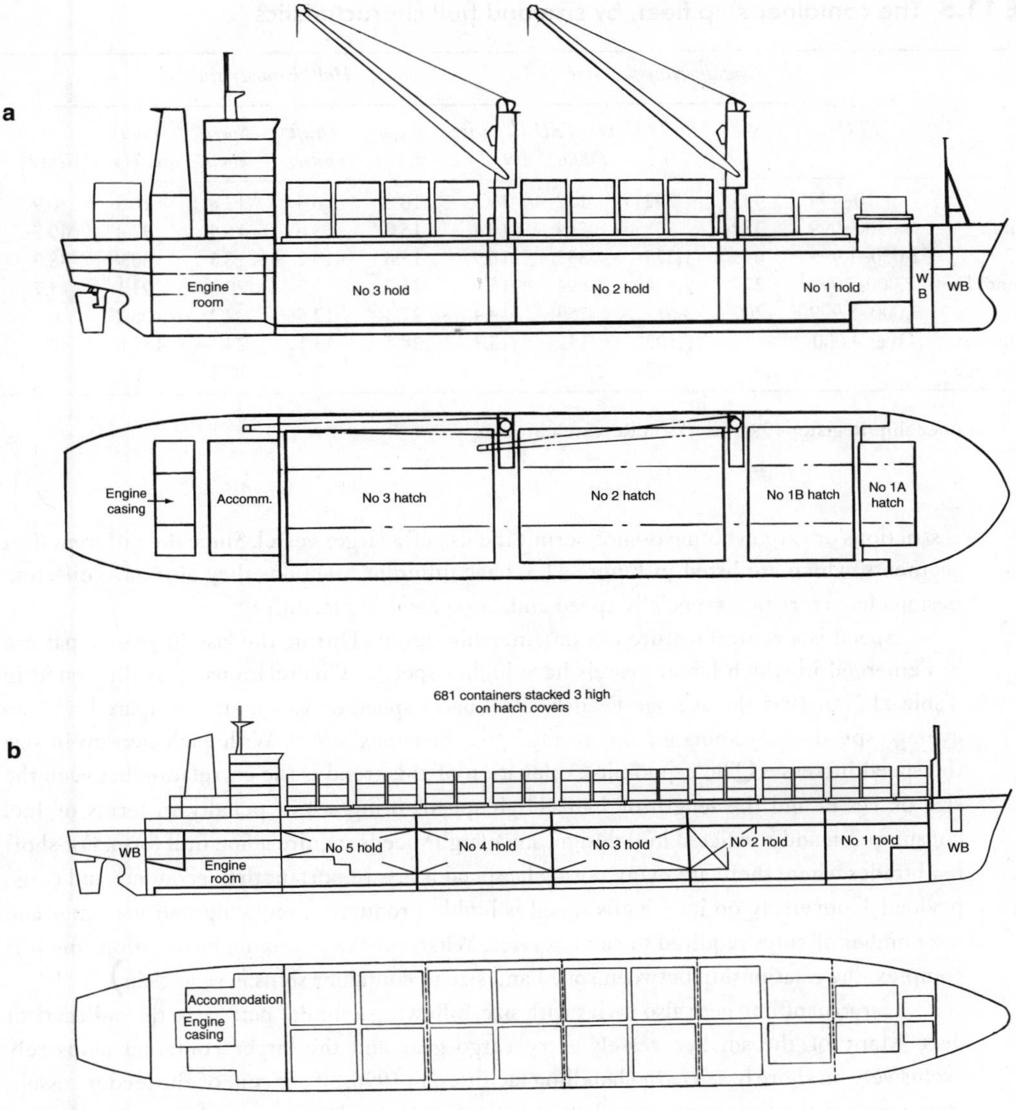

FIGURE 11.3 Container ship

generally used on short haul operations. They distribute the containers brought to regional load centres by the deep sea services and carry coastal traffic. The larger vessels, over 2,000 TEU, are used on long haul trades where they spend up to 80 per cent of their time at sea. There are three groups of these vessels, referred to as Sub-Panamax (2–3,000 TEU), Panamax (3–4,000 TEU) and post-Panamax (over 4,000 TEU). Between the large and the small container ships is a sizeable fleet of Handy vessels which are small enough to be used intra-regionally, but large enough to be used in the North–South trades where port

TABLE 11.5 The container ship fleet, by size and hull characteristics

	Ship size TEU	*Containership fleet size*			*Hull characteristics*					
		No	*Av. TEU*	*Tot. TEU ('000s)*	*Capacity dwt/TEU*	*Beam metres*	*Draft metres*	*Speed knots*	*Cons. t/day*	*% Geared*
Feeder	0–499	443	292	132	19.5	10.8	6.3	13.8	16.8	30.9
Feedermax	500–999	352	738	254	18.4	15.0	8.6	16.4	32.4	49.7
Handy	1,000–1,999	613	1,323	857	16.9	18.6	10.2	18.5	60.9	38.9
Sub-Panamax	2,000–2999	277	2,174	694	15.9	23.7	1.7	20.8	93.1	3.7
Panamax	3,000–3,999	207	3,617	754	14.4	27.3	12.5	22.2	108.2	0
Post-Panamax	Over 4,000	31	4,502	142	13.3	28.4	13.1	24	155.6	0
Total/average		1,923	1,473	2,832		25.5	9.5	18.2	59	

Source: Container ship Register 1996, Clarkson Research Studies

restrictions or cargo volume do not permit the use of a larger vessel. Since the different fleet segments, which are listed in Figure 11.3, have different functions they also have different design characteristics, especially speed and cargo handling facilities.

Speed is a central feature of containership design. During the last 20 years a pattern has emerged in which larger vessels have higher speeds. This relationship is illustrated in Table 11.5. In 1995 the average Feeder vessel had a speed of 13.8 knots, compared with an average speed of 24 knots for the average post-Panamax vessel. With each step up in size the speed increases. The economic explanation of this trend is the correlation between the size of vessel and the length of haul. High speeds bring a cost penalty in terms of fuel consumption and restricted hull design, since high speeds require a fine hull form. For short haul trades where there are many port calls speed is less important than economy and cargo payload. Conversely on long hauls speed is highly productive, reducing journey times and the number of ships required to run a service. Whatever the economic justification, and it is complex, the relationship between speed and size in container ships is very clear.

Cargo handling gear also varies with size, following a similar pattern to the bulk carrier fleet. Many of the smaller vessels carry cargo gear and the larger container ships rely exclusively on shore based cargo handling facilities. In 1996, 30 per cent of the feeder vessels, 49 per cent of the Feedermaxes and 39 per cent of the Handy container ships had cargo gear but only ten container ships over 2,000 TEU had their own cargo handling gear.

One of the most important ways of increasing containership versatility was the development of *refrigerated containers*, enabling the container companies to compete with reefer operators for the trade in meat, dairy products and fruit. This is achieved by insulating the containers and, where a substantial volume of reefer cargo is available (for example, on the Australia to UK route), incorporating a central refrigeration plant into the ship. This blows cold air through ducts into the insulated containers. At the loading and discharging ports the insulated containers are stored in special refrigerated reception facilities or, where none is available, a portable refrigeration plant is used. For small trades, containers incorporating their own refrigeration plant are used, obtaining their power from an electrical socket adjacent to the container slot. In addition to fast cargo handling, refrigerated containers offer shippers the benefit of precise temperature control through the whole journey and a better-quality product, which in the case of fruit and vegetables may result in a higher selling price.[4]

Finally, there has also been much research into developing containers suitable for the transport of small bulk cargoes. These include the use of ventilated containers for agricultural commodities such as coffee and cocoa beans, tank containers for bulk liquids, and containers with special loading and discharging facilities for the fast automated handling of minor bulk commodities. As we saw in chapter 10, bulk cargoes such as wool, rubber, latex, cotton and forest products are now containerized.

Ro-ro ships

In some cases, it is not feasible to containerize cargo. This confronted the shipping industry with the problem of finding a more efficient way of handling a mix of small bulk and heavy and awkward cargoes, which had moved in the traditional cargo liners but which could not be containerized. To combine fast cargo handling with greater cargo flexibility, in the late 1960s 'roll on, roll off' vessels were introduced into the deep sea trades. Several different designs were developed, but in concept the ro-ro is a cargo liner with through decks and roll-on access by means of ramps, rather than via hatches in the weatherdeck. This configuration is particularly suitable for carrying any cargo that can easily be handled by a fork-lift truck (pallets, bales, containers, packaged timber, etc.) and also for wheeled cargo (cars, loaded trucks or trailers, tractors, etc.). A major advantage of the ro-ro vessel is its ability to provide fast port turnaround without special cargo handling facilities.

Like many other shipping innovations, the roll on, roll off concept was first developed in the US domestic trade – in 1928 Seatrain introduced a service between Havana, East Coast ports and Gulf Coast ports carrying freight cars and vehicles. However, for many years the ro-ro was viewed as uneconomic in deep sea trades owing to the low utilization of cubic capacity. It was not until the late 1960s that the potential for using this type of vessel in the deep sea trades was fully appreciated and the first deep sea ro-ro service was introduced in 1969 by Scan Austral. The company had been operating a service between Europe and Australia using open-type liner ships of the Scandia class. Escalating cargo handling costs and slow port turnaround in Australia forced them to consider unitization, but a detailed cargo analysis revealed that only a small proportion of the trade could be containerized at that time. In volume terms, the southbound trade was dominated by forest products, cars and bulk liquids; while wool, hides, canned goods, fresh fruit and refined metals dominated the northbound passage. Overall, they found that only 40 per cent of the volume of cargo could be economically containerized. The choice of ro-ros followed logically, since containerized cargo could be carried but the mini-bulks could be handled in the most convenient form from pallets through to heavy lift units of 90 tons.

Although ro-ros have never been adopted on the scale of cellular container ships, they are still used in some trades. In 1984, Atlantic Container Lines (ACL) put five 34,000 dwt ro-ros into service. The ships were designed to be capable of carrying a cargo mix that includes containers, forest products, long steel items and every type of wheeled vehicle. There are container holds at the front of the ships and three ro-ro decks at the rear, accessed by a quarter stern ramp. Two of these decks have hoistable car decks, which can be adjusted to improve cargo stowage. On the weatherdeck there are permanent cell guides. This arrangement allows a high utilization to be obtained for vehicles or block stowage of unit cargo, combined with fast cargo handling for containers.

Although ro-ros have highly flexible cargo capacity, with an LCM coefficient of 6, and can handle cargo efficiently even in ports with very basic facilities, this flexibility has a price. Ro-ros have a lower stowage productivity than container ships and, since the cargo is more difficult and labour intensive to secure, the loading times are generally slower. In addition, ro-ros are very management intensive, requiring careful stowage planning.[5] However their greatest disadvantage is that they lack the simple integration with other transport systems which is the chief asset of the containership fleet. As a result the ro-ro fleet is very much smaller than the container fleet, and even on routes such as the West Africa trade where suitable conditions exist, ro-ros account for only about 10 per cent of the tonnage employed.[6]

Multi-purpose cargo liners

The traditional ship used in the liner services was the multi-deck cargo liner, of which a typical example is the *Ocean Priam* liner built in the early 1960s. These vessels had 'tween decks for mixed general cargo, tanks for carrying liquid parcels, and refrigerated capacity. They could also carry small bulk parcels (e.g. minor amounts of ore, copra, steel) in the lower hold and often had cargo handling gear with heavy lift ability. This type of ship is very effective in dealing with a wide range of cargo types, since general cargo, small bulk parcels, refrigerated cargo and small liquid parcels can all be accommodated within a single vessel. The major drawback is the time and labour required to load and discharge cargo. There are still a few of these vessels in operation, but there was no significant newbuilding beyond the 1970s.

Where there is a continuing demand for flexible liner tonnage, traditional cargo liners have mainly been replaced by 'multi-purpose' or lo-lo (lift on, lift off) vessels. Ships of this type are generally 15,000–22,000 dwt with four or five holds, each containing a 'tween deck. The main difference from earlier traditional liners is that they are designed to carry a full load of containers as well as general cargo. This is achieved by designing the lower hold and the 'tween deck with dimensions compatible with containers.

The details of two typical multi-purpose vessels are shown in Figure 11.4. The multi-purpose shown at the top of the figure is one of the simpler designs. It has dimensions selected to allow containers to be stacked in the holds and up to four high on the hatch covers. The emphasis on containers is also reflected in the length of holds, which are also designed to accommodate containers of 20 ft or 40 ft in length. In order to allow containers to be moved easily in or out, the hatches are much wider than in a traditional cargo liner or 'tweendeck

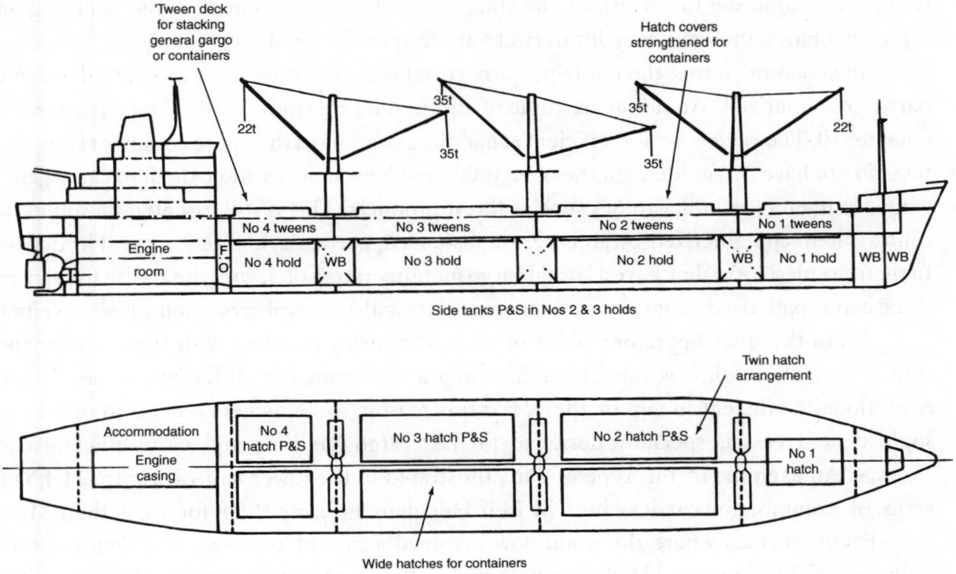

a Multi-purpose vessel

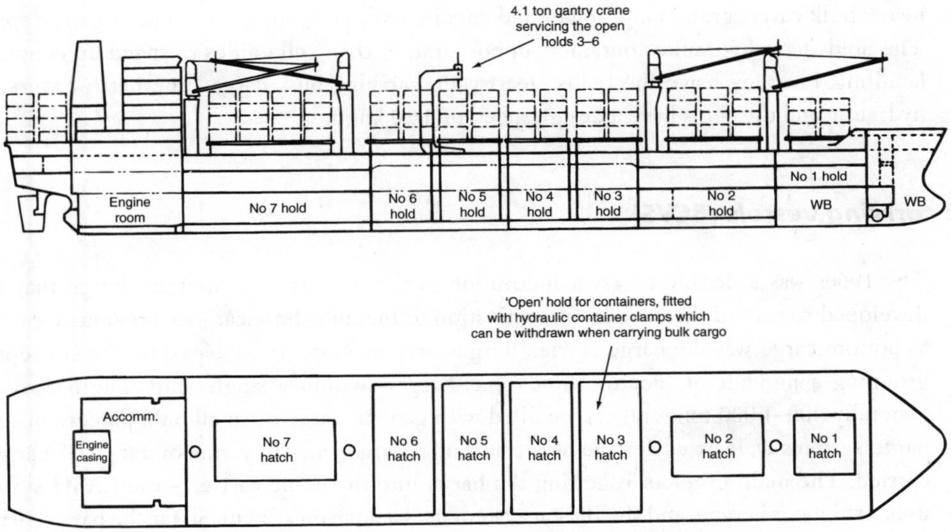

b Sophisticated multi-purpose vessel

FIGURE 11.4 Multi-purpose vessels

tramp, stretching the full width of the ship. As a rule there would be cargo handling gear, typically cranes, though heavy lift derricks are frequently fitted.

In economic terms, the multi-purpose vessel is a compromise for use in trades that are partly containerized. We saw an example of this in the case study of the West Africa trade in Chapter 10. The vessels are less efficient at handling containers than pure container ships, since they do not have cell guides, but the open holds and 'tween decks allow them to carry general cargo, containers or bulk cargoes such as forest products. This is still essential on some trade routes where containerized cargo is very unbalanced, particularly those in the Third World. In their simplest form they have a lateral cargo mobility rating of 5, with the ability to carry pre-slung cargo, palletized cargo, flats, containers, heavy and awkward cargo, and wheeled vehicles.

From the liner operator's point of view, the major problem with the multi-purpose ship is that, although it is capable of handling a wide range of different cargoes, it is not operationally efficient in any of these. For this reason, some owners choose to order more sophisticated vessels specially designed for fast cargo handling and more efficient cargo stowage. An example of this type of ship, illustrated in the lower half of Figure 11.4, is the series of 'combination carriers' built by Leif Hoegh in the early 1980s for use in their Middle East–Pacific service where the trade flow involved a mix of unitized, wheeled and minor bulk cargo. The ships are 42,000 dwt. with wide hatches giving a container capacity of 1,660 TEU and three holds (Nos 1, 2 and 7) with 'tween decks for break bulk cargo. Cargo handling gear includes four jib cranes and a 41-ton gantry crane making the vessel capable of loading heavy bulk cargo, grain, long timber and cars in 400 square metres of special garage space. The holds have hydraulic container supports rather than cell guides to speed up container handling, but they leave the holds clear when carrying bulk cargo. The hatch covers are hydraulic and the ships have a design speed of 16.0 knots.[7]

Barge carrying vessels (BCVS)

The 1960s was a decade of great innovation in the liner trades. Another design that was developed to extend the benefits of unitization to the mini-bulk cargoes previously carried as bottom cargo was the barge carrier. Barge-carrying systems are based on the concept of grouping a number of 'floating holds' (i.e. barges) within a single ship. The barges are generally 400–1,000 tons and can be filled with general cargo or small bulk parcels, making barge systems at least as flexible as a traditional cargo liner in terms of range of cargoes carried. The main problem is getting the barge into the barge carrier – the LASH system uses a shipboard crane, and the Baccat system uses a float-on system. So far the barge carrier has not been widely adopted in the West, but is used in Russia.

The 'tweendeck tramp

Finally, before moving on to a review of liner vessels, we come to the 'tweendecker tramp. These vessels are typically of 10,000–22,000 dwt and are designed with a 'tween deck that enables them to carry either a full load of general cargo or bulk cargoes such as grain. In some modern designs the 'tween deck is operated by hydraulics. Until the 1950s, 'tweendeckers dominated the dry bulk market and many were employed carrying general cargo from Western Europe to the developing countries and bulk cargo on the return journey – one of the classics was general cargo from the UK to South America, with a return cargo of grain from the River Plate. This flexibility was highly efficient at a time when the size of vessel used in the bulk trades was broadly similar to that used in the liner trades, enabling the owner to move freely between the two market sectors. Since the mid-1950s, the rapid growth of parcel size in the bulk trades has resulted in the 'tweendecker being squeezed out by the general-purpose bulk carrier, which has no 'tween deck.

11.5 Ships for the dry bulk trades

In the bulk cargo market, the focus is on low cost transport. The bulk carrier fleet (Table 11.6) consists of 5,014 vessels of 230 m.dwt. The fleet falls into four main parts generally referred to as Handy bulk carriers (10–29,999 dwt), Handymax bulk carriers (30–49,999 dwt), Panamax (50–79,999 dwt) and Capesize (over 80,000 dwt). These ships carry a wide spectrum of bulk cargoes ranging from grain, phosphate rock, iron ore and coal, to toxic chemicals, with a premium on economy and flexibility.

TABLE 11.6 Bulk carrier fleet, January 1996 by size and hull characteristics

	Bulk carrier fleet size			*Hull characteristics*					
	No	*Av. dwt (Mill)*	*Tot. dwt*	*Length metres*	*Beam metres*	*Draft metres*	*Speed knots*	*Cons. t/day*	*Per cent geared*
Handy									
10–19,999	686	16,223	11.1	147	21.6	8.9	14.3	24.6	73
20–24,999	563	23,074	13.0	165	23.5	9.8	14.6	29.3	70
25–29,999	850	27,511	23.3	174	24.4	10.1	14.6	32.5	85
Handymax									
30–39,999	979	35,981	35.2	189	27.3	10.9	14.6	34.8	76
40–49,999	603	44,003	26.5	181	30.3	11.2	14.5	34.2	67
Panamax									
50–59,999	195	55,318	10.8	218	31.7	12.4	15	47.5	15
60–79,999	715	68,023	48.6	223	32.1	13.1	14.5	43.0	8
Capesize									
80–99,999	38	87,603	3.3	245	37.1	13.3	14.5	50.1	0
100–149,999	260	137,150	35.7	266	42.2	16.6	14.4	56.5	0
150,000+	125	179,777	22.4	287	46.8	17.8	13.9	58.5	0
Total/average	5,014	45,901	230.1	189	28.1	11.2	14.5	36.0	57

Source: Bulk Carrier Register 1996, Clarkson Research Studies

The bulk carrier

Nowadays the major bulk cargoes and the great majority of minor bulk cargoes are transported in bulk carriers of the type shown in Figure 11.5, which provides examples of three different designs, a small 35,000 dwt geared bulk carrier, a 45,000 dwt open hatch bulk carrier and a 66,000 dwt Panamax bulk carrier. These are all single-deck ships with a double bottom, vertical cargo access through hatches in the weatherdeck and a speed generally in the range of 13–16 knots, though the average for most sizes is about 14.5 knots. Since the mid-1960s there has been a steady upward trend in the size of ship used in most bulk trades. For example, in 1969 only about 5 per cent of the iron ore was shipped in vessels over 80,000 dwt, but by the early 1990s over 80 per cent of the trade was shipped in vessels of this size. Having made this point, the statistics of the bulk carrier fleet in Table 11.6 show that the ships in the bulk carrier fleet are spread fairly evenly across the size range, with the greatest concentration in the smaller sizes.

Bulk carriers are generally designed for cheapness and simplicity. Key design features are cubic capacity, access to the holds, and cargo handling gear. Hold design is important because cargoes such as grain can easily shift and, if unchecked, can capsize a ship. To prevent this bulk carriers generally have self-trimming holds in which the topside wing tanks are sloped in such a way that granular cargoes can be loaded by gravity without having to trim the cargo out into the wings of the hold.

On conventional bulk carriers, hatch openings are generally 45–50 per cent of the beam (width) and around 65–75 per cent of the hold's length (see Figure 11.5a). This arrangement has the disadvantage that hatch openings are too narrow to allow vertical access to all parts of the cargo hold, with the result that it is difficult to handle large cargo units such as rolls of paper, steel products, pre-slung timber, cars loaded in pallets or containers in a single operation. However, because the deck makes an important contribution to the structural strength of the ship, wider hatches can only be accommodated by adding structural steel to reinforce the vessel, thus increasing costs. The hatch widths described above represent a trade-off between cargo handling speed and building cost that has been found to work well in practice.

Most bulk carriers are fitted with steel hatch covers of which there are several designs available. The self supporting type is probably the most popular. Each cover is arranged in four to six sections which extend across the hatchway and have rollers which operate on a runway. The covers are opened by rolling them to the end of the hatch where they tip automatically into a vertical position. Another consideration is whether or not to fit cargo handling gear. Cargo handling gear is normally fitted to smaller bulk carriers, since they are more likely to operate into ports with inadequate shore based facilities. Table 11.6 shows that only 86 bulk carriers over 50,000 dwt have cargo handling gear, compared with 2,800 smaller vessels. This is because the ports deep enough to be accessed by the bigger ships almost always have shore based facilities.

The cargo handling gear may be cranes or derricks. Derricks are the traditional means of cargo handling on merchant ships. A derrick consists of an 'arm' supported by a rope anchored to a mast, with a winch providing the lifting power. The goods loaded onto the

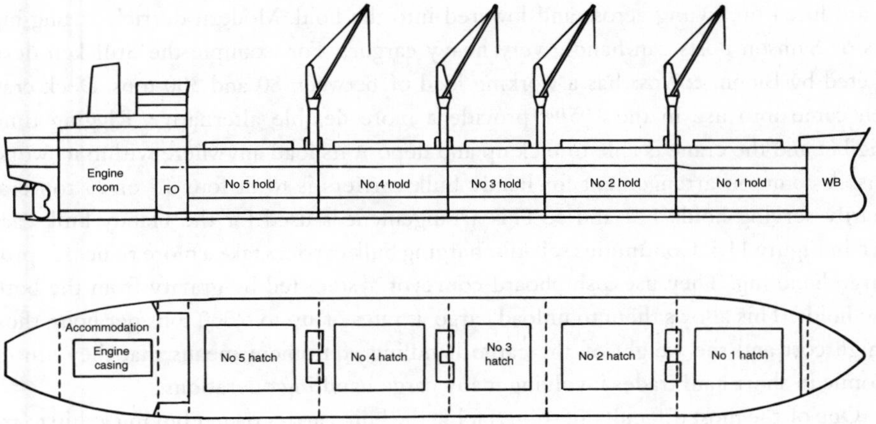

a 35,000 dwt bulk carrier

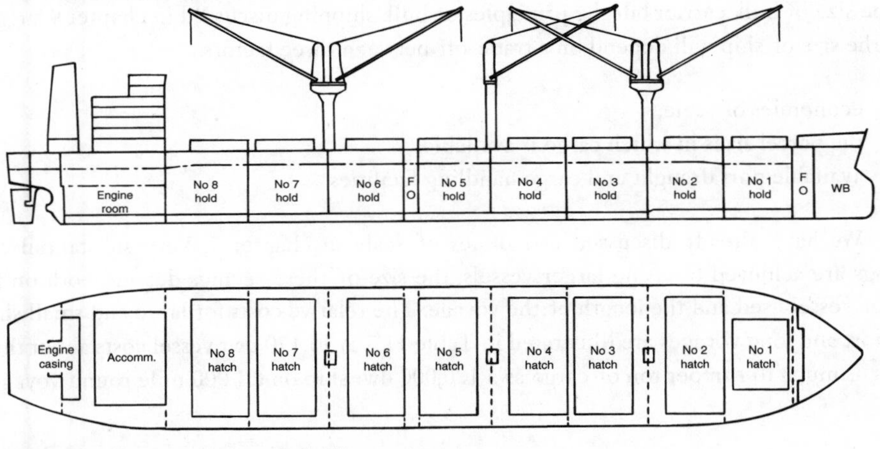

b 45,000 dwt open hatch bulk carrier

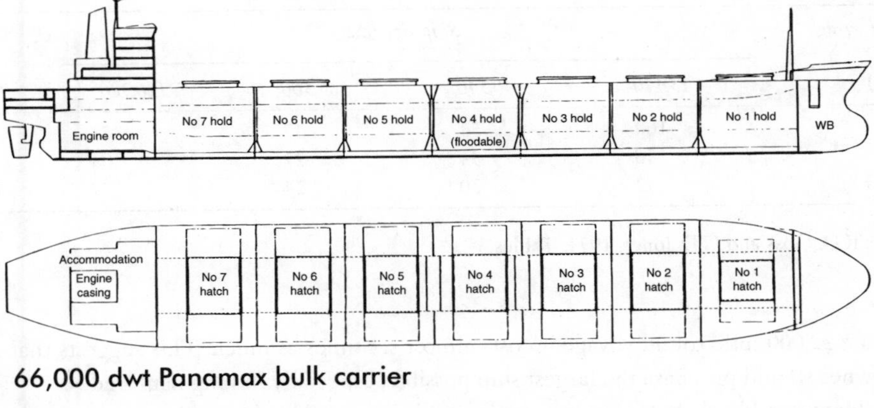

b 66,000 dwt Panamax bulk carrier

FIGURE 11.5 General purpose bulk carriers

ship are lifted up, swung across and lowered into the hold. Modern derricks, using bipod masts or Samson posts can handle very heavy cargoes. For example the Stulcken derrick marketed by Bloem & Voss has a working load of between 80 and 300 tons. Deck cranes, which came into use in the 1950s, provide a more flexible alternative. Rigging time is negligible and the crane is able to pick up and deposit its load anywhere within its working radius. A common arrangement for handy bulk carriers is to fit four 15 or 25 ton cranes primarily serving holds 1–4 and 5. This arrangement is used for the Handy bulk carrier shown in Figure 11.5. Continuous self-discharging bulk carriers take a more radical approach to cargo handling. They use a shipboard conveyor system fed by gravity from the bottom of the holds. This allows them to unload cargo at rates of up to 6,000 tons per hour, though the high cost and the weight of the cargo handling equipment means that they are most economic in short haul trades involving many cargo handling operations.

One of the most difficult questions facing the bulk carrier owner buying a ship to trade on the charter market is 'What size of vessel should I buy?' There are numerous influences on the size of bulk carrier but the principles of bulk shipping discussed in chapter 9 suggest that the size of ship will depend on a trade-off between three factors:

- economies of scale;
- the parcel sizes in which cargo is available;
- available port draught and cargo handling facilities.

We have already discussed economies of scale in chapter 5. Very substantial cost savings are achieved by using larger vessels; the size of these savings depend both on the size of vessel used and the length of the voyage. The relative costs for large and small ships on short and long voyages are illustrated in Table 11.7. A 15,170 dwt vessel costs about three times as much to run per ton of cargo as a 120,000 dwt ship on a 1,000 mile round voyage –

TABLE 11.7 Economies of scale in bulk shipping (per cent cost per ton mile)

Round voyage	*Ship size (dwt)*			
(miles)	*15,170*	*40,540*	*65,500*	*120,380*
1,000	100	53	47	37
6,000	56	34	27	20
22,000	52	30	24	17

Source: R.O. Goss and C.D. Jones, 1971: Tables 3

but on a 22,000 mile round voyage it costs almost six times as much. This suggests that the shipowner should purchase the largest ship possible, especially in long haul trades.

However, big ships face two important restrictions. The first is the maximum size of delivery that an industry is able or willing to accept at any one time. In some industries, stockpiles are only 10,000 or 15,000 tons and a delivery of 50,000 tons would be too large. Second, there is the constraint on ship size imposed by port draught since deep-draught vessels have access to fewer ports than shallow-draught vessels (see Table 11.8). Limits may also be placed on overall length or beam or both (either by ports or by canals). At the lower end of the scale, a small bulk carrier of 16,000 dwt is likely to have a draught of 7–9 metres and is able to access about three-quarters of the world's ports. As ships increase in size and draught, port access diminishes. When considering Table 11.8 it is necessary to bear in mind that ship designers can vary the draught/dwt ratio within certain limits. In addition, the measure of accessible ports is very crude since some ports are more important than others in the bulk trades and depth may vary substantially from berth to berth.

TABLE 11.8 Bulk carriers: the relationship between ship size, draught and port access

Ship draught		*Average size*	*Standard deviation**	*Per cent of world ports*	*Ship type (where*
feet	*metres*	*dwt*	*dwt*	*accessible*	*appropriate)*
25–30	7.6–9.1	16,150	3,650	73	Freedom (29')
30–35	9.2–10.7	23,600	3,000	55	B26 (35')
36–38	10.8–11.6	38,700	5,466	43	Bulk 35
39–44	11.7–13.4	61,000	5,740	27	Panamax
45–50	13.5–15.2	89,200	8,600	22	
51–55	15.3–18.5	123,000	9,000	19	B160

Source: Sample of bulk carriers from the Clarkson 'Bulk Carrier Register' and 'Ports of the World'
* The standard deviation shows the spread of the average size

To deal with these apparently conflicting requirements the bulk carrier market has evolved into several different size bands, each focusing on a different sector of the trade. At the smaller end of the range, 'Handy' bulk carriers of 10,000–30,000 dwt fill the role of highly flexible workhorses in trades where parcel size and draft restrictions demand small ships. Typically they carry minor bulks and smaller parcels of major bulks such as grain, coal and bauxite. As ports have improved over the last 20 years a new generation of larger 30–50,000 dwt handy bulkers has emerged, generally referred to as 'Handymax' bulk carriers. Like the Handy bulkers, these vessels are generally geared. In the centre of the market are the Panamax bulk carriers of 55,000–70,000 dwt, which service the trades in coal, grain, bauxite and the larger minor bulk parcels. The upper end is served by bulk carriers of 100,000–300,000 dwt, which are heavily dependent on the iron ore and coal trades. There is a good deal of interchange between these size groups and in the last resort the choice is a trade-off between unit cost and cargo flexibility: the small vessel is flexible but expensive to run, while the large vessels become progressively cheaper and more inflexible.

The open hatch bulk carrier (conbulker)

The 'open hold' bulk carrier offers a solution to the limited access to the hold provided by conventional bulk carriers. They have hatches the full width of the vessel, allowing large cargo units to be dropped into place, as shown in Figure 11.5b. This vessel has eight holds with hatch openings the full width of the vessel. This is particularly useful in the forest products trades where most of these vessels are employed. Where possible the holds/hatches are designed around standard cargo unit sizes with special attention paid to cargo handling gear. Often a gantry crane is fitted.

During the 1970s it also became apparent that the open hold bulk carrier had a role to play as a link between the dry bulk and liner sectors of the market. With the proliferation of containerized cargo across a wide range of general cargo trades, the opportunities for using open or wide hatch bulk carriers in the liner trades became apparent. They also offer the option to carry containers on the outward leg and dry bulk on the return leg. This is particularly useful for repositioning empty containers. Vessels built specifically for this type of trade are often known as 'conbulkers'.

11.6 Ships for the liquid bulk trades

The transportation of bulk liquids by sea generally requires the use of tankers. The main types of tanker are for the transport of oil products, crude oil, chemicals, wine, molten sulphur or liquid gas.

Oil tankers (Table 11.9) form by far the largest fleet of specialist bulk vessels, with a fleet of 3,130 vessels accounting for 37 per cent of the merchant fleet measured in tons deadweight. The size of individual tankers is up to 550,000 dwt; 1,200 feet (370 metres) in length; 130 feet (40 metres) in breadth; and drawing up to 75 feet (23 metres) of water. This fleet can usefully be subdivided into six segments, Handy (10–50,000 dwt), Panamax (50–70,000 dwt), Aframax (70–100,000 dwt), Suezmax (100–200,000 dwt, VLCC (200–300,000 dwt) and ULCCs (over 300,000 dwt). Each of these segments operates as a separate market and, from a ship design viewpoint, each has its own specific requirements. The smaller tankers under 50,000 dwt are mainly used for the transport of oil products (see the next section for details) and the larger vessels for the transport of crude oil.

There are two different designs for oil tankers, single hull and double hull. Until the 1990s almost all crude oil tankers had a single skin, using the hull as the main containment vessel and in 1996 86 per cent of the tanker fleet was single hull. The main features of the single hull design are shown by the hull cross section of a 38,000 dwt products tanker in Figure 11.6a. Two longitudinal bulkheads run the length of the ship from the bow to the engine room, dividing the hull into three sets of tanks, the port wing tanks, the centre wing tanks, and the starboard wing tanks. Transverse bulkheads running across the ship divide these three sets of tanks into separate cargo compartments. Tankers typically have five to seven transverse bulkheads dividing the cargo area into fifteen to twenty-four cargo

TABLE 11.9 The tanker fleet, January 1996 by size and hull characteristics

	Tanker fleet size			*Hull Characteristics*				
	No	*To dwt (million)*	*Av. dwt*	*Length metres*	*Draft metres*	*Speed knots*	*Cons. t/day*	*% D. hull*
Handy								
10–19,999	464	7.0	15,086	144	8.4	14.3	21.5	14
20–29,999	473	12.7	26,785	172	10.2	15.1	33.6	8
30–49,999	701	26.7	38,055	180	11.3	15	37.9	17
Panamax								
50–69,999	267	16.5	61,816	224	12.7	15.1	43.1	10
Aframax								
70–99,999	445	39.7	89,407	240	13.5	15.1	55.2	22
Suezmax								
100–199,999	347	47.0	134,219	269	16.2	15.1	70.9	18
VLCC								
200–249,999	125	30.8	248,401	326	19.6	14.9	83.5	1
250–299,999	254	71.8	284,184	329	20.9	15.1	87.5	11
ULCC								
300,000+	54	21.5	359,515	371	23.1	15.2	97.5	0
Total/average	3,130	273.7	72,872	217	13.0	14.9	45.7	14

Source: Tanker Register 1996, Clarkson Research Studies, London

compartments. In addition to strengthening the hull, the bulkheads restrict the movement of the cargo by the motion of the ship and limit the leakage of oil if the hull is damaged. In single hull vessels it is usual to allocate two of the wing tanks as 'segregated ballast tanks' (SBT), which means they are only used for ballast water.[8]

IMO Regulation 13F requires tankers ordered after 6 July 1993 to be of double hull construction as a protective measure against oil loss. A typical arrangement is shown in Figure 11.6a for a small tanker and Figure 11.6b for a large vessel. The regulations lay down precise rules regarding the width of the double side and the double bottom, but the principle is simple enough. There must be a second skin to limit the outflow of oil in the event of collision damage to the outer hull.

Cargo handling is an important aspect of tanker design. Rapid loading and discharge requires powerful pumps. Crude tankers rely on shore based facilities for locking, but carry their own cargo pumps for discharge. The pump room is generally located between the cargo tanks and the engine room. A network of pipes run along the deck, linking the cargo tanks to two banks of manifolds, one on each side of the ship. To load or discharge cargo the manifolds are connected to the shore based pipe system by flexible hoses, which are handled by the ship's cranes. The flow of oil is controlled by valves operated from a control panel on

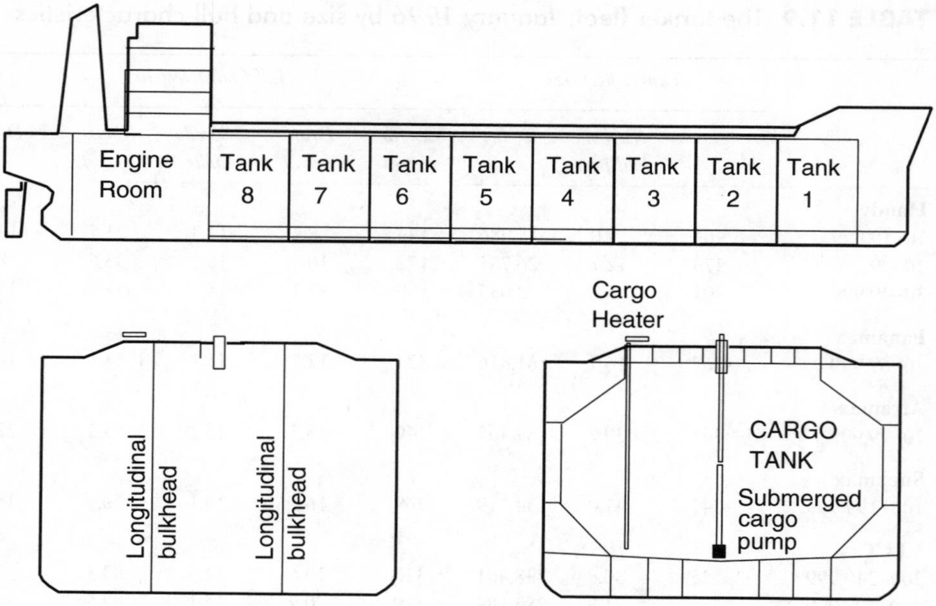

a 38,000 products tanker

Deadweight on scanting draft:	299,700 mt
Draft scanting mld:	21.60 m
Length overall:	343.71 m
Beam:	56.40 m
Dist. keel to top of mast:	66.44 m
Dist. keel to deck:	30.40 m
International gross tonnage:	158,475
International net tonnage:	94,891
Suez net tonnage:	149,067.35
Tons per cm immersion at SDWT (tpc):	171.5 mt

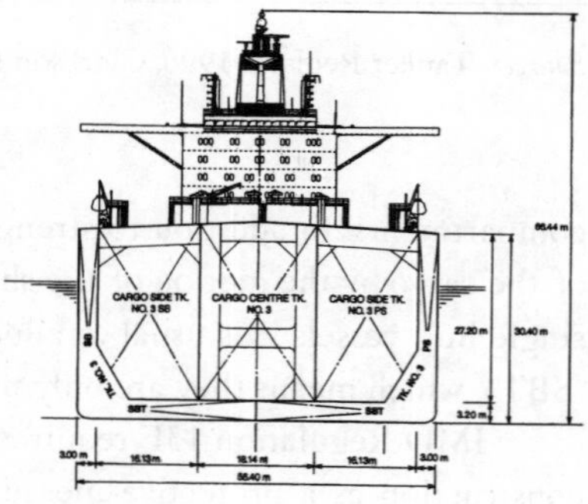

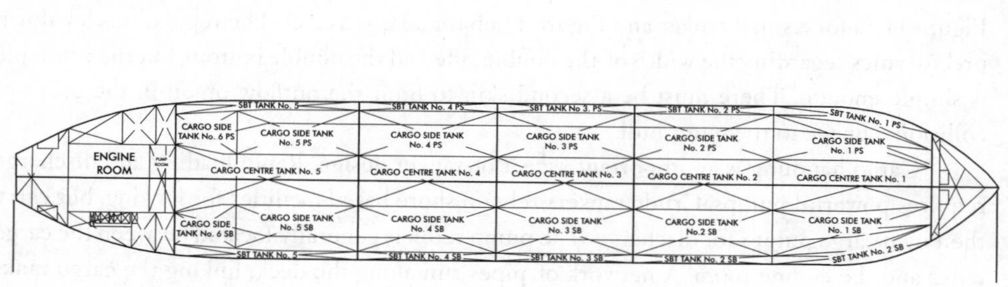

b 300,000 double hull crude tanker

FIGURE 11.6 Tanker design; (a) 38,000 products tanker; (b) 300,000 dwt double hull crude tanker

the bridge and must conform to a plan which minimizes stress on the hull (an incorrect load or discharge sequence can literally sink the ship!).

Products tankers

Within the oil tanker fleet *products tankers* form a separate category of vessel, but one which is not clearly defined in statistical terms because the distinction between crude and products tankers is blurred. Clean products tankers are similar to crude oil tankers but generally smaller. Most products tankers are 10–50,000 dwt, though there is a significant fleet of 50–80,000 dwt products tankers and two zinc coated vessels over 200,000 dwt. Figure 11.6a shows the outline design of a modern products tanker. This 38,000 dwt tanker has eight cargo holds with a cargo heating system for very heavy oils and a submerged cargo pump in each hold (deep well pump), allowing separate grades of cargo to be carried in each tank. Products tankers generally have tank coatings to prevent cargo contamination. Since these vessels can easily be used for crude trading, it is not a distinct category.

Chemical parcel tankers

One of the areas of innovation in recent years has been in the design of ships to carry small liquid bulk parcels of 2,000–6,000 tons. Typically these include products such as vegetable oils, lube oils, molasses, caustic soda, BTX, Styrene and a whole range of specialist chemicals. If a small chemical tanker of the appropriate size is used the freight cost is prohibitively high, on a long journey from Europe to the Far East reaching as much as $100 per ton. The alternative is to ship the cargo in a 'parcel tanker' designed to carry many small parcels within a single ship. Over the last 30 years a sophisticated transport system has developed to handle these small cargoes.

The structure of the transport system is illustrated in Figure 11.7. On the right are listed the various commodities which appear on the market in parcels of under 10,000 tons. On the left of the diagram are the two fleets which transport these parcels. First there is the parcel tanker fleet, consisting of 730 ships of 20 m.dwt, ranging in size from 10,000 dwt to as much as 50,000 tons incorporating 40 or 50 parcel segmentations. At the bottom of the chart on the left is the fleet 580 small tankers under 10,000 dwt which will offer transport on a one ship, one cargo basis. The organization of transport falls into three categories. At the top are the parcel tanker pools operated by companies like Stolt and Odfjell. They operate large fleets of parcel tankers which offer liner services for large parcels. They arrange transport on a contract of affreightment basis, with regular port itineraries worked out to meet the needs of the trade. However, they also take cargoes from the spot market where these are available at an acceptable rate and when the destination fits in with the vessel operating pattern. The second group consists of tramp parcel tankers. These are medium sized parcel vessels, often 10,000–20,000 dwt which operate on the spot market, grouping together several spot parcels on a voyager by voyage

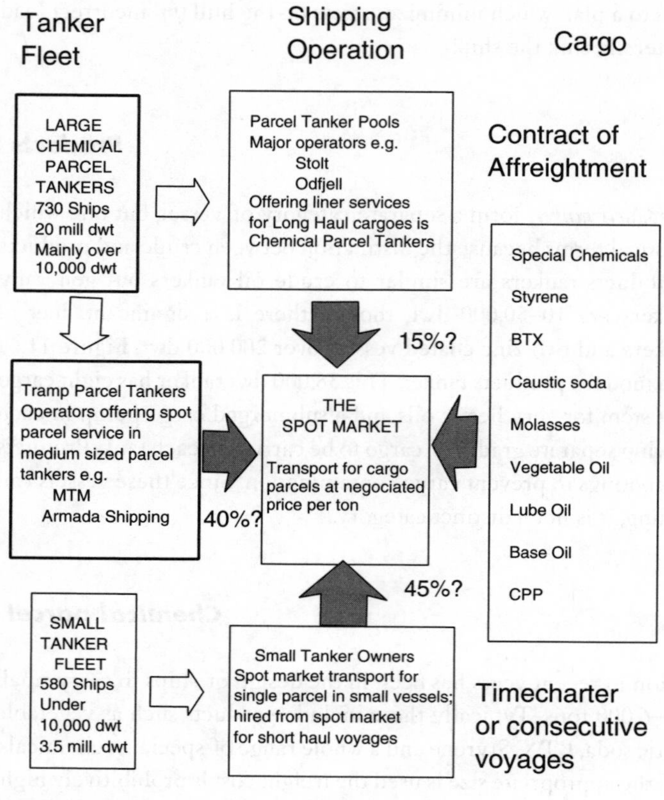

FIGURE 11.7 Small parcel market
Source: Martin Stopford, 1997

basis. Finally, there are the small tanker operators who generally operate on the spot market, picking up whatever parcels are available, but may be engaged on a time charter or a consecutive voyage basis. These small vessels tend to operate within the regions, particularly Europe and Asia.

The design of chemical parcel tankers is regulated by the IMO Convention on the Carriage of Dangerous Chemicals by Sea. This divides potentially dangerous cargoes into three categories, referred to as IMO Type I, Type II, and Type III. The most hazardous liquids must be carried in Type I tanks. These are the chemicals which are not biodegradable in the sense that once they are released in the sea they build up in marine organisms. Parcel tanks approved for the carriage of these chemicals must have double bottoms and be located not less than one-fifth of the ship's breadth from the ship's sides measured at the water line. This means that IMO Type I tanks are generally located in the centre of the ship. Type II tanks must also have a double skin protecting them from collision damage. Finally IMO Type III cargoes can be carried in standard tankers.

A separate issue is the protection and cleaning of the tanks. There are three methods commonly used in parcel tankers, stainless steel for corrosive cargo and zinc silicate or epoxy coatings which suit most others. The chemical tanker shown in Figure 11.8a has thirty-seven parcel tanks, of which twenty-nine are stainless steel and eight are zinc silicate. The size of the tanks varies a great deal. The smallest are 359 cubic metres, while the largest are 2,491 cubic metres. Finally the ship must have a flexible cargo handling system with the ability to handle the contents of each tank separately, usually by means of a separate deep well pump in each tank.

Solvents carriers are the simplest and oldest chemical tankers and some are classified as products tankers. The 'solvents' they carry are mainly the refinery products – naptha, benzene, toluene, xylene, alcohols and their derivatives. If there is no suitable solvent cargo available, the vessels will try to 'downgrade' to carry clean petroleum products. *Specialized chemical tankers* include the relatively sophisticated vessels specifically designed for a particular trade. They usually carry lubricating oils, vegetable oils or molasses. *Molten sulphur carriers* are a separate entity as they carry only sulphur, which needs much higher temperatures (80+ °C) than the other cargoes. The ships have special equipment including heating coils, stainless steel tanks, special valve gear and inert gas systems to prevent explosions. Special loading and discharging facilities are required, so the trade is generally conducted under long-term contract mainly for the export trades of liquid sulphur from the USA, France and Poland.

Liquid gas tankers

Liquid gas tankers are a comparatively recent development. The two main types used are LNG carriers and LPG carriers. The difference between LNG and LPG carriers is essentially one of temperature. Liquefied petroleum gas and the chemical gases that are shipped in LPG carriers do not need the extremes of refrigeration (– 163°C) or equivalent pressure required for the transport of liquefied natural gas. Most of the gases they carry need at most –51°C or equivalent pressure. There is one exception, ethylene, which needs –104°C and usually travels in small ethylene carriers. There are, however, large ethylene carriers, which are hybrid ships capable of carrying LNG and/or LPG.

LNG carriers are almost always purpose-built for a specific trade route. The gas is liquefied by refrigeration and is transported at atmospheric pressure in insulated tanks. Several different designs are currently in use. Owing to the high cost of shore-based liquefaction and handling facilities, LNG carriers generally form part of a carefully planned through transport operation. They range in size up to 125,000 cubic metres.

The majority of the LPG carriers are employed in carrying liquefied petroleum gases (propane, butane, propane/butane mix and isobutane), which make up by far the largest seaborne trade. Other less important gas cargoes are ammonia, ethylene, propylene, butadiene and vinyl chloride. LPG accounts for an even greater share of the ship demand because of the large volume shipped on long haul routes, especially from the Arabian Gulf to Japan. The ships have pressurized and insulated cargo tanks.

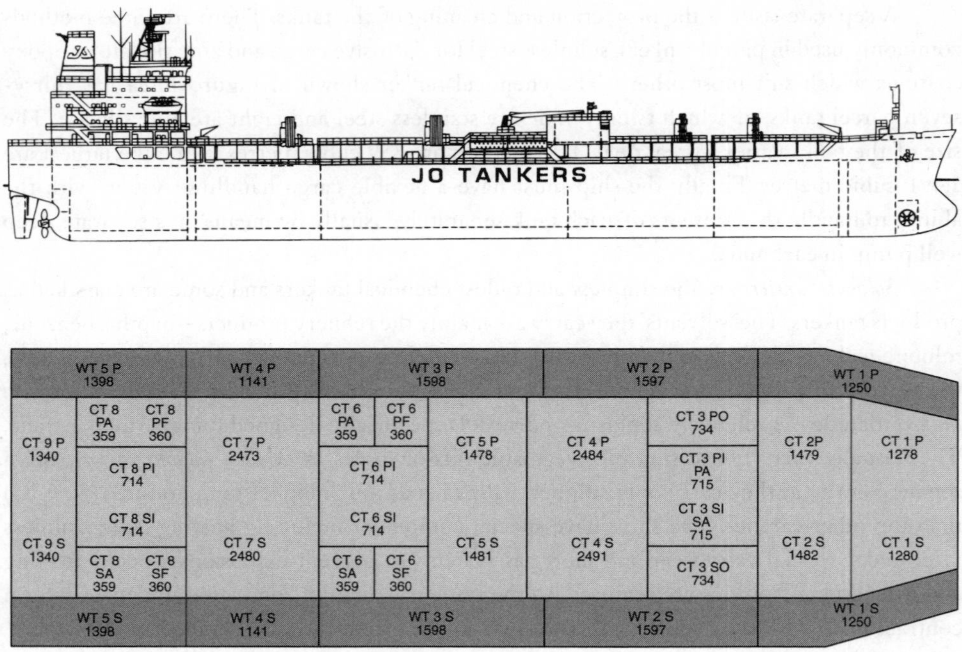

a 40,000 dwt chemical parcel tanker

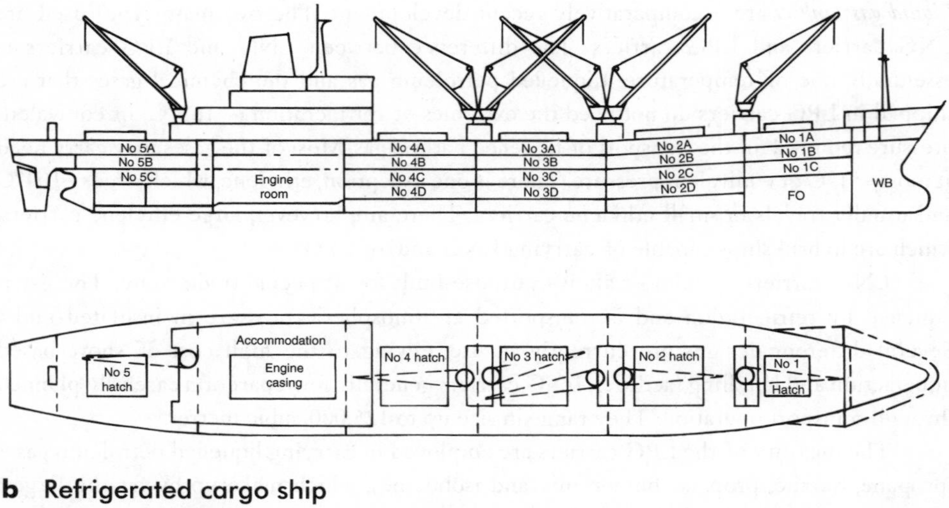

b Refrigerated cargo ship

FIGURE 11.8 Parcel tanker

11.7 Combined carriers

Combined carriers, OBOs

Combined carriers deserve a section to themselves, if only as an example of the pitfalls awaiting investors who abandon the KISS principle (see section 11.3). To give greater flexibility, oil/bulk/ore carriers often referred to as OBOs or 'combined carriers', are designed to carry a full cargo of dry bulk, e.g. ore, coal, grain, phosphates, etc., or a liquid cargo such as crude oil. This offers shipowners the opportunity to switch between the tanker and dry bulk markets when there is a rate advantage to be gained, or to reduce ballast time by carrying dry and liquid cargoes on alternate legs ('triangulation voyages'). In practice the rewards for flexibility have been slim.

The concept of carrying oil and dry cargo in the same ship can be traced back to the early days of the oil trade. The first ocean-going tank steamer, the *Vaderland* (1872), was designed to carry passengers from Belgium to the United States and return with a cargo of petroleum. The owners were not able to obtain a licence to carry passengers and oil in the same ship so the Vaderland ended up carrying general cargo in the petroleum tanks.[9] In the 1920s two ore/oilers, the *Svealand* and the *Amerikaland* were designed to carry iron ore from Peru to Baltimore, returning with a cargo of oil. Again the plan was frustrated, this time by the high transit charges for the Panama Canal. In the 1950s and 1960s combined carriers achieved greater success, capitalizing on the newly emerging oil and dry cargo trades.

Two different designs were used. The first to enter service in the 1950s were the ore/oilers. These vessels had holds in the centre of the ship to carry the high density iron ore, with side and bottom tanks designed to carry a full cargo of oil. The use of separate compartments avoided the need for cleaning between cargoes, but was wasteful of space and the dry leg was limited to high density iron ore. The second design, which appeared in the mid-1960s, was the OBO (oil/bulk/ore) which carried oil or dry bulk in the same cargo spaces. Typically these vessels have double bottoms and eleven holds to carry oil, of which seven can be used for ore or dry bulk. Hatch covers are oil-tight and gas-tight. Because the combined carriers were able to switch between wet and dry markets, they made handsome profits during the three tanker booms in 1967, 1970 and 1973 (see Chapter 2).

So great was the enthusiasm for combined carriers that by the mid-1970s a fleet of 49 m.dwt had been built. The capacity of this fleet so exceeded the available combined cargo voyages that the competitive advantage was lost. The indifferent commercial performance of combined carriers was compounded by the fact that the ships were complex to build, maintain and operate, costing about 15 per cent more to run than a comparable tanker or bulk carrier. In the early 1990s operators of combined carrier fleets were reporting a 10–15 per cent revenue premium (say $2,000–3,000/day), which paid the extra cost of operating the ship, but left little surplus to cover the higher capital cost. To make matters worse, the large combined carrier fleet ensured that surplus capacity was transmitted between the tanker and dry bulk markets, helping to moderate market peaks. As a result from the mid-1970s onwards few new ships were ordered and by the mid-1990s the combined carrier fleet had fallen below 20 m.dwt. In retrospect the commercial failure of the combined carrier fleet had less to do with the concept, which was perfectly sound, than the method of implementation which was not.

11.8 Ships designed for a single commodity

A number of dry bulk cargoes present stowage or handling problems which have resulted in specialist ships being built. Many ships could be included within this category, but the main ones are ore carriers, forest products carriers, woodchip carriers, cement carriers, vehicle carriers, refrigerated vessels and heavy lift vessels.

Ore carriers

Ore carriers originally found a market because of the high density of iron ore, which stows at approximately 0.5 cubic metres per ton, compared with a normal bulk carrier's capacity of 1.3–1.4 cubic metres per ton. In the last decade, general-purpose bulk carriers with strengthened holds or combined carriers have generally been preferred owing to their more flexible trading opportunities, though a few very large ore carriers have been built.

Forest products carriers

Forest products are another difficult commodity in terms of bulk transportation. Cargo can stow at anything from 2.3 cubic metres per ton for pre-slung timber to 2.8 cubic metres per ton for logs and the heavy units are difficult to handle in a conventional bulk carrier or 'tweendecker. Until the 1960s most forest products travelled by liner but, as the volume of trade increased and conventional liners were replaced by container ships on key routes such as Europe–Far East and the North Atlantic, much of the trade moved into bulk vessels.

Initial attempts to use general-purpose bulk carriers for forest products proved unsatisfactory owing particularly to the problems of cargo handling. This led to the construction of large, open hold bulk carriers, which allowed pre-slung timber, pulp and paper to be loaded and stowed by crane. Extensive shipboard cargo handling gear is generally fitted and sizes range up to 55,000 dwt. Woodchip carriers have a high internal cubic capacity to accommodate the low-density woodchips. Woodchip vessels may be fitted with gantry cranes, though shore-based pneumatic handling equipment is often used.

Cement carriers

Cement is a difficult and dusty cargo to handle, and some specialist cement carriers have been built. They incorporate pneumatic cargo handling gear with totally enclosed holds and moisture control systems. In principle, they can be used for any cargo with a fine particle size.

Vehicle carriers

Another problem area is wheeled cargo. Initially cars were shipped in cargo liners but, as the volume of seaborne trade increased in the 1960s, bulk shipment became possible. The first development was to fit bulk carriers with car decks that could fold up to allow other bulk cargoes to be carried – a classic combined voyage was cars from Emden to San Francisco with cars, returning with grain to Rotterdam. However, the low carrying capacity of car bulkers (one car per 13 dwt), combined with the additional weight of the decks, the slow loading and a high risk of damage in transit, made them a poor compromise. As the car trade grew in size in the 1970s, purpose-built vehicle carriers were built to carry new cars and small commercial vehicles, such as vans and pick-ups. They have multiple-decks (anything from four to ten depending on size) with a high cubic capacity to dwt ratio (e.g. one car per 3 dwt), high speed (around 20 knots for the bigger ones), roll-on, roll-off loading/discharging facilities and internal decks and ramps carefully designed to speed cargo handling and minimize damage. Lloyd's Register separates them from other vessels with ro-ro facilities by ruling that ro-ros carry vehicles (including trains) as conveyances of passengers or cargo, whereas in vehicle carriers the payload is the vehicles themselves.

The fleet varies in size and operation from ships of 499 grt with four decks each, carrying 500 cars in the European short sea trades up to Wallenius' *Madame Butterfly* of 27,779 dwt carrying 6,200 cars world-wide. Specialization brought a cost in terms of restricting the cargo to motor cars and light trucks. With the more volatile market of the late 1970s there was a move towards developing vehicle carriers capable of handling a wider range of cargo. The *Hual Trotter* (1983) can carry 3,710 cars on ten decks but decks three, five and seven are strengthened for unit loads of up to 150 tons, and height is adjustable by hoisting decks four, six and eight. This allows bulk parcels of cars to be supplemented by consignments of large vehicles such as trucks, buses and agricultural machinery, which cannot be accommodated between the narrow decks of a conventional car carrier.

Refrigerated vessels

Refrigerated vessels (reefers) were developed in the late nineteenth century for the carriage of meat from New Zealand and Australia to the United Kingdom. The first shipowner to use this process is reputed to have used wool to insulate the holds and when the vessel docked in London to have sold the wool as well as the meat cargo. Reefer cargo is either frozen or chilled, in which case the temperature is maintained just above freezing. To achieve this reefer vessels have insulated cargo holds with cargo handled horizontally through side ports and vertically through hatches.

Modern vessels, an example of which is illustrated in the lower half of Figure 11.8b, have their cargo spaces designed for palletized cargo and there may also be reefer container capacity on deck or in the holds. This particular vessel of 500,000 cubic feet has five holds with four decks in three holds and three decks in the other two. Size varies enormously, ranging up to 700,000 cubic feet in the deep sea trades (about 15,000 dwt). For fruit and vegetables the cargo continues to ripen during transit, so the refrigeration system must maintain a precisely controlled temperature in all parts of the cargo spaces. Since fruit cargoes such as bananas are frequently loaded in developing countries with poor port facilities, there is often a need to make the ships self-sufficient in terms of cargo handling. Cars are often carried as a backhaul.

Although reefers still dominate the refrigerated cargo trade, frozen foods are also transported in a wide range of other ship types, particularly reefer containers carried in container ships, ro-ros, or cargo liners. This makes the trade difficult to analyse as a whole.

Heavy lift vessels

Multipurpose vessels with heavy lift capacity and ro-ros can carry unit loads of up to 100 tons, but there is a demand for small vessels capable of carrying much larger loads (e.g. up to 500 tons) or on routes where liner companies do not offer heavy lift capabilities. Many different designs are used, including float-on and conventional crane loading using Stulken cranes.

11.9 Marine service vessels

Non-cargo and service vessels cover a wide variety of ships from a 200 grt tug to a 70,000 grt passenger liner. Statistics are sketchy and classification difficult because of the multitude of uses to which the small vessels can be put. This makes it difficult to analyse the demand for each type with any authority. Although these vessels represent only 7 per cent of the fleet in gross tonnage terms, they are much more important to the industry in value and number. Over 70 per cent of non-cargo carrying vessels may be under 500 grt, but by number they make up nearly half of the world's shipping fleet.

The fishing fleet

Fishing vessels account for nearly half the non-cargo carrying fleet by tonnage. The fleet includes both fishing vessels and fish factories. The world fishing fleet grew rapidly at 15 per cent per annum in the 1960s and then started to stabilize in the face of overfished oceans, escalating costs and the uncertainty of offshore limits.

Supply ships and tenders

Supply ships and tenders are used in the offshore industry in oil and gas. With the increasing depth and distance from shore at which the work is taking place, proportionally more and larger vessels are needed. There has also been a trend towards building more highly powered, sophisticated, multi-purpose vessels, especially for use in the bad weather areas of the North Sea and Gulf of Alaska.

Tugs and dredgers

Tugs and dredgers form part of the fleet related to the seabed activity and there has also been a growing demand from harbour and canal authorities. One of the reasons for the faster growth was the change in trading patterns towards the developing countries and the use of larger ships. The growing interest in the resources of the seabed also generated a growing market for research, survey vessels and icebreakers.

Passenger vessels

Passenger vessels suffered in the 1960s when air transport practically killed demand for regular services of large passenger liners. Because existing vessels were too large and fast to be economic as cruise ships, the mid-1970s saw a steady decline in the number of liners operating, with ships even less than 10 years old being taken out of service and often converted to vehicle carriers. However, the 1980s and 1990s brought a revival of the cruise market.

11.10 Economic criteria for evaluating ship design

So far we have discussed the options that may confront a shipowner contemplating an investment decision. For the many practical reasons discussed it is not easy to evaluate these options in financial or economic terms, and there is a temptation to suggest that ship design is a matter for commercial flair or 'gut feeling' rather than rigorous economic analysis. However, in all but a very few cases, the commercial world demands that decisions of this type should be supported by economic analysis.

There is substantial literature on the evaluation of alternative ship designs.[10] For practical purposes, the analysis needs to be carried out at two levels, which we will refer to here as market research and operational analysis.

Market research

Market research is concerned with analysing the economic performance of the ship within the company's overall shipping activities. For a charter market operator this analysis might involve an examination of the type of vessel that will be easy to charter and its potential resale value. A liner operator might study the type of ship required to handle changes in the pattern of trade or competition on major routes. This is closely aligned to the market research analysis described in Chapter 14. Through market research the owner can develop a specification for the type of shipping operation in which the vessel is to be used and the performance parameters that the vessel must satisfy.

Operational analysis

The next step is to identify the ship design that meets the performance requirements most effectively, using some form of economic measure of merit. For example, the designer may be told that the owner requires a product tanker with the following features:

- a draught of not more than 10 metres;
- a length of not more than 170 metres;
- ability to carry simple chemicals such as caustic soda;
- cargo tanks that are cheap to clean;
- an operating speed of 14 knots;
- about 35,000–40,000 dwt cargo capacity for products.

Although this list of requirements appears to be highly specific, in practice there may not be a unique solution. On examination, it may transpire that some of the requirements are inconsistent or very difficult to achieve. For example, it may be difficult to achieve the design draught within the other specified parameters, or doing so may result in a vessel with poor fuel economy. The cost of developing a 'clean tank' design may also turn out to be very considerable, involving double skin construction. Did the shipowner appreciate this when he laid down the specification and is he prepared to pay the cost? These are all issues that have to be tackled at the operational analysis stage.

The task of the ship designer is to evaluate the various options in economic terms to see which gives the best overall result, recognizing both cost and operational performance. Buxton suggests two different ways of doing this, depending on the circumstances:[11]

1 *Net present value (NPV).* This technique involves setting up a projected cashflow for each of the options under consideration. Revenues and costs are projected on an annual basis over the life of the ship and the net cashflow in each year is calculated, taking account of capital payments, trading income and expenditure, and probably the final resale value of the vessel. These annual cashflows are then discounted back to the present (using a minimum acceptable interest rate) and summed, giving the net present value of each of the options. The option giving the highest NPV is generally preferred.

This technique is widely used in business for evaluating capital expenditure projects, and many companies incorporate it as part of their capital expenditure system. The advantage is that it takes account of both the cost and revenue flows, and produces a single figure, which makes the comparison of options a simple matter. On the negative side, the revenue flow may in some cases be extremely difficult to project and arbitrary assumptions about the potential earning power of the vessel may give a distorted result.

For this reason, the NPV approach is most satisfactory for evaluating ships being constructed for a long-term time charter.

2 *Required freight rate (RFR).* This method avoids the problem of cost of the predicting revenue by comparing the relative unit transport different ship types. The RFR is calculated by computing the annual average cost of running the ship (operating plus voyage costs), adding the capital costs and dividing by the annual tonnage of cargo transported. There are several different ways of carrying out this calculation, but all aim to show which ship design will give the lowest unit transportation cost within the parameters specified by the owner.

There are several variations on these two methods, notably the yield or internal rate of return, which is closely related to the NPV method (being the interest rate that produces an NPV of zero), and the permissible price, which can be derived from either method.

11.11 Summary

This chapter has reviewed ships used in the shipping business. We started with two important observations. First, because the demand for merchant ships is derived from the demand for transport, we cannot determine the demand for merchant ships simply by examining the cargo flows. Shipowners are free to use whatever ships they think will provide the service most profitably. We must consider a wider range of economic factors which include the type of cargo, the type of shipping operation and the owner's commercial philosophy. Second 'ship types' should not be viewed in terms of physical design characteristics. From the shipowner's point of view ships of the same type are substitutes in the market place. In particular, size plays an important part in determining ship type.

An examination of the relationship between cargo units and ship types shows that some ships, such as the multi-purpose cargo liners or ro-ros, are highly flexible and capable of carrying six or seven different types of cargo units, while others, such as the container ship, the gas carrier or the crude oil tanker, are highly specialized and are capable of carrying only one cargo. In terms of the revenue maximization calculations described in chapter 3, the flexible ship has a better chance of achieving a high level of loaded days at sea and deadweight utilization because it is capable of carrying many different cargo types. The cost of this flexibility occurs in terms of higher capital cost and, in some cases, lower operating efficiency than the more specialized vessel. Recently the trend has been decisively towards specialized ships with low LCM ratios.

In the liner business, the three main types of purpose-built vessels are container ships, multi-purpose cargo ships and ro-ros. Most of the ships employed in the liner trades are purpose built within these general categories. There used to be an enormous number of different and unique ship specifications designed to fit particular trades, but containerization has brought a high degree of standardization to ships used in the liner trades. There are still a few ships in the fleet designed for cargo flexibility, notably the multi-purpose and 'tweendeckers which can switch between general cargo and dry bulk. The popularity of these ships with investors declined during the 1980s and the fleets are declining.

In the dry bulk market, the trend towards single purpose vessels continues. The general-purpose bulk carrier dominates the business, despite being restricted to the carriage of dry bulk cargoes. More flexible dry bulk vessels are the 'tweendecker which can trade either in bulk or general cargo; the open hold bulk carrier which can trade in homogeneous dry bulk, containers and specialized bulks such as forest products; and the combined carrier which can alternate between dry bulk and crude oil and other liquids. All have been losing market share, especially the combined carrier.

Finally, there is a range of specialist ships designed for the bulk transport of specific cargoes. The most prominent of these are liquefied gas carriers, refrigerated cargo ships, car carriers, heavy lift ships, and cement carriers. In some cases, such as gas carriers, these ships are totally specialized and are in competition only with other ships of the same type, whereas others, such as the refrigerated cargo ship, the car carrier or the heavy lift vessel, face competition from multi-purpose vessels.

The key point in all of this is that most cargoes can be transported in several different types of ship. In the last resort, the ship in which the cargo travels is determined by commercial performance rather than its specific technical design characteristics.

Chapter 12

The regulatory framework of maritime economics

Whosoever commands the sea commands the trade; whosoever commands the trade of the world commands the riches of the world and consequently the world itself.

(*Judicious and Select Essays and Observations by that Renowned and Learned Knight Sir Walter Raleigh, upon the First Invention of Shipping,* London, H. Moseley, 1650)

12.1 How maritime regulation affects maritime economics

Shipowners, like most businessmen, find that regulation often conflicts with their efforts to earn a reasonable return on their investment. When Captain Plimsoll first started his campaign against the notorious 'coffin ships' in the 1870s, British shipowners argued that the imposition of loadlines would put them at an unfair competitive advantage. Fayle observes that:

> In their efforts to raise both the standard of safety and the standard of working conditions afloat, the Board of Trade frequently found themselves, during the last quarter of the nineteenth century, at loggerheads with the shipowners. They were accused of cramping the development of the industry by laying down hard-and-fast rules which in effect punished the whole of the industry for the sins of a small minority, and hampering British shipping in international competition, by imposing restrictions from which foreign ships were free, even in British ports.[1]

The same, sometimes legitimate, resistance to regulation is found in most industries, but the world's oceans provide the shipping industry with an unrivalled opportunity to bypass the clutches of regulators and thereby gain an economic advantage. The goal of maritime regulators is to close the net. As a result, in the last 50 years the regulatory regime has become a central factor in the economics of the shipping market.

It would, however, be wrong to think that the regulatory process is just concerned with pursuing villains. A few regulations are made in response to particular incidents. The *Titanic*, the *Torrey Canyon*, the *Herald of Free Enterprise* and the *Exxon Valdez* all provoked a public outcry which led to new regulations. However these are the exceptions. Over the last century the shipping industry and the maritime states have evolved a complex regulatory system which impacts on all aspects of the economics of operating ships. The design of the ship, maintenance standards, crewing costs, operating standards, company overheads, taxation, commercial confidentiality, pollution liability, and cartels are all subject to regulation. As we shall see in the course of this chapter, there are many more examples. Thus a knowledge of maritime regulation has become an essential part of the maritime economist's toolkit.

The aim of this chapter is to discuss the international regulatory framework of maritime economics and the legal and political issues that have influenced, and in some cases dominated, the maritime scene since the mid-1960s. The chapter seeks to answer three questions:

1. *Who* regulates shipping and commerce?
2. *What* do they regulate?
3. *How* do regulations affect shipping economics?

The intention is simply to gain an understanding of the areas of shipping which these regulations affect, and the general procedures by which they are made and changed. We also address the question of ownership of the world fleet and the major issue of flags of registration.

12.2 The institutions that regulate shipping

The three regulatory regimes

The first step is to identify the regulators. In an ideal world we might expect there to be a supreme legislative body which makes laws and an international court that tries cases against them. Unfortunately reality does not live up to this ideal and probably never will. Indeed some experts doubt whether what passes for international law is really 'law' at all.[2] There is an International Court of Justice, but its rulings on shipping matters are purely advisory. We should not be surprised at this state of affairs. There are 163 countries with interest in shipping, each with its own national priorities.[3] Gaining agreement on a body of international law, far less approving an international executive to enforce the laws, is hardly likely to succeed.

As a result, the regulatory system we discuss in this chapter is a second best solution. It consists of an *ad hoc* mix of rules and regulations enacted and enforced by three different regulatory authorities:[4]

1 *The classification societies.* The shipping industry has its own system for regulating the technical and operational standard of ships. The *classification societies* make rules for ship construction and maintenance and issue a 'class certificate' to reflect compliance.
2 *The flag states.* The primary legal authority governing the activities of merchant ships is the state in which the ship is registered, the *flag state.* By custom this state is responsible for regulating all aspect of the commercial and operational performance of the ship. International laws are developed by the participation of flag states in treaties or conventions.
3 *The coastal states.* A ship is also subject to the laws of the *coastal state* in whose waters it is trading. The extent of each state's territorial waters and the scope of regulation varies from one country to another.

In the following sections we will consider each of these regulatory regimes.

12.3 Self-regulation and the classification societies

The shipping industry's own regulatory system arose from the efforts of insurers to establish that the vessels for which they were writing insurance were sound. In the middle of the eighteenth century they formed the first Classification Society and classification societies have now become an integral part of the maritime regulatory scene. During the intervening period their activities have become so closely involved with the regulatory activities of governments that it is often difficult to separate the two. In this section we will focus exclusively on the role of classification societies as non-legal bodies. We will try to define why they were set up, how they have evolved, the scope of their functions today and the impact which this has on maritime economics.

Origin of the classification societies

Like many other shipping institutions the classification societies are very much a product of their past. Knowing something of their history helps to explain the current structure. Lloyds Register of Shipping (LR), the first classification society, can trace its origins back to Lloyds Coffee House in the early 1700s. The proprietor, Edward Lloyd, presumably in an effort to attract clients, started to circulate lists giving details of vessels which might appear for insurance.[5] The next step came in 1764 when a committee of London insurers and insurance brokers published the first Register of ships. This register 'classified' ships according to their quality. It listed a grade 'conferred on the ship by the Committee's appointed surveyors'.[6]

The 'green book', as it was known, was compiled by insurers for the sole use of members of the society and contained details of 15,000 ships. All went well until the 1797–8 register when a new grading system was introduced. The new system based the ship's class on the river of build, favouring the Thames. This grading system was disputed by shipowners and in 1799 they published a rival register, the *New Register Book of Shipping*, known as 'red book'. There followed a period of punitive competition which brought both registers close to bankruptcy. In 1834 the differences were settled and a new society was set up to produce a shipping register which was acceptable to all sections of the industry. The new publication was *Lloyds Register of British & Foreign Shipping*. Its governing body had twenty-four members, eight each from among the merchants, the shipowners, and the underwriters, making it representative of the shipping industry as a whole.[7]

The new society had sixty-three surveyors and a system of regular inspection for ships was instituted. The main function continued to be the production of a register grading ships, but a new classification system was introduced:

Class A: The ship had not passed a prescribed age and had been kept in the highest state of repair.
Class E: Ships which, though not fit for carrying dry cargo, were considered perfectly safe for carrying cargoes not damaged by the sea.
Class I: Ships unsuitable for dry cargo, but fit for short voyages (not out of Europe)

The condition of the anchors, cables and stores when satisfactory was indicated by 1 and when unsatisfactory by 2. This system gave rise to the familiar expression 'A1 condition'. In the first five years 15,000 vessels were surveyed and 'classed'.

As the class movement developed in the nineteenth century, the role of classification societies changed. At first the main job was to grade ships. As time passed they started to set the standards to which ships should be built and maintained. Blake (1960) comments: 'As its authority grew, the Committee took upon itself something like disciplinary powers. Any new vessel for which an A1 classification was sought must undergo *a survey under construction*, which meant in effect that its progress was closely inspected at least three times while the hull was still on the stocks.' A1 became a requirement rather than a grade in a scale.

Technical committees were set up to write rule books setting the precise standards to which merchant ships should be built and maintained. These rules set the standards and the society policed them through their network of Ships Surveyors.

Other classification societies were set up in the nineteenth century. The American Bureau of Shipping (ABS) has its origins in the American Ship Masters Association which was organized in 1860 and incorporated in 1862 through an Act of Legislature of the State of New York. Like LR it is a non-profit making organization with general management vested in the membership comprising individuals prominent in the marine and off-shore industries and related fields. Most were non-profit making organizations managed by Boards drawn from all parts of the maritime industry – ship builders, shipowners, insurers, etc. Although underwriters still participate in general management through membership of these boards, the classification societies can no longer be seen as acting exclusively for the insurers.

The classification societies today

Today the main job of the classification societies is to 'enhance the safety of life and property at sea by securing high technical standards of design, manufacture, construction and maintenance of mercantile and non-mercantile shipping'. The Classification Certificate remains the mainstay of their authority. A shipowner must class his vessel to obtain insurance and in some instances a government may require a ship to be classed. However, the significance of the Classification Certificate extends beyond insurance. It is the industry standard for establishing that a vessel is properly constructed and in good condition.

Although the major societies do not distribute profits, they depend on client revenue to cover their costs and are subject to commercial pressures. As self-funding organizations, their survival depends on maintaining a sufficiently large fee paying membership to recover their costs. There is, therefore, intense competition between classification societies to attract members, leading to the anomaly that they are paid by the same shipowners on whom they have to impose financial penalties through their regulatory inspections. This led to criticism that shipowners were avoiding carrying out essential maintenance by re-classing to a society with less exacting standards.

Most of the large classification societies also supplement their income by undertaking technical inspection work on behalf of governments. Since government regulations cover much of the same ground as class rules, this leads to the confusion of the role of the class societies and government regulators. There are currently more than fifty classification societies operating world-wide, some large and prominent, others small and obscure. The list of the larger societies and the number of cargo ships they class, shown in Table 12.1 gives a rough idea of the relative prominence of the various institutions. These are all well-known names in shipping circles and together they cover over 90 per cent of the cargo and passenger fleet (note that these numbers do not include the many small non-cargo carrying vessels which the societies also class). Because they developed independently, the classification societies do not have common rulebooks. At one level this is a source of inconvenience. A repeat design built for one class society may have to be reworked to meet the requirements of another. Differences in rules can increase the building cost of a ship by millions of dollars. As governments have also become active in setting technical standards for ship construction, particularly through the International Maritime Organization, the need for co-ordination has increased.

To address this problem, in 1968 the International Association of Classification Societies (IACS) was set up. Its eleven members hold about 90 per cent of the world market for classification and statutory services and includes the ten societies listed in Table 12.1. The association has two aims. The first is to introduce an element of uniformity into the rules developed by class societies. The second is to provide a representative group who could interface with other major rule-setting organizations, principally IMO.

TABLE 12.1 The major classification societies, January 1997

Classification society	*Ships classed*	*'000 dwt(million)*	*% No.*
Lloyd's Register of Shipping	3,912	153,246	17.5
Nippon Kaiji Kyokei	3,854	142,483	17.2
American Bureau of Shipping	3,685	132,035	16.5
Det Norske Veritas	2,657	113,651	11.9
Bureau Veritas	1,837	43,185	8.2
Germanischer Lloyd	1,802	25,999	8.1
China Class Society	1,005	19,560	4.5
Korean Register of Shipping	431	14,680	1.9
Russian Maritime Register of Shipping	1,002	13,625	4.5
Registro Italiano Navale	543	10,924	2.4
Others	1,657	23,465	7
Totals	22,385	692,853	100

Note: The statistics cover only vessels included in Clarkson Registers

Source: Clarkson Research Studies

Over the last 30 years IACS has developed more than 160 sets of unified requirements. These relate to many factors of which a few are minimum longitudinal strength, loading guidance information, the use of steel grades for various hull members. Another function of IACS is to collaborate with outside organizations and in particular IMO. To enable IACS to carry out this role more effectively, in 1969 IMO granted IACS 'consultative status'. The fact that it is the only non-governmental organization with observer status at the IMO neatly illlustrates the ambiguous position of the class societies, hovering somewhere between the commercial shipping industry and governments.

In addition to their role as regulators, the major classification societies represent the largest single concentration of technical expertise available to the shipping industry. An example of a classification society helps to illustrate the nature of the structure. Lloyds Register, the largest classification society, has over 3,900 people, of whom half are qualified engineers, operating from 260 offices world-wide. These staff perform classification against its own rules (around 6,600 ships annually); statutory certification against international conventions, codes and protocols; quality services; and a range of engineering services. The American Bureau of Shipping (ABS) has a world-wide staff of 1,475 including 300 engineers located in 15 offices world-wide and 425 exclusive surveyors in 160 locations. For comparison the International Maritime Organization (IMO) has a secretariat staff of about 300. Many important bulk shipping companies have less than 100 shore-based staff. In these circumstances it is easy to see why, in addition to the classification role, the class societies have developed a major role as technical advisers to shipowners and governments.

The regulatory activities of the classification societies

Despite their obvious importance, the classification societies have no legal authority. There is no requirement for a shipowner to obtain classification, but classification is generally necessary to obtain insurance, and a ship would have little value without it. The voluntary nature of classification means that classification societies compete with each other to offer classification services to shipowners and do so on the value of their rules and their ability to implement them efficiently. The service they offer today has two fundamental aspects, developing rules and implementing them.

First, the continuous updating of rules to reflect changes in marine technology. Procedures vary, but most societies develop their rules through a committee structure, involving experts from various scientific disciplines and technical activities including naval architect, marine engineers, underwriters, owners, builders, operators, materials manufacturers, machinery fabricators and individuals in other related fields. This process takes into account the activities of IMO and IACS unified requirements.

The second stage involves the application of the rules to practical shipbuilding and shipping. This is a three-step procedure:

1. *A technical plan review.* The plans of the ship are submitted to the classification society for inspection, to ensure that the mechanical structural details in the design of the ship conforms to the rules. If the plans are found satisfactory they are passed and construction can proceed. Sometimes modifications are required, or explanations required on certain points.
2. *Surveys during construction* to verify that the approved plans are implemented, good workmanship practices are employed and that rules are followed. This includes the testing of materials and major components such as engines, forgings and boilers.
3. *Periodic surveys* for the maintenance of class. Merchant ships are required to undergo a scheme of surveys while in service to verify their acceptability for classification.

The classification procedures for classing existing ships are, in general terms, agreed by IACS for members and associates. The regulations imposed by Lloyds Register are; hull and machinery special survey – five years; dry-docking survey – two-and-a-half-years; hull and machinery annual survey – one year; tail shaft inspection – five years; boiler survey – two-and-a-half years. The hull and machinery survey is very demanding, involving detailed inspection and measurement of the hull.

As the ship grows older, the scope of this inspection widens to cover those areas of the ship which are vulnerable to ageing. For example, as oil tankers grow older the area of the deck plate is subject to tests for corrosion increases. To avoid the inconvenience and time out of service the classification societies allow a *continuous survey.* Under this arrangement the ship is subject to a programme of rolling inspections, with one-fifth of the ship being covered each year.

As more governments have acquired flag state regulatory authority over the last 30 years, the role of classification societies as representatives of governments has increased. The most common authorizations are in connection with tonnage measurement and loadlines; SOLAS, MARPOL and IMO standards on the transportation of dangerous goods. In carrying out statutory work, the classification society applies the standards relevant to the country of registry.

12.4 The law of the sea

Why the law of the sea matters

We now move on to the international legal system. Since maritime law is made and enforced by nation states, we must briefly examine the legal framework which determines the rights and responsibilities of nations for their ocean going merchant ships. There are two specific questions which arise when we start discussing how the law affects shipping economics. First, which nation's law applies to a ship? Second, what are the rights of other nations over that ship as it moves about the world? As we will see, these are very practical questions, the answers to which can make a great deal of difference to the cost of running ships. Over the centuries the world has evolved a set of customary rules for dealing with these questions, known as the 'law of the sea'.

The law of the sea: flag state versus coastal state

The debate over the legal responsibility for ships stretches back to the era when naval power was the deciding factor. A country's navy protected the ships flying its flag. This established the principle, which survives today, of flag state responsibility. However, coastal states also have a claim over ships visiting their ports or sailing in their coastal waters. Early writers suggested that the distance controlled by shore based canons should be the criterion for determining these rights of the coastal states. In a world of rapidly growing commerce, agreeing the respective rights of the the flag and coastal states has become a major issue. Can a country ban alcohol on board foreign ships in its territorial waters? Or if it considers a

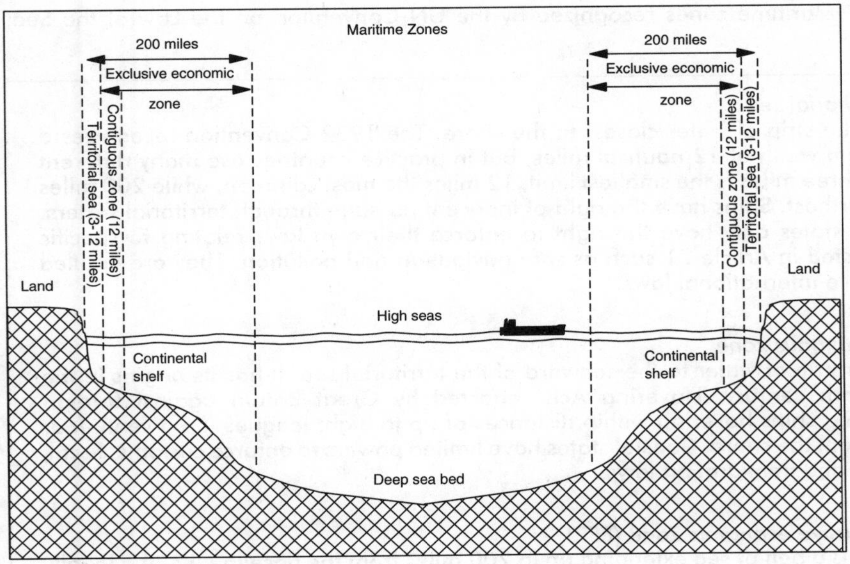

FIGURE 12.1 Maritime zones

Source Martin Stopford, 1997

foreign ship unsafe, has it the right to detain it? The answers to these questions, in so far as there are answers, are to be found in three conventions on the law of the sea, referred to as UNCLOS I in 1958, UNCLOS II in 1960 and UNCLOS III in 1973.

In 1958 the United Nations called the first United Nations Law of the Sea Conference (UNCLOS I). Eighty-six states attended. The aim was to define the fundamental issues of the ownership of the sea, the right of passage through it and the ownership of the sea bed. The latter issue has become increasingly important with the growing interest in offshore oil resources. Four conventions were eventually finalized, dealing with the Territorial Sea and Contiguous Zone, the High Seas, the Continental Shelf and Conservation of Fisheries.

A second conference, UNCLOS II, was called in 1960 to follow up on some items not agreed in UNCLOS I. In the 1960s the growing awareness of the mineral wealth on the sea bed placed new significance on the law of the sea and in 1970 the United Nations convened a third conference to produce a comprehensive Convention on the Law of the Sea. Work started in 1973 (UNCLOS III), attended by 150 states. With so many participants, discussion was extended. It was not until 1982 that the UN Convention on the Law of the Sea 1982 was finally adopted, to enter into force twelve months after it had been ratified by sixty states. It finally came into force on 16 November 1994, at last providing a 'comprehensive framework for the regulation of all ocean space . . . the limits of national jurisdiction over ocean space, access to the seas, navigation, protection and preservation of the marine environment'.[8]

As far as the flag of registration is concerned the 1982 Convention endorses the right of any state to register ships, provided there is a 'genuine link' between the ship and the state.

BOX 12.1 Maritime zones recognized by the UN Convention on the Law of the Sea, 1982

The territorial sea
This is the strip of water closest to the shore. The 1982 Convention recognizes a maximum width of 12 nautical miles, but in practice countries use many different limits. Three miles is the smallest limit, 12 miles the most common, while 200 miles is the furthest. Ships have the right of innocent passage through territorial waters. Coastal states only have the right to enforce their own laws relating to specific topics listed in Article 21 such as safe navigation and pollution. They are entitled to enforce international laws.

The contiguous zone
This is a strip of water to the seaward of the territorial sea. It has its origins in the eighteenth century 'Hovering Acts' enacted by Great Britain against foreign smuggling ships hovering within distances of up to eight leagues (i.e. twenty-four miles) from the shore. Coastal states have limited powers to enforce customs, fiscal, sanitary and immigration laws.

The exclusive economic zone (EEZ)
The EEZ is a belt of sea extending up to 200 miles from the baseline (i.e. the legally defined shoreline). It is mainly concerned with the ownership of economic resources such as fisheries and minerals. Within this zone third parties enjoy freedom of navigation and the laying of cables and pipelines. From a shipping viewpoint the EEZ is more like the high seas. However, the exception concerns pollution. Article 56 confers on the coastal state 'jurisdiction as provided for in the relevant provisions of this convention with regard to the protection and preservation of the marine environment'. The 'relevant provisions' relate to the dumping of waste and other forms of pollution from vessels. This gives the coastal state the right to enforce oil pollution regulations in the EEZ, a matter of major economic importance for shipowners.

The high seas
The high seas are 'all parts of the sea that are not included in the exclusive economic zone, in the territorial sea or the internal waters of a state'. In this area vessels flying a particular flag may proceed without interference from other vessels. This convention establishes the basis on which nationality can be granted to a merchant ship and the legal status of that ship. Article 91 of the 1982 Convention on the High Seas states that:

> Each state shall fix the conditions for the grant of its nationality to ships, for the registration of ships in its territory, and for the right to fly its flag. Ships have the nationality of the state whose flag they are entitled to fly. There must exist a genuine link between the state and the ship.

This paragraph was unchanged from the 1958 Convention and was the end-product of a heated debate about whether countries such as Liberia and Panama had the right to establish open registries. Since the Convention does not define what constitutes a 'genuine link' between state and ship, it was left to each state to define this link for itself.

TABLE 12.2 Limits of territorial sea

Distance miles	*Number countries*
3	20
4	2
6	4
12	81
15	1
20	1
30	2
35	1
50	4
70	1
100	1
150	1
200	13
None	5
Total	137

Source: Churchill and Lowe, (1983), Appendix

Since the flag state can define the nature of this link, in practice it can register any ship it chooses. Once registered, the ship becomes part of the state for legal purposes. The 'flag state' has primary legal responsibility for the ship in terms of regulating safety, labour laws and on commercial matters. However the 'coastal state' also has limited legal rights over any ship sailing in its waters.

The rights of the coastal states are defined by dividing the sea into the 'zones' shown in Figure 12.1, each of which is treated differently from a legal point of view. The territorial sea (the strip closest to land), the contiguous zone and the exclusive economic zone. The fourth zone is the high seas which nobody owns. None of the zones are precisely defined. Although the 1982 Convention fixes the limit to the territorial sea at 12 miles, Table 12.2 shows that many different limits are in use. The most common is 12 miles, but a few countries have adopted much more extensive limits. The contiguous zone and the exclusive economic zone are mainly of interest to shipowners because pollution control and prevention rights are granted to the coastal states in these areas. These zones are briefly defined in Box 12.1.

12.5 The regulatory role of the flag state

Economic implications of flag state regulation

In no area of maritime law has there been greater interplay between economics and regulation than flag state issue. When a ship is registered in a particular country (the 'flag state'), the ship and its owner become subject to the laws of that state. Registration makes the ship an extension of national territory while it is at sea. It also qualifies for its protection. Because of the interdependence between legal regulation and ship operating economics, the choice of register has become a major issue for shipowners, as has the drive to extend and tighten the control imposed by maritime law on shipping operations through international conventions.

There are four principal consequences of choosing to register in one state rather than another:

1 *Tax, company law and financial law.* A company that has registered a ship in a particular country becomes subject to that country's commercial laws. These laws will determine the company's liability to pay tax and may impose regulations in such areas as company organization, auditing of accounts, employment of staff and limitation of liability. All of these affect the economics of the business.

2 *Compliance with maritime safety conventions.* The ship is subject to any safety regulations laid down for the construction and operation of ships. Registration under a flag state that has ratified the 1974 Safety of Life at Sea (SOLAS) Convention and rigidly enforces it leaves the shipowner with no choice but to maintain high standards in the operation of his vessel. Conversely, registration under a flag state that has not ratified SOLAS, or does not have the means to enforce it, may allow shipowners to cut corners, thereby saving on equipment and maintenance.

3 *Crewing and terms of employment.* The company is subject to flag state regulations concerning the selection of crew and their terms of employment. Some flag states, for example, insist on the employment of nationals.

4 *Naval protection.* The oldest reason for adopting a flag was to benefit from the protection of the flag state. Although less important today, there were examples during the war between Iran and Iraq in the 1980s when shipowners changed to the US flag to gain the protection of US naval forces in the Gulf.

Any of these factors may be sufficient to motivate shipowners to seek a commercial advantage by changing their flag of registry. Table 12.3 shows that this has a long history, and one that has gathered momentum during the twentieth century as taxation and regulation have come to play an increasing part in the shipowner's commercial operations. This naturally raises the question, 'Is a shipowner free to change his flag?' To answer this question we need to look briefly into the procedure by which ships are registered. In some countries the shipowner is subject to the same legal regime as any other business, while in others special legislation is introduced covering merchant shipping companies.

Registration procedures

If a ship is to trade freely into the major ports of the world without encountering overwhelming difficulties with the authorities, it must have a nationality to identify it for legal and commercial purposes. That nationality is obtained by registering the ship. The way registration works varies from one country to another, but the British regime may be taken as an illustration.

Under the Merchant Shipping Act 1894, British ships must be registered within Her Majesty's dominions (in practice, because of the constraints presented by the legislation of UK Dependent Territories, that registration may have to be in the UK). A peculiarity of British registration is that the ship is divided into sixty-four shares. For the purposes of registration, thirty-three of these shares must be owned by a British subject or by a company established under the law of some part of Her Majesty's dominions and having its principal place of business in those dominions.[9] Because, under the UK Companies Acts, any person of any nationality may register and own a company in the United Kingdom, it follows that a national of any country may own a British ship.

Interestingly, there are no legal penalties for failing to register a ship in this way, possibly because it was felt that the practical penalties are such that no legal enforcement is

TABLE 12.3 History of open registry

Period	*Flag of registry*	*Motivation*
16th century	Spanish	English merchants circumvented restrictions limiting non-Spanish vessels from West Indies trade.
17th century	French	English fishermen in Newfoundland used French registry as a means to continue operation in conjunction with British registry fishing boats.
19th century	Norwegian	British trawler owners changed registry to fish off Moray Firth.
Napoleonic War	German	English shipowners changed registry to avoid the French Wars blockade.
	Portuguese	US shipowners in Massachusetts changed registry to avoid capture by the British.
1922	Panamanian	Two ships of United American Lines changed from US registry to avoid laws on serving alcoholic beverages aboard US ships.
1920–1930	Panamanian	US shipowners switched registry to reduce operating costs by employing cheaper shipboard labour.
1930s	Panamanian	Shipowners with German-registered ships switched to Panamanian registry to avoid possible seizure.
1939–1941	Panamanian	With encouragement from the US government, shipowners switched to Panamanian registry to assist the Allies without violating the Neutrality Laws. European shipowners also switched to Panamanian registry to avoid wartime requisitioning of their vessels.
1946–1949	Panamanian	More than 150 ships sold under the US Merchant Sales Act of 1946 were registered in Panama – as it offered liberal registration and taxation advantages.
1949	Liberian	Low registration fees, absence of Liberian taxes, absence of operating and crewing restrictions made registry economically attractive.
1950–late 1970		As registry in US and other countries became increasingly uneconomical, many countries competed to become 'flags of convenience' for ship registrations; only a few succeeded in attracting significant tonnage.

Source: Cooper (1986)

required to provide an additional inducement. A ship thus registered within Her Majesty's dominions becomes eligible to fly the British flag, i.e. the Red Ensign, although it is not obliged to do so. Nor is there any legal constraint on a British subject or British companies registering ships outside Her Majesty's dominions if they wish to do so. All that is necessary is for the requirements of the recipient register to be met.

There is much variation in the requirements for registration. Some flag states require the ship to be owned by a national. This is the case in Liberia, but the requirement is easily met by setting up a Liberian company which qualifies as a national for the purposes of registration. Panama has no nationality requirements, while the Greek flag falls somewhere between the two, requiring 50 per cent ownership by Greek citizens or legal entities.[10]

Types of registry

Ship registers can be broadly divided into two groups – national registers and open registers.

- *National registers* treat the shipping company in the same way as any other business in the country. Certain special incentives or subsidies may be available but, broadly speaking, the shipping company is subject to the full range of national legislation covering financial, company and employment regulations.
- *Open registers* have been set up with the specific aim of offering shipowners a registration service, often as a means of earning revenue for the flag state. The terms and conditions offered by open registers vary considerably, depending upon the policy of the country concerned. Some are highly professional and enforce international conventions on safety, while others are less vigilant, allowing shipowners to cut corners. However, all aim to offer terms that are favourable to an international shipowner.

The distinction here is one of policy rather than access to the flag. Most national registers are open to any shipowner, whatever his nationality, who wishes to apply for registration and satisfies the necessary conditions. For example, the United Kingdom is open to any Greek, Norwegian or Danish shipowner who wishes to register his vessels under the UK flag, provided he satisfies certain requirements.

In this chapter we are concerned with open registers, because these are the ones whose policy is to develop a regulatory regime which is explicitly designed to attract shipowners. Confronted with a choice of flags under which he can register his ship, the shipowner must weigh up the relative advantages and disadvantages of each of the alternatives.

The economic role of open registers

The movement towards open registers started in the 1920s, when US shipowners saw registration under the Panamanian flag as a means of avoiding the high tax rates in the United States, while at the same time registering in a country within the stable political orbit of the United States. There was a spate of registrations during this period, but the real growth came after the Second World War when the US government sold off Liberty ships to US owners. Anxious to avoid operation under the American flag, US tax lawyers approached Liberia to set up an advantageous regime for ship registration, and the registration conditions in Liberia were developed specifically to attract shipowners to register under that flag on the payment

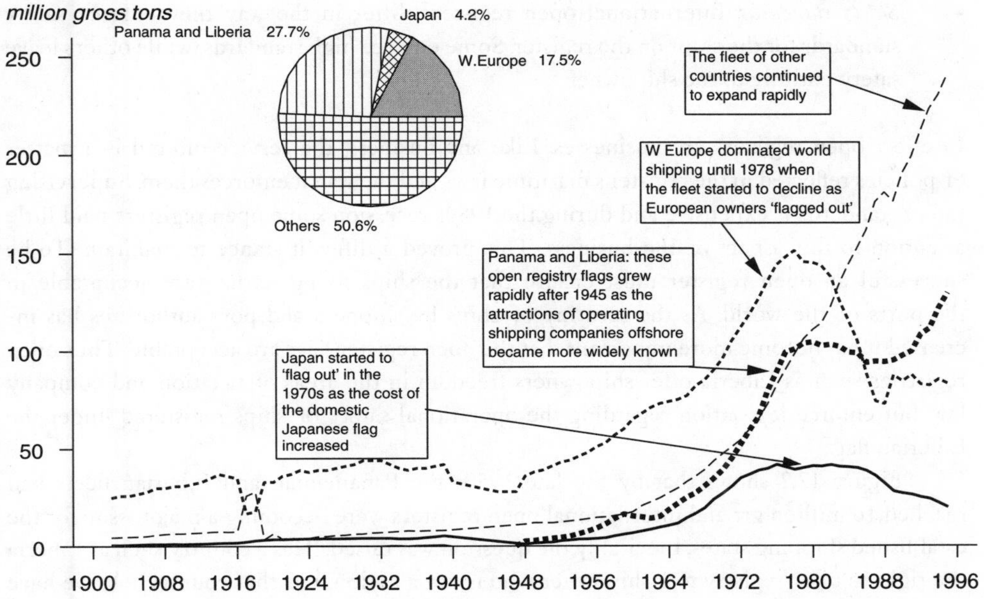

FIGURE 12.2 World merchant fleet by flag
Source: Lloyd's Register of Shipping

of an annual fee.[11] Shortly afterwards, Panama adapted its laws to attract shipowners from anywhere in the world, and thus the two major international open registers were established.

The use of an open register generally involves payment of an initial registration fee and an annual 'tonnage tax', which enables the register to cover its costs and make a profit. In return, the register offers regulations designed to suit a legal and commercial environment specially designed to suit a shipowner trading internationally. There are major differences in the way registers approach this task, but in general the areas addressed are:

- *Tax.* There are generally no taxes on profits or fiscal controls. The only tax is the subscription tax per net registered ton.
- *Crewing.* The shipping company has complete freedom to recruit internationally. There is no requirement to employ high-wage nationals, as either officers or crew. However, regulations regarding crew standards and training may be enforced, depending on the policy of the register.
- *Company law.* As a rule, the shipping company is given considerable freedom over its corporate activities. For example, ownership of the stock in the company need not be disclosed; shares are often in 'bearer' form, which means that they belong to the person who holds them; liability can be limited to a one-ship company; and the company is not required to produce audited accounts. There are generally few regulations regarding the appointment of directors and the administration of business.

- *Safety standards.* International open registers differ in the way they enforce safety standards for the ships on the register. Some enforce high standards, while others leave safety entirely to the shipowner.

In effect open registers are businesses. Like any business, the service offered is a matter of policies reflected in the register's maritime laws and the way it enforces them. Supervising safety standards is expensive and during the 1980s recession some open registers paid little attention to this aspect of the business. This proved a difficult stance to maintain. To be successful an open register must ensure that the ships flying its flag are acceptable in the ports of the world. As the scrutiny of ships by shippers and port authorities has increased it has become more important that the open register flags are acceptable. Thus open registries such as Liberia offer shipowners freedom in the areas of taxation and company law, but enforce legislation regarding the operational safety of ships registered under the Liberian flag.

Figure 12.2 shows that by the late 1950s the Panamanian and Liberian fleets had reached 16 million grt and international open registers were becoming a major issue for the established shipping states. Inevitably the question was raised: 'Has a country such as Liberia the right to offer registry to a shipowner who is not a national of that country?' As we have already seen, this issue was discussed at the first United Nations Law of the Sea Conference (UNCLOS I), which was held in 1958.

The issue was formally put to the test in 1959 when the first assembly of the newly formed Inter-governmental Maritime Consultative Organization (IMCO) met in London and elected its Maritime Safety Committee (MSC). The terms of the election of the MSC stated that eight members of the committee should be the largest shipowning nations. Initially the eight nations elected were the United States, the United Kingdom, Norway, Japan, Italy, the Netherlands, France and West Germany. However, objections were raised that Liberia, which ranked third in world tonnage, and Panama, which ranked eighth, should have been elected instead of France and Germany.

The dispute was finally submitted to the International Court of Justice for an opinion on whether the election was legal in terms of the 1948 Convention that established IMCO.[12] It was argued by the European shipowners that for a ship to register in a country there had to be a 'genuine link' between registration and ownership, and that in the case of international open registry flags this link did not exist. Predictably Liberia, Panama, India and the USA took the opposite view. The European argument was not accepted by the international court and by a 9 to 5 vote the court held that, by not electing Liberia and Panama to the MSC, the IMCO assembly had failed to comply with Article 28(a) of the 1948 Convention. As a result, international open registry flags were legitimized in international law.

Shipping is particularly well suited to offshore registration and once this facility became available it was widely adopted. Today about half the world merchant fleet is registered under open registers. The principal open registry flags, Liberia, Panama, Cyprus, Bahamas, Malta, Bermuda, and Vanuatu are listed in Table 12.4 which also shows the tonnage registered under these flags. The fact that virtually no domestic shipowners use the flags confirms their status as open registries (see Table 12.4, column 3). The exceptions are the two registries set up by Scandinavian governments, the Norwegain International Ship Registry (NIS) and the Danish International Registry. These were set up to provide a national alternative for domestic shipowners and are extensively used in this way. There is a stark contrast between the open registries, which have few nationals using their flag, and the national registers shown at the bottom of Table 12.4 where most of the tonnage registered belongs to domestic shipowners.

TABLE 12.4 World merchant fleet by ownership and registration, December 1995 (gross tonnage)

Country of registry	*For each flag state listed in the table...*		
	Total registered tonnage	*Tonnage owned by nationals*	*% owned by nationals*
Open-registry flag*			
Panama	98,409	0	0.0
Liberia	92,291	0	0.0
Cyprus	36,604	999	2.7
Bahamas	34,787	205	0.6
Norwegian Int. Registry	29,151	25,992	89.2
Malta	25,610	214	0.8
Danish Int. Registry	7,117	6,949	97.6
Bermuda	4,751	0	0.0
Vanuatu	2,077	0	0.0
Total	330,797	34,359	
National flag**			
Greece	52,065	50,880	97.7
Japan	28,784	23,429	81.4
United States	21,243	13,675	64.4
Norway	32,867	28,575	86.9
China	24,934	23,166	92.9
Hong Kong	15,257	6,987	45.8
United Kingdom	8,558	5,196	60.7
Republic of Korea	10,637	9,721	91.4
Russian Federation	15,794	14,319	90.7
Germany	6,600	6,168	93.5
Sweden	2,384	2,136	89.6
Singapore	21,021	7,867	37.4
India	11,614	11,208	96.5
Denmark	7,617	7,204	94.6
Other national flag	90,131	68,237	75.7
World total	671,184	313,307	50.0

Source: United Nations *Review of Maritime Transport*, 1995
* Data taken from Table 12, p. 26 of source
** Data taken from Table 10, p. 23 of source, excepting 'Total tonnage registered in the country' figures which were taken from Annex III(b), p. 143

All the major shipping nations make use of open registers, though the practice varies considerably. Despite the attractions of open registry, many shipowners in Greece, Japan, and the United States continue to register under their domestic flag (Table 12.4). Because the use of open registers gives shipowners greater freedom in their crewing arrangements, the system has been opposed by the seamen's unions, particularly the International Transport Workers' Federation (ITF). The ITF produces a recommended wage scale and issues a blue card to the master of ships employing crews paid on this scale. If the master cannot produce the blue card, the unions may attempt to black the ship. This has been relatively successful in persuading the owners of open registry flag vessels to observe pay scales. Although open registry developed a mixed reputation in the 1980s, the commercial pressures to 'flag out' have continued and many large shipping corporations eventually, and often reluctantly, abandoned their national flag in favour of open registers. In some cases the national flag responded to this trend by setting up its own open register. Thus, in the 1990s open registers have, for the main part, fallen in line with regulatory practice and this form of ownership has become accepted practice.

Dual registration

In some circumstances it is possible for a shipowner to register a ship under two flags. The ship is first registered in country A. A bare boat charter is then granted and this is registered in country B which accepts this structure for registration purposes. This device may be used to circumvent certain restrictive regulations in country A, for example crewing regulations.

Company structures associated with ship registration

The use of open registers in shipping has given rise to a distinctive structure of company organization designed to protect the 'beneficial owner'. A typical company structure is shown in Figure 12.3. There are four active components:

1. *The beneficial owner.* The ultimate controlling owner who benefits from any profits the ship makes. He may be located in his home country or an international centre such as Geneva or Monaco.
2. *One-ship company.* A company, usually incorporated in an open registry country, set up for the sole purpose of owning a single ship. It has no other traceable assets. This protects the other assets of the beneficial owner from claims involving the one ship company.[13]
3. *Holding company* Holding companies are often incorporated in a favourable tax jurisdiction for the purpose of owning and operating ships. The only assets of this company are the shares in each one-ship company. The shares in this company are held by the beneficial owner, which could be a company or an individual.
4. *Management company.* Day-to-day management of the ships is carried out by another company established for this purpose. Usually this company is located in a convenient shipping centre such as London or Hong Kong.

Beneficial ownership of the shipowning, management and holding companies takes the form of bearer shares. This device helps to insulate the beneficial owners of the ships from authorities seeking to establish tax and other liabilities. Its use is not universal and depends on the relative merits of the domestic flag. If we take the twenty largest shipowning nations, which are shown listed in order of the size of their fleets in Figure 12.4, we find that the proportion of the fleet registered under foreign flags in 1995 varies considerably. Greece, the nation with the biggest merchant fleet, had 58 per cent of the tonnage registered abroad, leaving 42 per cent under the domestic flag. In contrast Japan and the United States, both exceptionally high cost flags, had almost three-quarters of their fleets registered abroad. Sweden and Saudi Arabia both had over 80 per cent flagged out. Norway was the exception with only 41 per cent flagged out. The explanation is that in 1987 the Norwegian

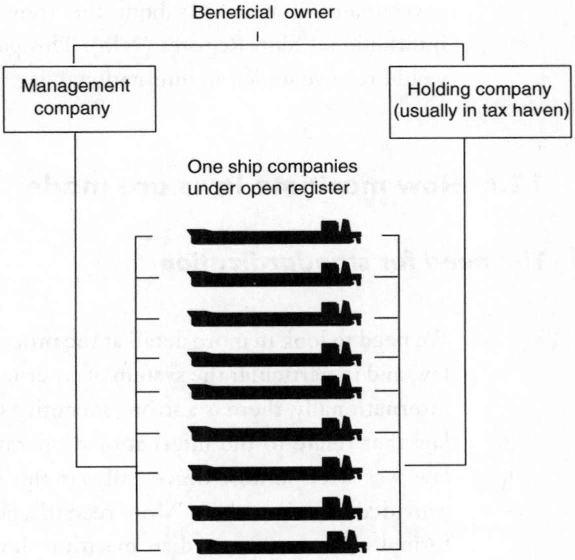

FIGURE 12.3 Shipping company structure
Source: Martin Stopford, 1997

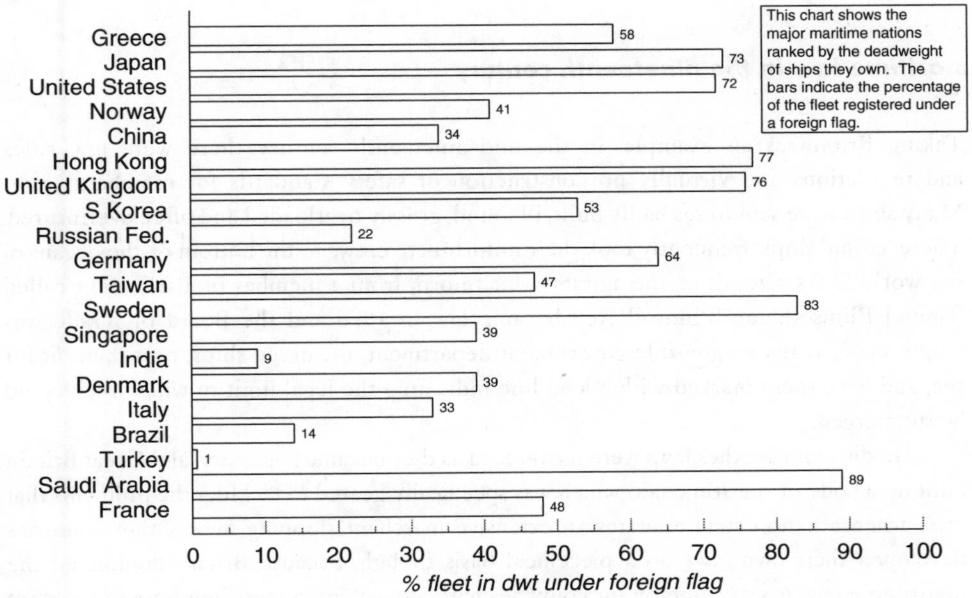

FIGURE 12.4 Principal merchant fleets using open-registry flags
Source: *Review of Maritime Transport* 1995, UNCTAD, Geneva, Table 10

government, concerned about the trend towards flagging out, set up the Norwegian International Ship Register (NIS). This gave Norwegian owners most of the benefits they would receive under an international flag.

12.6 How maritime laws are made

The need for standardization

We need to look in more detail at the procedures by which countries develop their maritime law, and in particular the system of international maritime conventions. Because ships trade internationally, there is a strong incentive to standardize those aspects of national maritime law that relate to the international operation of ships. In the nineteenth century, British law was used almost universally as the framework for national maritime law and this provided a common base. More recently, governments of maritime nations have taken more formal steps to standardize maritime law. This is achieved by means of international 'conventions', which are jointly drawn up between maritime states, setting out agreed objectives for legislation on particular issues. Each country can, if it wishes, introduce the measures set out in these conventions into its own national law. All nations that do this (known as signatories to the convention) have the same law on the subject covered by the convention.

British maritime law in the nineteenth century

Taking Britain as an example, in the mid-nineteenth century there were few rules and regulations and virtually no construction or safety standards for merchant ships. Many ships were sent to sea badly built, ill found, grossly overloaded and often overinsured. These 'coffin' ships 'frequently took their unfortunate crews to the bottom of the oceans of the world'.[14] As a result of the agitation for reform from a member of Parliament called Samuel Plimsoll, the 'Plimsoll Act' became law in 1876 and the Board of Trade was empowered, as the responsible government department, to survey ships, pass them fit for sea, and have them marked with a load line indicating the legal limit to which they could be submerged.

In due course other laws were introduced as they became necessary, and Great Britain built up a body of maritime law, which was specifically geared to tackling the problems that arise when a nation state operates an extensive merchant shipping fleet. Other countries developed their own laws on a piecemeal basis though, because Britain dominated the maritime scene, it was common for countries with a developing maritime interest to adopt British law as a basis for drafting their own legislation. Thus, British rules and regulations came to apply much more widely than in the United Kingdom.

International conventions for shipping

This approach was essentially *ad hoc*. The first step towards an international system for drawing up internationally accepted regulations (conventions) came in 1889 when the United States government invited thirty-seven states to attend an international maritime conference. On the agenda at this conference was a list of problem areas in the maritime industry where it was felt that the standardization of the international regulations would be an advantage. The agenda described in the Protocol of Proceedings of the International Marine Conference (1889) included:

- rules for the prevention of collisions;
- regulations to determine the seaworthiness of vessels;
- draught to which vessels should be restricted when loaded;
- uniform regulations regarding the designation and marking of vessels;
- saving life and properties from shipwrecks;
- necessary qualifications for officers and seamen;
- lanes for steamers; and frequented routes;
- night signals for communicating information at sea;
- warnings of approaching storms;
- reporting, marking and removing dangerous wrecks and obstructions to navigation;
- notice of dangers to navigation;
- the uniform system of buoys and beacons;
- the establishment of a permanent international maritime commission.[15]

In fact the conference succeeded in dealing with only the first item on the agenda, but the full agenda neatly illustrates the areas that were thought to be important and that were addressed by subsequent international conferences and conventions. What is manifestly clear is that many of these impact upon shipping economics and the opportunities for shipowners to reduce costs by 'cutting corners'. This conference set the pattern for the the present in which maritime laws are developed by consensus.

Procedures for making maritime conventions

The building blocks of maritime law are 'conventions'. Strictly speaking these are not laws. They are internationally accepted 'templates' from which individual nations can develop their own national maritime legislation. Whilst this does not guarantee that every country will have exactly the same maritime law, it means that most countries will have the same law on key issues. It also helps to avoid badly thought out or inconsistent maritime legislation. The procedure for making or changing a maritime convention involves four steps, which are broadly summarized in Box 12.2.

An example of this process is provided by the Law of the Sea Convention 1982 discussed in section 12.4. The convention was instigated by UN General Assembly resolution

BOX 12.2 Four steps in making a maritime convention

Step 1: Consultation and drafting conventions. The problem requiring legislation is identified by interested governments. If there is enough support in an appropriate agency such as the International Maritime Organization a convention is drafted by some suitably qualified technical body (e.g. of IMO or ILO) defining in detail the regulations to be applied.

Step 2: Adoption of draft convention. The conference is then reconvened to consider the draft convention and when agreement has been reached on the text, the convention is adopted by the conference. The discussion at the conference serves the dual purpose of showing whether or not there is a consensus that the regulations are required and indicating what form the regulations should take.

Step 3: The convention is 'opened for signature' by the governments; this indicates their intention to ratify the convention by making it legally binding in their own country.

Step 4: Ratification. Each signatory country ratifies the convention by introducing it into its own domestic legislation so that it becomes part of the law of the country or dominions. As a rule, the convention comes into force only when a certain number of states have completed this process – the precise terms and conditions will have been agreed as part of the original adoption of the convention. Once the necessary conditions have been met, the convention has the force of law in those countries that have ratified it. It does not apply in countries where it has not been ratified and any legal cases must be tried under the prevailing national law.

2749. This resolution noted the 'political and economic realities' of the preceding decade and 'the fact that many of the present State Members of the United Nations did not take part in the previous United Nations Conferences on the law of the sea'. It called for a new conference on the law of the sea. The conference was convened in 1973 and discussions continued until 30 April 1982 when the draft convention was adopted by vote (130 in favour, 4 against, with 17 abstentions). The convention was opened for signature in Montego Bay, Jamaica on 10 December 1982. On the first day signatures from 117 states were appended. In addition one ratification was deposited.

For this process to work, a considerable investment of time and effort is required in the organization of conferences, the drafting of conventions and subsequent action to ensure that they remain up to date. In the case of shipping conventions this service has devolved to three agencies of the United Nations – the International Maritime Organization (IMO), the International Labour Organization (ILO) and the Shipping Committee of UNCTAD. Each of these organizations deals with a particular range of maritime affairs as detailed in the following sections.

The work of these three organizations is constantly evolving. Although in the present context some of these conventions are of only passing interest, the key issues of maritime safety, pollution control and conditions of employment strike at the heart of ship operating economics. Further details of some of the more important conventions are summarized at the end of the chapter.

The conventions developed by these organizations are, in effect, statements of objectives that are acceptable to a majority of the states that have convened to discuss them. However, a state is not bound by the terms of a convention until it has itself ratified it and ratification has been secured from a defined proportion of the participants – usually two-thirds. Once a state has ratified a convention, and the convention has itself become effective because it has secured the prescribed number of ratifications or acceptances, all ratifying states have an obligation to enact the necessary national legislation to give the convention effect. The convention, when enacted in national law, provides the regime of constraint within which shipowners are required to operate. The following sections review the basic conventions on safety, pollution, conditions of seafarers' employment, and the UNCTAD Code of Conduct for Liner Companies.

12.7 The International Maritime Organization and its conventions

History and organization of IMO

The Inter-governmental Maritime Consultative Organization (IMCO) came into operation in 1958, with responsibility for adopting legislation on matters relating to maritime safety and pollution prevention on a world-wide basis and acting as the custodian of a number of related international conventions. Subsequently, in 1982, IMCO changed its name to the International Maritime Organization (IMO). It has been responsible for developing a large number of conventions, ranging from the Convention for the Safety of Life at Sea (SOLAS) to conventions on tonnage measurement and oil pollution.

IMO has 155 member states and two associate members. Its main objective, particularly in the early years, was to develop a comprehensive body of conventions, codes and recommendations which could be implemented by member governments. The most important conventions are now accepted by countries whose combined merchant fleets represent 98 per cent of the world total. A list of its most important conventions is shown in Table 12.5.

The governing body of IMO is the Assembly, which meets every two years. In between Assembly sessions a Council, consisting of thirty-two member states elected by the Assembly, acts as the governing body. The technical and legal work is carried out by five committees:-

- *The Maritime Safety Committee (MSC)* deals with a whole range of issues concerning safety at sea. Sub-committees deal with a wide range of issues which cover safety of navigation; radio communications and life-saving; search and rescue; standards of training and watchkeeping; ship design and equipment; life-saving appliances; fire protection; stability and load lines; fishing vessel safety; carriage of dangerous goods, solid cargoes and containers; carriage of bulk liquids and gases; and flag state implementation.

- *The Marine Environment Protection Committee (MEPC)* deals with all issues relating to pollution, particularly oil.
- *The Technical Co-operation Committee (TC)* handles the technical co-operation programme which is designed to help governments implement the technical measures adopted by the organization.
- *The Legal Committee* is responsible for considering any legal matters within the scope of the organization.
- *The Facilitation Committee* is concerned with easing the flow of international maritime traffic by reducing the formalities and simplifying the documentation required of ships when entering or leaving ports or terminals.

TABLE 12.5 Major IMO conventions relating to maritime safety and pollution prevention for merchant shipping, as at March 1997

No.	*Instrument*	*Date of entry into force*
1	SOLAS: International Convention for the Safety of Life at Sea, 1974* as amended, and its Protocols (1978, 1988)	25 May 1980
2	SAR: International Convention on Maritime Search and Rescue, 1979	22 June 1985
3	INTERVENTION: International Convention relating to Intervention on the High Seas in Cases of Oil Pollution Casualties, 1969, and its Protocol (1973)	6 May 1975
4	MARPOL: International Convention for the Prevention of Pollution from Ships, 1973, and its Protocol (1978) Annex I (2 Oct. 1983); Annex II (6 April 1987) Annex III (1 July 1992); IV; Annex V (31 Dec. 1988)	2 October 1983
5	OPRC: International Convention on Oil Pollution Preparedness, Response and Co-operation, 1990	13 May 1995
6	LC: Convention on the Prevention of Marine Pollution by Dumping of Wastes and Other Matter, 1972 as amended, and its Protocol (1996)	30 August 1975
7	COLREG: Convention on the International Regulations for Preventing Collisions at Sea, 1972, as amended	15 July 1977
8	FAL: Convention on Facilitation of International Maritime Traffic, 1965, as amended	5 March 1967
9	STCW: International Convention on Standards of Training, Certification and Watchkeeping for Seafarers, 1978, as amended	28 April 1984
10	SUA: Convention for the Suppression of Unlawful Acts against the Safety of Maritime Navigation, 1988, and its Protocol (1988)	1 March 1992
11	LL: International Convention on Load Lines, 1966, as amended and its Protocol (1988)	21 July 1968
12	TONNAGE: International Convention on Tonnage Measurement of Ships, 1969	18 July 1982
13	CSC: International Convention for Safe Containers, 1972 as amended	6 September 1977
14	SALVAGE: International Convention on Salvage, 1989	14 July 1996

Source: International Maritime Organization (London)

To support these committees IMO has a secretariat of nearly 300 civil servants located in London. Although in the early days the emphasis was on drafting conventions, since the early 1980s the focus has changed. By that date IMO had developed a comprehensive series of measures covering safety, pollution prevention, liability and compensation. It was recognized that legislation is of little value unless it is enforced so, in 1981, the Assembly adopted resolution A500(XII) which redirected activity towards the effective implementation of the conventions. This resolution was reaffirmed for the 1990s and 'implementation' has become the major objective of IMO.[16] To promote the task the MSC established the sub-committee on Flag State implementation.

The coverage of the conventions are briefly described in the following paragraphs.

The safety of life at sea convention (solas)

The first conference organized by IMO in 1960 adopted the International Convention for the Safety of Life at Sea, 1960, which came into force in 1965 and covered a wide range of measures designed to improve the safety of shipping. The provisions of the convention cover: the design and stability of passenger and cargo ships; machinery and electrical installations; fire protection; life-saving appliances; radio communications; navigational safety; and the carriage of dangerous goods. SOLAS was updated in 1974 and now incorporates an amendment procedure whereby the convention can be updated to take account of changes in the shipping environment without the major procedure of calling a conference. The 1974 SOLAS Convention entered into force on 25 May 1980 and at 31 December 1996 had been ratified by 132 states. A protocol relating to the Convention in 1978 entered into force on 1 May 1981.

With the growing recognition that loss of life at sea and environmental pollution are influenced by the way companies manage their fleets, in the 1990s IMO took steps to regulate the standards of management in the shipping industry. At the SOLAS Conference held in May 1994, the International Safety Management (ISM) Code was formally incorporated in chapter IX of the SOLAS Regulations. The Code requires shipping companies to develop, implement and maintain a Safety Management System (SMS) which includes:

1 A company safety and environmental protection policy.
2 Written procedures to ensure safe operation of ships and protection of the environment.
3 Defined levels of authority and lines of communication between, and among, shore and shipboard personnel.
4 Procedures for reporting accidents and non-conformities (i.e. errors which occur).
5 Procedures to prepare for and respond to emergency situations.
6 Procedures for internal audits.

The ISM Code becomes mandatory for passenger ships and cargo ships over 500 gross tons on 1 July 1998, by which time 30,000 ships and 7,000 shipping companies are required to comply. In the past safety regulations have tended to focus on the physical rather than the managerial aspects of the shipping business, so the ISM Code represents a new direction in maritime regulation. Inevitably it raises many new problems over implementation and policing of such a complex system.

Collision avoidance at sea

One of the most common causes of accidents at sea is collisions. Measures to prevent these occurring were included in an Annex to the 1960 Safety of Life at Sea Convention, but in 1972 IMO adopted the Convention on the International Regulations for Preventing Collisions at Sea, 1972. Included in this convention were regulations to introduce traffic separation schemes in congested parts of the world. By 31 December 1996 the convention, which was amended in 1981, had been ratified by 128 states. These 'rules of the road' have substantially reduced the number of collisions between ships[17].

Ships' load lines

The problem of dangerously overloading ships encountered in the nineteenth century was referred to earlier in the chapter. In 1930 an International Convention on Load Lines was adopted, setting out standard load lines for different types of vessels under different conditions. A new updated convention was adopted in 1966. The International Convention on Load Lines, 1966 came into force in 1968 and by the end of 1996 had been ratified by 139 states.

Convention on tonnage measurement of ships, 1969

Although this might seem an obscure subject for an international convention, it is one of great interest to shipowners because ports, canals and other organizations fix their charges on the basis of the ship's tonnage. This created an incentive to manipulate the design of ships in such a way as to reduce the ship's tonnage while still allowing it to carry the same amount of cargo. Occasionally this was at the expense of the vessel's stability and safety.

In 1969 the first International Convention on Tonnage Measurement was adopted. It proved to be so complex and so controversial that it required twenty-five states with not less than 65 per cent of the world's gross merchant tonnage to ratify it before it became law. The required number of acceptances was not achieved until 1980 and the Convention came into force in 1982. The convention establishes new procedures for computing the gross and net tonnages of a vessel. At the end of 1996 116 states had ratified it.

Convention on standards of training, certification and watchkeeping for seafarers (STCW), 1978

The aim of this convention was to introduce internationally acceptable minimum standards for the training and certification of officers and crew members. It came into force in 1984 and by the end of 1996 had been ratified by 120 states. Amendments in 1995 sought to complement the ISM Code initiative by establishing verifiable standards, structured training, and shipboard familiarization.

Convention for the prevention of pollution from ships (MARPOL)

With the development of bulk shipping and the carriage of very large quantities of toxic materials by sea, marine pollution has increasingly become the subject of international regulations. The process of developing legislation started with a conference held in London in 1952, and this led to the 1954 Convention for the Prevention of Pollution of the Sea by Oil (OILPOL). The problem addressed by the convention was that, when oil tankers carry ballast water in their cargo tanks that they then discharge to reload cargo, it inevitably contains a certain amount of crude oil, which pollutes the sea. The convention established 'prohibited zones' extending at least 50 miles from the nearest land. These regulations were progressively updated during the next 20 years.

As the pressure on the marine environment increased during the 1960s, the need was seen for a more broadly based convention on marine pollution, and in 1973 the International Convention for the Prevention of Pollution from Ships (MARPOL) was adopted. This convention deals with all forms of marine pollution except the disposal of land-generated waste. It covers such matters as: the definition of violation; certificates and special rules on the inspection of ships; enforcement; and reports on incidents involving harmful substances. For example, tankers must be fitted with oil discharge and monitoring equipment, and they must have slop tanks. New oil tankers of over 70,000 dwt must be provided with segregated ballast tanks of sufficient capacity to enable them to operate on ballast voyages without using oil tanks for water ballast except in very severe weather conditions. At the next international conference on tanker safety and pollution prevention in 1978 additional measures were added in the form of a protocol to the 1973 convention. The lower limit for tankers to be fitted with segregated ballast tanks was reduced from 70,000 dwt to 20,000 dwt and existing tankers were required to fit crude oil washing equipment.

In the early 1990s attention turned to measures to reduce the spillage of oil in the event of a tanker collision or grounding. Annex I to MARPOL (73/78) included two regulations, adopted on 1 July 1992, concerning the construction standards for new tankers (Regulation 13F) and upgrading the safety standards of existing tankers (Regulation 13G).

Regulation 13F deals with the design of new ships. Tankers ordered after 6 July 1993 are required to have a double hull or an equivalent, though unspecified, design. Attention is given to the precise design of the double hull, particularly the requirement that vessels over 30,000 dwt must have a two-metre space between the cargo tanks and the hull. Regulation

13G was even more controversial because it deals with existing ships. As adopted, Regulation 13G creates two age 'hurdles' for tankers. At 25 years tankers must allocate 30 per cent of the side or the bottom area of the vessel to cargo-free tanks. This is a defensive measure against oil spills. At 30 years of age all tankers must comply with Regulation 13F and fit a double hull.

The international convention for the prevention of pollution from ships as modified by the Protocol of 1978 relating thereto has been ratified by 97 states.

12.8 The International Labour Organization

The ILO is one of the oldest inter-governmental agencies now operating under the United Nations. It was originally set up in 1919. Its principal interest is in maritime labour problems and in this context it has been involved in developing a broad range of conventions dealing with working conditions on board ocean-going ships. These include provisions on manning, hours of work, pensions, vacation, sick pay and minimum wages. Since crewing costs account for a high proportion of total ship operating costs, the work of the ILO is of considerable importance in ship operating economics.

The terms and conditions of employment for seafarers have a direct impact upon ship operating economics. Since the 1920s the regulatory framework within which shipowners must operate has steadily expanded. Between 1920 and 1981 a total of thirty-two maritime labour conventions concerning seafarers were adopted, in addition to twenty-five maritime labour recommendations. A list of the conventions is shown in Table 12.6 along with the number of ratifications. The coverage of the conventions is briefly described in the following paragraphs.

Convention concerning minimum standards in merchant ships (1976)

This important convention, which came into force in November 1981, requires countries that ratify it to have laws or regulations laying down, for ships registered in their territory:

1 Safety standards including standards of competency, hours of work and manning, so as to ensure safety of life on board ship.
2 Social security measures.
3 Shipboard conditions of employment and shipboard living arrangements.

These laws and regulations must broadly conform to the standards set out in other ILO conventions. Countries that ratify the convention are also required: to set up the necessary machinery to ensure that the national laws or regulations dealing with these topics are adequately enforced; to ensure that seafarers are properly qualified or trained; to verify by inspection that ships comply with the international labour conventions that it has ratified; and to hold an official enquiry into any serious marine casualty involving ships registered in its territories. This convention has been ratified by most of the major flags, including Norway, France, West Germany, Greece, Italy, Liberia, Spain and the United Kingdom.

TABLE 12.6 Major ILO conventions relating to working and living conditions at sea

No.	*Instrument*	*No. Ratifications at 26 December 1993*
7	Minimum Age (Sea), 1920	50
8	Unemployment Indemnity Shipwreck, 1920	57
9	Placing of Seamen, 1920	37
15	Minimum Age (Trimmers and Stokers), 1921	67
16	Medical Examination of Young Persons (Sea), 1921	76
22	Seamen's Articles of Agreement, 1926	56
23	Repatriation of Seamen, 1926	43
53	Officers' Competency Certificates, 1936	32
54**	Holidays with Pay (Sea), 1936	6
55	Shipowners' Liability (Sick and Injured Seamen), 1936	16
56**	Sickness Insurance (Sea), 1936	18
57**	Hours of Work and Manning (Sea), 1936	4
58	Minimum Age (Sea) (Revised), 1936	50
68	Food and Catering (Ships' Crews), 1946	22
69	Certification of Ships' Cooks, 1946	34
70**	Social Security (Seafarers), 1946	7
71	Seafarers' Pensions, 1946	13
72**	Paid Vacations (Seafarers), 1946	5
73	Medical Examinations (Seafarers), 1946	40
74	Certification of Able Seamen, 1946	26
75**	Accommodation of Crews Convention, 1946	5
76**	Wages, Hours of Work and Manning (Sea), 1946	1
91†	Paid Vacations (Seafarers) (Revised), 1949	23
92	Accommodation of Crews (Revised), 1949	39
93**	Wages, Hours of Work and Manning (Sea) (Revised), 1949	6
108	Seafarers' Identity Documents, 1958	52
109**	Wages, Hours of Work and Manning (Sea) (Revised), 1958	15
133*	Crew Accommodation on Board Ship (Supplementary Provisions), 1970	25
134	Prevention of Occupational Accidents to Seafarers, 1970	26
145	Continuity of Employment (Seafarers), 1976	17
146	Seafarers Annual Leave with Pay, 1976	12
147	Merchant Shipping (Minimum Standards), 1976, and its Protocol (1996)	29
163	Seafarers' Welfare at Sea and in Port, 1987	10
164	Health Protection and Medical Care of Seafarers, 1987	6
165	Social Security for Seafarers (Revised), 1987	2
166	Repatriation of Seafarers (Revised),1987	4
178*	Labour Inspection (Seafarers), 1996	–
179*	Recruitment and Placement of Seafarers, 1996	–
180*	Seafarers' Hours of Work and the Manning of Ships, 1996	–
	All workers including seafarers:	
87	Freedom of Association and Protection of the Right to Organize, 1948	
98	Right to Organize and Collective Bargaining, 1949	
130	Medical Care and Sickness Benefits, 1969	
138	Minimum Age, 1973	

Source: International Labour Office, *Chart of Ratifications of International Labour Conventions* (Geneva, 1993).

* Conventions that have not yet received the required number of ratifications for entry into force.

** Conventions which did not receive the requisite number of ratifications.

† Conventions which are closed to ratification.

General conditions of employment

There are four conventions under this heading: Wages, Hours of Work and Manning (Sea); Paid Vacations (Seafarers), 1949; Repatriation of Seamen, 1926; and Seafarers Annual Leave with Pay, 1976. These controversial conventions deal with such key issues as minimum wage rates, hours of work on board ship, the circumstances under which seamen are entitled to repatriation expenses and the minimum entitlement to annual leave. The Convention on Wages, Hours of Work and Manning has not received sufficient ratifications to come into force.

Safety, health and welfare

The three principal conventions under this heading are: Food and Catering (Ships' Crews), 1946; Crew Accommodation on Board Ship (Supplementary Provisions), 1970; and the Prevention of Occupational Accidents to Seafarers, 1970. The first deals with regulations for ensuring that there are adequate catering facilities on board ship and that sufficient supplies of food and water are made available. The convention on crew accommodation (not in force) sets out minimum standards for sleeping accommodation, mess rooms and the provision of services, lighting and recreation facilities. In the same vein, the convention on the prevention of accidents requires minimum safety standards for the ship, its equipment and machinery, backed up by procedures for inspection, enforcement and the collection of statistics about accidents.

Conditions for admission to employment

Under this heading there are five conventions dealing with the minimum age for employment on board a ship (15 years) and the requirement for employees to produce a medical certificate attesting to their fitness for work.

Certificates of competency

The Officers' Competency Certificates Convention, 1936, requires masters, navigating officers, chief engineers and engineering officers to hold a certificate of competency. The terms on which these certificates may be awarded are also specified. The Certification of Ships' Cooks Convention, 1946, requires the cook to hold a certificate indicating that he has passed a practical test in the preparation of meals. A third convention deals with the qualifications required by able seamen (1946).

The extent to which conventions have been ratified varies widely between countries. For example, France, Norway, Italy and Spain have all ratified more than twenty ILO conventions, whereas the USA has ratified only four and Cyprus only two.

12.9 UNCTAD conventions

The UN Conference on Trade and Development (UNCTAD) was established in 1964. The Committee on Shipping is one of five standing committees of the Conference; it has a professional staff. Since the mid-1960s it has been particularly involved with the maritime interests of developing countries. The best known of its conventions is the Code of Conduct for Liner Conferences.

During the 1960s the newly independent developing countries faced various difficulties in establishing liner shipping operations. The struggle to develop an international convention confirming their right to participate in the transportation of their own trade became one of the major political issues of the 1960s and 1970s.

The issue was raised at the first UNCTAD conference in Geneva in 1964 and the consultation debate was further developed at the second UNCTAD conference in New Delhi in 1966. By 1972, when the third UNCTAD conference met at Santiago de Chile, a draft Code of Conduct for the Liner Conference System was issued to delegates and in the ensuing debate obtained almost total support from the Group of 77, though it met with strong opposition from many of the developed countries.

The vote was carried, the draft convention was approved and the UN General Assembly requested the Secretary General of the United Nations to convene, under the auspices of UNCTAD, a conference of plenipotentiaries[18] to consider and adopt a convention on a code of conduct for liner conferences. The conference was held in two parts in late 1973 and early 1974, and the Convention on a Code of Conduct for Liner Conferences was adopted by a vote of 72 to 7, with 5 abstentions. Details of the convention can be found on p. 350.

The convention was opened for signature in New York from 1 July 1974 to 30 June 1975 and was to enter into force six months after the date on which not less than twenty-four states with a combined tonnage of at least 25 per cent of the world's general cargo fleet had become contracting parties to it.[19] These criteria were met after the ratification of the convention by the Federal Republic of Germany and the Netherlands as 57th and 58th contracting parties, altogether owning 28.7 per cent of the relevant tonnage, on 6 April 1983.[20] Seventeen problems were encountered by the EEC countries in ratifying this convention because in restricting competition, it was held to be contrary to the Treaty of Rome.

Eventually a compromise was worked out known as the 'Brussels Package', whereby EEC countries ratified the convention on the understanding that there would be free competition in trade between EEC countries. In total this highly controversial convention had taken almost 20 years.

The UNCTAD Convention on Conditions for Registration for Ships

In the early 1980s UNCTAD convened a conference on conditions for registration of ships, attended by representatives from 109 states. Like other UNCTAD conventions, this appears to have been motivated by the Group of 77 with the aim of widening their maritime control. The final convention was agreed on 7 February 1986. Article I of the convention defines the objective as being to strengthen the genuine link between a state and ships flying its flag, in order to give more effective control of the identification and accountability of shipowners and operators especially in administrative, technical, economic and social matters.[21]

The convention defines the responsibility of the flag state to set up an adequate national maritime administration to ensure that ships flying its flag comply with the law (Article 5) and to ensure that the owner of the ship can be identified and held accountable where necessary (Article 6). The convention also specifies the information about the ship and its owner that should be entered in the state's national ship register (Article 11). Although it provides a formal statement of the main issues concerning the registration of ships, it is not generally regarded as having introduced any major changes in ship registration.

12.10 The regulatory role of the coastal states

Now we come to the 'coastal states' and the part they play in regulating merchant shipping. As the wider use of flags of convenience has diluted the supervisory role of the flag states, the coastal states have played an increasingly important part in the regulatory system. The 1982 Law of the Sea Convention permits coastal states to legislate for the 'good conduct' of ships in their territorial seas, but otherwise not to interfere with them. The Convention lists eight specific areas in which legislation is permitted. The main ones are safety of navigation; protection of navigational aids; preservation of the environment and prevention, reduction and control of pollution; and the prevention of infringement of customs and sanitary laws, etc. From an economic viewpoint the two areas in which legislation has been most significant are safety and pollution.

Port state control

As far as safety is concerned, the main vehicle is *port state control.* As we have already seen the safety of ships is governed by the law of the flag state and the Classification Societies. Article 21 of Law of the Sea specifically protects shipowners from unilateral regulations by coastal states concerning the design and construction of ships. It states that the legislation of coastal states 'shall not apply to the design, construction, manning or equipment of foreign ships, unless they are giving effect to generally accepted international rules or standards'. This is intended to prevent a 'nightmare scenario' in which ships are subject to different construction standards in different territorial waters. However, it does endorse the coastal state's right to enforce international regulations in its territorial waters. This right has given rise to the port state control movement under which some coastal states inspect ships entering their ports and detain any which do not meet international standards for construction, maintenance and safety equipment.

The US Oil Pollution Act 1990

Pollution is the other area in which coastal states are very active. One of the most forthright initiatives in recent years is the US Oil Pollution Act (1990). This legislation was formulated in response to the public concern caused by the grounding of the *Exxon Valdez* in the Prince William Sound, Alaska in March 1989.

The Act applies to oil spills in US inland waters; up to three miles off shore; and the 'exclusive economic zone' up to 200 miles to sea from the shoreline. The LOOP Terminal is not included. It lays down wide ranging regulations for the handling of oil spills. The 'responsible party' is defined as the owner or operator of the tanker. The responsible party is required to pay for the clean-up, up to a liability limit of $10 million. or $1,200 per gross ton, whichever is the greater. However, if there has been gross negligence these limits do not apply.

In addition to making shipowners responsible for the cost of pollution incidents, the Act laid down specific requirements for ships operating in US waters. These include requirements that ships should carry a certificate of financial responsibility, demonstrating that they have sufficient financial means to pay a claim. There is also a requirement that vessels ordered after 30 June 1990 or delivered after 1 January 1994 should have double-hulls and a schedule for phasing out single hull tankers by 2010. The coastguard is required to evaluate the manning standards of foreign vessels and to ensure that these are at least equivalent to US law. All tankers are required to carry a contingency plan for responding to an oil spill.

This legislation, particularly the requirement for double-hulled tankers, caused great controversy. However, the effect was to focus the attention of the shipping community far more rigorously on the risks associated with oil pollution. In particular, for the first time, shipowners were faced with the possibility of unlimited liability for the cost of any oil spill they are involved in. The high cost of cleaning up after the *Exxon Valdez* spill put a financial dimension on the possible scale of this problem.

12.11 Summary

In this chapter we have moved outside the conventional framework of market economics to examine the regulatory system that has played such a vital part in the shipping industry over the last 20 or 30 years. We started by identifying three regulatory regimes which operate in the shipping industry, the Classification Societies, the flag states and the coastal states.

The Classification Societies are the shipping industry's internal regulatory system. The mainstay of their authority is the Class Certificate which is issued when the ship is built and updated by means of regular surveys throughout the life of the ship. Without a Class Certificate a ship cannot obtain insurance and has little commercial value.

Flag states make the laws which govern the commercial, and civil activities of the merchant ship. Because different countries have different laws, the flag of registration makes a difference. Registers can be subdivided into national registers, which treat shipping companies in the same way as other national industries, and open registers (flags of convenience) such as Liberia and Panama, which are set up with the specific objective of earning revenue by offering commercially favourable terms of registration as a service to shipowners. With the increasing globalization of the maritime industry, open registers have become more prominent and half the world merchant fleet is now registered under a foreign flag, which in practice usually means a flag of convenience.

Although each nation makes its own maritime laws, there are areas where it is very advantageous if all countries have the same laws. On matters such as safe ship design, collision avoidance, load lines, pollution, tonnage measurement and certificates of competency it would be hopelessly impractical if each country had different laws. Developing a standard framework of international law which avoids this problem is achieved by means of international conventions. Maritime nations meet to discuss a draft convention, which is finally agreed. Each country then ratifies it and thereby undertakes to incorporate the terms of the convention into its own national legislation. International conventions drawn up since the mid-1960s cover a wide range of different subjects including the safety of life at sea, load lines, crew training, tonnage measurement, terms and conditions of employment of crew, oil pollution and the conduct of liner conferences. The three organizations active in developing these conventions are IMO, ILO and the Shipping Committee of UNCTAD.

Some countries do not ratify the conventions or allocate sufficient administrative resources to enforcing them, leaving 'loopholes' in the system. Shipowners registered in these countries are, in principle, able to operate outside the convention.

This brings us to the third form of regulation, the coastal state in whose waters the ship is trading. The Law of the Sea permits coastal states to pass legislation concerning the 'good conduct' of ships in its territorial waters. One important area of legislation is pollution control, notably the US Oil Pollution Act 1990. In addition there has been a recent trend towards 'port state control', whereby countries enforce safety standards on the ships using their ports.

Chapter 13

The economics of shipbuilding and scrapping

> The shipbuilding industry is characterised by an extraordinary pattern of switch-back production, moving from peak to trough and back to peak again within a decade . . . if only a more stable level of output could have been achieved, many of the problems in the industry, particularly in labour relations could have been avoided.
>
> (David Dougan, *The Shipwrights*)

13.1 Role of the merchant shipbuilding and scrapping industries

The job of the shipbuilding industry is to supply new ships, while shipbreakers are the last resort buyers of old ships when it is no longer possible to operate them profitably in the shipping market. In terms of their economic structure, the two industries are very different. Shipbuilding is a heavy engineering business, selling a large and sophisticated product built mainly in facilities located in the industrialized countries of Japan, Europe, South Korea, China and Taiwan. It requires substantial capital investment and a high level of technical expertise to design and produce a merchant ship. The ship scrapping industry, in contrast, is located mainly in the developing countries of the Indian subcontinent and is one of the world's most labour-intensive industries – in some countries ship scrapping takes place on the beach, with labour equipped with only the most primitive of hand tools and cutting equipment.

In the first part of the chapter we will examine the regional distribution of shipbuilding capacity in the 1980s and the relationship between the level of shipping and shipbuilding activity. We then consider shipbuilding market economics, looking in particular at the shipbuilding market cycle, the price mechanism and the influences on the supply of and demand for shipbuilding output. The section on shipbuilding ends with a discussion of competitiveness and the related issues of capacity measurement, the production process and international comparisons of productivity. The second part of the chapter discusses the process by which ships are scrapped, the market for scrap products and the international structure of the ship scrapping industry. Finally, in this chapter we introduce a new unit of measurement, the compensated gross ton (cgt). The cgt of a ship is derived from its gross tonnage (gt), but weighted to take account of the work content of that particular ship type – detailed definitions can be found in Appendix 2.

13.2 Regional structure of world shipbuilding

Who builds the world's merchant ships?

About thirty countries have a significant merchant shipbuilding industry (see Table 13.1). Their production fell from 27.5 m gt in 1977 to 13 m gt in 1980, then increased to 22.45 m gt in 1995. This volatility was accompanied by a re-alignment of regional shipbuilding capacity. Europe's market share fell from 41 per cent to 17 per cent, while the Far East grew from 46 per cent to 75 per cent. Japan and South Korea now dominate the industry, between them producing two-thirds of the world's ships. The other production is spread over many countries, mainly in Eastern and Western Europe. The shipbuilding output of most European countries declined during the 1980s, though only Sweden completely stopped building ships. South Korea and China both grew rapidly despite the general market problems in the shipbuilding industry.

Shipbuilding is a long cycle business. Ships take several years to deliver, and once built they remain in service for 24 or 30 years. Since ships trickle in and out of the merchant fleet at only a few per cent a year, the pace of change in shipbuilding demand is slow. Trends

TABLE 13.1 Merchant ships completed during years 1977–95

	1977	*1980*	*1985* *000 gt*	*1990*	*1995*	*% share 1995*
Europe						
Belgium	132	138	133	60	11	0
Denmark	709	208	458	408	1,003	4
France	1,107	283	200	64	254	1
Germany F.R.	1,595	376	562	874	1,120	5
German D.R.	378	346	358	In Germany F.R.		0
Greece	81	25	37	19	0	0
Irish Republic	40	1	0	0	0	0
Italy	778	248	88	392	395	2
Netherlands	240	122	180	190	205	1
Portugal	98	11	41	74	18	0
Spain	1,813	395	551	366	250	1
UK	1,020	427	172	126	126	1
Finland	361	200	213	256	317	1
Norway	567	208	122	91	147	1
Sweden	2,311	348	201	27	29	0
Total AWES	11,230	3,336	3,316	2,945	3,875	17
	41%	25%	18%	18%	17%	
Far East						
Japan	11,708	6,094	9,503	6,663	9,263	41
South Korea	562	522	2,620	3,441	6,264	28
Chinese PR	110	na	166	404	784	3
Taiwan	196	240	278	685	488	2
Singapore				49	99	0
Total Far East	12,576	6,856	12,567	11,242	16,898	74
	46%	52%	69%	70%	75%	
Eastern Europe						
Bulgaria	144	206	173	92	92	0
Poland	478	362	361	141	524	2
Romania	296	170	204	175	229	1
USSR	421	460	229	430		0
Yugoslavia	421	149	259	462		0
Russia					83	0
Ukraine					185	1
Croatia					179	1
Total	1,760	1,347	1,226	1,300	1,291	5
	6%	10%	7%	8%	6%	
Others						
Brazil	380	729	581	255	172	1
USA	1,012	555	180	23	7	0
Other countries	573	278	286	288	225	1
Total	1,965	1,562	1,047	566	404	2
	7%	12%	6%	4%	2%	
World total	27,531	13,101	18,156	16,053	22,468	98

Source: Lloyd's Register of Shipping Annual Summaries

develop over decades rather than years, and we need to step well back to see them. Nowhere is this more apparent than in the changing regional location of shipbuilding activity shown vividly in Figure 13.1. A century ago, shipbuilding was dominated by Great Britain. Gradually Continental Europe and Scandinavia squeezed Britain's share down to 40 per cent. Then in the 1950s Japan overtook Europe, achieving a market share of 50 per cent in 1969.

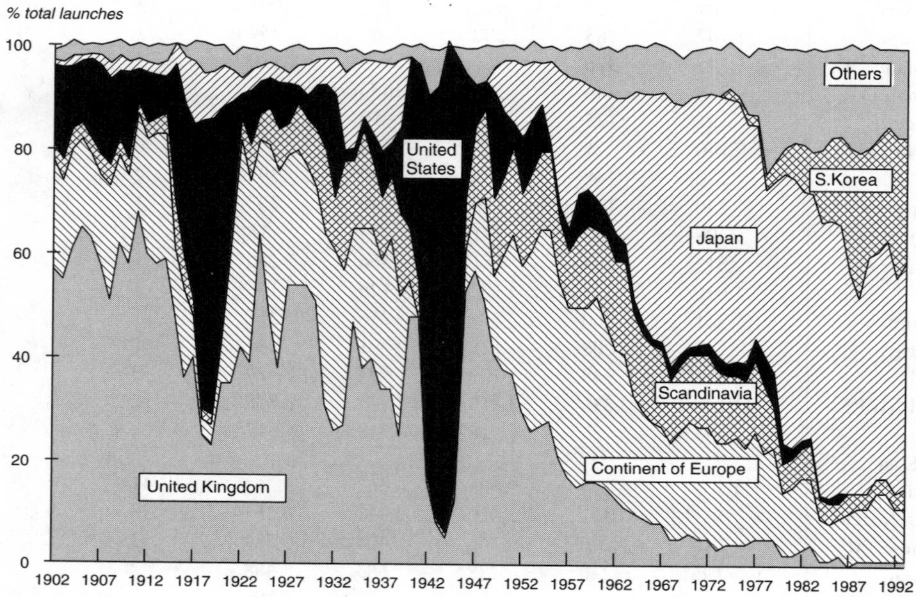

FIGURE 13.1 Shipbuilding market shares
Source: Lloyd's Register of Shipping

In the 1980s the South Korean industry grew rapidly, challenging Japan's dominant position and finally establishing the Far East as the centre of world shipbuilding. In the 1990s China was increasing in importance. Following this sequence of events we might ask what it is about shipbuilding that enables a single country to obtain the commanding position achieved by Britain, Japan, and South Korea and why the balance has changed so much over the years. To answer this question it is instructive to take a brief look at the recent history of the shipbuilding industry, and in particular the relationship between the shipping and shipbuilding industries.[1]

The decline of British shipbuilding

In 1892–4 Britain produced over 80 per cent of the world total gross tonnage and owned half the world fleet. In 1918 the Departmental Committee on Shipping and Shipbuilding commented 'there are few important industries where the predominance of British manufacture has been more marked than shipbuilding and marine engineering'.[2] Britain held this dominant place in the shipbuilding market until 1950 when, for a couple of years, it regained its 60 per cent market share, but when we examine Figure 13.2 the downward trend is apparent, as is the close correlation with the decline of the UK merchant fleet. At the beginning of the twentieth century, the UK merchant fleet had a 45 per cent market share and shipbuilding about 55 per cent.

It is not difficult to explain how British shipping achieved this dominant position. Britain controlled massive trade flows. The Empire was at its height and the shipping companies controlled major liner routes in the Atlantic and Pacific, particularly between the Dominions. In the tramp shipping market, Britain – an island nation – was the major importer of raw materials and foodstuffs such as grain, while the export trade in manufactures and coal was equally prominent. As the control of trade slipped away, so did shipping. With each world war the British Empire diminished in size, the merchant marine was weakened by wartime losses and trading partners became better able to carry their own trade.[3] By 1960 the UK fleet accounted for only 20 per cent of world tonnage and British shipbuilding for about the same proportion of world shipbuilding output. Thirty years later the market shares of both industries had fallen below 2 per cent.

One reason that has been put forward for the decline of British shipbuilding was its failure to graduate from a production process based on manual skills to the more closely integrated production technology[4] that was developed in Sweden and Japan during the twentieth century. It is, however, difficult to separate this effect from the link between the fortunes of shipping and shipbuilding. Discussing the rise of the British shipbuilding industry during the nineteenth century, Hobsbawm argues strongly for the existence of this link in the following terms:

> During the age of the traditional wooden sailing ship Britain had been a great, but by no means unchallenged producer. Indeed her weight as a shipbuilder had been due not to her technological superiority, for the French designed better ships and the USA built better ones . . . British shipbuilders benefited rather because of the vast weight of Britain as a shipping and trading power and the preference of British shippers (even after the abrogation of the Navigation Acts, which protected the industry heavily) for native ships.[5]

This link between trade, shipping and shipbuilding was crucial. In Britain a relationship existed between shipowners and shipbuilders that went beyond normal competitive ties. Many of the great British shipping lines had a longstanding association with particular shipyards, which seems to have reinforced the tradition of building at home. Even in the 1970s there were shipyards in Britain that built exclusively for a single owner. As we shall see when we look at other regions, this was not a uniquely British state of affairs. Despite the international nature of the shipbuilding market and the absence of trade barriers such as tariffs and transport costs, the concept of a home market seems to be very strongly established in the shipbuilding industry. Even in the intensely competitive world of the 1990s, shipbuilders are very dependent upon the fortunes of their home fleet.

European shipbuilding 1902–94

In mainland Europe, shipbuilding went through much the same cycle of growth and decline as the UK. No individual country achieved prominence in the shipbuilding market on a scale comparable with Japan or Great Britain, but European shipyards as a whole accounted for 20–40 per cent of shipbuilding output during the first half of the twentieth century. The position is best analysed by distinguishing the continental shipbuilders of West Germany, France, Belgium, the Netherlands, Italy and Spain from those in Scandinavia.

During the period 1902–80, the six continental shipbuilding countries maintained a market share of around 20 per cent, reaching 40 per cent in some years. This is shown in Figure 13.2c along with the market share of their shipping fleets, which was 5–10 per cent lower for most of the period after 1945. With the exception of the immediate post-war years, the correlation between shipping and shipbuilding is close. Between 1902 and 1939 the market share of continental shipbuilders averaged around 23 per cent, while their merchant fleet accounted for approximately 23 per cent of world shipping. The decline of the shipping fleet in the 1960s and 1970s is mirrored by a decline in the market share of shipbuilding – by the mid-1990s the market share of the continental yards had fallen below 10 per cent.

The experience of the Scandinavian shipbuilding industry is shown in Figure 13.2d. The main producers in this region are Denmark, Norway, Sweden and Finland. Although none of these countries has sufficient population or heavy industry to make them major participants in seaborne trade, they have a strong maritime tradition. In this sense, the Scandinavian fleets may be regarded as part of the international shipping industry, in much the same way as Greece. At the start of the period in 1902 the Scandinavian shipbuilding industry had only a 3 per cent market share, well below the 10 per cent share of the Scandinavian merchant fleet. The reason why shipbuilding capacity lagged behind the merchant fleet during this period appears to have been the difficulty that the Scandinavian shipbuilding industry had in switching from wooden shipbuilding to the more capital-intensive process of building steel ships. Petersen comments:

> In the 1870s Norway had a large number of small shipyards employing expert master carpenters and experienced workers. These men were able to build all the sailing ships Norway needed, using only simple tools and home grown timber. The building of steam ships, on the other hand, demanded the import of raw materials and the erection of large shipyards with expensive, heavy machinery, and cranes. Steamship building did not gain momentum until the 1890s.[6]

Shipbuilding output in Scandinavia remained nominal until the First World War, when the industry started a rapid growth that eventually reached a peak market share of 21 per cent in 1933. This position was maintained until the early 1970s when a decline in the market share of the Scandinavian fleet coincided with a fall in the market share of Scandinavian shipbuilding. The fall in the Scandinavian fleet may be explained partly by the transfer of registration to flags of convenience that occurred during this period; however, the decline in the shipbuilding market share both here and in continental Europe undoubtedly reflects the growing competitive strength of the Japanese industry.[7]

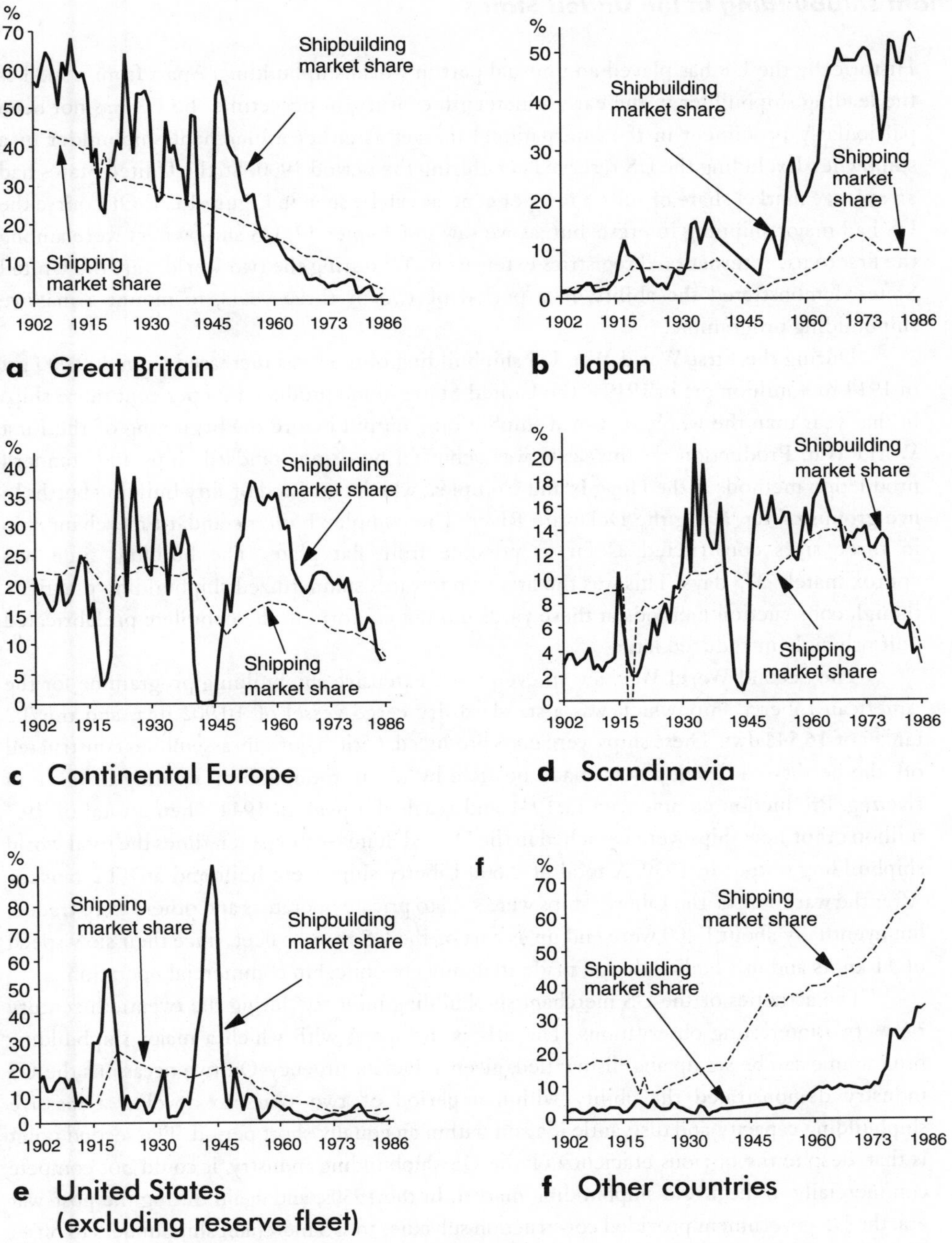

FIGURE 13.2 The link between shipping and shipbuilding market shares by region

Source: Lloyd's Register of Shipping, statistical tables

Note: The figure shows, for each region, the merchant fleet as a percentage of the world fleet, and shipbuilding output as a percentage of world shipbuilding output.

Merchant shipbuilding in the United States

Historically the US has played an unusual part in world shipbuilding. Apart from a spell as the leading shipbuilder in the early nineteenth century, in peacetime the US has not been particularly prominent in the international market as either a merchant shipbuilder or a shipowner. Excluding the US reserve fleet, during the period 1900–86 the United States had an average market share of only a few per cent, as can be seen in Figure 13.2e. Of course the US had major shipping interests but, as we saw in Chapter 12, US shipowners were among the first to use international registries extensively. Yet during the two world wars the United States demonstrated the ability, in a period of two or three years, to mount a massive shipbuilding programme.

During the First World War, US shipbuilding output was increased from 200,000 grt in 1914 to 4 million grt in 1919 – the United States alone produced 30 per cent more ships in that year than the whole of world shipbuilding output before the beginning of the First World War. Production on this scale was achieved by using standard ships and standard production methods at the Hogg Island Complex, which consisted of fifty building berths in five groups of ten along the Delaware River. The complex built a standard merchant ship in three sizes constructed as far as possible from flat plate. The building time was approximately 275 days. This was the first step towards standardized shipbuilding practices, though construction methods at these yards did not conform to the complete prefabricated unit principle introduced later.

The Second World War saw an even more extensive shipbuilding programme for the American Liberty ship, which was a standard dry cargo vessel of 10,902 dwt, and the T2 tanker of 16,543 dwt. These ships were mass produced, with major sub-assemblies constructed off the berths – a development made possible by the introduction of welding in place of riveting. Production commenced in 1941 and reached a peak in 1944 when a total of 19.3 million grt of new ships were launched in the United States – almost ten times the total world shipbuilding output in 1939. A total of 2,600 Liberty ships were built and 563 T2 tankers. After the war some of the Liberty ships were sold to private operators and others were traded, but eventually about 1,400 were laid up as part of the US reserve fleet, since their slow speed of 11 knots and full-bodied design made them uneconomical in commercial operation.

The activities of the US merchant shipbuilding industry during the twentieth century raises two interesting observations. The first is the speed with which a major shipbuilding programme can be set up and dismantled, given sufficient urgency. On two occasions the US industry demonstrated the ability within a period of two years to develop a massive shipbuilding capacity and dismantle it again within an equally short period. The second point is that, despite the obvious efficiency of the US shipbuilding industry, it could not compete commercially in the world shipbuilding market. In the 1930s, and again during the post-war era, the US government provided construction subsidies to US merchant shipbuilders to offset the difference between the construction in American and foreign yards. At different times the levels of subsidy varied from 30 per cent to 50 per cent of the cost of construction.[8] We find a similar pattern in Sweden, which was generally considered during the 1970s to have the highest productivity of any shipbuilding country, but also incurred the highest level of subsidies.

The Japanese shipbuilding

The rise of Japan as a dominant force in the world shipbuilding market provides a rather different example of the link between shipbuilding and the general level of maritime activity. Like Britain, Japan is an island nation and the growth of the economy after the Second World War made intense demands on seaborne transport. Initially the development of the Japanese shipbuilding industry drew strength from a co-ordinated shipping and shipbuilding programme. For example, Trezise and Suzuki comment:

> In the early post war period . . . the industries selected for intensive governmental attention included the merchant shipping industry. A planned shipbuilding programme for the merchant fleet was instituted during the occupation, in 1947, and is still being pursued essentially along the lines laid down at this time. Each year the government – that is to say the Ministry of Transport – in consultation with its industry advisors in Shipping and Shipbuilding Rationalisation Council – decides on the tonnage of ships to be built, by type (tankers, ore carriers, liners, and so on) and allocates production contracts and the ships among the applicant domestic shipbuilders and shipowners. The selected shipping lines receive preferential financing and in turn are subject to close government supervision.[9]

During the period 1951–72, 31.5 per cent of the total loans made by the Japan Development Bank were for marine transportation. This domestic shipbuilding programme undoubtedly contributed to the success of the Japanese shipbuilding industry, but the Japanese merchant marine never achieved the degree of market domination that the British merchant fleet had established in the nineteenth and early twentieth century. Figure 13.2b shows that, although the market share of the Japanese fleet increased from 1 per cent in 1948 to 10 per cent in 1984, this fell well short of the 50 per cent market share achieved by Japanese shipbuilders.

There are two explanations for this. One is that the Japanese flag was uncompetitive and many of the ships commissioned for the carriage of Japanese trade were purchased by international owners in Hong Kong or Greece and registered under flags of convenience. In 1995 73 per cent of the Japanese-owned fleet was operating under foreign flags (see Figure 12.4), so the shipping market share in Figure 13.2b is misleadingly low. The second is that the Japanese shipbuilding industry became highly competitive and obtained a high penetration of the export market, particularly the market for large tankers sold to independent owners.

The strategy followed by the Japanese in developing their shipbuilding industry was similar to their approach in other major industries – building large modern shipyards and using the domestic market as the volume baseload for selling highly competitively into the export market. There was heavy investment in new facilities, particularly in large modern shipyards with building docks capable of mass producing VLCCs and large bulk carriers at a rate of five or six vessels per annum. Some shipyards were built in the main industrial centres – for example the Mitsui Shipyard at Chiba, the IHI Shipyard at Yokohama and the Kawasaki Shipyard at Sakaide; others were in remote areas – for example the Mitsubishi Shipyard at Koyagi.

The rise of South Korean shipbuilding

The entry of South Korea into the world shipbuilding market was, like that of its near-neighbour Japan, the result of a carefully planned industrial programme. In the early 1970s, a major investment programme was planned, starting with the construction of the world's largest shipbuilding facility by Hyundai at Ulsan, with a 380 metre dry dock capable of taking vessels up to 400,000 dwt. Later in the decade a second major facility was built by Daewoo, with a 530 metre dry dock capable of taking vessels up to 1 m.dwt. This started production in the early 1980s. Two other South Korean industrial groups, Samsung and Halla Engineering built new shipbuilding facilities and by the mid-1990s South Korea had a 25 per cent market share and four out of the world's five largest shipyards.[10]

Perhaps the most interesting aspect of the expansion of South Korean shipbuilding capacity is that the growth has been far more heavily dependent upon the export market than was the case for either Britain or Japan, both of which based their initial expansion programmes upon the domestic fleet. Whilst South Korea has a rapidly growing economy, this remains very much smaller than the Japanese or European in terms of trade volume. The success of Korean shipbuilding almost certainly reflects the growing internationalization of the bulk shipping industry where, with the development of international registries and multinational companies, the link between ship, shipowner and national interest is increasingly tenuous.

Taiwan, China and other countries

It seems to be a feature of the shipuilding industry that there are always new entrants preparing to challenge the market leaders. Taiwan and the People's Republic of China, with a combined output in excess of 1.3 million gt in 1995, had both grown in importance during the previous decade. Eastern Europe is gradually becoming established in the world shipbuilding market. There are a few other countries in the shipbuilding market. In 1995 they accounted for 2 per cent of world output.

13.3 Shipbuilding market cycles

The changes in the regional structure of the shipbuilding market produced long periods of intense competition as each new entrant, Continental Europe, Scandinavia, Japan and then South Korea, fought for market share. This intense competition sets the scene for a harsh commercial climate, which is intensified by the cyclical nature of shipbuilding demand. Over the last century it is possible to identify eleven separate cycles, as shown in Table 13.2. The course of these cycles is charted in Figure 13.3. The average reduction in output from peak to trough was around 50 per cent and the maximum peacetime reduction was 84 per cent during the recession of the early 1930s. Superimposed on to these short term cycles were four longer cycles, or phases.

The first period lasted from 1886 to 1919 and was a period of 'cyclical growth', with output growing progressively at each peak, interspersed with periods of recession. As we saw in chapter 2, this was a period of very rapid technical change as steel hulled steamships of rapidly increasing size and efficiency replaced sail. The shipbuilding cycles seem to have followed the world trade cycles and the level of output responded sharply to each change in the market. During this period the cycles drove investment by drawing in a flood of new ships with the latest technology during the market peaks and then driving out the old and technically obsolete vessels during the lengthy troughs. A crude but effective way of adopting new technology, while deriving the maximum economic value from the existing stock of ships.

TABLE 13.2 Shipbuilding cycles 1902–81

Cyclical peak	*Output '000 grt*	*Duration peak (years) to peak*	*% Reduction peak to trough*
1901	2,617	5	24
1906	2,919	7	44
1913	3,332	6	64
1919	7,144	6	78
1924	2,193	5	24
1930	2,889	6	84
1938	3,023	8	42
1943	13,880	5	85
1958	9,269	15	10
1975	35,897	17	60
1981	16,900	16+	38
Average		8 Years	50

Source: Compiled from Lloyd's Register Statistocs

During the second period from 1920 to 1942 the industry faced acute and persistent market problems dominated by the 1931 depression. At the outset there was a massive shipbuilding capacity, which had been developed to meet wartime shipping requirements – in 1919 the industry was capable of producing 7 m. grt of ships a year, three times the underlying level of demand. In addition, several European governments had been convinced by the war of the importance of having a domestic maritime

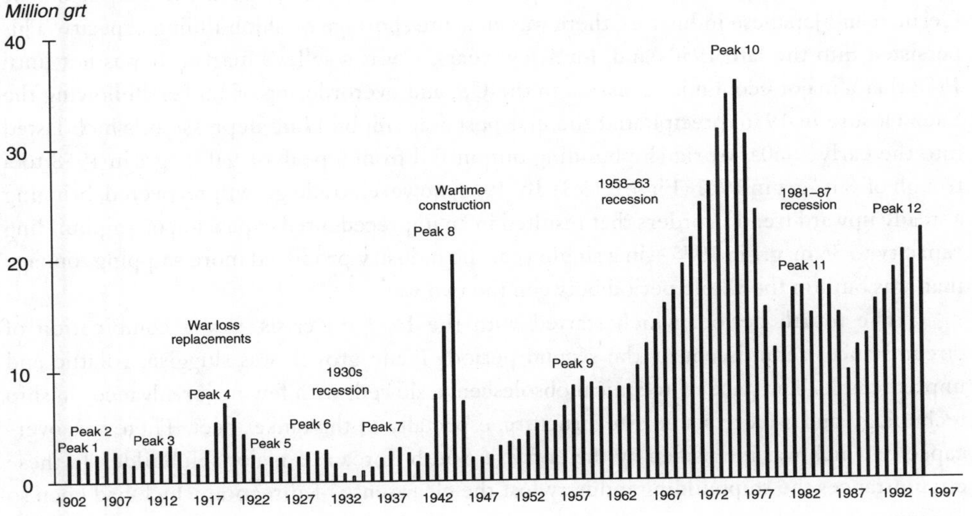

FIGURE 13.3 World shipbuilding launches 1902–95
Source: Lloyd's Register of Shipping

capability and devoted public funds to building up their industries. When combined with volatile trade, these supply side conditions set the scene for two decades of almost continuous overcapacity, interspersed by periods of moderate market improvement. Contemporary press statements illustrate the mood of the period. For example:

- In the early part of 1924 it was generally believed that depression in the shipbuilding industry had touched its lowest point. It could not be imagined that the signs of revival would be so short lived . . . the immediate outlook is now exceedingly grave.[11]
- The year 1926 was one of great depression in shipbuilding.[12]
- As far as shipbuilding is concerned 1930 has been a most trying time . . . only one berth in four occupied.[13]
- The year 1935 in the shipbuilding industry may be regarded as a year of marking time with only one-third of the greatly reduced capacity being utilised.[14]

In Britain, which dominated the shipbuilding market at that time, shipbuilding employment fell steadily from 300,000 in 1920 to 60,000 in 1931.[15] Unlike the pre-war period, this was not simply cyclical unemployment that was soon absorbed by the next boom; it was a steady downward trend. The scarcity of orders created intense international competition, indicated by 'incidents' such as a Furness Withy order placed in Germany in 1926 at a price 24 per cent below the lowest British price with marginal overhead recovery.

The third period, covering the two decades after the Second World War, was one of exceptional growth. Although the industry started with output of 7 m. grt (more than six times the pre-war level of demand – Figure 13.3), three-quarters was built under the US wartime construction programme, and at the end of the war the US effectively withdrew from the world shipbuilding market. Since war damage had reduced the output of the German and Japanese industries, there was an acute shortage of shipbuilding capacity. This persisted into the late 1950s and, for a few years, it was a seller's market. It was not until 1958 that a major economic recession in the US, and overordering of tankers following the Suez closure in 1956, precipitated the first post-war shipbuilding depression, which lasted into the early 1960s. World shipbuilding output fell from a peak of 9.0 m. grt in 1958 to a trough of 8 m. grt in 1961 (Figure 13.3). By 1963, however, trade growth recovered, bringing a steady upward trend in orders that resulted in an unprecedented expansion of shipbuilding capacity to 36 m. grt in 1975 – in a single year the industry produced more shipping tonnage than was built in the whole period between the two wars.

The fourth period, which started with the 1973 oil crisis, saw a combination of circumstances reminiscent of the second period. Trade growth was sluggish, volatile and unpredictable. The pace of technical obsolescence slowed, with few major advances in ship technology and a more stable size structure, especially in the tanker fleet. There was over-capacity which was intensified by the entry of South Korea as a major shipbuilder. In these circumstances the shipbuilding industry lost the clear sense of direction which had been so apparent during the previous period.

The period started in 1975 with peak world shipbuilding output of 36 m. grt, representing 50–100 per cent over-capacity. After two decades of continuous growth, seaborne trade first stagnated and then declined abruptly, particularly in the oil sector, with the result that the demand for new ships fell sharply from the pre-1975 level. This already difficult situation in the shipbuilding market was further aggravated by the entry of South Korea with a bid for a major share of the world market, with the result that there was a three-way battle between Japan, Korea and Western Europe for a share of the diminishing volume of orders.

During the late 1970s there was a major cutback in shipbuilding capacity, many shipyards were closed and output fell by 60 per cent to 14 m. grt in 1979. The time taken for this decline to occur reflects the large orderbook held by the world shipbuilding industry in 1974. A recovery in the world economy during the late 1970s brought renewed trade growth which, combined with the sizeable reduction in world shipbuilding capacity, was sufficient to produce a brief recovery in the world shipbuilding market. Laid-up tonnage fell to a minimal level, and during 1980–1 the world shipbuilding industry enjoyed something approaching a newbuilding boom. However, following the market peak of 1980–1, there was a sharp decline in the fortunes of the shipbuilding industry, fuelled primarily by the collapse of world seaborne trade. During the period 1979–83 the volume of seaborne trade fell from 3.8 bt to 3.3 bt, a reduction of 13 per cent. Severe downward pressure on shipbuilding prices and new ordering drove shipyard output in 1988 to a trough of 10.8 million gross tons, the lowest since 1962. Employment in the world shipbuilding industry halved[16] and many of the marginal shipyards were closed.

Finally, the 1990s saw renewed growth as the replacement of the fleet built during the 1970s boom fell due. By the mid-1990s the volume of output had doubled from the 1988 trough. South Korea had consolidated its position as a major shipbuilder, and Taiwan, China and East European shipyards were becoming established in the international market-place, opening the way for the next phase of competition.

In a century of shipbuilding it is difficult to find many 'normal' years. The combination of shipping market cycles and a constantly changing competitive structure, ensures that this business, even more than the shipping business, is in a constant state of change.

13.4 The economic principles

Causes of the shipbuilding cycle

It is not too difficult to understand why the shipbuilding market is so volatile when we examine the supply and demand mechanism that drives it. This is best illustrated with a simple example. If the active merchant fleet is 700 m.dwt, as it was in the mid-1990s, and seaborne trade grows by 5 per cent per annum, this will generate demand for an additional 30 m.dwt of new ships each year. If, in addition, 20 m.dwt of ships are scrapped each year, the total requirement for new vessels will be 50 m.dwt each year.

If, however, instead of growing by 5 per cent seaborne trade remains at the same level for 2 years running then there will be no need to expand the fleet and demand in each year will be only 20 m.dwt. Taking the argument a step further, if seaborne trade falls by 5 per cent there will not be any demand for new ships. In short, a small change in the growth rate of seaborne trade has a greatly magnified effect on shipbuilding demand. Falls of 5 or 10 per cent in seaborne trade are by no means unusual – much larger swings were experienced, for example, in 1975 and in the early 1980s.

Another problem with the structure of the shipbuilding market is the protracted delay before supply responds to a change in demand. Since it often takes more than a year to build a merchant ship, and in some cases two or three years, to keep supply and demand in balance shipowners need to predict the change in demand two or three years ahead, a skill that has been manifestly lacking. As we saw in our discussion of market cycles in chapter 2, the usual pattern is for ordering to build up to a peak at the top of the cycle, and for ships to be delivered two years later when the market is already declining, creating a greater surplus of shipping capacity and reducing the level of new orders.

The supply-side problem is further intensified by various 'rigidities' that prevent the supply of shipbuilding capacity responding quickly to a downswing in demand. Undoubtedly the most important rigidity derives from government policy to maintain employment. Many shipyards, particularly in Western Europe and Japan, are located in areas with few alternative employment opportunities, so that politicians often intervene to prevent closures. As a result, it now takes longer for shipbuilding capacity to respond to a major fall in demand than was the case in the 1930s.

This reasoning suggests that shipbuilding cycles are close relatives of the shipping cycles discussed at length in chapter 2, but with special features due to the industry's different economic structure. Volk (1994), in a lengthy study of shipbuilding cycles, takes much the same view, concluding that:

> Shipbuilding is characterised by heavy fluctuations of demand over the short-term and by high inertia of supply. This fact leads to brief phases of prosperity and long phases of depression.[17]

In one sense, this is all there is to be said. Until the demand for ships becomes regular or shipyards find a way of disappearing when they are not needed, the shipbuilding industry must live with cycles. From an economic perspective, however, this is just the beginning of our study. In the previous section we saw that over the course of the last century this simple mechanism has produced radically different commercial environments. Applied economists in shipping or shipbuilding who understand the underlying relationships can recognize the way a particular market is likely to develop. This is what we will focus on in the remainder of this chapter, starting with the general economic relationships followed by a discussion of the microeconomic aspects of shipyard production.

How shipbuilding prices are determined

Shipbuilding cycles are controlled by the price mechanism, and this is where we must start. Shipbuilding is one of the world's most open and competitive markets. Shipowners invariably take several quotations before ordering a ship and there are not the usual trade barriers in

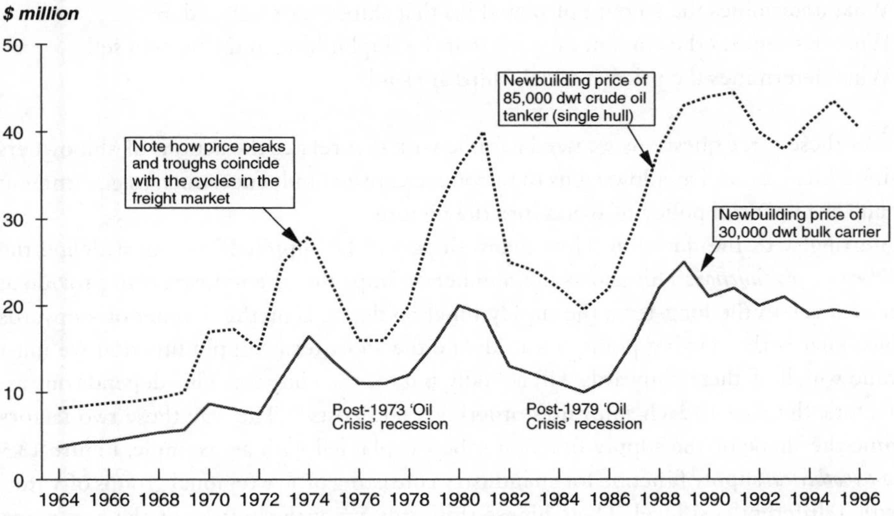

FIGURE 13.4 World shipbuilding prices 1964–96
Source: Clarkson Research Studies

the form of distance, transport costs and tariffs to provide shipbuilders with a protected home market. Prices swing violently upwards or downwards depending upon the number of shipyards competing for a given volume of orders.

This point can be illustrated by following the development of the contract price for a 30,000 dwt bulk carrier and an 85,000 dwt tanker during the thirty years 1964–96 (Figure 13.4). If we start in 1969, when a 85,000 dwt tanker cost $10 million, we see a sequence of price fluctuations on a scale which few other capital goods industries can match. The price of the ship almost trebled to $28 million in 1974; fell to $16 million in 1976; increased to $40 million in 1981; fell to $20 million in 1985; increased to $43 million in 1990 and then edged down to $40 million in 1996. Faced with such volatile prices it is hardly surprising that shipbuilders and their customers have difficulty in planning for the future. Because price movements for different types of ships are closely correlated – when the price of tankers goes up, so does the price of bulk carriers and ro-ros – there is no real refuge in finding market 'niches'. Most shipbuilders can compete for a wide range of ship types, and if their orderbook is short will bid for ships they would not normally consider building.

What determines the level of shipbuilding prices? One obvious answer is freight rates. A comparison of the cyclical peaks and troughs in shipbuilding contract prices with those in freight rates suggests that the freight market is an important influence, but this is certainly an oversimplified view. Although the economic structure of the shipbuilding market is closely linked to that of the shipping market, for the reasons discussed in chapter 3 shipbuilding is a separate market and events in the shipbuilding market do not always mirror those of the shipping market. In explaining the workings of the shipbuilding market, we are confronted with three basic questions:

- What determines the amount of new ships that shipowners will order?
- What determines the amount of ships that the shipbuilding industry will sell?
- What determines the price at which ships are sold?

To answer these three questions we need a framework that relates the actions of shipowners and shipbuilders, as well as allowing us to introduce external influences such as government policy and the financial policy of banks into the picture.

Starting with the question 'How many ships will be supplied?' we must define the *shipbuilding supply function.* This shows the number of ships that the industry will provide at each price level. In the long-term the supply function depends on the number of shipyards available. That is the starting point, but to define the short term supply function we must determine which of these shipyards will actually bid for the contract. This depends on two other factors, the size of each shipyard's orderbook and costs.[18] The way these two factors determine the shape of the supply function is best explained with an example. Figure 13.5 shows a *hypothetical* supply function for an industry consisting of five regional groups of yards, each with a different cost level. The Chinese shipyards are at the bottom of the cost range and the high cost yards are at the top. The yards supply one ship type, a capesize bulk carrier and the supply function shows how many ships they will offer at each price. At the lower price of $40 million only the Chinese yards are prepared to bid, and they only have space for two million deadweight. At $42 million the Korean yards bid and the supply jumps to seven million deadweight. Progressively as the price rises, the orderbooks of the most competitive shipyards fill up, making them unable to bid. With no low cost yards bidding, the less competitive yards can win orders at higher prices which cover their costs. Such a situation is described as the 'short-run supply function' because it refers to the shape of the supply function during a period of time when the basic parameters of shipbuilding capacity and performance are fixed.

This is very much the situation that applies during shipbuilding cycles. At any time there is a spectrum of yards with different cost levels – the familiar battle between the new entrants and the established builders. Five hundred years ago it was the Dutch versus the Venetians. Later it was the Japanese versus the Europeans and the South Koreans versus the Japanese. The high cost yards have to survive on the orders they can win during booms when the low cost yards have full orderbooks. If they are lucky they can survive by limping from one market peak to another, but they are very vulnerable to recessions. As time goes by the most expensive yards give up, making way for the low cost newcomers. Government subsidies often play a part in the process by allowing high cost shipyards to quote at lower price levels. If, for example, European governments provide their yards with a 13 per cent subsidy, the European yards are able to bid competitively with the Japanese large yards at $47 million. This creates a 'subsidy kink' in the shipbuilding supply curve. With the existing data it is not possible to define the shipbuilding supply function in numerical terms, but there are good reasons for believing that it would take approximately the shape shown in Figure 13.5.

Whereas the world shipbuilding industry offers more ships for sale at higher prices, the opposite is likely to be true for the *shipbuilding demand function* which describes the way shipowners buying those ships respond to price changes. As prices rise the financial case for

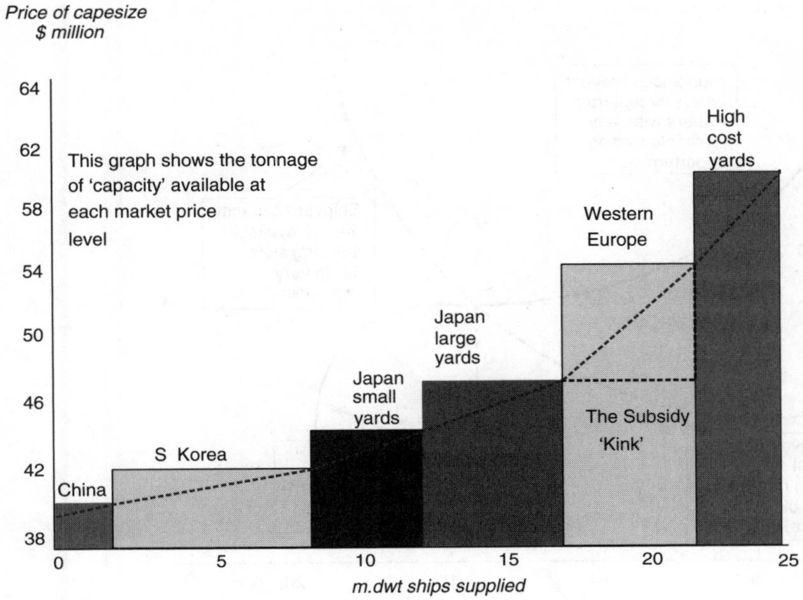

FIGURE 13.5 Shipbuilding supply function
Source: Martin Stopford, 1997

investment weakens and only those investors with a very profitable market opportunities or an urgent need for an new ship are willing to pay, so the number of orders shrinks. At these high prices it becomes cheaper for owners to extend the life of their existing ships, especially since rising prices are generally associated with a long delivery date. Conversely, as the price falls the financial case for new orders improves and the demand for new ships increases until, at some point, constraints on finance or market expectations limit the number of new orders placed and no further ships are ordered however low the price falls.

Equilibrium is achieved at the price where the demand for new ships equals the supply offered by shipbuilders. This is illustrated in Figure 13.6. At a price of $1,000 per cgt the 14.5 million cgt offered by the shipyards exactly matches the 14.5 million cgt the owners are willing to buy. If the shipyards try to increase prices to $1,400 per cgt, demand falls to only 4.5 million cgt, leaving shipyards with 10 million cgt of unutilized capacity. Conversely, at $750 per cgt the owners would want to order 19 million cgt, but the shipyards would offer only 11.5 million cgt of ships. There would be a shortage of berths and the price would be bid up. In this way the price mechanism matches capacity to demand.

Long term supply/demand functions

The supply and demand functions shown in Figure 13.6 assume that shipbuilding capacity is fixed. Given enough time, capacity will adjust to prices as new low cost shipyards are built

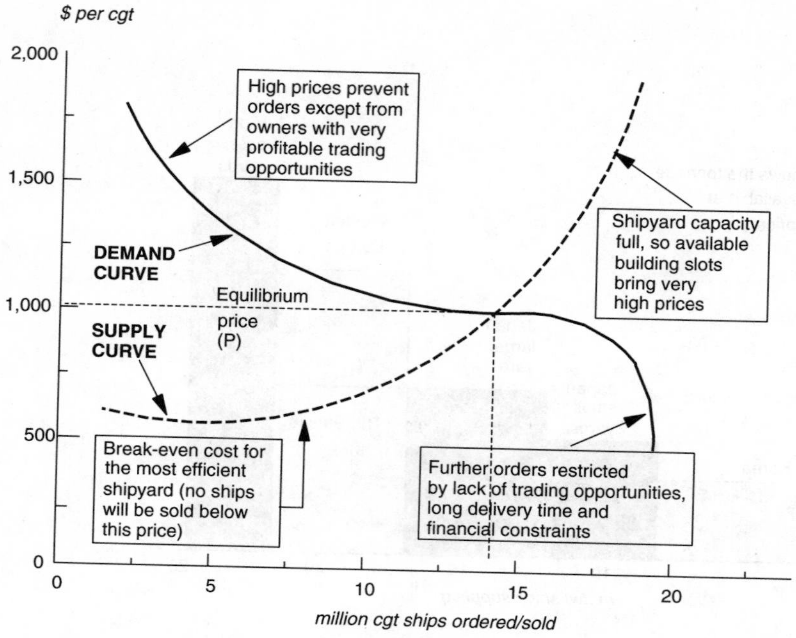

FIGURE 13.6 Supply and demand function
Source: Martin Stopford, 1997

and high cost yards are closed. For example, in Figure 13.7a we see an initial supply function (S1) where prices settle at a price of p1. At this price the low cost shipyards are making excess profits, so they open new yards and expand the existing ones. This new capacity moves the supply curve to the right and, with no change in the demand curve, the price falls from p1 to p2. A move in the demand function also affects prices. For example, the demand curve D1 in Figure 13.7b might represent a situation when the trend rate of fleet growth is 3 per cent a year, requiring q1 quantity of new ships each year. If fleet growth increases to 3.5 per cent per annum, the demand curve moves to D2, so prices increase to p2. Higher prices encourage low cost shipyards to expand their capacity, prices fall and so the cycle continues.

The shipbuilding market supply/demand model

The supply/demand analysis of the shipbuilding market provides a valuable starting point, but to relate it to the real world we must look more closely at the forces which drive the supply and demand functions. From the experience of the last two decades the following six influences can be expected to have particularly important roles to play in explaining the supply and demand functions for merchant ships:

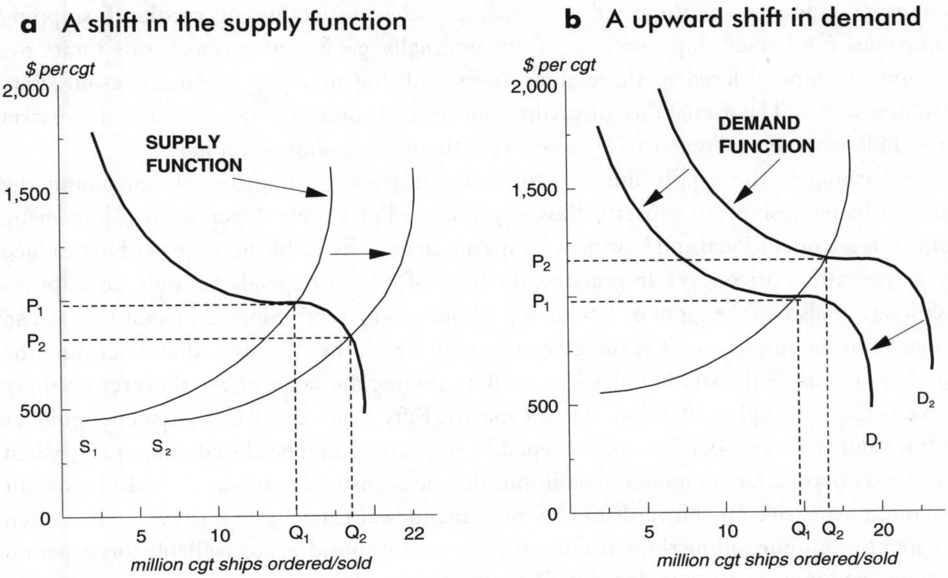

FIGURE 13.7 Effect on price of a movement in shipbuilding supply and demand functions

Source: Martin Stopford, 1997

Demand influences:

- shipping freight rates
- market expectations
- credit availability

Supply influences:

- shipbuilding capacity
- shipyard unit costs
- production subsidies

As far as the demand function is concerned, the role of freight rates in generating ship orders is easy to understand – high earnings encourage shipowners to order more ships and thereby increase their profits. If high freight rates persist for a considerable time this has the secondary effect of generating internal funds to help finance new ships. Historically there has been a close relationship between peaks in the freight market and peaks in ordering new ships. However, because of the time-lag between ordering a ship and taking delivery and the long service life of ships once it has been delivered, current freight rates will only be a partial influence on newbuilding demand. The key question facing the shipowner is what level of freight rates will prevail during the years following delivery of the vessel, and this introduces market expectations as the second major influence on newbuilding demand. The third important influence on shipbuilding demand is the availability of credit. If shipping companies fund their ship purchases from internally generated revenue, this limits the amount of ships ordered to those shipowners with the necessary financial resources to purchase a ship. The availability of credit removes this constraint and broadens the market to include many entrepreneurial shipowners without large sums of capital.

Turning to the supply function for new buildings, we immediately encounter the difficult issue of shipyard capacity. Basically, the level of supply depends upon how many shipyards are operational and how many ships it is financially viable for each yard to produce at the prevailing price level. In practice, the level of output depends not only on shipyard facilities but also on the input of labour and labour productivity. Shipyard facilities place an upper limit on output, but it is the efficiency with which they are used that determine the number of ships built. Another major factor determining the shape of the short term supply curve is the inflexibility of shipbuilding capacity. Fifty years ago, when personnel policies of 'hire and fire' were socially more acceptable, shipyards could be closed temporarily when there was no work. Under modern conditions the social costs of redundancy make it difficult and often expensive for shipyards to vary their manpower capacity in this way, so it is often cheaper to continue selling ships at a loss. If government subsidies are available this situation may persist for years, or even decades, flattening the supply curve.

Shipyard costs depend on labour costs, labour productivity, material costs, exchange rates, and subsidies (which determine whether the shipyard is able to sell at prices below an acceptable return on capital). Given a fixed level of capacity, costs and government subsidies, we can, in principle, define the shipbuilding supply function for an individual shipyard. At the lower end of this function there is a cut-off price below which no ships will be supplied – no shipyard is likely to sell a ship if it cannot expect to pay for the material and labour costs involved in building it. As prices rise, the supply of ships is likely to increase very sharply until a cut-off point is reached where capacity is fully utilized and additional production can be obtained only by high-cost measures such as extensive overtime working.

13.5 The shipbuilding production process

For a better understanding of the supply/demand model, we must now turn to the production process. Currently there are over 250 merchant shipyards world-wide employing about 200,000 workers. The number of docks/berths and the layout and equipment of the shipyard place an upper limit on the number of vessels which can be built per annum. There is great diversity. Some yards are fully operational, while others are uncompetitive and under-utilizing their facilities.

Categories of shipyard

Although modern shipyards are highly flexible in the type of ship they build, physical and commercial factors tend to subdivide the shipbuilding market into a number of sectors. The world shipyards today fall broadly into three categories – small, medium and large.

Small shipyards specialize in vessels below about 6,000 dwt. These facilities generally have a workforce of below 1,000 employees, sometimes as few as 100–200. Some specialize in particular ship types, such as dredgers or offshore supply craft, but the product range is very wide, comprising small cargo ships, mini-bulkers, chemical tankers and a whole range of service craft such as tugs and dredgers. Consequently, most small shipyards tend to be very versatile in their product range. This sector is comparatively self-contained and it is unusual to find large shipyards competing for orders in the small ship market.

Medium-sized shipyards build vessels in the size range 6,000–40,000 dwt, although some may take vessels up to Panamax size. The constraint is usually the size of berth/dock and the facilities to process large quantities of steel. Typically, medium-sized shipyards have a workforce of about 500 to 1,500, though this varies greatly. In product terms the mainstay of these yards are container ships, bulk carriers and small tankers. More sophisticated yards handle vessels such as short sea ro-ros, ferries and gas tankers.

Finally, some very large shipyards have docks capable of accommodating tankers of up to 1 m.dwt and in a few cases a workforce of 10,000 or more. These facilities generally have highly automated equipment for steel preparation and assembly. The shipyard in Figure 13.8 was developed to handle cargo and specialist vessels up to 30,000 dwt.

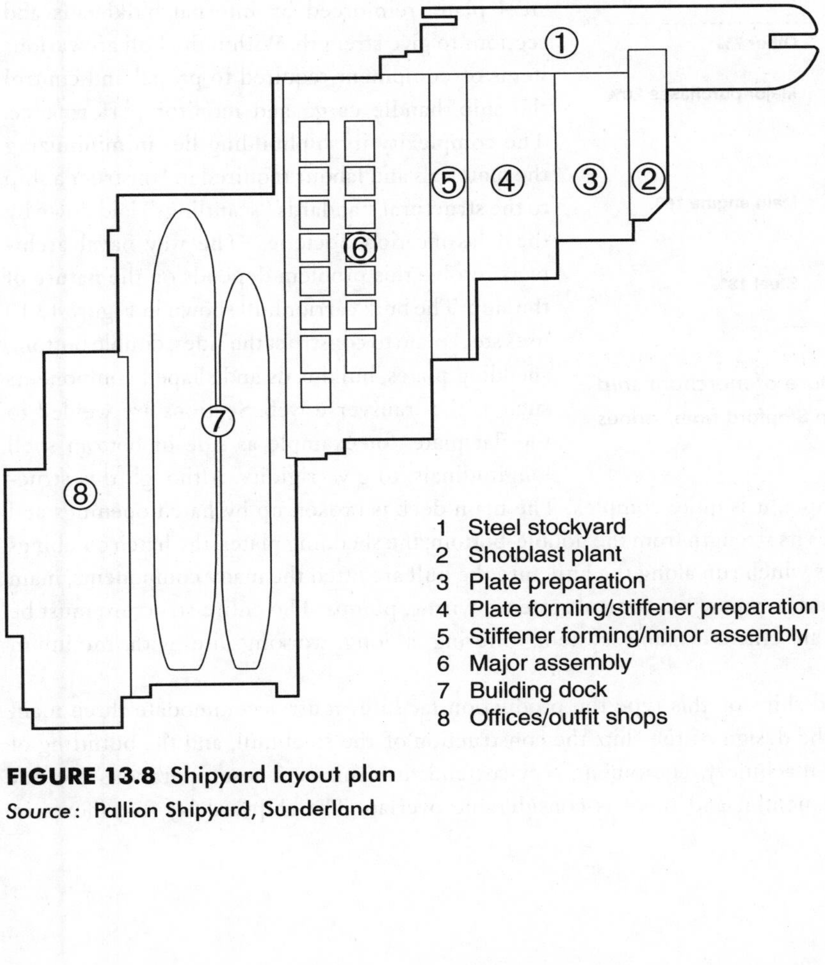

FIGURE 13.8 Shipyard layout plan
Source: Pallion Shipyard, Sunderland

Shipbuilding facilities and the production process

The merchant ship is the world's largest factory-produced product. A 30,000 dwt bulk carrier might typically contain 5,000 tons of steel and 2,500 tons of other components ranging from the main engine to many thousands of minor items of cabling, pipes, furniture and fittings – and, by modern standards, this is a comparatively small vessel. Over half of the cost of the ship is materials. Figure 13.9 shows a rough breakdown of the main items. Steel represents about 13 per cent of the cost, the main engine 16 per cent and other materials 25–35 per cent. The remainder of the cost is direct labour and overhead. The material content is higher for high outfit ships like cruise liners and lower for simple cargo ships such as large bulk carriers. Because of their size and value, virtually all merchant ships are built to order and the construction period is a long one, falling anywhere in the range 12 months to 3 years, depending on the ship size and the length of orderbook held by the shipbuilders.

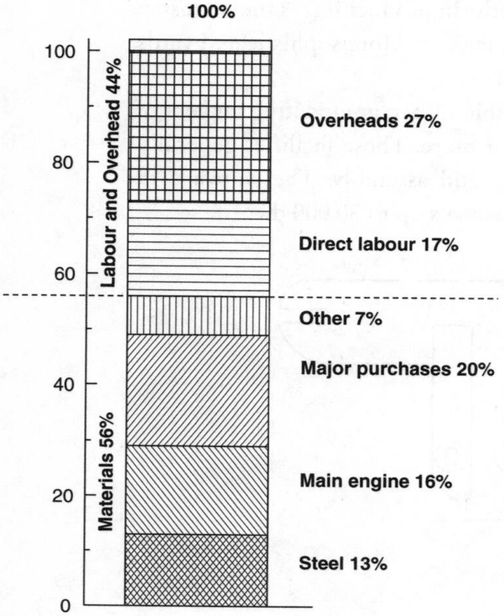

FIGURE 13.9 *Cost structure of merchant ship*
Source: Compiled by Martin Stopford from various sources

The basic structure of the ship is, in some ways, quite simple. The hull is a box built from thin steel plate, reinforced by internal bulkheads and sections to give strength. Within the hull are various items of equipment required to propel and control the ship, handle cargo and monitor performance. The complexity in shipbuilding lies in minimizing the materials and labour required to construct a ship to the structural standards ('scantlings') laid down by the Classification Societies. The way naval architects resolve this problem depends on the nature of the ship. The bulk carrier hull shown in Figure 13.10 uses steel plate to construct the sides, double bottom, shedding plates, bulkheads and shaped components such as the transverse web. Sections are welded to the flat plate, for example as side or bottom shell longitudinals, to give rigidity. Although this structure looks simple, it is quite complex. The main deck is broken up by hatch openings and the hull derives its strength from the double-bottom, the shedding plates, the hatch combings and the frames which run along the hull. Into the hull are fitted the many components, main engine, auxiliaries, pipework, control systems, wiring, pumps. The entire structure must be coated with an efficient paint system, offering a long working life with minimum maintenance.

To build ships of this type the production facilities must accommodate three main operations – the design of the ship, the construction of the steel hull, and the outfitting of the hull with machinery, equipment, services and furnishings. These operations are not necessarily sequential and there is considerable overlap. The shipyard lay-out shown in

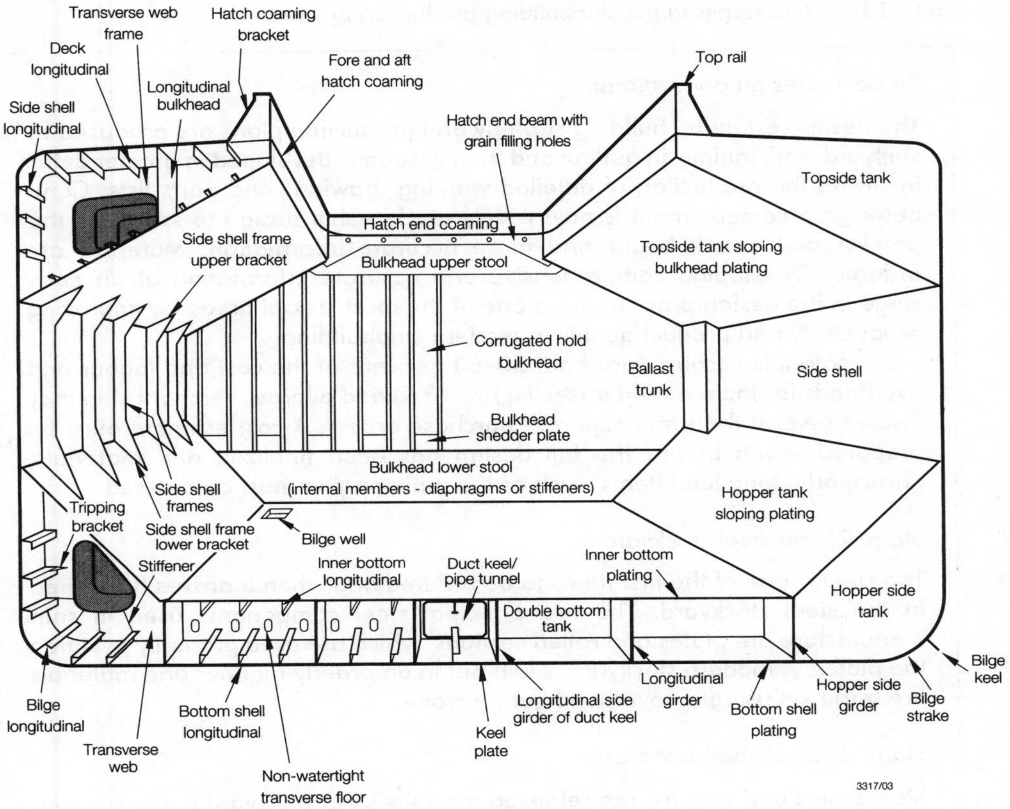

FIGURE 13.10 Cross-section of bulk carrier hull
Source: Lloyd's Register of Shipping

Figure 13.8 illustrates the way work flows through the shipyard from the steel stockyard through to the assembly of the ship in the dock. Although this shipyard layout illustrates the different stages unusually well, few shipyards are designed in such a logical way. It is more usual to find these facilities spread around the yard, with units moved from one location to another with low loaders. The nine manufacturing stages are itemized in Box 13.1.

The production process is essentially one of assembly, and few of the individual tasks require sophisticated technical skills. The skill comes in planning and implementing the tens of thousands of operations that contribute to the production of a merchant ship – materials must be ordered and arrive on time; steel parts, fabrication and pipework must fit accurately without the need for re-work. All of this requires considerable effort at the design and planning stage along with a production capability to manage material handling and production planning.

BOX 13.1 Nine stages in the shipbuilding production process

Stage 1: Design and estimating

The design, estimate, building strategy and production plans are produced by shipyard staff, initially in outline and then gradually developed in greater detail involving the production of detailed working drawings and parts lists. Computer graphic equipment is now widely used in ship design to speed up this process and create better and more accurate information. Materials are ordered. Developing comprehensive and accurate information at an early stage in the design programme is one of the most crucial areas for improving productivity and product quality in modern shipbuilding.

Materials account for about 50–60 per cent of the cost and labour and overheads for the remainder (see Figure 13.9) and a large merchant ship may involve several thousand separate purchase orders. A cost estimate must be prepared, often before the full design has been finalized and materials, particularly 'long lead items' such as the main engine must be ordered.

Stage 2: The steel stockyard

The steel is one of the first items to be ordered and when it arrives it is stored in the steel stockyard. The two principal steel components used in ship manufacture are plates and rolled sections, which are used primarily to stiffen the plates. A modern stockyard is laid out in an orderly manner and materials are retrieved using an overhead gantry crane.

Stage 3: Steel shotblast plant

Steel plates and sections are retrieved from the steel stockyard and processed through the steel shotblast plant. This involves rolling plates and straightening sections to ensure that they are true, followed by shotblasting to remove rust and priming to protect the plate from further rusting and provide a foundation for paint.

Stage 4: Plate and stiffener preparation

The primed steel plates are cut to the precise required size using profile burning machines. Any plates that do not need cutting are transferred to the flame planer to have their rough edges removed, and create the proper edge profile for welding. If required, they are bent to shape using a press or rolls. Framing members are prepared from steel sections, cut to size and then bent to shape using a frame-bending machine. By this process the many thousands of steel components for constructing the ship's hull are prepared, cut to size and numbered in accordance with the drawings. In practice, this is a flow process with a steady stream of components moving through the steel preparation bays.

Stage 5: Assembly

The next stage is to assemble the steel components into the 'building blocks' from which the ship will be constructed in the dock. Shaped steel is formed into 'minor assemblies', typically weighing less than half a ton. The larger plates that make up most of the hull are transferred to the panel assembly line where framing members are welded in place to form 'panel assemblies'. Finally, the minor assemblies and the sub- and panel assemblies are welded together into major three-dimensional (block) assemblies using various types of welding equipment.

Stage 6: Pre-outfitting

The hull must be fitted with tens of thousands of 'outfit' items such as pipes, electrical cables, switchboards, furnishings and machinery. During the various stages of assembling steelwork, advance outfitting is carried out. This involves the installation of as much pipework and equipment as is possible at the earliest practical stage in production. To achieve high levels of advanced outfitting requires large amounts of information, accuracy and organization. Plans must be made, materials ordered and delivered to the work zone when they are required, so that assembly can proceed smoothly. When the materials arrive they must be precisely as specified and fit into the assembly without adjustment or re-work. This sounds easy, but calls for great care in planning and accuracy control.

Stage 7: Coating

Traditionally painting was carried out at a late stage in production and often became a production bottleneck. In recent years coatings has become increasingly prominent in the production operation. There are two factors driving this. First, effective corrosion protection is now required by customers, as a way of reducing maintenance costs. Second, modern coatings are technically demanding and must be applied under controlled conditions, ideally in a properly designed paint cell. These requirements have led to the careful integration of paintwork into the production operation. Wherever possible outfitted steel units will be blasted and painted in dedicated paint cells before final assembly.

Stage 8: Assembly on berth

Finally, prefabricated sections of the ship, together with those items of outfitting already installed, are lifted into the assembly dock where they are carefully aligned, then welded into position. Outfit installations such as pipe runs are also linked up.

Stage 9: Outfit at outfit quay

When the hull is complete, the dock is flooded and the vessel is floated to an outfit quay where the outfitting of the ship is completed, systems are commissioned to ensure that on-board systems are operating correctly, and basin (or dock) trials of the main engines.

The major steps forward in shipbuilding techniques have been in these areas – for example, the introduction of pallets for material handling and the extensive pre-outfitting and painting of assemblies before installation in the ship. The application of these techniques yields dramatic results. For example, a shipbuilder using these techniques may take only half the manhours required by more traditional methods to build the same ship. In short, the key to modern shipbuilding is organization.

13.6 Shipbuilding costs and competitiveness

Because shipbuilding involves a complex production process the level of efficiency and costs varies considerably from one yard to another. Although attention often focuses on the shipyard facilities as the main determinant of competitiveness, in reality there are many factors to consider. Broadly speaking the price competitiveness of a shipyard depends on the six key variables summarized in Figure 13.11 – material supply, facilities, skilled labour, wages, labour productivity, exchange rates and, in some cases, subsidy all play a part in determining how many ships are produced, how much they cost and the revenue received by the shipbuilder.

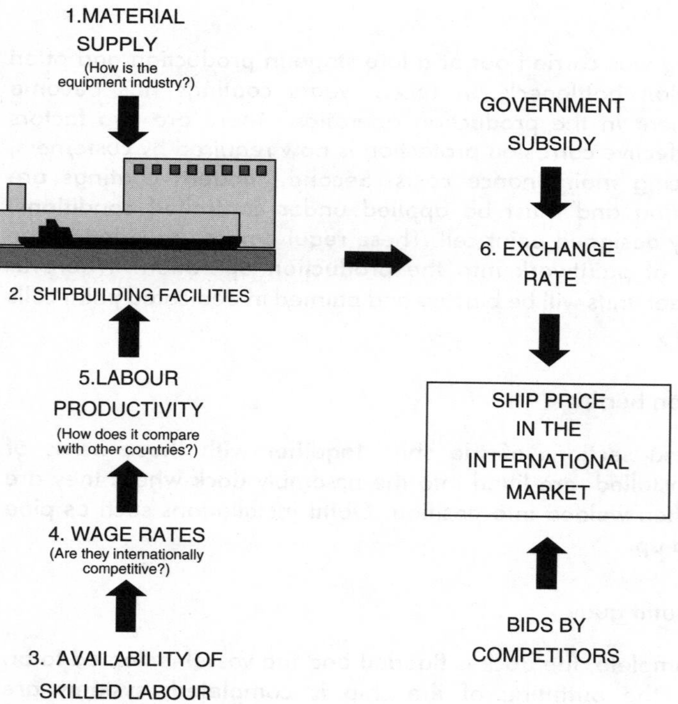

FIGURE 13.11 Influences on shipbuilding competitiveness

Source: Martin Stopford, 1997

Material costs

Material cost and availability is significant. Very large shipbuilding countries such as Japan and South Korea can support a full range of material suppliers, including engine builders, equipment manufacturers, subcontractors and manufacturers of specialist items such as stern frames. Long production runs give these suppliers a competetive advantage and the ability to deliver a wide range of quality components from stock. Shipyards in areas with little shipbuilding activity have a more difficult time. Even if they are able to obtain supplies abroad, the complexity of the assembly operation can make this a difficult strategy to implement.

Shipbuilding facilities and productivity

There are enormous differences in the productivity of shipyards around the world. Facilities play a part in explaining these differences in the sense that they set an upper limit on the size and volume of ships that can be built during a year. However output is far more dependent upon the productivity of the shipyard. Unlike a 'process' industry where achieving maximum production merely involves switching on the machinery and feeding in the required volume of raw materials, building a merchant ship requires highly sophisticated managerial skills in terms of planning, organization and control. Ultimately the maximum throughput will depend not just upon the size of the facilities, but upon the efficiency with which they are used. Some shipyards take ten times as many manhours as others to build the same ship.

This naturally raises the question: 'How can productivity be measured?' As a rule, labour productivity is measured in terms of manhours per unit of output. Unfortunately there are practical difficulties in applying this formula to measuring and comparing shipyard productivity on an international basis. This arises from a lack of detailed statistics about the labour used and, more importantly, the difficulty of measuring output in an industry where the product consists of large units, most of which are different. There are four main problems:

- *Output measurements.* It is extremely difficult to establish a reliable standard unit of production by which the output of different shipyards can be measured. Although there have been a few successful standard ship designs such as the SDI4, the majority of ships are not standard. Even where ships have an apparently similar specification, for example Panamax bulk carriers, there is considerable scope for varying the design, machinery and general quality of finish. The best measure currently available is compensated gross tons (cgt, or previously cgrt), but this has limited value when dealing with sophisticated or complex ships.
- *Differences in subcontracting.* The shipyard production process involves many stages, and different shipyards have different conventions about the work that is subcontracted – for example, some shipyards subcontract electrical and joinery work while others do

not. The accounting practice of most shipyards is to treat subcontract labour as 'outside goods and services' and to include it in material costs. As a result, a comparison of manhour productivity between two ships would be distorted if such differences in subcontracting were not taken into account, and this is extremely difficult to do at an international level.

- *Delivery peaks and troughs.* Ship deliveries from a yard may not represent the underlying level of production owing to the size and mix of ships. It is possible for a shipyard to be productively employed all year but not actually deliver any ships because of the irregular distribution of delivery dates. For this reason, throughput needs to be calculated from several years' deliveries if an accurate figure is to be obtained.
- *Joint product manufacture.* There are considerable practical difficulties in measuring employment engaged on merchant shipbuilding because many shipyards undertake other activities such as warship-building, offshore and ship repair.

For these reasons any calculation of shipbuilding productivity and cost competitiveness is subjective. However, to illustrate the general method involved, Table 13.3 shows the calculation of average shipbuilding productivity for some of the major shipbuilding countries in the early 1980s. The first column shows the estimated numbers of employees engaged on merchant shipbuilding at the end of 1982, while the second and third columns show the tonnage completed in each country in 1982 and 1983 (an average is more reliable than a single-year figure). Productivity measured in cgrt/man is calculated in column 4 by dividing the average completions in 1982 and 1983 by employment at end 1982. For the reasons mentioned above, the productivity figures cannot be regarded as definitive, but they provide a broad estimate of the differences between countries.

TABLE 13.3 Merchant shipbuilding productivity by country

Country	*Numbers employed on merchant new work, end 1982* (1)	*Tonnage completed 1982 ('000 cgrt)* (2)	*Tonnage completed 1983 ('000 cgrt)* (3)	*Productivity (cgrt/manyear)* (4)
Denmark	10,340	384	334	29.9
France	14,800	393	379	26.1
Germany	26,607	763	925	31.7
Spain	31,950	542	465	15.8
Japan	164,000*	5,811	4,908	32.6
S. Korea	e.55,000	880	986	17.0
Total	302,697	8,773	7,997	25.5

Source: Numbers employed, tonnage completed – Association of Western European shipbuilders/various

* Including 51,000 sub-contract jobs.

Labour costs and competitiveness

Labour accounts for 40–50 per cent of the cost of the ship, so wages have a major impact on competitiveness. The labour cost determines the total wage bill for producing the ship and depends upon the basic wage, to which must be added overtime payments and any bonuses paid to the workforce. In order to compare hourly wage costs it is necessary to convert them to a common currency; for present purposes, the US dollar has been used. There are significant differences in the wage rate in different countries, as can be seen in Table 13.4. Applying the labour cost per man year to the cgrt productivity per man year gives an estimate of the labour cost per cgrt, which is shown in the final column of Table 13.2. Differences in the productivity of various countries are to some extent offset by different wage rates.

TABLE 13.4 Shipbuilding unit labour cost by country

Country	*Productivity (cgrt/ man year)*	*Labour cost per man hour (local currency)*	*Exchange rate $ (average 1984) Currency*	*Value*	*Hours worked per man year*	*Labour cost per man year $*	*Labour cost per cgrt $*
	(1)	(2)	(3)	(4)	(5)	(6) (2 ÷ 4) × (5)	(7) (6) ÷ (1)
Denmark	29.9	90.92	Dkr.	10.3	1,709	15,086	505
France	26.1	73.40	F	8.7	1,709	14,418	552
Germany	31.7	28.52	DM	2.8	1,728	17,600	555
Spain	15.8	881.49	Pes.	159.8	1,737	9,582	606
Japan	32.6	1,986	Yen	236.0	e.1,800	15,147	465
S. Korea	17.0	1,616	Won	825.0	e.2,332	4,568	269
Average	25.5					12,733	492

Source: Compiled from various sources

Currency movements and competitiveness

Although currency movements are far removed from the shipyard, they are the single most important factor in determining the cost competitiveness of a shipbuilder. Since the world economy moved on to a floating exchange rate system after the breakdown of the Bretton Woods system in 1971, shipbuilders have faced a major problem with exchange rates. Unit labour costs vary proportionately with the exchange rate, and given the volatility of exchange rates during the 1980s and 1990s this is clearly a very major factor in determining shipbuilding cost competitiveness.

An example illustrates the point. A shipyard was negotiating the sale of a small bulk carrier. The yard's cost was £10 million and the exchange rate was $/£1.4, so the best price they could offer was $14 million. Unfortunately the owner would not pay more than $10 million, so to win the order the shipyard needed to cut its price by 30 per cent. Since bought-in materials accounted for 60 per cent of the shipyard cost, there was no way they could possibly close such a large gap by cost cutting. The negotiation dragged on over a period of six months and the exchange rate fell to $/£1.06. At this exchange rate the shipyard was competitive and the contract was signed. Although such large currency movements are relatively uncommon, it demonstrates just how vulnerable shipyards are to exchange rate fluctuations.

As we pull all of these factors together we build up a picture of how the competitive structure of the world shipbuilding industry really operates. At one extreme there are shipyards with low productivity but wages so low that manhours hardly matter. They can undercut allcomers. At the other there are the high productivity yards, with even higher wage costs which are slowly going out of business. This happened to the Swedish shipyards in the early 1980s, despite the fact that they had the highest productivity in the world. Between lie a whole range of shipyards with different combinations of wage costs and productivity. Washing over the whole industry are the waves of exchange rate movements that can sweep shipyards up and down the competitiveness league table in a matter of months. All of this combines to make shipbuilding a tough business that requires a reliable home market, great management skill and a great deal of tenacity. Despite all these problems, or perhaps because of them, shipbuilders are some of the most tenacious businessmen in the maritime industry.

13.7 The shipbreaking industry

Compared with shipbuilding, shipbreaking is an rough business. Most of the world's ship scrapping industry use manual labour to break ships in whatever facilities are available, often a suitable beach. Although it is possible to increase productivity by using mechanized shipbreaking methods, these are capital intensive and require special investment, which is not easily justified given the small margin in the shipbreaking business.

The process of non-mechanized shipbreaking falls into three stages. At the preparatory stage, the owner of the vessel undertakes various operations including stopping up all intake apertures; pumping out all bilge water; blocking off intakes and valves; and removing all non-metal objects together with potentially explosive materials. If the vessel is a tanker it must be cleared of potentially explosive gas. This work is often subcontracted.

The next stage is to beach the ship and remove large metal structures such as masts, pipes, superstructure, deck equipment, main engine, ancillary equipment of machinery room, decks, platforms, transverse bulkheads, propeller shafts, propeller shaft bearings, upper hull sections, bow and stern end sections. The remainder of the ship is then hauled or lifted on to dry land by means of slipways, ramps or dry docks and cut into large sections. In some of the less sophisticated shipbreaking operations the vessel is simply winched on to the beach. Although this process can be undertaken satisfactorily on a beach or alongside a quay, the availability of a dry dock is a considerable advantage, in terms of both efficiency and safety.

Finally, the panels and sections obtained from the ship are cut into smaller pieces as required, using manually operated acetylene cutters. The scrap is then assembled for transport to its ultimate destination.

The market for scrap products

Steel scrap obtained from the shipbreaking process is of comparatively high quality, especially from tankers that have large flat panels. In developing countries, the scrap is simply heated and rerolled into concrete reinforcing rods for sale to the construction industry. Rerolled steel is also ideal for sewage projects, metal roads and agricultural needs. Smaller pieces are melted down. Much of the shipbreaking industry is located in the Far East and Indian subcontinent where there is a sizeable market for reprocessed steel scrap products of this type. In the advanced countries of Europe, scrap is generally completely melted down to make fresh steel.

Although the scrap steel provides most of the value of the ship, the most lucrative return comes from the 2 per cent of non-ferrous items. Diesel engines, generators, deck cranes, compasses, clocks and furniture can also be resold. Again, the market for such equipment is more readily available in developing countries than in the developed countries where technical standards are more demanding and the costs of refurbishing are higher.

Who scraps ships?

For all these reasons most of the shipbreaking industry is located in developing countries where shipbreakers sell their products to the construction industry. This is a relatively mobile industry. Table 13.5 shows that in the mid-1980s almost three-quarters of the shipbreaking industry was located in Taiwan, China and South Korea. Ten years later Taiwan and South Korea had left the industry. China's market share had fallen to 9 per cent and India, Bangladesh and Pakistan had taken over as market leaders.

TABLE 13.5 Shipbreaking (by country) (1985–95)

	1986		*1991*		*1995*	
	GT	*%*	*GT*	*%*	*GT*	*%*
Taiwan	7,773	38	48	2	—	0
China	4,567	23	172	7	754	9
S.Korea	2,658	13	8	0	3	0
Pakistan	861	4	445	19	1,670	20
Japan	770	4	81	3	146	2
India	636	3	695	29	2,809	33
Spain	581	3	13	1	40	0
Turkey	418	2	77	3	207	2
Italy	311	2	8	0	1	0
Bangladesh	268	1	512	22	2,539	30
Others	1,444	7	306	13	354	4
Total	20,287	100	2,365	100	8,523	100

Source: Lloyd's Register of Shipping

The explanation is that this very basic industry gravitates towards countries with low labour costs. Taiwan's development as a shipbreaker illustrates the point. Demolition started with the dismantling of ships damaged during the Second World War and expanded rapidly after import controls were lifted in 1965. Encouraged by the government to meet rising domestic scrap demand and benefiting from a purpose-built site and from plentiful cheap labour, the industry established itself as the world's leading shipbreaker, with highly efficient facilities. Demolition took place in two state-owned sites at the deep-water port of Kaohsiung, using specially built berths and dockside cranes. The ships to be demolished were moored two abreast along the keyside and systematically dismantled, with a breaking cycle of 30 to 40 days. With each decade the working conditions improved.[19] As the economy grew and labour costs increased, shipbreaking became less attractive and in the early 1990s Taiwan closed the demolition yards and replaced them with a container terminal. South Korea was a more recent entrant to the Far East scrapping business, but the story is much the same. In the 1980s South Korea was the third biggest shipbreaker with a 13 per cent market share, mainly carried out in two demolition yards owned by Hyundai. As wages rose in the late 1980s and the shipbuilding industry expanded, the demolition yards were closed.

The People's Republic of China entered the ship demolition market in the early 1980s and rapidly became the world's second largest buyer of ships for scrap. There is a considerable domestic demand for steel products and, in fact, the China Steel Corporation was already importing a considerable amount of scrap steel from Taiwan. Although China continued to operate demolition yards in the 1990s, the scale of the business was restricted by government regulations controlling currency for the purchase of ships and strict environmental regulations, and China's market share fell from 23 per cent in 1986 to 9 per cent in 1995.

In the 1990s the growth areas for demolition were India, Bangladesh, and Pakistan (Table 13.4). Pakistan has one of the world's largest scrapping sites at Gandani Beach, with over 100 scrapping plots fully operational, each plot covering 2,500 square yards. Gandani Beach has no electricity supply or water mains and only a few plots have electric generators. Ship demolition takes place on the most basic level. Ships are driven on to the beach where an army of workers dismantle them. During busy periods, up to 15,000 labourers are employed breaking up the ships with the aid of very little mechanization. Much of the scrap material is still moved manually, with assistance of king posts, blocks and pulleys, but the more profitable plots have now moved into mechanization and are using fork lifts and mobile hydraulic cranes.

Little shipbreaking is carried out in Western Europe, owing to high labour costs and the lack of a ready market for scrap steel. There are also various difficulties associated with health and safety legislation and environmental protection, both of which are more prominent than in Third World countries. The only European countries with any significance in breaking activity in the recent past were Spain, Italy and Turkey. There are, however, a number of small shipbreaking companies scattered around the UK and continental Europe, mainly with 10–100 employees specializing in breaking warships and other high-value vessels.

13.8 Summary

In this chapter we have discussed the international shipbuilding and scrapping industries. Although shipbuilding is closely aligned to shipping, it operates in a totally different competitive environment that is highly volatile and shipbuilders are constantly under pressure to expand or contract their output. During the twentieth century there have been eleven major market cycles of this type.

The market operates through international competition, which forces change through the price mechanism. It is common for shipbuilding market prices to vary by as much as 60 per cent in a period of two or three years. Prices rise when there is a shortage of capacity to meet the new ordering demand of shipbuilders, and they fall when there is overcapacity.

Because of the continuous adjustment process in the level of shipbuilding output, the measurement of capacity has always been a contentious issue in the shipbuilding industry. There is no accurate way of measuring capacity, since the level of output depends upon physical facilities (which ultimately limit the maximum number of ships that can be built), the level of employment, the productivity of those employees, and the type of ship being built. Thus, it is possible for a modern shipyard with a highly productive workforce to produce twice as many ships as a shipyard of similar physical dimensions and the same number of employees but lower productivity.

The shipbuilding production process is simple in principle but complex in practice. It involves assembling many thousands of different components, each of which must be accurately produced and arrive at the workstation at the correct time. To achieve this, a shipyard must have effective systems for generating information, developing production plans, controlling materials and achieving high standards of accuracy in the production of components. For this reason, productivity in shipbuilding is heavily dependent upon management and organization skills.

For various practical reasons it is difficult to measure shipbuilding productivity accurately, but there is clear evidence that levels of productivity vary substantially between countries from around 15 cgt per employee at the lower end of the scale to around 40 cgt per employee at the upper end. Competitiveness does not just depend upon productivity; it also depends on unit costs, which include materials costs, labour costs and the exchange rate. Differences in these areas mean that some countries such as Sweden and the United States, which have high levels of physical productivity, are internationally uncompetitive, whereas others such as South Korea, which have comparatively low productivity, are very competitive.

Although the regional distribution of shipbuilding capacity depends upon competitiveness, there is clearly a close link between shipping and shipbuilding activities. The decline of the shipbuilding market share of Great Britain from 60 per cent to 1 per cent closely followed a similar decline in the market share of the British merchant fleet. Similarly, Japan's emergence as a major force in the shipbuilding market occurred during a period of major expansion of maritime activities under either the Japanese flag or international flags. The market share of shipbuilding in continental Europe and Scandinavia has generally conformed to the shipping market share achieved in these areas.

In conclusion, shipbuilding is a fascinating industry, but not an easy one to study. In nearly every area we find difficulties in measuring output, productivity, or competitiveness, while historically the industry has swung from periods of euphoria to gloom. Only one thing is certain: as long as there is seaborne trade and salt water, there will be shipbuilders.

Chapter 14

Maritime forecasting and market research

If a man will begin with certainties, he shall end in doubts; but if he will be content to begin with doubts, he shall end in certainties.

(Francis Bacon (1561–1626), *Advancement of Learning,* I.v.8)

14.1 The approach to maritime forecasting

One of the most common applications of maritime economics is in the preparation of forecasts and market research studies. Because the shipping industry is international in its operations and highly complex in its economic structure, the task facing the maritime researcher is extremely demanding. Many of the problem areas have been discussed in earlier chapters of this book; the intention in this chapter is to develop a practical approach to the preparation of forecasts and market research reports that will be of value to decision-makers. Before doing so, however, we shall briefly examine the purpose for which forecasts are produced and the obvious difficulty of achieving reliable results in an uncertain world.

The poor track record of forecasts

To be realistic, forecasting has a poor reputation in maritime circles. The argument that forecasts are never right is often put forward with great conviction by shipowners who have been far too successful in business to have their opinions taken lightly. Moreover, it is not a view that is confined to shipowners. Peter Beck, Planning Director at Shell UK, came to the same conclusion when trying to find forecasts for the oil industry:

> When looking at forecasts made in the 1960s and early 1970s, one can find many failures but few successes. Indeed one may be shocked at the extent to which the most important forecasts and their surrounding assumptions had turned out to be wrong.[1]

In the shipping and shipbuilding industries the success rate has been no better. Some forecasts have proved to be wildly wrong, while others were right, but only by combining a series of wildly inaccurate assumptions.

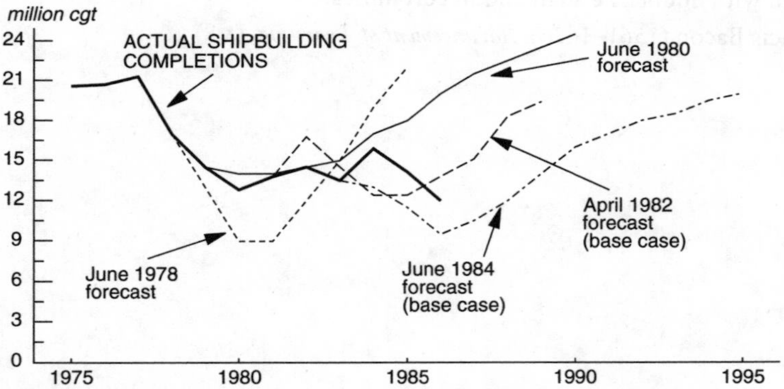

FIGURE 14.1 Comparison of forecasts of world shipbuilding completions

Source: Compiled by Martin Stopford from various sources

Note: This graph illustrates the way that group of experts progressively changed their view of the future over a period of six years.

As an example, we can take four forecasts of the demand for new ships produced between 1978 and 1984, summarized in Figure 14.1. Each successive forecast predicted a different pattern of demand over the next 7 years. The 1980 forecast predicted 50 per cent more demand in 1986 than the 1982 forecast, and even this proved to be too optimistic. In defence of the experts who produced these forecasts, there were developments in the world economy and the oil trade that they could not reasonably have anticipated. However, the fact remains that the forecasts were consistently wide of the mark.

Later in the chapter we shall review past economic forecasts that show how inaccurate some predictions for the 1980s, made in the mid-1960s, proved to be. They predicted widespread supersonic air travel but gave the computer only a passing mention and completely misjudged the two major economic developments of the 1970s – inflation and unemployment. With such a poor track record it is difficult not to agree with Peter Drucker that, the further ahead we try to predict, the more tenuous the forecasts become:

If anyone suffers from the delusion that a human being is able to forecast beyond a very short time span, look at the headlines in yesterday's paper, and ask which of them anyone could have possibly predicted a decade or so ago . . . we must start out with the premise that forecasting is not a respectable human activity and not worthwhile beyond the shortest of periods.[2]

The forecasting paradox

On this evidence, the case against forecasting seems formidable. The paradox is that decision-makers continue to ask for forecasts, and many maritime forecasts are produced each year, a strange state of affairs when there appears to be conclusive evidence that forecasting is a fruitless occupation.

The explanation of the 'forecasting paradox' is that most of the important decisions made by executives in the shipping market demand a view of the future, so they cannot avoid looking ahead. Questions like: Is now the right time to buy? Is now the right time to sell? Should the company move out of dry bulk shipping? Should we re-tonnage with Handymax bulk carriers, or geared Panamaxes? have very large sums of money riding on them and, faced with these questions, it is natural that decision-makers seek whatever advice they can, if only in the hope that it will confirm their own opinion. In economic terms, the demand for forecasts is derived from this need to make decisions which concern the future. It is derived demand. What matters is not whether the forecast is right, but whether the decision is right. If forecasts can contribute to better decisions, they are adding value.

Faced with the necessity of looking ahead, we must ask the question: What can the analyst can do to help the decision-maker to make better decisions? Beck and Drucker suggest that forecasting should be used as a way of helping decision-makers to think through the future implications of their decisions. Drucker argues this point as follows:

> Decisions exist only in the present. The question that faces the strategic decision-maker is not what the organisation should do tomorrow. It is 'What do we have to do today to be ready for an uncertain tomorrow?' The question is not what will happen in the future. It is, 'What futurity do we have to build into our present thinking and doing, what time spans do we have to consider, and how do we use this information to make a rational decision now'.[3]

This changes the emphasis. If this is the aim then the forecaster's job is not to define certainties but to seek out and evaluate risks against which the business should be protecting itself. If the shipowner buys bulk carriers, what is the chance of a protracted recession? Will he have the cash flow to survive such a depression? How will operating costs compare with competitors? What profits might be made by selling vessels at the top of the market and how would this compare with probable losses during a recession? These are all issues that are very much concerned with the future, but the part played by the forecaster is more like the poker player calculating the odds than the magician predicting the cards drawn from a pack.

Three principles of forecasting

All this sounds fine in theory, but how do we set about producing a research study that will actually be helpful to decision-makers? The first point to recognize is that, if the results of the study are to be used in making a decision, and because there are so many different decisions to be made, no single methodology will produce a useful result in every case. There are, however, three principles or criteria that can be used to judge whether a forecast is likely to be useful.

- Principle 1 relevance. The forecast must be relevant to the decision. For example, a shipbuilding market forecast that predicts the level of shipbuilding output five years ahead will not necessarily be relevant to a European shipbuilder trying to draw up a five-year corporate plan. What he needs to know is the prices at which ships will be sold so that he can calculate whether he can make a profit, and what share of the market he might win, which depends on the activities of competitors. In this case a relevant forecast would concentrate on price and competitor activity as well as the demand for new ships.
- Principle 2 rationale. There should be some reason why the forecast will happen – in other words, the conclusion should be based upon some consistent line of rational argument. Without this the forecaster is in the business of prophecy rather than economic analysis (although in the past many important decisions have been made after consulting oracles, entrails or fortune tellers).[4]
- Principle 3 significance. The forecast must be researched at a significant level of detail relative to the subject in hand. Unfortunately it is all too often the case that the most important variables in a forecast have not actually been researched at all in any

normal sense of the word. Just like any other job in business, forecasting requires an adequate input of skilled man-hours.

In short, companies in the maritime industry have to take decisions about the future and these three principles establish the minimum requirements for producing forecasts to support these decisions. We now move on to look at each part of this process in a little more detail.

14.2 Preparing for the forecast

Three practical steps must precede the forecast. The first is to define the decision to be made; the second, to determine who is qualified to make the forecast; and the third is to establish the things we are trying to forecast are really predictable.

Defining the decision

The range of decisions to which forecasts can contribute is extraordinarily wide, particularly if we take into account the decisions made by banks, governments, port authorities, shippers and other organizations with an interest in the shipping market. Each decision-maker has his own quite different need, as the following brief review suggests.

- *Shipowners.* All shipping companies have to make major decisions about the sale and purchase of ships, ordering newbuildings and whether to enter into long-term contractual agreements. These decisions depend crucially upon how the market develops in future in terms of freight rates, newbuilding prices and second-hand prices. Liner companies need to decide when to replace their vessels, what type to order and what policy to follow over using chartered tonnage. The view taken over the future volume and mix of cargo will crucially influence these decisions.
- *Shipbuilders.* Shipbuilders are concerned with future development in the world shipbuilding market, particularly prices, as well as with the demand for particular ship types as a basis for product development and future competition from other shipbuilders. The decisions taken by shipbuilders are principally concerned with whether to expand or reduce capacity and whether to invest in new product development in certain areas.
- *Bankers.* As we saw in chapter 3, much of the finance for new and second-hand ship purchases comes from commercial banks. Bank lending officers must make decisions about whether to approve a loan application and the level of security required. This involves decisions about whether a ship is a good investment, and whether the shipowner has the financial and managerial skills to survive a protracted recession; often the question being asked is: How bad could things get? If, in due course, the shipowner fails to service his loan owing to a protracted depression, then the banker faces another decision: Should I foreclose now and take a loss on the ships or wait in the hope that

the market will improve? Since bankers are working at narrow margins, these decisions depend upon a view of the relative probability of certain events occurring.

- *Governments.* The area of the industry in which governments are most extensively involved is shipbuilding. For most of the twentieth century, government ministers in Europe, North America and, more recently, Japan have been confronted by a continuous series of difficult decisions about the shipbuilding industry. These decisions involve issues such as whether or not to provide subsidy and whether or not to cut capacity. Many Third World governments are heavily involved in shipping policy, confronted with such decisions as whether or not to set up a national shipping line and how to manage it. All these decisions involve weighing short-term benefits against long-term risks. If a minister decides to subsidize a shipyard rather than allow it to close, he avoids a short-term political problem, but ties himself into a longer-term problem if, in fact, the shipyard remains unprofitable.
- *Port authorities.* Since the Second World War there have been enormous changes in the volume of cargo transported and the type of ships used. There is intense competition between ports to attract cargo by offering advanced cargo handling facilities for containers, large bulk carriers and specialist product terminals. The provision of these facilities involves major capital investment in terms of civil engineering, cargo handling equipment and dredging. As a result, decisions about port development depend crucially upon traffic forecasting to find out the volume of cargo, the way it will be packed and the ship types used. For example, the decision on whether or not to invest in a specialist container terminal involves such questions as: How much container cargo will be moving through our part of the coast? What volume of this cargo can we attract through our port? What facilities will we need to offer in future to attract this share of the cargo?
- *Machinery manufacturers.* By any standards, merchant ships are massive engineering structures and, with a total fleet of 72,000 vessels, there is an enormous industry world-wide manufacturing components for fitting into new ships – engines, generators, winches, cranes, navigation equipment, etc. – and spare parts and equipment to upgrade the existing fleet. Producers of this type of equipment are faced with decisions about what type of products to develop and how to manage their capacity. This involves looking at trends in ship construction, future developments in operational management of ships, ship operating economics and the activity of competitors.
- *Shippers.* The majority of shippers simply expect the maritime industry to be there when they want to use it, but some major companies may ship cargo in sufficient volume to be concerned about securing their future transport costs. For example, the major oil companies have traditionally met a proportion of their shipping requirements by running their own ships, and using the charter market to meet fluctuations in demand. Once this approach has been adopted, the companies are faced with decisions about the size and type of fleet to maintain.
- *International organizations.* Organizations such as the OECD, EU, the Association of Western European Shipbuilders (AWES), IMO, UNCTAD, and the Shipbuilders Association of Japan (SAJ) do not actually make commercial decisions, but they are

invariable drawn into the discussion of maritime policy. For example, the European Union produces Directives on Aid to Shipbuilding and has commissioned forecasts for this purpose.[5]

Each decision will be different and forecasting requirements must be carefully defined – it is unlikely that a 'general-purpose' forecast will meet the specific need of the decision-maker, though it may set the scene for the more specific work.

Who makes the forecast?

Although all of these decision-makers are obliged to take a view of the future when they make their decisions, it is clear that some are better equipped to do so than others. In general, by the time shipowners reach the position of making key decisions, they have achieved a great deal of knowledge about the shipping market and practical experience in judging the way events will develop. In these circumstances, it is entirely logical that the decision-maker should take his own view of the future. In many cases it would be extremely difficult to hire someone with the equivalent skills to do it for him. However, such experienced individuals make up only a small proportion of the key decision-makers in the maritime market. Bankers, government officials, shipbuilding executives and board members of major oil companies and shipping conglomerates are confronted by decisions concerning a complex industry that they may have neither the experience nor the time to study in depth. These decision-makers can hardly be expected to take their own view of the future, and in such cases a professional forecast is essential.

The need for a professional forecast also increases as more people are involved in making the decision. In the case of an independent shipowner buying a ship with his own cash for registration in Liberia, there is only one person involved in the decision – himself. If, however, he wishes to raise finance there are the bank lending officer and the bank's credit control department to convince. If the ship is to be purchased by the shipping division of a large group, there are the divisional board, the corporate board and the bank to consider, so that in some cases a very large number of people will be involved in deciding whether or not to buy the ship. Where large organizations are involved, it is extremely difficult to gain agreement to a decision resting entirely on the judgement of a single individual. Decision-makers need to be able to study the evidence and, if they know little of the subject, to have it checked by independent experts. In such cases a forecast becomes essential. Returning to our original question: Who makes the forecast? the answer is that ideally the decision-maker should do so, but if he lacks either the time or the experience to study the matter properly, or if he has a large group of other individuals to carry with him in the decision, then the forecast should be made by suitably qualified experts and written up in a report.

Identifying the economic model

There is one more technical point to clarify before we can proceed to the practicalities of making maritime forecasts; this is the thorny question of deciding what is actually predictable. It is important because, however much we dress up our forecasts in terms of scenarios or probabilities, they will only be of value to the decision-maker if the advice offered is right more often than it is wrong, and the fact is that some things are unpredictable. The classic illustration is the forecasting agency that predicts that there will be a boom in tanker freight rates. Shipowners see the forecast and order tankers, with the result that freight rates fall owing to oversupply. The forecast is proved wrong simply because shipowners believed that it would be right. The moral of this story is that not everything is predictable and we must approach the forecasting process with this firmly in mind.

To develop this line of thought we need to be clear about the rationale used in forecasting. We constantly make forecasts in our everyday life using the principle of 'constant conjunction' first observed by the eighteenth-century philosopher, David Hume, in his *Treatise on Human Nature.* Hume concluded that we conduct our lives on the assumption that future events will generally follow the patterns we have observed in the past.

For example, we expect it to rain because it is cloudy and, from past experience, we associate clouds with rain. In shipping, we may predict that trade will increase when the world economy recovers because this has always happened in the past. This form of verbal reasoning is the basis of most economic analysis. For example, we might extend the simple weather analysis by taking account of additional relationships. Are some types of cloud more likely to produce rain than others?

Once we start asking questions like this, the problem becomes more complex, and to deal with this economists use the concept of a *model.* The first step is to specify the precise nature of the model by identifying the variables which we believe are related and, from what we know, guessing the nature of the relationship between them. In the case of the weather model, one variable might be the percentage of blue sky visible in the morning and the other the hours of rain during the day. If we can quantify these two variables, for example by keeping records of their values every day for a year, we can analyse the data to measure the relationship (the number relating the variables is known as a *parameter*) and test the relationship. The point of the test is to see whether the relationship between them is significant (are the variables really related?) and stable (will the parameter keep changing?). If the model does not pass these tests we might try a different specification. Other variables affecting the weather might be the temperature and the barometric pressure. If a more consistent relationship emerges, we have the basis for making a more authoritative forecast – If the pressure is falling and there is 100 per cent cloud cover, we can expect five hours rain. Although they are not always correct, such forecasts can be helpful to us in taking day-to-day decisions like whether to wear a raincoat. Precisely the same principles apply in making business forecasts, but the time-scale is longer and there are many more variables to analyse, with the result that it requires more skill to draw a conclusion.

Identifying an economic model and measuring the relationship between the variables, is a challenging task. In reality some variables are more predictable than others and successful modelling depends on recognizing the nature of the variables and applying the appropriate analytical techniques. There are four different types, which we can refer to as 'tangible', 'technological', 'behavioural' and 'wild card'. Each of these has a different character:

- *Tangible variables.* These are physically verifiable and thus, in theory, have a high degree of predetermination. For example, the world's oil reserves, the calorific content of an oilfield and the maximum operating speed of an oil tanker can all be precisely defined, given sufficient information. For this reason, tangible variables tend to be reasonably predictable provided sufficient research is carried out – we are talking here about predicting such factors as future achievable oil production rates from the North Sea, though not actual output, which will depend on many other variables such as the oil price. Unfortunately the information about this type of variable can sometimes be inaccurate or misleading.
- *Technological variables.* A typical technological parameter is the amount of energy used per unit of industrial output. These relationships are often treated as parameters in forecasting models, but they can change substantially over time. In the early 1970s forecasters were confronted with the problem of predicting how the world economy would respond to higher oil prices, raising questions such as: Will the automobile industry be able to make vehicles more fuel efficient? The rate at which innovation could be introduced in response to a major price change is difficult to predict; nevertheless, with careful research, it is possible to form a reasoned view.
- *Behavioural relationships.* These depend primarily upon the way people behave. They can be very difficult to predict and in some cases attempts to predict them are self-defeating, as we saw in the case of the oil tanker forecast. Consequently the approach to forecasting is very different. For example, in a forecast of shipbuilding prices, a major factor determining the speed at which prices recover after a fall in demand is the extent to which shipbuilders reduce their capacity. In fact the question facing the forecaster is: How much will country X reduce capacity? and this depends on decisions still to be made. Behaviourals of this type are not predictable in the normal sense.
- *Wild cards.* Finally, there will be sudden departures from the established 'norm'. By definition they are unpredictable and there is really very little that can be done about them – life is, by its nature, a risky business.

Setting aside the problem of wild cards, the approach to predicting tangible and technological variables is quite different from the approach to predicting behavioural variables. In the former case, the emphasis is on careful research to establish the true facts of the matter. This is not always easy, since information treated as factual often turns out to be highly subjective. What is clear, however, is the need for painstaking research. Behavioural variables, in contrast, are subjective and the requirement is to understand and, if necessary, influence the way people behave in certain circumstances. How will shipowners behave when they see freight rates rising after a long recession? How will the Japanese shipbuilding industry respond to a long-standing overcapacity? These are difficult questions, but in some cases they will be of crucial importance in determining how events develop.

14.3 Forecasting methodologies

Market forecast or market research?

We now come to the practical issue of how to produce a maritime forecast. As we have seen, there are as many forecasts as there are decisions, so it is not possible to establish procedures that will apply in every case. What we can do is examine the general methodology and, in particular, the techniques that have been found to work in a variety of different circumstances.

It is useful to start by drawing the general distinction between market forecasts and market research. In the present context, these terms can be defined as follows:

- A shipping *market forecast* is concerned with the future of the market as a whole, or major parts of the market such as tankers and bulk carriers. It predicts the external environment within which a company's strategy will be implemented.
- Shipping *market research* is concerned with a specific commercial decision. In the case of shipping, this means studying the prospects for a specific ship, ship type, trade flow or business unit.

The distinction is important because of the basic differences in methodology and research techniques between the two types of analysis.

Figure 14.2 summarizes some of the practical differences between market forecasts and market research. In terms of objectives, market forecasts often have rather general terms of reference, whereas market research is generally linked to a defined business decision. The methodology of the market forecast tends to be dominated by statistical analysis, since statistics are the best way of representing large groups where the 'law of large numbers' can be assumed to apply. Consequently, analysis is numerical and often involves computer modelling. In contrast, market research tends to be more closely concerned with technical and behavioural variables, which are less easily represented in statistical terms – models can be used to establish the framework, but the central issues are questions like: How will competitors or charterers react? which are best dealt with by research into the current views and behaviour patterns of the relevant decision-makers. Numerical analysis is still important but is generally of a financial nature.

In preparing a market research study it is generally necessary to narrow down the area of analysis to make the task manageable in terms of the volume of information to be handled. This leads to one of the most important functions of the market forecast, which is to 'set the scene' for the more detailed market research study. However thorough the market research may be, it cannot afford to ignore trends in the market as a whole. If we take an analogy from road transport, the market forecast is equivalent to the road map that establishes where the main roads go, while the market research is equivalent to the route plan a driver prepares before setting out on a long journey. He will certainly refer to the road map, but his route plan will be unique. It will deal with a specific journey and, to be successful, must take account of such details as expected traffic density, speed limits, short cuts and road repair work which might cause delays, none of which are shown on the map. Of course motorists going on long journeys do not have to consult maps, or prepare route plans. Many just set off and follow the road signs, hoping not to get lost. Much the same is true of decision-makers in the shipping market.

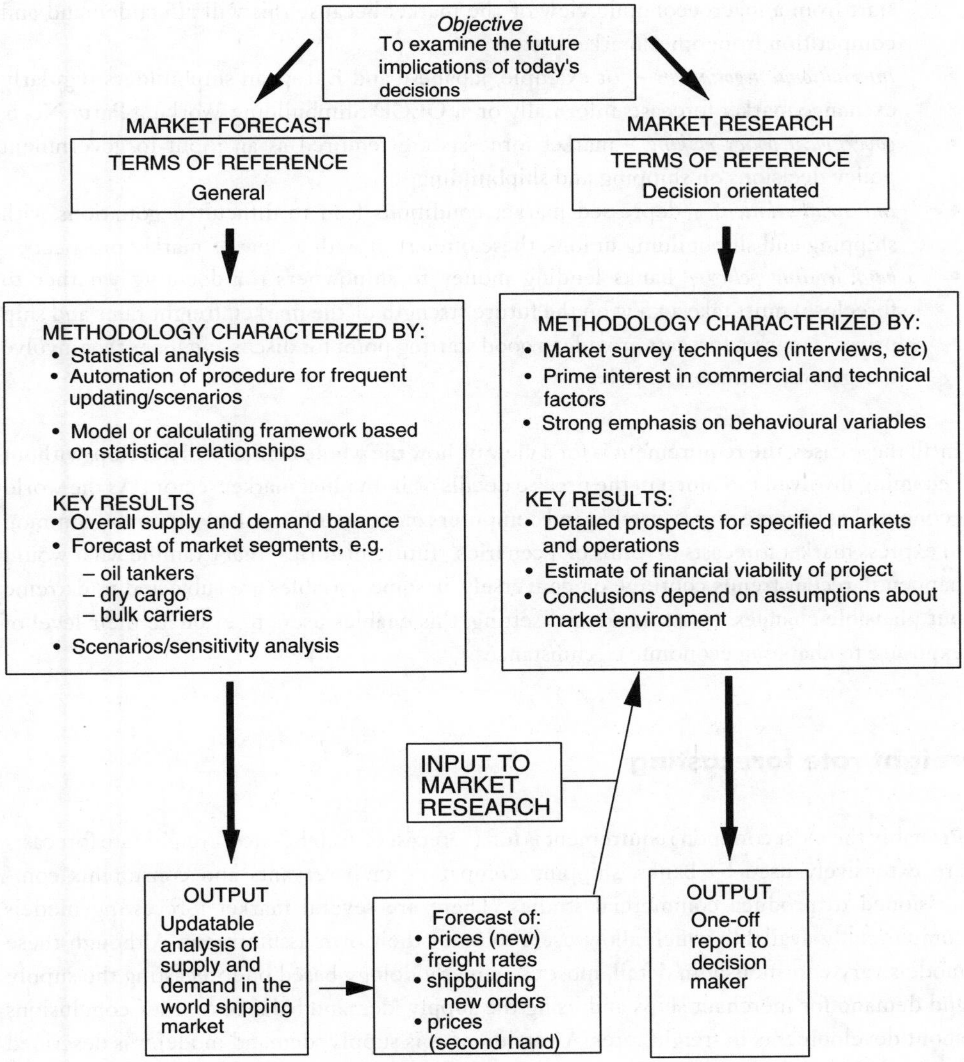

FIGURE 14.2 Differences between maritime market forecasting and market research

Source: Compiled by Martin Stopford from various sources

Market forecasting methodology

Having said this, market forecasts are widely used in the shipping industry. Some of the more important uses are:

- *strategic and corporate planning* – shipping companies use a market forecast/scenario to 'set the scene' for their corporate plan;
- *product market analysis* – although microeconomic in character, product forecasts must start from a macroeconomic view of the market because this will affect demand and competition from other market sectors;
- *international negotiations* – for example, Japanese and European shipbuilders regularly exchange market forecasts informally or at OECD Shipbuilding Working Party No. 6;
- *government policy-making* – market forecasts are required as an input to government policy decisions on shipping and shipbuilding;
- *industrial relations* – depressed market conditions lead to difficult negotiations with shipping and shipbuilding unions; these often start with a view of market prospects;
- *bank lending policy* – banks lending money to shipowners (or deciding whether to foreclose) must take a view on the future strength of the market, freight rates and ship prices; a market forecast provides a good starting point for discussing loans that involve a degree of commercial risk.

In all these cases, the requirement is for a view of how the whole market will develop, without becoming involved too much in the precise details of individual market sectors. As the world economy has become more unstable and computers more readily available, it is now common to express market forecasts in terms of 'scenarios' (future histories) that examine what would happen if recent trends continue or, conversely, if some variables are subjected to extreme but plausible changes. In a commercial setting, this enables users to evaluate their level of exposure to changing economic circumstances.

14.4 Freight rate forecasting

Probably the most common requirement is for a forecast of freight rates. Freight rate forecasts are extensively used by banks, shipping companies, civil servants and consultants commissioned to produce commercial studies. There are several market forecasting models commercially available which allow users to enter their own assumptions. Although these models vary enormously in detail, most use a methodology based on forecasting the supply and demand for merchant ships and using the supply/demand balance to draw conclusions about developments in freight rates. A version of this supply/demand model was described in chapter 4 and provides a consistent framework for preparing a market forecast of the shipping market. To assist analysts wishing to pursue this technique further, Appendix 1 contains a description of the arithmetic structure of the model. It must be emphasized that this model is only a framework, which needs to be developed in greater detail in order to produce forecasts that are significant for particular purposes.

The practical procedure for producing a forecast using the Shipping Market Model (SMM) described in Appendix 1 involves working through eight separate stages.

Stage 1: Economic assumptions

The first step is to decide what period the forecast is to cover and to discuss what assumptions should be made about the way in which the world economy will develop during this period. Specific requirements of the forecasting model are an assumption about the rate of growth of gross domestic product (GDP) and industrial production (IP) in the main economic regions. Deciding which regions to include, and in how much detail is a key task. Oil prices will also play an important part, as will views on such issues as political instability, passage through the Suez Canal, etc.

Stage 2: The seaborne trade forecast

The next step is to forecast seaborne trade during the period under review. The simplest method is to use a regression model[6] of the following type:

E14(1)

$$ST = f\ (IPt)$$

where: ST = seaborne trade
IP = industrial production
t = year subscript.

Suppose, for example, we assume that there is a linear relationship between seaborne trade and industrial production. The linear equation which represents this model is:

E14(2)

$$ST_t = a + bX_t$$

This model suggest that the two variables seaborne trade (ST) and industrial production (X) move together in a linear way. For example if industrial production increases by $1 billion, seaborne trade increases by 100,000 tons, etc. The precise nature of the relationship is measured by the two parameters a and b. Using past data, and linear regression technique we can estimate the value of the two parameters a and b. As an example, Figure 14.3a shows this model fitted to data for the period 1963–80 using a linear regression:

E14(3)

$$ST_t = -802.8 + 45.59X_t$$

What does this model tell us? The estimate for *b* shows us that during the period 1963 to 1980, for each 1 point increase in the industrial production index, seaborne trade increases by 45.59 mt. The 'fit' of the equation is excellent, with a correlation coefficient of 0.99, which means that changes in industrial production 'explain' 99 per cent of the changes in sea trade. If we accept the model, a forecast of seaborne trade can then be made by substituting an assumed value of industrial production for *X* and calculating the associated level of seaborne trade.

How reliable is this model? One way to test it is by carrying out a simulation analysis. We feed the actual industrial production index for the years 1981 to 1996 into the model and compare the predicted level of sea trade with the actual trade volume. The result shown, in Figure 14.3(a), is disappointing. Anyone who used this model to forecast trade volume would have been wide of the mark. In 1986, six years into the projection period, the forecast of seaborne trade is 4.3 bt but by that year actual sea trade had only reached 3.4 bt, a 26 per cent error. Clearly the underlying relationship has changed and the model no longer works.

The problem with very simple models of this type is that we have no way of knowing why the relationship has changed. A more thorough approach, which helps to overcome this problem, would be to subdivide the trade into separate commodities, e.g. crude oil, oil products, iron ore, coal, grain, etc., and to develop a more detailed model of the type discussed in Chapter 7 (section 7.6), for each commodity trade. For example we might start by splitting seaborne trade into dry cargo and oil and estimating the regression model separately for each commodity, again using data for the period 1963 to 1980.

The results of this analysis for dry cargo analysis is shown in Figure 14.3b. For the years 1963 to 1980 we estimate the relationship between the tonnage of dry cargo trade each year and OECD industrial production. Once again the fit is excellent, with a regression coefficient of 0.98. When we use the equation to project seaborne trade through to 1996 using actual OECD industrial production the forecast proves to be very accurate. The model predicts seaborne dry cargo trade of 2.7 bt in 1996, compared with actual trade of 2.87 bt. A 6 per cent error over 16 years is a far better result than most economists would dare to hope for. This model has certainly worked in the past, though this is no guarantee that it will continue to work in the future.

When we extend the exercise to the oil trade the result is much less satisfactory, as can be seen in Figure 14.3c. Although the model fits well during the base period 1963 to 1980, the projection for 1996 is 50 per cent too high. Clearly this is where the inaccuracy of the original trade model originated. When the oil price increased in 1989 many power stations switched from oil to coal and the oil trade declined. A properly specified model of the type discussed in Chapter 7 (section 7.6) would incorporate a price variable to pick up this substitution effect, thus providing a more reliable basis for making forecasts – provided you can predict when oil prices are going to rise.

Some of the more sophisticated market forecasting models subdivide trade into many commodities and forecast each commodity trade using a set of equations. In theory more information should lead to a more reliable result. The danger is that it is very time-consuming and can easily generate so much detail that the underlying rationale of the forecast is lost. The key issue is to identify a significant level of detail to work at.

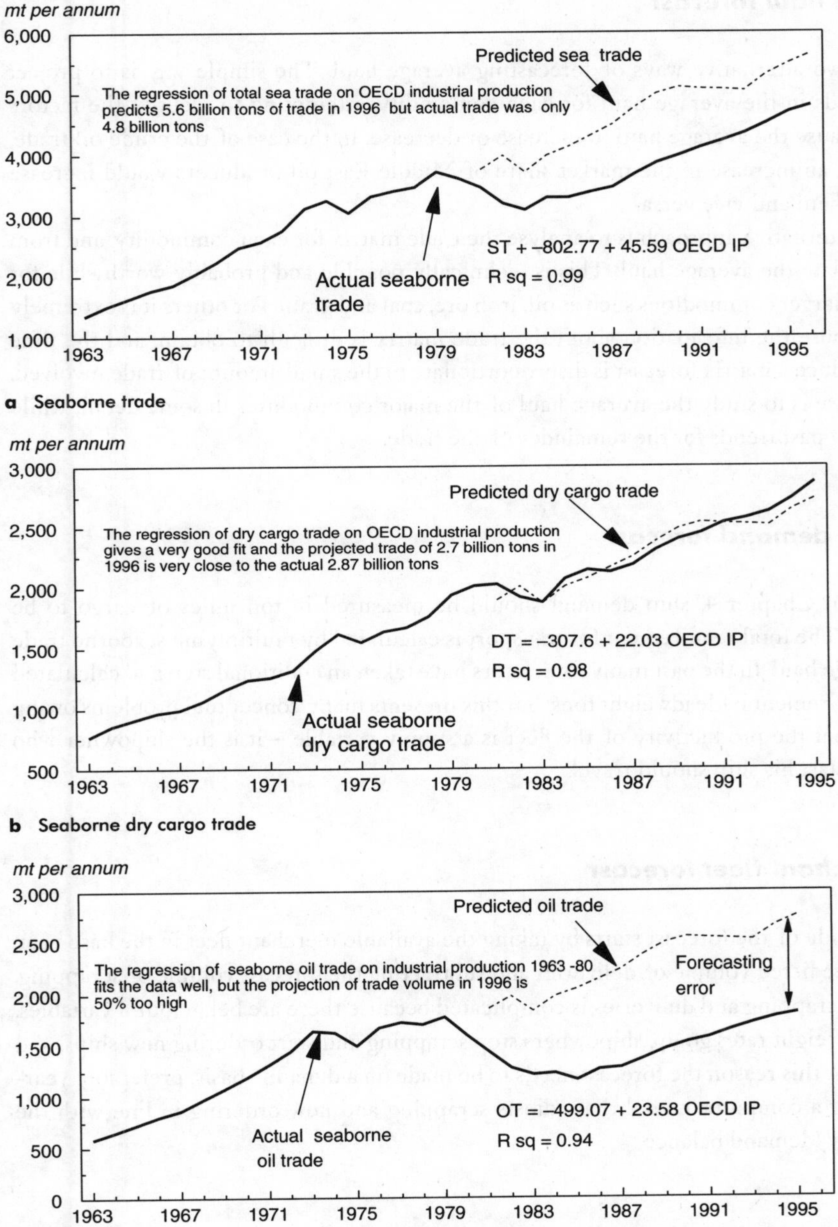

c Seaborne oil trade

FIGURE 14.3 Seaborne trade models (calculated by taking regression of seaborne trade on OECD industrial production 1963–80, with prediction for trade 1981–96)

Source: Fearnleys Annual Review, various editions

Stage 3: Average haul forecast

There are two alternative ways of forecasting average haul. The simple way is to project historic trends in the average haul for each commodity, attempting to identify the factors that might cause the average haul to increase or decrease. In the case of the crude oil trade, for example, an increase in the market share of Middle East oil producers would increase the average haul and vice versa.

The alternative approach is to analyse the trade matrix for each commodity, and from this to calculate the average haul. This is technically possible and probably worthwhile for some of the larger commodities such as oil, iron ore, coal and grain. For others it is extremely difficult because the information about the trade matrix is difficult to obtain, and the time taken to produce a matrix forecast is disproportionate to the small amount of trade involved. A compromise is to study the average haul of the major commodities in some detail, while extrapolating past trends for the remainder of the trade.

Stage 4: The ship demand forecast

As we saw in Chapter 4, ship demand should be measured in ton miles of cargo to be transported. The total requirement for transport is calculated by multiplying seaborne trade by the average haul. In the past many forecasters have taken an additional step and calculated the ship requirement in deadweight tons, but this presents many conceptual problems owing to the fact that the productivity of the fleet is a supply variable – it is the shipowner who decides how fast his ship should travel.

Stage 5: The merchant fleet forecast

The supply side of the forecast starts by taking the available merchant fleet in the base year, adding the predicted volume of deliveries and subtracting the forecast volume of scrapping. Forecasting scrapping and deliveries is complicated because these are behavioural variables. The minute freight rates go up, shipowners stop scrapping and start ordering new ships, and vice versa. For this reason the forecast needs to be made on a dynamic basis, preferably year-by-year using a computer model that adjusts scrapping and new ordering in line with the overall supply/demand balance.

Stage 6: Ship productivity forecast

As we saw in Chapter 4, the productivity of a ship is measured by the number of ton miles of cargo carried per deadweight of merchant shipping capacity per annum. There are two forecasting methods. The simplest is to take a statistical series of the past productivity of the merchant fleet (see Figure 4.8) and project this forward, taking account of any changes of trend that may be thought appropriate. Since productivity depends on market conditions, the forecast needs to be developed on a dynamic basis that recognizes that when market conditions improve the fleet will speed up and vice versa. A more sophisticated methodology is to build up the forecast of productivity using an equation of the type described in equation E5(7) in Chapter 5.

Stage 7: The shipping supply forecast

Finally, the available shipping supply is calculated in ton miles by multiplying the available deadweight tonnage of ships by their productivity. By definition, supply must equal demand. If supply is greater than demand, the residue is assumed to be laid up; if supply is less than demand, the fleet productivity must be increased.

Stage 8: The balance of supply and demand

As we have already stressed, the process of developing a supply/demand forecast of this type depends on behavioural variables, namely the scrapping and investment decisions of shipowners. This is the most difficult part of the model. By definition we know that supply must equal demand, and if the forecast level of supply does not match the forecast level of demand, then we must go back through the whole process again and make the adjustments that we believe the market would make in response to financial stimuli such as asset prices and freight rates and market sentiment.

Stage 9: Freight rates

Now we come to the heart of the forecast, the level of freight rates which will accompany each level of supply and demand. We discussed the relationship between supply, demand and freight rates in chapter 4, relating demand to the shipping supply function and showing how prices are established in different time frames. This is the method which should be used. From a technical viewpoint the most difficult element to model is the 'hockey stick' shape of the supply curve accurately. Regression equations relating freight rates to laid up tonnage do not generally work very well due to the difficulty of finding a functional form which picks up the 'spiky' shape of freight graph. Simulation models offer a more satisfactory solution.

A typical market forecast generally includes predictions of the rate of growth of ship demand, the requirement for newbuilding tonnage and the overall balance of supply and demand. There may also be scenarios of freight rates and prices.

Finally a word of caution. Analysts who successfully design and use a model of this type will learn an important lesson about the freight market which only becomes obvious when the relationships are quantified. As the market modelled approaches balance, the freight rates become so sensitive to small changes in assumptions that the only way to produce a sensible forecast is to adjust the assumptions until the model predicts a level of freight rates which is determined by the forecaster. That is the nature of the market. When there are two ships and two cargoes freight rates are determined by market sentiment at auction, a process which defies prediction. At their best shipping market models are educational in the sense that they help decision-makers to understand in simple graphic terms what could happen, but when it comes to predicting what will actually happen they are very blunt instruments.

14.5 Market research methodology

Market research studies focus on a particular part of the market, usually in connection with some specific commercial project involving investment in fixed assets or in the development of new products or services. For example, a banker deciding whether to finance a fleet of products tankers; a bulk operator deciding whether to order a 35,000 dwt general-purpose bulk carrier or a 45,000 dwt shallow-draft vessel; a port authority deciding how much to

BOX 14.1 Suggested procedure for a market research study

1 *Establish terms of reference*
- 1.1 Discuss decision to which study will contribute with decision-maker.
- 1.2 Identify type of information required.
- 1.3 Specify means by which results are to be presented.
- 1.4 Make realistic estimate of time and resources required for study.
- 1.5 Ensure resources are available.

2 *Analyse past trends*
- 2.1 Define market structure/segmentation.
- 2.2 Identify competition.
- 2.3 Compile database and tabulate.
- 2.4 Calculate trends and analyse their causes.
- 2.5 Extract cyclical effects.

3 *Survey competitors' plans and opinions of experts*
- 3.1 Identify main competitors.
- 3.2 Survey opinions of experts on future developments.
- 3.3 Survey plans of companies operating in market.
- 3.4 Prepare summary of the industry's view of the business.

4 *Identify key variables that will influence future market development*
- 4.1 Determine future market environment (from market forecast).
- 4.2 List key factors that will influence future outcome.
- 4.3 Prioritize variables in terms of their potential future impact on the market (e.g. on scale 1–10).

5 *Combine information into scenarios*
- 5.1 Identify scenario themes (e.g. What is the worst that can happen? What is the best that can happen?).
- 5.2 Develop detailed scenarios for each theme.
- 5.3 Write scenarios as clearly as possible.

6 *Present results*
- 6.1 Executive summary
- 6.2 Detailed report.
- 6.3 Verbal presentation.

invest in upgrading container handling facilities; a shipyard interesting in entering the chemical tanker market.

For each of these decision-makers better information can help to reduce the risk of making a bad investment. The banker is interested in the commercial future for tankers of a specific size, age and design so that he does not end up financing a fleet of ships which turn out to be very difficult to charter. Similarly, the bulk operator needs to evaluate details such as size trends, fuel economy, the options for automation, cargo handling gear, prices on offer, 'charterability of the vessel', resale value and what his competitors are doing. The port authority needs to know what aspects of a container terminal are most important to operators.

This type of market research requires a combination of commercial and economic knowledge. The statistical techniques that are so useful in market forecasting can often be omitted; the emphasis is on identifying the factors that will significantly influence the success or failure of the commercial decision, gathering information and assessing how these may develop. A major part of the task in carrying out the market research study is therefore deciding what the scope of the study should be. For example, a shipowner thinking of buying a chemical tanker obviously needs to consider the future growth and development of the chemical trade, but he must also look at a wide range of factors such as the commercial strength and plans of existing operators in that trade. A systematic procedure for carrying out a market research study is illustrated in Box 14.1, which lists the six main tasks involved.

The first step is to establish the terms of reference of the study. The researcher has to answer the question: What decision is to be made, and how will the study contribute? A great deal depends upon the stage of thinking that has been reached. For example, a liner company considering setting up a new service would need to decide what type of operation to set up and how much to invest in it. In this case some of the questions it must answer are:

- What is the size of the market that is accessible to me and what share might I win?
- How will freight rates develop on that route?
- What aspects of the service will be most important in achieving future sales?
- What ship type will be most cost effective in providing this service?
- How will competitors react to a new entrant to the trade?

Setting out the terms of reference in this way makes it clear that the decision-maker is seeking much more than a simple forecast of the trade on a particular route. He needs advice on how the competitive position is likely to develop and how the commercial environment in which he will be operating will change.

The next step is to assemble whatever information is readily available on the current position and to analyse past trends. Defining the market segment can often be quite difficult because it may be one of the issues that the study is expected to help resolve. For example, a shipowner considering the purchase of a small products tanker for trading on the charter market may not be sure precisely what type of vessel is required. Should it be able to trade in chemicals? Is it for clean or dirty products? How much attention should be given to tank cleaning?

Once the market segment has been defined, the next step is to identify the competition, since in the shipping market strongly growing demand does not necessarily bring commercial success – the shipowner may find himself squeezed out of the market by cut-throat competition. In the case of a shipbuilding company, this may involve identifying other shipyards with a known capability in the market segment and assembling information about their commercial performance. In a bulk shipping project, it may involve identifying the fleet of ships able to trade in this market and analysing the future orderbook and financial position of other operators. An integral part of this whole process is to compile a database drawing together as much information about market trends as is readily available.

The compilation of the database should be done in such a way that it illustrates the main trends affecting the trade. Often this is difficult because information is incomplete or unavailable, but it should aim to provide an overview of what is happening in the market, which the analyst can then investigate and explain. A final step is to consider any cyclical effects which may be at work – for example, recent strong growth may be due to the economic business cycle rather than a long-term trend.

Although statistics provide an overview, at best they record only the recent past and often give little indication of changes which are too recent to appear as a statistical trend. For example, a firm of consultants commissioned to produce a forecast of the shipping market in the mid-1960s produced an elegant mathematical model based on statistics. Unfortunately, as industry commentators were quick to point out, they made no mention of containerization, at a time when the first services were at the advanced planning stage. Had they interviewed experts this development would soon have been drawn to their attention.

To avoid this type of error it is important to survey the opinions of people involved in business and the plans of companies operating in the relevant market segment. This involves:

- identifying the relevant experts to question;
- deciding on a list of the questions that need to be answered;
- selecting the most appropriate method of surveying opinions.

There are many established techniques for surveying opinion, ranging from the personal interview to the general questionnaire.[7] For example, an opinion survey of the ferry market revealed that the commercial trend was strongly towards treating the ship as a 'floating hotel' in order to maximize on-board expenditure by passengers. This provided the basis for a new line of investigation about how this trend would develop over the next decade.

The first three stages of the research procedure outlined in Box 14.2 lay the foundation for the study by defining its aims, analysing statistical trends, obtaining the views of experts, and identifying the plans of competitors operating in the market. It remains to draw up the report, and this is subdivided into three steps. The first is to decide what the future market environment is likely to be and how sensitive the market sector is to these trends. This involves asking questions like: How sensitive is this market to commercial conditions in other sectors of the shipping market? For example, during the 1970s the market for small products tankers proved to be comparatively robust against the surplus of very large crude carriers

(VLCCS) that developed in the second half of the decade. Conversely, in the dry bulk carrier market there was a tendency for a surplus of large combined carriers to push down into the Panamax market, forcing them into the handy bulk carrier markets. The next two steps are to single out the factors that are likely to be most important in determining the future outcome for the project and to examine how these will develop. For example, a study concerning the purchase of an oil products tanker might identify as a key factor the development of export refineries in oil-producing countries and look into this.

Finally, a valuable presentation technique is to draw up several alternative scenarios of how the project may develop under different circumstances. The aim of this approach is to enable the decision-maker to think through the implications of his decision under a variety of different circumstances. For example, suppose some of the key influences on the market develop unfavourably, what would happen and how would the company be able to react? Suppose, for example, the company buys products tankers and the Middle East refineries are cancelled. Would it matter? Is there any action that can be taken now to guard against such an event? This is not nearly as easy to carry out in practice as it sounds, but it is preferable to the 'spot prediction' technique.[8]

14.6 Forecasting problems

Problems with model specifications and assumptions

There are many obstacles to producing a worthwhile forecast and it is useful to round off our discussion of forecasting methods with a review of some of the errors that can easily trap the unwary. One obvious danger area is in developing the framework (or model) and deciding what assumptions to use. The following problems often occur:[9]

1. *Incorrect or superficial model specification.* The forecast may analyse and measure only surface factors and ignore important underlying forces. For example, when considering the future of the seaborne coal trade, it is important to take account of new technology which may, for example, change the type or volume of coal used in steelmaking. In the previous section we saw the consequences of not taking account of oil prices when forecasting the oil trade.
2. *Consensus assumptions.* P.W. Beck, Planning Director for Shell UK Ltd, points out one problem – the absence of independent forecasts among rival forecasters. Beck found that there were few 'uncorrelated estimates' in the work done by so-called independent forecasters, all of whom tend to make use of the same assumptions, statistics and theories.[10]
3. *Consensus results.* When uncertain what to predict, forecasters often check their results against other forecasts, with the result that predictions made at a particular point in time are all very similar, and are not really independent.
4. *Too much detail.* There is a research rule of thumb that the researcher will identify 80 per cent of the facts in 20 per cent of the time required to obtain 100 per cent of the

facts. Put another way, it is easy to spend a long time investigating interesting but unimportant matters and lose sight of the overall objective.

5 *Unchallenged preconceptions.* It is all too easy to assume that certain assumptions or relationships are correct and to accept them without question. Careful examination may show that under some circumstances they may be wrong (look how often forecasters have been caught out by oil price changes).

6 *Attempting to predict the unpredictable.* Some variables, such as the actions of small groups of people, are intrinsically unpredictable and to attempt to predict them can create a false sense of security for decision-makers who assume that the forecast has a 'scientific' basis.

The forecaster needs constantly to ask the question: Am I falling into one of these traps?

The problem of monitoring results

When we look at past forecasts, we see just how difficult forecasting really is. Even deciding whether a forecast was right is not as easy as it seems. The problem was neatly summarized in an article reviewing the forecasting record of the UK National Institute of Economics and Social Research over a period of 23 years.[11] The article comments:

> It might be imagined that it must be possible, after a certain time has elapsed, to conclude in an unambiguous way whether a forecast has turned out to be correct or not. Unfortunately, the comparison of forecasts with actual results is not nearly as straightforward as it sounds. The first difficulty is that official statistics often leave a considerable margin of doubt as to how big the increase or decrease in output has been. The three measures of GDP (from expenditure, income and output) often give conflicting readings. Moreover the estimates are frequently revised, so that a forecast which originally appeared wrong, may later appear right and vice versa. Another difficulty is that forecasts, which were pre-budget, were conditional on unchanged policies. Since policies often did change it would be inappropriate to compare the forecasts directly with what actually happened.

These comments apply to forecasts of gross domestic product one year ahead. Assessing the accuracy of shipping forecasts presents just as many problems. In some cases we find that the forecasts are of ship demand, but there are no published statistics of ship demand with which we can compare the forecasts to judge their accuracy. In others, the statistical data base has been so manipulated that it requires a considerable effort to reduce currently available statistics to a form comparable with the forecast.

The difficulty of making accurate comparisons of the predictions with actual events led M. Baranto to comment 'The analysis of forecasting errors is not a simple process – ironically it is as difficult as making forecasts.'[12] Care is needed to produce forecasts that are capable of being monitored quickly and easily by users.

The problem of escaping from the present

Perhaps the greatest challenge facing any forecaster is to escape from the present. An illuminating example of this is provided by a forecast of the British economy in 1984, which was published in the early 1960s. The study is of particular interest because it was so wide-ranging and explicit in both its assumptions and its predictions. Reviewing the book 20 years later, Prowse[13] draws the following conclusions:

- Some of the basic assumptions that appeared unquestionable at the time have proved to be very wide of the mark. For example, the study contains the passage: 'It has been assumed throughout that no Government in power will permit unemployment to rise above 500,000 (2 per cent of the labour force) for any length of time.' In a similar vein, it assumed that there would be an 'average rise in retail prices of 1–2 per cent per annum.' Neither of these assumptions looked unreasonable in terms of the statistical trends evident in 1964. In fact, by 1984 Britain had unemployment of 10–15 per cent in many areas of the country, while a reduction of the inflation rate to 5 per cent per annum was regarded as a major achievement.
- In the area of technological change, the forecasts proved to be equally wide of the mark. Written at a time when the Concorde supersonic liner project was at the development stage, the study anticipated the use of vertical take-off passenger airliners crossing the Atlantic in one-and-a-half hours. As it turned out the airlines, like shipping, preferred economies of scale to cutting edge technology. In 1984 no new Concordes had been built, and transit times had hardly changed, but 'Jumbo Jets' had made cheap air travel available on an unprecedented scale. In the motor industry it was the same story. The study anticipated the replacement of the petrol engine by the fuel cell. By 1984 the cars were still basically the same as in the 1960s, but their design had evolved, making them more fuel efficient, better built and relatively cheaper. In all these cases revolution was predicted, but the commercial world chose evolution. Yet some revolutions were overlooked. The potential of computers was recognized in the statement 'By 1984 the electronic computer will have come into its own', but the study did not anticipate the revolutionary impact which the microchip revolution has had on almost every area of business.
- Another area where problems arose was in the long-term projections of economic growth. The study predicted that UK productivity would increase by 2½ per cent per annum, and taken together with a 17 per cent rise in the labour force it was expected that real GDP would double by 1984. As it turned out, the stagnation of demand during the 1970s and the failure of productivity increases to materialize meant that the increase in output was only about one-third during the period.

At the time these forecasts were prepared, inflation was running at 1 per cent and within living memory prices had actually fallen; Concorde was the big technical phenomenon; and the first generation of nuclear power stations had been highly successful. In short, the forecasts seemed reasonable and it is easy to see the problems of following any alternative line of thought. A forecast in the mid-1960s that anticipated inflation rates of 20 per cent, or the virtual stagnation of the nuclear power programme, would have been extremely difficult to justify. The one certainty is that things will change and we must not be surprised by surprises.

14.7 Summary

Market forecasting and market research are the areas where maritime economics can make a direct contribution to business decision-making. We started this chapter by discussing the poor track record of forecasting in the maritime business and drawing attention to the paradox that, despite poor performance, decision-makers continue to regard forecasts as an essential part of the decision process. The explanation of this paradox lies in the fact that some of the most important decisions facing executives in the maritime industry demand judgement of future events. Where individuals do not have the knowledge or experience to make such judgements themselves, or where several different people are involved in making the decision, it is logical to ask for a forecast prepared by an independent expert.

All forecasts should satisfy three simple criteria – they should be *relevant* to the decision for which they are required; they should be *rational* in the sense that the conclusion should be based upon a consistent line of rational argument; and the findings should be based upon *research* at a significant level of detail.

Forecasts fall into two categories, market forecasts and market research. Market forecasts are concerned with the shipping market as a whole and typically take the form of supply/demand projections for major market sectors such as crude oil tankers, combined carriers and other vessels. They may also include forecasts of freight rates and ship prices. An eight-step programme for producing a maritime market forecast was discussed, using the supply/demand analysis developed in chapter 2 and described in mathematical form in Appendix 1.

Market research is generally linked to a specific commercial decision. For this reason each study must be planned to meet the information requirements of the decision-maker. We discussed a six-stage procedure for planning and developing a study of this type.

In the last section of the chapter we discussed forecasting problems. Many difficulties arise in specifying the 'model' underlying the forecast and selecting appropriate assumptions. All forecasts are based on some form of implicit and explicit model; in some cases, the problem is that the model is developed in insufficient detail, while in others the model becomes too large and complex to be manageable.

Another problem area is in monitoring forecasts against actual developments. This can prove to be difficult, particularly for statistical forecasts, unless care is taken to ensure that predictions are made in a form that is directly comparable with regularly published information.

Finally, we discussed the problem of being too strongly influenced by current events, and saw how easy it is for assumptions that appear unquestionable to prove to be wide of the mark. This problem is so obvious, and so serious, that it reinforces the argument for extreme caution in making forecasts far ahead. In the last resort, forecasting requires equal measures of technical expertise and common sense in judging what can reasonably be predicted with any degree of confidence.

Appendix 1

An Introduction to ship market modelling

Introduction

The first three chapters of the book, and particularly Chapter 4, were devoted to a discussion of the economic principles that underlie the shipping market. With the increasing power of microcomputers it has become possible to develop shipping market models that can assist in judging future trends in the shipping market. This appendix provides a brief description of the basic supply/demand framework, using numerical examples. This is not intended to be a complete model, but rather a skeleton that can then be developed in a number of different ways.

A supply/demand model of the shipping market

Since for most cargoes there is no viable alternative to ships on deep sea routes, the supply and demand for sea transport can be defined in the following way:

$$DD_t = f(CT_t, AH_t) \qquad \text{EA1(1)}$$

$$SS_t = f(MF_t, P_t) \qquad \text{EA1(2)}$$

where: DD = demand for seaborne transport (ton miles)
CT = tons of cargo transported in time period
AH = average haul of cargo (miles)
SS = supply of seaborne transport (cargo ton miles)
P = ship productivity (ton miles cargo/dwt/annum)
MF = merchant fleet (dwt)
t = year subscript.

Demand, measured in ton miles of transport required, is determined by the tonnage of cargo to be moved and the average distance over which each ton of cargo is transported. The supply of shipping capacity, measured in cargo ton miles, is determined by the merchant fleet capacity measured in deadweight tonnage and fleet performance, i.e. the average ton miles of cargo delivered per deadweight, per annum.

These definitions are highly simplified, but they make the important point that in economic terms, although the physical supply of ships is fixed at a given point in time, the available transportation capacity is flexible. As we saw in Chapter 4 transport supply depends on fleet performance, which is in turn is determined partly by market variables and partly by physical characteristics of the ships in the fleet.

Building on the definition of supply and demand in EA1(1) and (2), we can specify the basic structural equations of the macro model as follows:

Demand equations

$$CT_{tk} = f(E_t, \text{etc.}) \qquad \text{EA1(3)}$$

$$CT_t = \sum_k (CT_{tk}) \qquad \text{EA1(4)}$$

$$DD_{tk} = CT_{tk} \cdot AH_{tk} \qquad \text{EA1(5)}$$

$$DD_{tm} = \sum_k (A_{tkm} \cdot DD_{tk}) \qquad \text{EA1(6)}$$

$$A_{tkm} = \frac{DD_{tkm}}{DD_{tk}} \qquad \text{EA1(7)}$$

Supply equations

$$MF_{tm} = MF_{(t-1)m} + D_{tm} - S_{tm} \qquad \text{EA1(8)}$$

$$AMF_{tm} = MF_{tm} - L_{tm} \qquad \text{EA1(9)}$$

$$SS_{tm} = AMF_{tm} \cdot P_{tm} \qquad \text{EA1(10)}$$

Equilibrium condition

$$SS_{tm}(FR_{tm}) = DD_{tm}(FR_{tm}) \qquad \text{EA1(11)}$$

where: E = indicator of economic activity
A = market share of ship type (m)
D = deliveries of merchant ships in year (m.dwt)
S = scrapping of merchant ships in year
P = ship productivity (ton miles/dwt/annum)
AMF = active merchant fleet (m.dwt)
L = laid-up tonnage
FR = freight rate
m = ship types (e.g. tankers, etc.)
k = commodity (e.g. oil).

Dealing first with the demand side of the model, in EA1(3) and (4) we define seaborne trade as the aggregate of k individual commodity trades. The simplest forecasting model would treat seaborne trade in aggregate, as we did in the example in Chapter 14. This simulation analysis emphasized the importance of treating major commodity trades separately. Clearly the oil trade should be modelled separately in a way which takes account of developments in the energy market such as changing energy prices. A more detailed discussion of the approach to specifying the form of the functions in EA1(3) is discussed in Chapter 7. If this approach is followed the trade model can become complex and very time consuming to update. Alternatively, the volume of seaborne trade by commodity may be treated as an erogenous variable, and obtained from some other source, for example by using forecasts of trade published by consultancy organizations.

Moving on to EA1(5), the volume of ship demand generated by each commodity, k, and measured in ton miles is the product of the tonnage of cargo of each commodity and its average haul. At this stage, demand is expressed in terms of the total ton miles of demand generated by each commodity, k, and it is still necessary to transform this into demand by ship type, m. This is done in EA1(6), which shows that the demand for ship type m is defined as the market share of that ship type in each commodity trade, summed over all commodities. This is a simple relationship to write in algebraic terms, but is much more difficult to define in practice. In reality trade will be carried in whatever ships are available, which depends on what shipowners order, so analysing investment trends may be the answer.

We pick this up on the supply side of the model in EA1(8) which defines the fleet of ship type m as equalling the fleet in the previous year, plus deliveries and less scrapping during the year. This fleet includes all vessels of type m potentially available, but at any given time part of the fleet will not be trading. EA1(9) derives the active merchant fleet (AMF) by deducting laid-up tonnage from the total merchant fleet. This equation could be extended to include other categories of inactive tonnage, for example oil tankers in storage. Finally, EA1(10) shows that the supply of shipping capacity for ship type *m* is determined by the product of the active fleet and the productivity of that fleet, measured in ton miles of cargo delivered per annum.

The balancing condition in the model is shown in EA1(11), which specifies that the available ton mile supply of transport capacity of type *m* equals the ton mile demand at the equilibrium freight rate (FR). If too much supply is available, the freight rate will fall until equilibrium is achieved, by additional vessels being laid up or reduced steaming speeds. Conversely, if there is too much demand, the freight rate will rise until the demand is satisfied, though in the extreme case this may not be possible owing to the time-lag in delivering new ships.

The simple model set out in equations EA1(4–11) is deterministic, in the sense that the key equations take the form of simple algebraic identities. The model is also 'closed' in the sense that any change in demand must be matched by an identical change in supply, and vice versa. As a practical illustration of the basic shipping market model, we can take the three market segments for oil tankers, combined carriers and dry cargo vessels. The model, calculations are shown for tankers in Table A1.1, for dry cargo vessels in Table A1.2. Taking tankers as an example, the calculations can be, briefly summarized as follows:

1. Starting from the oil trade in column 1 and average haul in column 2, the oil trade is calculated in btm in column 3. A forecast would require predicting both of these variables exogenously.
2. Oil tanker demand in column 5 is calculated by deducting combined carrier cargo (column 4) from oil trade (column 3). This calls for a judgement about how the combined carrier fleet will change is size and how it will be distributed between the oil and dry cargo trades. This is usually a matter of relative freight rates, which means that so long as there is a combined carrier fleet the tanker market cannot be treated in isolation from the rest of the market.
3. The supply of tanker capacity starts from the total fleet in column 11, deducts tankers in grain (a rarity nowadays), tankers in oil storage (column 9) and tankers laid up (column 8), deriving the active tanker fleet in column 9.
4. Fleet performance is shown in column 7 in ton miles/dwt and tanker supply in column 6 in btm. As a 'memo' item column 8 show the tons per deadweight carried by the tanker fleet. This is another way of viewing productivity.

The statistics in these tables provide historical trends showing the relationships between the variables and the way they have changed in the past. To make a forecast requires input assumptions for the tanker fleet, trade and the combined carrier fleet in oil. From these variables surplus tonnage can be calculated as the balancing item, on the assumption that supply must equal demand. Substituting these into the model, the volume of surplus tonnage can be calculated. For good order Table A1.3 shows the underlying supply/demand model for the combined carrier fleet. The three supply/demand models in Tables A1.1–A1.3 can be progressively enlarged so that it generates its own forecasts of the key assumptions, for example by introducing equations to predict the future level of oil trade, average haul, fleet growth, etc. (see Chapter 14). Since the variables on the supply side include behavioural variables, automating them is very difficult.

Once the level of surplus tonnage has been established, an estimate can be made of the level of freight rates. In extreme cases where there is a very large surplus this is easy. We know that freight rates will fall to operating costs. The difficulty lies in modelling market behaviour when the demand curve is hovering in the 'kink' of the supply curve. Sometimes this is done with regression equations, but a simulation model is likely to work better. Whatever method is used, the first lesson modellers learn is that when the market is close to balance, tiny changes in supply or demand send rates shooting up or down, which makes forecasting very difficult. Unfortunately that is how the shipping market works. If it was easy to predict, there would be no need for a market.

TABLE A1.1 Supply/demand model – tanker fleet

	Tanker demand						*Tanker fleet*					
	Crude and products trade							*Less*				
Year	*Trade volume mt*	*Av. haul miles*	*Transport required btm*	*Less combined carriers btm*	*Oil tanker demand btm*	*Tanker fleet productivity tm dwt per annum*	*Active tanker Fleet m. dwt*	*Laid up m. dwt*	*Stor-age m. dwt*	*In grain m. dwt*	*Total tanker fleet m. dwt*	*Year*
	(1)	(2)	(3)	(4)	(5)	(6)	(7)	(8)	(9)	(10)	(11)	
1963	582	4,210	2,450	0	2,450	37,348	65.6	0.7		1.0	67.3	1963
1964	652	4,248	2,770	0	2,770	39,180	70.7	0.5		1.7	72.9	1964
1965	727	4,292	3,120	24	3,096	40,365	76.7	0.4		3.4	80.5	1965
1966	802	4,151	3,329	53	3,276	38,271	85.6	0.4		3.4	89.4	1966
1967	865	4,775	4,130	162	3,968	41,077	96.6	0.3		1.4	98.3	1967
1968	975	5,074	4,947	358	4,589	42,649	107.6	0.2		0.6	108.4	1968
1969	1,080	5,197	5,613	400	5,213	42,660	122.2	0.2		0.7	123.1	1969
1970	1,193	5,438	6,487	465	6,022	43,386	138.8	0.2		0.8	139.8	1970
1971	1,317	5,660	7,454	714	6,740	42,390	159.0	1.2		0.4	160.6	1971
1972	1,446	5,982	8,650	920	7,730	43,525	177.6	1.4		0.7	179.7	1972
1973	1,640	6,230	10,217	1255	8,962	44,877	199.7	0.3		1.4	201.4	1973
1974	1,625	6,536	10,621	1084	9,537	40,966	232.8	0.7		0.7	234.2	1974
1975	1,496	6,504	9,730	826	8,904	36,358	244.9	26.8		1.1	272.8	1975
1976	1,670	6,676	11,149	841	10,308	38,766	265.9	38.5		2.2	306.6	1976
1977	1,724	6,614	11,403	912	10,491	35,527	295.3	30.3		1.6	327.2	1977
1978	1,702	6,196	10,546	676	9,870	33,732	292.6	32.8	4.0	0.5	329.9	1978
1979	1,776	5,910	10,497	635	9,862	33,844	291.4	14.8	21.0	0.4	327.6	1979
1980	1,596	5,789	9,239	404	8,835	28,417	310.9	7.9	8.0	0.0	326.8	1980
1981	1,437	5,701	8,193	368	7,825	26,136	299.4	13.0	11.0	0.0	323.4	1981
1982	1,278	4,915	6,282	389	5,893	22,850	257.9	40.8	12.0	0.0	310.7	1982
1983	1,212	4,586	5,558	328	5,230	23,516	222.4	52.4	15.0	0.0	289.8	1983
1984	1,227	4,603	5,648	285	5,363	24,817	216.1	46.0	10.5	0.0	272.6	1984
1985	1,159	4,450	5,157	304	4,853	25,745	207.4	34.9	9.6	0.0	251.9	1985
1986	1,263	4,675	5,905	479	5,426	28,070	197.6	20.8	14.6	0.0	233.0	1986
1987	1,265	4,668	5,905	480	5,425	25,895	205.8	11.0	11.9	0.0	228.7	1987
1988	1,367	4,770	6,520	355	6,165	27,412	218.0	4.0	10.4	0.0	232.4	1988
1989	1,460	4,984	7,276	316	6,960	29,467	229.1	2.3	7.9	0.0	239.3	1989
1990	1,526	5,125	7,821	445	7,376	30,695	231.7	2.3	12.4	0.0	246.4	1990
1991	1,573	5,268	8,287	403	7,884	31,261	246.7	2.2	6.1	0	255.0	1991
1992	1,648	5,217	8,597	398	8,199	32,140	250.1	5.8	4.6	0	260.5	1992
1993	1,714	5,345	9,162	431	8,731	34,633	255.7	4.5	5.3	0	265.5	1993
1994	1,755	5,316	9,329	328	9,001	35,451	254.7	3.5	3.7	0	261.9	1994
1995	1,808	5,155	9,320	234	9,086	36,041	252.3	3.1	5.7	0	261.1	1995

Source:
1 Fearnleys Review, Table 1 – Oil + Oil Products
2 (3)/(1)*1,000
3 Fearnleys Review, Table 2 – Oil + Oil Products
4 Fearnleys World Bulk Trades, Table 2
5 (5)(3) – (4)
6 (5)/(7)*1,000
7 (11) – (10) – (9) – (8)
8 Fearnleys Review Table 7, at 31 Dec.
9 Fearnleys Review Table 8, at 31 Dec.
10 John I. Jacobs Review
11 Fearnleys Review Table 3, at 31 Dec.

TABLE A1.2 Supply/demand model – dry cargo fleet

	Dry cargo demand					*Dry cargo fleet productivity*	*Dry cargo fleet*					
	Dry cargo trade								*Add*			
Year	*Trade volume mt*	*Av. haul miles*	*Transport required btm*	*Less comb. carriers btm*	*Dry cargo demand btm*	*Tm/dwt per annum*	*Active dry cargo fleet m. dwt*	*Less laid up m. dwt*	*Tankers in grain m. dwt*	*'Other' fleet m. dwt*	*Total bulker fleet m. dwt*	*Year*
	(1)	(2)	(3)	(4)	(5)	(6)	(7)	(8)	(9)	(10)	(11)	
1963	768	2,930	2,250	92	2,158	21,303	101.3	1.3	0.0	85.5	17.1	1963
1964	858	3,019	2,590	115	2,475	23,023	107.5	0.7	1.7	87.2	19.3	1964
1965	913	2,990	2,730	138	2,592	22,442	115.5	0.4	3.4	88.3	24.2	1965
1966	968	3,006	2,910	155	2,755	22,545	122.2	0.6	3.4	88.9	30.5	1966
1967	995	3,116	3,100	132	2,968	23,242	127.7	0.8	1.4	88.4	38.7	1967
1968	1,065	3,221	3,430	95	3,335	24,414	136.6	0.5	0.6	89.1	47.4	1968
1969	1,160	3,241	3,760	184	3,576	24,730	144.6	0.3	0.7	90.0	54.2	1969
1970	1,240	3,363	4,170	280	3,890	25,525	152.4	0.4	0.8	91.3	60.7	1970
1971	1,260	3,397	4,280	170	4,110	25,528	161.0	3.0	0.4	94.3	69.3	1971
1972	1,317	3,379	4,450	204	4,246	24,600	172.6	1.6	0.7	94.9	78.6	1972
1973	1,481	3,504	5,190	316	4,874	25,953	187.8	0.5	1.4	97.5	89.4	1973
1974	1,623	3,555	5,770	678	5,092	25,861	196.9	1.3	0.7	99.7	97.8	1974
1975	1,551	3,630	5,630	718	4,912	24,281	202.3	7.4	1.1	102.9	105.7	1975
1976	1,642	3,575	5,870	782	5,088	23,033	220.9	5.3	2.2	107.4	116.6	1976
1977	1,675	3,612	6,050	734	5,316	22,095	240.6	5.4	1.6	114.8	129.6	1977
1978	1,764	3,617	6,380	822	5,558	22,091	251.6	4.3	0.5	120.5	134.9	1978
1979	1,938	3,617	7,010	1,000	6,010	23,009	261.2	2.1	0.4	125.2	137.7	1979
1980	2,010	3,667	7,370	1,165	6,205	23,196	267.5	1.8	0.0	127.2	142.1	1980
1981	2,024	3,690	7,469	1,150	6,319	22,512	280.7	2.5	0.0	128.5	154.7	1981
1982	1,921	3,757	7,217	921	6,296	22,438	280.6	18.4	0.0	129.8	169.2	1982
1983	1,878	3,739	7,022	688	6,334	21,610	293.1	16.8	0.0	131.8	178.1	1983
1984	2,065	3,767	7,778	902	6,876	22,102	311.1	10.2	0.0	133.5	187.8	1984
1985	2,134	3,706	7,908	888	7,020	21,747	322.8	9.7	0.0	135.0	197.5	1985
1986	2,122	3,747	7,951	465	7,486	23,256	321.9	9.1	0.0	135.0	196.0	1986
1987	2,178	3,751	8,170	473	7,697	23,100	319.4	6.0	0	132.2	193.2	1987
1988	2,308	3,808	8,790	636	8,154	23,099	325.3	3.1	0	132.9	195.5	1988
1989	2,400	3,792	9,100	916	8,184	23,099	335.6	1.9	0	134.8	202.7	1989
1990	2,451	3,798	9,310	938	8,372	23,102	346.6	2.2	0	137.7	211.1	1990
1991	2,537	3,780	9,590	719	8,871	23,102	353.8	2.9	0	140.8	215.9	1991
1992	2,573	3,747	9,640	646	8,994	23,097	357.4	3.3	0	144.1	216.6	1992
1993	2,625	3,722	9,770	581	9,189	23,181	365.0	3.5	0	147.9	220.6	1993
1994	2,735	3,755	10,271	580	9,691	21,797	377.8	3.8	0	152.8	228.8	1994
1995	2,870	3,787	10,870	616	10,254	22,606	395.7	3.3	0	158.0	241.0	1995

Source:
1 Fearnleys Review, Table 1 – Total Dry Cargo
2 (3)/(1)*1,000
3 Fearnleys Review, Table 2 – Total Dry Cargo
4 Fearnleys World Bulk Trades, Table 2
5 (3) – (4)
6 (5)/(7)*1,000
7 (11) + (10) + (9) – (8)
8 Fearnleys Review Table 7, at 31 Dec.
9 John I. Jacobs Review
10 Fearnleys Review Table 3, at 31 Dec.
11 Fearnleys Review Table 3, at 31 Dec.

TABLE A1.3 Supply/demand model – combined carrier fleet

	Combined carrier transport				*Combined carrier fleet*			
Year	*Dry bulk btm*	*Oil and products btm*	*Total cargo btm*	*Combined carrier fleet productivity tm/dwt per annum*	*Active fleet m. dwt*	*Less laid up m. dwt*	*Total combo fleet m. dwt*	*Year*
	(1)	*(2)*	*(3)*	*(4)*	*(5)*	*(6)*	*(7)*	*(8)*
1963	92	0	92	38,333	2.4	0.0	2.4	1963
1964	115	0	115	41,071	2.8	0.0	2.8	1964
1965	138	24	162	47,647	3.4	0.0	3.4	1965
1966	155	53	208	48,372	4.3	0.0	4.3	1966
1967	132	162	294	38,182	7.7	0.0	7.7	1967
1968	95	358	453	44,412	10.2	0.0	10.2	1968
1969	184	400	584	47,869	12.2	0.0	12.2	1969
1970	280	465	745	47,756	15.6	0.0	15.6	1970
1971	170	714	884	41,896	21.1	0.0	21.1	1971
1972	204	920	1,124	38,759	29.0	0.0	29.0	1972
1973	316	1,255	1,571	42,005	37.4	0.0	37.4	1973
1974	678	1,084	1,762	41,853	42.1	0.0	42.1	1974
1975	718	826	1,544	34,932	44.2	0.0	44.2	1975
1976	782	841	1,623	37,921	42.8	4.0	46.8	1976
1977	734	912	1,646	39,190	42.0	6.3	48.3	1977
1978	822	676	1,498	32,923	45.5	3.2	48.7	1978
1979	1,000	635	1,635	34,277	47.7	0.5	48.2	1979
1980	1,165	404	1,569	33,454	46.9	0.4	47.3	1980
1981	1,150	368	1,518	34,112	44.5	0.8	45.3	1981
1982	921	389	1,310	35,310	37.1	6.0	43.1	1982
1983	688	328	1,016	28,066	36.2	6.0	42.2	1983
1984	902	285	1,187	30,436	39.0	2.1	41.1	1984
1985	888	304	1,192	34,451	34.6	1.0	35.6	1985
1986	473	479	952	29,202	32.6	0.8	33.4	1986
1987	636	480	1,116	33,818	33.0	0.7	33.7	1987
1988	916	355	1,271	38,632	32.9	0.4	33.3	1988
1989	938	316	1,254	39,188	32.0	0.3	32.3	1989
1990	719	445	1,164	37,428	31.1	0.4	31.5	1990
1991	646	403	1,049	34,281	30.6	0.1	30.7	1991
1992	614	398	1,012	35,017	28.9	2.3	31.2	1992
1993	581	431	1,012	35,760	28.3	0.7	29	1993
1994	580	328	908	35,058	25.9	0.1	26	1994
1995	616	234	850	35,565	23.9	0.1	24	1995

Source: 1 Fearnleys World Bulk Tades, Table 2
2 Fearnleys World Bulk Trades, Table 2
3 (1) + (2)
4 (3)/(5)*1000
5 (7) – (6)
6 Fearnleys Review Table 7, at 31 Dec.
7 Fearnleys Review Table 3, at 31 Dec.

Appendix 2

Tonnage measurement and conversion factors

A problem that recurs frequently in the shipping industry is the need to measure the size of a ship or the size of a fleet of ships. One reason for doing this is to measure the cargo carrying capacity, but there are many other commercial reasons. For example, port authorities will wish to charge large ships higher wharfage fees than small ships, and the same applies to the Panama and Suez Canal Authorities. To meet these needs a whole range of different measurement units have been developed in the shipping industry, each adapted to some particular need. In this section we briefly review the principal units currently in use.

Gross registered tonnage (grt)

One major issue of concern to shipowners, particularly liner companies handling low-density cargo, is the internal volume of the ship, and this is recorded by the gross registered tonnage. The grt is a measure of the total permanently enclosed capacity of the ship and consists of:

- underdeck tonnage
- 'tweendeck tonnage
- superstructures
- deckhouses and other erections.

Certain spaces such as navigational spaces (wheelhouse, chart rooms, etc.), galleys, stairways, light and air spaces are exempted from measurement, in order to encourage their adequate provision. The official gross tonnage of a vessel is calculated by the Government Surveyor when it is first registered. One ton equals 100 cubic feet of internal space.

Gross tonnage (gt)

The 1969 IMO Tonnage Convention introduced a new simplified standard procedure for calculating gross tonnage, and this is now used in all countries that are signatories to the convention. Instead of going through the laborious process of measuring every open space in the ship, the gross tonnage is calculated from the total volume of all enclosed spaces, measured in cubic metres, using a standard formula. For some ship types, especially those with complex hull forms, the gt and the grt may be significantly different.

Net registered tonnage (nrt)

Under the existing rules, nrt is supposed to represent the cargo volume capacity of the ship and is obtained by deducting certain non-revenue-earning spaces from the grt. The net registered tonnage is expressed in units of 100 cubic feet.

Net tonnage (1969)

A formula introduced by the 1969 Tonnage Convention gives net tonnage (1969) as a function of the moulded volume of all the ship's cargo spaces, with corrections for draughts less than 75 per cent of the ship's depth and for the number of berthed and unberthed passengers. The net tonnage so calculated cannot be less than 30 per cent of gt. The net tonnage is also dimensionless.

Deadweight (dwt)

In many trades the principal concern is with measuring the cargo-carrying capacity of a fleet of ships, and for this purpose deadweight tonnage is used. The deadweight of a ship measures the total weight of cargo that the vessel can carry when loaded down to its marks, including the weight of fuel, stores, water ballast, fresh water, crew, passengers and baggage.

As a rule, the non-cargo items account for about 5 per cent of the total deadweight in medium-sized ships, although the proportion is lower in large vessels. As an example, a 35,000 dwt bulk carrier would probably be able to carry about 33,000 deadweight of cargo.

Deadweight can also be measured as the difference between the loaded ship displacement and its lightweight (see below for definition).

Compensated gross tonnage (cgt)

This unit of measurement was developed for the totally different purpose of measuring the level of shipbuilding output. In the early 1970s, shipbuilders in Europe and Japan had reached the conclusion that inter-country comparisons of shipbuilding output, measured in deadweight or gross registered tonnage, were unreliable because some ships had a much higher work content per gross ton than others. For example, a passenger ferry of 5,000 gross tons may involve the shipbuilder in as much work as a bulk carrier of 15,000 gross tons. To overcome this problem, a new standard unit called compensated gross registered tonnage (cgrt) was developed. The cgrt of a ship was calculated by multiplying the grt of a ship by an appropriate conversion ship factor for that ship type. A set of standard conversion factors was agreed at the OECD in 1977. In 1984, to take account of the move to gross tonnage, a new set of conversion factors was agreed at the OECD and some examples are summarized in Table A2.l. Under this system a VLCC of 250,000 dwt with a gross tonnage of 125,000 gt would have a cgt of 31,250.

TABLE A2.1 Average cgt coefficients

Ship type	*Ship size (dwt)*							
	100 gt–4,000	*4,000–10,000*	*10,000–30,000*	*30,000–50,000*	*50,000–80,000*	*80,000–160,000*	*160,000–250,000*	*250,000 and over*
Crude oil carriers	1.70	1.15	0.75	0.60	0.50	0.40	0.30	0.25
Product carriers and chemical carriers	2.30	1.60	1.00	0.75	0.55	0.50		
Bulk carriers	1.60	1.10	0.70	0.60	0.50	0.40	0.30	

Source: Selected cgt coefficients proposed and agreed by experts of the Shipbuilder's Association of Japan and Association of Western European Shipbuilders
Note: The cgt of a ship is calculated by multiplying the gross tonnage by the appropriate factor shown in the above table.

As a basis for estimating the average relationship between gross tonnage, deadweight tonnage and compensated gross tonnage, Table A2.2 shows the actual conversion factors for vessels completed in 1984.

TABLE A2.2 Conversion factors: Average conversion factors for dwt, grt and cgt (based on all ships delivered in 1984)

Ship type	*Average ship size*			*Conversion factor*	
	g(r)t 000s	*cg(r)t 000s*	*dwt 000s*	*cg(r)t/ g(r)t*	*dwt/ g(r)t*
Tankers, crude	20.0	9.8	35.9	0.49	1.79
Tankers, products and chemical	6.6	6.1	11.6	1.07	1.75
Combined carriers	17.8	11.4	29.0	0.63	1.62
Dry bulk carriers	24.4	13.9	41.7	0.57	1.70
ro-ro	11.1	13.7	12.0	1.22	1.07
Vehicle carriers	19.5	20.4	8.8	1.04	0.45
General cargo ships	3.5	4.7	5.1	1.33	1.44
Full container and HS liners	22.4	19.0	21.6	0.85	0.96
LPG carriers	9.1	10.7	11.0	1.17	1.20
LNG carriers	82.7	49.5	61.3	0.59	0.74
Ferries	0.7	2.4	0.3	3.26	0.47
Passenger ships	10.4	21.5	3.7	2.05	0.35
Fishing vessels	0.5	2.0	0.2	3.50	0.49
Other non-cargo vessels	1.1	3.7	0.9	3.19	0.85

Lightweight (lwt)

A ship's lightweight is the weight of the vessel as built, including boiler water, lubricating oil and the cooling system water.

Standard displacement (sd)

This is the theoretical but accurate weight of the vessel fully manned and equipped with stores and ammunition but without fuel or reserve feed water.

Suez and Panama tonnages

For ships transiting the Suez and Panama Canals, different systems of measurement are used to assess the dues payable. All ships have to be specially measured for the assessment of their dues when passing through these areas.

Notes

1 The economic organization of the shipping market

1 Radcliffe (1985).
2 Drury and Stokes (1983), 28, discuss the case of Tidal Marine, which collapsed in 1972, raising many questions about the basis on which loans had been obtained.
3 One Greek shipowner vividly summarized his philosophy in the following way: 'Shipping is our hobby. We have been rewarded unusually well in the past and we shall be in the future. The odds are for us, gentlemen, in shipping.'
4 See chapter 12 for a discussion of the influence of the colonial on the maritime industry in the nineteenth and early twentieth century.
5 Cippola (1968).
6 Smith (1983), p. 122.
7 Graham and Hughes (1985).
8 The rail freight for coal shipped by rail from West Virginia's Ashland Coal to Jacksonville Electric Authority in Florida is reported as $17.2 per ton in *International Bulk Journal*, May 1986, p. 27. On 27 August 1986, Lloyd's List reported a charter from Hampton Roads to Japan, a voyage of over 9,000 miles, at $6.50 per ton.
9 This trade hardly existed at the beginning of the period, so for the period 1950–60 the transport cost is estimated from the transport costs of other deep sea trades, which should give a sufficiently reliable guide for this purpose.

10 The prices in this table were based on a survey carried out by *The Economist*. To allow a comparison with the $ freight costs for coal and oil the £ sterling prices were converted into US dollars using an exchange rate of £/$ of 0.3567 in 1960 and 0.556 in 1990.

11 Rochdale Report (1970).

12 Neresian, R. (1981), p. 75, discusses the importance of flexibility in ship types. See also the discussion in chapter 7 of this text.

13 Despite the long distances, the use of big ships offering economies of scale means that the cost of deep sea shipping is very low. The ships used range in size from 10,000 dwt at the lower end to tankers capable of carrying 400,000 tons of cargo. Typical shipping costs in 1993 were $12 to ship a ton of coal from the USA to Japan or $500 to ship a container carrying 10 tons of cargo from the USA to Europe. The transport cost for a ton of oil over the 11,000 miles from the Middle East to the USA was only $4.

14 'Short-Sea Bulk Trades' David Tinsley, Fairplay Publications Ltd, London 1984

15 An Integrated Transport System consists of a series of components (e.g. road, sea, rail) which are designed for the efficient transfer of cargo from one system to another. Intermodalism refers to the specific elements in this system concerned with the transfer of cargo from one mode to another.

16 The statistics in Table 1.1 are taken from the United Nations Maritime Transport Study. These statistics provide an unrivalled source of detailed information about the type of commodity moving by sea. Unfortunately the UN discontinued the collection of these statistics in 1990 and the most recent available data is 1986. In the absence of any alternative source it remains the most recent information available on seaborne commodity trades.

17 For a more extensive discussion of the PSD function see Stopford (1979a) particularly Appendix C, 'A model of dry cargo ship demand' (pp. 366 onwards), which analyses the PSD function for fifty-five commodity groups.

18 Rochdale Report (1970).

19 Graham and Hughes (1985), p. 17, discuss the problems faced by conventional liner owners in the 1960s.

20 Lloyd's Shipping Economist, 'Steel trades: the choice of ship type', July 1984, p. 16, provides a well documented example of the shipment of steel products in containers, bulk carriers, ferries and ro-ros.

21 The *John Bowes* (1852) and the *Agamemnon* (1865) are considered to be forerunners of the modern bulk carrier and cargo liner.

22 H. Clarkson & Co., Tanker Register (1997 and earlier copies) provides a listing of tankers by size and age.

23 Dunn (1975), p. 196.

24 Fearnleys, World Bulk Trades 1969, p. 13, shows that in 1969 61 per cent of the grain trade was in vessels below 25,000 dwt and only 1 per cent in vessels over 60,000 dwt. The 1985 edition of the same reports shows 40 per cent of all shipments in vessels over 60,000 dwt.

25 John 1. Jacob's, *World Tanker Fleet Review* January–June 1995 page 34.

26 Neresian (1981), Ch. 14, gives a particularly vivid account of the debate over whether an oil company should buy its own ships.

27 Lloyd's Shipping Economist, 'Mitsui, OSK', March 1981, p. 37.

28 Rochdale Report (1969).

2 The shipping market cycle

1 This comment was made in conversation with the owner of a North American shipowning company in Spring 1995.

2 Chida and Davis (1990) p. 177.

3 Rochdale Report (1970) para. 565.
4 Xenon S. Xannetos 'Market and Cost Structure in Shipping' in Lorange and Norman 1973, p. 41.
5 These comments apply principally to charter market operations where the decisions are few but the consequences of errors are large. In liner companies, a multitude of decisions have to be made daily, but for the most part the consequences of error are less onerous.
6 Braudel (1985) Vol. III chap. 1.
7 Gould and Angier (1920).
8 Kircaldy (1913), pp. 174 and 208.
9 Fayle (1933) page 276.
10 Cufley, (1972), p. 408.
11 Hampton (1991) suggests that the shipping market has a short cycle of three to four years and a longer cycle of about twenty years, with an 8–12 year build up phase, followed by an 8 to 12 year 'correction'.
12 Hampton, (1991), p. 2.
13 Schumpeter (1939).
14 Braudel (1985) Vol. III chap. 1.
15 The rate for a coal cargo from South Wales to Singapore confirms the trend. In 1869 the freight was 27 shillings/ton, but by 1908 it had fallen to a low of 10 shillings (before decimalization in 1972, the English pound (£) was divided into 20 shillings. Thus 27 shillings was equivalent to £1.35).
16 The early steam engines had worked at 6 lbs/in pressure and consumed 10 lbs of coal/horsepower hour. They could carry little but bunker coal. By 1914, pressures had increased to 165 lbs/in and coal consumption had fallen to 1½lbs/horsepower hour, giving the steamer a decisive economic advantage, despite its high capital costs.
17 Smith, and Holden (1946).
18 These fleet figures understate the true growth of shipping supplies. According to contemporary estimates, the productivity of a steamer was four times as high as a sailing ship, so in real terms the available sea transport capacity increased by 460 per cent. No doubt much of this was absorbed by increasing tonmiles as more distant trades were opened up, though unfortunately no tonmile statistics were collected at this time.
19 The brokers' reports for the forty-five-year period paint a consistently gloomy picture. There are only a handful of years that do not warrant a complaint about the state of the market. As time progresses the complaints about over-building intensify. A comment on 1884 from Gould and Angier (1920) is typical 'This state of things was brought about by the large over-production of tonnage during the three previous years, fostered by reckless credit given by the banks and builders and over-speculation by the irresponsible and inexperienced owners'.
20 MacGregor (1961) p. 149.
21 Gould, Angier & Co. (1920).
22 Given that the freight index fell to 80 in the 1930s' recession, and assuming that this represented the operating cost of the marginal ship, the operating margin for capital in the 1920s must have been about 30 points.
23 Jones 1957, Table V p. 31.
24 Angiers Report for 1936 published in Fairplay.
25 Jones (1957) p. 57.
26 Platou (1970) p. 158.
27 Platou (1970) p. 162.
28 Platou (1970) p. 200.
29 Tugendhat (1968) pp. 186–7.
30 Tugendhat (1968) p. 186.
31 Hill and Vielvoye (1974).
32 Fearnleys Annual Review 1974, p. 8.

33 Fearnleys Annual Review 1977 p. 9.
34 Fearnleys Annual Review 1981 p. 9.
35 Fearnleys Annual Review 1982 p. 9.
36 The 1982 built 64,000 dwt *Pacific Prosperity* sold in August for $6.2 million.
37 This is not to suggest that individual companies did not make good returns. We are concerned here with market averages.
38 Tramp Shipping Administrative Committee, 1936.
39 Committee of Enquiry into Shipping May 1970, CMND 4337 para 1275.
40 The Rochdale Report (1970) thought that one reason for the poor performance of British shipowners was their unwillingness to borrow. In 1969 the companies surveyed had only £160 million debt compared with £1,000 million of assets.
41 Ibbotson and Sinquefield (1986).
42 Brealey and Myers (1988) p. 136.
43 Smith (1983) B 1 Chap. X.
44 Alderton (1973) p. 92.
45 'We have a saying in Greek "we get the light from above" ... when we buy we buy because a vessel is cheap, that is the main consideration: when we consider it a bargain' (statement by Greek shipowner).
46 Websters dictionary offers two definitions, one of which implies regularity and the other does not. The first focuses on regular time intervals and defines a cycle as 'an interval of time during which one sequence of a *regularly* recurring sequence of events or phenomena is completed'. For example we talk of the 'special survey cycle' of a ship, meaning a sequence of ship inspections and dry dockings in accordance with a regular timetable. However there is another meaning of the word which has nothing to say about timing or regularity. It defines a cycle as 'a recurrent sequence of events which occur in such an order that the last event of one sequence precedes the recurrence of the first event in the new series'. For example when we discuss the building cycle of a ship (i.e. keel lay, launch, sea trials, delivery, etc.) we make no comment on how long each of these stages will take. It depends on the shipbuilder. Knowing that the keel has been laid is little help in predicting the launch date.
47 Kepner and Tregoe (1982).

3 The four shipping markets

1 Jevons W.S. Theory of Political Economy, 1871 Chap. IV.
2 At least that is the case if there is no bank lending. If the buyer borrows 60 per cent of the purchase price of the ship, repayable over five years, this increases the short-term liquidity of the shipping industry. For example, if an owner purchases a $10 m. tanker and finances the transaction with a $6 m. loan plus $4 m. of his own equity, the effect is to increase the industry's short-term cash balance by $6 m. If we look at the industry balance sheet as a whole, the effects of this sale and purchase transaction is to increase the current assets by $6 m., which is precisely offset by a $6 m. increase in net liabilities.
3 The S&P market has an important economic role as the mechanism used by the market to filter out unsuccessful shipowners. During recessions the financially weak owners are obliged to sell to the financially strong at bargain prices.
4 Ihre and Gordon (1980) provide a more detailed discussion of the charter-party practices.
5 A new Norwegian Sales Form was issued in 1993, but is less widely used than the 1987 version which is shorter and well tested in law.
6 Fairplay 15 July 1920 p. 221 'Fluctuations in Shipping Values'.
7 Based on statistical analysis of Lloyd's Register of Shipping, Casualty Return.

4 Supply, demand and freight rates

1 Isserlis (1938).
2 Samuelson (1964), p. 263.
3 Pigou (1927).
4 Samuelson (1964), p. 251.
5 Isserlis (1938), p. 76.
6 In fact the standard deviation of the average elasticity, a statistical measure of volatility, doubled from 0.6 in the first period to 1.2 in the second.
7 Maizels (1962).
8 Stopford (1979a).
9 European Commission (1985), p. 18.
10 Kindleberger (1967), p. 24.
11 MARPOL Paragraph 13G.
12 Platou (1970), p. 180.
13 Platou (1970), p. 183.
14 In the present context the 'productivity' of a fleet can be defined as the total ton miles of cargo shipments in the year divided by the deadweight fleet actively employed in carrying the cargo.
15 'VLCC Investment; a Scenario for the 1990's' Clarkson Research Studies Ltd, London 1993.
16 op cit, p. 52
17 Webster's dictionary defines a retailer as someone who sells small quantities direct to the ultimate consumer at a price customarily charged by the retailer.
18 In this section the discussion is restricted to a graphical discussion of the supply/demand model. A mathematical treatment can be found in Evans and Marlow (1990) chapter 6.
19 Evans and Marlow (1990), chapter 7.
20 A notable exception to this is the oil trader who operates on small margins and whose market activity may be very sensitive to freight rates.
21 One possible solution to forcing up freight rates at this stage in the market is the formation of a cartel. However efforts by owners to control the market by forming 'Stabilization Pools' of vessels that remain permanently out of the market have never been successful.
22 For the reasons discussed in the previous section, freight rates and supply should be expressed per ton mile.
23 M. Hampton 'Long and Short Shipping Cycles: The Rhythms and Psychology of Shipping Markets', 3rd Edition, Cambridge Academy of Transport Cambridge, March 1991.
24 Smith, A. (1776), p. 160.
25 Marshall, A. (1994 edition), p. 289.

5 Costs, revenue and financial performance

1 See 'Capesize Quality Survey', Clarkson Research Studies, London 1994, p. 181
2 The daily cost referred to here covers both operating and voyage costs. Normally time charter rates do not cover fuel costs, since these are paid by the charterer. Since fuel costs are different we need to take this into account.
3 This is evident in the USA where the domestic market was for many years closed off from the world shipping market by the Jones Act. Faced with high replacement costs and little change in size, ships often trade to thirty or forty years of age.
4 The first steps in ship automation were made in the early 1960s, and in 1964 the East Asiatic vessel *Andorra* was the first vessel to go into service without an engineroom watch below. To facilitate

this, the ship had an elaborate system of malfunction alarms with indicators relayed to strategic points in the accommodation. At this time the main emphasis was on improving crew conditions and freeing them from the unproductive routine task of engineroom watchkeeping in order to carry out maintenance work elsewhere on the vessel.

5 Defining the sea margin is very subjective. Some brokers add 'one day per ocean' as a rule of thumb. Others cut the speed by 5 per cent.

6 Financing ships and shipping companies

1 According to 'World Shipyard Monitor' published by Clarkson Research Studies, in 1994 the bulk shipping industry invested \$13.6 bn in new ships and \$7.5 bn in second-hand vessels.

2 Select Committee on Employment of British Shipping 1844 D111Q55.

3 G. Atkinson 'The Shipping Laws of the British Empire' (1854) p. 122, quoted in A. Palmer (1972) p. 49.

4 S.A. Palmer (Investors in London Shipping, 1820–50 in Maritime History, Vol. 2 (1) April 1972.

5 A.M. Northway 'The Tyne Steam shipping Co: a late nineteenth-century shipping line' in Maritime History Vol. 2 No. 1 1972, p. 71.

6 Hyde (1967), p. 99.

7 Sturmey (1962). p. 398.

8 Rochdale Report (1970), para. 1270.

9 op. cit., para. 1270.

10 Olsen & Ugelstad 1915–1965, Grondahl & Sons, Oslo, 1965, p. 35.

11 See Petersen (1955) p. 197. Owners applying for a licence to build abroad were required to obtain foreign currency loans.

12 Sturmey (1962), p. 223.

13 'Bankers view of ship finance' presented by Finn W. Arnesen, Director of Hambros Bank Ltd at Seatrade Money and Ships Conference 26 March 1973.

14 Examples of this practice were provided verbally by the head of a major shipping bank active at the time in ship finance.

15 These investors are spread around the financial centres of Europe, North America and the Far East. Their investment behaviour is restricted and to some extent determined both by the regulatory framework within which they operate (which is different in Tokyo, London and New York) and the policies implicit in their own particular business. For example, liquidity is less important to institutions such as life insurance companies which invest huge amounts of money for the 'long haul'. On the contrary, liquidity will be of prime importance to the corporate treasurer investing spare cash which he may need to draw on at any time. Other complications are the currency in which assets are held and commitments must be paid.

16 For example treasury bills, short term tax exempts, certificates of deposit, commercial paper, bankers acceptances or short-term euro currency deposits. Because it is an efficient market, at any given time there is a standard price for a given combination of liquidity, risk and yield.

17 If we lived in a world without regulation and taxes the two markets would be the same – the interest rate on a Eurodollar loan would have to be the same as an equivalent domestic dollar loan, etc. This is not the case because governments use domestic interest rates to regulate domestic bank lending, resulting in pools of currency held off-shore where rates are determined by supply and demand.

18 To achieve this there are various regulatory requirements designed to provide security for the purchaser of the bonds. In order to issue the bonds a company must have a credit rating, for example, by Standard and Poors in the USA. The quality of this rating determines the risk associated with the bonds – bonds issued by companies rated less than BBB are popularly known

as 'junk bonds' and they attract higher rates of interest. Naturally, many financial institutions hold portfolios of long dated bonds.

19 Usually this demands evidence that the company has a profitable trading record in an industry which is considered to have a profitable future.

20 According to the FT/S&P Acturies World Indices in 1996 the value of equity markets was £8.455 trillion, of which 0.18 per cent was transport. Note that debt is not included.

21 Stokes, P. (1992), p. 179.

22 The liability of the general partner is unlimited, but for equity partners it is limited to the sum committed.

23 To avoid having any assets held by the general partner, his capital is often provided as a loan from the organizer.

24 Recently there have been moves to limit the K/S system. In November 1989 the 'Aarbakke-committee' recommended that the depreciation rate in the K/S should be reduced to 10 per cent and the classification fund provision should not be allowed. In June, 1991 it was announced that the cutback would be to 20 per cent.

25 The fund was marketed in Europe and South East Asia but according to the organizers, interest from South East Asia was virtually nil, and it was not much better in Norway. Eventually a total of $21.25 million was raised mainly from UK institutions, but with the help of two substantial subscriptions from Germany and Saudi Arabia.

26 see Chapter 12 for a discussion of ship registration.

27 A 'basis point' is 100th of a per cent. For example 150 basis points is 1.5 per cent etc.

28 The placement was in two tranches, $96 million with a 7-year term and $79 million with a 10-year term.

29 Brealey R. and Myers S. (1988), chapt. 8.

7 The economic principles of maritime trade

1 Two important countries which are not included in this list are the USSR and China.

2 David Hume *Political Discourses* (1752) reprinted in Meek (1973), p. 61.

3 Smith (1776) 1961 reprint, p. 434.

4 The factors of production required to produce a product are the costs which the manufacturer must pay, organized into convenient groups. In a very general way labour and capital are the main factors

5 Winters (1991), p. 31. Three other assumptions are: perfect competition in factor markets; no impediments to trade such as tariffs or transport costs; and that there are two factors and two countries.

6 Rostow (1960).

7 Maizels (1971), p. 30.

8 The discussion of this function can be found in Henderson and Quandt (1971), chap. 2.

8 The global pattern of maritime trade

1 Brodel (1979), p. 49.

2 Haws and Hurst (1985), p. 15.

3 McEvedy (1967), p. 26.

4 Haws and Hurst (1985), p. 18.

5 Lindsay (1874), Vol. 1, p. 4.

6 McEvedy (1967), p. 44.
7 Haws and Hurst (1985), Vol. 1, p. 36. Heroditus described the Greek trading methods in a detailed account written in c.620 BC.
8 McEvedy (1961), p. 58.
9 According to Lindsay (1874), Vol. I p. 549, the merchants of the Mediterranean were 'too desirous of retaining in their own hands the monopoly of the Indian trade to encourage expeditions which had for their object merely the extension of geographical knowledge'. Indeed there seems to have been a conspiracy of silence in which the merchants and seamen were induced to restrict their knowledge of the size and extent of Asia to their own classes.
10 Lindsay, Vol 1, p. 549.
11 McEvedy (1972), p. 38.
12 Van Cauwenbergh, George 1983, Antwerp, Portrait of a Port, Lloyd Anversois S.A. p. 16.
13 Haws and Hurst (1985), p. 270.
14 McEvedy (1961), p. 38.
15 Lindsay (1874), Vol II, p. 184.
16 Rogers (1898), Vol 1, p. 101.
17 Beenstock (1984) argues the case for the transition theory.
18 Mangone (1977), p. 88.
19 Jantscher (1975).
20 Ibid., p. 5.
21 UNCTAD Review of Maritime Transport 1995, Table 10.
22 'Dry Cargo Ship Demand to 1980' Maritime Transport Research, London, 1977.
23 Statistics published by the United Nations show that in 1985 the West Coast North American trade accounted for 30 per cent of exports and 12 per cent if imports by the region.
24 Containerisation International Yearbook 1994.
25 The dimensions of the locks are length 233.48 m; width 24.38 m; depth over sill 9.14 m.
26 The Gulf Intracoastal Waterway comprises large sheltered channels running along the coast and intersected by many rivers giving access to ports a short distance inland. New Orleans is reached by the Tidewater Ship Canal, a more direct and safer waterway than the Mississippi Delta. The Pacific coast canals are not linked with the national network.
27 These percentages, and others given later in the chapter are based on the United Nations 'Maritime Transport Study' 1985.
28 Note that the trade data in Figure 8.5C are slightly different from Table 8.3 because they include W. Coast S. America and come from a different source.

9 The global pattern of maritime trade

1 McEvedy (1967), p. 70.
2 McCord (1979), p. 113.
3 Craig, Robin (1980) The Ship: Steam Tramps and Cargo Liners 1850–1950 (National Maritime Museum, London).
4 The United Nations' annual 'Maritime Transport Study', published until 1986, use a commodity classification developed specially for maritime transport statistics. It subdivides commodities into Dry Bulk, Liquid Bulk, Refrigerated Foods, General Cargo and Other Dry Cargo. See also A.C. Handy (1926), p. 2.
5 Comment by P. J. Raleigh of Falconbridge Nickel Mining in Kirschenbaun and Argall (eds), vol. 2, p. 127. 1
6 H.E. Tanzig, 'Imaginative bulk parcel ocean transportation', in Kirschenbaun and Argall (eds), vol. 2, p. 290.

7 A typical sample consists of a scoop which is quickly swung through the material on the belt and deposits its contents into a sample box for analysis.
8 McCord (1979), p. 130.
9 Dunn, Lawrence (1956) 'The World's Tankers' (Adlard Coles, London), p. 18.
10 Dunn (1956), p. 19.
11 Blake, George (1960), 'Lloyds Register of Shipping 1760–1960', p. 83. Unfortunately this clever idea did not work. The Belgian authorities refused permission for storage tanks and the American authorities refused a licence for passenger carriage. When the *Vaderland* arrived in Philadelphia, the pumping apparatus was not ready, so they loaded general cargo. The owners then got a mail contract from the Belgian Government and the ships never traded in oil.
12 The *Loutsch* was still trading in Russian hands in the early 1950s.
13 Kirkaldy (1913), p. 126.
14 Strictly speaking the first 'oil company' to get involved with tankers was the Swedish Nobel brothers, of explosives fame. They exported oil from the Russian oilfields, which involved a difficult journey to the Caspian Sea, down the Volga and through the Black Sea to Europe. Starting with barges and sailing ships on the Volga, in 1878 they built the *Zoroaster*, a tank steamer that burned fuel oil and carried 250 tons of kerosene in twenty-one vertical cylindrical tanks. By 1882 they had twelve tank steamers trading in the Caspian.
15 Hunting (1968) and Dunn (1956).
16 Howarth (1992), p. 23.
17 Howarth (1992), p. 29.
18 Tugenhat (1968), p. 187.
19 At the time tanker owning was not particularly risky because most of the tanker owning industry's revenue was covered by long-term contracts. In 1972 Professor Zenon S. Zannetos confirmed this view by stating 'I know of few industries which are less risky than the oil tank transportation industry'. 'Market and Cost Structure in Shipping' Bergen 1972 (Conference proceedings).
20 This chart compares the actual tanker fleet (the top line) with the demand for tankers based on the oil trade and the peak efficiency of 44,000 ton miles per dwt achieved in 1973.
21 For example the thermal coal trade for power stations increased from almost nothing in 1971 to current 236 mt.
22 Odell (1981) p. 13.
23 Odell (1981) p. 120.
24 At this temperature the gas is reduced to 1/630th of its original volume.
25 Estall and Buchanan (1966), p. 156.
26 Bernham and Hoskins (1943), p. 104.
27 Dunn (1973), p. 195.
28 International Iron and Steel Institute, Steel Statistical Yearbook (1985), Table 9.
29 Maritime Transport Research (1976), vol. 3, Appendix E.
30 Steven (1969), p. 108.
31 Stopford (1979b).
32 Fearnleys, World Bulk Trades (1985), Table 12.
33 Ibid., p. 23.
34 OECD (1968), Annex 5, Table 1.
35 Morgan (1979), p. 137.
36 Income/consumption curves showing income on one axis and consumption on the other are often referred to as 'Engel Curves'. Typically calorie intake rises from a subsistence level of 2,000 calories to reach a plateau at around 3,500 calories per day.
37 Inferior goods are the cheapest commodities with an income elasticity below zero – consumption declines as income rises; necessities are commodities with an income elasticity between zero and one – consumption increases with income, but at a slower rate of growth; and luxuries with an income elasticity in excess of 1 so consumption grows faster than income.

38 Maritime Transport Research (1972), p. 36.
39 Lloyd's Shipping Economist, 'Steel trades: the choice of ship type', July 1984, p. 16.

10 The general cargo and the economics of liner shipping

1 Drewry Shipping Consultants 'Global Container Markets' (July 1996) p. 6, estimates liner freight at $80–90 billion per annum.
2 Jennings (1980), p. 16.
3 Kirkaldy (1914), p. 179.
4 Griapios, pages 38–39.
5 McKinsey (1967).
6 'A Commemoration of 40 Years of Containerisation', Containerisation International, April 1996, p. 65.
7 'A Commemoration of 40 Years of Containerisation' Containerisation International, April 1996, p. 9.
8 Meek, M 'Operational experience of large container ships', paper to Institute of Engineers and Shipbuilders in Scotland, 1985.
9 This definition is an updated version of the definition given in *A Short History of the World's Shipping Industry* Fayle, p. 253.
10 Strictly speaking we should also include the various administrative costs of running a liner business in this item, although doing so would not alter the principles we are discussing.
11 Marriner and Hyde (1967), p. 141.
12 Jennings (1980), p. 23.
13 Deakin and Seward (1973), p. 24.
14 Sturmey (1962), p. 324.
15 Briggs and Jordan (1954), p. 295.
16 Deakin and Seward (1973), p. 1.
17 *China Mail*, Hong Kong, 22 November 1879.
18 Sturmey (1962), p. 327.
19 One freight forwarder interviewed in this survey commented: There are not many shippers left who would say that they are 100 per cent loyal to the conferences they have signed for. The problem is that it is such a difficult thing for the conference to police. Bird, J. (1988) p. 119.
20 Bird, J. Freight Forwarders speak: the perception of route competition via seaports in the European Communities Research project – Part II Maritime Policy and Management, 1988, Vol. 15 (2), 107–125, p. 121.
21 Some years ago the United Nations developed a Maritime Transport Classification (MTC) which divided commodity trades into 'bulk' and 'general' cargo. 'International Sea-borne Trade Statistics Yearbook 1984–1985 UN Statistical Papers Series D lists over sixty commodity groups.
22 Collinson, F.M., 'Market segments for marine liner service', *Transportation Journal*, Vol 24, pp. 40–54
23 Brooks, Mary R. 'Understanding the ocean container market – a seven country study' *Maritime Policy and Management*, 1995, vol 22, no1, 39–49
24 Bird, op. cit., p. 111.
25 Bird, op. cit., p. 111.
26 'Container Lines: Could Do Better' *Lloyds Shipping Economist* March 1995, p. 20. The ports surveyed were Busan and Singapore in the Far East and Hampton Roads and Los Angeles/Long Beach in North America. The survey covered 995 arrivals.
27 Containerisation International, 'Lifting the lid on the chocolate box', May 1983, p. 67.
28 Containerisation International (1985), p. 51.
29 Drewry (Shipping Consultants) Ltd (1979). p.51.

30 Drewry Shipping Consultants Ltd (1979), Table 4.1.
31 Clarkson Research (1996) The Containership Register (Clarkson Research, London).
32 Deakin and Seward (1973), p. 54.

11 The economics of ships and ship designs

1 For a discussion of the techniques for this analysis see Buxton (1987) or Benford (1983a,b).
2 Benford (1983a), p. 2.
3 Buxton, Daggitt, and King (1978), p. 25. This book provides a detailed technical discussion of many of the design features discussed in chapter 7.
4 Containerisation International, 'UNCTAD reviews the banana trade and favours boxes'. August 1982, p. 41.
5 Graham and Hughes (1985), p. 20.
6 'West Africa – a difficult market for ro-ros', Lloyd's List, 13 May 1986, p. 8, contains a discussion of the use of containers in the West African trade.
7 'Multi stacking tween deck covers on new design', *MacGregor News*, No. 102, April 1984, p. 30.
8 MARPOL (78) required SBT to be fitted to all new tankers over 20,000 dwt.
9 Dunn, Laurence 1956 *The world's tankers* London *Adlard Coles*.
10 See, for example, Buxton (1987) and Benford (1983a).
11 Buxton (1987).

12 The regulatory framework of maritime economics

1 Fayle (1933) 2nd impression 1934, p. 285.
2 'International Law of the Sea' John Hopkins, Senior Tutor, Downing College, Cambridge March 1994, Cambridge Academy of Transport.
3 In 1997 there were 155 IMO members and 8 non-IMO members which were parties to IMO conventions.
4 The term 'regulatory authority' is used here to indicate an institution which creates rules and has the capacity to enforce them.
5 The earliest list in existence dates from 5 October 1702 'Lloyds Register of Shipping 1760–1960' p. 3.
6 Blake (1960), p. 5. The ships were graded according to hull condition and equipment standard. The hull of ships were classified A, E, I, O or U according to the excellence of their construction and their continuing soundness, or otherwise. Equipment was G, M or B – simply good, middling or bad. Any ship classified AG was thus as sound as it could be, while one rated UB was obviously a bad risk from the underwriter's point of view
7 Blake, G (1960), p. 22.
8 *Law of the Sea* (1983) p. XXV.
9 Stephenson Harwood, (1991), page 202
10 Stephenson Harwood, (1991), chap. 9.
11 Cooper (1986).
12 Gold (1981), p. 258.
13 The International Convention relating to the Arrest of Seagoing Ships provides that '... a claimant may arrest either the particular ship in respect of which the maritime claim arose, or any other ship which is owned by the person who was, at the time when the maritime claim arose, the owner of the particular ship ...' Stephenson Harwood (1991), p. 10.

14 Gold (1981), p. 119.
15 Protocol of Proceedings of the International Marine Conference 1889, 3 vols (Washington DC: US Government Printing Office, 1890), Vol. 1, pp. ix–xiii.
16 'World Trends in Regulation of Safety at Sea and Protection of the Environment' E.E.Mitropoulos Sea Japan Conference Paper 9 March 1994
17 E.E Mitropoulos (1985), p. 11.
18 A government official or representative authorized to sign a treaty or convention on behalf of the government.
19 The relevant tonnage was to be based on figures contained in Lloyd's Register, Statistical Tables 1973, Table 2.
20 Faust (1983), p. 3.
21 United Nations Convention on Conditions for Registration of Ships, TD/RS/Conf./22, 7 February 1986, Article 1.

13 The economics of shipbuilding and scrapping

1 A more detailed discussion can be found in Stopford and Barton (1986).
2 Board of Trade, Departmental Committee on Shipping and Shipbuilding, Report (1918), pp. 35–6.
3 Sturmey (1962), particularly chap. 2, provides a vivid description of the link between British shipping and trade.
4 Svensson (1986) puts forward this explanation of the decline in British shipbuilding.
5 Hobsbawm (1968), pp. 178–9.
6 Petersen (1955), p. 47.
7 Stopford and Barton (1986), pp. 34 and 35, discuss the competition between Japan and Europe in the 1960s.
8 Jones (1957), p. 72.
9 Trezise and Suzuki (1976).
10 World Shipyard Monitor, published by Clarkson Research, London, February 1996, p. 12.
11 Glasgow Herald Trade Review, 31 December 1924.
12 Glasgow Herald Trade Review, 31 December 1924.
13 'Shipbuilding notes', Shipbuilding Employers' Federation, press release, December 1930 (unpublished).
14 'Shipbuilding Notes', Shipbuilding Employers' Federation, December 1936 (unpublished).
15 Shipbuilders' and Repairers' National Association employment statistics (unpublished).
16 See 'Yard Capacity – is it enough to meet future needs?' by Martin Stopford, Fairplay Magazine, 15 December 1988, p. 22.
17 Volk, (1994).
18 For a discussion of the principles of supply/demand analysis see Evans and Marlow (1986), chap. 5.
19 Geff Walthow, a demolition broker dealing with Taiwan from the early 1950s to 1994, describes how the living standards of workers at the Kaohsiung yard gradually improved from a shanty town to purpose-built apartments.

14 Maritime forecasting and market research

1 Beck (1983).
2 Drucker (1977).
3 ibid., p. 119.

4 Temple (1984) provides a discussion of the use of these techniques in decision-making.
5 Stopford and Barton (1986).
6 A discussion of the procedure for fitting a regression model can be found in Evans and Marlow (1986), Ch. 10.
7 For a detailed discussion of these techniques see Tull and Hawkins (1980), particularly Ch.10.
8 For a discussion of scenario techniques see Beck (1983) and Linnerman (1983), p. 94.
9 Moyer (1984), p. 17 contains a more detailed discussion of these problems.
10 Beck (1983)
11 Savage (1983)
12 Baranto (1977)
13 Prowse (1984)

References and recommended reading

Abrahamsson, B.J. (1980) *International Ocean Shipping: Current Concepts and Principles* (Boulder, Col.: Westview Press).

Alderton, P.M. (1973) *Sea Transport Operation and Economics* (London: Thomas Reed).

Baranto, M. (1977) 'How well does the OECD forecast real GNP?' *The Business Economist*, Vol. 9.

Batty, J. (1982) *Management Accountancy* (Plymouth: MacDonald & Evans).

Beck, P.W. (1983) 'Forecasts: opiates for decision-makers', a lecture to the Third International Symposium on Forecasting, 5 June, Philadelphia.

Beenstock, M. (1984) *The World Economy in Transition* (London: Allen & Unwin).

Benford, H. (1983a) *A Naval Architect's Introduction to Engineering Economics* (Ann Arbor, Mich.: University of Michigan, College of Engineering) No. 282.

—— (1983b) *The Blacksmith Ship Economist* (Ann Arbor, Mich.: University of Michigan, College of Engineering) No. 270.

—— (1985) 'Ship's capital costs: the approaches of economists, naval architects and business managers', *Journal of Maritime Policy and Management* (Swansea), Vol. 12(1), pp. 9–25.

Bergstrand, S. and Doganis, R. (1986) *The Impact of Soviet Shipping* (London: Allen & Unwin).

Bernham, T.H. and Hoskins, G.0. (1943) *Iron and Steel in Britain 1870 to 1930* (London).

Beth, H.L., Hader, A. and Kappel, R. (1984) *25 Years of World Shipping* (London: Fairplay Publications).

Bird, J. (1988) 'Freight forwarders speak: the perception of route competition via seaports in the European Comunities Research project – Part II' *Maritime Policy and Management* Vol. 15(2), 107–25).

Blake, G. (1960) *Lloyds Register of Shipping 1760–1960* (London: Lloyds Register of Shipping).

Branch, A.E. (1981a) *Elements of Shipping*, 5th editiion (London: Chapman & Hall).

—— (1981b) *Economics of Shipping Practice and Management*, 1st edition (London: Chapman & Hall)

Braudel, F. (1985) *Civilisation and Capitalism, 15th–18th Century, Volume III The Perspective of the World* (London: Fontana Press).

Brealey R.A. and Myers, S.C. (1988) *Principles of Corporate Finance*, 3rd edition (New York: McGraw-Hill).

Briggs, M. and Jordan, P. (1954) *The Economic History of England* (London: University Tutorial Press).

Brodel, F. (1979) *Civilisation and Capitalism 15th–18th Century: The Perspective of the World*, Vol. 3 (London: Fontana.

Brooks, M.R. (1995) 'Understandng the ocean container market – a seven country study', *Transportation Journal*, Vol. 22(1), pp. 33–49.

Buxton, I.L. (1987) *Engineering Economics and Ship Design*, 3rd edition (Wallsend: British Maritime Technology).

Buxton, I.L., Daggitt, R.P. and King, J. (1978) *Cargo Access Equipment for Merchant Ships*, (London: E&FN Spon).

Cheng, P.C. (1979) *Financial Management in the Shipping Industry* (Ithaca, NY: Cornell Maritime Press).

Chiang, A.C. (1974) *Fundamental Methods of Mathematical Economics* (Tokyo: McGraw Hill).

Chida, T. and Davies, P.N. (1990) *The Japanese Shipping and Shipbuilding Industries* (London: The Athlone Press).

Chilton, M. (1976) *What Goes on in Shipbuilding?* (Cambridge: Woodhead-Faulkner).

Chrzanowski, I. (1985) *An Introduction to Shipping Economics* (London: Fairplay Publications).

Churchill R.R and Lowe A.V. (1983) *The Law of the Sea* (Manchester: The Manchester University Press).

Cippola, C. (1968) *The Economic History of World Population* (London: Pelican)

Collinson, F.M. (1984) 'Market segments for marine liner service', *Transportation Journal*, Vol. 24, pp. 40–54.

Containerisation International (1985) 'Brazil/US bulk coffee trial report', August, p. 51.

Cooper, G.B.F. (1986) *Open Registry and Flags of Convenience* (Cambridge: Seatrade Academy, March).

Craig, R (1980) *The Ship: Steam Tramps and Cargo Liners 1950–1950* (London: National Maritime Museum).

Cufley, C.F.H. (1972) *Ocean Freights and Chartering* (London: Staples Press).

Deakin, B.M. and Seward, T. (1973) *Shipping Conferences: A Study of their Development and Economic Practices* (Cambridge: Cambridge University Press).

Douglas, P. (1984) Proceedings of International Shipping Seminar (Haifa University, May).

Drewry (Shipping Consultants) Ltd (1996) *Global Container Markets: Prospects and Profitability in a High Growth Era* (London: Drewry Shipping Consultants).

—— (1979) *West African Liner Shipping* (London).

—— (1984) *Dry Bulk Operating Costs, Past, Present and Future* (London, May).

Drucker, P.F. (1977) *Management: Tasks, Responsibilities, Practices* (New York: Harpers College Press).

Drury, C. and Stokes, P. (1983) *Ship Finance: The Credit Crisis* (London: Lloyd's of London Press).

Dunn, L. (1956) *The World's Tankers* (London: Adlard Coles).

—— (1973) *Merchant Ships of the World in Colour 1910 to 1925* (London: Blandford Press).

—— (1975) *Merchant Ships of the World* (London: Blandford Press).

Estall, R.C. and Buchanan, R.O. (1966) *Industrial Activity and Economic Geography* (London: Hutchinson).

European Commission (1985) Progress towards a Common Transport Policy: Maritime Transport, Commission to Council, Com (85)90 Final (Brussels, March).

Evans, J.J. and Marlow, P.B. (1990) *Quantitative Methods in Maritime Economics* (London: Fairplay Publications), 2nd edition..

Faust, P. (1983) *The United Nations Convention on a Code of Conduct for Liner Conferences* (Geneva: UNCTAD).

Fayle, E.C. (1933) *A Short History Of the World's Shipping Industry* (London, George Allen & Unwin).

Gilman, S. (1983) *The Competitive Dynamics of Container Shipping* (London: Gower Press).

Gold, E. (1981) *Maritime Transport: The Evolution of International Maritime Policy and Shipping Law* (Lexington, Mass.: D.C. Heath).

Goss, R.0. (1982) *Advances in Maritime Economics* (Cambridge: Cambridge University Press).

Gould, J.C. Angier & Co., Ltd (1920) 'Fifty Years' Freights' (A series of Articles in Fairplay Magazine published during 1920).

Graham, M.G. and Hughes, D.O. (1985) *Containerisation in the Eighties* (London: Lloyd's of London Press).

Grammenos, C.T. (1979) *Bank Finance for Ship Purchase* (Cardiff: University of Wales Press).

Gripaios, H. (1959) *Tramp Shipping* (London: Thomas Nelson).

Hampton, M. (1986) 'Shipping cycles', *Seatrade*, January.

Hampton, M.J. (1989) *Long and Short Shipping Cycles* (Cambridge: Cambridge Academy of Transport), 3rd edition 1991.

Handy, A.C. (1926) *Bulk Cargoes* (London: Chapman and Hall Ltd).

Haws, D. and Hurst, A.A. (1985) *The Maritime History of the World*, 2 vols (Brighton: Teredo Books Ltd).

Henderson, J.M. and Quandt, R.E. (1958) *Microeconomic Theory: A Mathematical Approach*, 2nd edition 1971, (New York: McGraw Hill).

Hill, P. and Vielvoye, R. (1974) *Energy in Crisis* (London: Robert Yateman Ltd).

Hobsbawm, E.J. (1968) *Economic History of Britain, Vol. 3: Industry and Empire* (London: Penguin).

Hunting, P. (1968) *The Group and I*, (London: John Wallis).

Hyde, F.E. (1967) *Shipping Enterprise and Management* (Liverpool: Liverpool University Press).

Ibbotson R.G. and Sinquefield R.A. (1986) *Stocks, Bills and Inflation* (Chicago: Ibbotson Associates).

Ihre, R. and Gordon, L. (1980) *Shipbroking and Chartering Practice* (London: Lloyd's of London Press).

Isserlis, L. (1938) 'Tramp shipping, cargoes and freights', *Journal of the Royal Statistical Society*, Vol. 101.

Jantscher, G.R. (1975) *Bread upon the Water: Federal Aids to the Maritime Industries* (Washington, DC: Brookings Institute).

Jennings, E. (1980) *Cargoes: A Centenary Story of the Far East Freight Conference* (London: Meridian).

Jevons, W.S. (1871) *Theory of Political Economy*, Chap.IV.

Jones, J.J. and Marlow, P.B. (1986) *Quantitative Methods in Maritime Economics* (London: Fairplay Publications).

Jones, L. (1957) *Shipbuilding in Britain: Mainly between the Wars* (Cardiff: University of Wales Press).

Kepner, C.H. and Tregoe, B.B. (1982) *The New Rational Manager* (London: John Martin Publishing).

Kindleberger, C.P. (1967) *Foreign Trade and the National Economy* (New Haven, Conn.: Yale University Press).

Kirkaldy, A.W. (1914) *British Shipping* (London: Kegan Paul Trench Trubner & Co. Ltd.), reprinted Augustus M. Kelly, New York 1970.

Kirschenbaun, N.W. and Argall, G.O. (eds) (1975) *Minerals Transportation*, Vol. 2 (San Francisco: Miller Freeman).

Kondratieff, N.D. (1935) 'The long wave in economic life', *Review of Economic Statistics*.

Kummerman,. H. and Jacquinet, R. (1979) *Ship's Cargo, Cargo Ships* (London: E&FN Spon).

Law of the Sea (1983) Official text of the United National Convention on the Law of the Sea with Annexes and Index (New York: United Nations).

Lindsay, W.S. (1874) *History of Merchant Shipping and Ancient Commerce*, 4 Vols (London: Simpson Low, Marston, Low and Searle).

Linnerman, R.E. (1983) 'The use of multiple scenarios by US industrial companies: a comparison study 1971–1981', *Long Range Planning*, Vol. 6.

Lobo, G.A. (1981) 'Hong Kong shipping: the inside story', *Lloyd's Shipping Economist* (London).
Lorange, P. and Norman, V.D. (eds) (1973) *Shipping Management* (Bergen: Institute for Shipping Research).
McCord, N. (1979) *North East England: The Region's Development 1760 to 1960* (London: Batsford).
McEvedy, C. (1961) *The Penguin Atlas of Medieval History* (Harmondsworth: Penguin Books).
—— (1967) *The Penguin Atlas of Ancient History* (Harmondsworth: Penguin Books).
—— (1972) *The Penguin Atlas of Modern History* (Harmondsworth: Penguin Books).
MacGregor, D.R. (1961) *The China Bird, The History of Captain Killick and the firm he founded* (London: Chatto and Windus).
Maizels, A. (1962) *Growth and Trade* (Cambridge: Cambridge University Press).
—— (1971) *Industrial Growth and World Trade* (Cambridge: Cambridge University Press).
McKinsey and Company (1967) *Containerisation: The Key to Low Cost Transport* (London: British Transport Docks Board).
Mangone, G.J. (1977) *Marine Policy for America: The United States at Sea* (Lexington, Mass.: D.C. Heath).
Maritime Transport Research (1972) *The Sea Trades in Grain* (London: MTR).
—— (1976) *Dry Cargo Ship Demand to 1985*, Vol. 3: Raw Materials (London: Graham & Trotman).
—— (1977) *Dry Cargo Ship Demand to 1985*, Vol. 6: Ship Demand (London: Graham & Trotman).
Marriner, S. and Hyde, F. (1967) *The Senior John Samuel Swipe 1925–98: Management in Far East Shipping Trades* (Liverpool: Liverpool University Press).
Marshall, A. (1920) *Principles of Economics*, 8th edition (London: The Macmillan Press, reprinted 1994).
Meek, R.L. (1973) *Precursors of Adam Smith 1750–1775* (London: J.M. Dent & Sons).
Metaxas, B.N. (1971) *The Economics of Tramp Shipping* (London: Athlone Press).
Mitropoulos, E.E. (1985) 'Shipping and the work of IMO related to maritime safety and pollution prevention', paper presented at Maritime Economists' Conference on the State and the Shipping Industry, London, 1–2 April.
—— (1994) 'World Trends in Regulation of Safety at Sea and Protection of the Environment', paper presented at Sea of Japan Conference, Yokahama, 9 March.
Morgan, D. (1979) *Merchants of Grain* (London: Weidenfeld & Nicolson).
Moyer, R. (1984) 'The futility of forecasting', *Long Range Planning*, Vol. 17(1), February, pp. 65–77.
Neresian, R. (1981) *Ships and Shipping: A Comprehensive Guide* (New York: Penwell Press).
Northway, A.M. (1972) 'The Tyne Steam Shipping Co: a late nineteenth-century shipping line', *Maritime History*, Vol. 2(1).
Odell, P.R. (1981) *Oil and World Power* (London: Pelican).
OECD (1968) *Agricultural Commodity Projections 1975 and 1985: Production and Consumption of Major Foodstuffs* (Paris: OECD).
'Olsen & Ugelstad 1915–1965' (1965) (Grondahl & Sons, Oslo.)
Packard, W.V. (1979) *Voyage Estimating*, lst edition (London: Fairplay Publications).
—— (1980) *Laytime Calculating*, 1st edition (London: Fairplay Publications).
Palmer, A. (1972) 'Investors in London Shippping, 1820–50 in Maritime History', Vol. 2(1), April.
Patrick, H. and Rosovsky, H. (1976) *Asia's New Giant* (Washington, DC: The Brookings Institution).
Pearson, R. and Fossey, J. (1983) *World Deep Sea Container Practice* (London: Gower Press).
Petersen, K. (1955) *The Saga of Norwegian Shipping* (Oslo: Dreyers Foriag).
Pigou, A.C. (1927) *Industrial Fluctuations* (London: Macmillan).
Platou, R.S. (1970) 'A survey of the tanker and dry cargo markets 1945–70', *Norwegian Shipping News*, No. 10c, pp. 109–86.
Prowse, M. (1984) 'The future that Britain never had', *Financial Times*, 17 August.
Radcliffe, M.A. (1985) *Liquid Gold* (London: Lloyd's of London Press).
Riddle, I. (1983) *Shipbuilding Finance* (Cardiff: University of Wales Press).
Robicheck, A.A. and Myers, S.C. (1965) *Optimal Financing Decisions* (New Jersey: Prentice Hall).
Rochdale Report (1970) Committee of Enquiry into Shipping, Cmnd 4337 (London: HMSO).
Rogers, J.E. (1898) *The Industrial and Commercial History of England*, Vol. I (London: T. Fisher Unwin).

Rostow, W.W. (1960) *Stages of Economic Growth* (Cambridge: Cambridge University Press).
Samuelson, P.A. (1964) *Economics: An Introductory Analysis* (London: McGraw Hill).
Savage, D. (1983) 'The assessment of the National Institute's forecasts of GDP, 1959–1982', *National Institute Economic Review*, No. 105, August.
Schmitthoff, C.M. (1976) *The Export Trade*, 8th edition (London: Sweet & Maxwell).
Schumpeter, J.-A. (1939) *Business Cycles: A Theoretical, Historical and Statistical Analysis of the Capitalist Process* (New York: McGraw Hill).
Sletmo, G.K. and Ernest, L.V.W. (1981) *Liner Conferences in the Liner Age* (London: Macmillan).
Sloggett, J.E. (1984) *Shipping Finance* (London: Fairplay Publications).
Smith, A. [1776](1983) *The Wealth of Nations* (London: Penuin English Library).
Smith, J.W. and Holden, T.S. (1946) *Where Ships are Born, Sunderland 1346–1946. A History of Shipbuilding on the River Wear* (Sunderland: Thomas Reed and Company).
Stephenson H. (1991) *Ship Finance* (London: Euromoney Books).
Steven, R. (1969) *Iron and Steel for Operatives* (London: Collins).
Stokes, P (1992) *Ship Finance: Credit Expansion and the Boom–Bust Cycle* (London, Lloyd's of London Press Ltd).
Stopford, R.M. (1979a) 'Inter regional seaborne trade – a disaggregated commodity study', London University PhD thesis.
—— (1979b) 'New designs and newbuildings', paper given at Commodities and Bulk Shipping in the '80s Conference', London (Lloyd's of London Press), December.
—— (1991) 'The Return on Investment in Shipping', paper presented at the Admiralty Finance Forum, London, 5 November. 1991.
—— (1995) When Will the Return on Investment Return? Paper presented at the Seatrade Tanker Convention, London, 20 February, 1995.
Stopford, R.M. and Barton, J.R. (1986) 'Economic problems of shipbuilding and the state', *Journal of Maritime Policy and Management* (Swansea), Vol. 13(1), pp. 27–44.
Sturmey, S.G. (1962) *British Shipping and World Competition* (London: Athlone Press).
Svensson, T. (1986) 'Management strategies in shipbuilding in historical and comparative perspective'. Lecture to the Fourth International Shipbuilding and Ocean Engineering Conference, Helsinki', 8 September.
Temple, K.G. (1984) *Conversations with Eternity* (London: Ryder).
Tinsley, D. (1984) *Short-Sea Bulk Trades* (London: Fairplay Publications Ltd).
Trezise, P.H. and Suzuki, Y. (1976) 'Politics, government and economic growth in Japan' in Patrick and Rosovsky (1976).
Tugendhat, C. (1968) *Oil: The Biggest Business*, 2nd edition (London: Eyre & Spottiswoode).
Tull, D.S. and Hawkins, D.L. (1980) *Marketing Research* (London: Collier Macmillan).
UNCTAD (1985) *Port Development: A Handbook for Planners in Developing Countries*, 2nd edition, Sales No. E84.1l.Dl.
Van Cauwenbergh, G. (1983) *Antwerp, Portrait of a Port* (Lloyd Anversois SA).
Volk, B. (1994) *The Shipbuilding Cycle – A Phenomenon Explained* (Bremen: Institute of Shipping Economics and Logistics).
Winter, L.A (1991) *International Economics* 4th edition (London: Harper Collins).
Zannetos, Z.S. (1966) *The Theory of Oil Tankship Rates* (Cambridge, Mass.: MIT Press).
Zannetos, Z.S. (1972) 'Market and Cost Structure in Shipping', Proceedings of shipping management seminar (Bergen: Institute of Shipping Research).

Magazines and Periodicals

Containerisation International (monthly) – the best international publication devoted to the container trades. Many detailed articles and each year the July edition contains world statistical container survey.

Cargo Systems International (monthly) – valuable source of information on the container industry and inter-modalism.
Fairplay (weekly) – old established practical shipping journal.
International Bulk Journal (monthly) – in-depth articles on the bulk trades and bulk handling; particularly good on minor bulks.
Lloyd's List (daily) – newspaper covering shipping and the transport industry; essential reading for keeping up-to-date; also includes many supplements, features, articles and conference reviews.
Lloyd's Shipping Economist (monthly) – an excellent source of statistics and feature articles for the practical shipping economist.
Marine Money (monthly) – newsletter specializing in ship finance and investment-related topics.
Maritime Policy and Management (quarterly) – a wide-ranging academic quarterly.
Motor Ship (monthly) – mainly technical, provides detailed design drawings of ships and also feature articles.
OECD, Maritime Transport (annual, Paris) – annual review of maritime industry,
Petroleum Economist (monthly) – definitive journal dealing with the oil industry and oil trade by sea; includes statistics of oil production and prices.
Seatrade Week (weekly) – newssheet focusing on people and business news.
Seatrade (monthly) – shipping magazine particularly strong on US and Pacific affairs.
Shipping Intelligence Weekly – authoritative source of shipping market statistics published by Clarkson Research Studies.
Shipping News International (monthly) – international shipping journal; formerly Norwegian Shipping News
Tradewinds – colourful and lively weekly shipping newspaper containing news, features and an extensive range of shipping statistics.
UNCTAD, Review of Maritime Transport (annual), United Nations E.86.1l.D3 – annual review of shipping industry.
World Shipping Monitor – comprehensive monthly statistics on the world shipbuilding industry, published by Clarkson Research Studies.

Maritime Geography and Ports

Guide to Port Entry (Shipping Guides Ltd, Reigate, UK) – re-issued annually; provides extensive details of ports.
Maritime Atlas (Lloyd's of London Press, 1986) – details of port, terminal and trade of ports, by country.
Times Atlas of the Oceans (Times Press, London).
World Ports Directory (Fairplay, London) – annual.

Maritime Statistics

British Petroleum Ltd, *Statistical Review of the World Energy Industry*, annual (London: BP).
Calvert, J. and McConville, J. (1983) *Shipping Industry Statistical Sources* (Sir John Cass Faculty of Transport, City of London Polytechnic).
Clarkson, H. and Company Ltd, *Tanker Register*, annual (12 Camomile Street. London EC3A 7BP).
—— *Bulk Carrier Register*, annual (12 Camomile Street, London EC3A 7BP).
—— *Liquid Gas Carrier Register*, annual (12 Camomile Street, London EC3A 7BP).

—— *Offshore Service Vessel Register*, annual (12 Camomile Street, London EC3A 7BP).
Containerisation International Yearbook (National Magazine Company, London) – contains detailed statistics of world container industry.
Fairplay Int., Shipping Weekly, 'World Ships on Order' – quarterly supplement to the magazine.
Fearnleys, *Annual Review*, annual (PO Box 1158 Sentrum, 0107 Oslo 1, Norway) – provides a range of up-to-date shipping statistics.
—— *World Bulk Fleet*, bi-annual (PO Box 1158 Sentrum, 0107 Oslo 1, Norway).
—— *World Bulk Trades*, annual (PO Box 1158 Sentrum, 0107 Oslo 1, Norway) – provides statistics of shipments in bulk carriers over 40,000 dwt.
International Iron and Steel Institute, *World Steel Statistics and Steel Statistical Yearbook*, annual (IISI, Brussels).
Jacobs, John I., *World Tanker Fleet Review*, bi-annual (John I. Jacobs PLC, 5 Devonshire Square, London) – authoritative source of tanker fleet statistics plus commentary.
Lloyd's Register of Shipping, *Register of Ships*, 3 vols (London) – containing details of all ships in the fleet.
Lloyd's Register, *Casualty Return* (London) – details of ships totally lost, broken up, etc.
—— *Statistical Tables* (London) – annual summary of world merchant fleet.
OECD, *Main Economic Indicators* (OECD, Paris)
Platou, R.S., *The Platou Report*, annual (R.S. Platou, Oslo) – source of second-hand price statistics.
United Nations, 'Maritime Transport Study', annual, Statistical Papers, Series D, Vol. XXIX–XXXII, no. 2.
—— *Monthly Bulletin of Statistics* (United Nations, New York).
—— *Statistical Yearbook* (United Nations, New York) – many useful background statistics.

General Publications

Drewry Shipping Consultants Ltd – consultant company specializing in shipping economics; many regular publications on shipping topics.
OECD, *Maritime Transport* – annual review of shipping industry produced by OECD Maritime Transport Secretariat; good introduction to recent trends.
Thomas, O.O., *Thomas' Stowage: The Properties and Stowage of Cargo*, 6th edition (Glasgow: Brown Son and Ferguson).

Index

Note: Entries in Italics are for references to figures and tables found in the text.